THE FALKLAND ISLANDS

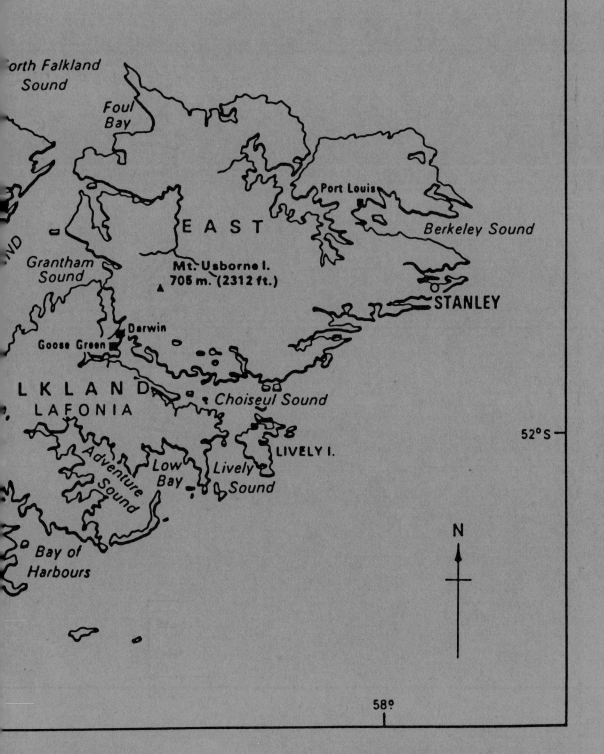

THE FALKLAND ISLANDS DISPUTE IN INTERNATIONAL LAW AND POLITICS:
A DOCUMENTARY SOURCEBOOK

THE FALKLAND ISLANDS DISPUTE

JASON ISLANDS

Keppel Sound

SAUNDERS I.

PEBBLE I.

North Falkland Sound

KEPPEL I.

Four Bay

Byron Sound

Mt. Adam
▲ 700 m. (2297 ft.)

King George Bay

W E S T

SOUND

Grantham Sound

F A L K L A N D

FALKLAND

Goose Green

BEAVER I.

Queen Charlotte Bay

Fox Bay East

F A L K L A N

WEDDELL I.

Fox Bay West

LAFONIA

Adventure Sound

SPEEDWELL I.

Bay of Harbours

Eagle Passage

IN INTERNATIONAL
LAW AND POLITICS:
A DOCUMENTARY SOURCEBOOK

BY

RAPHAEL PERL

With an Historic Chronology and Bibliography by
EVERETTE E. LARSON

OCEANA PUBLICATIONS, INC/LONDON · ROME · NEW YORK

The viewpoints expressed here are solely the personal ones of the author and should not be construed as representing the viewpoints or endorsement of his employer, or of the persons from whom he has received assistance.

Library of Congress Cataloging in Publication Data

Perl, Raphael.
    The Falkland Islands dispute in international law
& politics.

    Bibliography: p.
    1. Falkland Islands—International status.
2. Great Britain—Foreign relations—Argentina.
3. Argentina—Foreign relations—Great Britain.
4. Falkland Islands War, 1982.   I. Larson, Everette E.
II. Title.
JX4084.F34P47   1983   327.41082   82-25972 √9|83
ISBN 0-379-11251-5

Manufactured in the United States of America

TABLE OF CONTENTS

v

LIST OF DOCUMENTS

This conflict poses a particularly acute problem for persons and nations who love peace...

We have all come to appreciate how deep the roots of the conflict are. Britain, in peaceful possession of the Falkland Islands for 150 years, has been passionately devoted to the proposition that the rights of the inhabitants should be respected in any future disposition of the Islands. No one can say that this attitude, coming from a country that has granted independence to more than 40 countries in a generation and a half, is a simple reflex to retain possession.

Yet we know too how deep is the Argentine commitment to recover islands they believe were taken from them by illegal force. This is not some sudden passion, but a long sustained national concern that also stretches back 150 years, heightened by the sense of frustration at what Argentina feels were nearly 20 years of fruitless negotiation...

That a conflict of such dimensions should take place, and that it should occur here, in the Western Hemisphere—whose countries have long shared a particular commitment to each other, to their mutual welfare and to peace—causes us the deepest concern. This conflict, however urgent, cannot be permitted to obscure the common engagement of all American states to the rule of law and to the well-being of this hemisphere.

AMBASSADOR JEANE J. KIRKPATRICK
United States Representative to the
United Nations in the Security Council,
on the question concerning the
situation in the region of the Falkland
Islands (Islas Malvinas) May 22, 1982

ACKNOWLEDGEMENTS

The author would like to express his appreciation to Dr. Everette E. Larson, who prepared the chronology and bibliography for this book, and to all others who were instrumental in assisting him on the preparation of this work.

In particular, he would like to thank Senator Alphonse D'Amato of New York and his Legislative Assistant for National Security Affairs, Michael Hathaway, who originally requested a study, the outgrowth of which is this book.

Special acknowledgment is also due Dr. Eduardo Jantus, Press Attache, Embassy of the Argentine Republic, in Washington, D.C.; and Nigel Ellacott, Assistant Information Officer, British Embassy, Washington, D.C.

Marjorie Browne, Robert Schaaf, Daniel Zahfren, Marie-Louise Bernal, and Richard Duquette of the Library of Congress also provided valuable assistance.

Finally, the staff of Oceana Publications, Inc., in particular Vince O'Brien with his editorial assistance, made the technical aspects of producing this book an enjoyable experience, indeed.

Raphael Perl

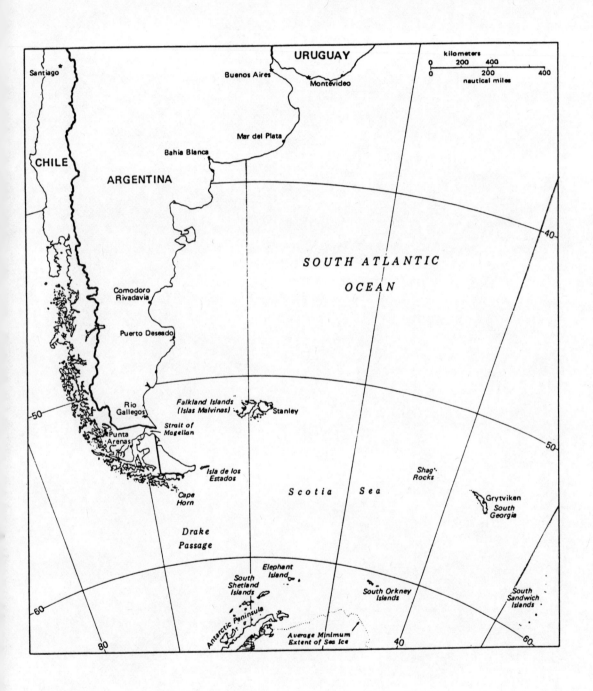

I. INTRODUCTION

The military confrontation between Argentina and the United Kingdom on the issue of territorial sovereignty over the Falkland/Malvinas Islands 1/ that recently riveted the world's attention stems from a dispute that has smoldered for quite some time and leaves in its aftermath numerous and complex legal as well as political issues. An understanding of the issues involved is complicated by sharply differing accounts not only of historical events but of the legal significance ascribed to those events by the two belligerents and by scholars. Thus a researcher looking for definite answers is faced with the difficult task of finding principles or rules of international law applicable to opposing perceptions of fact. Questions to be considered include those concerning rights historically awarded to nations as a result of certain types of prolonged occupation or presence and those rights, if any, of self-determination for a "population" numbering approximately eighteen hundred and situated on a relatively small territory.

The events leading up to this dispute have transpired in a highly charged political atmosphere. 2/ They have transpired in a world that is seeing a rapid growth in the power and international standing of former colonies, with regionalism being strengthened by economic and political ties. The economic/strategic stakes in the present controversy have become higher in light of the discovery of oil and mineral deposits off the Falklands.

There exist supportable arguments on both sides as to who is the rightful sovereign of the Islands. Furthermore, although the public generally envisions such rights of sovereignty as applying to the Islands and their Dependencies as a group, it is not at all clear from the legal point of

----

1/ Because this study is written in English, the designation "Falklands" or "Falkland Islands" will predominate, but its use is merely for linguistic convenience and does not signify any bias for Great Britain's claim to the area. Similarly, analysis of the issues in terms of the categories the "Islands" (East and West Falkland) and the "Dependencies" (the other islands) is for functional purposes only and is not to be construed as favoritism towards British administrative designations or acts.

2/ Note also the similarity of the instant dispute with the situation the United Kingdom faces in a much more strategically situated colony which is also claimed by another nation in close proximity to it. Consider the implications that the loss of the Falklands might have on British efforts to retain Gibraltar, a crown colony of similar legal status.

view that this is the case. The Islands, in contrast to the Dependencies, are distinct entities with distinct histories.

This dispute between Argentina and the United Kingdom regarding sovereignty over tne Falklands and their Dependencies was recognized by the United Nations General Assembly in Resolution 2056 (XX) of December 16, 1965, which invited both sides to proceed with negotiations for a peaceful solution to the problem. 3/ However, because no final and binding international agreement, adjudication, or arbitration resulted in this case, the use of military force prevailed. This study attempts to present a comprehensive compilation of information related to the legal aspects of this territorial sovereignty issue and to analyze these sources from the viewpoint of international law and practice. The study will not discuss the question of the lawful use of force, however. 4/

II. GEOGRAPHY AND TERMINOLOGY

The Falkland/Malvinas Islands, situated in the South Atlantic about 480 miles northeast of Cape Horn, consist of about 200 islands, the two largest being East and West Falkland. There is only one town, Stanley (pop. 1,813) and the next largest settlement (pop. 95) is Goose Green, both on East Falkland. The total land area of the Islands is approximately 4,700 square

---

3/ U.N. Res. A/2065 (XX), 20 U.N. GAOR Supp. (No. 14) at 57 (1966) and U.N. Res. A/3160 (XXVIII), 28 U.N. GAOR Supp. (No. 30) at 108-109 (1974). Note also that the South Shetland Islands and Graham Land are also claimed by Chile. See Great Britain, Government Overseas Information Services, Reference Division, Central Office of Information, The Falkland Islands Dependencies, 9 (April 1956), hereafter cited as "Central Office of Information" and I.C.J. Pleadings, Antarctica Cases (United Kingdom v. Argentina; United Kingdom v. Chile) at 64-65, hereafter cited as "Pleadings."
The Falklands-Malvinas dispute is but one of many international conflicts concerning disputed territorial sovereignty. Today there are a number of active island disputes and hundreds of such land and sea boundary disputes. See John Norton Moore, "The Inter-American System Snarls in Falklands War" 76 Am. J. Int'l L. 830-31 (1982).

4/ For a discussion on the lawful use of force in the current Falkland Islands situation, including tne issue as to whetner or not the U.N. prohibition against the use of force applies to a "re-taking" of one's own territory, see Daniel Hill Zafren, "The Falkland Islands (Malvinas) Situation: Some International Law Issues," Congressional Research Service, Library of Congress, Washington, D.C., June 14, 1982.

miles. There are few trees, substantial grassland, diverse bird and marine mammal life, and no native land mammals. 5/

The principal territories of the Islands are the Orkneys, the South Shetlands, the mainland peninsula of Graham Land, and a segment of the Antarctic mainland delineated according to the sector principle. They have been defined as including all lands and islands south of latitude 58 degrees South between longitudes 50 degrees and 80 degrees West. 6/ With the exception of South Georgia, which has an area of approximately 1,450 square miles, the other Islands are entirely arctic in character, although none of the Islands lies within the Antarctic Circle. The five territories listed above were formally designated by the United Kingdom as the Dependencies of the Colony of the Falkland Islands in 1908 and 1917. 7/ On March 3, 1962, the British designated and created the British Antarctic Territory, which included the area previously known as the Falkland Islands Dependencies, absent the Island of South Georgia and the South Sandwich Islands. 8/ Thus, the Islands' current geographical designations, as set out by the British, consist of:

1) the Falkland/Malvinas Islands (East and West Stanley and surrounding smaller islands); and

----

5/ Central Office of Information, supra note 3, at 3, and see also Bill Hezlep, "Geographical Fact Sheet on the Falklands Islands, South Georgia Island," and the South Sandwich Islands (INR/GE/CA) 1982. U.S. Dept. of State, Office of the Geographer.

6/ Falkland Island Letters of Patent of July 21, 1908 (1912), 101 British and Foreign State Papers (hereafter cited as B.F.S.P.) 76 (1907-08) as amended by the Letters of Patent of March 28, 1917 (1912), 111 B.F.S.P. 16 (1917-18).

7/ Id. and Great Britain, Colonial Office, Colonial Office List," 1966 102 (London, 1966), hereafter referred to as "Colonial Office List" and Great Britain, Reference Services, Central Office of Information, "The Falkland Islands and Dependencies" 7 (April 1982), hereafter cited as "British Reference Services."

8/ British Antarctic Order in Council, 1962, issued February 26, 1962, 1962 Stat. Instr. No. 400, hereafter cited as "Order in Council," and Colonial Office List, id., at 82. See also British Antarctic Territory/ Report for the Years 1961 to 31st March 1967 1 (London, 1967). By means of a similar act, Argentina established tne "National Territory of Tierra del Fuego, Antarctica and South Atlantic Islands." This included the Falklands, Georgias and the South Sandwich Islands. Decree Law No. 2.191, Boletin Oficial de la Republica Argentina 19/III/ 57 (1957).

2)   the Dependencies, which were split up by the British and incorporated into two groups:

   a)   the Falkland Island Dependencies (South Georgia and South Sandwich Islands); and

   b)   British Antarctic Territory, which includes the Orkneys, the South Shetlands, the main peninsula of Graham Land, and a segment of Antarctica delineated by sector.

III. HISTORY

A. The Islands

In April 1502 the Islands were probably sighted by a Portuguese sea captain and were noted at the time in the record of Amerigo Vespucci. 9/ Other sightings were subsequently recorded, and by 1550 these Islands off the Patagonian coast were known to Spanish, Portuguese, and English navigators. British sources stress a probable first British sighting by the English Captain John Davis in 1592 and other sightings by Sir John Hawkins in 1594 and a Dutch sailor, Sebald de Weert, in 1600. British sources maintain that the first recorded landing occurred in 1690 by Captain John Strong, who named the Islands after Viscount Falkland, then Treasurer of the English Navy. They assert that the Spanish designation of the Islands--"las Islas Malvinas" --derives from the name given them by French seal hunters of the eighteenth century who called the Islands "les Iles Malouines," after the port of St. Malo. 10/

Argentine sources note the designation of the Islands on numerous Spanish maps, the first of which appeared in 1522, but they attribute the first discovery to Esteban Gomez of Magellan's expedition in 1520. They note that in 1580 Sarmiento de Gamoba took symbolic possession of the Straits of Magellan (and the adjacent Islands) and founded a settlement there. As do the British, the Argentinians note the sighting by the Dutch navigator Sebald

----

9/   V.F. Boyson, _The Falkland Islands_ 15 (Oxford, 1924).

10/ British Reference Services, _supra_ note 7, at 2, and Great Britain, Foreign and Commonwealth Office, _The Falkland Islands, The Facts_ 2 (London, May 1982), hereafter cited as "The Facts."

de Weert in 1600. However, the Argentinians reject the alleged British discovery by Davis (1592) and Hawkins (1594) and cite the absence of any
reference to the island in the British cartography of the period. 11/

Both sides agree that in February 1764 Louis Antonine de Bougainville
established a French colony at Port Louis and that in April 1767 the French
ceded Port Louis to the Spanish, who then renamed it Port Soledad. Both
parties agree that in 1766 the British established a settlement on Saunders
Island, which they called Port Egmont, although the Argentinians refer to
this expedition as a "clandestine" one. 12/ Both parties agree that in 1770
Spain forced Britain to abandon Port Egmont, but, by a declaration made in
the name of Spain on January 22, 1771, the British were permitted to re-
establish their settlement. This declaration contained the condition that
the restoration was not in any way to affect the question of prior sovereign
rights over the Islands. 13/ In 1774, Britain left the Islands, allegedly
because the settlement was a financial burden, although the Argentinians
argue it was because of a secret promise to do so which had been part of the
1771 agreement. 14/ In any case, the British left behind a plaque claiming
the territory for themselves. The wording of the plaque is in dispute. The
Argentinians claim that it referred to "Falkland's Island" in the singular, 15/

11/ Statement by the Representative of Argentina, H.E. Dr. José Maria
Ruda, Before the Subcommittee III of the Special Committee on the Situation
with Regard to the Implementation of the Declaration on the Granting of
Independence to Colonial Countries and Peoples, "Malvinas Islands," 2-3 (New
York, Sept. 9, 1964), hereafter cited as "Malvinas Islands' Statement."

12/ Id. at 4.

13/ For the text of the declaration, see 22 B.F.S.P. 1387 (1832-34).
See also, Malvinas Islands' Statement, supra note 11, at 6.

14/ 22 B.F.S.P. 1388 (1832-34); Malvinas Islands' Statement, supra note 11, at
2; Julius Goebel, The Struggle for the Falkland Islands, Ch. 7 (New York,
1971 reprint of 1927 ed.), hereafter cited as "Goebel"; and José Arce, The
Malvinas (Our Snatched Little Isles) 79 (Madrid, 1951), hereafter cited as
"Arce."

15/ Malvinas Islands' Statement, supra note 11, at 6.

whereas Julius Goebel maintains that the plural, "Falkland Islands," was used. 16/

The Spanish subsequently withdrew their settlement on East Falkland in 1811, although Boyson sets the date at 1808. 17/ By the Declaration of Independence of July 9, 1816, the United Provinces of Rio de la Plata, with its seat of government at Buenos Aires, declared independence from Spain. 18/ In 1820, the Buenos Aires Government sent a ship to the Islands to proclaim its sovereignty over them, and in 1823 appointed its own governor over the Islands. A fishery and livestock concession was granted to Don Jorge Pacheco and Luis Vernet that same year. 19/ In 1826, a settlement was established, under the leadership of Vernet, 20/ and in June 1829, Vernet was appointed Commandant of the newly created Political and Military Commandancy of the Islands. 21/

16/ Goebel, supra note 14, at 410. For one version of the plaque's entire text, see infra note 33, at 50.

17/ Boyson, supra note 9, at 77-82; Goebel, supra note 14, at 433 and British Reference Services, supra note 7, at 2.

18/ Boyson, id.

19/ Goebel, supra note 14, at 434-436.

20/ Id. at 435.

21/ The text of the decree establishing Vernet's appointment is as follows:

> El gobierno de Buenos Aires:
>
> Habiendo resuelto por decreto de esta fecha que las Islas Malvinas y las adyacentes al Cabo de Hornos en el mar Atlántico sean regidas por un Comandante politico y militar, y teniendo en consideración las calidades que reune Don Luis Vernet, á tenido á bien nombrarlo como por el presente lo nombra para el expresado cargo de Comandante Politico y Militar de las Islas Malvinas, delegando en su persona toda authoridad y jurisdicción necesaria al efecto.
>
> Dado en Buenos Aires, á diez de junio de mil ochocientos veinte y nueve.
>   MARTIN RODRIGUEZ.
>   SALVADOR MARIA DEL CARRIL

(Source: E.J. Fitte, La Agresión norteamericana a las Islas Malvinas, Crónica documental 17 (Buenos Aires, 1966)).

In exercising his newly granted authority as Military Commandant, Vernet notified the masters of any alien vessels found seal fishing in the area about the new regime and asked them to cease operations under penalty of being sent to Buenos Aires for trial. His warnings were apparently not taken seriously, violations continued, and on July 30, 1831, the first of three American schooners was seized. 22/ The United States responded to the seizure of the three ships by sending the U.S.S. Lexington to Port Soledad/ Louis. The ship arrived on December 28, 1831, apparently under French flag, and a classic instance of "gun boat diplomacy" ensued. The ship's captain, Commander Duncan, destroyed the settlement and sailed away with one of Vernet's lieutenants--whom Duncan had invited on board--and five of his compatriots, in irons. Before his departure, Duncan declared the Islands free of all government. 23/ The British later dispatched two warships to the Falklands. One, the Clio, arrived at Port Egmont on December 20, 1832, made repairs to the old fort, and affixed a notice of possession. On January 3, 1833, the Clio appeared at Port Louis/former Port Soledad. The next day a force was landed and the British flag was raised, over the protests of the commander of the Argentine armed schooner, the Sarandi, who had just quashed a revolt of the colonists on the Island. 24/ The Sarandi departed several days later, her departure having been delayed by stormy weather. On January 3, 1833, the second British ship, the Tyne, visited Port Egmont, and a symbolic flag raising took place. 25/

For the text of the decree establishing the political and military commandancy, see 20 B.F.S.P. 314-315 (1832-33) and Malvinas Islands' Statement, supra note 11, at 10.

22/ Goebel, supra note 14, at 438 and British Reference Services, supra note 7, at 2.

23/ Goebel, id., at 454-455, and British Reference Services, id.

24/ Goebel, id., at 454-455. According to Boyson, supra note 9, at 96-98, the Argentine Government wanted "to make the islands a presidio (a term having the double significance of a frontier garrison and penal settlement); and the men were for the most part deportees, serving a term of punishment. Either unjustly treated or insufficiently guarded they revolted in December 1832."

25/ Boyson, id. at 98, and Great Britain, Foreign Office, Falkland Islands, Kerguelen 14 (London, 1920) hereafter cited as "Foreign Office Handbook No. 138." Argentina protested British actions by note of Don Manuel

In January 1834, a British naval officer was placed in charge of Port Louis, and the Islands remained under the British Admiralty until January 1842, when a Lieutenant-Governor, who was appointed by the Colonial Office in August 1841, reached Port Louis. 26/ In 1843, an Act of Parliament put the Islands' civil administration on a permanent footing. Under this act, letters of patent were issued in June of 1844, and the Falkland Islands became a crown colony of the ordinary type with a governor, legislative council, and executive council, in 1845. This system continues as such to the present time. 27/

Britain approved a grant-in-aid to the colony, which continued until 1881. A grant-in-aid for a mail service continued until 1884-85, when the colony became self-supporting. 28/

B. The Dependencies

The history of the Dependencies, their being primarily arctic, is not as easily ascertainable. Britain defined the Dependencies in letters of patent in 1908 and 1917. 29/ In March of 1962, the British retained South Georgia and the South Sandwich Islands as "dependencies" and severed the South Orkney and South Shetland Group, including them in the newly created

----

Moreno of June 17, 1833--see 22 B.F.S.P. 1384 (1832-34) for the text, as well as Argentine Republic, Protestation au Gouvernment des Provinces Unites du Rio de la Plata par son Ministre Plenipotentiaire à Londres (Londres, 1833), and the British reply at 22 B.F.S.P. 1384 (1832-34). Since that date, Argentina has maintained an "unbroken position of protest" against the British taking, according to Malvinas Islands' Statement, supra note 12, at 1, and Organization of American States, Inter-American Juridical Committee, "Work Accomplished by the Inter-American Juridical Committee During Its Regular Meeting, January 12-February 13, 1976, O.A.E./Ser. QIV.12.CJI-27 (hereafter cited as "Juridical Committee"), at 20.

26/ Foreign Office Hand Book No. 138, supra note 25, at 16.

27/ Id. at 15.

28/ Colonial Office List, supra note 7, at 102.

29/ Letters of Patent, supra note 6.

administrative designation "British Antarctic Territory." 30/ The British claim the first landing by Captain James Cook in 1775 on South Georgia and the first discovery of the South Sandwich Islands by him the same year. 31/ They note that sealers of many nationalities visited the Islands and state that the principal development took place in 1903 when C.A. Larsen founded the first modern whaling company in South Georgia. 32/ There were intermittent establishments of such shore factories until about 1920 when technology permitted the increased use of ships which operate continuously on the open ocean during the whaling season. After World War II, two shore stations were worked out of South Georgia but all stations ceased operation in 1965. 33/ For administrative purposes, the British have maintained a government station at King Edward Point at South Georgia, since 1909. This office had an administrative officer and an official staff, including customs and police officials; in 1912 a post office was added. After 1969, the administrative officer position was replaced by that of the Base Commander of the British Antarctic Survey, who became magistrate of the area. 34/

Britain sent magistrates to the South Shetlands and Graham Land at various times and maintained a post office at Port Foster, Deception Island, from 1912-1930. 35/ There were sporadic visits of the British Magistrate to the South Orkneys before 1928. 36/ Since 1944, the United Kingdom has sent ships to the South Shetlands, South Orkneys, and Graham Land every summer and

----

30/ Order in Council, supra note 8.

31/ Pleadings, supra note 3, at 11.

32/ It was, incidentally, an Argentine company, id. at 14.

33/ British Reference Services, supra note 7, at 6 and Great Britain, Foreign and Commonwealth Office, Falkland Islands and Dependencies, Report for the Years 1970 and 1971 68 (London, 1973), and Dependencies, Report for the Years 1970 and 1971 68 (London, 1973), hereafter cited as "Report."

34/ Id. and Pleadings, supra note 3, at 18. See also F.M. Auburn, Antarctic Law and Politics 48 (Bloomington, 1982), hereafter cited as "Auburn."

35/ Pleadings, supra note 3, at 18-19.

36/ Id.

has carried out extensive explorations and surveys of the territories through a special organization, the Falklands Islands Dependencies Survey. 37/ The British claim discovery, landing, and symbolic possession of the South Shetland Islands by William Smith, who discovered the Islands on February 18, 1819, and planted a British flag on them in October 1819, taking possession in the name of King George III. On February 4, 1820, a similar act was performed by Edward Bransfield, R.N., who was accompanied by William Smith, on the easternmost island of the group, the same act having been performed by two other Englishmen on the largest Island in the center of the group on January 16, 1820. Discovery and symbolic possession of the South Orkneys is laid to the British sealing Captain, George Powell, on December 6, 1821. First discovery of Graham Land is attributed to Bransfield, on January 30, 1820. Symbolic possession for the Crown was subsequently taken by a number of different British nationals. 38/

Argentina has run an observatory at Laurie Island in the South Orkneys since 1904, 39/ and since that date, "the Argentine colors have flown over the Island." Argentina also established a post office on the South Orkneys. 40/

In 1942, an Argentine naval transport installed a lighthouse on Lambda Island in the Melchior Archipelago, and in 1943, the same transport made topographic surveys of the area. On March 9, 1947, a luminous buoy was installed on Graham Land by the personnel of an Argentine-sponsored expedition, and on March 14, 1947, a similar beacon was installed on Duomer Island, at 64 degrees 32 latitude South. 41/ On March 26, 1947, a meteorological

----

37/ Id. at 19.

38/ Id. at 11-12.

39/ Marjorie M. Whiteman, 2 Dig. Int'l L. 1061 (Washington, Govt. Print. Off., 1963); Auburn, *supra* note 34 at 48, and Arce, *supra* note 14 at 113.

40/ Arce, id. at 112.

41/ Id. at 118-119.

station, equipped with radio-telegraphic installations, was inaugurated by Argentina on Gamma Island in the Melchior Archipelago. [42]/

By 1974, considerable interest had developed in the hydrocarbon reserves of the continental shelf of the Islands and Dependencies. Numerous license requests have been made, [43]/ and the Falkland Islands Legislative Council urged that they be granted. [44]/ In 1978, the United Kingdom reported that two private companies had completed seismic surveys in the waters surrounding the Islands. Press reports characterized the survey results as being "more encouraging than discouraging," and in mid-February 1981, it was announced that the largest Argentine offshore oil strike had been made near the Patagonian coast by the Shell Oil Company. The discovery resulted in a well whose flow rate is approximately 2,000 barrels a day. It was later reported that concessionary licenses were being sought for an area within 154 kilometers of the Falkland Islands, which includes an area that straddles what the United Kingdom regards as the "putative" line between Argentina and British territory. [45]/ Moreover, there is a strong likelihood that sizeable copper deposits are present on the Antarctic mainland. [46]/ The Antarctic

----

[42]/ Id. at 111 and 119.

[43]/ R.L. Fabrney, "Status of an Island's Continental Shelf Jurisdiction: A Case Study of the Falkland Islands (1979),"10(4) J. Mar. L. Com., 539.

[44]/ U.N. Doc. A/10023/Add.8 (Part III) (31 October 1975).

[45]/ U.N. General Assembly, Special Committee on the Situation with Regard to the Implementation of the Declaration on the Granting of Independence to Colonial Countries and Peoples, "Falkland Islands (Malvinas)," Working paper prepared by the Secretariat, p. 9, U.N. Doc. A/AC.109/670 (5 August 1981).

[46]/ Statement provided by Dr. James E. Mielke, Senior Analyst, Science Policy Resources Division, Library of Congress:

> The area of Antarctica where the claims of Argentina, Chile, and Great Britain overlap includes the Antarctic Peninsula. Geologically, the Antarctic Peninsula and the adjacent islands are the southern extension of the Andean Orogen of South America. The Andean zone of South America contains many, and in some cases large, ore deposits. These deposits include ores containing copper, molybdenum, iron, gold, tin, silver and other metals. Although there has been a paucity of mineral occurrences reported in the Antarctic Pensinsula, it would appear to be perhaps the most favorable region for mineral exploration in Antarctica. In addition, the higher proportion of exposed ice-free land area in the region would favor mineral exploration and discovery. Relative to more inland points, the potential for possible future

krill also represent a significant natural resource in the area. [47]/ It is against this economic backdrop that the Falklands dispute must be viewed.

IV. MODES OF ACQUISITION AND LOSS OF TERRITORIAL SOVEREIGNTY UNDER CUSTO-MARY INTERNATIONAL LAW

A. Modes of Acquisition

Sovereignty is considered to be one of the fundamental principles of customary international law. [48]/ Sovereignty has been defined as (1) the right to exercise state functions over territory to the exclusion of any other states and is described as follows in the words of Judge Huber in the Island of Palmas case:

> ...sovereignty in relation to a portion of the surface of the globe is the legal condition necessary for the inclusion of such portion in the territory of any particular State....
> Sovereignty in the relations between States signifies independence. Independence in regard to a portion of the globe is the right to exercise therein, to the exclusion of any other State, the functions of a State. [49]/

----

development would also be enhanced by the proximity of the ocean for potential port or shipping points.

As to the possible mineral potential in the region, the U.S. Geological Survey has performed a statistical analysis of the mineral potential of Antarctica based largely on geologic inference and analogy to related areas of the surrounding continents [see N.A. Wright and P.L. Williams, Mineral Resources of Antarctica, U.S. Geological Survey Circular 705, 1974]. This analysis suggests that the total number of mineral deposits that can be expected in the Andean geologic province would be around 380, of which only 16 would likely be in exposed areas. The mineral resource potential is further reduced, however, because the results of past exploration indicated that only a very small fraction of the mineral occurrences studied will likely have any signficant resource potential.

[Sept. 1982]

[47]/ Note that krill in the south Atlantic Ocean is the world's largest supply, see Auburn, supra note 34, at 205.

[48]/ G. Schwarzenberger, A Manual of International Law 35-36 (1976).

[49]/ Island of Palmas, 2 R.Int'l Arb. 829, 838 (1928).

Another commentator calls sovereignty "The freedom of a State from outside control in the conduct of its internal and external affairs." 50/ In the eyes of another scholar, it is regarded as "the supreme power of the State over its territory and inhabitants, and independence of any external authority." 51/

No unanimity exists as to the modes of acquiring territory (or losing it) in the international community; however, scholars traditionally seem to recognize five modes of acquisition. They are: cession, occupation, accretion, subjugation, and prescription. 52/

1. Cession

Cession is title derived from another state by the transfer of sovereignty of territory by the owner state to another state. Cession, however, can be effected only in a treaty between the ceding and the acquiring states. Cession may frequently be the outcome of a war, the result of a gift, sale, or exchange. Cession also requires possession or occupation by the new owner, unless the owner immediately cedes the territory to a third state. When such occupation takes place, the subjects domiciled in the newly acquired territory become subjects of the acquiring state, absent agreement to the contrary. There is, however, precedent in the several treaties of session concluded during the nineteenth century that cession should only be valid provided the inhabitants consented to it through a plebiscite. 53/ Assuming an agreement of session permits inhabitants the option of retaining

---

50/ M. Gamboa, A Dictionary of International Law and Diplomacy 244 (Quezon City, 1973).

51/ M. Korowicz, "Some Present Aspects of Sovereignty in International Law," 102 Recueil des Cours 1 at 108 (1961).

52/ L. Oppenheim (ed. by H. Lauterpacht), 1 International Law 546 (London, 1955). Whiteman, supra note 39, at 1028 also lists "discovery" as a primary mode.

53/ Oppenheim, id. at 551, note 6 citing Rivier, 1 Principes du droit des gens 210 (1896).

their old citizenship, the acquiring state has the right to expel such persons, absent an express stipulation to the contrary. Another option may be the option to emigrate within a certain period of time. 54/

International law prescribes no set format for cession to occur. What is essential, however, is that it take place with the full "consent of the governments concerned." 55/

2. Occupation

Occupation is the act of appropriation of territory which is not at the time under the sovereignty of another state (res nullius). It differs from subjugation in that in the case of subjugation, the territory acquired previously belongs to another state. 56/ For example, an uninhabited island not considered to be part of a state would be a classic example of a territory ripe for appropriation by occupation. However, once occupied, if later abandoned, it would again be vulnerable for occupation by another state.

Occupation must be effective occupation for a state to acquire territory. It requires both possession and administration. Possession would require the presence of a settlement coupled with some formal act such as a flag raising or formal proclamation to indicate that the possessor intends to keep the territory under his sovereignty. The requirement of administration is met by establishing some sort of administration that exercises governing functions. However, before the eighteenth century, a real taking of possession was not necessary, and it was possible to acquire sovereignty by means of symbolic acts. 57/ Thus, today, although discovery does not constitute acquisition through occupation, it does confer an inchoate title and acts as a temporary bar to occupation by another state for a period of time which would reasonably permit occupation to take place. If such occupation does not take place, the inchoate title dies. Finally, it is important to note

----

54/ This was a right guaranteed by Article 2 of the Peace Treaty of Frankfurt, 1871, which ended the Franco-Prussian War and ceded Alsace and Lorraine to Germany. See Oppenheim, id. at 553.

55/ Whiteman, supra note 39, at 1088.

56/ Oppenheim, supra note 52, at 555.

57/ Id. at 558.

that occupation of a territory does not extend sovereignty over neighboring territories. 58/

3. Accretion

Accretion is the term given to an increase in existing land masses by new geological changes, such as the formation of a new island in a river. 59/ As this form of acquisition of territory is not relevant to the Falkland case, it need not be discussed further here.

4. Subjugation

Conquest which has been firmly established and is followed by formal annexation constitutes the acquisition of title by subjugation. Before the Covenant of the League of Nations, subjugation was a widely recognized form of acquisition of territory. 60/ In order for subjugation to take effect, there must be an end to the state of war, either by a formal peace treaty or by simple cessation of hostilities. Annexation that takes place during a war does not constitute a firmly established conquest, which is a necessary prerequisite for acquisition of title through subjugation. 61/

5. Prescription

Prescription is a means of acquiring territory which is subject to the sovereignty of another state.

> Prescription in International Law may be defined as the acquisition of sovereignty over a territory through continuous and undisturbed exercise of sovereignty over it during such period as is necessary to create under the influence of historical development the general conviction that the present condition of things is in conformity with international order. Thus, prescription in International Law has the same

---

58/ Id. at 450. However, Lord Palmerston in 1834 appears to have suggested that the proximity of Lobos Island to Peru gave Peru prima facie title to it. J. Moore, 4 International Arbitrations 3554 (1898); see also 31 B.F.S.P. 1097 (1842-43).

59/ Oppenheim, supra note 52, at 563.

60/ Id. at 570.

> rational basis as prescription in Municipal
> Law--namely, considerations of stability and
> order...<u>62</u>/

However, despite the recognition of the United States Supreme Court
of this principle, it cannot be said that any general rule exists as to
length of time or other circumstances necessary to create a title by prescription. <u>63</u>/ Schwarzenberger, for example, appears to place heavy emphasis on
recognition as a means of establishing the validity of a new title in relation to other states. He notes that:

> A State may perfect a title to a territory
> by exercising peaceful and effective juris-
> diction over the territory for a prolonged
> period. By virtue of the rules governing the
> principle of good faith, prolonged inaction on
> the part of third States which, at one time,
> might have been in a position to contest the
> claims of the State in effective occupation,
> gradually comes to be viewed as acquiescence.
> Then, such States are estopped from contesting
> the occupant's title. This title to terri-
> tory, known traditionally as <u>acquisitive pre-
> scription</u>, is actually a title with multiple
> roots and is based on the interplay of the
> rules underlying the principles of sover-
> eignty, consent and good faith. [Citations
> omitted.] <u>64</u>/

It is important to note that the Spanish-American republics have
adopted a principle related to prescription, in contrast to the aforementioned principle, which has not been generally accepted by other nations. <u>65</u>/
This principle, <u>uti possidetis</u>, does not require occupation as a basis for
sovereignty and has been characterized as an expression of the will of those
Latin American countries which had formed part of the Spanish Colonial Empire
to have their frontiers follow the former administrative colonial frontiers.
Thus, territories which have never been occupied by Spain or any of the Latin
American states were considered occupied by legal fiction by these states

----

<u>62</u>/ Oppenheim, <u>supra</u> note 52, at 576, cited from Arkansas v. Tennessee
310 U.S. 563 at 570 (1940).

<u>63</u>/ <u>Id</u>. at 575-576.

<u>64</u>/ Schwarzenberger, <u>supra</u> note 48, at 98.

<u>65</u>/ Whiteman, <u>supra</u> note 39, at 1068.

from the first hour. This rule also functioned as a "pre-Monroe Doctrine" doctrine by excluding recognition to territory which non-American states might desire to acquire on the American continent. 66/ This differing perception of applicable rules complicates even further the resolution of the Falkland Islands sovereignty dispute.

In this context, the following observation takes on added meaning:

> On winning independence from Spain, Argentina automatically became heir to all Spanish dominions within the area which had been the vice royalty of Rio de la Plata. As the southern limits of this vice royalty have never been specified, Argentina claims her dominion toward the south is unlimited. 67/

Therefore, as a corollary to the aforementioned concept of uti possidetis, comes the Latin American view which does not recognize effective occupation as the criterion for sovereignty. Thus again, European and North American views differ with those of Latin America on wnat rules govern. The language of one scholar summed up this issue as follows:

> While Europeans and North Americans on the whole regard effective occupation as the criterion of sovereignty, no Latin American government or jurist will admit that mere physical occupation of a territory can constitute valid title to sovereignty. 68/

Finally, although no general rule can be laid down on the length of time or other circumstances necessary to create title by prescription, if other states protest and pursue claims, the actual exercise of sovereignty over the territory is not undisturbed nor is there the prerequisite conviction that the status quo is in conformity with international order. 69/

66/ Id. at 1079.

67/ Id. at 1060.

68/ J. Daniel "Conflict of Sovereignties in the Antarctic," Y. B. World Aff. 252, at 262 and 268 (1949).

69/ Oppenheim, supra note 52, at 577. Note also, pursuant to a treaty between Great Britain and Venezuela on February 2, 1897, it was agreed that "Adverse holding or prescription during a period fifty years shall make good title." Id. at 477, note 2.

B. Modes of Loss of Territorial Sovereignty Under Customary Inter-national Law

Sovereignty may be lost in the five corresponding ways in which it is acquired, namely, cession, derelection (abandonment of occupation), opera-tions of nature, subjugation, and prescription. Property may also be lost by revolt when the state which has broken off from another has established it-self safely and permanently. 70/

The six modes described above are basically self explanatory; how-ever, derelection requires special attention in the context of this study. As occupation requires physical possession and intent to acquire sovereignty, so derelection requires physical abandonment plus lack of will or ability to repossess. If and when territory becomes derelect, another state may acquire it through occupation. However, when occupation of a territory deemed to be derelect occurs, it is not uncommon for the former owner to protest and to try to prevent the new occupier from acquiring it. 71/

V. UNITED STATES POLICY ON SOVEREIGNTY OVER THE FALKLANDS

In his testimony before the House Foreign Affairs Subcommittee on Inter-American Affairs, Assistant Secretary of State for Inter-American Affairs Thomas O. Enders emphatically re-affirmed United States policy on the Falkland's sovereignty issue:

> The United States takes no position on
> the merits of the competing claims to
> sovereignty, nor on the legal theories on
> which the parties rely. 72/

70/ Id. at 578-579.

71/ Id. at 580. For a more detailed discussion of the means of acquisi-tion and loss of territory, see Whiteman, supra note 39, at 1028-1132.

72/ Prepared Statement of Thomas O. Enders, Assistant Secretary of State for Inter-American Affairs Before the Subcommittee on Inter-American Affairs, U.S. House of Representatives, Washington, D.C., August 5, 1982, hereafter cited as "Enders Statement." Note: this statement is consistent with decisions of the United States Courts' which recognized that the United States Government did not support the sovereignty claims of Argentina to the Falklands. See Williams v. Suffolk Insurance Company 38 U.S.(13 Pet.) 415 (1839). (However, non-recognition of Argentine sovereignty does not necessarily imply recognition of British sovereignty.) In another case, Davidson v. Seal-Skins, 2 Paine 324, 7 Fed. Cas. 192 (C.C.D. Conn, 1835) (No. 3,661), the Court noted that a dispute existed between the United States and Buenos Aires as to whether or not American citizens had a right to take seals upon the Falkland

This statement is in line with the conclusions reached in an internal Department of State research project conducted in 1947. The study confirmed that neither British nor Argentine claims were admitted as being valid or determinative of the sovereignty issue and stressed that such policy was consistent with the United States policy of non-intervention in foreign controversies. After a detailed historical analysis, the study summarized the current (1947) United States policy regarding conflicting British-Argentine claims as follows:

> (a) The United States accepts and works with the de facto situation; (b) it accepts tacitly but by unmistakable implication the de jure sovereignty of the United Kingdom over the Islands, although there has been a tendency even in intra-departmental statements to avoid clear cut, categorical recognition of British sovereignty; (c) It seeks to avoid exacerbating Argentine sensibilities by refraining so far as possible from public explicit commitment on the dispute. 73/

The latter statement regarding "exacerbating Argentine sensibilities," would seem to imply that if the United States were to have made a public commitment on the issue in 1947, it would have been unfavorable to the Argentinians. In

----

Islands but noted clearly that: " these islands were held in the possession and under the jurisdiction of the Buenos Ayrean government, and Vernet's establishment then was under the authority and protection of that government." (7 Fed. Cas. 192, 196). For a brief history of U.S. claims to prescriptive fishing rights on and near the Falklands, see H.D. Reid, International Servitudes in Law and Practice, 64-68 (Chicago, 1932). See also 82 Dep't St. Bull. 81-89 (June 1982) for U.S. policy generally.

73/ U.S. Department of State, "The United States Position Respecting Argentine-British Claims to the Falkland Islands," Research Project No. 55 (6/24/47) p. 8, hereafter cited as "United States Position." Note, however, that this paper does not have any official standing as a formal Department of State viewpoint and represents only the personal viewpoints of the researcher whose position with the Department of State at the time was not one at a policy-making level. It is of interest, however, from the historical viewpoint, within the context of these limitations. Recent United States support for a General Assembly Resolution (Agenda item no. 135, 37th Session, U.N. Doc. A/37/L.3/Rev 1), introduced by Argentina, is not on its face, despite British protests, inconsistent with U.S. policy to remain neutral on the sovereignty issue. The resolution, introduced well after the latest cesssation of armed hostilities, called for negotiations between the parties and was passed by a final vote of 90 to 12, with 53 abstentions. See also Michael J. Berlin, "U.N. Backs Talks on Falklands," Wash. Post, November 5, 1982, at 1.

fact, a world map prepared for the Department of State by the American Geographical Society in 1947 portrayed the Islands as "(U.K.) (Claimed by Argentina)." An internal Department of State memorandum at the time commented on this indication as follows: "This makes it clear that we regard the Islands as British, but wish to indicate the Argentine claim." This memorandum was cleared and apparently was regarded "as an official, although not public, expression of policy." 74/

An argument could be made that, on its face, the United States position might appear to be a violation of the Monroe Doctrine by permitting intervention or domination by a non-hemispheric state and by condoning an extension of a portion of the European system to the Western Hemisphere. However, the United States position has been that as British presence on the Islands had predated the doctrine, it was inapplicable to the controversy. Material submitted by Secretary Enders addresses the issue as follows:

> United States neutrality is also reflected in the United States position on the non-applicability of the Monroe Doctrine. Because the dispute over the Islands predated the Monroe Doctrine, and because the United States took no position on the dispute over sovereignty, the State Department long ago expressed the view that the reinsertion of a British presence on the Islands in 1833 was not a new attempt at colonization, and that the Doctrine is thus inapplicable. 75/

74/ Id. at 6. For U.S. policy relating to self-determination in general, see E.S. Lent, "American Foreign Policy and the Principle of Self-Determination," 133 World Affairs 293-303 (March 1971), and for U.S. policy relating to colonial territories and peoples in general, see S.M. Finger, "United States Reviews Question of Colonial Territories and Peoples, " 60 Dep't St. Bull. No. 1561, 452-454.

75/ See "Legal Aspects of Falkland/Malvinas Crisis Negotiations," attached to Enders Statement, supra note 72, at 1, which states that the United States considers the Monroe Doctrine a statement of policy which could be renounced unilaterally, although Latin American jurists tend to disagree. See Whiteman, supra note 39, at 1061. Note also that the terms of the doctrine specifically preclude any retroactive operation. See Goebel, supra note 14, at 464.

Furthermore, it is interesting to note that the Inter-American treaty
of Reciprocal Assistance (Rio Treaty of 1947), 76/ under Article 4, extends
to the South Pole, and because south of South America, the boundaries are 90
degrees West and 24 degrees West, the Treaty text might be interpreted as
preventing the United States from supporting Great Britain in the event of an
armed confrontation between it and South American countries over the Falklands or the Dependencies. 77/ However, as a U.S. declaration to the treaty
stated that the Treaty had no effect on the status of sovereignties in the
region, a better position would be to hold it inapplicable to the current
conflict between Britain and Argentina.

VI.   THE ARGENTINE POSITION
The crux of the Argentine position lies with rights claimed by virtue
of Argentina's succession to Spanish sovereignty over the Malvinas. Spanish
rights, it is argued, go back to the Pontifical Concession of May 4, 1493,
when Pope Alexander VI promulgated the Bull _Inter Caetera_, awarding to the
Crown of Castile all the mainland and the islands of the sea, discovered and
to be discovered in the future, beyond the imaginary line dividing the world
at the time 78/ and the subsequent redivision between Spain and Portugal by

---

76/   21 U.N.T.S. 78.

77/   Auburn, _supra_ note 34, at 57, note 80. Certainly an Argentine
attack against the United Kingdom proper, under Articles 5 and 6 of the North
Atlantic Treaty of April 4, 1949, would be considered an attack against all
N.A.T.O. signatories, including the United States. It is interesting to
speculate, however, whether an Argentine attack against a British vessel in
the North Atlantic or in a British port might have been grounds for invoking
the treaty.

78/   Boniface del Carril, _The Malvinas/Falklands Case_ 34 (Buenos Aires,
1981).

the Treaty of Tordesillas in 1494. 79/ Furthermore, according to the Argentine view, Article 8 of the second Peace Treaty of Utrecht (1713) between Britain and Spain guaranteed Spanish possessions in the Americas against further British action. Consequently, in 1770, Spain compelled British settlers to leave the Islands. 80/ Such a view is further reinforced by the fact that the Saint Lawrence Convention of 1790 appears to have prohibited either Britain or Spain from establishing new settlements on islands adjacent to the coasts of South America, thereby preserving the status quo at the

----

79/   C.H.M. Waldock, "Disputed Sovereignty in the Falkland Islands Dependencies," 25 B.Y.I.L. 311 at 319 (1948). Under that agreement, however, it appears that Spain purported to get rights west of the 48th parallel and Portugal to the east of it. According to such a reading, South Georgia, the South Sandwich and the South Orkney Islands would be under Portuguese sovereignty and not Spanish sovereignty. Furthermore, it is maintained that these documents define respective spheres of annexation between the parties only.

80/ For the text of Article 8, see Goebel, supra note 14, at 166, and 28 Parry's T.S. 325,328. See also Auburn, supra note 34, at 52.

time. 81/   An outline of the Argentine position prepared by the Argentine
Embassy in Washington bases the Argentine claim to sovereignty over the
Malvinas primarily on the following:

1) discovery by Spain;

2) France and England expressed recognition of Spanish sovereignty
    by many treaties;

3) peaceful occupation and administration by 19 Spanish governors
    since 1774 until Argentina's independence;

4) succession of states;

5) recognition of Argentina's independence by Britain in 1825 with-
    out any claim to the Islands, which were then under the ruling of
    an Argentine governor living in the Islands; and

6) peaceful and undisputed occupation and administration by five
    Argentine governors (in the Lexington incident, Argentine rights
    to the Islands were never at stake).

81/ Malvinas Islands Statement, supra note 11, at 7-8. Note that a whole
series of other agreements may be interpreted as British agreement not to
challenge the Spanish sphere of influence in the Western Hemisphere, i.e.,
between Spain and Great Britain:
     a) Article 8, Treaty of Peace and Friendship Between Great Britain
and Spain, signed at Madrid 13(23) May 1667, 10 Parry's T.S. 63, incor-
porating the provisions of the Treaty of Peace Between Spain and the
Netherlands signed at Muster, 30 January 1648, 1 Parry's T.S. 1.
     b) Articles 1 and 7, Treaty Between Great Britain and Spain, signed
at Westminster (Madrid?), 8(18) July 1670, 11 Parry's T.S. 383.
     c) Article 14, Preliminary Treaty of Peace Between Great Britain and
Spain, signed at Madrid, 27 March 1713, 27 Parry's T.S. 455 and the Treaty
of Peace and Friendship Between Great Britain and Spain, signed at
Utrecht, 13 July 1713, 28 Parry's T.S. 295.
     d) Treaty of Peace, Union, Amity and Mutual Defence Between France,
Great Britain and Spain, signed at Seville, 9 November 1929, 33 Parry's
T.S. 253.
     e) Definitive Treaty of Peace Between France, Great Britain and
Spain, signed at Paris, 10 February 1763, 42 Parry's T.S. 251. For the
text of Articles V and XVII, see 20 B.F.S.P. 426-427 (1832-33).
     f) Convention Between Great Britain and Spain (Saint Lawrence Con-
vention) signed at the Escurial, 28 October 1790, 51 Parry's T.S. 67.
     For a detailed reasoning of this point, see Arce, supra note 14, at
147-154. See also Malvinas Islands Statement, supra note 11, at 7-8, and
C.P. Preece et al., "The Falkland/Malvinas Islands Crisis, Appendix," Congressional Research Service, Issue Brief No. IB82052 (1982), Library of Congress, Washington, D.C.

Under the Argentine line of reasoning, the British displacement of the Argentinians from the Islands in 1833 was "an act of usurpation of its [Argentina's] national territory, usurpation carried out by unacceptable and illegal means," as asserted recently by Argentine Foreign Minister Costa Mendez, speaking before the U.N. Security Council:

> ...the reason for the calling of these meetings lies in the Malvinas Islands, which is [sic] part of Argentine territory and which was illegally occupied by the United Kingdom in 1833 by an act of force which deprived our country of that archipelago.
>
> The British fleet in 1833 displaced by force the Argentine population and the authorities which were exercising the legitimate rights that belonged to the Republic at that time as the heir to Spain.
>
> Legally speaking, that act of force cannot give rise to any right at all, and politically the events of 1833 were one more reflection of the imperialist policy which the European States carried out in the nineteenth century at the expense of America, Africa, and Asia. Hence, we can say today that this is a colonial problem in the most traditional sense of that political and economic phenomenon.
>
> Since 1833, the Republic of Argentina has been claiming reparation from the United Kingdom for the great wrong done. The Republic of Argentina has never consented to that act of usurpation of its national territory, usurpation carried out by unacceptable and illegal means. All the successive Governments of Argentina, regardless of party or faction, have remained united and steadfast in their position during those 149 years of strongly protesting against that arbitrary occupation. [Translation from the Spanish.] 82/

Argentine authorities staunchly reject the concept that the principle of self-determination should be applied to the inhabitants of the Malvinas and note that the South Sandwich and South Georgia Islands have no real population to speak of. The Argentine Foreign Minister has expressed this viewpoint in the following words:

> ...As the President of my country has said, we are ready to guarantee all the individual rights of the inhabitants. But we cannot allow anyone to use those 1,800 persons as something enshrined in international law as a "population." 83/

82/ U.N. Security Council, Doc. S/PV. 2350, 3 April 1982.

83/ Id. at 7. Contrast the Argentine position with that reportedly taken by Argentina at the 1940 Inter-American Meeting in Havana:

This position was expounded in further detail by the Argentine Embassy in Washington as follows:

> De facto and de jure, the islands belonged to the Argentine Republic in 1833 and were governed by Argentine authorities and occupied by Argentine settlers. These authorities and these settlers were evicted by violence and not allowed to return to the territory. On the contrary, they were replaced, during those 149 years of usurpation, by a colonial administration and a population of British origin, now numbering some 1800 inhabitants. It is basically a temporary population that occupies the land and one that cannot be used by the colonial power in order to claim the right to apply the principle of self-determination.
>
> Therefore, this principle would be ill-applied in cases like this, where part of the territory of an independent state has been wrested--against the will of its inhabitants--by an act of force, by a third State, without there being any subsequent international agreement to validate the de facto situation and where on the contrary, the aggrieved state has constantly protested the situation. [84]/

An important issue at [this Meeting] in Havana, Cuba, was the question of European colonies in the Western Hemisphere. The United States favored a collective trusteeship over colonies of metropolitan nations conquered by the Axis powers. It was Argentina that opposed the plan, insisting that any decisions on the transfer of sovereignty of those colonies should rest with the inhabitants of those territories themselves.

(Anthony P. Maingot, "The Falklands for the Falklanders," Miami Herald, April 25, 1982, at 3E.)

[84]/ Untitled 6-paged memo on the Malvinas Islands and its dependencies, distributed by the Embassy of Argentina, Washington, D.C., July 26, 1982.

Thus, under the Argentine view, "...British presence on the Islands is an anachronism and must be eliminated." 85/

Argentina's position on the sovereignty issue has received support in the international legal community. 86/ In the April 3, 1982, Security Council debate, the Argentine assertion of the validity of Argentine claim to sovereignty over the Malvinas received support from the following nations: Bolivia, Brazil, Panama, Paraguay, Peru, Uganda. 87/

On January 16, 1976, the Inter-American Juridical Committee (a consultative body to the OAS on juridical matters established by the OAS Charter (arts. 105-111)) came out in full support of the Argentine position: 88/

> Recalling the just title the Republic of Argentina possesses to sovereignty over the Malvinas Islands, based on the international rules in force at the time the dispute began; that the archipelago appears in the nautical charts of the South Atlantic prepared by the cartographers of the Casa de Contratacion of Seville (1522-23), in connection with the voyage of Magellan; that the first effective occupation of the aforementioned islands, made by a group of French colonists, concluded with the agreement of 1767 by which they handed over those islands to the Spanish authorities under the Government

----

85/ Malvinas Islands Statement, supra, note 11, at 15. Note: this statement covers in great detail the Argentine position and is thus an indispensable source. Also not to be overlooked is the letter to the Editor of the Wash. Times, July 9, 1982, at 7A, entitled "Argentina's case for sovereignty," by Estaban A. Takacs, the Argentine Ambassador to Washington, and Sumner Welles, "Falklands Dispute, Job for Pan-American Consultation," Wash. Post, March 2, 1948, at 11, as well as Pablo D. Valle, "The Falklands Dispute; an Argentine View," Christian Sci. Mon., April 28, 1982, at 22.

86/ See Goebel, supra, note 14; Carril, supra note 78; Arce, supra note 14; Welles, id., and Valle, id.

87/ Security Council Provisional Verbatim Record, supra note 82, at 32 (Bolivia) 21 (Brazil), 343-45 (Panama), 63-65 (Paraguay), 33-35 (Peru), 91 (Uganda). Council Debates: It is interesting to note that neither China nor the USSR came out in support of the Argentine position on sovereignty. The USSR supported an end to the colonial status of the Islands (p. 96) and China favored negotiations, taking note, that the non-aligned nations have supported the Argentine claims (id. at 106), although not themselves offering formal support to the Argentinians. (For a chronology of non-aligned national support, see id. at 36). The Falklands situation poses a dilemma for nations which espouse both an end to colonialism and at the same time the principle of self-determination of peoples. To give support to the latter principle in this case might be considered tantamount to support of colonial actions.

88/ Juridical Committee, supra note 25.

and Captaincy General (Capitania General) of Buenos Aires; that the occupation of the Malvinas Island by the English was only partial, since it was confined to Puerto Egmont, and temporary, since after eight years (1766-74) it was abandoned; that by decree of June 10, 1829, the Government of the United Provinces of the River Plate (Provincias Unidas del Rio de la Plata) established a political and military government in the Malvinas Islands, under the Civil and Military commandant Louis Vernet; that on January 3, 1833, the English corvette Clio violenty dislodged the Argentine authorities there established and proceeded to illegitimate occupation by the United Kingdom; that the Argentine Government has constantly maintained its claim to its right since the first moment of the dispute (note from the Argentine Minister in London dated June 17, 1823) and during all the time since;... 89/

In conclusion, as its first declaration, the Committee declared as follows:

DECLARES:

1. That the Republic of Argentina has an undeniable right of sovereignty over the Malvinas Islands, for which reason the basic question to be resolved is that of the procedure to be followed for restoring its territory to it... 90/

Furthermore, the OAS, in its Twentieth Meeting of Consultation of Ministers of Foreign Affairs, which took place in Washington, D.C., on April 26, 1982, in a resolution transmitted to the President of the U.N. Security Council, took note of the 1976 Declaration of the Inter-American Juridical Committee relating to Argentina's "undeniable right of sovereignty over the Malvinas Islands." 91/ Thus, the group resolved, among other items:

3. To urge those governments [the United Kingdom and Argentina] immediately to call a truce that will make it possible to resume and proceed normally with the negotiation aimed at a peaceful settlement of the conflict, tak- ing into account the rights of sovereignty of the Republic of Argentina over the Malvinas (Falkland) Islands and the interests of the islanders [emphasis provided]. 92/

89/ Id. at 18 and 20.

90/ Id. at 21. The authority of the committee to deal with this issue and to approve such a declaration as a "judicial" body has been questioned by at least one of its eleven members. S.J. Rubin, "The Falklands (Malvinas), International Law, and the O.A.S.," 76 Am.J.Int'l L. 594 (1982).

91/ For text, see U.N. Security Council Document S/13008, Annex, p. 1 or OEA/Ser. F/II.20, Doc. 28/82, rev. 3, 28 April 1982. See also B. Crossette, "O.A.S. Backs Argentine on Sovereignty," N.Y.Times, April 29, 1982, at A.19.

92/ Document, id.

VII. THE BRITISH POSITION

The current British position on the British claim to sovereignty over the Falklands is rooted in the following sequence of events:

1) Early and probably first sighting and discovery (sighting by John Davis in 1592 and Sir John Hawkins in 1594).

2) The first known landing in 1690 by Captain John Strong who named the Islands after Viscount Falkland, then Secretary of the Navy.

3) Establishment in 1766 of a settlement of about 400 people at Port Egmont, West Falkland (in 1770, the Spanish forced the British to leave but allowed reestablishment of the settlement in (1771). This settlement remained until 1774 when the British withdrew on grounds of economy but left a plaque declaring the Falkland Islands to be British property.)

4) Withdrawal of the Spanish settlement on West Falkland in 1811.

5) British protests to the fact that Luis Vernet was appointed governor of the Falkland Islands by the Buenos Aires Government noticing the Spanish restitution of Port Egmont and asserting that the British evacuating of 1774 had not constituted abandonment.

6) British repossession of Port Egmont in 1832 and occupation of Port Louis in 1833.

7) Open, continuous, effective, and peaceful, occupation since 1833 [emphasis provided]. 93/

Thus, the British position as stated in 1829 94/ was one to the effect that Britain's claim had been recognized by Spain in 1771 and that Britain had not legally abandoned her claim to the territory when she left the Islands in 1774. Modern British sources also state that Argentina's claim is based mainly on her claim to have been the successor to the Spanish Viceroyalty of the River Plate and emphasize that the Viceroyalty also

----

93/ British Reference Services, supra note 7, and The Facts, supra note 10.

94/ 20 B.F.S.P. 346 (1832-33).

governed most of what is today the countries of Uruguay, Paraguay, Bolivia, and Chile. 95 /

British sources also claim that South Georgia and the South Sandwich Islands are legally distinct from the Falkland Islands and that "the root of British title to them is different from that to the Falkland Islands themselves." 96/ A summary of the British position on the Dependencies reads as follows:

> South Georgia and the South Sandwich Islands are British Dependent Territories, legally distinct from the Falkland Islands; but for convenience they are administered by the Falkland Islands Government which is empowered to legislate for them. Captain Cook landed and took formal possession of South Georgia in 1775. The Island became a centre for sealing and whaling from the nineteenth century; but all shore stations ceased operations by December 1965. In 1908 the British Government annexed South Georgia by Letters Patent; since then the Island has been under continuous British administration. A magistrate, who is also the Base Commander of the British Anarctic Survey Stations, resides at King Edward Point in South Georgia.
>
> The South Sandwich Islands were discovered by Captain Cook on the same voyage in 1775; they were similarly annexed in 1908 and have been under continuous British administration since that date.
>
> The first Argentine claim to South Georgia dates only from 1927; they made no claim to the South Sandwich Islands before 1948. The two groups of Islands lie about 1800 and 2300 km from Argentina. Before their annexation by the British, the Dependencies were never occupied by Argentina. The root of British title to them is different from that to the Falkland Islands themselves. Whatever claim Argentina may have to the Falkland Islands cannot apply to the Dependencies. In 1947 and subsequently, Britain offered to submit the dispute over the Dependencies to the International Court of Justice. In 1955 the British Government applied unilaterally to the Court for redress against encroachments on British sovereignty by Argentina, which, however, declined to submit to the Court's jurisdiction in the matter. 97/

95/ The Facts, <u>supra</u> note 10, at 2.

96/ <u>Id</u>. at 4.

97/ <u>Id</u>. at 5.

The modern British position also argues for the rights of the people of the Falkland Islands, outlined as follows in the words of spokesman Sir Anthony Parsons before the U.N. Security Council:

> The Foreign Minister of Argentina argued that the people of the Falkland Islands are not a population in international law. Those 1,800 or 1,900 people are not recent arrivals in the Islands. The vast majority of them were born there to families which had been settled there for four, five, six generations since the first half of the nineteenth century. In the judgment of my government, whether they are 1,800 or 18,000 or 18 million, they are still entitled to the protection of international law and they are entitled to have their freely expressed wishes respected. 98/

VIII. ANALYSIS OF SOVEREIGNTY RIGHTS

A. The Islands

1. Argentina v. Britain. Both British and Argentine sources appear to be in agreement that the first physical occupation of the Islands took place in 1764 when a small French colony was established by de Bougainville in East Falkland. 99/

Again, both sides appear to be in agreement that Spain's title to the Islands was obtained from (or re-affirmed by) the French by virtue of a treaty of succession of 1766. 100/ Thus, Spanish title in 1766 appears not to be contested.

The same sources confirm that in 1766 the British established a settlement at Port Egmont and that they were forced to leave the Island by the Spanish in 1770. By declaration of January 22, 1771, 101/ the Spanish returned Port Egmont to Britain. The text of this declaration included a statement to the effect that such restitution would not affect the question of the prior

----

98/ Provisional Verbatim Record, supra note 82, at 72; see also Maingot, supra note 83.

99/ Malvinas Island Statement, supra note 11, at 4 and British Reference Service, supra note 7.

100/ 22 B.F.S.P. 1383 (1832-34); Goebel, supra note 14, at 228; Malvinas Islands Statement, supra note 11, at 4; British Reference Services, supra note 7, at 2; and Carril, supra note 78, at 40.

101/ 22 B.F.S.P. 1387 (1832-34).

right of sovereignty over the Islands. 102/ It is uncontroverted that the British left the Islands on May 20, 1774. They left behind a lead plaque with an inscription purporting to reserve the Island for Britain. 103/

Thus it would appear that in 1774 the British abandoned their settlement in West Falkland while the Spanish kept their settlement on East Falkland until 1811. 104/

In summary, therefore, the situation at least from 1766 onward was one as follows: Spain had sovereignty from the French; Spain expelled the British in 1770; Spain permitted the British to re-occupy Saunders Island (West Falkland) (1771); Great Britain did so but left again in 1774, leaving Spain again in control of the Islands. Even though Great Britain had left, leaving behind a symbolic reservation of her rights, this did not affect the

----

102/   Goebel, supra note 14, at 358-360. It was subsequently argued by Don Manuel Moreno in 1833 that in the 1771 declaration contained a secret oral understanding that the British would later abandon the Islands and that British evacuation in 1774 confirmed this. However, no concrete evidence of such an agreement could be located. See 22 B.F.S.P. 1377, 1388 (1832-34) and also 20 B.F.S.P. 411-412 (1832-33).

103/   See supra page 5 and notes 14-16 concerning how each side claims the plaque was worded.

104/   In the words of the noted British scholar, M.F. Lindley:

> In 1832 Great Britain again took possession of the Islands, in spite of the vigorous protests of the Argentine Republic. But it cannot be said that the notice left on the fort, which, moreover, appears to have been destroyed in 1781, was sufficient evidence, over the whole intervening period, of her intention to retake the island, and it would appear that any rights she may have had in 1774 had been abandoned long before 1832
>
> (M.F. Lindley, The Acquisition and Government of Backward Territory in International Law 51 (London, 1926)).

For additional support for the contention that British actions in 1774 constituted an "abandonment," see "The Argentine Claim to the Falkland Islands," The Review No. 28, at 29 (1982).

Note also that the British similarly evacuated Santa Lucia but attempted to maintain ongoing claims to it, Oppenheim, supra, note 52, at 580. Note further that a finding to the effect that British actions in 1774 formed the basis for an abandonment of the Islands would give Argentina a strong link in her claim to subsequent title.

validity of the Spanish title. 105/ The reason for this conclusion is that nothing in the compromise of 1771 removed title from Spain, the country which legally had it then. In 1820 when the Islands had been vacant for 9 years, the Spanish having left in 1811, the Buenos Aires Government--which had declared its independence from Spain in 1816--sent a ship to the Falkland Islands to claim sovereignty for the Government. A governor was appointed in 1823. 106/ However, no permanent occupation occurred until 1826 when Louis Vernet established a settlement at Port Soledad, on the Islands. 107/ By decree of June 10, 1829, Vernet was appointed Governor of the Islands and of the large Island of Tierra del Fuego, as well. 108/

When the decree became known in Buenos Aires, Woodbine Parish, the British Chargé d'Affaires, delivered a formal protest against the decree, noting that "the Argentine Republic, in issuing this Decree, [has] assumed

----

105/ Goebel, supra note 14, at 411.

106/ Malvinas Islands Statement, supra note 11, at 9.

107/ British Reference Service, supra note 7, at 2 and Goebel, supra, note 14, at 434.

108/ For text of Vernet's appointment, see 20 B.F.S.P. 314-315 (1832-33). Note further that it appears that Vernet's settlement-- which was established in 1826--was established under a concession granted in 1823 by the Argentine Government but not on behalf of or for the Argentine Government. It was only in 1829 by decree that for the first time a military commandancy (colony) was established and Vernet appointed Commandant. See Goebel, supra note 14, at 434 and H.A. Smith, Great Britain and the Law of Nations 59 (London, 1935; New York, reprint 1975).
   Tierra de Fuego is approximately 300 miles from the Falklands and title to it was for a long time in dispute between Chile and Argentina. This dispute was settled in 1881 by a treaty giving the greater part of the Island to Chile. Smith, id. at 58 and Auburn, supra note 34, at 57. This decree claimed title from Spain and dated Argentine independence from 1810. However, in 1810, the Government of Buenos Aires controlled only part of the territory of the Spanish Viceroyalty of Rio de la Plata; this territory including the republics of Bolivia, Paraguay, and Uruguay as well. Thus it has been said that any of these governments might have had as good a claim as the Government of Buenos Aires to succeed to Spanish title in the Falklands. Smith, id. at 58. Chilean claims to the South Shetlands and Graham Land have an entirely different basis. Pleadings, supra note 3, at 64.

authority incompatible with His Britannic Majesty's rights of Sovereignty over the Falkland Islands," citing as he did so, British rights from discovery and the restoration of occupation in 1771. 109/

In July of 1831, Vernet seized the first of three American whaling vessels and imprisoned their crews. The U.S. responded by sending the U.S.S. Lexington, under Commander Duncan, to the Islands. On December 31, 1831, the colony was broken up, leaving the Falklands administratively unoccupied until January 1833 when the British took possession. 110/

The case is strong that the Spanish withdrawal of their settlement in 1811 or earlier, constituted an abandonment, leaving the territory res nullius. 111/ Spanish withdrawal took place at a time when Spain was losing her colonies in the Western Hemisphere, and the fact that no record of Spanish protest has surfaced protesting either the subsequent Argentine occupation or the subsequent British one is a further indication that Spain had abandoned her claims to the Islands. Thus, when Argentina claimed and subsequently occupied the Islands and established a settlement there, she acquired de facto sovereignty and an inchoate claim to sovereignty based on expectancy. Argentina attempted to perfect her claim but was prevented from doing so by both the United States and England. 112/ Also, it appears that Argentine

----

109/   20 B.F.S.P. 346 (1832-33).

110/   Smith, supra note 108, at 59-60 and Goebel, supra note 14, at 438-459.

111/   However, one might also contend that Spanish abandonment took place much later, in light of a potential Spanish claim going back to 1493, and clear Spanish title dating from 1766. A nine-year withdrawal (1811 until 1820 when the Buenos Aires Government sent its first ship to proclaim sovereignty) by the Spanish (in light of the peculiar history of these islands) could not be considered derelection, absent a clear showing of intent of giving up sovereignty. Such a position might be supported by the decision of the Permanent Court of International Justice in Legal Status of Eastern Greenland (1933) P.C.I.J., Ser. A/B, No. 53, 45-46, in which Denmark was held to have possessed sovereignty over the disputed territory during long periods when no settlements existed at all and even during the more contemporary period when Denmark's rival Norway had established settlements on the Island. See also Oppenheim, supra note 52, at 580.

112/   Note that a contemporary U.S. court decision recognized that Vernet was appointed pursuant to a governmental act, but that the United States did not recognize the Argentine claim to sovereignty over the Islands, supra note 72. The Argentine claim of sovereignty, it was claimed, infringed on alleged prescriptive whale and seal fishing rights of U.S. citizens. This administrative control over the Islands under Vernet from 1826 to 1829 was weak, if it existed at all. Vernet, in a report to Buenos Aires, noted that the establishment of the colony was his own work, that he received no salary as Governor, that he received no assistance from the Argentine Government, and that he collected no taxes. 113/ The absence of any evidence of an exercise of Argentine state functions is problematic for the Argentine claim in light of the decision of the P.C.I.J. in the Island of Palmas case. 114/ In that case, which dealt with an island inhabited by native tribes, the establishment of a special administration on the island to maintain a claim of sovereignty was held unnecessary. What was necessary, however, was the actual, continuous, and peaceful display of state functions over the territory in question, 115/ and such activity would prevail over a prior inchoate title. 116/

If one examines the Argentine declaration of 1829, one sees that it amounts to a declaration of right. No formal cession was made or acknowledged by Spain. Thus the territory was not formally ceded to the Argentine Republic, but the declaration meant merely that the Islands were under the Command of the Governor and that the Laws of the Republic were to be applied

----

position was taken by U.S. Secretary of State Livingston, who wrote in 1832 that actions taken in the area by Vernet, pursuant to a claim of sovereignty and of authority from Argentina, infringed on alleged prescriptive whale and fishing rights of U.S. citizens. See Instructions of January 26, 1832 to Baylies, the charge at Buenos Aires, text in 1 Moore's Dig. Int'l L. 877 (1906). See also Goebel, supra note 14, at 448.

113/ 20 B.F.S.P. 374-80 (1832-33), and Smith, supra note 108, at 58.

114/ Tne Island of Palmas (1928). 2 R. Int'l Arb. Awards 831 (1928): 22 Am. J. Int'l L. 867 (1928).

115/ 2 R. Int'l Arb. Awards 831 at 839-840 and 22 Am. J. Int'l L. 867 (1928). Note, however, that the standard applied by the Tribunal as to the establishment of sovereignty over a territory will vary. The exercise of state functions must be appropriate to the circumstances of the territory. Thus, in the Clipperton Island case (26 Am. J. Int'l L. 390 (1932)) a symbolic annexation as opposed to actual occupation formed the original basis of the French claim which was upheld by the Tribunal. (Clipperton Island (1931), 2 R. Int'l Arb. Awards 1105, 26 Am. J. Int'l L. 390 (1932)).

116/ 2 R. Int'l Arb. Awards 831 (1928).

to the citizens. 117/ This declaration, coupled with possession, established Argentina as a de facto regime with an inchoate title to future rights of possession. Therefore, it appears that when Britain ousted Argentina from the Islands in 1833, the Argentine claim was based on expectancy only and not fully vested. This delayed any acquisition of title by Britain, and title was not conferred when Britain occupied the Island in 1833, because she was not a good faith occupier, as had been the case with Argentina. Furthermore, when Britain occupied the Island in 1833, Spain did not protest nor did she cede the territory. Thus when Britain occupied the Island in 1833, it appears that her claim was also based only on expectancy. 118/ However, Britain, being the stronger, was able to remain on the island long enough seemingly to perfect her title, despite Argentine protests. Given Spanish silence for a prolonged period of time, given Britain's exercise of uninterrupted posses- sion and authority since that time, given formal designation of the Falklands as a crown colony on April 11, 1843, 119/ and given appointment of a Governor in June of 1843, and British administration to date, the case appears strong but not conclusive that British title to the Falklands vested.

This is not to neglect the possible conclusion that Argentina, find- ing the territory res nullius, was the power which, beginning in 1820, took steps in accordance with the practice of the times to perfect her title, which she did by her full exercise of state functions during the period 1829- 1833. Most probably had both the United States and Great Britain permitted Argentina to continue to exercise and to perfect the sovereign rights she claimed over the territory, she would have continued to do so and would govern the Falkland Islands today. But the actions and text of the corre- spondence at the time indicate that the United States and Great Britian did not take the newly independent rebel government of Argentina seriously in her declarations and attempts to establish sovereignty over the islands. It

----

117/ The one-sidedness of this declaration was also challenged by Chile because it purported to apply also to Tierra del Fuego, but Argentina settled this dispute with Chile by giving Chile the greater part of that Island in 1881, see supra note 108, and text, supra, note 21.

118/ H. Weber, Falkland-Islands oder Malvinas? 86 (Frankfurt, 1977).

119/ Colonial Office List, supra note 7, at 102, and Foreign Office Handbook No. 138, supra note 25, at 16.

was only when Argentina began to exercise her claim to sovereign rights to the exclusion of other nations--e.g., by seizing infringing foreign ships--that other nations responded. The United States initially responded to Argentine actions as it would have to actions taken by pirates. The whole essence of sovereignty appears to be the exercise of state acts to the exclusion of any contrary actions by other nations and as soon as Argentina tried actively to do this, she was prevented from doing so and thus from practically perfecting her claim.

2. <u>Self-determination right of the population</u>. In 1833, when Britain took possession of the Falkland Islands, the principle of self-determination of peoples was not a principle which received general recognition. However, Article 73 of the U.N. Charter requires:

> ...those members which have or assume responsibilities for the administration of territories whose peoples have not yet attained a full measure of self-government...to develop self-government, to take due account of the political aspirations of the peoples, and to assist them in the progressive development of their free political institutions... 120/

Furthermore, U.N. General Assembly Resolution 1514, the Declaration on the Granting of Independence to Colonial Countries and Peoples, established a set of obligations for non-self governing territories which were not covered by trusteeship arrangements. It provided that "all peoples have the right to self-determination," that "repressive measures of all kinds directed against dependent peoples shall cease in order to enable them to exercise peacefully and freely their right to complete independence," and that "[i]mmediate steps shall be taken...to transfer all powers to the peoples of those territories, without any conditions or reservations, in accordance with their freely expressed will and desire, without any distinctions as to race,

----

120/ United Nations Charter, Article 73(b). Note also that the Commission of the European Communities, by statement of 6 April 1982, condemned Argentine actions as..."an intervention committed in violation of international law <u>and the rights of the inhabitants of the Falkland Islands</u>." [Emphasis added] 15 Bull. Eur. Communities 7 (1982). For a step-by-step chronology of Community action from 2 April through 12 July 1982, <u>see</u> <u>Europe 82</u>, No. 9, 15 (Sept. 1982).

creed or color, in order to enable them to enjoy complete independence and freedom." 121/

However, the term "peoples" is circumscribed by language in paragraph 6 that reads "any attempt aimed at the partial or total disruption of the national unity and the territorial integrity of a country is incompatible with the purposes and principles of the Charter of the United Nations." 122/

To give effect to these precepts, a special committee was created to assume the same responsibilities towards such non-self governing territories as had been exercised by the Trusteeship Committee in regard to trust territories. 123/ This special committee regularly investigates the situation in such territories and reports to the General Assembly on compliance and non-compliance with United Nations' policies. 124/ Interestingly enough, before Great Britain held a referendum in Gibraltar on September 10, 1967, for residents to choose between British or Spanish sovereignty, the Special Committee adopted a resolution 125/ that the holding of the referendum would contradict the provisions of General Assembly Resolution 2231 (XXI) which asked the "administrative power to expedite, without any hindrance and in consultation with the government of Spain, the decolonization of Gibraltar..." 126/ Later

----

121/ G.A. Res. 1514 (XV). 15 U.N. GAOR Supp. 16, at 66-67, U.N. Doc. A/4684 (1960).

122/ T. Franck and P. Hoffman, "The Right of Self-Determination in Very Small Places, " 8 N.Y.U. J. Int'l L. Pol. 333 (Winter 1976). See also Z. Mustafa, "The Principle of Self-Determination in International Law," 5 Int'l Law. 479 (July 1971). For a discussion on the applicability of paragraph 6 specifically to the Falklands' situation, see Gerard Cohen Jonathan, "Les Isles Falkland (Malouines)," 18 Annuaire Français de Droit International 249-254 (1972).

123/ The Special Committee on the Situation with Regard to the Implementation of the Declaration on the Granting of Independence to Colonial Countries and Peoples, established by G.A. Res. 1654. 16 U.N. GAOR Supp. 17, at 65, U.N. Doc. A/5100 (1961), hereafter cited as "Special Committee."

124/ See, for example, Working Paper, supra note 45, and Report of the Special Committee, U.N. Doc. A/36/23 (Part V), 29 September 1981, pp. 39-40.

125/ Report of the Special Committee, 22 U.N. GAOR, Annexes, Addendum to Agenda Item No. 23 (Part II), at 238, U.N. Doc. A/6700/Rev. 1 (1967).

126/ G.A. Res 2231, 21 U.N. GAOR Supp., 16, at 74, U.N. Doc. A/6316 (1966).

that year, the General Assembly adopted a nearly identical resolution by vote of 73 to 19, with 27 abstentions. The preamble of this resolution applied Resolution 1514 (XV), paragraph 6, (territorial integrity provisions), 127/ to the Gibraltar situation. 128/ What this means is that, at least in Gibraltar, consulting the people of a territory as to their own wishes was found to violate the prohibition against disruption of territorial integrity and national unity. 129/ This is particularly important in light of the similarities between the situation in Gibraltar and in the Falklands. 130/ However, a significant distinction can be drawn between these two territories. Thus, Crawford observes that international practice applies the principle of self-determination to "colonial enclaves" only in very limited circumstances, but that Gibraltar seems to fit those circumstances, while the Falkland Islands would not. Crawford argues that the principle is applied only:

> to "enclaves" of the claimant State, which are ethnically and economically parasitic upon or derivative of that State, and which cannot be said in any legitimate sense to constitute separate territorial units. Such a category would include Gibraltar.... It would not include island territories --which are by definition not enclaves: the General Assembly has given only lukewarm support to Argentina's claim to the Falkland Islands. 131/

Both Gibraltar and the Falkland Islands have been classified as non-self-governing territories. 132/ Apparently in both countries the inhabitants

----

127/ Supra note 121.

128/ G.A. Res. 2353, 22 U.N. GAOR Supp. 16, at 53, U.N. Doc. A/6716 (1967).

129/ See J. Crawford, The Creation of States in International Law 381 (Oxford, 1979). Contrast, however, the Case of the Cook Islands. This small entity was a non-self governing territory administered by New Zealand. In 1965 it requested to have the United Nations supervise an act of self-determination. The Islanders subsequently "dumbfounded a substantial portion of the Organization by rejecting independence in favor of a state of 'free association' with New Zealand." M.M. Gunter, "Self-Determination in the Recent Practice of the United Nations," 137 World Affairs 155 (Fall 1974).

130/ Franck and Hoffman, supra note 122, at 379.

131/ Crawford, supra note 129, at 384.

132/ Id. at 358.

wish to remain linked to Britain and Britain has formally pledged to respect
that wish. 133/ Both territories are considered by the British to be crown
colonies; both were at some point conquered by Great Britain, both are non-
contiguous to Britain, and both have pro-British populations. 134/ The similarities in the situations of both territories have received detailed treatment by a team of scholars who capsulized the situation in the Falkland's
dispute as follows:

> The role of the U.N. in this dispute differs little
> from its role vis-à-vis Gibraltar. General Assembly
> resolutions since 1965 have essentially sided with
> Argentina's claim and against Britain's position in
> terms almost identical to the Gibraltar resolutions,
> calling for negotiations between Argentina and Britain
> to terminate the colonial presence, while merely
> "bearing in mind" the interest of the local popula-
> tion...245/ Neither the Gibraltar resolutions nor the
> Falkland Island resolutions, however, include provi-
> sions calling for self-determination. Indeed in 1973
> the Assembly passed a new resolution in which it ex-
> plicitly accepted the Argentinian contention that "the
> way to put an end to this colonial situation is the
> peaceful solution of the conflict of sovereignty" (i.e.
> the transfer of sovereignty to Argentina) and expressed
> the Assembly's "gratitude for the continuous efforts
> made by the Government of Argentina, in accordance with
> the relevant decisions of the General Assembly, to
> facilitate the process of decolonization..." 246
> Argentina's position is initially based on a claim
> to historic title originating prior to 1833 (when the
> islands became a British colony), and leads to the by
> now familiar invocation of paragraph 6 of Resolution
> 1514--the "territorial integrity" clause. Second,
> Argentina contends that the population now living in
> the islands has no right to self-determination because
> they are a settler population who replaced the legi-
> timate previous Argentinian inhabitants. These argu-
> ments have received overwhelming endorsement in the
> General Assembly. 247

245. G.A. Res. 2065. 20 U.N. GAOR Supp. 14, at 57, U.N.
Doc. A/6014 (1965); Consensus, 21 (U.N. GAOR, Annexes, agenda
item No. 23, at 31. U.N. Doc. A/6628 (1966), noted by the

133/ Concerning Gibraltar, see Franck and Hoffman, supra note 122, at
374, note 208. Concerning the Falklands, see British Reference Services,
supra note 7, at 1.

134/ Franck and Hoffman, id. at 371 and 375, and Foreign Office Handbook,
No. 138, supra note 25, at 16.

General Assembly in 21 U.N. GAOR 1500, at 1 (1966); Consensus, 22 U.N. GAOR Supp. 16, at 57 c. U.N. Doc. A/6716
(1967); Consensus, 24 U.N. GAOR Supp. 29, at 111-112. U.N.
Doc. A/8429 (1971).
   246. G.A. Res. 3160, 28 U.N. GAOR Supp. 30, at 109. U.N.
Doc. A/9030 (1973).
   247. The vote on Resolution 2065 (XX) was 94 to 0, with 14
abstentions—all these being Western European or white Commonwealth countries and South Africa. 20 U.N. GAOR 1398, at
9 (1965).

_____   135/

   Thus it seems evident that current prospects for the United Nations
finding that the Falklanders have a right to determine their sovereignty
status appear bleak.

   B. The Dependencies
   The possibility of sovereignty over polar regions presents issues
which are related but not identical to those of sovereignty rights over the
Falkland Islands themselves. In addition, at least one new claimant--Chile--
enters the picture. 136/ In 1955 Great Britain, in recognition of this situation, unilaterally submitted the dispute on the issue of the Dependencies to
the International Court of Justice. However, both Argentina and Chile declined to submit to the Court's jurisdiction. 137/
   At present, occupation in the traditional sense is not feasible for
such territories; however, the British base their claims upon the discovery
of South Georgia and South Sandwich in 1775 and upon their continuous administration of the Dependencies since and before their annexation in 1908. 138/
Argentine claims are based upon claimed inheritance of title from Spain and

----

135/ Franck and Hoffman, id. at 380-381.

136/ Pleadings, supra note 3.

137/ Pleadings, id. and Antarctica Case (United Kingdom v. Argentina),
Order of March 16, 1956, I.C.J. Reports 1956, p. 12.

138/ See supra note 6. The Facts, supra note 10, and Pleadings, id.

proximity to Argentina as part of its continental shelf 139/ and upon continuous occupation of the South Orkneys since 1904. 140/

The implications of the dispute over the Dependencies and the Islands
proper are directly related. In the words of one scholar:

> Disputed sovereignty in the Falklands is directly
> related to Antarctica. Argentina regards the islands
> as situated on its continuous continental shelf which
> by parity of reasoning extends to South Georgia, the
> South Sandwich and South Orkneys groups. Argentina
> puts forward a legal argument that these islands are
> a geological continuation of the Andes reappearing as
> the Antartandes. In geopolitical terms the Southern
> Atlantic and Antarctic are seen as a single region.
> Within a year of the Antarctic Treaty coming into
> force, the United Kingdom detached the area south of
> 60 degrees S from the Falkland Islands Dependencies
> to form the British Antarctic Territory insulating
> its Antarctic claim from the effect of any future
> settlement with Argentina in the Falklands. In
> practice a transfer of sovereignty over the islands
> would tend to weaken Britain's position in South
> Georgia leading to a ripple effect. Much of the
> United Kingdom's case for the Antarctic depends on
> administrative acts carried out in the Falklands.
> [Footnotes omitted.] 141/

Unfortunately, only the British submitted formal pleadings to the
International Court of Justice, and thus the record contains no formal Argentine response to Britain's claim to the Dependencies.

The British pleadings stress that:

> 12. ...from very early dates varying between
> 1775 and 1843, Great Britain possessed, on the
> basis of discovery, accompanied by a formal

139/ British Reference Services, supra note 7, at 7, and Auburn, supra
note 34, at 55.

140/ Britain claims that when it handed over to the Argentinians the
operation of the meteorological station on Laurie Island in the South
Orkneys, it was with the understanding that the islands were a British
possession and that in 1907 a note was sent to this effect to avoid possible
misunderstandings. Pleadings, supra note 3, at 22. Thus, Argentina claims
that she is the only one that maintains in real form the rule of her
sovereignty in the lands of the Antarctic. Whiteman, supra note 39, at
1061. For a summary of the parties' Antarctic claims, see Auburn, id., at
49-61.

141/ Auburn, supra note 34 at 55.

claim in the name of the British Crown, an original root of title to all territories concerned. 142/

and furthermore contend that:

the United Kingdom, by its continued display of
State activity; by protests or counter-measures,
which were always prompt, and evidence of the
exercise of due vigilance; by attempts to settle
the dispute through diplomatic negotations; by
actively seeking to bring the dispute to arbitration or judicial settlement, had energetically
prosecuted its case, upheld its sovereignty, and
maintained its rights and titles. 143/

The primary British contention was summarized in the following
words:

(1)   that by reason of historic British discoveries
of certain territories in the Antarctic and
sub-Antarctic; by reason of the long-continued
and peaceful display of British sovereignty
from the date of those discoveries onwards in,
and in regard to, the territories concerned; by
reason of the incorporation of these territories in the dominions of the British Crown;
by virtue of their formal constitution in the
Royal Letters Patent of 1908 and 1917 as the
British Possession called the Falkland Islands
Dependencies: the United Kingdom possesses, and
at all material dates has possessed, the sovereignty over the territories of the Falkland
Islands Dependencies, and in particular the
South Sandwich Islands, South Georgia, the
South Orkneys, South Shetlands, Graham Land and
Coats Land. 144/

Britain argues to the effect that four specific decisions of international
tribunals in four cases clarify the change in the concept of effective occupation which has taken place in the past century and that these cases support the British sovereignty position. These four cases are the following:

The Island of Palmas (1928) 2 **Reports of International
Arbitral Awards**, 831;

142/   Pleadings, supra note 3, at 13.

143/   Id. at 33.

144/   Id. at 37.

Clipperton Island (1931), 2 **Reports of International Arbitral Awards,** 1105;

Legal Status of Eastern Greenland (1933) **Series**A/B 53;

Minquiers and Ecrehos. **I.C.J. Reports**, 1953, p. 47. 145/

In both the cases concerning the Islands of Palmas 146/ and Eastern Greenland, 147/ a display of sovereignty at irregular but comparatively long intervals was held sufficient to constitute effective occupation, so long as there was an intention and will to act as a sovereign in conjunction with some actual exercise or display of sovereignty. The Clipperton Island case, which involved a desolate reef, came close to outrightly attributing to a symbolic annexation of an uninhabited territory the full force of effective occupation, provided that such annexation is not disputed at the time. 148/ Judge Huber in the Island of Palmas case commented thus:

> Although continuous in principle, sovereignty cannot be exercised in fact at every moment on every point of a territory. The intermittance and discontinuity compatible with the maintenance of the right necessarily differ according as inhabited or uninhabited regions are involved, or regions enclosed within territories in which sovereignty is incontestably displayed, or again regions accessible from, for instance the high seas."
> [as quoted in 22 Am. J. Int'l L. 867 (1928).

Minquiers and Ecrehos, 149/ the fourth and most recent case cited by Britain, dealt with disputed sovereignty between France and the United Kingdom over two groups of inlets and rocks close to the Isle of Jersey. The Court in its decision concluded that sovereignty belonged to the United Kingdom and stressed that historically the territory was treated and considered part of territory held by the British King and placed heavy reliance upon state functions exercised by Britain in the nineteenth and twentieth centuries.

145/   Pleadings, supra note 3 at 33, and Whiteman, supra note 39, at 1036-38.

146/   Island of Palmas, supra note 114.

147/   Legal Status of Eastern Greenland, supra note 111.

148/   Clipperton Island, supra note 115.

149/   Minquiers and Ecrehos (France/United Kingdom, Judgment, November 17, 1953), 1953 I.C.J. 47.

>The Court, being now called upon to appraise the
relative strength of the opposing claims to sovereignty over the Ecrehos in the light of the facts
considered above, finds that the Ecrehos group in
the beginning of the thirteenth century was considered and treated as an integral part of the fief
of the Channel Islands which were held by the
English King, and that the group continued to be
under the dominion of that King, who in the beginning of the fourteenth century exercised jurisdiction in respect thereof. The Court further finds
that British authorities during the greater part of
the nineteenth century and in the twentieth century
have exercised State functions in respect of the
group. The French Government, on the other hand,
has not produced evidence showing that it has any
valid title to the group. In such circumstances it
must be concluded that the sovereignty over the
Ecrehos belongs to the United Kingdom. 150/

In response to claims that British title also was based on a medieval
land grant, the court emphasized: "What is of decisive importance...is not
indirect presumptions deduced from events in the Middle Ages, but the evidence which related directly to the possession of the Ecrehos and Minquiers
groups." 151/

Unfortunately, the rules governing sovereignty over such polar regions are far from clear. 152/ Effective occupation as a sole criterion makes
little practical sense, and if one attempts to base claims on administration
alone, the question arises as to how far does or can effective administration
extend. In addition, technology for extending control is constantly advancing, and the time it takes to travel great distances is greatly diminishing.
Today, it is possible by assistance of radio contact, air routes, and even
satellite monitoring to claim administration of large (primarily unpopulated)
areas. However, the advance of technology will also work against these areas'
remaining unpopulated. Thus if and when exploitation of polar regions
becomes economically and technically feasible, polar regions may indeed be
inhabited and may be located only a short distance away--in terms of time--an

----

150/ Id. at 67.

151/ Id. at 57. See also Schwarzenberger, "Title to Territory: Response to
a Challenge," 51 A.J.I.L. 315-316 (1957).

152/ See Whiteman, supra note 39, at 1263 ff.

even shorter hop from traditionally inhabited areas. Thus, one day in the future, should the equivalent of the great Gold Rush take place by Latin pioneers, for example, in well-insulated polar clothing and living in special solar enclaves, the concept of administrative "control" or exercise of state acts by a far-away power such as Britain may be totally meaningless as a practical matter. These postulations are not totally absurd given the rapid pace of technology to exploit natural resources and the fact that "some degree of family life in now possible in Antarctica." 153/

The legal issues concerning the Dependencies, in the conclusion of one scholar, "are exceedingly complex and much of the original evidence necessary for reaching final findings of fact is not available." 154/ The British claim of exercise of state activity even before Great Britain's annexation of the Dependencies, is a strong one, but it is not an exclusive one in light of a long line of Argentine and Chilean activity. 155/ The problem arises when one attempts to ascertain the legal significance of such activity. No clear rules exist; the case law relied on by Britain tends to be over 30 years old, and absent a negotiated agreement among the parties or voluntary submission of the dispute to an arbitral tribunal or to the International Court, the issue of sovereignty over the Dependencies will not be resolved.

IX. RECENT HISTORICAL PRECEDENTS IN INTERNATIONAL LAW

It is important that the Falkland Islands controversy be viewed in the context of previous successful efforts by other countries to regain claimed territory by the use of force. Three examples, those of Goa, the Spanish Sahara, and East Timor, provide important precedents which should be considered.

153/ Auburn, *supra* note 34, at 42. Since 1977, Argentine soldiers' wives and children have been present at Esperanza Base. In 1975, a plane landed at Spitsbergen, carrying officials, and a group of Soviet women with double beds, and some Soviet wives and children have also lived in subarctic South Georgia, *id.* at 42.

154/ Waldock, *supra* note 82, at 353.

155/ *Id.* at 331-332 and Pleadings, *supra* note 3, at 25 ff. *See also* Central Office of Information, *supra* note 3, at 9, for a summary of Chilean claims.

A. The Case of Goa

The case of Goa may be taken as a territorial dispute somewhat analogous to the Falklands situation. On December 18, 1961, an Indian military force numbering approximately 45,000 troops set in motion an attack which overwhelmed the 3,500 Portuguese defenders of the Portuguese territories of Goa, Damao, and Diu. 156/ India subsequently annexed the territories and allotted them two representational seats in the House of People. 157/ What happened in Goa was a relatively straightforward solution to the problem of what has been termed the "colonial enclave"..."the small territory claimed by a neighbouring state, for whatever reason. Without regard to the principle of self determination." 158/

The Indian position in the debate before the Security Council at the time of the attack stressed that part of its territory had been illegally occupied for 450 years by the Portuguese as a result of their conquest and that such occupation was illegal in light of Security Council Resolution 1514, and that India's taking its own territory could in no way constitute aggression. 159/ The Portuguese response was to argue that the right of sovereignty should be respected and that armed aggression was not a legitimate means of transferring the territories. 160/ The United States position was to avoid the merits of the issue of sovereignty and to stress that such use of armed force is an act clearly forbidden by the U.N. Charter. 161/ Two U.N. Security Council Draft resolutions were introduced and neither was adopted. The first, S/5032, would have rejected the Portuguese complaint of aggression against India and called upon Portugal to cooperate with India in liquidation of her colonial possessions in India. It was defeated by a vote of 7 to 4. The second, S/5033, called for a cessation of hostilities, withdrawal of

----

156/ *Congressional Record*, House, p. 23744-46, of December 18, 1963.
Whiteman, *supra* note 39, at 1140-44. Crawford, *supra* note 129, at 112-13.

157/ Gazette of India, March 28, 1962, Pt. II, S. 1, Ext., pp. 8, 19, and Whiteman, *id*. at 1144-45.

158/ Crawford, *supra* note 129, at 377.

159/ Whiteman, *id*. at 1140-44.

160/ *Id*. at 1141-42.

161/ *Id*. at 1142-43.

Indian forces and urged the parties to work out a permanent peaceful solution. This draft resolution received 7 votes in favor and 4 against, but was vetoed by the Soviet Union. 162/

The similarities between the Indian actions in Goa and Argentine actions vis-à-vis the Falklands are strong. In both cases the "reclaiming" power moved against a colonial territory with a long history of European (non-local) administration. In both cases historical claims were stressed by the "reclaiming" power, and in both cases the defending power was geographically a distant one. Finally, in both cases self-determination rights, if any, of the local population were not considered at the time to be an overriding issue by the claiming state.

B. The Case of Spanish Sahara

The successful Indian use of force to take control of Goa may be taken as a precedent for Third World states to pursue their national interests through military means rather than through law and peaceful diplomacy, regardless of any self-determination rights local populations of coveted territories may have. Thus, one finds the experience of the Goa situation echoed in the Moroccan/Mauritanian takeover of Spanish Sahara and the Indonesian takeover of East Timor, and, of course, in Argentine military actions aimed at obtaining control of the Falklands. In observing this trend in the context of the Spanish Sahara takeover, it is interesting to note that in 1966 one scholar touched on the possibility of its becoming a precedent for a flood of other claims:

> The "settlement" of the Saharan issue in favor of
> Morocco's claim of historic title and the denial of
> self-determination to the Sahrawi people radically
> departs from the norms of decolonization established
> and consistently applied by the United Nations since
> 1960. This is bound to have an important signif-
> icance for numerous other irredentist territorial
> claims such as those of Guatemala on Belize, Somalia

162/ For the debate of the Council on the Indian Action and the two proposed draft resolutions, see: Verbatim Record of the Security Council, 987th meeting, December 18, 1961, S/PV, 987, pp. 26-27, Verbatim Record of the Security Council 988th meeting, December 18, 1961, S/PV, 988, pp. 32-33, 40-41, 86-86. It is interesting to speculate what United Nations action might have been had Argentina prevailed militarily. For additional background material on the Goa dispute, see T.B. Cunha, Goa's Freedom Struggle (Bombay, 1961) and A. Menezez, 1 Goa - Historical Notes (1978).

on Djibouti, and Argentina on the Falklands. [Emphasis added; footnotes omitted.] 163/

Spanish (Western) Sahara is about the size of Colorado, with an indigenous Sahrawi population of about 75,000 persons; it is rich in phosphate and iron, and until 1974 it was a Spanish colony to which both Morocco and Mauritania had expressed historic claims. 164/ U.N. General Assembly resolutions had regularly called upon Spain to implement the population's right to self-determination which Spain agreed to do under U.N auspices in the first half of 1975. 165/ Faced with the prospect of the territory's becoming independent, Morocco obtained a majority vote of the General Assembly in December 1974 to solicit an advisory opinion on the issue of whether the territory had belonged to either the Moroccan empire or the Mauritanian entity prior to its colonization by Spain 166/ The Court, in deciding that Western Sahara had not belonged to the Moroccan Empire not the Mauritanian "entity," noted that this would not "affect the application of Resolution 1514 (XV) in the decolonization of Western Sahara and, in particular, ...the principle of self-determination through the free and genuine expression of the will of the peoples of the Territory. 167/

Furthermore, the U.N. Mission sent to visit the non-self governing territory found "that there was an overwhelming consensus among Sahrawis

---

163/ T.M. Franck, "The Stealing of the Sahara," 70 Am. J. Int'l L. 694 (1976). For a comprehensive study of this dispute and the issues involved, see also Abigail Byman, "The March on the Spanish Sahara a Test of International Law," 6 Denver J. Int'l L. Pol'y 95 (1976).

164/ Franck and Hoffman, supra note 122, at 335-336.

165/ For a list of applicable General Assembly Resolutions, see Franck and Hoffman, id. at 336.

166/ Id. at 339.

167/ Advisory opinion on Western Sahara (1975), I.C.J. Rep. 12, at 68. For a discussion of the opinion, see Franck, supra note 162, at 709-11. See also: Gary J. Levy, "Advisory Opinion on the Western Sahara," 2 Brooklyn J. Int' Law 289-307 (Spring, 1976); Mark W. Janis, "The International Court of Justice: Advisory Opinion on the Western Sahara," 17 Harv. Int'l L. J. 609-621 (1976).

within the Territory in favor of independence and opposing integration with any neighboring country." 168/

Faced with these two adverse determinations, Morocco announced on October 18, 1975, that a massive march (the "Green March") of 350,000 unarmed civilians would enter the Sahara to gain recognition of Morocco's right to national unity and territorial integrity. 169/ The Spanish response to the invasion which followed was to accede to the claims of Morocco and Mauritania; an agreement was reached among the parties which partitioned the territory between Morocco and Mauritania and left Spain 35 percent interest in FOSBUCRAA, a successful Saharan phosphate company. 170/ Algeria declared that it would not recognize the agreement and recognized a Saharan government in exile. 171/ The U.N. response was to pass two resolutions. The first one reaffirmed the self-determination rights of the people of Spanish Sahara and called upon the Secretary General to make arrangements to supervise the act of self-determination. 172/ The second one recognized the tripartite agreement concluded, and the three-year interim administration it established and called upon the administration to permit "free consultation" with the population. 173/

168/ Report of the United Nations Visiting Mission to Spanish Sahara, 1975, in The Report of the Special Committee on the Situation with Regard to the Implementation of the Declaration on the Granting of Independence to Colonial Countries and Peoples, U.N. Doc. A/10023/Add. 5, Annex. (1975) at 48.

169/ Letter from the Permanent Representative of Morocco to the United Nations to the President of the Security Council, October 18, 1975, U.N. Doc. S/11852 (1975). Note: The United Nations deplored the march and called upon Morocco to withdraw. See Resolution 380, 1975, adopted by the Security Council at its 1854th meeting on November 6, 1975.

170/ Franck and Hoffman, supra note 122, at 341.

171/ Third Report by the Secretary-General of Security Council Resolution 379 (1975) relating to the situation concerning Western Sahara. U.N. Doc. S/1180. Annex IV, p. 2-3.

172/ G.A. Res. 3458A (XX) of December 10, 1975.

173/ G.A. Res. 3458B (XX) of December 10, 1975. See also Report by the Secretary-General in pursuance of Security Council Resolution 384 (1975) U.N. Doc. S/12011, Annex, at 3 (1976). Note that the Moroccan action did not prevent the U.S. sale of 24 F-5E jetfighters to that country in February 1976. See Franck, supra note 163, at 696.

The precedent established by the success of the Western Sahara seizure has potentially far-reaching implications, as outlined in the words of Franck:

> The easy success of Morocco and Mauritania in the Sahara (and, concurrently, of Indonesia in Timor) against wholly ineffectual UN opposition <u>cannot but change the odds and encourage more vigorous pursuit of other territorial claims</u>. Nor is there any reason to believe that this renewed tendency to assert claims of historic title can be limited to issues of decolonization. The arguments successfully used yesterday to justify the deployment of Moroccan forces against the colony of Spanish Sahara can as well be used tomorrow to legitimate the use of force to reassert Morocco's historic title to the independent state of Mauritania. [Emphasis added.] 174/

Such reasoning is persuasive, and the future implications of these events on the existing international order are explicit. However, it is possible that British resolve to reverse such a trend in the Falklands will provide a model for a contrary trend in the future.

C. The Case of East Timor

A detailed examination of the complex factual background leading to Indonesia's formal incorporation of East Timor as its twenty-seventh province on July 17, 1976, would involve extensive research that is beyond the scope of this study. 175/ What is important, however, is the international response and in particular the U.S. response to this incorporation. East Timor had been a Portuguese colony since the sixteenth century. In 1893, the Island was divided by agreement between Portugal and the Netherlands, Portugal retaining the east part. 176/ Of a population numbering approximately 650,000 persons, only about 600 persons are of European origin. 177/ In 1974, the new

----

174/ Franck, <u>supra</u> note 163, at 720.

175/ For background information, <u>see</u> Roger S. Clark on the "decolonization" of East Timor and the United Nations' norms on self-determination and aggression, 7 Yale J. World Pub. Ord. 244 (1980).

176/ P.D. Elliott, "The East Timor Dispute," 27 Int'l Comp. L. Q. 238 (1978).

177/ Franck and Hoffman, <u>supra</u> note 122, at 343.

Portuguese government provided for the decolonization of Portuguese territories by constitutional amendment and recognized their people's right to self-determination. 178/ A number of political parties became active, civil war broke out, and by November 28, 1975, one party (FRETILIN) declared East Timor independent. Two days later, the other parties also declared independence and the integration of the territory with Indonesia. On December 7, 1975, Indonesian troops entered the territory, and, on December 17, 1975, the pro-Indonesian integration coalition parties established a provincial government. On May 31, 1976, a People's Assembly was constituted and Indonesia was formally requested to accept the Assembly's request for integration, which it did on July 17, 1976. 179/

The United Nations response was a series of proclamations which deplored the military intervention of Indonesia, called for the withdrawal of Indonesian troops, called upon all states to respect the right of the people of Portuguese Timor to self-determination, and called for the appointment of a special fact-finding representative, who was then appointed. 180/

These activities culminated in the passing of General Assembly Resolution 31/53 of December 17, 1976, which among other things called upon Indonesia to withdraw from the territory inasmuch as the people of the territory had not been able to freely exercise their independence. 181/ It further rejected the claim that East Timor had been integrated into Indonesia.

The Indonesian taking of East Timor differs from the previous examples cited (Goa and Spanish Sahara) in that it is not fully clear what form

----

178/ Elliott, supra note 176, at 238.

179/ Id. at 238-240.

180/ (1) G.A. Res. 3485 (XX) of December 12, 1975, U.N. Doc. A/RES/3485 (XX). (2) Security Council Res. 384 of December 12, 1975. Report of the Security Council of June 16, 1975-June 15, 1976, 31 GAOR Supp. No. 2, Ch. 4: U.N. Doc. A/31/23 Add. 6. See also Report by the Secretary-General in pursuance of Security Council Resolution 384 (1975), U.N. Doc. S/12011, Annex, at 3 (1976). (3) Security Council Res. 389 of April 22, 1976, contained in U.N. Doc. S/12011, id. (4) See also: U.S. Department of State, Dig. U.S. Prac. Int'l L., 1976, 15-16 (Washington, 1977), and General Assembly Resolution 3153 of December 17, 1976. U.N. Doc. A/RES/31/53. The vote was: 68 in favor; 20 against; 49 abstentions.

181/ G. A. Res. 31/53, id.

of self-determination the population wanted or would have chosen had it been given the choice. However, there appears no evidence that continued status as a Portuguese colony was not one of the favored options. This being the case, the issue, as addressed by the Special U.N. Representative, was not so much one of Indonesia's seizing the colony from Portugal, as primarily a question of whether or not Indonesia might have seized the territory from its inhabitants. The answer to this question was unclear, as the special U.N. Representative found it was impossible to assess accurately the prevailing situation in East Timor. 182/

The United States position on the events in East Timor is interesting in that it seems to add particular importance to the accomplishment of a fait accompli. George H. Aldrich, Deputy Legal Adviser of the Department of State, outlined this position on July 19, 1977:

> The United States Government did not question the incorporation of East Timor into Indonesia at the time. This did not represent a legal judgment or endorsement of what took place. It was, simply, the judgment of those responsible for our policy in the area that the integration was an accomplished fact, that the realities of the situation would not be changed by our opposition to what had occurred, and that such a policy would not serve our best interests in light of the importance of our relations with Indonesia. It was for these reasons that the United States voted against United Nations General Assembly Resolution 31/53 of December 1, 1976, which rejected the incorporation of East Timor into Indonesia and recommended that the Security Council take immediate steps to implement its earlier resolutions to secure exercise by the people of East Timor of their right of self-determination... 183/

> ...

> In the case of East Timor, the policy judgment has been made by this Administration, as stated by Deputy Assistant Secretary [Robert B..] Oakley last March, that our interest would not be served by seeking to

----
182/ U.N. Doc. S/12106. 1,4.

183/ Human Rights in East Timor, Hearings before the Subcommittee on International Organizations of the Committee on International Relations of the House of Representatives, 95th Cong., 1st Sess. (June 28-29, 1977), 46-48. Testimony partially reproduced in U.S. Department of State, Dig. U.S. Prac. Int'l L. 1977, 11 (Washington, 1978).

reopen the question of Indonesian annexation of East
Timor. Instead, we have directed our efforts to
urging Indonesia to institute a humane administration
in East Timor and to accept an impartial inspection
of its administration by the International Committee
of the Red Cross. It is believed that these measures
represent the most effective way we can promote the
human rights of the inhabitants of East Timor in the
present circumstances. [184]/

In his testimony, Aldrich stressed that he did not see U.S. policy in
the East Timor case as setting a legal precedent for the future, [185]/ but one
cannot help but speculate as to whether similar weight might have been given
to a successful Argentina fait accompli in the Falklands had Argentina
provided a humane administration for the Islanders. [186]/

XI. CONCLUSION

It is impossible to arrive at a definitive answer as to who has the
right of sovereignty over the Falkland Islands. However, an examination of
historic events and often differing principles of international law could
lead to a conclusion that insofar as concerns the two major Islands, East
and West Falkland, the case is strong--but far from conclusive--that original
sovereignty rested with the Spanish and that this sovereignty was not compromised by the British establishment of a settlement at Port Egmont in 1766,
as the British were subsequently forced out by the Spanish in 1770. Nor was

----

[184]/ Digest, id. at 12. For background on the subsequent humaneness of the
Indonesian administration the U.S. Department of State had desired to
promote, see: Arnold S. Kohen, "The Cruel Case of Indonesia: U.S. Diplomacy
and Human Rights," 225 Nation 553-557 (November 26, 1977); Arnold S.
Kohen, "The Politics of Starvation," 3 Inquiry (San Francisco) 18-22
(February 18, 1980); U.S. Congress, House, Committee on Foreign Affairs,
Subcommittee Asian and Pacific Affairs, Famine Relief for East Timor.
Hearings, 96th Cong., 1st Sess., December 4, 1979. Washington, U.S. Govt.
Print. Off., 1980; Denis Freney, "US-Australian Role in East Timor Geno-
cide," 4 Counterspy 10-21 (Spring 1980); Arnold S. Kohen, "Invitation to
a Massacre in East Timor," 232 Nation 136, 138-139 (February 7, 1981);
Henry Kamm, "The Silent Suffering of East Timor," N.Y. Times (Magazine)
Feb. 15, 1981, at 34-35, 56, 58, 60-63; and Jack Anderson, U.S.Ignores '75
Massacre of East Timorese," Wash. Post, Oct. 12, 1982, at B-2.

[185]/ Digest, supra note 181, at 11.

[186]/ It is further interesting to note that U.S. military assistance
to Indonesia was temporarily suspended for six months following Indonesia's
taking of East Timor. Digest, supra note 183 at 991-92.

Spanish sovereignty compromised when Spain permitted the British to re-occupy Port Egmont in 1771, nor during the British stay there until 1774.

Furthermore, it appears that the Islands were abandoned in 1811 and that therefore Argentina, not having acquired the Falklands from the Vice-royalty of Rio de la Plata prior to Spanish abandonment, subsequently laid claim to abandoned territory. Thus, Argentina, when she occupied the Islands in the 1820s, obtained an inchoate title to the Islands, based on expectancy. Subsequently, Argentina attempted to perfect her title by actively exercising her authority to the exclusion of other powers, but was prevented from doing so by her clash with the United States and later ouster by the British in 1833. One can conclude that when Great Britain ousted the Argentinians in 1833, her title was also one based on expectancy and that British title at the time was not as good as the Argentine title, which was a prior one. However, Great Britain is able to make a strong case that she perfected her title by continuous and effective occupation and subsequent formal incorporation of the Island into the British Colonial Empire.

Insofar as the Dependencies are concerned, the situation is very unclear. The Dependencies are primarily polar regions which defy traditional rules of acquisition of territory. British activity in the area is noteworthy, but Argentine and Chilean activity and claims cannot be ignored.

Additionally, potentially controlling international case law tends to be more than thirty years old, and law is to some degree an evolutionary process. Thus, until some clearer body of law evolves to apply to such situations, it is impossible to speculate the outcome. Britain has offered to help make such law by submitting the issue to the International Court. Certainly, if Chile and Argentina were to agree, they could assist in making such law, although the mere passage of time might prove more favorable to them than a court decision--in general the British record of decolonization has been an impressive one.

As to the issue of the rights of the Islanders to determine their own future, the prospects seem bleak that the United Nations would sanction such British efforts on their behalf, in view of the United Nation's failure to sanction the British referendum on this issue in Gibraltar. General Assembly Resolutions on the Falklands recognize the "interests" of the population but not their wishes, as the Argentine government is quick to point out. Moreover, it is questionable whether rights of self-determination apply to small island territories of this type.

Finally, it is important from the political viewpoint to consider that there are marked similarities between the status of the Falklands and that of Gibraltar. Thus, British attempts to preserve sovereignty in the Falklands must be seen in the light of a desire to avoid the creation of an unfavorable precedent which might later be applied to more strategically located territory. The probable presence of oil around the Islands, and the fact that British claims to Antarctica and its resources are based in part on their claim to sovereignty in the Falklands should not be overlooked in attempting to understand the actions of the parties to this dispute. In addition, the fact that India was successful in taking the Portuguese territories of Goa, Damao, and Diu without regard to the wishes of their populations might be seen by Argentina and other nations as a precedent and an international "green light" to successful seizures of the type Argentina recently came close to achieving. The same may be true of the examples set by Moroccan and Mauritanian actions vis-a-vis Western (Spanish) Sahara and by the Indonesian incorporation of East Timor.

As a practical matter, there are few territories which are not or could not be claimed (justly or unjustly) by persons other than their current inhabitants or by the regimes other than those presently governing them. Thus, the concept of pure historical title to national territory is often a fiction. Ultimately, somewhere, sometime, someone displaced somebody else. Just recently, the response of the international community was to tacitly permit claimant states to acquire territory by the use of or threat of force in the cases of Goa, Western Sahara, and East Timor. In the case of the Falklands, however, with their sector proximity to the Antarctic mainland, their mineral resources, and their similar status to strategically important Gibraltar, Argentina tread on sensitive ground and was repelled. Whether or not the example of Britain's willingness to defend a small, but important territory at high cost proves to be the start of a new international trend remains to be seen.

CHRONOLOGY

A CHRONOLOGY OF EVENTS RELATING TO
THE FALKLAND ISLANDS AND ITS DEPENDENCIES

Compiled by Everette E. Larson

1493
05/04
Issuance of the Papal Bull Inter Caetera of
Alexander VI drawing a line of demarcation between
the Spanish and Portuguese areas of discovery 100
leagues west of the Cape Verde Islands.
> Frances Gardiner Davenport. European
> Treaties bearing on the History of the
> United States and its Dependencies to
> 1648. Washington, Carnegie Institution,
> 1917. pp. 71-78.

1494
07/02
Treaty of Tordesillas signed between Spain and
Portugal accepting the line of demarcation of Pope
Alexander VI but moving it 370 leagues west of the
Cape Verde Islands [between 48 degrees and 49
degrees west latitude of Greenwich]. Spain was
acknowledged to have rights to the West of the
line. [One should note that South Georgia is East
of this line].
> Francis Gardiner Davenport. European
> Treaties bearing on the History of the
> United States and its Dependencies to
> 1648. Washington, Carnegie Institution,
> 1917. pp. 84-100.

1502
04/07
Amerigo Vespucci sighted land which was probably
the South Georgias at 52 degrees south latitude.
> Ernesto J. Fitte. La disputa con Gran
> Bretaña por las islas del Atlántico sur.
> Buenos Aires, Emecé Editores, 1968. pp.
> 9-19, & 37.

1506
01/24
Papal sanction given to the change of the line of
demarcation as amended by the Treaty of Tordesillas in the Bull Ea Quae.
> Francis Gardiner Davenport. European
> Treaties bearing on the History of the
> United States and its Dependencies to
> 1648. Washington, Carnegie Institution,
> 1917. pp. 107–111.

1520

In the Mapa Mundi of Petro Apiano there is a large
island with several smaller ones in the middle of
the South Atlantic and another smaller one off the
coast of South America between 50–60 degrees South
latitude and 340 degrees (with 0 degrees at Ferro
ascending towards the East).
> Reproduction in the Geography and Map
> Division, Library of Congress.

1522

The map of Pedro Reinel shows islands off of the
southern coast of South America. "The chart
records only the information brought back by
Estevão Gomes [Esteban Gomes] when, after
deserting Magellan, he arrived in Sevilla on 6 May
1521."
> Armando Cortesão. Portvgaliae Monvmenta
> Cartographica. Lisboa, 1960. vol. I, p.
> 40.

1592
08/14
Sir Thomas Cavendish, sailing from England in the
Desire, captained by John Davis "discovered"
[i.e., sighted] the Falkland Islands.
> Great Britain. Colonial Office. Falkland
> Islands and Dependencies. Report for the
> years 1970 and 1971. London, HMSO, 1973,
> p. 48.

1594
02/02
Sir Richard Hawkins sighted what many feel was the
Falkland Islands and named them Hawkin's Maidenland.
> Great Britain. Colonial Office. Falkland
> Islands and Dependencies. Report for the
> years 1970 and 1971. London, HMSO, 1973,
> p. 48 and José A. Landeiro. Malvinas;
> cronología de un despojo. Buenos Aires,
> Adrogue Gráfica Editora, 1982, p. 20.

1600
01/24
Sebald de Weert, a Dutchman, sighted the north-
western part of the Falkland Islands.
> Great Britain. Colonial Office. Falkland
> Islands and Dependencies. Report for the
> years 1970 and 1971. London, HMSO, 1973,
> p. 48. See also Malvinas Islands.
> Statement by the Representative of
> Argentina, H.E. Dr. José María Ruda,
> before the Subcommittee III of the
> Special Committee on the situation with
> regard to the implementation of the
> declaration on the granting of
> independence to colonial countries and
> peoples. New York, 9 Sept., 1964, p. 3.

1675

British expedition by Antonio de la Roché
"probably" discovered South Georgia.
> Brian Roberts. "Chronological list of
> Antarctic expeditions," The Polar
> Record, v. 9, no. 59 (May, 1958),
> p. 98.

1690
01/27
Captain John Strong of the Welfare landed on the
Falklands and named the sound between the two
major islands "Falkland Sound".
> Great Britain. Colonial Office. Falkland
> Islands and Dependencies. Report for the
> years 1970 and 1971. London, HMSO, 1973,
> p. 48.

1713
07/13
Second treaty of Utrecht subscribed to by the
British and Spanish, article 8, according to the
Argentine position, purports to guarantee Spanish
possessions in America against further British
Action.
> Julius Goebel. The struggle for the
> Falkland Islands; a study in legal and
> diplomatic history. Port Washington,
> N.Y., Kennikat Press [1971] p. 166.

1756

The Spanish ship León sighted and circumnavigated
South Georgia.
> Brian Roberts. "Chronological list of
> Antarctic expeditions," The Polar
> Record, v. 9, no. 59 (May, 1958), p.
> 98.

1764
02/03
Bouganville with colonialists from Saint-Malo in
France establishes Fort (Port) Louis in Berkeley
Sound. This is the first settlement on the Falk-
lands.
> Ernesto J. Fitte. Crónicas del Atlántico
> sur; Patagonia, Malvinas y Antártida.
> Buenos Aires, Emecé Editores, 1974.,
> p. 191.

1765
01/23
John Bryon discovered what he called Port Egmont
on Saunder's Island near West Falkland and claimed
it for Britain.
> Ernesto J. Fitte. Crónicas del Atlántico
> sur; Patagonia, Malvinas y Antártida.
> Buenos Aires, Emecé Editores, 1974.,
> pp. 191-192.

1766
01/08
British settlement established at Port Egmont on
the Falklands.
> José A. Landeiro. Malvinas; cronología
> de un despojo. Buenos Aires, Adrogue
> Gráfica Editora, 1982, p. 36.

1766
10/04
Spain obtains the settlement Fort (Port) Louis
from the French Compagnie de St. Malo upon payment
of compensation. Spanish Naval Capt. Felipe Ruiz
Puente named by a Real Cédula, of this date, as
governor of the Falkland Islands dependent upon
the government and Captain General of the province
of Buenos Aires, subject to the jurisdiction of
the Viceroy.
> Ernesto J. Fitte. Crónicas del Atlántico
> sur; Patagonia, Malvinas y Antártida.
> Buenos Aires, Emecé Editores, 1974., p.
> 192 and 194, see also Great Britain.
> Foreign Office. British and Foreign

State Papers. vol. XXII, 1833-1834.
London, James Ridgway and Sons,
Piccadilly, 1847, p. 1372.

1766
10/04
Spanish government declared the Falkland Islands
to be dependencies of the Captaincy General of
Buenos Aires.

> Malvinas Islands. Statement by the
> Representative of Argentina, H.E. Dr.
> José María Ruda, before the Subcommittee
> III of the Special Committee on the
> situation with regard to the implemen-
> tation of the declaration on the
> granting of independence to colonial
> countries and peoples. New York, 9
> Sept., 1964, p. 4.

1767
04/01
Ceremony held in Port Louis confirming the French
transfer of the Falklands to the Spanish. The
name of the town was subsequently changed to
Puerto Soledad.

> Malvinas Islands. Statement by the
> Representative of Argentina, H.E. Dr.
> José María Ruda, before the Subcommittee
> III of the Special Committee on the
> situation with regard to the implemen-
> tation of the declaration on the
> granting of independence to colonial
> countries and peoples. New York, 9
> Sept., 1964, p. 4.

1770
07/10
British garrison was evicted from Port Egmont on
Saunder's Isle in the Falklands by "Spanish forces
of the Rio de la Plata Fleet under command of the
governor of Buenos Aires, Buccarelli."

> Malvinas Islands. Statement by the
> Representative of Argentina, H.E. Dr.
> José María Ruda, before the Subcommittee
> III of the Special Committee on the
> situation with regard to the implemen-
> tation of the declaration on the
> granting of independence to colonial
> countries and peoples. New York, 9
> Sept., 1964, p. 5.

1771
01/22
Diplomatic negotiations restores only Port Egmont
to the British. However, the Spanish reserve
their prior right to sovereignty.

> Great Britain. Foreign Office. British
> and Foreign State Papers. vol. XXII,
> 1833-1834. London, James Ridgway and
> Sons, Piccadilly, 1847, p. 1387.

1774
02/11
British decide to withdraw their forces from the
Falkland Islands for economical reasons "leaving
there the proper marks or signals of possession."

> Great Britain. Foreign Office. British
> and Foreign State Papers, vol. XXII,
> 1833-1834. London, James Ridgway and
> Sons, Piccadilly, 1847, p. 1393.

1774
05/20
British leave Port Egmont in the Falklands leaving
behind a plaque claiming the Falklands for
Britain.

> José A. Landeiro. Malvinas; cronología
> de un despojo. Buenos Aires, Adrogue
> Gráfica Editora, 1982, p. 45.

1775
01/17
Capt. James Cook, R.N., landed at three places on
South Georgia and took possession of the island
for Great Britain.

> I.C.J. Pleadings, Antarctica Cases
> (United Kingdom v. Argentina), p. 11.

1775
01/31
Capt. James Cook, R.N., sighted a group of islands
which he called the Sandwich Land.

> I.C.J. Pleadings, Antarctica Cases
> (United Kingdom v. Argentina) , p. 11

1806
06/25
British troops land and approach Buenos Aires. The
Viceroy flees to Cordoba.

> Frederick Alexander Kirkpatrick. A
> History of the Argentine Republic.
> Cambridge, University Press, 1931, pp.
> 46-47.

1806
06/27
British take Buenos Aires.
      Frederick Alexander Kirkpatrick. A
      History of the Argentine Republic.
      Cambridge, University Press, 1931, p. 47.

1806
08/12
British troops in Buenos Aires surrender.
      Frederick Alexander Kirkpatrick. A
      History of the Argentine Republic.
      Cambridge, University Press, 1931, p.50.

1806
08/??
The Viceroy resigned his military command in
Buenos Aires to Liniers [the effective leader of
the volunteer troops opposing the British] and
the political government to the Audiencia due to
public pressure for his failure to defend the
city. "In effect Liniers became civil and
military Governor of Buenos Aires, the Cabildo
acting as Parliament and War Council...."
      Frederick Alexander Kirkpatrick. A
      History of the Argentine Republic.
      Cambridge, University Press, 1931,
      p. 51.

1807
06/28
British land troops to try a second time to take
Buenos Aires.
      Frederick Alexander Kirkpatrick. A
      History of the Argentine Republic.
      Cambridge, University Press, 1931, p. 53.

1807
07/06
British troops capitulate.
      Frederick Alexander Kirkpatrick. A
      History of the Argentine Republic.
      Cambridge, University Press, 1931, p. 57.

1810
05/25
The Provisional Governing Junta of the Provinces
of the Rio de la Plata is formed to administer the
viceroyalty in the name of Ferdinand VII pending
his restoration. This was in opposition to
Napoleon's brother, Joseph Bonaparte, who was
placed on the Spanish throne in 1808. The last
Viceroy resigned the next day.

> Frederick Alexander Kirkpatrick. A
> History of the Argentine Republic.
> Cambridge, University Press, 1931, p. 72.

1810
05/30
The Governing Junta of the Provinces of the Rio de
la Plata receives a request for payment from
Spanish naval officer Gerardo Bordas for his
service as commandant in the Falklands.

> Ernesto J. Fitte, "La Junta de Mayo y
> su autoridad sobre Las Malvinas."
> Historia, No. 46 (enero—marzo 1967), pp.
> 28-29.

1811
01/08
The Spanish garrison on the Falkland Islands was
removed under orders from Gaspar Vigodet in
Montevideo for reasons of economy. A plaque was
left behind stating that the islands were
Spanish.

> Ernesto J. Fitte, "La Junta de Mayo y su
> autoridad sobre Las Malvinas." Historia,
> No. 46 (enero—marzo 1967), pp. 34-35.

1816
07/09
Argentina declares its independence from Spain.

> Henry Stanley Ferns. Argentina. New
> York, Frederick A. Praeger, 1969, p. 62.

1819

"The first British [sic] sealing vessel known to
have visited the South Shetland Islands" was the
Espirito Santo, from Buenos Aires.

> Brian Roberts, "Chronological list of
> Antarctic expeditions," The Polar
> Record, v. 9, no. 59 (May, 1958), p. 102.

1819

British sealing expedition of the ship Admiral
visited South Georgia.
>   Brian Roberts, "Chronological list of
>   Antarctic expeditions," The Polar
>   Record, v. 9, no. 59 (May, 1958), p. 102.

1819

The first ship to have taken Fur Seals in the
South Shetland Islands was the Argentine San Juan
Nepomuceno.
>   Brian Roberts, "Chronological list of
>   Antarctic expeditions," The Polar
>   Record, v. 9, no. 59 (May, 1958), p. 102.

1819
02/18
Capt. William Smith, sighted the islands which
he revisited in October of the same year, planting
the British flag and naming them New South Britain
(this was later changed to South Shetlands).
[Fitte cites the almost simultaneous appearence of
the Espirito Santo, the Hersilia, and Smith's
ship at these islands in October or November of
1819.]
>   I.C.J. Pleadings, Antarctica Cases
>   (United Kingdom v. Argentina) , p. 11.
>   Cf. Ernesto J. Fitte. La disputa con
>   Gran Bretaña por las islas del Atlántico
>   sur. Buenos Aires, Emecé Editores, 1968.
>   pp. 11-13.

1819
12/22
The Russian expedition of Bellingshausen extended
Cook's survey of the South Sandwich Islands naming
a number of previously undiscovered islands.
>   Brian Roberts. "Chronological list of
>   Antarctic expeditions," The Polar
>   Record, v. 9, no. 59 (May, 1958), p. 103
>   and Ernesto J. Fitte. La disputa con
>   Gran Bretaña por las islas del Atlántico
>   sur. Buenos Aires, Emecé Editores, 1968,
>   pp. 132-134.

1820
01/??
James P. Sheffield and his second mate N. B.
Palmer of the U.S. sealing ship Hersilia (from
Stonington) visited the South Shetland Islands.
    Brian Roberts. "Chronological list of
    Antarctic expeditions," The Polar
    Record, v. 9, no. 59 (May, 1958),
    p. 102. Cf. Ernesto J. Fitte. La
    disputa con Gran Bretaña por las islas
    del Atlántico sur. Buenos Aires, Emecé
    Editores, 1968, pp. 11-13.

1820
01/28
The Russian expedition of the ships Vostok and
Mirnyy lead by Thaddeus Bellinghausen surveyed the
South Shetland Islands.
    Brian Roberts. "Chronological list of
    Antarctic expeditions," The Polar
    Record, v. 9, no. 59 (May, 1958), p. 103.

1820
01/30
Edward Bransfield, R.N., sighted what he called
Trinity Land, Hope Island, and Tower Island. This
area is now known as Graham Land and is the
northern extremity of the Antarctic continent.
    I.C.J. Pleadings, Antarctica Cases
    (United Kingdom v. Argentina), p. 1

1820
02/22
James Weddell of the sealer Jane visited and named
the South Orkney Islands.
    Brian Roberts. "Chronological list of
    Antarctic expeditions," The Polar
    Record, v. 9, no. 59 (May, 1958), p. 108.

1820
11/06
U.S. citizen Daniel Jewett, in the service of
Argentina, commanding the frigate Heroina arrived
at the Falkland islands, raised the Argentine flag
and claimed the islands for Argentina.
    José A. Landeiro. Malvinas; cronológia
    de un despojo. Buenos Aires, Adrogue
    Gráfica Editora, 1982, p. 48.

1821
12/06
Capt. George Powell discovered the South Orkney
Islands. The following day he landed on the
largest and claimed them for Britain.
>I.C.J. Pleadings, Antarctica Cases
>(United Kingdom v. Argentina),
>pp. 11-12.

1823

Pablo Areguati designated governor of the Falkland
Islands by the government of Buenos Aires.
>Malvinas Islands. Statement by the
>Representative of Argentina, H.E. Dr.
>José María Ruda, before the Subcommittee
>III of the Special Committee on the
>situation with regard to the implemen-
>tation of the declaration on the
>granting of independence to colonial
>countries and peoples. New York, 9
>Sept., 1964, p. 9.

1823
12/02
Monroe Doctrine first enunciated by President
James Monroe.
>James Monroe. Message from the
>President of the United States, to both
>Houses of Congress, at the commencement
>of the First Session of the Eighteenth
>Congress. Washington, Gales & Seaton,
>1823.

1829
06/10
Decree of the provisional governor of Buenos Aires
establishes a Political and Military Commandancy in
Puerto de la Soledad in the Falklands with jurisdiction over the Falklands and "those adjacent to
Cape Horn in the Atlantic."
>Ernesto J. Fitte. La disputa con Gran
>Bretaña por las islas del Atlántico sur.
>Buenos Aires, Emecé Editores, 1968.
>p. 234.

1829
06/10
Luis Vernet is named Commandant of the Political
and Military Commandancy of the Falkland Islands.
>Malvinas Islands. Statement by the
>Representative of Argentina, H.E. Dr.
>José María Ruda, before the Subcommittee
>III of the Special Committee on the
>situation with regard to the implemen-
>tation of the declaration on the
>granting of independence to colonial
>countries and peoples. New York, 9
>Sept., 1964, p. 10.

1829
11/10
Britain protested the establishment of the Political and Military Commandancy in the Falklands,
stating that this was "an authority that is incompatible with the Sovereign Rights of His Britannic
Majesty over the Islands."
>Malvinas Islands. Statement by the
>Representative of Argentina, H.E. Dr.
>José María Ruda, before the Subcommittee
>III of the Special Committee on the
>situation with regard to the implemen-
>tation of the declaration on the
>granting of independence to colonial
>countries and peoples. New York, 9
>Sept., 1964, p. 10.

1831
06/30
U.S. schooner Harriet seized by Luis Vernet who
claimed he was acting under authority of the
government of Buenos Aires.
>Williams v. Suffolk Insurance Company,
>13 Peters 415 (1839) at 416.

1831
08/18
U.S. schooner Breakwater seized by Luis Vernet at
the Falklands again claiming his authority from
the government of Buenos Aires.
>Williams v. Suffolk Insurance Company,
>13 Peters 415 (1839) at 416.

1831
08/19
The cargo of seal skins from the U.S. schooner
Superior was confiscated by Luis Vernet on the
Falkland Islands.
>Davison v. Seal-skins. [2 Paine, 324]
>Circuit Court, D. Connecticut (1835)
>[7 Fed. Cas. pp. 192-197].

1831
12/07
Letter from Silas Duncan of the U.S. Lexington to
the Argentine Minister for Foreign Affairs
concerning to the "plunder [of] the American
schooner Harriet...while lying at the Falkland
Islands." Duncan requests that "Lewis Vernet
having been guilty of piracy and robbery be
delivered up to the U. States to be tried, or that
he be arrested and punished by the laws of Buenos
Ayres."

> Argentine Republic. Ministerio de
> Relaciones Exteriores. Papers relative
> to the origin and present state of the
> questions pending with the United States
> of America, on the subject of the
> Malvinas, (Falkland Islands)....
> Buenos-Ayres, Gaceta Mercantil, 1832. p. 14.

1831
12/30
A U.S. corvette, the Lexington, flying the French
flag and carrying signals asking for pilots headed
for the wharf of Puerto Soledad in the Falklands.
In this fashion, U.S. sailors landed, destroyed
the settlement, and captured many of the
inhabitants, including Vernet.

> Malvinas Islands. Statement by the
> Representative of Argentina, H.E. Dr.
> José María Ruda, before the Subcommittee
> III of the Special Committee on the
> situation with regard to the implemen-
> tation of the declaration on the
> granting of independence to colonial
> countries and peoples. New York, 9
> Sept., 1964, p. 11.

1832

Argentina returned to settle in Puerto Soledad.

> Malvinas Islands. Statement by the
> Representative of Argentina, H.E. Dr.
> José María Ruda, before the Subcommittee
> III of the Special Committee on the
> situation with regard to the implemen-
> tation of the declaration on the
> granting of independence to colonial
> countries and peoples. New York, 9
> Sept., 1964, p. 12.

1832
01/26
Letter of the U.S. Secretary of State to the U.S.
Charge d'Affaires at Buenos Aires puts forth the
U.S. position regarding Vernet, the seizure of U.
S. vessels, the right of fishery, orders for the
recapture of the vessels and orders to "break up
the settlement and bring him [i.e. Vernet] to
Buenos Aires for trial. The U. S. had doubts as
to the authenticity of a decree of Vernet's to the
masters of vessels arriving at the Falklands. The
result of these doubts prompted the following
statement:"With these reasons for believing the
pretence of a decree a mere color for piratical
acts, the President [Jackson] has directed the
Secretary of the Navy to send all the force he
could command to those seas...."

> William Ray Manning. Diplomatic cor-
> respondence of the United States;
> Inter-American Affairs 1831-1860. vol.
> I: Argentina. Washington, Carnegie
> Endowment for International Peace, 1932,
> pp. 4-12 passim.

1832
02/21
John Biscoe in the Tula from London annexed Graham
Land for the British.

> Brian Roberts. "Chronological list of
> Antarctic expeditions," The Polar
> Record, v. 9, no. 59 (May, 1958), p. 111.

1832
04/24
U.S. Commodore Rodgers wrote to the Argentine
Ministry of Foreign Affairs explaining Capt.
Duncan's conduct in breaking up the Falkland
Island settlement. "From this correspondence thus
far, it is evident that Capt. Duncan, when he went
to the Falkland Islands, and broke up Vernet's
establishment, was under the impression that they
were a nest of pirates; and that Commodore
Rodgers, as soon as he found this to be a mistake
... discharged the prisoners, disclaiming to hold
them as pirates; and there is no pretence, in any
of this correspondence, that Capt. Duncan, in this
particular act, was pursuing any special order of
the government of the United States; but he was,
no doubt, acting in good faith, under what he
considered his duty, in protecting the rights of
American citizens."

> Davison **v** Seal-skins. [2 Paine, 324]
> Circuit Court, D. Connecticut (1835)
> [7 Fed. Cas. at 196].

1833
01/03
The British evicted the Argentines from Puerto
Soledad.

> Malvinas Islands. Statement by the
> Representative of Argentina, H.E. Dr.
> José María Ruda, before the Subcommittee
> III of the Special Committee on the
> situation with regard to the implemen-
> tation of the declaration on the
> granting of independence to colonial
> countries and peoples. New York, 9
> Sept., 1964, p. 12.

1833
01/15
Argentina protested the eviction of its colony in
the Falklands to the British Chargé d'Affairs in
Buenos Aires who replied that he lacked instructions.

> Malvinas Islands. Statement by the
> Representative of Argentina, H.E. Dr.
> José María Ruda, before the Subcommittee
> III of the Special Committee on the
> situation with regard to the implemen-
> tation of the declaration on the
> granting of independence to colonial
> countries and peoples. New York, 9
> Sept., 1964, p. 13.

1833
01/22
Argentina again protested the eviction and the
British Chargé d'Affairs renewed his "passive
stand."

> Malvinas Islands. Statement by the
> Representative of Argentina, H.E. Dr.
> José María Ruda, before the Subcommittee
> III of the Special Committee on the
> situation with regard to the implemen-
> tation of the declaration on the
> granting of independence to colonial
> countries and peoples. New York, 9
> Sept., 1964, p. 13.

1833
04/24
Argentine representative in London, Manuel Moreno,
filed a protest to the British over the Falklands
eviction.

> Malvinas Islands. Statement by the
> Representative of Argentina, H.E. Dr.
> José María Ruda, before the Subcommittee
> III of the Special Committee on the
> situation with regard to the implemen-

tation of the declaration on the
granting of independence to colonial
countries and peoples. New York, 9
Sept., 1964, p. 13.

1833
06/17
Argentine representative in London, Manuel Moreno,
reiterated his protest of 24 April 1833 in a
lengthy memorandum.

> Great Britain. Foreign Office. British
> and Foreign State Papers. vol. XXII,
> 1833-1834. London, James Ridgway and
> Sons, Piccadilly, 1847, p. 1366-1384.

1834
01/08
Viscount Palmerston replied to the Argentine
representative in London, that the rights of
Britain "were based on the original discovery and
subsequent occupation of the said Islands."

> Malvinas Islands. Statement by the
> Representative of Argentina, H.E. Dr.
> José María Ruda, before the Subcommittee
> III of the Special Committee on the
> situation with regard to the implemen-
> tation of the declaration on the
> granting of independence to colonial
> countries and peoples. New York, 9
> Sept., 1964, p. 13.

1834
12/29
Argentine representative Moreno rejected
Palmerston's arguments.

> Malvinas Islands. Statement by the
> Representative of Argentina, H.E. Dr.
> José María Ruda, before the Subcommittee
> III of the Special Committee on the
> situation with regard to the implemen-
> tation of the declaration on the
> granting of independence to colonial
> countries and peoples. New York, 9
> Sept., 1964, p. 13.

1839
01/??
U.S. Supreme Court adjudicates the case of Charles
L. Williams vs. The Suffolk Insurance Company
regarding the seizure of the schooners Harriet and
Breakwater by the authorities of Buenos Aires on
the Falklands. The court would not question the
Executive Authority's position "...that the Falkland islands do not constitute any part of the
dominions within the sovereignty of Buenos
Ayres...."
> Williams v. The Suffolk Insurance
> Company, 13 Peters 415 (1839) at 415-
> 422.

1843
06/23
Royal Letters Patent issued by the British providing for the government of the "Settlements in
the Falkland Islands and their Dependencies."
> I.C.J. Pleadings, Antarctica Cases
> (United Kingdom v. Argentina), p. 13.

1847
11/27
George Rennie appointed as British Governor and
Commander in Chief in the Falkland Islands and
their Dependencies.
> I.C.J. Pleadings, Antarctica Cases
> (United Kingdom v. Argentina), p. 45.

1876
04/28
British Letters Patent of 23 June 1843 revised.
> Brian Roberts. "Chronological list of
> Antarctic expeditions," The Polar
> Record, v. 9, no. 59 (May, 1958), p. 115

1892
02/25
British Letters Patent of 28 April 1876 revised.
> Brian Roberts. "Chronological list of
> Antarctic expeditions," The Polar
> Record, v. 9, no. 59 (May, 1958), p. 115

1902
04/??
The Norwegian C.A. Larsen explored Cumberland bay
and named a smaller adjacent bay Grytviken which
in Norwegian means "Bay of Pots" because he found
several large ones used to rend blubber left there
by previous expeditions.
> Ernesto J. Fitte. La disputa con Gran
> Bretaña por las islas del Atlántico sur.

Buenos Aires, Emecé Editores, 1968.
p. 78.

1903
02/25
W.S. Bruce , with his Scottish scientific expedition to the South Orkneys, arrived at Laurie
Island and established Copeland Observatory, a
meteorological station which was entrusted to the
Argentine meteorological Office in the following
year.

Ernesto J. Fitte. La disputa con Gran
Bretaña por las islas del Atlántico sur.
Buenos Aires, Emecé Editores, 1968.
p. 165. See also I.C.J. Pleadings,
Antarctica Cases (United Kingdom v.
Argentina), p. 14.

1904

The Norwegian Capt. Larsen, formed the Compañia
Argentina de Pesca in Buenos Aires and established
a whaling station at South Georgia.

I.C.J. Pleadings, Antarctica Cases
(United Kingdom v. Argentina), p. 14

1904
01/04
Argentine Ministry of Agriculture granted permission by the Argentine government to take possession of the meteorological station in the South
Orkneys offered by W.S. Bruce.

Ernesto J. Fitte. La disputa con Gran
Bretaña por las islas del Atlántico sur.
Buenos Aires, Emecé Editores, 1968. p. 181.

1904
01/04
The Argentine Hugo A. Acuña, one of the four
Argentines to be sent to man the Laurie Island
meteorological station is given charge of the
South Orkneys postal branch.

Ernesto J. Fitte. La disputa con Gran
Bretaña por las islas del Atlántico sur.
Buenos Aires, Emecé Editores, 1968.
p. 176.

1904
02/22
The meteorological station at Laurie Island in the
South Orkneys was "entrusted to the Argentine
meteorological office."
>   I.C.J. Pleadings, Antarctica Cases
>   (United Kingdom v. Argentina), p. 14,
>   and Ernesto J. Fitte. La disputa con
>   Gran Bretaña por las islas del Atlántico
>   sur. Buenos Aires, Emecé Editores, 1968.
>   p. 173.

1904
11/16
Three ships of the Compañia Argentina de Pesca
arrived at uninhabited Grytviken in South Georgia
to begin construction of a whaling station.
>   Ernesto J. Fitte. La disputa con Gran
>   Bretaña por las islas del Atlántico sur.
>   Buenos Aires, Emecé Editores, 1968. p. 82.

1905
01/01
The Argentine Ministry of Agriculture authorized
the Compañia Argentina de Pesca to establish a
meteorological station in Grytviken in the South
Georgias. Observations from this station continued
until 1943.
>   Ernesto J. Fitte. La disputa con Gran
>   Bretaña por las islas del Atlántico sur.
>   Buenos Aires, Emecé Editores, 1968.
>   p. 91.

1906
01/01
The British granted the Compañia Argentina de
Pesca a lease for 500 acres of land in the South
Georgias.
>   I.C.J. Pleadings, Antarctica Cases
>   (United Kingdom v. Argentina), p. 17.

1906
08/23
British government sends letter to the Argentine
government to clarify that the South Orkneys are
British.
>   Ernesto J. Fitte. La disputa con Gran
>   Bretaña por las islas del Atlántico sur.
>   Buenos Aires, Emecé Editores, 1968.
>   p. 180-181.

1908

British send a magistrate to Grytviken, South
Georgias.

> Ernesto J. Fitte. La disputa con Gran
> Bretaña por las islas del Atlántico sur.
> Buenos Aires, Emecé Editores, 1968. p. 119

1908

British establish a post office in Grytviken and a
police constable.

> Ernesto J. Fitte. La disputa con Gran
> Bretaña por las islas del Atlántico sur.
> Buenos Aires, Emecé Editores, 1968. p. 119.

1908
06/21
"South Georgia, the South Orkneys, the South
Shetlands, the Sandwich Islands and the territory
of Graham Land were by Royal Letters Patent
formally constituted Dependencies of the Colony of
the Falkland Islands...."

> I.C.J. Pleadings, Antarctica Cases
> (United Kingdom v. Argentina), p. 15.

1908
07/21
British Letters Patent of 25 February 1892 revised
to claim for Britain all lands south of"the 50th
parallel of south latitude, and lying between the
20th and the 80th degrees of west longitude."

> I.C.J. Pleadings, Antarctica Cases
> (United Kingdom v. Argentina), p. 39.

1913
07/05
Negotiations were begun for the British cession of
the South Orkneys to Argentina. The talks
stalemated because Argentina wanted its previous
claims to these islands recognized and Britain
would not do so. [The British position holds that
the terms of the draft treaty is an indication
that Argentina recognized British claims.]

> I.C.J. Pleadings, Antarctica Cases
> (United Kingdom v. Argentina), p. 23.
> Cf. Ernesto J. Fitte. La disputa con
> Gran Bretaña por las islas del Atlántico
> sur. Buenos Aires, Emecé Editores, 1968,
> pp. 179-204.

1917
03/28
British Letters Patent of 21 July 1908 revised.
[This corrected the embarassing 1908 inclusion of
Southern Chile and Argentina within the British
claim.]
> I.C.J. Pleadings, Antarctica Cases
> (United Kingdom v. Argentina), pp.
> 40-41.

1920

The British granted a lease in the South Orkneys
of 500 acres to a Norwegian company, the A/S
Tönsberg Hvalfangeri.
> I.C.J. Pleadings, Antarctica Cases
> (United Kingdom v. Argentina), p. 18.

1925

Argentina began construction of a wireless station
on Laurie Island in the South Orkneys. Argentina
then applied for a call sign from the
International Telegraph Bureau at Berne.
> I.C.J. Pleadings, Antarctica Cases
> (United Kingdom v. Argentina), p. 25.

1926
04/14
Britain protested the Argentine call sign of the
Laurie Island wireless station reiterating British
sovereignty over the South Orkneys.
> I.C.J. Pleadings, Antarctica Cases
> (United Kingdom v. Argentina), p. 25.

1927
09/08
Britain protested the assumption of Argentine
sovereignty over Laurie Island.
> I.C.J. Pleadings, Antarctica Cases
> (United Kingdom v. Argentina), p. 25.

1927
09/14
The wireless station on Laurie Island was put into
operation with the Argentine call sign.
> I.C.J. Pleadings, Antarctica Cases
> (United Kingdom v. Argentina), p. 25.
> Cf. Ernesto J. Fitte. La disputa con
> Gran Bretaña por las islas del Atlántico
> sur. Buenos Aires, Emece Editores, 1968,
> p. 241.

1927
12/15
Argentina sought to reopen negotiations regarding
the 1931 proposed cession of the Orkneys but
nothing occurred.
>   Ernesto J. Fitte. La disputa con Gran
>   Bretaña por las islas del Atlántico sur.
>   Buenos Aires, Emecé Editores, 1968,
>   pp. 206-207.

1928
01/20
Argentina responded to the British protest of 08
Sept. 1927 stating that she claimed the South
Orkneys on the grounds of "first occupation
constantly maintained."
>   I.C.J. Pleadings, Antarctica Cases
>   (United Kingdom v. Argentina), p. 25.

1947
03/??
The Argentine Ministry of the Treasury sent an
inspector to verify and stamp an alcoholic dis-
tillery in Grytviken which he accomplished.
>   Ernesto J. Fitte. La disputa con Gran
>   Bretaña por las islas del Atlántico sur.
>   Buenos Aires, Emecé Editores, 1968. p. 123.

1947
08/29
The Argentine delegation to the Inter-American
Conference for the Maintenance of Continental
Peace and Security [i.e. the Rio Treaty] requested
that the following appear in the minutes of the
session: "The Argentine Delegation declares that
within the waters adjacent to the South American
continent, along the coasts of the Argentine
Republic in the so-called security zone, it does
not recognize the existence of colonies or
possessions of European colonies and adds that it
especially reserves and maintains intact the
legitimate title and rights of the Republic of
Argentina to the Falkland (Malvinas) Islands, the
South Georgia Islands, the South Sandwich Islands,
and the lands included in the Argentine Antarctic
sector, over which the Republic exercises the
corresponding sovereignty."
>   OEA/Ser.A/1/CRJ/125/CII/19

1947
08/30
U.S. Delegation suggests a clarification in the
sense of the Rio Treaty that it does not affect
questions of sovereignty.
>   OEA/Ser.A/1/CRJ/130.CII/24.

1947
10/02
The Inter-American Treaty of Reciprocal
Assistence, or The Rio Treaty, was signed at Rio
de Janeiro.
> OEA/Ser.A/1/CRJ/131.CC/27-30/8

1950
01/01
The British seized the Argentine meteorological
station at Grytviken, South Georgias, and sent the
instruments to the Compañia Argentina de Pesca by
way of Montevideo.
> Ernesto J. Fitte. La disputa con Gran
> Bretaña por las islas del Atlántico sur.
> Buenos Aires, Emecé Editores, 1968.
> p. 125.

1956

A group of Argentine naval personnel spent the
summer on one of the islands of Southern Thule in
the South Sandwich Islands.
> Ernesto J. Fitte. La disputa con Gran
> Bretaña por las islas del Atlántico sur.
> Buenos Aires, Emecé Editores, 1968. p. 139.

1957

The Argentine Prefectura General Marítima sent an
officer to Grytviken, South Georgia, to investigate a suspected source of contraband alcohol. The
British refused to let him land without a
passport.
> Ernesto J. Fitte. La disputa con Gran
> Bretaña por las islas del Atlántico sur.
> Buenos Aires, Emecé Editores, 1968. p. 124.

1957
02/28
Argentine Decree Law No. 2.191 established the
"National Territory of Tierra del Fuego,
Antarctica and South Atlantic Islands." This
included the Falklands, Georgias and the South
Sandwich Islands.
> Ernesto J. Fitte. La disputa con Gran
> Bretaña por las islas del Atlántico sur.
> Buenos Aires, Emecé Editores, 1968. p. 237.

1960
12/14
U. N. Resolution A/1514 (Declaration on the
granting of independence to colonial countries and
peoples) declares, among other things, that "All
peoples have the right to self-determination; by
virtue of that right they freely determine their
political status and freely pursue their economic,
social and cultural development.

> G.A. Res. 1514, 15 U.N. GAOR Supp. (no.
> 16) at 66-67. U.N. Doc. A/4684 (1961).

1962
03/03
British Order in Council established the separate
colony of British Antarctica Territory.

> I Stat. Instr., 1962, No. 400.

1964
03/06
British landed a platoon of Marines who camped on
one of the South Sandwich Islands until the 22nd
of March of 1964.

> Ernesto J. Fitte. La disputa con Gran
> Bretaña por las islas del Atlántico sur.
> Buenos Aires, Emecé Editores, 1968. p. 139.

1964
09/09
Argentine statement to a U.N. subcommittee
submitted regarding the Falklands as an integral
part of Argentine territory.

> Malvinas Islands. Statement by the
> Representative of Argentina, H.E. Dr.
> José María Ruda, before the Subcommittee
> III of the Special Committee on the
> situation with regard to the implemen-
> tation of the declaration on the
> granting of independence to colonial
> countries and peoples. New York, 9
> Sept., 1964. 21 pp.

1966
01/04
U.N. Resolution A/2065, invites Britain and
Argentina to begin negotiations in order to find a
peaceful solution to the dispute between them
regarding the Falklands.

> G.A. Res. 2065, 20 U.N. GAOR Supp. (no.
> 14) at 57. U.N Doc. A/6015 (1966)

1974
01/29
U.N. Resolution A/3160 again invites Britain and
Argentina to arrive at a peaceful solution.
        G.A. Res. 3160, 28 U.N. GAOR Supp. (no.
        30) at 108-109. U.N. Doc. A/9030 (1974).

1976
01/16
The Inter-American Juridical Committee of the
Organization of American States declared "that the
Republic of Argentina has an undeniable right of
sovereignty over the Malvinas Islands...."
        OEA Serie Q/IV.12.CJI-2, pp. 17-22.

1976
02/04
Argentine destroyer <u>Almirante Storni</u> fires on and
chases the unarmed British research ship
<u>Shackleton</u> 400 miles off Argentine coast, 78 miles
from Falkland Islands. Argentina claims the
<u>Shackleton</u> was in Argentine territorial waters.
        Times of London, 6 February 1976.

1976
10/??
President of Colombia solicits help of Spanish
King Juan Carlos regarding claims of sovereignty
of Falklands.
        Times of London, 13 October 1976.

1976
12/??
British protest the Argentine establishment of a
scientific base on southern Thule in the South
Sandwich Islands.
        Times of London, 10 May 1978.

1977
07/??
Secret talks between Britain and Argentina take
place in Rome concerning the future of the
Falkland Islands.
        Times of London, 14 July 1977.

1977
12/??
Representatives from Britain and Argentina meet in
New York to discuss Falklands.
        Times of London, 13 December 1977.

1978
05/10
Britain and Argentina continue discussion over
Argentine scientific base on southern Thule in the
South Sandwich Islands.
> Times of London, 10 May 1978.

1980
11/27
British Foreign Secretary Lord Carrington confirms
that discussions concerning the Falklands are
taking place, but denies that sovereignty might be
transferred to Argentina.
> Times of London, 27 November 1980.

1982
03/19
Argentine workers land on South Georgia to
dismantle an old whaling station. They did not
secure necessary visas and work permits. They
raise the Argentine flag.
> Times of London, 23 March 1982.

1982
03/20
In response for the scrap workers raising the
Argentine flag in the South Georgias, a group of
Falkland Islanders invaded the offices of the
Argentine State Airline (LADE) in Stanley,
exchanging the Argentine flag for the Union Jack
and painting the office with toothpaste.
> Convicción (Buenos Aires), 27 March
> 1982.

1982
04/02
Argentina seizes the Falkland , the South
Georgias, and the South Sandwich Islands.
> New York Times, 3 April 1982.

1982
04/25
Argentine troops surrender to British at South
Georgia.
> New York Times, 26 April 1982.

1982
04/28
A resolution is adopted by the Organization of
American States Ministers of Foreign Affairs
regarding the Falklands underscoring the
Declaration of the Inter-American Juridical
Committee on 16 January 1976.
> OEA/Ser.F/II.20 Doc.28/82 rev. 3.

1982
06/14
All Argentine land, sea and air forces in the
Falkland Islands surrender to the British.
> Text of Argentine Surrender Document in
> Daily Report; Western Europe. [Washing-
> ton], FBIS, June 17, 1982. pp. Q4-Q5.

1982
06/20
Argentine personnel on Thule Island, South Sandwich Islands, surrender to British.
> Daily Report; Western Europe. [Washing-
> ton], FBIS, June 21, 1982. p. Q2.

DOCUMENTS

PRIMER PERÍODO.

ROMA Y ESPAÑA.

~~~

BULA DEL PAPA ALEJANDRO VI,

Haciendo donacion de la América á los reyes católicos Fernando ó Isabel, en 4 de mayo de 1493.

Cuando Colon hubo descubierto las Indias occidentales, Fernando, rey de Castilla, obtuvo su concesion del papa Alejandro VI. Ella dió lugar á una discusion entre la España y el Portugal, que fué sometida á la decision del soberano Pontífice. Cristóbal Colon habia seguido el curso del sol, miéntras que Vasco de Gama navegó en rumbo opuesto cuando descubrió las Indias. Para conciliar los intereses de ambas partes, la Santa Sede propuso dividir el globo terrestre en dos porciones iguales, y por esta bula acordó á la España todo lo que pudiera descubrir al Oeste de una primera línea meridiana colocada á cien leguas al Oeste de una de las islas Azores ó del Cabo Verde (San Antonio, la mas setentrional, 36° al O. de Lisboa); y al Portugal, el país que reconociese al E. de ese meridiano, con tal que no hubiese sido ocupado por ningun príncipe cristiano ántes del dia de Noel del mismo año. Esa línea, llamada la *Línea de marcacion*, separó el Brasil de la América meridional.

El rey D. Juan, que reclamaba la posesion de las islas Molucas, protestó contra esa bula. No obstante, para allanar las dificultades que podrian suscitarse en el porvenir entre las dos coronas de Castilla y Portugal, se convino en someterla á la decision de tres comisarios de cada nacion, que se reunieron en Tordesillas el siete de junio de mil cuatrocientos noventa y tres (1). Estos trazaron una nueva línea llamada *Línea de demarcacion*, porque destruía la otra, llevándola á doscientas setenta leguas mas al Oeste : y se convino en que todos los países situados al O. de ese meridiano, pertenecerian á la España, y los al E. al Portugal. Esta decision fué aprobada el 2 de julio, en Arévalo, por el rey de España; y el 25 de febrero del siguiente año, en Évora, por el de Portugal (2).

(1) Véase el tratado de Tordesillas, página 19.
(2) Herrera, dec. I, lib. II, cap. 4, 5, 8 y 10. — Gomara, lib. I, cap. 19. — Lafitau, *Histoire des découvertes*, tom. I, liv. I. — Torquemada, *Monar. Indiana*, lib. XVIII, cap. 3.

DOCUMENTO.

1493. *Alexander Episcopus, servus servorum Dei, charissimo in Christo filio Ferdinando Regi, et charissimæ in Christo filiæ Elisabeth, Reginæ Castellæ, Legionis, Aragonum, Siciliæ et Granatæ, illustribus: Salutem et apostolicam benedictionem.*

Inter cætera divinæ Majestatis beneplacita opera, et cordis nostri desiderabilia, illud profectò potissimum existit, ut fides catholica et christiana religio, nostris præsertim temporibus, exaltetur, ac ubilibet amplietur et dilatetur, animarumque salus procuretur, ac barbaricæ nationes deprimantur, et ad fidem ipsam reducantur. Undè, cùm ad hanc sacram Petri Sedem, divinâ favente clementiâ, meritis licet imparibus, evecti fuerimus, cognoscentes vos tanquam veros catholicos Reges et Principes, quales semper fuisse novimus, et à vobis præclarè gesta toti penè jam orbi notissima demonstrant, nedùm id exoptare, sed omni conatu, studio et diligentiâ, nullis laboribus, nullis impensis, nullisque parcendo periculis, etiam proprium sanguinem effundendo efficere, ac omnem animum vestrum, omnesque conatus ad hoc jamdudum dedicasse, quemadmodùm recuperatio regni Granatæ à tyrannide Saracenorum hodiernis temporibus per vos, cum tantâ divini nominis gloriâ, facta testatur; dignè ducimus non immeritò, et debemus illa vobis etiam spontè et favorabiliter concedere, per quæ hujusmodi sanctum et laudabile ab immortali Deo cœptum propositum in dies

TRADUCCION.

(Del ejemplar impreso en Lisboa el año de 1750.)

Alejandro obispo, siervo de los siervos de Dios. Á nuestro muy
amado en Cristo hijo Fernando, y á nuestra muy amada en
Cristo hija Isabel, Rey y Reina ilustres de Castilla, Leon,
Aragon, Sicilia y Granada : Salud y apostólica bendicion.

1493.

Entre todas las obras que se ha dignado crear la divina Ma-
jestad y que nuestro corazon desea mas ardientemente, figura
á la verdad como primordial la exaltacion de la fe católica y de
la Religion cristiana, con especialidad en nuestros tiempos, y
su difusion y propagacion por todas partes ; como igualmente
la de trabajar en la salvacion de las almas y en someter á las
naciones bárbaras para reducirlas á la misma fe. Así es que
habiéndonos favorecido la clemencia divina con nuestra exaltacion á la silla de Pedro, aunque con méritos desiguales, y
conociendo que vosotros sois, como hemos reconocido que lo
habeis sido siempre, unos Reyes y Príncipes verdaderamente
católicos, como elocuentemente lo demuestra ya, á la faz de
casi todo el orbe, la notoriedad de vuestros hechos ; y que no
tan solo habeis tenido este vehemente deseo, sino que lo habeis
puesto por obra, empeñando en ello, hace ya mucho tiempo,
todo vuestro espíritu y todos vuestros conatos, con el mayor
esfuerzo, cuidado y diligencia ; sin omitir, hasta conseguirlo,
ningun linaje de trabajos y gastos, y aun despreciando todos
los peligros, incluso el de la efusion de vuestra propia sangre,

1493.   ferventiori animo ad ipsius Dei honorem, et imperii christiani propagationem prosequi valeatis.

Sanè accepimus quòd vos dudum animum proposueratis aliquas insulas et terras firmas remotas et incognitas, ac per alios hactenùs non repertas, quærere et invenire, ut illarum incolas et habitatores ad colendum Redemptorem nostrum, et fidem catholicam profitendam reduceretis, sed hactenùs in expugnatione et recuperatione ipsius regni Granatæ plurimùm occupati hujusmodi sanctum et laudabile propositum vestrum ad optatum finem perducere nequivistis, sed tandem sicut Domino placuit, regno prædicto recuperato, volentes desiderium adimplere vestrum, dilectum filium Christophorum Columbum, virum utique dignum et plurimùm commendandum, ac tanto negotio aptum, cum navigiis et hominibus ad similia instructis, non sine maximis laboribus et periculis ac expensis destinatis, ut terras firmas et insulas remotas et incognitas hujusmodi, per mare ubi hactenùs navigatum non fuerat, diligenter inquireret.

Qui tandem (divino auxilio factâ extremâ diligentiâ in mari Oceano navigantes) certas insulas remotissimas, et etiam terras firmas, quæ per alios hactenùs repertæ non fuerant, invenerunt, in quibus quamplurimæ gentes pacificè viventes, et, ut asseritur, nudi incedentes, nec carnibus vescentes inhabitant, et, ut præfati Nuntii vestri possunt opinari, gentes ipsæ in insulis et terris prædictis habitantes credunt unum Deum Creatorem in cœlis esse, ad fidem catholicam amplexendam, et bonis moribus imbuendum satis apti videntur, spesque habetur quòd si erudirentur, nomen Salvatoris Domini nostri Jesu Christi in terris et insulis prædictis faterentur, ac præfatus Christo-

como lo comprueba la recuperacion que con tanta gloria del nombre divino habeis hecho, en estos tiempos, del reino de Granada, de la tiranía de los Sarracenos: con razon y dignamente juzgamos de nuestro deber concederos, favorablemente y de buena voluntad, todas aquellas cosas por cuyo medio podais proseguir, con ánimo de dia en dia mas fervoroso, y en obsequio de Dios mismo, el propósito que habeis comenzado, santo y laudable á los ojos del Dios inmortal, de propagar el imperio cristiano.

En efecto, hemos sabido que vosotros habiais concebido el designio de buscar y encontrar algunas islas y tierras firmes distantes y desconocidas, y hasta ahora no encontradas por otros, para reducir á sus moradores y habitantes á rendir culto á nuestro Redentor y á profesar la fe católica, pero que hasta el presente no pudísteis llevar al deseado término vuestro santo y laudable propósito, por encontraros muy ocupados en combatir por la recuperacion del mismo reino de Granada; el que recuperado al fin, como á Dios plugo, y persistiendo vosotros en cumplir vuestro deseo, destinásteis á nuestro predilecto hijo Cristóbal Colon, varon verdaderamente digno y tan recomendable como capaz para un asunto de tamaña magnitud, proveyéndole de naves y de hombres, aprestados para ese objeto con supremos trabajos, peligros y gastos, á fin de que buscase con el mayor empeño las tierras firmes é islas remotas y desconocidas, por un mar en que hasta ahora no se habia navegado.

Los que por fin (habiendo navegado en el mar Océano, con el auxilio divino y á merced de un cuidado grandísimo) encontraron ciertas islas muy remotas, y tambien tierras firmes que hasta ahora no habian sido encontradas por otros, en las cuales habitan muchísimas gentes que viven pacíficamente, y las que, como se asegura, andan desnudas y no se alimentan con carne; y, segun pueden opinar vuestros referidos nuncios, esas mismas gentes que moran en las mencionadas islas y tierras creen que existe un Dios Criador en los cielos, y parecen suficientemente aptas para abrazar la fe católica y para ser imbuidas en las buenas costumbres, y hay la esperanza de que si

1493.   phorus in ..nâ ex principalibus insulis prædictis, jam unam
turrim satis munitam, in quâ certos christianos, qui secum
inerant, in custodiam, et ut alias insulas et terras firmas, remotas et incognitas inquirerent, posuit, construi et ædificari
fecit.

In quibus quidem insulis et terris jam repertis, aurum, aro-
mata, et aliæ quamplurimæ res pretiosæ diversi generis, et
diversæ qualitatis reperiuntur.

Undè omnibus diligenter, et præsertim fidei catholicæ exal-
tatione et dilatatione (proùt decet catholicos Reges et Principes) consideratis, more progenitorum vestrorum claræ memo-
riæ Regum, terras firmas et insulas prædictas, illarumque
incolas et habitatores vobis, divinâ favente clementiâ, subjicere,
et ad fidem catholicam reducere proposuistis.

Nos igitur hujusmodi vestrum sanctum et laudabile propositum plurimùm in Domino commendantes, ac cupientes ut
illud ad debitum finem perducatur, et ipsum nomen Salvatoris nostri in partibus illis inducatur, hortamur vos quamplu-
rimùm in Domino, et per sacri lavacri susceptionem, quâ man-
datis apostolicis obligati estis, et viscera misericordiæ Domini
nostri Jesu Christi attentè requirimus, ut cùm expeditionem hujusmodi omninò prosequi et assumere probâ mente orthodoxæ
fidei zelo intendatis, populis in hujusmodi insulis et terris
degentes ad christianam Religionem suscipiendam inducere
velitis et debeatis, nec pericula, nec labores ullo unquàm tempore vos deterreant, firmâ spe fiduciâque conceptis, quòd Deus
omnipotens conatos vestros feliciter prosequetur.

Et ut tanti negotii provinciam apostolicæ gratiæ largitate
donati liberiùs et audaciùs assumatis, motu proprio, non ad
vestram vel alterius pro vobis super hoc nobis oblatæ peti-

se instruyesen reconocerian el nombre del Salvador nuestro 1493. Señor Jesucristo en las indicadas tierras é islas; y que el expresado Cristóbal hizo ya construir y edificar, en una de las principales islas mencionadas, una torre bien fortificada, en la cual situó á varios cristianos que con él habian entrado, para que la custodiasen y para que se informasen de otras islas y tierras firmes, remotas y desconocidas.

En cuyas islas, por cierto, y tierras ya descubiertas, se encuentra oro, aromas, y muchísimas otras cosas preciosas de diverso género y de diversa cualidad.

De donde provino que, teniendo vosotros cuidadosamente en consideracion estas circunstancias, y con especialidad la exaltacion y propaganda de la fe católica (cual conviene á Reyes y Príncipes católicos), os propusísteis, segun la costumbre de vuestros progenitores, — Reyes de ilustre recordacion, — someter á vuestro dominio las tieras firmes é islas precitadas, y, favorecidos por la divina clemencia, convertir á la fe católica á sus moradores y habitantes.

Nosotros, pues, recomendando mucho al Señor vuestro santo y laudable propósito, y deseando que se lleve á debido término, y que el nombre mismo de nuestro Salvador se lleve á aquellas regiones, os exhortamos encarecidamente en el Señor, y os pedimos con especialidad, que, tanto con el auxilio del sagrado bautismo, al cual os obligan los mandatos apostólicos, como por las entrañas de misericordia de nuestro Señor Jesucristo, cuando intenteis proseguir esa expedicion y tomarla á cargo vuestro con el recto designio de fomentar el celo de la fe ortodoxa, sea de vuestra voluntad y deber inducir á los pueblos que de tal suerte pasan la vida en esas islas y tierras, á que abracen la Religion cristiana; y jamas ni en tiempo alguno os amedrenten los peligros y trabajos, sino ántes bien reposad en la firme esperanza, y en la confianza de que el Dios omnipotente proseguirá felizmente vuestros esfuerzos.

Y para que con mayor libertad y valor os apodereis de una provincia de tanta importancia, concedida por la liberalidad de la gracia apostólica, de *motu proprio*, y no á instancia vuestra

1493.   tionis instantiam, sed de nostrâ merâ liberalitate, et ex certâ scientiâ, ac de apostolicæ potestatis plenitudine, omnes insulas et terras firmas inventas et inveniendas, detectas et detegendas versùs Occidentem et Meridiem, fabricando et construendo unam lineam à polo arctico, scilicet Septentrione, ad polum antarcticum, scilicet Meridiem, sive terræ firmæ et insulæ inventæ et inveniendæ sint versùs Indiam, aut versùs aliam quamcumque partem, quæ linea distet à quâlibet insularum, quæ vulgariter nuncupantur *de los Azores y Cabo Verde*, centum leucis versùs Occidentem et Meridiem, ita quòd omnes insulæ et terræ firmæ repertæ et reperiendæ, detectæ et detegendæ, et præfata linea versùs Occidentem et Meridiem, per alium Regem aut Principem christianum non fuerint actualiter possessæ usque ad diem Nativitatis Domini nostri Jesu Christi proximè præteritum, à quo incipit annus præsens millesimus quadringentesimus nonagesimus tertius, quando fuerunt per nuntios et capitaneos vestros inventæ aliquæ prædictarum insularum, auctoritate omnipotentis Dei Nobis in beato Petro concessâ, ac vicariatus Jesu Christi, quâ fungimur in terris, cum omnibus illarum dominiis, civitatibus, castris, locis, juribusque et jurisdictionibus, ac pertinentiis universis, vobis hæredibusque et successoribus vestris (Castellæ et Legionis Regibus) in perfectum tenore præsentium donamus, concedimus et assignamus. Vosque et hæredes ac successores præfatos illarum dominos cum plenâ, liberâ et omnimodâ potestate, auctoritate et jurisdictione, facimus, constituimus et deputamus.

Decernentes nihilominùs per hujusmodi donationem, concessionem et assignationem nostram nulli christiano Principi, qui actualiter præfatas insulas et terras firmas possederit usque ad dictum diem Nativitatis Domini nostri Jesu Christi, jus quæsitum sublatum intelligi posse, aut auferri debere. Et insuper mandamus vobis in virtute sanctæ obedientiæ (sicut pollice-

sobre esto, ni á peticion alguna que otro por vos nos haya hecho, sino por un acto de pura liberalidad nuestra, con ciencia cierta y en plenitud de la potestad apostólica, Nosotros, usando de la autoridad del Dios omnipotente, que Nos ha sido concedida en el bienaventurado Pedro, y de la cual gozamos en la tierra en desempeño del vicariato de Jesucristo, por el tenor de las presentes os damos, concedemos y asignamos á perpetuidad á vosotros y á vuestros herederos y sucesores (los Reyes de Castilla y de Leon) con todos sus dominios, ciudades, fortalezas, lugares, derechos y jurisdicciones, y con todas sus pertenencias, todas aquellas islas y tierras firmes encontradas y que se encuentren, descubiertas y que se descubran hácia el Occidente y el Mediodía, imaginando y trazando una línea desde el polo ártico, esto es, desde el Septentrion, hasta el polo antártico, esto es, el Mediodía, ó sea las tierras firmes é islas encontradas y por encontrar que estén hácia la India, ó hácia cualquiera otra parte, cuya línea distará de cualquiera de las islas que vulgarmente se llaman *de los Azores y Cabo Verde*, cien leguas hácia el Occidente y Mediodía, con tal que todas las islas y tierras firmes encontradas y que se encuentren, descubiertas y que se descubran, y la referida línea hácia el Occidente y Mediodía, no hayan sido poseidas actualmente por otro Rey ó Príncipe cristiano hasta el dia de la Natividad de nuestro Señor Jesucristo, próximo pasado, en cuyo dia principia el presente año de mil cuatrocientos noventa y tres, cuando fueron encontradas por vuestros nuncios y capitanes algunas de las islas precitadas. Y os hacemos, constituimos y consagramos señores de todas ellas, tanto á vosotros como á vuestros precitados herederos y sucesores, con plena, libre y omnimoda potestad, autoridad y jurisdiccion.

Decretamos, sin embargo, que por esta nuestra donacion, concesion y asignacion no pueda entenderse quitado, ni deba quitarse, ningun derecho adquirido, á ningun príncipe cristiano que actualmente poseyere las predichas islas y tierras firmes hasta el dicho dia de la Natividad de nuestro Señor Jesucristo. Y por las presentes os mandamos, en virtud de santa obediencia

1493.

1493. mini, et non dubitamus pro vestrâ maximâ devotione et regiâ magnanimitate vos esse facturos) ad terras firmas et insulas prædictas viros probos et Deum timentes, doctos, peritos, et expertos, ad instruendum incolas et habitatores præfatos in fide catholicâ, et bonis moribus imbuendum destinare debeatis, omnem debitam diligentiam in præmissis adhibentes.

Ac quibuscumque personis cujuscumque dignitatis, etiam imperialis et regalis, statûs, gradûs, ordinis vel conditionis, sub excommunicationis latæ sententiæ pœnâ, quam eo ipso si contrafecerint incurrant, districtiùs inhibemus ne ad insulas et terras firmas inventas et inveniendas, detectas et detegendas versùs Occidentem et Meridiem, fabricando et construendo lineam à polo arctico ad polum antarcticum, sive terræ firmæ et insulæ inventæ et inveniendæ sint versùs aliam quamcumque partem, quæ linea distet à quâlibet insularum, quæ vulgariter nuncupantur *de los Azores y Cabo Verde*, centum leucis versùs Occidentem et Meridiem, ut præfertur, pro mercibus habendis, vel quâvis aliâ de causâ, accedere præsumant absque vestrâ ac hæredum et successorum vestrorum prædictorum licentiâ speciali.

Non obstantibus constitutionibus et ordinationibus apostolicis, cæterisque contrariis quibuscumque. In illo à quo imperia, et dominationes et bona cuncta procedunt confidentes, quòd dirigente Domino actus vestros, si hujusmodi sanctum et laudabile propositum prosequamini, brevi tempore cum felicitate et gloriâ totius populi christiani, vestri labores et conatus exitum felicissimum consequentur.

Verùm, quia difficile foret præsentes litteras ad singula quæque loca, in quibus expediens fuerit deferri, volumus, ac motu et scientiâ similibus decernimus, quòd illarum transumptis manu publici notarii rogati subscriptis, et sigillo alicujus personæ in ecclesiasticâ dignitate constitutæ, seu curiæ ecclesiasticæ munitis, ea prorsùs fides in judicio et extra, ac aliàs ubilibet adhibeatur, quæ præsentibus adhiberetur, si essent exhibitæ vel ostensæ.

(como lo teneis prometido, y no dudamos lo cumplireis por vuestra suprema devocion y real magnanimidad), que debeis destinar á las enunciadas tierras firmes é islas varones probos y dotados del temor de Dios, doctos, sabios y de experiencia, para que instruyan en la fe católica á los predichos moradores y habitantes, y para que los imbuyan en las buenas costumbres; en todo lo cual debeis poner toda la atencion que es debida.

Y prohibimos muy estrictamente á cualesquiera personas de cualquiera dignidad,—aun la imperial y régia,—estado, grado, órden ó condicion, bajo pena de excomunion *latæ sententiæ*, en la cual incurrirán por el simple hecho de la contravencion, que se atrevan á acercarse, con objeto de especular ó con otro motivo cualquiera, sin especial licencia vuestra ó la de vuestros predichos herederos y sucesores, á las islas y tierras firmes encontradas y que se encuentren, descubiertas y que se descubran hácia el Occidente y Mediodía, imaginando y trazando una línea del polo ártico al polo antártico , ó sea las tierras firmes ó islas encontradas y por encontrar que estén hácia cualquiera otra parte, cuya línea distará de cualquiera de las islas que vulgarmente se llaman *de los Azores y Cabo Verde*, cien leguas hácia el Occidente y Mediodía, como ántes se ha dicho.

No obstarán á esto ningunas constituciones y ordenaciones apostólicas, ni otros actos cualesquiera en contrario. Confiamos en aquel de quien emanan los imperios y dominaciones y todos los bienes, que, dirigiendo el Señor vuestros pasos, si proseguis en ese santo y laudable propósito, en breve tiempo y con felicidad y gloria de todo el pueblo cristiano, vuestros trabajos y esfuerzos serán coronados con el éxito mas venturoso.

Pero como será difícil exhibir las presentes letras en cada lugar en que sea menester producirlas, queremos y decretamos con igual voluntad y conocimiento, que á sus compulsas suscritas por mano de notario público rogado al efecto, y con el sello de cualquiera persona constituida en dignidad eclesiástica, ó de la Curia eclesiástica, se les dé entera fe dentro y fuera de juicio, y en otros actos en cualquiera parte, lo mismo que si se exhibiesen y mostrasen las presentes.

1493.   Nulli ergò omninò hominum liceat hanc paginam nostræ com-
mendationis, hortationis, requisitionis, donationis, concessio-
nis, assignationis, constitutionis, deputationis, decreti, mandati,
inhibitionis et voluntatis infringere, vel ei ausu temerario contraire. Si quis autem hoc attentare præsumpserit, indignatio-
nem omnipotentis Dei, ac beatorum Petri et Pauli apostolorum
ejus, se noverit incursurum.

Dat. Romæ apud S. Petrum, anno Incarnationis dominicæ,
millesimo quadringentesimo nonagesimo tertio, quarto nonas
maii, Pont. nostri anno primo.

Á ningun hombre, pues, sea lícito en manera alguna infrin-   1493.
gir ó contrariar con temeraria osadía esta página de nuestra
recomendacion, exhortacion, peticion, donacion, concesion,
asignacion, constitucion, deputacion, decreto, mandato, prohi-
bicion y voluntad. Pero si alguno imaginase intentarlo, tenga
como cierto que ha de incurrir en la indignacion del Dios omnipotente, y de los bienaventurados Pedro y Pablo sus apóstoles.

Dadas en Roma, en San Pedro, en el año de la Encarnacion'
del Señor mil cuatrocientos noventa y tres, á cuatro de mayo,
en el año primero de nuestro pontificado.

PRIMER PERÍODO.

ESPAÑA Y PORTUGAL.

～〜✺〜～

TRATADO DE TORDESILLAS,

Firmado solemnemente el 7 de junio de 1494, y aprobado por el Rey de España el 2 de julio.

1494. Á consecuencia de este arreglo, ambas potencias convinieron en enviar cuatro embarcaciones con astrónomos, navegadores y geógrafos, con el fin de establecer la línea divisoria y determinar los territorios pertenecientes á cada corona. Este tratado tomó un carácter mas inviolable aún por la sancion del papa Julio II, cuya bula, de 24 de enero de 1506, fué comunicada por el arzobispo de Braga y el obispo de Viseo, á sus respectivos soberanos.

Segun el informe de doce cosmógrafos castellanos y portugueses, nombrados para fijar esa línea de límites, los primeros tomaron por base la isla de San Antonio, la mas occidental de las del Cabo Verde ; los segundos, la de Sal, la mas oriental de dichas islas. No se habia indicado el valor de las leguas, y los instrumentos de los geógrafos eran muy imperfectos, por con-

secuencia los comisarios diferian mucho entre sí, quedando 1494.
sin ejecucion la operacion. No obstante, los hidrógrafos portugueses pretendian que el Portugal tenia derecho á doscientas
leguas de terreno en el Brasil, pasando la línea de demarcacion
por el rio de la Coroa, cerca de Maranháŏ y no distante de San
Vicente (1).

El 6 de setiembre de 1522, regresó de su viaje el buque
« Victoria, » durante el cual habia descubierto las islas Molucas. Cada príncipe pretendia que esas islas estaban comprend-
didas en su reparticion. En la misma época, se descubrian varios otros territorios en la costa austral y meridional de la
América, que comprendia el meridiano supuesto de la demarcacion.

Deseando llegar á una conciliacion, se decidió (1524) que se
nombrarian plenipotenciarios por ambas partes y se reunirian
en el puente del rio Caya, limítrofe entre Badajoz y Yélves,
para determinar el meridiano de Tordesillas, y otros á su
nadir ó punto diametralmente opuesto. La imperfeccion de los
globos, cartas é instrumentos astronómicos impidieron á esos
comisarios que se entendiesen. Pasaron su tiempo discutiendo
si las 370 leguas comenzarian de la mas occidental ó de la mas
oriental de las islas del Cabo Verde, y se separaron sin tomar
ninguna resolucion (2).

Dos años despues, nuevos árbitros y comisarios se reunieron
en Sevilla : por parte del Portugal, el embajador de esta
corona con el jurisconsulto Azevedo ; y por la del empera-
dor, el obispo de *Osma*, presidente del consejo de las Indias,
el Dr. *Lorenzo Galindes*, del mismo consejo, D. *Garcia
de Padilla*, gran comendador de la órden de Calatrava, con la
intervencion del gran canciller y del nuncio apostólico *Mercurio
Gatinara*. Despues de muchas conferencias y de una larga negociacion, en donde se encontraron jurisconsultos, geógrafos y

---

(1) *Comunicacion de D. Juan Bautista de Gesio.* Madrid, 24 de noviem-
bre de 1579. El original existe en el *archivo general de Indias de Sevilla.*
(2) *Herrera*, déc. III, lib. vi, cap. 6, 7 y 8.

1494. frailes, dice Argensola, que en vez de resolver las dificultades no hicieron mas que aumentarlas, no resultando de su negociacion, en España, mas que alegatos, compromisos y proyectos inútiles; y en Asia, combates entre las flotas y los ejércitos de ambos monarcas (1).

En cuanto á la línea de demarcacion americana, los cosmógrafos españoles y portugueses, guiados por cartas náuticas y derroteros particulares; y no por observaciones astronómicas, llegaron á resultados muy diferentes. Segun los primeros, la extension del continente entre Porto Veio, en el mar del Sur, y el cabo San Agustin en el del Norte, era de 51°; segun los últimos, comprendia 55°. Se trató de establecer la línea de demarcacion por la embocadura del rio Maranháõ de un lado, y del otro por la del San Antonio y Órganos, comprendiendo el rio de la Plata, y toda la costa hasta la bahía de San Vicente.

Los cosmógrafos portugueses insistieron, diciendo, que si ese meridiano caía por la boca del Maranháõ, deberia pasar mucho mas allá de la bahía de San Vicente, porque entre el cabo de San Agustin y el Maranháõ hay 14° y 2/3 de distancia, y entre el mismo cabo y esa bahía, no hay mas que 10°; y que por consecuencia, la línea de demarcacion no podia pasar por ambos puntos. Entre la isla de San Antonio y el cabo San Agustin, se cuentan mas ó ménos 3°, y 14° dos tercios entre el cabo San Agustin y el Maranháõ, los que, reunidos, hacen 17° dos tercios. Faltaban casi 5° para completar el número de 22° un tercio, ó de 370 leguas concedidas á la corona de Portugal.

Desde entónces una extension considerable de continente situado entre el Plata y la bahía de San Vicente, fué reclamada por cada una de las potencias, hasta que la reunion de los dos reinos bajo el mismo monarca (1580) puso fin á la discusion. Fué ese (dice Solorzano, cap. 6, n° 74) un efecto de la Providencia, á fin de que bajo la direccion de un solo rey, se propagase con mas libertad, entre las naciones bárbaras, la luz del Evan-

(1) *Conquista de las islas Molucas.*

gelio, como tambien para evitar las discusiones ocasionadas por el descubrimiento de las Filipinas, á las que tenian los Portugueses mas derechos que los Castellanos.

1494.

DOCUMENTO.

(Tomado de la Coleccion de Tratados de Castro, tomo III, p. 52.)

Don Fernando y doña Isabel, por la gracia de Dios rey y reyna de Castilla, de Leon, de Aragon y de Sicilia, de Granada, de Toledo, de Valencia, de Galicia, de Mallorca, de Sevilla, de Cerdeña, de Córdova, de Córcega, de Murcia, de Jahen, del Algarbe, de Algezira, de Gibraltar, de las islas de Canaria, conde y condesa de Barcelona, y señores de Viscaya y de Molina, duques de Aténas y de Neopatria, condes de Rossellon y de Cerdaña, marqueses de Oristan y de Goceano, en una con el príncepe don Juan, nuestro muy caro y muy amado hijo, primogénito heredero de los dichos nuestros reynos y señoríos. Por quanto, por don Henrique Henriques, nuestro mayordomo mayor, y don Guterre de Cárdenas, comisario mayor de Leon, nuestro contador mayor, y el doctor Rodrigo Maldonado, todos del nuestro consejo, fué tratado, assentado y capitulado por nos, y en nuestro nombre, y por virtud de nuestro poder, con el sereníssimo don Juan, por la gracia de Dios rey de Portugal y de los Algarbes, de aquende y de allende el mar, en África señor de Guinea, nuestro muy caro y muy amado hermano, y con Ruy de Sosa, señor de Usagres y Berengel, y don Juan de Sosa su hijo, almotacen mayor del dicho sereníssimo rey nuestro hermano, y Arias de Almadana, corregidor de los fechos civiles de su corte y del su desembargo, todos del consejo del dicho sereníssimo rey nuestro hermano, en su nombre, y por virtud de su poder, sus embaxadores que á nos vinieron, sobre la diferencia de lo que á nos y al dicho sereníssimo rey nuestro hermano pertenece, de lo que hasta siete dias deste mes de

Consideracion
preliminar.

1494. junio, en que estamos, de la fecha desta escriptura está por descubrir en el mar Océano, en la qual dicha capitulacion los dichos nuestros procuradores, entre otras cosas, prometieron que dentro de cierto término en ella contenido, nos otorgaríamos, confirmaríamos, juraríamos, ratificaríamos y aprovaríamos la dicha capitulacion por nuestras personas ; é nos queriendo complir, é compliendo todo lo que asy en nuestro nombre fué assentado, é capitulado, é otorgado cerca de lo susodicho, mandamos traer ante nos la dicha escriptura de la dicha capitulacion y asiento para la ver y examinar, y el tenor della de *verbo ad verbum* es este que se sigue :

Trascricion de una escritura de capitulacion. *En el nombre de Dios Todopoderoso, Padre y Fijo y Espírito Santo, tres personas realmente distintas y apartadas, y una sola esencia divina* (1).

Manifiesto y notorio sea á todos quantos este público instromiento vieren, como en la villa de Tordesillas, á siete dias del mes de junio, año del nascimiento de nuestro Señor Jesu Christo de mil é quatrocientos é noventa é quatro años, en presencia de nos los secretarios y escrivanos, é notarios públicos de yuso escritos, estando presentes los honrados don Henrique Henriques, mayordomo mayor de los muy altos y muy poderosos príncipes, señores don Fernando y doña Isabel, por la gracia de Dios rey y reyna de Castilla, de Leon, de Aragon, de Sicilia, de Granada, etc., é don Guterre de Cárdenas, contador mayor de los dichos señores rey y reyna, y el doctor Rodrigo Maldonado, todos del consejo de los dichos señores rey y reyna de Castilla, é de Leon, de Aragon, de Sicilia, é de Granada, etc., sus procuradores bastantes de la una parte, é los honrados Ruy de Sosa, señor de Usagres é Berengel, é don Juan de Sosa su hijo, almotacen mayor del muy alto y muy excelente señor don Juan, por la gracia de Dios rey de Portugal, é de los Algarbes, de aquende é de allende el mar, en África señor de Guinea, é Arias de Al-

(1) Véase la nota del tratado de 1681, y el artículo XXI del tratado de 1º octubre de 1777.

madana, corregidor de los fechos civiles en su corte, é del su desembargo, todos del consejo del dicho señor rey de Portugal é sus embaxadores é procuradores bastantes, segund amas las dichas partes lo mostraron por las cartas é poderes, é procuraciones de los dichos señores sus constituyentes, de las quales su tenor *de verbo ad verbum* es este que se sigue :

Don Fernando y doña Isabel, por la gracia de Dios rey y reyna de Castilla, de Leon, de Aragon, de Sicilia, de Granada, de Toledo, de Valencia, de Galicia, de Mallorca, de Sevilla, de Cerdeña, de Córdova, de Córcega, de Murcia, de Jahen, del Algarbe, de Algezira, de Gibraltar, de las islas de Canaria, conde y condesa de Barcelona, é señores de Viscaya é de Molina, duques de Aténas é de Neopatria, condes de Rossellon é de Cerdaña, marqueses de Oristan é de Goceano. Por quanto el serenissimo rey de Portugal, nuestro muy caro é muy amado hermano, embió á nos por sus embaxadores é procuradores á Ruy de Sosa, cuyas son las villas de Usagre é Berengel, é á don Juan de Sosa su almotacen mayor, é Arias de Almadana su corregidor de los fechos civiles en su corte é del su desembargo, todos del su consejo, para platicar é tomar asiento é concordia con nos, ó con nuestros embaxadores é procuradores, en nuestro nombre, sobre la diferencia que entre nos y el dicho serenissimo rey de Portugal nuestro hermano, é sobre lo que á nos y á él pertenece de lo que hasta agora está por descubrir en el mar Océano ; por ende confiando de vos don Henrique Henriques nuestro mayordomo mayor, é don Guterre de Cárdenas comisario mayor de Leon, nuestro contador mayor, é el doctor Rodrigo Maldonado, todos del nuestro consejo, que sois tales personas, que guardareis nuestro servicio, é bien, é fielmente hareis lo que por nos vos fuere mandado é encomendado, por esta presente carta vos damos todo nuestro poder complido, en aquella mas apta forma que podemos é en tal caso se requiere, especialmente para que por nos y en nuestro nombre é de nuestros herederos, é subcesores, é de todos nuestros reynos é señorios, súbditos é naturales dellos, podais tratar, concordar é asentar, é fazer trato é concordia con los dichos embaxadores

1494.

Plenipotenciarios
de la España.

1494. del dicho sereníssimo rey de Portugal nuestro hermano, en su nombre, qualquier concierto, asiento, limitacion, demarcacion é concordia sobre lo que dicho es, por los vientos en grados de Norte, é del Sol, é por aquellas partes, divisiones, é lugares del cielo, é de la mar, é de la tierra, que á vos bien visto fueren, é asy vos damos el dicho poder, para que podais dexar al dicho rey de Portugal, é á sus reynos é subcesores todos los mares é islas, é tierras que fueren é estovieren dentro de qualquier limitacion é demarcacion, que con él fincaren é quedaren; é otrosy vos damos el dicho poder, para que en nuestro nombre, é de nuestros herederos é subcesores, é de nuestros reynos é señorios, é súbditos é naturales dellos, podades concordar, é asentar, é recebir, é aceptar del dicho rey de Portugal, é de los dichos sus embaxadores, é procuradores en su nombre, que todos los mares, islas é tierras que fueren é estovieron dentro de la limitacion é demarcacion de costas, mares é islas, é tierras, que quedaren é fincaren con nos é con nuestros subcesores, para que sean nuestros é de nuestro señorío é conquista, é asy de nuestros reynos é subcesores dellos, con aquellas limitaciones é excepciones, é con todas las otras divisiones é declaraciones, que á vosotros bien visto fuere ; é para que sobre todo lo que dicho es, é para cada una cosa é parte dello, é sobre lo á ello tocante, ó de ello dependiente, ó á ello anexo é conexo en qualquier manera, podais fazer é otorgar, concordar, tratar é recebir, é aceptar en nuestro nombre, é de los dichos nuestros herederos é subcesores, é de todos nuestros reynos, señorios, é súbditos é naturales dellos, qualesquier capitulaciones é contractos, escripturas, con qualesquier vínculos, abtos modos, condiciones, bligaciones é estipulaciones, penas é submisiones, é renunciaciones, que vosotros quisierdes é bien visto vos fuere, é sobre ello podais fazer é otorgar, é fagais, é otorgueis todas las cosas, é cada una dellas, de qualquier naturaleza é calidad, gravedad é importancia que sean, ó ser puedan, aunque sean tales, que por su condicion requieran otro nuestro señalado é especial mandado, é de que se deviese de fecho é de derecho fazer singular é espresa mencion, é que nos seyendo presentes

podríamos fazer é otorgar, é recebir; é otrosy vos damos poder   1494.
complido, para que podais jurar, é jureis en nuestra ánima,
que nos é nuestros heredores é subcesores, é súbditos, é naturales, é vassallos adqueridos é por adquerir, ternemos, guardaremos é compliremos, é que ternán, guardarán é complirán
realmente é con efecto todo lo que vosotros asy asentardes, capitulardes, é jurardes, é otorgardes, é firmardes, cesante toda
cautela, fraude é engaño, ficcion, simulacion, é asy podais en
nuestro nombre capitular é segurar, é prometer, que nos en
persona seguraremos, juraremos é prometeremos, é otorgare-
mos é firmaremos todo lo que vosotros en nuestro nombre,
cerca lo que dicho es, segurardes é prometierdes é capitulardes,
dentro de aquel término de tiempo que vos bien pareciere, é
que lo guardaremos é compliremos realmente é con efecto, so
las condiciones é penas é obligaciones contenidas en el contracto de las paces entre nos y el dicho serenésimo rey nuestro
hermano fechas é concordadas, é so todas las otras que vosotros
prometierdes é asentardes, las quales desde agora prometemos
de pagar, si en ellas incorriéremos, para lo qual todo é cada
una cosa é parte dello, vos damos el dicho poder con libre é
general administracion, é prometemos, é seguramos por nuestra
fe y palabra real, de tener é guardar é complir nos é nuestros
heredores é subcesores, todo lo que por vosotros, cerca de lo
que dicho es, en qualquier forma é manera fuese fecho é capitulado é jurado, é prometido, é prometemos de lo haver por
firme, rato é grato, estable é valedero agora é en todo tiempo
jamas; é que no iremos ni vernemos contra ello ni contra
parte alguna dello, nos, ni nuestros heredores é subcesores, por
nos, ni por otras interpósitas personas, directe, ni indirecte, so
alguna color, ni causa en juicio, ni fuera dél, so obligacion expresa, que para ello fazemos de todos nuestros bienes patrimoniales é fiscales, é otros qualesquier de nuestros vassallos, súbditos, é naturales, muebles y raizes, havidos é por haver. Por
firmeza de lo qual mandamos dar esta nuestra carta de poder,
la qual firmamos de nuestros nombres, é mandamos sellarla con
nuestro sello, dada en la villa de Tordesillas á cinco dias del

1494. mes de junio, año del nascimiento de nuestro Señor Jesu Christo de mil quatrocientos é noventa é quatro años. — Yo el rey. — Yo la reyna. — Yo Fernan Dalvres de Toledo, secretario del rey é de la reyna nuestros señores la fize escrivir por su mandado.

Plenipotenciarios del Portugal. Don Juan, por la gracia de Dios rey de Portugal, é de los Algarbes, de aquende, de allende el mar en África, é señor de Guinea. Á quantos esta nuestra carta de poder é procuracion vieren, fazemos saber, que por quanto por mandado de los muy altos, y muy excelentes, é poderosos príncepes, el rey don Fernando, é reyna doña Isabel, rey é reyna de Castilla, de Leon, de Aragon, de Sicilia, de Granada, etc., nuestros muy amados é preciados hermanos, fueron descobiertas é halladas nueva- mente algunas islas, é podrian adelante descobrir é hallar otras islas é tierras, sobre las quales unas é las otras halladas, é por hallar, por el derecho é razon que en ello tenemos, podrian sobrevenir entre nos todos, é nuestros reynos é señoríos, súbdi- tos é naturales dellos, debates é diferencias, que nuestro Señor no consienta, á nos plaze, por el grande amor é amistad que entre nos todos ay, é por se buscar, procurar, é conservar mayor paz, é mas firme concordia, é asuciego, que el mar en que las dichas islas están, y fueren halladas, se parta é demarque entre nos todos en alguna buena, cierta é limitada manera; y porque nos al presente no podemos en ello entender en persona, con- fiando de vos Ruy de Sosa, señor de Usagres é Berengel, y don Juan de Sosa, nuestro almotacen mayor, y Arias de Almadana, corregidor de los fechos civiles en la nuestra corte, é del nuestro desembargo, todos del nuestro consejo, por esta presente carta vos damos todo nuestro complido poder, abtoridad, é especial mandado, é vos fazemos é constituimos á todos juntamente, é á dos de vos é á uno in solidum si los otros en qualquier ma- nera fueren impedidos, nuestros embaxadores é procuradores, en aquella mas abta forma que podemos, é en tal caso se requier, general y especialmente, en tal manera, que la gene- ralidad no derrogue á la especialidad, ni la especialidad á la generalidad, para que por nos, y en nuestro nombre é de nuestros heredoros é subcesores, é de todos nuestros reynos é señorios, súbditos é naturales dellos podais tratar, concordar, asentar é fazer, trateis, concordeis, é asenteis, é fagais con los dichos rey é reyna de Castilla nuestros hermanos, ó con quien para ello su poder tenga, qualquier concierto, asiento, limitacion, demarcacion, é concordia sobre el mar Océano, islas, é tierra firme, que en él estovieren por aquellos rumos de vientos, é grados de Norte é de Sol, é por aquellas partes, divisiones é lugares del cielo é del mar, é de la tierra, que vos bien parecier, é asy vos damos el dicho poder para que podais dexar, é dexeis á los dichos rey é reyna, é á sus reynos é subcesores, todos los mares, islas, é tierras, que fueren é estovieren dentro de qualquier limitacion, é demarcacion, que con los dichos rey é reyna quedaren, é asy vos damos el dicho poder para en nuestro nombre, é de nuestros herederos é subcesores, é de todos nuestros reynos é señorios, súbditos é naturales dellos, podais con los dichos rey é reyna, ó con sus procuradores, concordár, asentar, recebir, é aceptar, que todos los mares, islas, é tierras, que fueren é estovieren dentro de la limitacion, é demarcacion de costas, mares, islas, é tierras que con nos é nuestros subcesores fincaren, sean nuestros é de nuestro señorío é conquista, é asy de nuestros reynos é subcesores dellos, con aquellas limitaciones é excepciones de nuestras islas, é con todas las otras cláusulas é declaraciones que vos bien parecier. El qual dicho poder damos á vos los dichos Ruy de Sosa, é don Juan de Sosa, é Arias de Almadana, para que sobre todo lo que dicho es, é sobre cada una cosa, é parte dello, é sobre lo á ello tocante, ó dello dependiente, ó á ello anexo é conexo en qualquier manera, podais fazer é otorgar, concordar, tratar é distratar, recebir é aceptar en nuestro nombre, é. de los dichos nuestros herederos é subcesores, é de todos nuestros reynos é señorios, súbditos é naturales dellos, qualesquier capítulos é contratos é escripturas, con qualesquier vínculos, pactos, modos, condiciones, obligaciones, é estipulaciones, penas, é submisiones, é renunciaciones, que vos 'quisierdes, é á vos bien visto fueren, é sobre ello podais fazer é otorgar, é fagais é otorgueis todas las cosas, é cada una dellas de qualquier naturaleza, calidad,

1494.

1494.   gravedad é importancia que sean ó ser pueden, puesto que sean tales, que por su condicion requieran otro nuestro singular é especial mandado, é de que se deviesse de fecho é de derecho fazer singular é expresa mencion, é que nos siendo presentes podríamos fazer é otorgar é recebir ; é otrosy vos damos poder complido, para que podais jurar, é jureis en nuestra ánima, que nos é nuestros herederos é subcesores, súbditos é naturales é vassallos adquiridos, é por adquerir, ternemos, guardaremos, é compliremos, ternán, guardarán é complirán realmente, é con efeto, todo lo que vos asy asentardes, capitulardes, jurardes, é otorgardes, é firmardes, cesante toda cautela, fraude, engaño é fingimento, é asy podais en nuestro nombre capitular, segurar, é prometer, que nos en persona seguraremos, juraremos, prometeremos, é firmaremos todo lo que vos en el sobre dicho nombre, acerca de lo que dicho es, segurardes, prometierdes, é capitulardes, dentro de aquel tér- mino de tiempo que vos bien parecier, é que lo guardaremos é compliremos realmente, é con efeto, so las condiciones, penas, é obligaciones contenidas en el contracto de las paces entre nos fechas, é concordadas, é so todas las otras que vos prometierdes, é asentardes en el dicho nombre, las quales desde agora prome- temos de pagar, é pagaremos realmente, é con efeto, si en ellas incurriéremos, para lo qual todo, é cada una cosa, é parte dello, vos damos el dicho poder con libre é general adminis- tracion, é prometemos, é seguramos por nuestra fe real, de tener, guardar é complir, é asy nuestros herederos é subcesores, todo lo que por vos acerca de lo que dicho es, en qualquier forma é manera que fuere fecho, capitulado, jurado, é prometido, é prometemos de lo haver por firme, rato é grato, estable, é va- lioso de agora para todo siempre, é que no iremos, ni vernemos, ni irán, ni vernán contra ello, ni contra parte alguna dello en tiempo alguno, ni por alguna manera, por nos, ni por sí, ni por interpósitas personas directe, ni indirecte, so alguna color ó causa en juicio, ni fuera dél, so obligacion expresa, que para ello fazemos de los dichos nuestros reynos é señoríos, é de todos los otros nuestros bienes patrimoniales, fiscales, é otros quales-

quier de nuestros vassallos, súbditos é naturales, muebles é de   1494.
raiz, avidos é por aver ; en testimonio é fe de lo qual, vos mandamos dar esta nuestra carta firmada por nos, é sellada de
nuestro sello, dada en la nuestra cebdat de Lisbona á ocho dias
de marzo. — Ruy de Pina la fizo año del nascimiento de nuestro
Señor Jesu Christo, de mil é quatrocientos é noventa é quatro
años. — El rey.

É luego los dichos procuradores de los dichos señores rey é   Comienza la línea
reyna de Castilla, de Leon, de Aragon, de Sicilia, de Granada, etc.,   divisoria.
é del dicho señor rey de Portugal, é de los Algarbes, etc., dixe-
ron, que por quanto entre los dichos señores sus constituyentes
hay cierta diferencia, sobre lo que á cada una de las dichas
partes pertenece, de lo que fasta oy dia de la fecha desta capitulacion está por descubrir en el mar Océano ; por ende que ellos
por bien de paz é concordia, é por conservacion del debdo é
amor, qual dicho señor rey de Portugal tiene con los dichos
señores rey é reyna de Castilla, é de Aragon, etc., á Sus Altezas plaze, é los dichos sus procuradores en su nombre, é por
virtud de los dichos sus poderes, otorgaron é consintieron, que
se haga é señale por el dicho mar Océano una raya, ó línea derecha de polo á polo; convien á saber, del polo ártico al polo
antártico, que es de Norte á Sul, la qual raya ó línea se aya de
dar, é dé derecha, como dicho es, á trecientas é setenta leguas
de las islas del Cabo Verde, hácia la parte del Poniente, por
grados ó por otra manera como mejor y mas presto se pueda
dar, de manera que no sean mas, é que todo lo que hasta aquí
se ha fallado é descubierto, é de aquí adelante se hallare, é des-
cubriere por el dicho señor rey de Portugal, é por sus navíos,
asy islas como tierra firme, desde la dicha raya, é línea dada
en la forma susodicha, yendo por la dicha parte del Levante dentro de la dicha raya á la parte del Levante, ó del
Norte, ó del Sul della, tanto que no sea atravesando la dicha raya, que esto sea, é finque, é pertenezca al dicho señor
rey de Portugal é á sus subcesores, para siempre jamas, é que
todo lo otro, asy islas, como tierra firme, halladas y por hallar,
descubiertas y por descubrir, que son ó fueren halladas por los

1494.

dichos señores rey é reyna de Castilla, é de Aragon, etc., é por sus navíos desde la dicha raya dada en la forma susodicha, yendo por la dicha parte del Poniente, despues de pasada la dicha raya hácia el Poniente, ó el Norte, ó el Sul della, que todo sea, é finque, é pertenezca á los dichos señores rey é reyna de Castilla, de Leon, etc., é á sus subcesores para siempre ja-

Promesa recíproca de no enviar navíos.

mas. Item los dichos procuradores prometieron, é seguraron por virtud de los dichos poderes, que de oy en adelante no embiarán navíos algunos; convien á saber, los dichos señores rey é reyna de Castilla, é de Leon, é de Aragon, etc., por esta parte de la raya á la parte del Levante aquiende de la dicha raya, que queda para el dicho señor rey de Portugal é de los Algarbes, etc., ni el dicho señor rey de Portugal á la otra parte de la dicha raya, que queda para los dichos señores rey é reyna de Castilla, é de Aragon, etc., á descobrir é buscar tierras, ni islas algunas, ni á contratar, ni rescatar, ni conquistar en manera alguna; pero que si acaesciere, que yendo asy aquiende de la dicha raya los dichos navíos de los dichos señores rey é reyna de Castilla, de Leon é de Aragon, etc., fallasen qualesquier islas, ó tierras en lo que asy queda para el dicho señor rey de Portugal, que aquello tal sea, é finque para el dicho señor rey de Portugal, é para sus herederos para siempre jamas, é Sus Altezas gelo ayan de mandar luego dar é entregar. É si los navíos del dicho señor rey de Portugal fallaren qualesquier islas é tierras en la parte de los dichos señores rey é reyna de Castilla, é de Leon, é Aragon, etc., que todo lo tal sea, é finque para los dichos señores rey é reyna de Castilla, de Leon, é de Aragon, etc., é para sus herederos para siempre jamas, é que el dicho señor rey de Portugal gelo haya luego de mandar, dar é entregar. Item, para que la dicha línea ó raya de la dicha particion se aya de dar, é dé derecha, é la mas cierta que ser podiere por las dichas trecien-

Envío recíproco de carabelas, para reunirse en la Gran Canaria, con objeto de comenzar la operacion.

tas é setenta leguas de las dichas islas del Cabo Verde hácia la parte del Poniente, como dicho es, concordado, é asentado por los dichos procuradores de amas las dichas partes, que dentro de diez meses primeros siguientes, contados desde el dia de la fecha desta capitulacion, los dichos señores sus constituyentes hayan de enviar dos ó quatro caravelas, convien á saber, una ó dos de cada parte, ó ménos, segund se acordaren por las dichas partes que son necesarias, las quales para el dicho tiempo sean juntas en la isla de la gran Canaria; y embien en ellas cada una de las dichas partes, personas, asy pilotos como astrólogos, é marineros, é qualesquier otras personas que convengan, pero que sean tantos de una parte, como de otra; y que algunas personas de los dichos pilotos, é astrólogos, é marineros, é personas que sepan, que embiaren los dichos señores rey é reyna de Castilla, é de Leon, é de Aragon, etc., vayan en el navío ó navíos que embiare el dicho señor rey de Portugal é de los Algarbes, etc., é asy mismo algunas de las dichas personas que embiare el dicho señor rey de Portugal, vayan en el navío, ó navíos, que embiaren los dichos señores rey é reyna de Castilla, é Aragon, tanto de una parte como de otra parte, para que juntamente puedan mejor ver ó reconocer la mar, é los rumos, é vientos, é grados de Sol é Norte, é señalar las leguas sobredichas, tanto que para fazer el señalamiento é límite concurrirán todos juntos, los que fueren en los dichos navíos, que embiaren amas las dichas partes, é llevaren sus poderes; los quales dichos navíos, todos juntamente continúen su camino i las dichas islas del Cabo Verde, é desde allí tomarán su rota derecha al Poniente hasta las dichas trecientas é setenta leguas, medidas como las dichas personas, que asy fueren, acordaren que se deven medir, sin prejuicio de las dichas partes, y allí donde se acabaren se haga el punto, é señal que convenga, por grados de Sol ó de Norte, ó por singradura de leguas, ó como mejor se pudieren concordar. La qual dicha raya señalen, desde el dicho polo ártico al dicho polo antártico, que es de Norte á Sul, como dicho es, y aquello que señalaren lo escrivan, é firmen de sus nombres las dichas personas que asy fueren embiadas por amas las dichas partes, las quales han de llevar facultad é poderes de las dichas partes cada uno de la suya, para hacer la dicha señal é limitacion; y fecha por ellos, seyendo todos conformes, que sea avida por señal é limitacion perpetuamente para siempre jamas. Para que las dichas partes, ni

1494.

Comienza
la operacion
de señalar la raya.
Señalamiento
de pertenencias
reciprocas.

alguna dellas, ni sus subcesores para siempre jamas no la puedan contradecir, ni quitar, ni remover en tiempo alguno, ni por alguna manera que sea, ó ser pueda. É si caso fuere, que la dicha raya é límite de polo á polo, como dicho es, topare en alguna isla ó tierra firme, que al comienço de la tal isla ó tierra que asy fuere hallada donde tocare la dicha raya se haga alguna señal ó torre ; é que en derecho de la tal señal ó torre se continúe dende en adelante otras señales por la tal isla ó tierra en derecho de la dicha raya, los quales partan lo que á cada una de las partes perteneciere della, é que los súbditos de las dichas partes no sean osados los unos de pasar á la de los otros, ni los otros de los otros, pasando la dicha señal ó límite en la tal isla ó tierra.

Item por quanto para ir los dichos navios de los dichos señores rey é reyna de Castilla, de Leon, de Aragon, etc., de los reynos é señoríos á la dicha su parte allende de la dicha raya, en la manera que dicho es, es forzado que ayan de pasar por los mares desta parte de la raya que queda para el dicho señor rey de Portugal, por ende es concordado é asentado que los dichos navíos de los dichos señores rey é reyna de Castilla, de Leon, de Aragon, etc., puedan ir é venir, y vayan é vengan libre, segura é pacificamente sin contradiccion alguna por los dichos mares que quedan con el dicho señor rey de Portugal, dentro de la dicha raya en todo tiempo, é cada y quando Sus Altezas, é sus subcesores quisieren, é por bien tuvieren ; los quales vayan por sus caminos derechos, é rotas, desde sus reynos para cualquier parte de lo que está dentro de su raya é límite, donde quisieren embiar á descobrir, é conquistar ó contratar, é que lleven sus caminos derechos por donde ellos acordaren de ir para qualquier cosa de la dicha su parte, é de aquellos no pueden apartarse, salvo lo que el tiempo contrario los fiziere apartar ; tanto que no tomen ni ocupen ántes de pasar la dicha raya cosa alguna de lo que fuere fallado por el dicho señor rey de Portugal en la dicha su parte ; é si alguna cosa fallaren los dichos sus navíos ántes de pasar la dicha raya, como dicho es, que aquello sea para el dicho señor rey de Portugal, é Sus Altezas gelo ayan de man-

dar luego dar, é entregar. É porque podria ser que los navíos,   1494.
é gentes de los dichos señores rey é reyna de Castilla, é de Aragon, etc., ó por su parte avrán fallado hasta veinte dias deste
mes de junio en que estamos de la fecha desta capitulacion,
algunas islas é tierra firme dentro de la dicha raya, que se ha de
fazer de polo á polo por línea derecha en fin de las dichas trecientas é setenta leguas contadas desde las dichas islas del Cabo
Verde al Poniente, como dicho es; es concordado, é asentado,
por quitar toda dubda que todas las islas é tierra firme que
sean falladas, é descobiertas en qualquier manera hasta los dichos veinte dias desde dicho mes de junio, aunque sean falladas
por los navíos, é gentes de los dichos señores rey é reyna de
Castilla, é de Aragon, etc., con tanto que sea dentro de las docientas é cincuenta leguas primeras de las dichas trecientas é
setenta leguas, contadas desde las dichas islas del Cabo Verde
al Poniente hácia la dicha raya, en qualquier parte dellas para
los dichos polos, que sean falladas dentro de las dichas docientas
é cincuenta leguas, haciéndose una raya, ó línea derecha de polo á
polo donde se acabaren las dichas docientas é cincuenta leguas,
queden é finquen para el dicho señor rey de Portugal é de los Algarbes, etc., é para sus subcesores é reynos para siempre jamas.
É que todas las islas, é tierra firme, que hasta los dichos veinte
dias deste mes de junio en que estamos, sean falladas é descobiertas por los navíos de los dichos señores rey é reyna de Castilla, é de Aragon, etc., é por sus gentes, ó en otra qualquier
manera dentro de las otras ciento é veinte leguas, que quedan
para complimiento de las dichas trecientas é setenta leguas, en
que ha de acabar la dicha raya, que se ha de fazer de polo á
polo, como dicho es, en qualquier parte de las dichas ciento é
veinte leguas para los dichos polos que sean falladas fasta el
dicho dia, queden é finquen para los dichos señores rey é reyna
de Castilla é de Aragon, etc., é para sus subcesores, é sus reynos
para siempre jamas, como es, y ha de ser suyo lo que es ó fuere
fallado allende de la dicha raya de las dichas trecientas é setenta leguas, que quedan para Sus Altezas, como dicho es, aunque las dichas ciento é veinte leguas son dentro de la dicha raya

de las dichas trecientas é setenta leguas, que quedan para el dicho señor rey de Portugal , é de los Algarbes , etc., como dicho es. É si fasta los dichos veinte dias desde dicho mes de junio, no son fallados por los dichos navíos de Sus Altezas cosa alguna dentro de las dichas ciento é veinte leguas, é de allí adelante lo fallaren, que sea para el dicho señor rey de Portugal, como en el capítulo susoescripto es contenido. Lo qual todo que dicho es, é cada una cosa, é parte dello los dichos don Henrique Henriques, mayordomo mayor, é D. Guterre de Cárdenas, contador mayor, é doctor Rodrigo Maldonado, procuradores de los dichos muy altos é muy poderosos príncepes, los señores el rey é la reyna de Castilla, de Leon , de Aragon , de Sicilia, é de Granada, etc., é por virtud del dicho su poder que de suso va incorporado, é los dichos Ruy de Sosa , é don Juan de Sosa su hijo, é Arias de Almadana , procuradores é embaxadores del dicho muy alto é muy excelente príncepe el señor rey de Portugal é de los Algarbes, de aquende é allende , en África señor de Guinea, é por virtud del dicho su poder, que de suso va incorporado, prometieron é seguraron en nombre de los dichos sus constituyentes, que ellos é sus subcesores é reynos é señoríos para siempre jamas ternán é guardarán é complirán realmente, é con efecto, cesante todo frude y cautela, engaño, ficcion, é simulacion, todo lo contenido en esta capitulacion , é cada una cosa , é parte dello , é quisieron é otorgaron que todo lo contenido en esta dicha capitulacion, é cada una cosa, é parte dello sea guardado é complido é executado como se ha de guardar é complir, é executar todo lo contenido en la capitulacion de las paces fechas é asentadas entre los dichos señores rey é reyna de Castilla, é de Aragon , etc., é el señor don Alfonso rey de Portugal, que santa gloria aya, é el dicho señor rey, que agora es de Portugal, su fijo, seyendo príncipe, el año que pasó de mil é quatrocientos é setenta é nueve años , é so aquellas mismas penas, vínculos, é firmezas, é obligaciones, segund é de la manera que en la dicha capitulacion de las dichas paces se contiene, y obligáronse que las dichas paces ni alguna dellas, ni sus subcesores para siempre jamas no irán, ni vernán contra lo que

de suso es dicho y especificado, ni contra cosa alguna ni parte
dello directe, ni indirecte, ní por otra manera alguna en tiempo
alguno, ni por alguna manera pensada, ó non pensada, que sea
ó ser pueda; so las penas contenidas en la dicha capitulacion
de las dichas paces. É la pena pagada ó non pagada, ó gracio-
samente remetida, que esta obligacion, é capitulacion, é asiento,
quede é finque firme, estable, é valedera para siempre jamas,
para lo qual todo asy tener, é guardar, é complir é pagar los
dichos procuradores en nombre de los dichos sus constituyentes obligaron los bienes cada uno de la dicha su parte, muebles
é raizes, patrimoniales é fiscales é de sus súbditos é vassallos,
havidos é por haver, é renunciaron qualesquier leyes, é derechos
de que se puedan aprovechar las dichas partes, é cada una dellas, para ir ó venir contra lo susodicho, ó contra alguna parte
dello; é por mayor seguridad é firmeza de lo susodicho, juraron á Dios, é á santa María, é á la señal de la cruz, en que po-
sieron sus manos derechas, é á las palabras de los santos Evangelios de quier que mas largamente son escriptos, en ánima de
los dichos sus constituyentes, que ellos y cada uno de ellos ternán, é guardarán, é complirán todo lo susodicho, y cada una
cosa, é parte dello realmente, é con efecto, cesante todo fraude,
cautela, é engaño, ficcion, é simulacion, é no lo contradirán en
tiempo alguno, ni por alguna manera. So el qual dicho juramento juraron de no pedir absolucion, ni relaxacion dél á nuestro muy santo Padre, ni á otro ningun legado, ni prelado que
gela pueda dar, é aunque proprio motu gela dé, no usarán
della, ántes por esta presente capitulacion suplican en el dicho
nombre á nuestro muy santo Padre, que á Su Santidad plega
confirmar, é aprovar esta dicha capitulacion, segund en ella se
contiene, é mandando expedir sobre ello sus bulas á las partes,
ó á qualquiera dellas, que las pedieren, é mandando incorpo-
rar en ellas el tenor desta capitulacion, poniendo sus censuras
á los que contra ella fueren, ó pasaren, en qualquier tiempo
que sea, ó ser pueda. É asy mismo los dichos procuradores en
el dicho nombre se obligaron so la dicha pena, é juramento,
dentro de ciento dias primeros siguientes, contados desde el dia

1491.

Seguridades
y penas.

Canje
de las ratificaciones.

1494.   de la fecha desta capitulacion, darán la una parte á la otra, y la
otra á la otra aprobacion, é ratificacion desta dicha capitulacion,
escriptas en pergamino, é firmadas de los nombres de los dichos
señores sus constituyentes, é selladas con sus sellos de plomo
pendiente, é en la escriptura que ovieren de dar los dichos señores rey é reyna de Castilla, é Aragon, etc., aya de firmar, é
consentir, é otorgar el muy esclarecido, é ilustríssimo señor el
señor príncepe don Juan su hijo, de lo qual todo que dicho es,
otorgaron dos escripturas de un tenor tal la una como la otra,
las quales firmaron de sus nombres, é las otorgaron ante los
secretarios, é escrivanos de yuso escriptos, para cada una de
las partes la suya. É qualquiera que paresciere, vala como si
ambas á dos paresciesen; que fueron fechas, é otorgadas en la
dicha villa de Tordesillas el dicho dia, é mes, é año susodicho.
El comisario mayor don Henrique Ruy de Sosa, don Juan de
Sosa, el doctor Rodrigo Maldonado, licenciatus Arias, testigos
que fueron presentes, que vieron aquí firmar sus nombres á los
dichos procuradores, é embaxadores, é otorgar lo susodicho, é
fazer el dicho juramento el comisario Pedro de Leon, el comisario Fernando de Torres, vecinos de la villa de Vallid, el comisario Fernando de Gamarra comisario de Tagra é Senete,
contino de la casa de los dichos rey é reyna nuestros señores, é
Juan Soares de Seguera, é Ruy Leme, é Duarte Pacheco, conti-
nos de la casa del señor rey de Portugal para ello procurados.
É yo Fernan Dalvres de Toledo, secretario del rey é de la reyna
nuestros señores, é del su consejo, é escrivano de cámara, é
notario público en la su corte, é en todos los sus reynos é señoríos, fuy presente á todo lo que dicho es en uno con los dichos
testigos, é con Estévan Vaes, secretario del dicho señor rey de
Portugal, que por abtoridad que los dichos rey é reyna nuestros
señores le dieron para dar fe deste abçon en sus reynos, que
fué asy mismo presente á lo que dicho es, é á ruego é otorga-
miento de todos los dichos procuradores, é embaxadores, que
en mi presencia, é suya, aquí firmaron sus nombres, este público instromento de capitulacion fize escrevir, el qual va escripto en estas seis fojas de papel de pliego entero escriptas de

ambas partes con esta en que van los nombres de los sobredi-   1494.
chos , é muí signo; é en fin de cada plana va señalado de la
señal de mi nombre é de la señal dél dicho Estévan Vaes , é
por ende fize aquí mi signo, que es tal. En testimonio de verdad Fernan Dalvres. É yo el dicho Estévan Vaes , que por abtoridad que los dichos señores rey é reyna de Castilla, é de Leon,
me dieron para fazer público en todos sus reynos é señorios,
juntamente con el dicho Fernan Dalvres, á ruego , é requeri-
mento de los dichos embaxadores é procuradores á todo presente fuy, é por fe é certidumbre dello aquí de mi público señal la signé, que tal es.

La qual dicha escriptura de asiento, é capitulacion, é concordia suso incorporada, vista é entendida por nos, é por el dicho príncepe don Juan nuestro hijo, la aprovamos, loamos, é
confirmamos, é otorgamos, é ratificamos, é prometemos de tener,
é guardar, é complir todo lo susodicho en ella contenido, é cada
una cosa , é parte dello realmente é con efeto, cesante todo
fraude, é cautela, ficcion, é simulacion, é de no ir, ni venir
contra ello, ni contra parte dello en tiempo alguno, ni por alguna manera que sea, ó ser pueda ; é por mayor firmeza, nos, y
el dicho príncepe don Juan nuestro hijo juramos á Dios, é á
santa María, é á las palavras de los santos Evangelios do quier
que mas largamente son escriptas, é á la señal de la cruz, en
que corporalmente posimos nuestras manos derechas en presencia de los dichos Ruy de Sosa, é don Juan de Sosa, é licen-
ciado Arias de Almadana, embaxadores é procuradores del dicho sereníssimo rey de Portugal, nuestro hermano, de lo asy
tener é guardar, é complir, é á cada una cosa, é parte de lo que
á nos incumbe, realmente é con efeto, como dicho es, por nos
é por nuestros herederos é subcesores, é por los dichos nuestros
reynos é señoríos, é súbditos é naturales dellos, so las penas é
obligaciones, vínculos é renunciaciones en el dicho contracto de
capitulacion, é concordia de suso escripto, contenidas : por cer-
tificacion, é corroboracion de lo qual, firmamos en esta nuestra
carta nuestros nombres, é la mandamos sellar con nuestro sello
de plomo pendiente en filos de seda á colores. Dada en la villa

1494.   de Arévalo, á dos dias del mes de julio año del nascimiento de nuestro Señor Jesu Christo de mil quatrocientos noventa é quatro años.

YO EL REY. — YO LA REYNA. — YO EL PRÍNCIPE.

Y YO FERNAN DALVRES DE TOLEDO,

Secretario del rey é de la reyna nuestros señores, la fice escrebir por su mandado.

ASENSOS DOCTOR (1).

(1) Esta assignatura está tão inintelligvel no original, que pareceu declarar aqui por duvida á interpretação que se lhe deu.

Treaty of Peace between Spain and the Netherlands, signed at Munster, 30 January 1648

THE Latin text of this Treaty (taken from a version published by Aitzema in 1651 entitled *Tractatus Pacis inter Hispaniae et Unitum Belgium, Monasterii . . .*) includes the full powers of the plenipotentiaries of both parties, the ratifications (the Spanish undated, the Dutch dated 18 April 1648), and the form of proclamation of the Treaty by the Netherlands, which indicates that the exchange of ratifications was effected on 25 May 1648.

It includes also the lists of additional parties nominated for inclusion in the Peace in accordance with Article LXXII, as well as the Particular Article, concerning navigation and commerce, added to the Treaty on 4 February 1648. This Article was further explained by the Treaty of 17 December 1650.

The text reproduces also the Articles concerning the Prince of Orange of 8 January and 27 December 1647, which are incorporated into the Treaty by Article XLV. As to the implementation of the provisions by the handing over of Turnhout to Orange, see the Cession etc. of 26 October 1649. Further on the implementation of Article III etc. see the Treaty signed at Brussels between the parties on 20 September 1664.

The Latin text is to be found also in the *Theatrum Pacis*, vol. I, p. 3, and in Lündorp, *Acta Publica*, Part VI, p. 331.

The French translation given here is taken from Dumont, *Corps Universel Diplomatique du Droit des Gens*, vol. VI, Part I, p. 429, and by him (scil.) from Scheltus, *Recueil van de Tractaaten* etc. He records that it is to be found also in Aitzema, *Historia Pacis*, p. 687, and *Recueil des Traités de Confédération et d'Alliance entre la Couronne de France* etc. It exists also in German (*Theatrum Pacis, loc. cit., Theatrum Europaeum*, vol. VI, p. 460) and Italian (Siri, *Mercurio*, vol. XII, p. 158) translations. There is an abbreviated English translation in Jenkinson, *Treaties* etc., vol. I, p. 10. See also *Venezuela–British Guiana Boundary Arbitration*, Venezuelan Case, vol. III, p. 4.

Though not formally a component of the Peace of Westphalia (and thus, strictly, anterior to the present series) this Treaty is included here because of its general importance in European affairs of the succeeding decades.

té de leur part à l'Affemblée des Seigneurs Eftats Generaux; le Sieur François de Donia, Sieur de Hinnema, Hielfum, Deputé à l'Affemblée des Seigneurs Eftats Generaux, de la part de la Province de Frife; le Sieur Guillaume Ripperda, Sieur de Hengeloo, Boxbergen, Bobuloo & Ruffenbergh, Deputé de la Nobleffe de la Province d'Over-Yffel à l'Affemblée des Seigneurs Eftats Generaux; le Sieur Adrian Kland de Stedum, Sieur de Nitterfum &c. Deputé ordinaire de la Province de la Ville de Groningue & Ommelande à l'Affemblée des Seigneurs Eftats Generaux; Tous Ambaffadeurs extraordinaires en Allemagne, & Plenipotentiaires defdits Seigneurs Eftats Generaux, aux Traiétés de la Paix generale. Tous garnis de Pouvoirs fuffifans qui feront inferez à la fin des prefentes, lefquels affemblez en la Ville de Munfter en Weftphalie de commun concert deftinée au Traiété general de la Paix de la Chreftienté, en vertu de leursdits Pouvoirs, pour & au nom defdits Seigneurs Roy & Eftats, ont fait, conclu & accordé les Articles qui s'enfuivent.

I. Premierement declare ledit Seigneur Roy & reconnoit que lefdits Seigneurs Eftats Generaux des Pays-Bas Unis, & les Provinces d'iceux refpeétivement avec tous leurs Pays affociés, Villes & Terres y appartenans font libres & Souverains Eftats, Provinces & Pays, fur lefquels, ny fur leur Pays, Villes & Terres affociées, comme deffus, ledit Seigneur Roy ne pretend rien, & que prefentement ou cy-aprés pour foy mefme, fes Hoirs & Succeffeurs il ne pretendra jamais rien, & qu'enfuite de ce il eft content de traiéter avec lefdits Seigneurs Eftats, comme il fait par le prefent une Paix perpetuelle, aux Conditions cy-aprés efcrites & declarées.

II. A fçavoir, que ladite Paix fera bonne, ferme, fidelle & inviolable, & qu'enfuite cefferont & feront delaiffez tous aétes d'hoftilité, de quelque façon qu'ils foient entre lefdits Seigneurs Roi & Eftats Generaux tant par Mer, autres Eaux, que par Terre, en tous leurs Royaumes, Pays, Terres & Seigneuries, & pour tous leurs Sujets & Habitans de quelque qualité ou condition qu'ils foient, fans exception de lieux ny de Perfonnes.

III. Chacun demeurera faifi & joüira effectivement des Pays, Villes, Places, Terres & Seigneuries, qu'il tient & poffede à prefent, fans y eftre troublé ny inquieté directement ny indirectement, de quelque façon que ce foit; En quoy on entend comprendre les Bourgs, Villages, Hameaux & plat Pays, qui en dependent. Et en fuite toute la Meyerie de Boïfleduc, comme auffi toutes les Seigneuries, Villes, Châteaux, Bourgs, Villages, Hameaux & plat Pays, dependans de ladite Ville & Meyerie de Boïfleduc, Ville & Marquifat de Berges fur Zoom, Ville & Baronnie de Breda, Ville de Maftricht & reffort d'icelle, comme auffi le Comté de Vroonhoff, la Ville de Grave & Pays de Kuyk, Hulft & Baillage de Hulft & Hulfter Ambacht, & auffi Axele Ambacht, affis aux coftés Meridional & Septentrional de la Gueldre, comme auffi les Forts que lefdits Seigneurs Eftats poffedent prefentement au Pays de Waes, & toutes autres Villes & Places, que lefdits Seigneurs Eftats tiennent en Brabant, Flandres & ailleurs, demeureront auxdits Seigneurs Eftats en tous & mefmes Droits & Parties de Souveraineté & Superiorité, fans rien excepter, & tout ainfi qu'ils tiennent les Provinces des Pays-Bas Unis. Bien entendu, que tout le refte dudit Pays de Waes, exceptant lefdits Forts, demeurera audit Seigneur Roy d'Efpagne. Touchant les trois Quartiers d'outre Meufe, fçavoir Fauquemont, Dalem & Roleduc, ils demeureront en l'eftat auquel ils fe trouvent à prefent; Et en cas de difpute & controverfe elle fera renvoyée à la Chambre my-partie, de laquelle il fera parlé cy-aprés pour y eftre decidé.

IV. Les Sujets & Habitans des Pays defdits Seigneurs Roy & Eftats auront toute bonne Correfpondence & Amitié par enfemble, fans fe reffentir des offences & dommage qu'ils ont reçeus par le paffé; pourront auffi frequenter & fejourner és Pays l'un de l'autre, & y exercer leur Trafic & Commerce en toute feureté, tant par Mer, autres Eaux, que par Terre.

V. La Navigation & Trafique des Indes Orientales & Occidentales fera maintenuë, felon & en conformité des Octroys fur ce donnés, ou à donner cy-aprés; pour feureté de quoy fervira le prefent Traicté & la Ratification d'iceluy, qui de part & d'autre en fera procurée; Et feront compris fous ledit Traicté tous Potentats, Nations & Peuples, avec lefquels lefdits Seigneurs Eftats, ou ceux de la Societé des Indes Orientales & Occidentales en leur nom, entre les limites de leurfdits Octroys font en Amitié & Alliance; Et un chacun, fçavoir les fufdits Seigneurs Roy & Eftats refpectivement demeureront en poffeffion & jouïront de telles Seigneuries, Villes, Chafteaux, Fortereffes, Commerce & Pays és Indes Orientales & Occidentales, comme auffi au Brefil & fur les coftes d'Afié, Afrique & Amerique refpectivement, que lefdits Seigneurs Roy & Eftats refpectivement tiennent & poffedent, en ce compris fpecialement les Lieux & Places que les Portugais depuis l'an mil fix cent quarante & un, ont pris & occupé fur lefdits Seigneurs Eftats; compris auffi les Lieux & Places qu'iceux Seigneurs Eftats cy-aprés fans infraction du prefent Traicté viendront à conquerir & poffeder; Et les Directeurs de la Societé des Indes tant Orientales que Occidentales des Provinces-Unies, comme auffi les Miniftres, Officiers haut & bas, Soldats & Matelots, eftans en fervice actuel de l'une ou de l'autre defdites Compagnies, ou ayants efté en leur fervice, comme auffi ceux qui hors leur fervice refpectivement, tant en ce Pays qu'au Diftrict defdites deux Compagnies, continüent encor, ou pourront cy-aprés eftre employés, feront & demeureront libres & fans eftre moleftez en tous les Pays eftant fous l'obeïffance dudit Seigneur Roy en l'Europe, pourront voyager, trafiquer & frequenter, comme tous autres Habitans des Pays defdits Seigneurs Eftats. En outre a efté conditionné & ftipulé, que les Efpagnols retiendront leur Navigation en telle maniere qu'ils la tiennent pour le prefent és Indes Orientales, fans fe pouvoir eftendre plus avant, comme auffi les Habitans de ce Pays-Bas s'abftiendront de la frequentation des Places que les Caftillans ont és Indes Orientales.

VI. Et quant aux Indes Occidentales, les Sujets & Habitants des Royaumes, Provinces & Terres defdits Seigneurs Roy & Eftats refpectivement s'abftiendront de naviger & trafiquer en tous les Havres, Lieux & Places garnies de Forts, Loges, ou Chafteaux, & toutes autres poffedées par l'une ou l'autre Partie; fçavoir, que les Sujets dudit Seigneur Roy ne navigeront & trafiqueront en celles tenuës par lefdits Seigneurs Eftats, ny les Sujets defdits Seigneurs Eftats en celles tenuës par ledit Seigneur Roy, & entre les Places tenuës par lefdits Seigneurs Eftats feront comprifes les Places que les Portugais depuis l'an mil fix cent quarante & un ont occupé dans le Brafil fur lefdits Seigneurs Eftats, comme auffi toutes autres Places qu'ils poffedent à prefent tandis qu'elles demeureront auxdits Portugais; fans que le precedent Article puiffe deroger au contenu du prefent.

VII. Et pour ce qu'il eft befoin d'un affez longtemps pour advertir ceux qui font hors lefdites limites avec Forces & Navires, à fe defifter de touts actes d'hoftilité, a efté accordé, qu'entre les limites de l'Octroy cy-devant donné à la Societé des Indes Orientales du Pays--Bas, ou à donner par continuation, la Paix ne commencera pluftoft qu'un an aprés la date de la conclufion du prefent Traicté; Et quant aux limites de l'Octroy cy-devant donné par les Eftats Generaux, ou à donner par continuation à la Societé des Indes Occidentales, qu'auxdits Lieux la Paix ne commencera pas pluftoft que fix mois aprés la date que deffus. Bien entendu que fi l'advis de ladite Paix foit de la part du public de part & d'autre parvenu pluftoft entre lefdits limites refpectivement, que dés l'heure de l'advis l'Hoftilité ceffera auxdits Lieux; mais fi aprés le terme d'un an & de fix mois refpectivement dans les limites des Octroys fufdits fe fait aucun acte d'hoftilité, les dommages en feront reparés fans delay.

VIII. Les Sujets & Habitans des Pays defdits Seigneurs Roy & Eftats faifans Trafic aux Pays l'un de l'autre ne feront tenus de payer plus grands Droits & Impofitions, que les propres Sujets refpectivement, de maniere que les Habitans & Sujets des Pays-Bas Unis, feront & demeureront exempts de certains vingt pour cent, ou de telle moindre, plus haute, ou quelque autre Impofition, que ledit Seigneur Roy durant la Trefve de douze ans a levée, ou cy-aprés directement ou indirectement voudroit lever fur les Habitans & Subjets des Pays-Bas Unis, ou mettre à leur charge par deffus & plus haut qu'il ne feroit fur fes propres

Treaty of Peace and Friendship between Great Britain and Spain, signed at Madrid, 13(23) May 1667

THE Latin text and Spanish translation of this Treaty are taken from Abreu y Bertodano, *Colección de los Tratados de Paz* &c., vol. X, p. 145. The English translation is reproduced from *Hertslet's Commercial Treaties*, vol. II, p. 140, and the Cedulas referred to in the IXth Article from *British and Foreign State Papers*, vol. I, p. 582. The Treaty was ratified by Spain on 21 September and by Great Britain on 23 September 1667. It was renewed by the Treaties of 18 July 1670, 10 June 1680, 13 July 1713, 9 December 1713, 9 November 1729, 10 February 1748 and by the Additional Articles of 28 August 1814. With respect to Sicily, it must be considered to have been terminated by the Treaty of 26 September 1816 between Great Britain and the Two Sicilies. French and Latin versions are to be found in Bernard, *Recueil des Traitez de Paix*, vol. IV, p. 193 (French and, p. 228, Latin). A French version containing the Spanish and English full powers is printed in Dumont, *Corps Universel Diplomatique du Droit des Gens*, vol. VII, Part I, p. 27. Other English translations appear in Chalmers, *A Collection of Treaties between Great Britain and other Powers*, vol. II, p. 5; Davenport, *European Treaties* &c., vol. II, p. 94; Gostling, *Extracts from the treaties between Great Britain and other Kingdoms* &c., pp. 112 and 229; and *Marine Treaties* &c., p. 125.

vessels, with any things introduced into the Dominions or places of the Crown of Great Britain as prizes, and judged for such in the said Dominions and places, shall be taken for goods and merchandize of Great Britain, comprehended so by the intention of this Article.

VIII. That the subjects and vessels of the most Serene King of Great Britain may bring and carry to all and singular the Dominions of the King of Spain, any fruits and commodities of the East Indies, it appearing by testimony of the Deputies of the East India Company in London, that they are of, or have come from the English conquests, plantations or factories, with like privilege, and according to what is allowed to the subjects of the United Provinces, by the Royal *Cedulas* of *Contravando*, bearing date the 27th of June, and the 3d of July, 1663, and published on the 30th of June, and 4th of July, the same year. And for what may concern both the Indies, and any other parts whatsoever, the Crown of Spain doth grant to the King of Great Britain and His subjects, all that is granted to the United States of the Low Countries and their subjects, in their Treaty of Munster, 1648, point for point, in as full and ample manner as if the same were herein particularly inserted, the same rules being to be observed whereunto the subjects of the said United States are obliged, and mutual offices of friendship to be performed from one side to the other.

IX. That the subjects of the King of Great Britain, trading, buying, and selling in any of the Kingdoms, Governments, Islands, ports, or Territories of the said King of Spain, shall have, use, and enjoy all the privileges and immunities which the said King hath granted and confirmed to the English merchants that reside in Andalusia, by his Royal *Cedulas* or orders, dated the 19th day of March, the 26th day of June, and the 9th day of November, 1645. His Catholic Majesty by these presents reconfirming the same as a part of this Treaty between the two Crowns. And to the end that it be manifest to all, it is consented, that the said schedules (as to the whole substance thereof) be passed and transferred to the body of the present Articles, in the name and favour of all and singular the subjects of the King of Great Britain, residing and trading in any places whatsoever within His Catholic Majesty's Dominions.

Treaty between Great Britain and Spain, signed at Westminster, 8(18) July 1670

THE Latin text of this Treaty of peace and for settling all disputes in America, is reproduced from Dumont, *Corps Universel Diplomatique du Droit des Gens*, vol. VII, Part I, p. 137, who takes it from a copy printed in Madrid in 1670, recording that there exist also English and French versions. It is printed also in Bernard, *Recueil des Traitez de Paix*, vol. IV, p. 284, and, from the Spanish archives (together with a Spanish translation), in Abreu y Bertodano, *Colección de los Tratados de Paz* etc., vol. X, p. 498. The English translation given here is taken from Chalmers, *Treaties*, vol. II, p. 34. Other English versions, complete or partial, appear in *General Collection of Treatys*, vol. I, p. 162, Gostling, *Extracts from all the Treaties* etc., p. 125, Jenkinson, *Treaties*, vol. I, p. 197, *Marine Treaties*, p. 62, *British and Foreign State Papers*, vol. I, p. 668, *Hertslet's Commercial Treaties*, vol. II, p. 196, *Handbook of Commercial Treaties*, (3rd ed., 1924) p. 755, and Davenport, *European Treaties bearing on the History of the United States*, vol. II, p. 197.

The Treaty was ratified by Great Britain on 10 August and by Spain on 28 September 1670. It was renewed by the Treaties of 10 June 1680, 13 July 1713, 10 February 1763 and 3 September 1783, the Preliminary Articles of 30 April 1748 and the Additional Articles of 28 August 1814.

noftri nomine, locoque, necnon Hæredum, ac Succefforum ejus, dictum Nos Tractatum juxta formam,
& tenorem fuum conftanter, ac inviolabiliter obferva-
turos, & perfecturos, atque, ut obfervetur, & perfi-
ciatur, curaturos effe, eo modo ac fi eundem in propria perfona noftra tractaffemus, neque ulla quacumque
tandem ratione, five directa, five indirecta, contraven-
turos, neque ut ab aliis contraveniatur permiffuros effe:
Cum obftrictione in eum finem, atque obligatione dicti
Sereniffimi Regis Catholici Filii noftri chariffimi, atque
Hæredum, Succefforum, pofterorumque ejus, quin
etiam omnium, & fingulorum Regnorum, Regionum,
& Dominiorum noftrorum, nullis exceptis, ut & omnium aliorum Bonorum noftrorum præfentium, & fu-
turorum. Quo autem fupradicta Obligatio eo magis
confirmetur, Legibus, confuetudinibus, & exceptioni-
bus quibufcunque contra facientibus, vel adverfantibus
renuntiamus. In eorum autem omnium, quæ fupra
dicta funt, fidem, & teftimonium juffimus expediri
præfentes Literas propria noftra manu fubfcriptas, ac
Sigillo noftro fecreto munitas, manuque Secretarii nostri Status fubfignatas. Dabantur Matriti octavo die
menfis Octobris, anno Domini milleſimo fexcenteſimo
feptuageſimo. YO LA REYNA. Don Diego
de la Torre.

ENGLISH

TRANSLATION

WHEREAS, for many years paft, the good un-
derftanding and correfpondence between the Englifh
and Spanifh nations having been difturbed in America,
it pleafed the moft Serene and Powerful Prince Charles,

King of Great Britain, &c. in order to the reftoring
and regulating the fame for the future, to fend into
Spain his envoy extraordinary Sir William Godolphin, Knight, with full authority and power to make
any treaty convenient and proper for that end: and
likewife the moft Serene and Powerful Charles, King
of Spain, &c. and the Queen Regent Maria-Anna, &c.
for the carrying on a work of fo much piety and public
good, deputed on their part the Earl of Penaranda,
Counfellor of State, and Prefident of the Indies, to
confer, treat, and conclude thereupon with the. faid Sir
William Godolphin: at length they mutually refolved
and agreed upon the articles of the following treaty,
in virtue of their feveral commiffions.

I. Firft, it is agreed between the above-mentioned
plenipotentiaries, Sir William Godolphin and the Earl
of Penaranda, in the names of the moft Serene Kings
refpectively, their mafters, that the articles of peace
and alliance made between the crowns of Great Britain
and Spain, in Madrid, on the $\frac{13}{23}$ of May 1667, or
any claufe thereof, fhall in no manner be deemed or
underftood to be taken away or abrogated by this prefent treaty; but that the fame fhall remain perpetually
in their ancient force, ftability, and vigour, fo far forth
as they are not contrary or repugnant to this prefent
convention and articles, or to any thing therein contained.

II. That there be an univerfal peace, true and
fincere amity, in America, as in the other parts of the
world, between the moft Serene Kings of Great Britain
and Spain, their heirs and fucceffors, and between the
kingdoms, ftates, plantations, colonies, forts, cities,
iflands, and dominions, without any diftinction of place
belonging unto either of them, and between the people
and inhabitants under their refpective obedience, which
fhall endure from this day for ever, and be obferved
inviolably, as well by land as by fea and frefh-waters,
fo as to promote each the welfare and advantage of

the other, and favour and affift one another with mutual love; and that every where, as well in thofe remote countries as in thefe which are nearer, the faithful offices of good neighbourhood and friendfhip may be exercifed and increafe between them.

III. Alfo, that for the time to come, all enmities, hoftilities, and difcords, between the faid Kings, their fubjects and inhabitants, ceafe and be abolifhed: and, that both parties do altogether forbear and abftain from all plundering, depredation, injuries, and infeftation whatfoever, as well by land as by fea, and in frefh-waters, every where.

IV. The faid moft Serene Kings fhall take care that their fubjects do accordingly abftain from all force and wrong-doing: and they fhall revoke all commiffions and letters of reprifal and mart, or otherwife containing licence to take prizes, of what condition or kind foever, being to the prejudice of the one or other of the faid Kings, or of their fubjects, whether the fame have been given or granted by them unto fubjects or inhabitants, or unto ftrangers; and fhall declare the fame to be void and of no force, as by this treaty of peace they are declared fo to be: and whofoever fhall do any thing to the contrary, he fhall be punifhed not only criminally, according to the merit of his offence, but fhall alfo be compelled to make reftitution and fatisfaction for the loffes to the parties damnified, requiring the fame.

V. And furthermore, the faid Kings fhall denounce, as by the tenor of thefe prefents every of them hath and doth renounce, whatfoever league, confederation, capitulation, and intelligence, made by what manner foever, in the prejudice of the one or the other, which doth or may repugn againft this peace and concord, and all and fingular the contents thereof: all which and every of them, fo far as they do concern the effect aforefaid, they fhall annul and make void, and declare to be of no force or moment.

VI. The prisoners on both sides, one and all, of what degree or condition soever, detained by reason of any hostilities hitherto committed in America, shall be forthwith set at liberty, without ransom, or any other price of their freedom.

VII. All offences, damages, losses, injuries, which the nations and people of Great Britain and Spain have at any time heretofore, upon what cause or pretext soever, suffered by each other in America, shall be expunged out of remembrance, and buried in oblivion, as if no such thing had ever past.

Moreover, it is agreed, that the most Serene King of Great Britain, his heirs and successors, shall have, hold, keep, and enjoy for ever, with plenary right of sovereignty, dominion, possession, and propriety, all those lands, regions, islands, colonies, and places whatsoever, being or situated in the West Indies, or in any part of America, which the said King of Great Britain and his subjects do at present hold and possess; so as that in regard thereof, or upon any colour or pretence whatsoever, nothing more may or ought to be urged, nor any question or controversy be ever moved concerning the same hereafter.

VIII. The subjects and inhabitants, merchants, captains, masters of ships, mariners of the kingdoms, provinces, and dominions of each confederate respectively, shall abstain and forbear to sail and trade in the ports and havens which have fortifications, castles, magazines, or warehouses, and in all other places whatsoever possessed by the other party in the West Indies; to wit, The subjects of the King of Great Britain shall not sail unto, and trade in the havens and places which the Catholic King holdeth in the said Indies; nor in like manner shall the subjects of the King of Spain sail unto, or trade in those places which are possessed there by the King of Great Britain.

IX. But if, at any time hereafter, either King shall think fit to grant unto the subjects of the other, any general or particular licence or privileges of navigating unto, and trading in any places under his obedience who fhall grant the fame, the faid navigation and trade fhall be exercifed and maintained according to the form, tenor, and effect of the faid permiffions or privileges to be allowed and given ; for the fecurity, warrant, and authority whereof, this prefent treaty and the ratification thereof fhall ferve.

X. It is alfo agreed, that in cafe the fubjects and inhabitants of either of the confederates, with their fhipping (whether public and of war, or private and of merchants) be forced at any time through ftrefs of weather, purfuit of pirates and enemies, or other inconvenience whatfoever, for the feeking of fhelter and harbour, to retreat and enter into any of the rivers, creeks, bays, havens, roads, fhores, and ports belonging to the other in America, they fhall be received and treated there with all humanity and kindnefs, and enjoy all friendly protection and help : and it fhall be lawful for them to refrefh and provide themfelves, at reafonable and the ufual rates, with victuals and all things needful, either for the fuftenance of their perfons, or reparation of their fhips, and conveniency of their voyage ; and they fhall in no manner be detained or hindered from returning out of the faid ports or roads, but fhall remove and depart, when and whither they pleafe, without any let or impediment.

XI. Likewife, if any fhips belonging to either confederate, their people and fubjects, fhall, within the coafts or dominions of the other, ftick upon the fands, or be wrecked (which God forbid) or fuffer any damage, the perfons fhipwrecked and caft on the fhore fhall in no fort be kept prifoners, but, on the contrary, all friendly affiftance and relief fhall be adminiftered to their diftrefs, and letters of fafe-conduct given them for their free and quiet paffage thence, and the return of every one to his own country.

XII. But when it fhall happen, that the fhips of

either (as is above-mentioned) through danger of the sea, or other urgent cause, be driven into the ports and havens of the other, if they be three or four together, and may give juft ground of fufpicion, they fhall immediately upon their arrival acquaint the governor or chief magiftrate of the place with the caufe of their coming, and fhall ftay no longer than the faid governor or chief magiftrate will permit, and fhall be requifite for the furnifhing themfelves with victuals, and reparation of their fhips : and they fhall always take care not to carry out of their fhips any goods or packs, expofing them to fale, neither fhall they receive any merchandize on board, nor do any thing contrary to this treaty.

XIII. Both parties fhall truly and firmly obferve and execute this prefent treaty, and all and every the matters therein contained, and effectually caufe the fame to be obferved and performed by the fubjects and inhabitants of either nation.

XIV. No private injury fhall in any fort weaken this treaty, nor beget hatred or diffentions between the forefaid nations, but every one fhall anfwer for his own proper fact, and be profecuted thereupon; neither fhall one man fatisfy for the offence of another by reprifals, or other fuch like odious proceedings, unlefs juftice be denied, or unreafonably delayed, in which cafe it fhall be lawful for that King, whofe fubject hath fuffered the lofs and injury, to take any courfe according to the rules and method of the law of nations, until reparation be made to the fufferer.

XV. The prefent treaty fhall in nothing derogate from any pre-eminence, right, or dominion, of either confederate in the American feas, channels, or waters, but that they have and retain the fame in as full and ample manner as may of right belong unto them : but it is always to be underftood, that the liberty of navigation ought in no manner to be difturbed, where nothing is committed againft the genuine fenfe and meaning of thefe articles.

XVI. Laftly, The folemn ratifications of this prefent treaty and agreement, made in due form, fhall
be delivered on both fides, and mutually exchanged
within the fpace of four months from this day; and
within eight.months, to be computed from the faid exchange of the inftruments (or fooner if poffible) they
fhall be publifhed in all convenient places throughout
the kingdoms, ftates, iflands, and dominions of both
confederates, as well in the Weft Indies as elfewhere.

In teftimony of all and fingular the contents hereof,
we the above-mentioned plenipotentiaries have
figned and fealed this prefent treaty, at Madrid,
the $\frac{8}{18}$ day of July, in the year of our Lord
1670.

The Count of *Penaranda*,   *William Godolphin*,
              (L. S.)   (L. S.)

Treaty of Peace and Friendship between Great Britain and Spain, signed at Utrecht, 13 July 1713

THE Latin text of this, the Anglo-Spanish Treaty of Utrecht, is taken from Dumont, *Corps Universel Diplomatique du Droit des Gens*, vol. VIII, p. 393, who takes it from *Actes et Mémoires de la Paix d'Utrecht*, vol. V, p. 136, and the English translation from Jenkinson, *Treaties*, vol. II, p. 66. Other English versions are: Almon, *A Collection of all the Treaties of Peace* etc., vol. I, p. 168; Gostling, *Extracts from the Treaties*, etc., p. 130; *Marine Treaties* (1760), p. 49; Chalmers, *Treaties*, vol. II, p. 40; *Generall Collection of Treatys*, vol. III, p. 470; *Hertslet's Commercial Treaties*, vol. II, p. 199; *British and Foreign State Papers*, vol. I, p. 611 (extract only); *Handbook of Commercial Treaties* (3rd ed. 1924), p. 758; and Davenport, *European Treaties bearing on the History of the United States*, vol. III, p. 223 (who prints the original text, in part, from the Spanish ratification in the British archives: *S.P. 108/475*, adding a translation). Lamberty, *Mémoires pour Servir à l'Histoire du XVIII Siécle* (1735), vol. VIII, p. 375, has the Treaty in French and it appears in Spanish in *Colección de los Tratados de Paz* etc. vol. I (1796), p. 201, Del Cantillo, *Tratados, Convenios y Declaraciones de Paz y de Comercio*, p. 115, and Calvo, *Recueil complet des Traités etc. de L'Amerique*, vol. II, p. 115 (extract only). The Treaty, which was ratified by Great Britain on 31 July and by Spain on 4 August 1713, was renewed by the Treaties of 9 December 1713, 13 June 1721, 9 November 1729, 10 February 1763 and 3 September 1783, and the Preliminary Articles of 30 April 1748. Dumont's text includes, in addition to the Treaty, the British ratification, the Spanish full powers, the British full powers, the Separate Article respecting the observance of the Treaty of 27 March 1713 together with the British ratification thereof, the Second Separate Article concerning the provision made for the Countess Orsini, again with a British ratification, the Declaration of the plenipotentiaries, dated 12(23) February 1714, respecting ratification of the Treaty, the Certificate respecting exchange of ratifications of this Treaty and of the Treaty of 28 November (9 December) 1713, bearing the same date, and finally the Declaration of the Spanish envoys respecting the titles employed in the Spanish ratification. The translation does not extend to the full powers, or to the ratifications other than the British ratification of the Treaty itself,

or pretence should hereafter endeavour to oppose the said succession, either by open war, or by encouraging sedition, and forming conspiracies against such prince and princes, who are in possession of the throne of Great Britain, by virtue of the acts of parliament there made, or against that prince or princess to whom the succession to the crown of Great Britain shall belong, according to the acts of parliament, as abovesaid.

VII. That the ordinary distribution of justice be restored, and open again through the kingdoms and dominions of each of their royal majesties, so that it may be free for all the subjects on both sides, to prosecute and obtain their rights, pretensions and actions, according to the laws, constitutions and statutes of each kingdom. And especially if there be any complaints concerning injuries or grievances, which have been done contrary to the tenor of the treaties, either in time of peace, or at the beginning of the war lately ended, care shall be taken that the damages be forthwith made good, according to the rule of justice.

VIII. That there be a free use of navigation and commerce between the subjects of each kingdom, as it was heretofore, in time of peace, and before the declaration of this late war, in the reign of Charles II. of glorious memory, Catholic King of Spain, according to the treaties of friendship, confederation, and commerce, which were formerly made between both nations, according to ancient customs, letters patents, cedulas, and other particular acts; and also according to the treaty or treaties of commerce which are now, or will forthwith be made at Madrid. And whereas, among other conditions of the general peace, it is by common consent established as a chief and fundamental rule, that the exercise of navigation and commerce to the Spanish West-Indies, should remain in the same state as it was in the time of the aforesaid King Charles II. That therefore this rule may hereafter be observed with inviolable faith, and in a manner never to be broken, and thereby all causes of distrust and suspicion, concerning that matter may be prevented and removed, it is especially agreed and concluded, that no licence, nor any permission at all, shall at any time be given, either to the French, or to any nation whatever, in any

name, or under any pretence, directly or indirectly, to
fail, to traffick in, or introduce negroes, goods, merchandizes, or any things whatsoever into the dominions fubject to the crown of Spain in America, except what may
be agreed by the treaty or treaties of commerce abovesaid, and the rights and privileges granted in a certain
convention, commonly called *el Affiento de Negros*, whereof mention is made in the twelfth article; except also
whatsoever the said Catholic King, or his heirs or fucceffors, fhall promife by any contract or contracts for the
introduction of negros into the Spanifh Weft-Indies to
be made after that the convention, or the *Affiento de Negros* abovementioned fhall be determined. And that more
ftrong and full precautions may be taken on all fides, as
abovefaid, concerning the navigation and commerce to the
Weft-Indies, it is hereby further agreed and concluded,
that neither the Catholic King, nor any of his heirs and
fucceffors whatfoever, fhall fell, yield, pawn, transfer, or
by any means, or under any name, alienate from them,
and the crown of Spain, to the French, or to any other
nations whatever, any lands, dominions, or territories, or
any part thereof belonging to Spain in America. On the
contrary, that the Spanifh dominions in the Weft-Idies
may be preferved whole and entire, the Queen of Great
Britain engages, that fhe will endeavour, and give affiftance to the Spaniards, that the ancient limits of their dominions in the Weft Indies be reftored, and fettled as they
ftood in the time of the abovefaid Catholic King Charles
II. if it fhall appear that they have in any manner, or under any pretence, been broken into; and leffened in any
part, fince the death of the aforefaid Catholic King
Charles II.

IX. It is further agreed and concluded as a general
rule, that all and fingular the fubjects of each kingdom
fhall, in all countries and places on both fides, have and
enjoy at leaft the fame privileges, liberties and immunities,
as to all duties, impofitions, or cuftoms whatfoever, relating to perfons, goods, and merchandizes, fhips, freight,
feamen, navigation, and commerce; and fhall have the
like favour in all things, as the fubjects of France, or any
other foreign nation, the moft favoured, have, poffefs,

(11.)—*CONVENTION between Great Britain and Spain, relative to America.*—*Signed at the Escurial, the 28th of October,* 1790.

(Translation.)

LEURS Majestés Britannique et Catholique, étant disposées à terminer, par un accord prompt et solide, les différends qui se sont élevés en dernier lieu entre les 2 Couronnes, elles ont trouvé que le meilleur moyen de parvenir à ce but salutaire seroit celui d'une transaction à l'amiable, laquelle, en laissant de côté toute discussion rétrospective des droits et des prétentions des 2 Parties, réglât leur position respective à l'avenir sur des bases qui seroient conformes à leurs vrais intérêts, ainsi qu'au désir mutuel dont Leurs dites Majestés sont animées, d'établir entre elles, en tout et en tous lieux, la plus parfaite amitié, harmonie et bonne correspondance.

Dans cette vûe, elles ont nommé et constitué pour leurs Plénipotentiaires; savoir, de la part de Sa Majesté Britannique, le Sieur Alleyne Fitz-Herbert, du Conseil Privé de Sa dite Majesté dans la Grande Bretagne et en Irlande, et son Ambassadeur Extraordinaire et Plénipotentiaire près Sa Majesté Catholique; et de la part de Sa Majesté Catholique, Don Joseph Monino, Comte de Florida-blanca, Chevalier Grand Croix du Royal Ordre Espagnol de Charles III, Conseiller d'Etat de Sa dite Majesté, et son Premier Secrétaire d'Etat et del Despacho; lesquels, après s'être communiqués leurs Pleinspouvoirs respectifs, sont convenus des Articles suivans:

ART. I. Il est convenu que les Bâtimens et les Districts de Terrein, situés sur la Côte du Nordouest du Continent de l'Amé-

THEIR Britannic and Catholic Majesties, being desirous of terminating, by a speedy and solid agreement, the differences which have lately arisen between the 2 Crowns, have judged that the best way of attaining this salutary object would be that of an amicable arrangement, which, setting aside all retrospective discussion of the rights and pretensions of the 2 Parties, should fix their respective situation for the future on a basis conformable to their true interests, as well as to the mutual desire with which Their said Majesties are animated, of establishing with each other, in everything and in all places, the most perfect friendship, harmony, and good correspondence.

In this view, they have named and constituted for their Plenipotentiaries; to wit, on the part of His Britannic Majesty, Alleyne Fitz-Herbert, Esq., one of His said Majesty's Privy Council, in Great Britain and Ireland, and his Ambassador Extraordinary and Plenipotentiary to His Catholic Majesty; and on the part of His Catholic Majesty, Don Joseph Monino, Count of Floridablanca, Knight Grand Cross of the Royal Spanish Order of Charles III, Councillor of State to His said Majesty, and his Principal Secretary of State, and of the Despatches; who, after having communicated to each other their respective Full Powers, have agreed upon the following Articles:

ART. I. It is agreed that the Buildings and Tracts of Land, situated on the North-west Coast of the Continent of North Ame-

rique Septentrionale, ou bien sur des Iles adjacentes à ce Continent, desquels les Sujets de Sa Majesté Britannique ont été dépossédés, vers le mois d'Avril, 1789, par un Officier Espagnol, seront restitués aux dits Sujets Britanniques.

II. De plus, une juste réparation sera faite, selon la nature du cas, pour toute acte de violence ou d'hostilité qui aura pû avoir été commis, depuis le dit mois d'Avril, 1789, par les Sujets de l'une des 2 Parties Contractantes contre les Sujets de l'autre; et au cas que depuis la dite époque, quelques uns des Sujets respectifs aient été forcément dépossédés de leurs Terrains, Bâtimens, Vaisseaux, marchandises, ou autres objets de propriété quelconques, sur le dit Continent, ou sur les Mers ou Iles adjacentes, ils en seront remis en possession, ou une juste compensation leur sera faite pour les pertes qu'ils auront essuyées.

III. Et, afin de resserrer les liens de l'amitié, et de conserver à l'avenir une parfaite harmonie et bonne intelligence entre les 2 Parties Contractantes, il est convenu que les Sujets respectifs ne seront point troublés ni molestés, soit en naviguant ou en exerçant leur Pêche dans l'Océan Pacifique, ou dans les Mers du Sud, soit en débarquant sur les Côtes qui bordent ces Mers, dans des endroits non déjà occupés, afin d'y exercer leur commerce avec les Naturels du Pays, ou pour y former des Etablissemens. Le tout sujet néanmoins aux restrictions et aux provisions qui seront spécifiées dans les 3 Articles suivans.

rica, or ou Islands adjacent to that Continent, of which the Subjects of His Britannic Majesty were dispossessed, about the month of April, 1789, by a Spanish Officer, shall be restored to the said British Subjects.

II. And further, that a just reparation shall be made, according to the nature of the case, for all acts of violence or hostility which may have been committed, subsequent to the month of April, 1789, by the Subjects of either of the Contracting Parties against the Subjects of the other; and that, in case any of the said respective Subjects shall, since the same period, have been forcibly dispossessed of their Lands, Buildings, Vessels, merchandise, or other property whatever, on the said Continent, or on the Seas or Islands adjacent, they shall be re-established in the possession thereof, or a just compensation shall be made to them for the losses which they shall have sustained.

III. And in order to strengthen the bonds of friendship, and to preserve in future a perfect harmony and good understanding between the 2 Contracting Parties, it is agreed that their respective Subjects shall not be disturbed or molested either in navigating or carrying on their Fisheries in the Pacific Ocean, or in the South Seas, or in landing on the Coasts of those Seas, in places not already occupied, for the purpose of carrying on their commerce with the Natives of the Country, or of making Settlements there; the whole subject, nevertheless, to the restrictions and provisions specified in the 3 following Articles.

IV. Sa Majesté Britannique s'engage d'employer les mesures les plus efficaces pour que la Navigation et la Pêche de ses Sujets dans l'Océan Pacifique, ou dans les Mers du Sud, ne deviennent point le prétexte d'un commerce illicite avec les Etablissemens Espagnols; et, dans cette vûe, il est en outre expressément stipulé, que les Sujets Britanniques ne navigueront point, et n'exerceront pas leur Pêche dans les dites Mers, à la distance de 10 lieues maritimes d'aucune partie des Côtes déjà occupées par l'Espagne.

V. Il est convenu, que tant dans les endroits qui seront restitués aux Sujets Britanniques, en vertu de l'Article I, que dans toutes les autres parties de la Côte du Nord-ouest de l'Amérique Septentrionale, ou des Iles adjacentes, situées au Nord des parties de la dite Côte déjà occupées par l'Espagne, partout où les Sujets de l'une' des 2 Puissances auront formé des Etablissemens, depuis le mois d'Avril, 1789, ou en formeront par la suite, les Sujets de l'autre auront un accès libre, et exerceront leur commerce, sans trouble ni molestation.

VI. Il est encore convenu, par rapport aux Côtes tant Orientales qu'Occidentales de l'Amérique Méridionale, et aux Iles adjacentes, que les Sujets respectifs ne formeront à l'avenir aucun Etablissement sur les parties de ces Côtes situées au Sud des parties de ces mêmes Côtes, et des Iles adjacentes, déjà occupées par l'Espagne; bien entendu que les

IV. His Britannic Majesty engages to take the most effectual measures to prevent the Navigation and Fishery of his Subjects in the Pacific Ocean, or in the South Seas, from being made a pretext for illicit trade with the Spanish Settlements; and, with this view, it is moreover expressly stipulated, that British Subjects shall not navigate, or carry on their Fishery in the said Seas, within the space of 10 sea leagues from any part of the Coasts already occupied by Spain.

V. It is agreed, that as well in the places which are to be restored to the British Subjects, by virtue of the Ist Article, as in all other parts of the North-western Coasts of North America, or of the Islands adjacent, situated to the North of the parts of the said Coast already occupied by Spain, wherever the Subjects of either of the 2 Powers shall have made Settlements since the month of April, 1789, or shall hereafter make any, the Subjects of the other shall have free access, and shall carry on their trade, without any disturbance or molestation.

VI. It is further agreed, with respect to the Eastern and Western Coasts of South America, and to the Islands adjacent, that no Settlement shall be formed hereafter, by the respective Subjects, in such parts of those Coasts as are situated to the South of those parts of the same Coasts, and of the Islands adjacent, which are already occupied by Spain; pro-

dits Sujets respectifs conserveront la faculté de débarquer sur les Côtes et Iles ainsi situées, pour les objets de leur Pêche, et d'y bâtir des cabanes, et autres ouvrages temporaires, servant seulement à ces objets.

VII. Dans tous les cas de plainte, ou d'infraction des Articles de la présente Convention, les Officiers de part et d'autre, sans se permettre au préalable aucune violence ou voie de fait, seront tenus de faire un rapport exact de l'affaire, et de ses circonstances, à leurs Cours respectives, qui termineront à l'amiable ces différends.

VIII. La présente Convention sera ratifiée et confirmée dans l'espace de 6 semaines, à compter du jour de sa signature, ou plutôt si faire se peut.

En foi de quoi, nous Soussignés Plénipotentiaires de Leurs Majestés Britannique et Catholique, avons signées, en leurs noms, et en vertu de nos Pleinspouvoirs respectifs, la présente Convention, et y avons apposé les Cachets de nos Armes.

Fait à San Lorenzo el Real, le 28 Octobre, 1790.

(L.S.) ALLEYNE FITZ-HERBERT.

(L.S.) EL CONDE DE FLORIDABLANCA.

vided that the said respective Subjects shall retain the liberty of landing on the Coasts and Islands so situated, for the purposes of their Fishery, and of erecting thereon huts, and other temporary buildings, serving only for those purposes.

VII. In all cases of complaint or infraction of the Articles of the present Convention, the Officers of either Party, without permitting themselves previously to commit any violence or act of force, shall be bound to make an exact report of the affair and of its circumstances, to their respective Courts, who will terminate such differences in an amicable manner.

VIII. The present Convention shall be ratified and confirmed in the space of 6 weeks, to be computed from the day of its signature, or sooner if it can be done.

In witness whereof, we, the Undersigned Plenipotentiaries of Their Britannic and Catholic Majesties, have, in their names, and in virtue of our respective Full Powers, signed the present Convention, and set thereto the Seals of our Arms.

Done at the Palace of St. Lawrence, the 28th of October, 1790.

(L.S.) ALLEYNE FITZ-HERBERT.

(L.S.) EL CONDE DE FLORIDABLANCA.

Convention between Great Britain and Spain, signed at the Escurial, 28 October 1790

DAVENPORT, *European Treaties bearing on the History of the United States*, vol. IV, p. 169, takes from the Spanish ratification in the Public Record Office, London (F.O. 94/284(1)), dated 21 November 1790, the French text of this Convention relative to America, which was renewed by the Additional Articles of 28 August 1814. This text appears also in Martens, *Recueil des Principaux Traités* (1st ed.) vol. III, p. 184, (2nd ed.) vol. IV, p. 492; Ancell, *A Collection of Treaties between Great Britain and Foreign Powers, 1743–1803*, vol. II, No. 54; *British and Foreign State Papers*, vol. I, p. 663; *Hertslet's Commercial Treaties*, vol. II, p. 257; Del Cantillo, *Tratados, Convenios y Declaraciones de Paz y de Comercio*, p. 623; Calvo, *Recueil complet des Traités etc. de l'Amérique Latine*, vol. III, p. 356; Handbook of Commercial Treaties (1st ed., 1908), p. 868; Martens et de Cussy, *Recueil Manuel et Pratique des Traités*, vol. II, p. 33; and D'Hauterive et de Cussy, *Recueil des Traités de Commerce etc.*, Part II, vol. II, p. 500.

Article Secret.

Comme par l'article six de la presente convention il a été stipulé par rapport aux côtes tant orientales qu'occidentales de l'Amerique Meridionale, et aux isles adjacentes, que les sujets respectifs ne formeront à l'avenir aucun établissement sur les parties de ces côtes situées au sud des parties de ces mêmes côtes deja occupées par l'Espagne, il est convenu et arreté par le present article que cette stipulation ne restera en force qu'aussi longtems qu'aucun établissement ne sera formé dans les endroits en question par les sujets de quelqu'autre puissance. Le present article secret aura la meme force que s'il etoit inseré dans la convention.

En foi de quoi nous sous-signés plenipotentiaires de leurs Majestés Catholique et Britannique avons signé le present article secret, et y avons apposé les cachets de nos armes.

Fait à San Lorenzo el Real le vingt huit Octobre mille septcent quatre vingt dix.

El Conde de FLORIDABLANCA.   ALLEYNE FITZ-HERBERT.

18TH CONGRESS.]   No. 360.   [1ST SESSION.

MESSAGE OF THE PRESIDENT OF THE UNITED STATES, AT THE COMMENCEMENT OF THE FIRST SESSION OF THE EIGHTEENTH CONGRESS.

COMMUNICATED TO THE SENATE DECEMBER 2, 1823.

****

At the proposal of the Russian Imperial Government, made through the minister of the Emperor residing here, a full power and instructions have been transmitted to the minister of the United States at St. Petersburg, to arrange, by amicable negotiation, the respective rights and interests of the two nations on the northwest coast of this continent. A similar proposal has been made by his Imperial Majesty to the Government of Great Britain, which has likewise been acceded to. The Government of the United States has been desirous, by this friendly proceeding, of manifesting the great value which they have invariably attached to the friendship of the Emperor, and their solicitude to cultivate the best understanding with his Government. In the discussions to which this interest has given rise, and in the arrangements by which they may terminate, the occasion has been judged proper for asserting as a principle in which the rights and interests of the United States are involved, that the American continents, by the free and independent condition which they have assumed and maintain, are henceforth not to be considered as subjects for future colonization by any European powers.

p.246

****

It was stated at the commencement of the last session that a great effort was then making in Spain and Portugal to improve the condition of the people of those countries, and that it appeared to be conducted with extraordinary moderation. It need scarcely be remarked that the result has been, so far, very different from what was then anticipated. Of events in that quarter of the globe with which we have so much intercourse, and from which we derive our origin, we have always been anxious and interested spectators. The citizens of the United States cherish sentiments the most friendly in favor of the liberty and happiness of their fellow-men on that side of the Atlantic. In the wars of the European powers in matters relating to themselves we have never taken any part, nor does it comport with our policy so to do. It is only when our rights are invaded or seriously menaced that we resent injuries or make preparation for our defence. With the movements in this hemisphere we are, of necessity, more immediately connected, and by causes which must be obvious to all enlightened and impartial observers. The political system of the allied powers is essentially different in this respect from that of America. This difference proceeds from that which exists in their respective Governments. And to the defence of our own, which has been achieved by the loss of so much blood and treasure, and matured by the wisdom of their most enlightened citizens, and under which we have enjoyed unexampled felicity, this whole nation is devoted. We owe it, therefore, to candor, and to the amicable relations existing between the United States and those powers, to declare that we should consider any attempt on their part to extend their system to any portion of this hemisphere as dangerous to our peace and safety. With the existing colonies or dependencies of any European power we have not interfered and shall not interfere. But with the Governments who have declared their independence, and maintained it, and whose independence we have, on great consideration and on just principles, acknowledged, we could not view any interposition for the purpose of oppressing them, or controlling in any other manner their destiny, by any European power, in any other light than as the manifestation of an unfriendly disposition towards the United States. In the war between these new Governments and Spain we declared our neutrality at the time of their recognition, and to this we have adhered and shall continue to adhere, provided no change shall occur which, in the judgment of the competent authorities of this Government, shall make a corresponding change on the part of the United States indispensable to their security.

The late events in Spain and Portugal show that Europe is still unsettled. Of this important fact no stronger proof can be adduced than that the allied powers should have thought it proper, on any principle satisfactory to themselves, to have interposed, by force, in the internal concerns of Spain. To what extent such interposition may be carried, on the same principle, is a question in which all independent powers whose Governments differ from theirs are interested, even those most remote, and surely none more so than the United States. Our policy in regard to Europe, which was adopted at an early stage of the wars which have so long agitated that quarter of the globe, nevertheless remains the same, which is, not to interfere in the internal concerns of any of its powers; to consider the Government *de facto* as the legitimate Government for us: to cultivate friendly relations with it, and to preserve those relations by a frank, firm, and manly policy, meeting, in all instances, the just claims of every power; submitting to injuries from none. But in regard to these continents, circumstances are eminently and conspicuously different. It is impossible that the allied powers should extend their political system to any portion of either continent without endangering our peace and happiness; nor can any one believe that our southern brethren, if left to themselves, would adopt it of their own accord. It is equally impossible, therefore, that we should behold such interposition, in any form, with indifference. If we look to the comparative strength and resources of Spain and those new Governments, and their distance from each other, it must be obvious that she can never subdue them. It is still the true policy of the United States to leave the parties to themselves, in the hope that other powers will pursue the same course.

p.250

****

WASHINGTON, *December* 2, 1823.   JAMES MONROE.

___

MESSAGE of the Government to the Legislative Body of the Province of Buenos Ayres, transmitting Correspondence relative to the Misunderstanding with The United States, with respect to the Right of Fishery, &c., on the Coasts of the Malvinas, or Falkland Islands.—18th September, 1832.

___

(Translation.) *Buenos Ayres, 18th September, 1832.*

TO THE HON. HOUSE OF REPRESENTATIVES OF THE PROVINCE.

THE Delegate Government has the honour to inform the Gentlemen of the House of Representatives, that, in pursuance of the Communication made by His Excellency the Governor, in his Message, on the last opening of the Legislature, on the subject of the unpleasant occurrence which had taken place at the Island of La Soledad, (one of the Malvinas,) it has deemed it its duty to lay before them all the Papers relative to the origin and present state of the Negotiation carried on, in consequence thereof, prior to the departure of The United States Sloop of War *Lexington*, Captain Silas Duncan, from these roads for The Malvinas; and subsequently, from the arrival of the Minister of the Government of Washington till the moment of his receiving his Passport.

The Hon. Representatives of the Province, on perusing this Correspondence, will doubtless find, that, in this weighty and delicate affair, the Government has endeavoured to fulfil, as it promised, its resolution of sustaining its rights with firmness; seeking, by the pacific means which honesty, good faith, and sound reason suggest, reparation for the scandalous aggression and heinous outrage committed by an Officer of The United States Navy.

The Government flatters itself that the Cabinet of Washington will not sully its glory, nor cast a blot upon its fame, by refusing to make such redress as becomes the honor and dignity of the 2 Republics.

His Excellency the Governor has directed that such further information as may be required on the subject, shall be afforded your Hon. House, through the Minister of Foreign Relations, who will attend your Hon. House for that purpose.

The Undersigned has, on this occasion, the pleasure of saluting the Gentlemen of the House of Representatives with his highest consideration and respect.

MANUEL VICENTE DE MAZA.

(1.)—*The American Consul to the Buenos Ayres Minister.*

Buenos Ayres, 21st November, 1831.

THE Undersigned, Consul of The United States, has the honor to make known to His Excellency, the Minister for Foreign Affairs, that he has this moment been informed of the arrival in this Port yesterday, of the American Schooner, *Harriet,* Davison, Master, of Stonington, a Prize to this Government, forcibly taken at the Falkland Islands by order of Governor Vernet.

The Undersigned is at a loss to conceive upon what possible ground a *bonâ fide* American Vessel, while engaged in a lawful trade, should be captured by an Officer of a friendly Government, and with which The United States are happily on terms of the most perfectly good understanding and amity. And he cannot bring himself to believe that the Government of Buenos Ayres will sanction an act which, under its present aspect, must be viewed as one calculated materially to disturb them.

The importance of this subject has induced the Undersigned to lose not a moment in bringing it before His Excellency the Minister, with the earnest request, and in the confident expectation that he will with all convenient despatch inform him if this Government intends to avow and sustain the seizure of the aforesaid Vessel.

The Undersigned avails himself, &c.

H. E. Don Tomas de Anchorena.   GEO. W. SLACUM.

(2.) *The Buenos Ayres Minister to the American Consul.*

Department of Foreign Relations,

(Translation.) *Buenos Ayres, 25th Nov. 1831.*

THE Undersigned, Minister of Foreign Relations, has received the Note under date of the 21st instant, in which the Consul of The United States makes known to him that he has been informed of the arrival in this Port of the American Schooner *Harriet*, Davison, Master, of Stonington, a Prize taken on the Coasts of the Malvinas, by order of Governor Vernet, and requests to be informed whether this Government intends to avow and sustain the seizure of the aforesaid Vessel.

To reply duly to the Consul of The United States, the undersigned Minister can only state that the case of the before-mentioned Schooner, *Harriet*, is now in the Ministry of War and Marine, and that after the customary forms shall have been observed, it will be laid before the Government, whose resolution thereon will be in accordance with what the Laws of the Country prescribe.

The undersigned salutes the Consul, &c.

TOMAS MANUEL DE ANCHORENA.

The Consul of The United States.

––––––––

(3.) *The American Consul to the Buenos Ayres Minister.*

Buenos-Ayres, 26th November, 1831.

THE Undersigned, Consul of The United States, has the honor to acknowledge the Note of His Excellency, the Minister for Foreign Affairs, under date of yesterday, in answer to one from the Consulate, dated 21st instant, in which he is informed that " the subject of the American Schooner, *Harriet*, is actually before the Department of the Minister of War and Marine, and that after the customary forms shall have been observed, it will be placed before the Government, whose decision will be conformable to what the Laws of the Country prescribe."

This unexpected reply from His Excellency, the Minister, cannot be viewed by the Undersigned in any other light than as a virtual avowal, on the part of this Government, of the right of Mr. Lewis Vernet to capture and detain American Vessels engaged in the Fisheries at the Falkland Islands, and the Islands and Coasts about Cape Horn. It, therefore, only remains to him to deny, *in toto*, any such right, as having been, or being now vested in the Government of Buenos Ayres, or in any person or persons acting under its authority ; and to add his most earnest remonstrance against all measures which may have been adopted by said Government, including the Decree issued on the 10th of June, 1829,* asserting a claim to the before-mentioned Islands and

––––––––

* *Decree of the Government of Buenos Ayres.*

(Translation.) *Buenos Ayres, 10th June, 1829.*

When by the glorious Revolution of the 25th of May, 1810, these Provinces separated themselves from the Dominion of the Mother Country, Spain held the

Coasts, and the Fisheries appurtenant thereto, or any other Act or Decree having the same tendency, and also the Circular Letter of the said Vernet, issued in consequence of the same ; as well as against all such measures as may hereafter be adopted by said Government, or persons acting under its authority, which are calculated in the remotest degree to impose restraints upon the Citizens of The United States engaged in the Fisheries in question, or to impair their undoubted right to the freest use of them.

The Undersigned cannot but regret that a subject of so important and serious a nature should have arisen ; but nevertheless, his duty to his Government, as well as to the rights and interests of his Fellow-Citizens, impels him to request that His Excellency the Minister for Foreign Affairs will be pleased to receive this Communication as a formal Protest on the part of the Government of The United States against that of Buenos Ayres, and all and every person or persons acting under its authority, for the illegal and forcible seizure at the Falkland Islands aforesaid, by order of the said Vernet, of the American Schooner *Harriet,* as well as of the *Superior* and *Breakwater,* of which the Undersigned has also received information ;

---

important Possession of the Islands of the Malvinas, (Falkland Islands,) and of all the others which approximate to Cape Horn, including that known under the denomination of Tierra del Fuego : this Possession was justified by the right of being the first occupant, by the consent of the principal Maritime Powers of Europe, and by the proximity of these Islands to the Continent which formed the Viceroyalty of Buenos Ayres, unto which Government they depended. For this reason, the Government of the Republic, having succeeded to every right which the Mother Country previously exercised over these Provinces, and which its Viceroys possessed, continued to exercise acts of Dominion in the said Islands, its Ports, and Coasts, notwithstanding circumstances have hitherto prevented this Republic from paying the attention to that part of the Territory which, from its importance, it demands. Nevertheless, the necessity of no longer delaying such precautionary measures as shall be necessary to secure the rights of the Republic ; and at the same time to possess the advantages which the productions of the said Islands may yield, and to afford to the Inhabitants that protection of which they stand in need, and to which they are entitled ; the Government has ordered and decreed, as follows.

Art. I. The Islands of the Malvinas and those adjacent to Cape Horn in the Atlantic Ocean, shall be under the command of a Political and Military Governor, to be named immediately by the Government of the Republic.

II. The Political and Military Governor shall reside in the Island de la Soledad, on which a Battery shall be erected under the Flag of the Republic.

III. The Political and Military Governor shall cause the Laws of the Republic to be observed by the Inhabitants of the said Islands, and provide for the due performance of the Regulations respecting Seal Fishery on the Coasts.

IV. Let this be made public.

RODRIGUEZ.

SALVADOR MARIA DEL CARRIL.

as also for the violent arrest and imprisonment of their Officers and Crews, American Citizens : and for the consequences thereof.

The Undersigned, in performing this duty, begs, &c.

H. E. The Minister for Foreign Affairs.　　　　GEO. W. SLACUM.

(4.)—*The Buenos Ayres Minister to the American Consul.*

(Translation.)　　　　　　　　　*Buenos Ayres*, 3rd *December*, 1831.

THE Undersigned, Minister of Foreign Relations, has received the Note dated the 26th. uit., in which the Consul of The United States acknowledges the receipt of that which the Undersigned addressed to him, under date of the 25th of the same month, stating, in reply to a former Communication, that the Case of the capture and detention of the American Schooner *Harriet* is in the Ministry of War and Marine, and that, after the customary forms shall have been observed, it will be laid before the Government, whose resolution thereon will be in accordance with what the Laws of the Country prescribe; and then proceeds to state that, this answer being a virtual avowal on the part of this Government of the right of Mr. Lewis Vernet to capture and detain American Vessels engaged in the Seal-fishery at the Malvinas and the Islands and Coasts adjacent to Cape Horn, he finds himself under the necessity of denying, *in toto*, any such right as having been, or being now vested in the Government of Buenos Ayres, or in any person or persons acting under its authority ; and of adding his most earnest remonstrance against all measures which may have been adopted by the said Government, including the Decree issued on the 10th of June, 1829, asserting a claim to the before-mentioned Islands and Coasts, and the Fisheries appurtenant thereto, or any other Act or Decree having the same tendency, and also the Circular Letter of the said Vernet, issued in consequence thereof; as well as against all such measures as may hereafter be adopted by the said Government, or persons acting under its authority, which may be calculated in the remotest degree to impose restraints upon the Citizens of The United States engaged in the Fisheries in question, or impair their right to the freest use of them ; and concludes by requesting that the said Communication may be received by the Undersigned as a formal Protest on the part of the Government of The United States against that of Buenos Ayres, and all and every person or persons acting under its authority, for the illegal and forcible seizure at the Malvinas, by order of the said Vernet, of the American Schooner *Harriet*, as well as of the *Superior* and *Breakwater*, as also, for the violent arrest and imprisonment of their Officers and Crews ; and for the consequences thereof.

The aforesaid Note having been placed before the Delegate Government, the Undersigned has received directions to reply, as he now does, to the Consul of The United States, that the inquiry which this affair is still undergoing in the Ministry of War and Marine, is unconnected with the resolution it may come to upon the main point, and is only intended to enable the Government to arrive at the truth, in order to act as in justice bound: that it cannot admit the said Communication of the Consul of The United States as a formal Protest of his Government against that of this Province; as, besides its being untimely, the Consul does not make it appear that he is especially authorized for this purpose; and the Government considers that he is not, from his being only invested with the character of Consul, and the more so as it is an indubitable fact that the Government of The United States possesses no right to the aforesaid Islands or Coasts, nor to the Fisheries thereon, whilst that vested in this Republic is unquestionable; that consequently the Government might found a just ground of complaint on the Protest of the Consul; but it is willing to suppose him actuated by upright motives, and being fully convinced of the wisdom and justice which preside over the Councils of his Government, is desirous to avoid any serious measure; hoping that any question which may arise with the Government of The United States will be amicably arranged by a direct understanding between the 2 Governments.

The Undersigned avails himself, &c.

TOMAS MANUEL DE ANCHORENA.

The Consul of The United States.

(5.)—*The American Consul to the Buenos Ayres Minister.*

Buenos Ayres, 3rd *December,* 1831.

THE Undersigned, Consul of The United States, has the honor to transmit herewith to His Excellency the Minister for Foreign Affairs, a Copy of a Letter received yesterday from Silas Duncan, Esq. commanding The United States Ship *Lexington,* off this City.

The Undersigned avails himself, &c.

H. E. The Minister for Foreign Affairs.　　GEO. W. SLACUM.

(Enclosure.)—Commander Duncan to the American Consul.

United States Ship Lexington,

SIR,　　　　　*Off Buenos Ayres, River Plate,* 1st*. Dec.* 1831.

I HAVE received your Reply to my Communication of the 29th. ult., enclosing Copies of Documents in relation to the capture of several American Vessels at the Falkland Islands, while engaged in the Fisheries; and, having given them the proper consideration, I consider it to be my duty to proceed thither with the force under my command, for the protection of the Citizens and commerce of The United States engaged in the Fisheries in question.

I also learn, that, in consequence of these captures, 7 Americans have been abandoned upon the Island of Staten Land without the means of subsistence.

Under these circumstances, I have to request you will be pleased to communicate a Copy of this Letter to the Government of Buenos Ayres, under whose authority certain individuals have assumed to capture American Vessels, in order that no misunderstanding shall arise with respect to the object of my visit to the Falkland Islands, and in conformity with the open and candid mode in which the affairs of The United States are conducted.

I have the honor to be, &c.

Geo. W. Slacum, Esq.   S. DUNCAN.

---

(6).—*The Buenos Ayres Minister to the American Consul.*
(Translation.)   *Buenos Ayres, 6th December,* 1831.

THE Undersigned has received the Note which the Consul of The United States has addressed to him, under date of the 3rd. inst., transmitting Copy of a Letter which he has received from Mr. Silas Duncan, Commander of the Ship *Lexington*, in this Port.

The Undersigned has the honor to inform the Consul of The United States that this Note has been referred to the Minister of War, and avails himself of the opportunity, &c.

TOMAS MANUEL DE ANCHORENA.

The Consul of The United States.

(7.)—*The American Consul to the Buenos Ayres Minister.*
Buenos Ayres, 6th December, 1831.

THE Undersigned, Consul of The United States, has the honor to acknowledge the receipt of the Note of His Excellency the Minister for Foreign Affairs, under date 3d. instant.

In communicating with the Commander of The United States Ship *Lexington*, whose intention of immediately proceeding to the Falkland Islands, for the protection of American Citizens engaged in the Seal-fishery, has already been made known to His Excellency the Minister, he has suggested to the Undersigned the propriety, as indicating the frankness by which his measures will be governed, of proposing that he will delay his departure until the morning of the 9th. inst., in order to wait the receipt of any Communications which the Government of this Province may think fit to make, having reference to the immediate suspension of the exercise of the right of capture of the Vessels of The United States, which may be found fishing within the limits claimed to be subject to the jurisdiction or authority of Mr. Vernet. And also, coupling with such suspension the immediate restoration to the legitimate Owners or Agents, of the Schooner *Harriet* now detained as a prize to this Government at this Port, as well as of all the property illegally taken out of the said Schooner at the time of her capture or since; or from American Citizens, at the Falkland Islands or elsewhere, by the said Vernet or his Agents; and moreover, the placing them in the position in which they stood previous to the aforesaid captures, and the interference in the business in which they were lawfully engaged.

The Undersigned begs leave to suggest to His Excellency the Minister, that the shortness of the period within which the said Commander can wait for an answer from this Government to the aforesaid propositions, is in consequence of his anxiety to relieve as soon as may be, several distressed American Seamen, left by one of the captured Schooners, with a limited supply of provisions, on Staten Land, as well as to put an immediate stop to further captures which may be making at the said Falkland Islands, by the Agents of said Vernet, whom he left in command there, authorized to that effect.

The Undersigned is requested by the said Commander further to manifest to His Excellency the Minister, that the propositions above-mentioned are based upon the spirit of the friendly relations which are known happily to subsist between the Government of The United States and that of this Province,—and more especially, upon the suggestion contained in the Note of His Excellency the Minister, that it is the desire of this Government amicably to settle the question of right in relation to the afore-mentioned Fisheries, by a direct under-standing with the Government of The United States,—until which can take place, the Undersigned concurs in opinion with the said Commander, that the Citizens of The United States should be subject to no further molestation in prosecuting them.

In concluding this Note, the Undersigned, willing to remove any doubt as to his right to protest, would observe that, in so doing, he acted under authority from his Government; and that he cannot consent to its rejection or withdrawal, even had no such authority existed, as he has been considered, and treated with, by this Govern-ment, as the Representative of that of The United States, since the decease of the late Chargé d'Affaires: and he would not willingly believe that the Government of Buenos Ayres would at this time offer any denial of such right so as to preclude him from defending the interests of American Citizens.

The Undersigned trusts, that His Excellency the Minister will receive this communication as a continued earnest of his sincere desire to do all in his power to maintain unimpaired the present friendly relations of the 2 Governments.

The Undersigned avails himself of the occasion, &c.

H. E. The Minister for Foreign Affairs.   GEO. W. SLACUM.

(8.)—*Commander Duncan to the Buenos Ayres Minister.*

United States Ship Lexington,
SIR,   *Off Buenos Ayres, River Plate, 7th December,* 1831.

I HAVE it in proof, upon oath, that Lewis Vernet, now a resident at this place, did plunder the American Schooner *Harriet* of almost every article on board said Schooner while lying at the Falkland Islands.

The object of this Note is to request, that the said Lewis Vernet, having been guilty of piracy and robbery, be delivered up to The United States to be tried, or that he be arrested and punished by the Laws of Buenos Ayres.

I have the honor to be, &c.

H. E. Thomas Manuel de Anchorena.   S. DUNCAN.

(9.)—*The Buenos Ayres Minister to the American Consul.*
(Translation.)   *Buenos Ayres, 9th December,* 1831.

THE Undersigned, Minister of Foreign Relations, has the honor to inform the Consul of The United States, that the Minister of War and Marine has communicated to the Undersigned, under date of the 7th instant, that the Commandant of the Malvinas, Mr. Luis Vernet, having presented a Memorial soliciting that the departure of Mr. Gilbert Davison, Captain of the American Schooner *Harriet,* should be prohibited until he should leave an Agent duly authorized ; the said Memorial was referred to the Attorney-General, to whom the Papers relative to the Capture of the aforesaid Vessel had been transmitted ; and orders having been issued to the Captain of the Port to prevent the departure of the said Davison, that Officer returned for answer that having given the suitable directions to the Adjudant of the Port, the latter reported that, previously to their receipt, Captain Davison had embarked in a Boat of The United States Ship *Lexington,* to go on board that Vessel. And as such a step on the part of Captain Davison appears to be calculated to embarrass the legal proceedings and the just decision of the Case of the before mentioned Schooner *Harriet;* the Undersigned has received orders from the Government of this Province to require, as he now does, that the Consul of The United States will have the kindness to notify to Captain Gilbert Davison, not to absent himself from this Province without leaving an Agent duly authorized to represent him and act for him in the said affair ; with the understanding that his refusal or omission in this respect, will render him liable to all the damages resulting therefrom according to Law.

The Undersigned avails himself, &c.

TOMAS MANUEL DE ANCHORENA.

The Consul of The United States.

(10.)—*The Buenos Ayres Minister to the American Consul.*
(Translation.)   *Buenos Ayres, 9th December,* 1831.

THE Undersigned, Minister of Foreign Relations, received on the 7th instant, the Note of the Consul of The United States dated the day previous, which was immediately placed before the Government of the Province. Steadfast in the same views and principles which the Undersigned has manifested to the Consul of The United States on the subject to which his Note relates, the Government has observed with surprise, that, although aware of the multifarious, weighty and urgent attentions, by which it is notorious that this Government is at present surrounded, and that a religious solemnity being celebrated here yesterday, the Public Offices would be closed, he did not deem it a breach of propriety and decorum to propose to the Undersigned, for this day precisely, the decision of a private litigated affair, in which, for that reason, the Consul could have no right to interfere; and which, having to be investigated and decided conformably to the Laws of the Country, requires, from its nature, the course of various forms, and a serious and attentive consideration, in order nowise to defraud justice.

It is true that the Consul of The United States affirms, that the shortness of the period within which the Commander of The United States' Ship *Lexington* can await an Answer from this Government to the Propositions made by the Consul, is in consequence of his anxiety to relieve, as soon as possible, several American Seamen, left by one of the captured Schooners with a scanty supply of provisions in Staten Land, as likewise to put an immediate stop to such further Captures as may be making in the Malvinas, by the Agents whom Mr. Vernet left in command there, authorized for that purpose. But be that as it may, and waving the motives which the said Commander may have for proceeding to the aforesaid Islands, this does not give any right to the Consul of The United States to interpose himself before the Government of this Province in a private contentious affair, in which there are parties who can exercise their rights, either by themselves or through their Agents duly authorized to that effect. Nor will the Government ever deviate from the line of conduct which justice and its own dignity point out to it, whatever the aforesaid Commander may think or do; the Government not recognizing in him any right to interfere in affairs of this nature.

But, as it desires to preserve unimpaired the relations of friendship which it happily mantains with the Government of The United States, and is persuaded that hitherto no pretext has, in anywise, been afforded on its part for their interruption, it has directed the Undersigned to declare to the Consul of The United States, that, if the Commander of the *Lexington*, or any other person dependent on the said Government, should commit any act, or take any steps tending to set at naught the right which this Republic possesses to the Malvinas, and other Islands and Coasts adjacent to Cape Horn, and to prohibit the Seal Fisheries thereon, especially on the former,—the Government of this Province will address its formal complaint to that of The United States, in the firm confidence that it will be attended to as justice may direct, and it will use every means which it may deem expedient to assert its rights and cause them to be respected; as it is fully persuaded that the Government of The United States has not denied nor will deny those rights, and that, in case any other question connected with them should arise, it will not attempt to decide it by force, despoiling this Government of the possession which it holds.

For the rest, the Consul labors under a very remarkable mistake, in supposing that this Government has considered and treated him as the Representative of The United States since the decease of Mr. Forbes, Chargé d'Affaires near this Republic; and he ought to have known that it could not consider him as invested with any other character than that of simple Consul of the said United States in this Republic. Viewing him in this light, and the extent of the Consular functions being well known, the chief of which is to exert himself in order that his Fellow-Citizens respect the Laws and Authorities of the Country in which he resides; this Government hopes that he will henceforth circumscribe himself to those functions, and cease to persist in the Protest which he has made, against rights which have been, and are vested in this Government, and which no one as yet has called in question.

The Undersigned, after having discharged his duty in this Communication, has the honor to renew, &c.

TOMAS MANUEL DE ANCHORENA.
The Consul of The United States.

(11.)—*The American Consul to the Buenos Ayres Minister.*

Buenos Ayres, 15th December, 1831.

THE Undersigned, Consul of The United States, has the honor to acknowledge the receipt of the 2 Notes addressed to him by His Excellency the Minister for Foreign Affairs, under date of the 9th instant, and which were delivered into his hands at 5 o'clock P.M. of the same day.

In reply to that complaining of the conduct of Captain Davison, late of the Prize Schooner *Harriet,* in embarking to go on board of the United States' Sloop-of-War *Lexington,* for the purpose, as is assumed by His Excellency the Minister, embarrassing the proceedings which may be carrying on in the Tribunal here for procuring the condemnation of said Schooner, and in which it is urged upon the Undersigned to notify the said Captain Davison not to depart from the Province, without previously appointing an Attorney or Agent to represent him in the said prosecution; the Undersigned begs leave to say that it was matter of notoriety that the Sloop-of-War *Lexington,* weighed anchor and left this port, at 12 o'clock, M. of the 9th, several hours previous to the receipt of the said Note by the Undersigned; so that any efforts on his part to have detained the said Captain Davison, would have proved ineffectual, had he deemed it to be a part of his official duty to have made any, at the urgency of this Government, appearing to be solely founded upon a memorial or solicitude of Lewis Vernet.— Moreover, it had been communicated to His Excellency the Minister, that the *Lexington* would remain in port until the morning of the 9th, at which time it was to be presumed of course that she would sail, and it appears that the Government were advised of the said Captain Davison's having embarked to go on board of the said Sloop of War on the 7th, so that a sufficient time seems to have been afforded to this Government, to have served any notification upon him, which they might choose, without insinuating or charging upon him the intention of withdrawing from the Province, for any sinister purpose; or protesting against him for damages, for that act, or its results. But after all, the Undersigned does not perceive upon what principles this Government could have undertaken to detain the said Captain Davison, an American Citizen, already the victim of a protracted incarceration, with a view to coerce him to execute a Power of Attorney under any pretence or for any purpose, which might be alleged by the said Vernet; when he, the said Davison, has not thought proper to present himself in the Tribunals to litigate any question with the said Vernet, but to deny *in toto* the right of capture in this Government, of his Schooner, engaged in sealing at the Falkland Islands, and against which the Undersigned has protested, on his behalf, and that of those whom he represents; he, the said Davison, having, on his arrival here, thrown himself upon the Undersigned for protection and redress.

In replying to the other Note of His Excellency, the receipt of which is acknowledged as above, the Undersigned in the first place takes the liberty to remark, that he cannot assent to the propriety of any application to him of the strong expressions of His Excellency the Minister, if such was intended, in reference to any non-observance of the 8th as a day of religious solemnity, not being aware of any want of decorum in this respect on his part, as the Note communicating the propositions of the Commander of the *Lexington*, was handed to the Chief Clerk of the Ministry of Foreign Relations, on the morning of the 7th instant; and, if the interval from that time until 12 o'clock, M. of the 9th, when the Ship sailed, may have been deemed too short for this Government to resolve whether they would or would not restore the property of American Citizens, illegally seized upon by Lewis Vernet, at the Falkland Islands, it is proper for the Undersigned to observe, that this period, or its limit, which was the time of sailing of the *Lexington*, was not fixed by him, as it could not be, but by the Commander of the said Ship, and from motives of humanity, particularly in relation to Seamen left exposed on a desert Island, as explained in said Note. And here the Undersigned is constrained to note an error into which His Excellency, the Minister, appears to have fallen, in attributing to him the propositions referred to, when, on the contrary, they are declared by the Undersigned to have emanated from the Commander of the *Lexington*; and were communicated at his request; and in regard to these propositions, the Undersigned is not aware that they involved the "resolution of a private litigious affair," as is expressed by His Excellency, but on the contrary, nothing more than an assent or denial to restore property illegally captured at the Falkland Islands, from American Citizens, while engaged in a trade to which they have the most undoubted right; the claim to which, the Undersigned has authority from his Government to assert, as he has already made known to His Excellency, the Minister; and which raises a question to be settled, not by the Local Tribunal of this Country,—not by a private litigation between Mr. Vernet and Captain Davison, or any other private parties,—but by the Government of the Province and that of The United States, if not of the other maritime Nations, who are all interested in the free use of unappropriated Fisheries, as they are of the highway of the Ocean. And it was with the view that the question of right might so be referred, to be settled amicably, that the propositions before mentioned were made by the Commander of the *Lexington*, and which it was supposed would accord with the friendly feelings declared by His Excellency the Minister, to be entertained by this Government, towards that of The United States; and the result would have been, if fortunately the propositions had been admitted, the placing matters on the footing on which they stood previous to the outrages committed by the aforesaid Vernet. And in this connexion, the Undersigned will observe that, notwithstanding it was distinctly stated by him in his Note, dated the 6th. instant, which he had the honor to address to His Excellency the Minister, that in protesting against the captures of American Sealing Vessels at the Falkland Islands, &c., he acted under the authority of his Government, His Excellency, the Minister, has subsequently called it in question in his Note of the 9th.; therefore the Undersigned, in order to remove all further doubt from the mind of His Excellency, upon this part of the subject, altho' he deemed his first assertion of the fact sufficient, now begs leave to inform him, that, in consequence of indirect information being lately laid before his Government of the Decree of the 10th of June, 1829, asserting a right of Sovereignty to the Falkland Islands, &c., and of the exclusive use of the Fisheries appurtenant to them,—formal Instructions were sent out to the late Chargé d'Affaires of The United States, to address to this Government " an earnest remonstrance against any Measures that may have been adopted by it, including the Decree and Circular Letter referred to, if they be genuine, which are calculated in the remotest degree to impose any restraints whatever upon the enterprize of the Citizens of The United States engaged in the Fisheries in question, or to impair their undoubted right to the freest use of them ;"—the said Fisheries, having heretofore always been considered as free to all Nations whatever and the exclusive property of none.

That such remonstrance was not made by the late Chargé d'Affaires was probably owing to the circumstance that the Despatches did not reach this Country until a short time previous to his death.

In further answer to His Excellency the Minister, the Undersigned does not consider himself called upon to reply to anything contained in the Note now under consideration, which has reference to the motives of the Commander of the *Lexington* in proceeding with his Ship to the Falkland Islands, even if these had not been, as he deems they were, frankly expressed in the Communication transmitted, containing his Propositions; nor to the intimation of this Government, that it will pursue the course which it has marked out to itself, whatever the said Commander may think or do ; these being matters solely for his own consideration, for which the Undersigned is clearly not responsible : but the Undersigned cannot admit that he has " improperly interposed himself before the Public Authority of this Province,' as declared by His Excellency the Minister, in any thing that he had done, either in asking of this Government an avowal or disavowal of the Capture of the Schooner *Harriet* by Lewis Vernet, (styled by His Excellency the Minister, " Commandant of the Falkland Islands,") which was the purport of his first Note ; or in protesting against the same, as in his second Note; or in being the medium of communicating, in a sincere spirit of frankness, the amicable Propositions of the Commander of the *Lexington*, as in his late Note, in relation to this unpleasant business, which he cannot consider with His Excellency as a " private contentious affair," and " to be resolved by this Government conformably to what the Laws of the Country prescribe," but as one of a very different and very serious nature, involving an attack upon the " Rights and Privileges of his Nation and its Citizens," which it is his first and principal duty as Consul to endeavour at least to protect, although His Excellency seems to be of a different opinion ; and with the resolution of which the Municipal or Local Laws, or *trámites de estilo*, of this Province have no more to do than those of The United States. But perhaps the Undersigned ought to be delicate in expressing his opinion in regard to the nature and extent of his duties as Consul, seeing that he has been chided by His Excellency in that particular, and who has deigned to intimate to him, that the principal of those duties is, to maintain over his Fellow-Citizens a supervision in regard to their conduct in the Country in which he resides.

In conclusion, the Undersigned begs leave to say, that, while he is unaware of any want of decorum or of improper interference in his official capacity before the Authorities of this Province, in the course which he has taken in this affair, or the Correspondence to which it has given rise, he still deems it to be his duty to continue to insist upon the Protest which he has transmitted to this Government; which the nature of the transaction in question so imperiously demanded; and a failure in presenting which, would have been an omission of duty, and a relinquishment of an unalienable Consular Right.

This Protest is rejected by His Excellency the Minister, and if the Undersigned is not charged with having transcended the line of his duty, he is counselled to confine himself within it. But what are the facts which called for that Protest? Have not 3 American Vessels, while engaged in a lawful Trade been captured, and their Cargoes forcibly and illegally taken out of them and immediately appropriated to the use of the Captors; have not their Officers and Crews, American Citizens, been violently arrested and imprisoned; has not a part of them been sent to a foreign land and there thrown upon the bounty of strangers; while another part has been abandoned upon the distant and desolate Island of "Staten Land," without a supply of provisions, and this too by a person holding his authority under, and now protected by this Government, with which that of The United States is at peace; and has this not been done without any previous official notice having been given to the latter that the former had set up claims of sovereignty and exclusive jurisdiction to the Islands and Fisheries in question?

And is it under circumstances like these, that the Undersigned is told he shall not be heard in defence of the injured rights and interests of his Fellow-Citizens?

Responsible only to his own Government for his official conduct, he expects the full and free exercise of his public functions as Consul of The United States, so long as he shall continue within the line of his duty, and to observe a due courtesy and respect towards the Government near which he resides.

Having nothing further to add in the present stage of this business, the Undersigned will content himself by referring the whole matter to the consideration of his Government.

The Undersigned avails himself of this occasion, &c.

H. E. the Minister for Foreign Affairs.   GEO. W. SLACUM.

(12.)—*The Buenos Ayres Minister to the American Consul.*
(Translation.)   *Buenos Ayres, 14th February,* 1832.

The Undersigned, Minister of Foreign Relations, addresses Mr. George W. Slacum, Consul of The United States, in this City, for the

purpose of acquainting him, that the Government,—considering the
aberration of ideas and irregularity of language in his Official Notes,
relative to the occurrences with the American Fishing Vessels on the
Coasts of the Malvinas, belonging to and in possession of this Republic, and the prejudices his conduct has given rise to, especially since
the aggression perpetrated by the Commander of The United States'
Ship *Lexington,* at said Islands; and that the strong excitement
which that violence has produced, requires the careful removal of
every thing that can directly or indirectly sour the public mind, and
disturb the moderation and temperance with which affairs between
civilized and friendly Governments ought always to be conducted ;—
has judged it expedient and conducive to those ends, to suspend all official intercourse with Mr. Slacum, who can appoint any Person properly
qualified to substitute him in his Consular functions ; of which resolution due notice is given to the Government of The United States, who
will doubtless be satisfied, as well with the object, as the motives which
produce it.

The Undersigned, &c.

The Consul of The United States.   MANUEL J. GARCIA.

(13.)–*Proclamation of the Government of Buenos Ayres.*–14*th Feb.* 1832.

PROCLAMATION.

THE DELEGATE GOVERNMENT OF THE PROVINCE TO THE PEOPLE.

FELLOW CITIZENS !   (Translation.)

THE official details collected by the Government, have confirmed the
truth of the scandalous acts, stated to have been committed in the
Malvinas. The Commander of The United States' Ship *Lexington*
has invaded, in a time of the most profound peace, that, our infant
Colony; destroyed with rancorous fury the public property, and
carried off the effects legally deposited there at the disposal of our
Magistrates. The Colonists being unexpectedly assaulted under a
Friendly Flag, some of them fled to the interior of the Island; and
others violently torn from their homes, or deluded by deceitful artifices,
have been brought away and cast clandestinely upon the shores of the
Oriental State, which now extends to them a generous hospitality;
whilst others, Natives and Fellow-Countrymen of ours, are conducted
as Prisoners to The United States, for the ostensible purpose of being
tried there. The unanimous burst of indignation which this outrage
has produced in you, is fully justified; and the same feeling will
doubtless be evinced by men of honor in every part of the World,
when they hear of this transaction.

But, Citizens, it is as impossible that the Government of Washington should approve of such aggressions, as that your Government
should tolerate them in silence. The former, acting up to the principles of moderation and justice which characterize it, will doubtless

give satisfaction correspondent to the dignity of the 2 Republics. In the mean time, be assured that, whatever may be the issue of these unpleasant occurrences, your Government will maintain the inviolability of the Persons and Property of North American Citizens, with the same firmness as it will support its own rights, and in no case will stain itself with an ignoble reprisal of innocent men, who are under the safeguard of the national honor.

JUAN RAMON BALCARCE.

Buenos Ayres, 14th February, 1832.   MANUEL J. GARCIA.

(14.)—*The American Consul to the Buenos Ayres Minister.*

Buenos Ayres, 15*th February,* 1832.

THE Undersigned, Consul of The United States, has the honor to transmit to His Excellency the Minister of Foreign Affairs, Copy of a Note this moment received from the Commander of The United States' Ship *Lexington,* who writes to the Undersigned that he will await an answer from him, being on the eve of sailing for Rio de Janeiro.

The Undersigned has the honor, &c.

The Minister of Foreign Affairs.   GEO. W. SLACUM.

(Enclosure.)—*Commander Duncan to the American Consul.*

United States' Ship Lexington,

SIR,   *Off Montevideo,* 11*th February,* 1832.

I HAVE to state that I will deliver up or liberate the Prisoners now on board the *Lexington,* upon an assurance from the Government of Buenos Ayres that they have been acting by its authority.

I have the honor to be, &c.

Geo. W. Slacum, Esq.   S. DUNCAN.

(15.)—*The Buenos Ayres Minister to the American Consul.*

(Translation.)   *Buenos Ayres,* 15*th February,* 1832.

THE Undersigned, Minister of Foreign Relations, has received the Note of Mr. George W. Slacum, dated this day, transmitting Copy of a Letter from the Commander of the Ship *Lexington,* informing him that he will liberate the Prisoners he has on board, upon an assurance from this Government that they have acted under its authority.

The Undersigned in reply to Mr. Slacum, begs to state that Mr. Vernet was appointed Military and Political Commandant of the Malvinas, in virtue of the Decree of the 10th of June, 1829, published on the 13th of the same month; consequently the said Vernet and the individuals serving under him, can only be amenable to their own Authorities.

In the mean time, the Undersigned, &c.

The Consul of The United States.   MANUEL J. GARCIA.

(16.)—*The American Consul to the Buenos Ayres Minister.*

Buenos Ayres, 16*th February,* 1832.

THE Undersigned, Consul of The United States, has the honor to acknowledge the receipt of the Note of his Excellency the Minister of Foreign Affairs, under the date of the 14th instant; in which his Excellency makes known to him " that the Government, considering the irregularity of ideas and of language of the Official Notes of Sr. Consul relative to the occurrences with the American Fishing Vessels on the Coasts of the Malvina Islands, belonging to, and in possession of this Republic, and the prejudices his conduct has excited, especially since the aggression perpetrated by the Commander of The United States' Ship *Lexington,* at said Islands; and that the lively sensation which that violence has produced, requires the diligent removal of every thing that can sour minds, or disturb the moderation and temperance with which affairs between civilized and friendly Governments ought always to be conducted ; has judged it opportune and conducive to those ends, to suspend all official relation with Mr. Slacum, who can name, to substitute him in his Consular functions, any Person duly qualified: of which resolution, corresponding notice is given to the Government of The United States, which will, no doubt, be satisfied, as well with the object as the motives which produce it."

The Undersigned cannot refrain from expressing his surprise at so extraordinary a Communication ; and, in reply to that part of it which has reference to " the remarkable irregularity of ideas and of language in his Official Notes," he would observe, that his Correspondence upon the subject of the captured American Fishing Vessels was closed as early as the 15th of December last, in consequence of the Communication, under date of the 9th of that month from his Excellency the late Minister of Foreign Affairs, Señor D. Tomas Manuel de Anchorena, and the whole matter referred to the consideration of the Government of The United States, as there declared.

In further answer to his Excellency the Minister, the Undersigned cannot suppress the astonishment which he feels at the allusion made to his conduct after the result of the visit of the *Lexington* to the Falkland Islands was made known ; being entirely ignorant of any thing on his part which could possibly call for such intimation ; and in the belief that his Excellency labored under a remarkable misconception, he cannot but regret that his Excellency had not been so distinct as to have enabled the Undersigned to have formed some idea of what was intended, and to have left room for explanation.

However, this Government has thought fit to suspend the Consular functions of the Undersigned, and to deprive him of his public character; at the same time, to grant him permission to appoint some Person duly qualified to substitute him in the discharge of those functions.

The Undersigned will not allow himself to make any observations upon the novelty of this procedure, but will only say that he has not received instructions from his own Government to cease his Consular functions here, nor is he authorized, in such a case as this, to appoint a Person in his stead. He can, therefore, only leave to this Government the responsibility of the act of his suspension, and any, and all measures, which it may deem proper to pursue.

The Undersigned avails himself of this occasion, &c.

H. E. Don Manuel J. Garcia.   GEORGE W. SLACUM.

(17.)—*The American Chargé d'Affaires to the Buenos Ayres Minister.*

Buenos Ayres, 20*th June,* 1832.

THE Undersigned, Chargé d'Affaires from the United States of America near the Government of Buenos Ayres, has the honor to inform His Excellency the Minister of Grace and Justice, charged provisionally with the Department of Foreign Affairs, that he has been instructed by his Government to call the attention of this Government to certain transactions of Mr. Lewis Vernet, who claims, under a Decree of this Government, dated the 10th of June, 1829, to be " The Military and Civil Governor of the Falkland Islands, and all those adjacent to Cape Horn, (including Tierra del Fuego,) in the Atlantic Ocean."

Under color of this Decree, on the 30th day of July last, Gilbert R. Davison, a Citizen of The United States, and Master of a Vessel called the *Harriet,* sailing from Stonington, in the State of Connecticut, one of the said United States, and owned by Citizens of the said States,—in a time of profound peace, while pursuing lawful commerce and business, was forcibly arrested by a body of armed men, acting under the orders of the Governor Vernet, who at the same time, arrested his boat's Crew, placed him in close confinement,—subsequently seized the *Harriet,*—forced the Crew on shore and imprisoned them all, excepting the mate, cook and steward. The Papers of the *Harriet* and many articles on board were forcibly taken, and a part of the articles were sold by order of the Governor, without formal condemnation or any legal process whatever.

On the 17th day of August last, Captain Carew, a Citizen of The United States, and Master of the Schooner *Breakwater,* also sailing from Stonington, and owned by Citizens of The United States, in a time of profound peace, while on lawful business, was, by order of Governor Vernet, arrested and imprisoned at Port Louis, and the Vessel, which lay at St. Salvador, on the following day was forcibly seized, deprived of her Papers and detained. She was afterwards recaptured by the Crew, who regained their liberty by their courage and prowess, and reached their own Country in safety. The Master and

4 Men being left on the Islands, were compelled by the Governor to embark in a British Vessel, bound to Rio Janeiro, in Brazil, against the will of the Master, who was anxious to proceed to Buenos Ayres in the *Harriet.*

On the 19th of August last, Captain Stephen Congar, a Citizen of The United States, commanding the Schooner *Superior,* sailing from the City of New York, in the State of New York, one of The United States, belonging to Citizens of the said States, was also, in a period of profound peace, while engaged in lawful business, arrested and imprisoned; and subsequently, this Vessel also was forcibly seized and the Crew imprisoned, by order of Governor Vernet, and Vessel, Master, and Crew were forced into his service under the following circumstances. While the Captains, Davison and Congar, were Prisoners, closely guarded, the Governor, by operating on their fears, induced them to enter into an Agreement, which, among others, contained the following extraordinary provisions:

Having arrested and imprisoned them, in his capacity of Military and Civil Governor, for violating the Laws and the Sovereignty of this Republic—regardles of the high official character in which he acted, and the dignity of the Government under whose appointment he professed to act—instead of bringing them to trial for these offences, he endeavoured to compel them to enter his service, for purposes altogether personal, and to substitute himself forcibly in the place of their Owners; and, degrading the style and dignity of his high office, by calling himself a Director instead of a Military and Civil Governor, and by undertaking to transform himself into a Merchant; used his military and civil powers to extort from his Prisoners a written obligation in the shape of a mercantile contract, to go with one of their Vessels and its Crew, beyond his pretended jurisdiction, through the Straits of Magellan to the western Coast of South America, for the purpose of taking Seals on his account; for which service he afterwards selected the *Superior,* her Master and Crew.

In mockery of those usages regarded by all Christian Nations as solemn and sacred, he compelled these American Citizens, with minds depressed by imprisonment and sufferings, and all their prospects of fortune and competency blasted by his oppression, to bind themselves, *by oaths,* " to do nothing to compromise his interests;" and, in defiance of all legitimate authority and moral and patriotic obligations, compelled them also to agree, that any deviation from this compulsory contract should be considered as a " breach of faith," and that " no Laws should liberate them from the penalties and forfeitures" which he chose, under these circumstances, to impose upon them; thus attempting to secure his own piratical interests from the operation of the Laws, by oaths of his own devising.

The Schooner *Harriet* arrived here on the 20th of November last, under his charge, and is now detained (as the Undersigned has been informed,) by virtue of some process emanating from this Government, and her Crew, (with the exception of 5 who had been liberated by the Governor, on their Agreement to enter his service,) were put on board the aforementioned British Vessel, and sent with Captain Carew, and some of his Men, to Rio Janeiro.

Seven Men, being a part of the Crew of the *Superior*, had been left, previous to the Capture, on Staten Land, with provisions for 6 months; and, in consequence of the detention of that Vessel, were exposed, in that dreary and desolate Region, to the peril of dying from starvation, which would have been inevitable without accidental succour, inasmuch as Captain Congar was restricted, in the Agreement, to a direct voyage through the Straits of Magellan, to the West Coast of South America, and a direct return to Port Louis, and was obligated to avoid all communication with the Sealers, and no steps whatever were taken for their relief.

The Governor, Mr. Lewis Vernet, has endeavoured to seduce American Seamen from their own Flag, and to allure all who were so base as to renounce their Country, into his service, by the promise of extravagant wages.

Wholly regardless of the common rights of humanity, he has arrested and imprisoned Isaac S. Waldron, George Lambert, John Jones, and William Smyley, all Citizens of The United States, a part of the Crew of the Schooner *Belville* of Portland, in the State of Maine, commanded by Captain Bray; which Vessel was wrecked on the Coast of Tierra del Fuego.

He also forcibly seized a large number of seal skins, and a large quantity of whalebone, then in their possession—sold the stores to the Master of an English Vessel, and transported the whalebone to Buenos Ayres; and then compelled these friendless, unfortunate, shipwrecked, imprisoned Mariners, under threats of being sent to Buenos Ayres to be tried for their lives as Pirates, to sign an Agreement, in behalf of themselves and 5 Shipmates, who were then on Eagle Island occupied in building a shallop, in which they stipulated that the Shallop, when completed, should be employed in the Seal Fishery on his account, and should wear the Flag of this Republic.

Not satisfied with seizing their property and treating them as Slaves, he would complete the measure of their humiliation by reducing these American Citizens to a degree of moral debasement as low as his own, inasmuch as, in another article of this compulsory Agreement, after binding them by a mockery of terms " to act in every respect in an honorable manner as becomes good men," he would have seduced them to the commission of acts of violence and robbery on their own Countrymen, by engaging to share with them the profits arising from the plunder of the Vessels which they should capture !

In this mode, he has compelled individuals belonging to the captured American Vessels to engage in his service, and in some instances to assist in the capture of their own Countrymen; and, in one instance, finding an American Seamen, by the name of Crawford, refractory to his persuasions, heedless of his threats and unsubdued by imprisonment, he endeavored to force him into his service by depriving him of food—and this wretched Seamen would have died of hunger, had not relief been administered secretly by Captain Davison, in defiance of his orders.

The Undersigned would also call the attention of his Excellency the Minister of Foreign Affairs to certain declarations of Don Luis Vernet, important, as coming from a high Functionary of this Government, the Military and Civic Governor of an extensive Region; and if those declarations are to be considered as indicative of the sentiments and views of this Government, there would be just cause for apprehending that a Project was in contemplation, involving the destruction of one of the most important and valuable national interests of The United States—the *Whale Fishery*—for he declared to Captain Davison, that it was his determination to capture all American Vessels, including *Whaling-Ships*, as well as those engaged in catching Seals, upon the arrival of an armed Schooner, for which he had contracted, which was to carry 6 guns and a complement of 50 men.

The Undersigned would also call the attention of His Excellency the Minister to another declaration of the Governor, from which an inference is fairly to be deduced, that the Citizens of The United States were to be selected as the special victims of his power; while the Vessels and Seamen of other Nations were to be unmolested—inasmuch as, when he was told that the Crew of the *Adeona*, a British Vessel, had taken many Seals on the Islands, and some even on the Volunteer Rocks, at the mouth of the Sound on which his Establishment was placed—his reply was, "that he could not take an English Vessel with the same propriety that he could an American."

It may sometimes happen that Nations may mistake their rights, and may attempt to establish sovereign jurisdiction over unoccupied Territories not clearly their own, and to which their title may be disputed,—and other Nations, whose rights may be affected in consequence of such assumptions, are not necessarily obliged—perhaps, in the first instance—to regard acts enforcing such jurisdiction, as intrinsically and absolutely hostile, if their operation is equal and indiscriminate:—but, if the Citizens or Subjects of one Nation, only, are subjected to penalties and punishments for violations of sovereign jurisdiction so assumed, while the Subjects or Citizens of other Nations, committing the same violations, are unmolested—such partial selection is evidence of hostile feeling, at least, in the Officer to whom the Authority to punish is delegated—and the Government which justifies an Officer who thus favors and spares the one, and punishes the other, when both are *in pari delictu*, must be considered as avowing a preference, injurious and hostile to the Nation which suffers.

The Undersigned would also call the attention of his Excellency the Minister of Foreign Affairs to the period when the Governor began to capture American Vessels and American Citizens.—The Decree from which he pretends to derive his authority, bears the date of 10th of June, 1829, and it remained a dead letter, as to the North Americans, until the 30th day of July, 1831, more than 2 years from its date. It is a matter of public notoriety that the late Chargé d'Affaires of The United States near this Government, died in this City on the 14th day of June, 1831. When it was ascertained at the Falkland Islands that the American Representative was dead, this system of depredation on American property, and of outrage and violence on American Citizens, was commenced. It seems evident to the Undersigned, that the Governor was well convinced that such atrocities, if perpetrated previous to the death of the American Representative, must have roused him from his apathy, insensible, as he was, to the importance of this Decree, which has wrought so much mischief to his Countrymen, and of which his Government, to this day, have not been officially informed.

The Governor must have known (for he has resided many years in The United States, and is well acquainted with their Institutions and Laws, and with the temper and disposition of the People) that no distance could smother the voice of just complaint, when uttered by American Seamen: that it would have been heard, even from this remote Region, by a Government never deaf to their entreaties for protection—never insensible to their wrongs and injuries—and that its echo would have traversed back the wide expanse of the Ocean waters, which roll between the 2 hemispheres: he must have known that the American Representative here, would have been compelled to have told this Government these solemn truths—that the Flag of The United States must be respected, whether floating beneath the constellations of the North or the South—that the wrongs of every American Citizen must be redressed—and that certain vital national interests, amongst which is, the right of Free Fishery, can never be abandoned. Sensible of this, the Governor chose a time for the exercise of his power in acts of despotism, when no high Diplomatic Functionary was here to advocate and protect the interests and the rights of his Countrymen—and remained unchecked and uncontrolled, until an American Naval Commander was found, of sufficient energy and patriotism, to defend and protect those rights, on his own responsibility.

But had the Governor, in the exercise of his authority, confined himself merely to the capture of American Vessels, and to the institution of Processes before the regular Tribunals which administer the Laws in this Country, with the sole view of ascertaining whether transgressions against the Laws and the Sovereignty of this Republic had, or had not, been committed, and had he so done in strict pursuance of his delegated authority—yet, in the view of the Government of The United States, even an exercise of authority thus limited, would have been an essential violation of their maritime rights; and the Undersigned is instructed and authorized to say,—that they utterly deny the existence of any right in this Republic to interrupt, molest, detain or capture, any Vessels belonging to Citizens of the United States of America, or any Persons being Citizens of those States, engaged in taking Seals, or Whales, or any species of fish or marine animals, in any of the waters, or on any of the shores or lands, of any, or either, of the Falkland Islands, Tierra del Fuego, Cape Horn, or any of the adjacent Islands in the Atlantic Ocean.

In consequence of these repeated outrages on American property and American Citizens, it has become the solemn and imperative, but unpleasant duty of the Undersigned, as the Representative of the United States of America, to demand in their behalf, a restitution of all captured property belonging to Citizens of The United States, now in the possession of this Government, or in the possession of Don Luis Vernet, claiming under its appointment to be the Military and Civic Governor of the Falkland Islands, Tierra del Fuego, and all the Islands in the Atlantic Ocean adjacent Cape Horn—and ample imdemnity for all other property of American Citizens which has been seized, sold or destroyed by said Vernet, or persons acting under his orders; and full and ample immunity and reparation for all consequential injuries and damages arising therefrom, and full indemnity to all American Citizens for personal wrongs—whether from detention, imprisonment, or personal indignities.

The Undersigned would also call the attention of His Excellency the Minister of Foreign Affairs, to the case of the American Consul, whose functions have been suspended by this Government—not with a view to make any specific demand, because on this subject, he is not, as yet, specially instructed—but merely to suggest to His Excellency, that the Government of The United States, (in his opinion) if they do not view this act as absolutely hostile, (which he will not venture to affirm they do not,) yet they must consider it as evidence of unfriendly feelings. The Undersigned can find nothing in the conduct of the Consul (so far as he understands it) which will justify this Government in taking a step so strong and decisive as that of his suspension. Presenting his exceptionable acts to the consideration of his own Government, would have been the more expedient and friendly mode to obtain redress; inasmuch as that Government have always respected the feelings of the People among whom their Consuls reside.

The Undersigned would, with much respect, suggest for the consideration of His Excellency, the propriety of removing the obstacles which impede the exercise of the Consular functions of Mr. Slacum, until the views of the Government of The United States respecting this question, can be ascertained.

The Undersigned takes this occasion, &c.

FRANCIS BAYLIES.

H. E. Senor Dr. D. Manuel Vicente de Maza.

———

(18.)—*The Buenos Ayres Minister to the American Chargé d'Affaires.*
(Translation.)   *Buenos Ayres, 25th June,* 1832.

THE Undersigned, Minister of Grace and Justice, charged provisionally with the Department of Foreign Relations, has received and placed before His Excellency the Governor and Captain-General of this Province, the Note of the Chargé d'Affaires of The United States of America, dated the 20th inst., complaining of the proceedings of Mr. Louis Vernet in the Malvinas, and making statements, of a nature so serious and strange, that they require the most attentive consideration of the Supreme Authority of this Country. To the end, therefore, of inquiring into the complaints which the Chargé d'Affaires prefers against the said Vernet, and prior to answering the several points comprised in his Note, His Excellency has this day resolved that explanations be required from Mr. Louis Vernet, upon all and every one of those relative to his public conduct, in the cases which rest upon his responsibility. On view of them, and after the Government shall have formed its opinion, as well from the facts which Mr. Vernet may set forth, as from those on which the Chargé d'Affaires grounds his claim, His Excellency will discharge his duty, without attempting to impair the individual rights of the Citizens of The United States, who may prove to have been aggrieved or injured, and likewise without sacrificing to exorbitant pretensions the rights of Mr. Louis Vernet, nor the public ones, which by the common Law of Nations, belong to the Argentine Republic, as a sovereign and independent State.

The Undersigned, on acquainting the Chargé d'Affaires of The United States with the measure adopted by His Excellency, has the honor, &c.

MANUEL VICENTE DE MAZA.

The Chargé d'Affaires of The United States.

———

(19.)—*The American Chargé d'Affaires to the Buenos Ayres Minister.*
Buenos Ayres, 26th June, 1832.

THE Undersigned, Chargé d'Affaires from the United States of America, has the honor to acknowledge to his Excellency the Minister of Grace and Justice, charged provisionally with the Department of Foregn Affairs, the receipt of his Note of yesterday, from which he learns that his Communication of the 20th has been received.

He learns also with much pleasure that the Communication above mentioned has been placed in the hands of His Excellency the Govenor and Captain-General of this Province, as he is well persuaded from the high character which his Excellency the Governor universally sustains for wisdom and justice, that, when satisfied of the existence of wrong, he will never withhold redress.

His Excellency the Minister says that the complaints which the Undersigned, as the organ of his Government, has addressed to him are serious;—they are so, for they are preferred in behalf of American Citizens to obtain redress for aggravated injuries. His Excellency also says that they are strange ;—as to this also, the Undersigned has the honor to entertain a similar opinion, inasmuch, as nothing can be more strange to the Government and People of The United States, than that outrages and violences should have been committed upon the Persons and property of their Citizens, in a time of profound peace, under the sanction of the Government of Buenos-Ayres.

His Excellency has also been pleased to inform the Undersigned that explanations would be asked of Don Luis Vernet: the Undersigned will take the liberty to say that, as to the substantive matter of the complaint no further explanations are necessary, inasmuch as Don Luis Vernet has admitted, in the public newspapers of this City, under his own signature, that he has captured American Vessels, which admissions cannot be unknown to His Excellency ;—neither can it be unknown to him, that the Schooner *Harriet*, owned by Citizens of The United States and captured by the said Vernet, is now detained in this Port by virtue of a process issued by some Tribunal within the jurisdiction of this Government.

The aggravations with which these injuries on the Persons and property of American Citizens were accompanied, cannot affect the principle assumed by the Government of The United States, but are important only in ascertaining the measure and magnitude of those injuries—inasmuch as the Government of The United States not only deny any right in the said Vernet to capture, and detain, the property or the Persons of their Citizens engaged in Fishing at the Falkland Islands, Tierra del Fuego, Cape Horn, or any of the adjacent Islands in the Atlantic Ocean, but also any right or authority in the Government of Buenos Ayres so to do.

His Excellency has been pleased to say that " the public rights which, by the common Law of Nations, belong to the Argentine Republic as a Sovereign and Independent State, he will not pretend to sacrifice :"—to this the Undersigned can only say, that the Government which he represents has neither the intention or the disposition to bring into question any of the *rights* of the Argentine Republic—but they wish to know *distinctly* from this Government whether they claim, on their part, any right or authority to detain or capture, or in any way to molest, interrupt, or impede, the Vessels or the Citizens of The United States, while engaged in Fishing in the waters or on the shores of the Falkland Islands, and the other places already mentioned.

The Undersigned also takes the liberty to express to His Excellency the Minister, the hope that this inquiry may be answered as speedily as his convenience will permit,—and he has the honor to assure him, &c.

FRANCIS BAYLIES.

H. E. Señor Dr. Don Manuel V. de Maza.

(20.)—*The American Chargé d'Affaires to the Buenos Ayres Minister.*

Buenos Ayres, 10*th July*, 1832.

THE Undersigned, Chargé d'Affaires from the United States of America near this Government, has the honor to inform His Excellency the Minister of Grace and Justice, charged provisionally with the Department of Foreign Affairs, that he has received no answer to the inquiry which he had the honor to submit to him, in his Communication of the 26th ultimo, and which was of the following purport—that his Government wished to know, distinctly, from this Government, whether it claimed, on its part, any right or authority, to detain or capture, or in any way to molest, interrupt or impede, the Vessels or the Citizens of the United States of America, while engaged in Fishing in the waters or on the shores of the Falkland Islands, and the other places included in the Decree of June 10th, 1829.

It appeared to the Undersigned that no deliberation was necessary to enable the Government of this Republic to answer this plain question ; and, therefore, he expressed the hope that the reply might be speedy. But, inasmuch as several days have elapsed since it was made, he must take it for granted that the inquiry was considered futile by His Excellency—as the fact inquired of was of common notoriety; inasmuch as the rights claimed by the Argentine Republic had been asserted in the Decree of June 10th, 1829, and in the Correspondence between D. Tomas Manuel de Anchorena, formerly Minister of Foreign Affairs, and George W. Slacum, Esqr., Consul of The United States,—that Minister having, in his Communication to Mr. Slacum, of date December 3rd, 1831, denied the right of The United States to the Fisheries in question ; while he asserted the rights claimed by this Republic to be " unquestionable,"—and also having, in a Communication to the Consul subsequently made (viz. on the 9th of the same December) expressed the wish of his Government, that the Consul would refrain " from persisting in the Protest which he had made against rights which had been, and were, in possession of this

Government, and which (said the Minister) until this time, nobody has questioned,"—and inasmuch as, in a Proclamation issued by the Delegate Government on the 14th. of February last, the Falkland Islands are claimed as a " Colony" of this Province,—and, in a Circular issued by the same Delegate Government to the Provinces, Don Luis Vernet is styled the Political and Military Governor of the Falkland Islands, &c.,—and inasmuch as this Government now detains the American Schooner *Harriet*, captured by virtue of this assumed power.

The Decree of June 10th, 1829, the Proclamation of February 14th, 1832, and the Circular to the Provinces, and the Process against the Schooner *Harriet*, have never been communicated officially to the American Government or to their Representative here; and, although the same right was asserted, in behalf of this Government, by their Minister of Foreign Affairs, in the Correspondence with Mr. Slacum, the American Consul, yet, as the Diplomatic character of that Gentleman was positively denied, and as he was subsequently suspended from his Office by this Government—whatever was asserted in that Correspondence, is not perhaps to be considered of a character as solemn as that of direct assertions of this right, made to an accredited Representative of the American Government here.

Therefore, the Undersigned felt some solicitude to obtain an avowal of this claim, from a Minister of this Government, made distinctly to himself, as the accredited Representative of The United States.

But, as His Excellency has not, as yet, condescended to reply to the enquiry—the Undersigned thinks himself justified in the presumption that the power and authority described in his Application, are assumed by this Government. And, acting on this presumption, he will proceed to lay before His Excellency the views which his Government have taken of this question—and to present some facts, having relation to the question in issue, for the consideration of His Excellency, which he sincerely hopes may produce a happy termination of this unpleasant controversy.

To simplify the investigation upon which the Undersigned proposes to enter, he will, in the commencement, take the liberty to state the question, in this manner .—

The Argentine Republic claims sovereignty and jurisdiction over the Falkland Islands, Tierra del Fuego, Cape Horn and the Islands adjacent in the Atlantic Ocean, by virtue of having succeeded to the Sovereign rights of Spain over those Regions.

As these Sovereign rights thus claimed are altogether derivative from Spain—the first enquiry naturally divides itself into 2 branches :—

1st. Had Spain any Sovereign rights over the abovementioned Places?—

2nd. Did the Argentine Republic succeed to those rights?

If it can be shewn that Spain had no such rights, the question is terminated, unless the Argentine Republic should abandon all title under Spain, and claim an absolute vested Sovereignty, original in itself.

If it be shewn affirmatively, that Spain had such rights, then it must be as clearly shewn that the Argentine Republic succeeded to them; and if that can be shewn, then it must also be shewn that the Argentine Republic had authority to capture and detain American Vessels and American Citizens engaged in the Fisheries at those places, without notifying the American Government, or its Representative here, officially, of such assumptions and such claims.

It must be premised, that the United States of America claim no Sovereign jurisdiction or exclusive privileges over the water or the soil of these Regions. They only claim such privileges as they have been accustomed to exercise, in common with other Maritime Nations.

Civilized Nations have claimed title to Countries uninhabited, or inhabited only by savage Aboriginals, in three modes :-

1. By prior discovery.
2. By taking formal possession of such Countries.
3. By prior occupation.

It has sometimes been contended, that the first sight of Countries never before seen by civilized and Christian People, give to the Nation by whose Subjects such discovery was made, a preferable title; but it does not seem altogether reasonable that the discovery of a new Region by ignorant mariners, in consequence, perhaps, of a casual storm, or a trifling accident, should give to their Nations a solid title to valuable Territories. But, when skill and science are put in requisition, and expensive Expeditions prepared for the purpose of discovery, it would seem just that discoveries consequent on such enterprises, should be followed by some benefits to the Persons by whom they were made, and to the Nations by whom they were patronized.

It has also been contended, that no title can accrue from mere discovery, unless such discovery be accompanied by certain formal Acts, which generally are styled Acts of possession.

Formal possession of uninhabited and wild Countries has generally been taken by Naval Officers, and has always been attended with many ceremonies and solemnities; amongst which are—landing in state, under salutes—raising Flags—making inscriptions, and proclaiming formally that possession is taken in behalf of their Sovereign or Nation. If Catholics, crosses are sometimes reared—and, sometimes, coins are buried.

Some Nations have admitted rights in the savage Aboriginals of such Countries, and have claimed subsequently, on occupation, what may be called a pre-emptive right, that is, the right to extinguish the aboriginal title by voluntary agreement, to the exclusion of all other Nations.

Other Nations have denied the existence of any right or title to territory amongst uncivilized Tribes.

On this point, no question can arise when the Regions claimed are uninhabited.

In the discussion which took place in the British Parliament, with respect to the proceedings of the Spaniards at Nootka-Sound, Mr. Fox, who is justly ranked amongst the most illustrious of British Statesmen, denied that discovery furnished any ground of title whatever; and rested the British title to Nootka on occupation alone.

Prior occupation, according the more liberal and rational usages of modern times, is certainly the least impeachable title to Regions uninhabited, or inhabited only by Savages.

The title founded on occupation may be strengthened, however, by the collateral circumstances of prior discovery and the formal act of taking possession, especially when there has been an occupation nearly simultaneous by 2 Nations. A mere temporary occupation, without the intention of remaining, neither gives title, nor furnishes presumptive evidence of title;—there is scarcely a desolate Island in this hemisphere, that has not had its temporary occupants; but the occupation must be such as to furnish strong presumptive evidence of an intention to abide—and the evidence of the intention can hardly be controverted, if the occupation be effected in pursuance of the orders of the Constituted Authorities of a Nation, and if actual possession be taken by a military force.

Such being the general principles which the wisest Statesmen have adopted, with respect to Countries uninhabited, or inhabited only by Savages; it is proper, for the elucidation of the questions which have arisen between the United States of America and the Argentine Republic, touching the Falkland Islands, Cape Horn, Tierra del Fuego, and the adjacent Islands in the Atlantic Ocean, to ascertain, from historical facts, how these principles will apply.

The Undersigned dos not pretend to say that Ferdinand Magellan, a Subject of the King of Portugal, in the service of Charles V., Emperor of Germany and King of Spain, commenced the first voyage of circumnavigation on the 20th of September, 1519, about 27 years after the discovery of America by Columbus. Unfortunately he did not live to complete it—having been killed at the Ladrones, in 1521. In October, 1520, he entered the Straits which divide Patagonia and Tierra del Fuego: he was, unquestionably, the first discoverer of the northern coast of the latter Region. More fortunate than Columbus, he not only left an enduring name to the Strait which he traversed, but he has fixed it eternally in the celestial Regions of the Southern Hemisphere.

In 1527, Groca de Loaisa, a Knight of Malta, in the service of Spain, undertook, with a squadron of 7 Ships, to follow the route of

Magellan, and actually passed the Straits; but all his Vessels were lost on the voyage, and he, with the remnant of his Followers, perished in the East Indies.

Sebastian Cabot and Americo Vespuçci, names of note in American history, made abortive attempts to pursue the same route—as did Simon de Alcazara, whose crew, having mutinied before he reached the Straits, compelled him to return. But the failure of Cabot, a name equally to be venerated by North and South America, can scarcely be regretted; inasmuch as it enabled him to complete the discovery of the fine Country of the Rio de la Plata, and to explore, in several directions, those mighty waters, which flow through Regions of matchless beauty and fertility.

These repeated failures, disheartened the Spaniards, and they gave over all attempts at discovery in this Quarter, for many years.

On the 20th August, 1578, Sir Francis Drake, an Englishman, and the first Naval Commander who circumnavigated the World, entered the Straits of Magellan and named an Island, which he discovered there, Isabel, in honour of his Queen. After leaving the Straits, he was driven South by a succession of storms, as far as latitude 55°, where he discovered a cluster of Islands, anchored, and spent some days on shore. Leaving these Islands, he was assailed by another violent storm, and was driven farther South, even beyond the 57th degree, " where (says the writer of his voyage) we beheld the extremities of the American Coast, and the confluence of the Atlantic and Southern Oceans." This was on the 28th of October, 1578.

From these notices, it would appear that the Northern Coast of Tierra del Fuego was first discovered by Magellan, when in the service of Spain; and the South-western Coast and some Islands in that direction by Sir Francis Drake, in the service of England—who probably discovered the southern extremity of the American Continent, now called Cape Horn.

So little was known of the southern and eastern coast of Tierra del Fuego as late as the year 1774, that Cook, the greatest of English navigators, while on his second Voyage, when actually in sight of Cape Horn, could not ascertain whether it formed a part of that great Island, or whether it was a part of a smaller detached Island. Cook, however, by exploring the eastern and southern Coasts of Tierra del Fuego, and laying down with mathematical and geographical accuracy, their several headlands, bays and harbors, deserves the credit of an original discoverer; as he unquestionably brought many things to light which were not known before.

The Undersigned cannot discover from any evidence within his command, that any Nation has ever taken formal possession of Tierra del Fuego or any of the Islands adjacent—or attempted to establish any Settlements within their Territories, or occupied them in any way.

The savage Aboriginals of those inhabited, have always remained without interruption or molestation; and without having been required to yield even a nominal obedience or allegiance to any Sovereign or Nation whatever.

Although it is highly probable that Sir Francis Drake was the original discoverer of Cape Horn and the Island of which it forms the extremity—yet, that discovery has generally been assigned to Jacob Le Maire, a Dutchman, in the service of the States of Holland, who, in 1616, rediscovered that which Drake had discovered before, perhaps, and left the name of Hoorn (now corrupted to Horn) attached to the Cape, in honour of the Town of that name in Holland. Le Maire was the first European Navigator who, by finding a passage into the Pacific Ocean round this *terminus* of South America, thereby enabling Navigators to avoid the difficult and dangerous passage through the Strait of Magellan, has almost rivalled De Gama, who converted the Cape of Storms into the Cape of Good Hope, when the way was opened to those magnificent Oriental Regions, which, for so long a period, have poured their riches into the lap of Europe. It is immaterial, so far as respects rights resulting from original discovery, whether this Cape, or the Island of which it is a part, was first seen by Sir Francis Drake, the Englishman, or Jacob Le Maire, the Dutchman —the honor of the discovery was never claimed by Spain:—the discovery was followed neither by possession nor occupation, and the Natives still retain undisputed dominion over this wintry and storm-beaten Region.

To the Strait between Tierra del Fuego and Staten Land, Le Maire has attached his name; but Staten Land—still desolate and uninhabited—serves only to remind us of the ancient enterprize of ill-fated Holland.

It has been asserted, with confidence, that the first European who placed his eyes on the Falkland Islands, was Davies, an Englishman and an Associate of Cavendish, in his voyage to the South Seas, in 1592, during the reign of Queen Elizabeth. Driven by storms within view of them, so imperfect was the discovery that he left not even the frail memory of a name.

In 1594, Sir Richard Hawkins, an English Admiral, in the service of Queen Elizabeth saw these Islands, and, in honor of his mistress and himself, called them Hawkins' Maiden-land.

In 1598, the States of Holland despatched a Squadron to the South Seas under the command of Admiral Verhagen and Sabald de Wert. These Islands were seen by the Squadron and named Sabald Islands, under which appellation they appear in many ancient charts; and this, or a name so similar as to indentify them, was retained until the year 1683; for William Dampier, a celebrated English Seaman, in the fourth edition of the Relation of his Voyages, published in London, in

1699, says, that on the 28th January, 1683, " we made the Sibbel de Wards, which are 3 Islands lying in the latitude of 51 deg. 35 min. South, and longitude West from the Lizard in England, by my account, 57 deg. 28 min."—" These Islands of Sibbel de Wards were so named by the Dutch." In the Map prefixed to this edition of his Voyages, these Islands, which, from their position, must be the Falklands, are called Sibbel de Wards.

The name of Falkland, it is said, was first bestowed on these Islands by an English Navigator, Captain Strong, in 1689.

This name was subsequently adopted by all the English Geographers and men of science, particularly by Dr. Halley. The Journal of Strong yet exists, unprinted, in the British Museum.

Between the years 1700 and 1708, many French Ships from St. Maloes, sailed into the South Seas. By some of them these Islands were discovered and the French name of Malouines was attached to them—which name the Spaniards have adopted.

The French claimed the honor of having made the original discovery; but Frezier, a French author, whose relation of a voyage to the South Sea was published at Paris in 1716, admits that " *ces Isles sont sans doute les mêmes que celles que le Chevalier Richard Hawkins découvrit en* 1593," and his admission has been adopted by Malte-Brun, his countryman, the inimitable geographer of modern times.

There is not, on the part of Spain, the slightest pretence of having made the original discovery of these Islands. Spain, indeed, does not pretend to have made it—but has adopted even the French name.

In the year 1764, a Squadron was ordered to the South Seas by the King of Great Britain, George III., which Squadron was placed under the command of Commodore the Honorable John Byron, an illustrious name in the naval annals of Great Britain. What follows is extracted from his Instructions, dated June 17th, 1764, " and whereas His Majesty's Islands, called Pepy's Island and Falkland Islands, lying within the said track," (i. e. the track between the Cape of Good Hope and the Straits of Magellan) " notwithstanding their having been first discovered and visited by British Navigators, have never yet been so sufficiently surveyed as that an accurate judgment may be formed of their coasts and product, His Majesty, taking the premises into consideration, and conceiving no juncture so proper for enterprises of this nature as a time of profound peace, which his Kingdoms at present happily enjoy, has thought fit that it should now be undertaken.'

On the 23rd January, 1765, Commodore Byron went on shore at these Islands, with the Captains and Principal Officers of his Squadron, " where the Union Jack being erected on a high staff and spread, the Commodore took possession of the Harbor and all the neighboring

Islands for His Majesty King George III., his Heirs and Successors, by the name of Falkland's Islands. When the Colors were spread, a salute was fired from the Ship.''

Possession was thus taken, with all the usual formalities, in the name of the King of Great Britain.

On the 8th of January, 1766, Captain MacBride arrived at Port Egmont with a military force—erected a block-house, and stationed a Garrison. No traces of former habitations, cultivation, or people, were perceived, but the English made some attempts to cultivate; and, as there was no native wood, several thousand young trees, with the mould about their roots, were transported from Port Famine Bay, in one of the Ships of Commodore Wallis' Squadron, for the purpose of being re-set at the Falklands.

All this was done by the command of the King of Great Britain; and, as to all consequent rights, the occupation was complete.

It is true, that it is said that some Frenchmen had made a temporary establishment on one of the Falkland Islands, about this period; and that, in consequence of a remonstrance made by Spain, the King of France ceded all his right to those Islands to His Catholic Majesty. If the doctrine assumed by Spain was correct, that France had not even a colourable title, the cession was a nullity; and it is a fact that Spain so regarded it, and relied on her prior rights, alone, in her subsequent controversy with Great Britain.

On the 10th of June, 1770, a large Spanish Force, under the command of Admiral Madariaga, dispossessed the British of their establishment at Port Egmont, by force. The expedition by which this was achieved was put in motion by Buscarelli, the Viceroy of Buenos Ayres.

At the time of the forcible dispossession, the title of Great Britain was, certainly, placed on very strong foundations: she had prior discovery, formal possession, and actual occupation to urge; and there were no aboriginal rights to be extinguished.

The act of dispossession was disavowed by Spain, and the Territory restored by solemn Convention: she, however, reserved her prior rights. The reservation was a nullity; inasmuch as she had no claim, either by prior discovery, prior possession, prior occupation, or even the shadow of a name.

The restoration of Port Egmont, and the disavowal of the act by which she was temporarily dispossessed, after discussion, negotiation, and solemn agreement, gave to the title of Great Britain more stability and strength; for it was a virtual acknowledgement, on the part of Spain, of its validity. Great Britain might then have occupied and settled all the Islands, and fortified every harbor, without giving to Spain any just cause of umbrage.

With her rights again acknowledged, the emblems of sovereignty again reared, and possession resumed by a military and naval Force, Great Britain voluntarily abandoned these distant Dominions, taking every possible precaution, when she so did, to give evidence to the World, that, though she abandoned, she did not relinquish them.

It is true, that many years have elapsed since, under these circumstances, she ceased to occupy the Falkland Islands. But the lapse of time cannot prevent her from resuming possession, if her own maxim of Law be well founded—*nullum tempus occurrit regi*—and, that she persists in her claim, is evident, from the following Protest, communicated to the Undersigned officially by His Excellency, Henry S. Fox, now His Britannic Majesty's Minister Plenipotentiary and Envoy Extraordinary near this Government, and which is in the following words:—

> *The British Chargé d'Affaires to the Buenos Ayres Minister.*
>
> " *Buenos Ayres*, 19*th November*, 1829.

" THE Undersigned has the honor to inform His Excellency, the Minister of Foreign Affairs, that he has communicated to his Court the Official Document published by the Government of Buenos Ayres on the 10th of June last, containing certain provisions for the Government of the Falkland Islands.

" The Undersigned has received the order of his Court to represent to His Excellency, that the Argentine Republic, in issuing this Decree, have assumed an authority incompatible with His Britannic Majesty's rights of Sovereignty over the Falkland Islands.

" These rights, founded upon the original discovery and subsequent occupation of the said Islands, acquired an additional sanction from the restoration, by His Catholic Majesty, of the British Settlement, in the year 1771, which, in the preceding year, had been attacked and occupied by a Spanish Force, and which act of violence had led to much angry discussion between the Governments of the 2 Countries.

" The withdrawal of His Majesty's Forces from these Islands, in the year 1774, cannot be considered as invalidating His Majesty's just rights. That measure took place in pursuance of a system of retrenchment, adopted at that time by His Britannic Majesty's Government; but the marks and signals of possession and property were left upon the Islands: when the Governor took his departure, the British Flag remained flying, and all those formalities were observed which indicated the rights of ownership, as well as an intention to resume the occupation of the Territory, at a more convenient season.

" The Undersigned, therefore, in execution of the Instructions of his Court, formally protests, in the name of His Britannic Majesty, against the pretensions set up by the Government of Buenos Ayres, in their Decree of the 10th of June, and against all acts which have been, or may hereafter be, done, to the prejudice of the just rights of sovereignty which have heretofore been exercised by the Crown of Great Britain."

                              " The Undersigned, &c.

H. E. *Don Tomas Guido*.   " WOODBINE PARISH."

Although His Excellency, Don Tomas Manuel de Anchorena, formerly Minister of Foreign Affairs, has asserted, in his Communication to the American Consul, of date December 9th, 1831, that, until then, nobody had questioned the rights of this Government; yet, the Minister of Foreign Affairs must, certainly, have overlooked the Protest above-recited; for the Undersigned has in his hands a Copy of the official acknowledgment of its receipt, by His Excellency, Don Tomas Guido, formerly Minister of Foreign Affairs; which Copy has also been communicated to him officially by His Excellency, the British Envoy.*

After a dispassionate view of these historical facts, can it be contended that Spain, whose claim of title is restricted to the prior discovery of the Northern Coast of Tierra del Fuego—a discovery made more than 300 years ago, followed neither by the formal acts of possession nor actual occupation—who has always left that region of desolation as she found it, in the possession of its miserable Aboriginals—could have had the slightest justification for attempting to exclude the Citizens of the United States of America from the rights of free Fisheries in all these Island-regions? Spain did not attempt it; and although she has captured hundreds of American Vessels, and an amount of property for which she afterwards remunerated The United States, by paying to their Citizens the sum of 5,000,000 of Spanish dollars, it is not now recollected that a single Whale-ship or Sealing-vessel, was amongst those captures.

Can this Republic, then, claiming no original title or rights, but such only as are derivative, and which are derived altogether from

---

* *The Buenos Ayres Minister to the British Chargé d'Affaires.*

(Translation.)   *Buenos Ayres, 25th November,* 1829.

The Undersigned, Minister of Foreign Relations, has received and placed before his Government, the Communication which Woodbine Parish, Esq. His Britannic Majesty's Chargé d Affaires, has been pleased to address him, under date of the 19th Instant, remonstrating against the Decree issued on the 10th of June of the present year, whereby a political and military Commandant of Malvinas was appointed.

The Government intends to give an attentive consideration to the Note of Mr. Parish, and the Undersigned will be happy to communicate to him its Resolution, as soon as he shall receive orders so to do.

                    The Undersigned has the honor, &c.

                                        TOMAS GUIDO.

H. B. M. Chargé d'Affaires.

Spain—assume any higher titles than those which Spain herself assumed?—and Spain, certainly, never assumed any right to capture or detain American Vessels or American Citizens engaged in the Fisheries at the places above-mentioned.

And to shew that Spain had excluded herself from exercising any high rights of Sovereignty, by voluntary compact—the Undersigned would call the attention of His Excellency to the VIth Article of the Convention concluded between His Catholic Majesty and the King of Great Britain, at San Lorenzo el Real, October 28th, 1790, and ratified on the 22nd of November following ; and which is in the following words :—

"It is further agreed, also, that, as it respects the Eastern as well as the Western Coasts of South America and the adjacent Islands, that the respective Subjects of the 2 Powers shall not form, in future, any Settlements in any part of these Coasts, situated to the South of the Coasts and of the Islands adjacent thereto, already occupied by Spain ; it being well understood, that the respective Subjects of the 2 Nations shall have the power to land on the Coasts and Islands so situated, for the purpose of fishing, and to build cabins and other temporary works that may serve solely for these objects."

The Undersigned presumes that it will not be contended that any Settlements then existed at any of the Places included in the Decree of the 10th of June, 1829; and, by this Article, Spain and Great Britain both restricted themselves from forming any Settlements there.

Can it be supposed that Spain, a Nation jealous of her rights and sovereignty, and peculiarly sensitive on the subject of her South American Dominions, would have virtually abandoned her sovereign rights over these wide Regions, if she supposed her title to be well founded and free from doubt? There can be no dispute as to the real object of this Treaty, which was to leave an open Fishery in these Regions.

But, if it be hypothetically admitted that the full and entire right of sovereignty was possessed by Spain—has Spain renounced it? Has Spain ever, by any acknowledgement whatever, yielded the rights which she once possessed? Has Spain, as yet, relinquished, by any formal Act or acknowledgment, any part of her claim to supreme dominion over these Islands? If the rights of Spain are dormant, they are not extinct; and the Undersigned has little doubt of her ability to maintain her actual rights (if any) over the Falkland Islands: for, although some of the brightest jewels have been torn from her Crown, she is now a great and powerful Nation; and could her capacities be developed by free and liberal Institutions, she would soon resume much of her ancient grandeur.

But again—if the rights of Spain to these Islands were undoubted —and if, again, it be admitted hypothetically, that the ancient Vice

Royalty of the Rio de la Plata, by virtue of the Revolution of the 25th of May, 1810, has succeeded in full sovereignty to those rights; would that admission sustain the claim which the Province of Buenos Ayres, or, in other words, the Argentine Republic, sets up to Sovereignty and Jurisdiction?

In May, 1810, a Provisional Government was named at Buenos Ayres, who deposed the Spanish Vice Roy and sent him to Spain. Against this proceeding, some of the interior Provinces and the City of Montevideo protested.

Until the 9th day of July, 1816, Ferdinand VII was acknowledged as King at Buenos Ayres, and all official acts were promulgated in his name. During this period, had he assumed the Government of the Falkland Islands, would his Sovereign acts, orders or appointments, have been issued, proclaimed, or promulgated in his name and by his authority, as King of Spain and the Indies, or as King of Buenos Ayres or Rio de la Plata? Were not the proceedings of May, 1810, always received by the King as rebellious? In his estimation, was not this effort for liberty an insurrectionary movement; and did he not attempt to restore the ancient Dominion of Spain over the entire Vice Royalty?

Is it not a truth that Paraguay, one of the Provinces of the ancient Vice Royalty, has even refused to be united to Buenos Ayres, and has always remained a separate and independent Government?

The ancient Vice Royalty of the Rio de la Plata is now divided between several distinct Nations, having no dependency on each other —exercising all the powers of Sovereignty within their own limits, uncontrolled—and, with respect to the Argentine Republic, or the Province of Buenos Ayres, as entirely foreign and independent, as is the Republic of the United States of America. The Undersigned, therefore, asserts, that the Republic of Bólivia—the Province of Paraguay, and the Oriental Republic of the Uruguay, commonly styled the Banda Oriental—all included formerly in the Vice Royalty of the Rio de la Plata, have no political dependent connection with the Argentine Republic, or the Province of Buenos Ayres.

If, then, the sovereign rights of Spain to those Southern Islands, descended to the ancient Vice Royalty of the Rio de la Plata, by virtue of the Revolution—and if that Vice Royalty is now divided into several Sovereignties, independent of each other; to which one of these several Sovereignties shall these rights be assigned? Where are the title-deeds of the Argentine Republic? Where are the releases, of the other Nations of the Vice Royalty, to that Republic?

But again—if it be admitted hypothetically that the Argentine Republic did succeed to the entire rights of Spain over these Regions; and that, when she succeeded, Spain was possessed of sovereign rights; —the question is certainly worth examination, whether the right to exclude American Vessels and American Citizens from the Fisheries there, is incident to such a succession to Sovereignty.

The Ocean Fishery is a natural right, which all Nations may enjoy in common. Every interference with it by a Foreign Power, is a National wrong. When it is carried on within the marine league of the Coast, which has been designated as the extent of National Jurisdiction, reason seems to dictate a restriction, if, under pretext of carrying on the Fishery, an evasion of the Revenue Laws of the Country may reasonably be apprehended, or any other serious injury to the Sovereign of the Coast, he has a right to prohibit it; but, as such prohibition derogates from a natural right, the evil to be apprehended ought to be a real, not an imaginary one. No such evil can be apprehended on a desert and uninhabited Coast; therefore, such Coasts form no exception to the common right of Fishing in the Seas adjoining them. All the reasoning on this subject applies to the large Bays of the Ocean, the entrance to which cannot be defended ; and this is the doctrine of Vattel, ch. 23, § 291,* who expressly cites the Straits of Magellan, as an instance for the application of the rule.

As to the use of the Shores, for the purposes necessary to the Fishery ; that depends on other principles. When the right of exclusive Dominion is undisputed, the Sovereign may, with propriety, forbid the use of them to any Foreign Nation, provided such use interferes with any that his Subjects may make of them ; but where the Shore is unsettled and deserted, and the use of it, of course, interferes with no right of the Subjects of the Power to which it belongs, then it would be an infringement of the right to the common use of the Shores as well as of the Ocean itself, which all Nations enjoy, by the Laws of Nature, and which is restricted only by the paramount right which the Sovereign of the soil has to its exclusive use, when the convenience or interests of his Subjects require it ; or when he wishes to apply it to public purposes. It is true, that he is the judge of this interest, and of the necessity of using it for his public purposes—but justice requires, that where no such pretension can be made, the Shores, as well as the body of the Ocean, ought to be left common to all.

These principles seem to have dictated the Articles in the Treaties

---

* (Vattel, Chap. 23. § 291.) "All we have said of the parts of the Sea near the Coast, may be said, more particularly, and with much greater reason, of Roads, Bays, and Straits, as still more capable of being possessed, and of greater importance to the safety of the Country. But I speak of Bays and Straits of small extent, and not of those great tracts of Sea, to which these names are sometimes given, as Hudson's Bay, and the Straits of Magellan, over which the empire cannot extend, and still less a right of property. A Bay, whose entrance can be defended, may be possessed and rendered subject to the Laws of the Sovereign; and it is of importance that it should be so, since the Country might be much more easily insulted in such a Place, than on a Coast that lies exposed to the winds, and the impetuosity of the waves."

between The United States and Great Britain. The IIIrd Article of the Treaty of Peace of 1782, declares that the People of The United States shall continue to enjoy, unmolested, the right to take Fish on the Grand Banks, &c., and to dry and cure their fish in any of the unsettled Bays, Harbors, and Creeks, of Nova Scotia, Magdalen Islands, and Labrador, so long as the same shall remain unsettled; but that, when Settlements are made there, they cannot enjoy the right, without a previous agreement with the Inhabitants or possessors of the soil.

His Excellency will perceive, from the terms of this Treaty, that no rights of public sovereignty are claimed against The United States; but that the private rights of those who have settled and cultivated lands on the margin of the Ocean, are protected in such way as to secure their individual improvements from injury.

In the Treaty of Utrecht, too, France is allowed the use of the unsettled Shores, for the purpose of drying fish, by certain metes and bounds.

The Treaty concluded between Great Britain and Spain, in 1790, already alluded to, is to be viewed, in reference to this subject; because, both Nations, by restricting themselves from forming Settlements, evidently intended that the Fishery should be left open, both in the waters and on the Shores of these Islands, and perfectly free, so that no individual claim for damage, for the use of the Shores, should ever arise. That case, however, could scarcely occur, for Whales are invariably taken at sea, and generally without the marine league—and Seals, on rocks and sandy beaches, incapable of cultivation. The Stipulation in the Treaty of 1790 is, clearly, founded on the right to use the unsettled shores for the purpose of Fishery, and to secure its continuance.

When the unsettled Shore, although under the nominal sovereignty of a civilized Nation, is, in fact, possessed by independent, uncivilized Tribes, the right to exclude other Nations from the use of the Shores, is on a much less stable footing.

This is the case with all the Continent of South America, to its extremity from the Rio Negro in lat. 41°, and also with Tierra del Fuego and some of the adjacent Islands. On the Pacific side, the Araucanians; and on the Atlantic, the Puelches, Patagonians and other Tribes, are perfectly independent. To the common use of these Shores, therefore, there can be no reasonable objection.

The following conclusions, from the premises laid down, are inevitable:—

1. That the right of The United States to the Ocean Fishery, and in the Bays, arms of the Sea, gulfs and other inlets capable of being fortified, is perfect and entire.

2. That the right of the Ocean within a marine league of the Shore, where the approach cannot be injurious to the Sovereign of

the Country—as it cannot be on uninhabited Regions, or such as are occupied altogether by Savages—is equally perfect.

3. That the Shores of such Regions can be used as freely as the waters: a right arising from the same principle.

4. That a constant and uninterrupted use of the Shores for the purposes of a Fishery, would give the right, perfect and entire; although Settlements on such Shores should be subsequently formed or established.

That the Citizens of The United States have enjoyed the rights of free Fishery in these Regions, unmolested, is a fact which cannot be controverted. While they were yet Subjects of Great Britain, it was of such notoriety that it attracted the attention of an illustrious British Statesman and Orator, whose splendid panegyric, in the House of Commons, upon the maritime enterprise of the New-Englanders, will never be forgotten. " Pass by the other parts (said the Orator) and look at the manner in which the People of New-England have, of late, carried on the Whale-fishery. While we follow them among the tumbling mountains of ice, and behold them penetrating into the deepest frozen recesses of Hudson's Bay and Davis' Straits; whilst we are looking for them in the Arctic Circle; we hear that they have pierced into the opposite Region of polar cold,—that they are at the Antipodes and engaged under the frozen Serpent of the South. Falkland Islands, which seemed too remote and romantic an object for the grasp of national ambition, is but a stage and resting place in the progress of their victorious industry," &c.

It is of equal notoriety that from the period of the acknowledgement of their Independence by Great Britain, they have been in the unmolested enjoyment of the Whale and Seal Fishery in and about these Islands: that these Fisheries, with the full knowledge of Spain, have been prosecuted by them to an extent far exceeding the Fisheries of any and all other Nations. If long and uninterrupted use and possession can impart any right to Fisheries of the above description—the title of The United States is unimpeachable. And Vattel, Book I., chap. 23,, § 287, although he admits the right of Nations owning the Coasts to appropriate to themselves certain Fisheries on their Coasts—expressly excludes them under certain circumstances. " But if (says this Writer) so far from taking possession of it, the Nation has once acknowledged the common right of other Nations to come and fish there, it can no longer exclude them from it. It has left that Fishery in its primitive freedom, at least with respect to those who have been accustomed to take advantage of it. The English not having originally taken exclusive possession of the Herring Fishery on their Coasts, it has become common to them with other Nations." The acknowledgement spoken of, may be express or implied: a long continued use without interruption, is a virtual acknowledgement of the right to use; and in the instance cited (the Herring Fishery on the English Coast) there has been no formal acknowledgement, on the part of England, that other Nations have a right to use that Fishery: from the acquiescence of England, the acknowledgement is inferred.

Again—If it be admitted, hypothetically, that the rights of sovereign jurisdiction were vested in the Argentine Republic, by virtue of the Revolution of May, 1810, and that the right to exclude all Nations from the Fisheries of the Falklands and other Islands mentioned in the Decree of June 10th, 1829, was undoubtedly consequent to sovereign jurisdiction thus acquired; yet, some preliminary acts remained to be performed, before the capture and detention of the persons or property of Citizens of The United States of America engaged in the Fisheries, can be justified.

If Regions, never occupied or brought under any positive jurisdiction—without Garrisons, or Naval Forces, or Inhabitants—are to be occupied and brought under civil or military rule, and those who have enjoyed the privilege of a free Fishery there, are to be excluded from that privilege, it is incumbent on the Nation assuming such powers, to give official notice to the resident Representatives, or to the Governments, of all Nations with whom relations of amity are maintained, before any acts of violence, in assertion of such sovereign rights, can be justified. A warning to individuals is not enough—for that is not a general notice; and individuals not warned, may incur forfeitures and penalties, without any knowledge of their liabilities; and their Governments, equally ignorant, could take no preventive measures for their security.

In the Archives of the American Legation here, and of the Department of State at Washington, there is not the slightest trace of any Official Notice of the Decree of June 10th, 1829.

The Undersigned takes the liberty to say, that, on principles of common justice (and on such principles are the Laws of Nations based) a right enjoyed for more than half a Century—even if it was enjoyed by tacit permission, only—ought not to be denied or withdrawn without notice: and, surely, no penalty can be enforced, with justice, in such cases—unless the system of *ex post facto* Laws and Decrees is to be revived, in an age which boasts of its enlightened liberality and justice. Therefore, even on the supposition that the rights of the Argentine Republic are indisputable—yet, the seizure of American Vessels is a just cause of complaint, and the Government of The United States have a right to demand restoration and indemnity.

These remarks, touching the original rights of Spain and the derivative rights of the Argentine Republic; the rights of free Fishery, and the propriety of notice, when dormant and unclaimed rights are asserted and resumed; are offered for the consideration of His Excellency.

The Undersigned is well aware that the pending question involves important principles; and, although he may be satisfied as to the extent and character of the rights of The United States and the Argentine Republic, yet he freely admits that every Nation must decide, for herself, on all questions touching her dignity and her Sovereignty.

If the Argentine Republic can shew conclusively, that Spain was possessed of rights over the Falkland Islands, Tierra del Fuego, Cape Horn and the Islands adjacent in the Atlantic Ocean, of such a high and sovereign character as to justify the exclusion of the Citizens of the United States of America from the Fisheries there; if this Republic can shew that Spain has relinquished, renounced, or in any way lost her sovereign rights to the Regions above-mentioned, and that such Sovereignty has become absolutely vested in herself; and if she can further shew that, having acquired such rights, and being about to exercise them, by inflicting penalties and forfeitures upon the persons and property of the Citizens of a friendly Nation, for exercising privileges which they had been long accustomed to use—she is justified in witholding all official notice of the acquisition of such rights, and of her intention so to exercise them, from the Government or the resident Representative of such Nation—then, although the American Government might have some reason to complain of unceremonious and unfriendly treatment, there might, perhaps, have been no cause of complaint, on the ground of a violation of positive rights.

These questions, in controversy between the 2 Republics, involve principles which, in their applicability to the national rights of The United States, extend far beyond these Regions; and affect, in a most serious manner, their most important and vital interests.

It is the cause of deep regret to the People of those States, that circumstances should have compelled them to contend for these principles, with a People for whom they have ever cherished the most amicable sentiments—whose independence was recognized by them at an early period of their national existence; and the Undersigned takes the liberty to say, that this recognition was not occasioned by any anticipations of the advantages of a free commercial intercourse—but from sympathies, excited to enthusiasm, for a gallant People, who had won their freedom by their prowess and valor. Ere that recognition had passed through the forms of legislation, it was a Law in the hearts of the American People.

The Undersigned takes this occasion to inform His Excellency that he is instructed to say, " that the President of The United States is fully sensible of the difficult situation in which the internal troubles of this Republic have placed its Government, and that he does not attribute to any unfriendly disposition, acts, that, in ordinary times, might wear such an aspect; but he expects from the similarity of the Republican forms of the Governments of both Nations—and from a recollection of the early recognition of the Independence of this Republic by the Government of The United States, and their uniformly amicable disposition since, that, on consideration of their complaints, full justice will be done to the Citizens of The United States, and that measures will be taken to meet the disposition he feels for a strict commercial union, on principles of perfect reciprocity.

If the preliminary difficulties can be removed—the Undersigned has the pleasure to inform His Excellency that he is invested with Full Powers to conclude a Commercial Treaty with this Republic, on fair and reciprocal terms.

The Undersigned takes occasion, &c.

FRANCIS BAYLIES.

H. E. Senor Dr. Don Manuel V. de Maza.

(21.)—*The Buenos Ayres Minister to the American Chargé d'Affaires.*
(Translation.)   *Buenos Ayres,* 10*th July,* 1832.

WHEN the Undersigned, Minister of Grace and Justice, charged provisionally with the Department of Foreign Relations, acknowledged to the Chargé d'Affaires of The United States, the receipt of his Note dated the 20th ultimo, he expressed to him at the same time, that both with respect to the charges contained therein against Mr. Louis Vernet, and to the other points to which it referred, His Excellency the Governor would discharge his duty in a just and legal manner. Therefore, when the Government shall reply to the Chargé d'Affaires, on those subjects, it may then make the declaration which it may deem proper in behalf of its rights, without prejudice to those of any foreign, friendly or neutral Nations, or any of their Subjects. In the mean time, the Undersigned hopes that whatever may be the ideas which the Chargé d'Affaires of The United States entertains, respecting the conduct of Mr. Louis Vernet at the Malvinas, and the extent of the rights of the Argentine Republic, he will be aware that His Excellency the Governor cannot conscientiously form his opinion as to the nature of the facts, from isolated assertions, however respectable the party by whom they are advanced; and that he will much less judge it prudent to separate questions intimately connected, in order to anticipate an Answer, as the Chargé d'Affaires appears to desire in his Note of the 26th ult. The Undersigned, serving as a faithful organ to the wishes of his Excellency the Governor of this Province, cannot but assure the Chargé d'Affaires, that His Excellency, being resolved not to swerve from the principles of strict justice, which the patriotic and enlightened people of The United States will know how to appreciate, will conduct himself always with that pru-

dence and circumspection, which duty prescribes, in order in no instance to risk the correctness of his decisions.

The Undersigned, &c.

MANUEL VICENTE DE MAZA.

The Chargé d'Affaires of The United States.

(22.)—*The American Chargé d'Affaires to the Buenos Ayres Minister.*
Buenos Ayres, 11th July, 1832.

THE Undersigned, Chargé d'Affaires from the United States of
America near the Government of Buenos Ayres, has the honor to
acknowledge the receipt of the Communication from his Excellency
the Minister of Grace and Justice, charged provisionally with the
Department of Foreign Affairs, of yesterday's date.

Although under no obligation of courtesy so to do,—yet, before
the reception of the last Communication from His Excellency, the
Undersigned had prepared another Communication for his consideration; and had entertained the hope, that its contents when well considered, might lead to the adjustment of an unpleasant controversy,
on terms equally honorable to the Argentine Republic and the
United States of America.

As the object of the Undersigned is to make known, with perfect
frankness, the views of his own Government—and as he hopes to be
met with a corresponding spirit by this Government; although the
enquiry which he had the honor to make, in his Communication of
the 26th ultimo is not yet answered—yet, he now transmits the Communication which he had determined to place in his Excellency's
hands yesterday; and he takes the liberty to express the wish that the
final determination of the Government of the Argentine Republic may
be communicated to him, as speedily as the convenience of his Excellency will permit.

The Undersigned prays, &c.

H.E.Senor Dr. D. Manuel Vicente de Maza. **FRANCIS BAYLIES.**

(23.)—*The American Chargé d'Affaires to the Buenos Ayres Minister.*
Buenos Ayres, 6th August, 1832.

THE Undersigned, Chargé d'Affaires from the United States of
America near the Government of the Argentine Republic, takes the
liberty to remind His Excellency the Minister of Grace and Justice,
charged provisionally with the Department of Foreign Affairs, that, in
a Communication which he had the honor to submit to him, of date
June 20th—after a recapitulation of the outrages which had been
committed by the Military and Civic Governor of the Falkland Islands
and other Territories embraced in the Decree of June 10th, 1829, on
the persons and property of Citizens of the United States of America—he informed His Excellency that he was authorized and in-

structed by his Government to say, " that they utterly denied the
existence of any right in this Republic to interrupt, molest, detain, or
capture, any Vessels belonging to Citizens of The United States, engaged in taking Seals, or Whales, or any species of Fish or marine
animals, in any of the waters, or any of the shores or lands, of any, or
either, of the Falkland Islands, Tierra del Fuego, Cape Horn, or any
of the adjacent Islands in the Atlantic Ocean.''

The Undersigned also takes the liberty to represent—that, in
another Communication, of June 26th, he had also the honor to submit, on the part of his Government, an inquiry in simple and plain
terms, " wishing to know, distinctly, from the Government, whether
it claimed, on its part, any right or authority to detain or capture, or in
any way to molest, interrupt or impede, the Vessels or the Citizens of
The United States, while engaged in Fishing in the waters, or on the
shores, of the Falkland Islands and the other places already mentioned.".

This enquiry not being answered, the Undersigned, in another
Communication, of date July 10th, assumed the fact that the Argentine Republic did claim the right to exclude American Citizens from
the Fisheries of all the shores and seas included within the limits of
the civil and military Government of Don Louis Vernet; and, although
it was incumbent on this Government to take the affirmative and prove
their rights—inasmuch as force had been used in the assertion of those
rights—yet, to convince this Government of the amicable disposition
of the Government of The United States, and that the latter rested
their rights on principles from which they could not swerve—he
waved all technical advantages, and undertook to prove, that the Argentine Republic had not the rights which were claimed, and sub
mitted for the consideration of his Excellency, an argument founded
on the principles of international Law and on historical facts.

If the Undersigned has been so unfortunate as to fail to convince
His Excellency the Provisional Minister of Foreign Affairs, and the
Government whose organ he is, that the Argentine Republic has not
the rights which are claimed—he wishes to know it as speedily as the
convenience of His Excellency will permit; and if it is inconvenient
for His Excellency to reply at length to the several points which were
made in his Communication of July 10th—yet it will be satisfactory in
some respects (although unpleasant in others) to receive from His Excellency, as the organ of his Government, a formal and official assertion of this right to exclude American Citizens from the use of these
Fisheries, in terms as brief as His Excellency shall choose to make them.

If, on the other hand, the Undersigned should be so fortunate as
to find that his own opinions are in accordance with His Excellency's, and with those of the Government of the Argentine Republic,

touching these rights of Fishery—it would be satisfactory to him to know it.

The Undersigned takes this occasion, &c.

H. E. Dr. Don Manuel V. de Maza.   FRANCIS BAYLIES.

(24.)—*The Buenos Ayres Minister to the American Secretary of State.*
(Translation.)   *Buenos Ayres, 8th August,* 1832.

THE Undersigned, Minister of Grace and Justice, charged provisionally with the Department of Foreign Affairs of the Argentine Republic, has received orders from his Government to address the Secretary of State of the United States of North America, and manifest to him frankly and candidly, that from the time that, as a political step of paramount importance to the interest of both Countries, it resolved to suspend all official communication with Mr. George Washington Slacum, Consul of that Republic in this Capital, His Excellency the Governor deemed it his duty to make known to His Excellency the President of The United States, the motives which prompted that resolution. But the Ministers who had first intervened in the affair with Mr. Slacum having retired from Office, and the duties of the Department having subsequently devolved on other Members of the Administration, delay in the intended Communication became inevitable.

The Government of Buenos Ayres subsequently prepared to fulfil this duty, when, by the last Message of His Excellency the President of The United States, under date of the 6th December last, on the opening of Congress, received here on the 14th of February of the present year, it learned that a Minister from The United States was about to leave, for the purpose of "enquiring into the nature of the occurrences at the Malvinas." His Excellency the Governor then resolved to await the arrival of that Minister, confident that as soon as he should be enabled to judge from correct statements, of what had happened, and transmit to his Government the faithful result of his observations, the coolness of the conduct of the Buenos Ayres Government in its proceedings, with Mr. Slacum would not be misconstrued by the Cabinet of Washington, into a feeling unworthy of the Authorities of this Country.

The march of the Government had been so just and circumspect, and so imperious the necessity of refusing to Mr. Slacum his *accessit,* that it was desirous the whole affair should be closely examined into on the spot, in order to avoid that change of aspect it might otherwise be liable to at a distance, the which would tend to diminish the sympathy which His Excellency might otherwise expect from the wisdom and integrity of the Government of The United States.

But the opinions of Mr. Baylies, Chargé d'Affaires of The United States, in his first Note, rendered the hope remote, that he would admit the vindication of the Argentine Government to take precedence of the interest of a Person, to whom he appeared to have already listened with predilection, and whose restitution to the exercise of his Consular Office, he did not hesitate to demand 5 days after he entered on his Diplomatic Functions, apparently without having reflected on the danger attendant on precipitate and unmeditated demands. This being the case, it has become absolutely necessary for this Government to communicate directly with the Secretary of State of The United States, in order to place the facts before him in their true light.

As it will appear by the Copies, No. 1 to 9, herewith transmitted, Mr. Slacum, immediately on his becoming informed of the arrival of the American Schooner, *Harriet*, at this Port from the Malvinas, initiated before this Government an irregular question, and proposed to maintain the same on incorrect and indiscreet principles. The *Harriet*, with 2 other Schooners, the *Breakwater* and the *Superior*, had been detained by the Political and Military Commandant of the said Islands for having persisted in their Fishery, notwithstanding that since the year 1829 they had been formally notified that their Vessels and Cargoes would be confiscated if they continued to fish on the Coasts which were under the dominion of the Republic, and had been colonized under the protection of the Argentine Government. The *Harriet* was brought to this Port, not only for having infringed the public prohibition against Fishing within the jurisdiction of the Malvinas, but moreover by virtue of an express and solemn Agreement entered into between the Commandant of the Islands and Captain Davison, by which the latter bound himself to come and answer before the Government of Buenos Ayres, both for himself and as Representative of Captain Congar of the Schooner *Superior*, in the trial which should ensue, with regard to the seizure of their Vessels and Cargoes. The affair would necessarily be argued before the Tribunals of this Country, and no one without the most flagrant injustice could presume that an illegal decision would be given; or, that Captain Davison, or whoever else might be similarly situated, would be deprived of any means of defence, that might be adequate to the protection of their rights and interests. But Mr. Slacum, feigning to be ignorant of the principles on which this Government took upon itself to detain Captain Davison, an American Citizen, considered the act as calculated to disturb the friendship and good understanding existing with The United States.

The Government of Buenos Ayres had the strongest reasons for considering this step as preliminary to others, which might place it in the necessity of refusing every kind of interference on the part of Mr. Slacum, in the questions relating to the Malvinas. But for the present it limited itself solely to replying to him that the case of the *Harriet* was in a course of judicial procedure, and that it would be decided in conformity with the Laws of the Country.

After such a declaration, which involved a national responsibility as to the result of the trial thus initiated, with respect to the Case of the *Harriet* ; and since that, on the one side, the parties interested were secured from the damages, costs, and prejudices, that might arise thereon, and on the other there existed the express Deed of Agreement, which will be found in Paper No. 11 , it was not to be expected that Mr. Slacum would persist tenaciously in his interference.

But far from terminating here an affair which, from its nature, involved other questions of a higher order, the discussion of which solely belonged to the 2 Governments, or at least to Functionaries of a more elevated class than a mere Consul, Mr. Slacum went so far as not only to deny, *in toto*, that any right either has existed or does exist in the Republic to detain American Vessels engaged in the Fishery of Seals on the Malvinas, and the Islands and Coasts adjacent to Cape Horn ; but furthermore to protest formally against all the measures that in virtue of such right had been adopted, including the Decree published under date of the 10th June, 1829, by which the property in the Islands and Fisheries was asserted, and an Administrative Authority established in the name of the Republic, that is to say, denying the sovereignty which the Argentine Republic exercises over these Islands.

It is not necessary to comment on the terms of this Protest in order to estimate its importance. Many years had elapsed since that, under the very eye of a Chargé d'Affaires of The United States, the Colony in the Malvinas was founded by order of the Argentine Government. The Commission granted on the 10th of June, 1829, in favor of Don Luis Vernet, appointing him Military and Political Commandant of the said Islands, with competent authority and jurisdiction, was published in the Newspapers of this Capital, when neither Mr. Forbes thought proper to make the slightest objection thereto ; nor was any other individual of The United States hardy enough to call in question the right of the Republic to dispose, as it might deem proper, of a Territory belonging to the Argentine State, such as it had been acknowledged to be, without contradiction, by the Government of Washington itself.

But on what grounds could Mr. Slacum call this right a question ? Could he be ignorant that the Malvina Islands, Coasts of Patagonia and its adjacencies unto Cape Horn, were comprehended in the territorial delineations of the Kings of Spain, as constituting an integral part of the former Vice Royalty of Buenos Ayres, since erected into a Nation by the will and efforts of its Sons? Could Mr. Slacum doubt that the right acquired by the Court of Spain, to what it had discovered, conquered, possessed, and occupied, as well on the Continent as in the Islands adjacent to the aforesaid Vice Royalty, has descended, as a fundamental right to the Argentines, from the instant

they asserted their Nationality and Independence, and formed themselves into a Republic; in the same manner that the right to those
Territories which had been discovered, conquered, possessed, and occupied by England in North America, descended to its Sons with
jurisdictional authority, which the United States duly appropriated to
themselves? If Mr. Slacum has wished to deny the right of Spain to
the Sovereignty of the Malvinas, and the Islands adjacent, has he forgotten that, as often as they have been occupied by English or French
Colonists—so often have they again been given up, in virtue of remonstrances from the Court of Spain; and that, although the Fishery and
Traffic of these Islands was formerly an object of serious controversy,
Spain, nevertheless, was at all times firm in her resistance, which was,
at length, acquiesced in, from a just respect to the Sovereignty which
she exercised over them? Without adducing, for the present, those
reasons, which, in proper time, will completely elucidate this question,
it sufficed that the Government of Buenos Ayres had the power to impose or remove the restrictions which, of right, appertain to her to
adopt, as to the Fishery of amphibious animals in the Malvinas; it
was sufficient that the detention of the *Harriet*, and the other 2
Schooners alluded to, could be conciliated with the common Law of
Nations, to shew, that the Protest of Mr. Slacum was as extravagant
as it was foreign to his Consular functions. Nevertheless, the Government limited itself to signifying to Mr. Slacum, that the legal investigation which was in process, in the case of the *Harriet*, was only
intended to place it in possession of the truth, in order to decide as
justice might prescribe; and that it could not acknowledge that he, in
his Consular character, had authority to enter such Protest.

Thus far had the Ministerial Correspondence been carried on, when
Mr. Slacum transmitted, to the Department of Foreign Affairs, the
Letter of Mr. Duncan, Commander of the United States Ship, *Lexington*, announcing his intention to sail for the Malvinas, with the Force
under his Command, for the purpose of protecting the Citizens and
commerce of The United States in the Fishery in question; disguising,
under apparent candor, the perfidious machinations which were in con-
certation. Mr. Slacum's Note was dated the 3rd of December,—and
by another, under date of the 6th, he stated that Captain Duncan
would delay his departure, solely, until the morning of the 9th, in the
hope that, in the mean time, he might receive intelligence of the
Orders of this Government to leave unrestricted the right of free
Fishery to the North Americans; to restore to the Owners or Agents
of the Schooner, *Harriet*, the Vessel and Cargo; and, at the same
time, to withdraw from the Military and Civil Commandant of the
Malvinas all powers of interference in the Traffic in which the Citizens
of The United States were engaged on the Coasts thereof.

It now became easy to discover through the veil which disguised these demands, the strict connivance which existed between the Commander of the *Lexington* and Mr. Slacum, and that the latter, regardless of the unassuming pretensions of the Ministry, endeavored to give a dark coloring to the faithful picture which Commandant Vernet had pourtrayed in the publications made by him, relative to every thing connected with the detention of the Schooners in Malvinas. But the Government, firm in its resolution not to depart from a benevolent and equitable line of conduct, notified Mr Slacum, on the 9th of the same Month, that Mr. Gilbert Davison, of the *Harriet*, who had embarked on board the American Corvette, *Lexington*, ought not to absent himself without leaving some proper Person empowered to represent him; and urged him at the same time to make it known to the Party interested, as in the case either of his refusal or omission to do so, he would subject himself to all the damages, costs, and prejudices, consequent thereon. The Government took advantage of the opportunity thus afforded it, to advise Mr. Slacum, that, although it did not acknowledge the authority, which he wished to arrogate to himself since the death of Mr. Forbes, yet it could not do otherwise than make him sensible of the surprise it felt, that he should have desired to circumscribe to the precise time fixed for the departure of the *Lexington*, the decision of a private litigated affair, in which, in the exercise of his Consular functions, he could have no interference; and which, having to be tried and decided on, in conformity with the Laws of the Country, demanded a serious and lengthened consideration, in order to avoid committing any act of injustice. Above all, Mr. Slacum was informed that any proceeding that might have a tendency to disavow the right of the Argentine Republic to the Malvinas, and other Islands and Coasts adjacent to Cape Horn, would give rise to a formal remonstrance which the Government would make to that of The United States, under the firm conviction that it would meet with just attention.

Neither the repeated incivilities of Mr. Slacum—his continued transgression of the limits of his Consular duty, in endeavouring to turn the natural course of the affair of the Malvinas, already subject to legal procedure; nor, finally, the known circumstance of his mercantile connexion, so foreign to the duty of a Public Functionary, who nevertheless took part in these questions, could induce the Government to depart from the position it had taken, in order to give His Excellency the President of The United States an incontestible proof of the coolness and moderation by which the Administration of the Republic was regulated. Nevertheless, after all these unpleasant occurrences, it preserved towards Mr. Slacum the same immunities and acts of courtesy which it had paid to any other Consul resident in this Capital; because the wisdom, probity and circumspection of the Cabinet of Washington presented a pledge of confidence by far too respectable for it to doubt that, in its judgment, it would incline itself in favor of the rights and dignity of the Argentine Government, whose friendly disposition ought never to be doubted either by the Government or the People of North America. Thus elapsed more than 2 months, when the Government of Buenos Ayres was surprised by the receipt of the unexpected news of the attack made by the Ship-of-War *Lexington*, on the Colony established in Malvinas, on the Island of Soledad,—which was effected, without any resistance, on the 31st December last, by her Commander, Duncan, who spiked the artillery, fired the magazine, disposed of the public and private property, and carried on board, in arrest, the person entrusted with the preservation of the Colonial Fishery—loaded with irons 6 Citizens of the Republic, and atrociously destroyed the fruits of many years' honest industry— vulnerating at the same time the rights and respect due to a friendly Nation. This outrage, in the execution of which Mr. Duncan spared no means to render it as humiliating and scandalous as possible, in the eyes of the World, awakened a just resentment in a People jealous of their prerogatives—who were conscious of not having offended—and who, since their emancipation from Spain, had never omitted one single act of benevolence or generous hospitality towards the Citizens of The United States. It moreover compromised the highest duties of the Government, obliging it to coincide with the public opinion which designated Mr. Slacum, if not as the active coadjutor of this un- heard of aggression, at least as the blind tool of a misguided opinion, and whose example probably had stimulated Captain Duncan to perpetrate this shameful assault upon a peaceable Settlement, subject to the Authority and the Laws of the Argentine Republic.

From the moment this opinion with regard to Mr. Slacum became a National feeling—from the moment the Government was obliged to look upon him with displeasure and suspicion, he could no longer be a proper organ to promote the interests of his Country ; he could no longer be admitted in his public character without wounding the dignity of the Argentine Republic, nor without acting in opposition to the opinion of its Citizens, and consequently diminishing that confi- dence which it is the duty of the Authorities to inspire.

Acting upon this principle, on the 14th of February, it notified to Mr. Slacum the suspension of all Official Communication with him— inviting him to nominate some Person duly qualified to exercise his Consular Functions, as will appear by the authorized Copy No. 12,— and at the same time guarantying the Persons and Property of the North Americans with every security in the power of a civilized and humane Government.

From the candid exposition the Undersigned has thus made, by order of his Government, to His Excellency the Secretary of State of The United States, of the course the Ministerial Correspondence with

Mr. Slacum had taken, and the causes which have influenced the conduct of the Government, the Undersigned is persuaded—

1. That, in the mind of his Excellency the President of The United States, the motives for delaying this Communication, will be deemed justifiable.

2. That, during the progress of this disagreeable controversy, the Government has omitted no effort to bring the question to a legal issue.

3. That the refusal to hold further Communication with Mr. Slacum, was not only a consequence strictly allied to the dignity of the first Authority in the Country, but likewise that his Excellency, in making use of the rights inherent to his Office, and in all respects conformable with the customs of other Nations, has left nothing undone in order to secure the interests of the Americans.

The Undersigned, in renewing on this occasion the sincere wishes of his Government to maintain inviolate the friendship and good understanding between The United States and the Argentine Republic, permits himself to join his own to this national feeling, and salutes His Excellency the Minister, &c.

MANUEL VICENTE DE MAZA.

The Secretary of State of The United States.

(25.)—*The Buenos Ayres Minister to the American Chargé d'Affaires.*
(Translation.) *Buenos Ayres, 14th August, 1832.*

THE Undersigned Minister of Grace and Justice, charged provisionally with the Department of Foreign Relations of the Argentine Republic, has the honor to state, that Mr. Louis Vernet, Political and Military Commandant of the Malvina Islands, having rendered the Report which the Government had required from him, (an authorized Copy whereof is herewith transmitted,) relative to certain charges and complaints which the Chargé d'Affaires of The United States adduced in his first Note dated in this City the 20th of June last, His Excellency, the Governor of this Province, has taken into consideration, as well the before-mentioned Note as the 4 subsequent ones under the dates of 26th of the same month of June, 10th and 11th of July and 6th of the present month of August, which his Honor has been pleased to address to the Undersigned.

Having scrupulously examined and meditated on the contents of the before-mentioned Notes, he observes that, in the first, the Chargé d'Affaires of The United States proposed with earnest solicitude to draw the attention of His Excellency, principally and almost exclusively, towards certain proceedings of Mr. Louis Vernet, who claimed, under a Decree of the Government of this Province, dated June 10th,

1829, to be Civil and Military Commandant of the Malvina Islands and all those adjacent to Cape Horn (including Tierra del Fuego,) in the Atlantic Ocean; forming on such proceedings various complaints and charges against the aforesaid Commandant, and declaring himself authorized to utterly deny the existence of any right in this Republic to interrupt, molest, detain or capture any Vessel belonging to the United States of North America, or any Persons whatsoever, being Citizens of those States, engaged in taking Seals or Whales, or any species of fish or marine animal in any of the waters, or on any of the shores or lands of any or either of the Malvina Islands, Tierra del Fuego, Cape Horn, or any of the adjacent Islands in the Atlantic Ocean. In consequence thereof, and of the outrages committed by Mr. Louis Vernet on the Persons and property of American Citizens, his Honor demanded the restitution of all captured property belonging to the said Citizens, which may be at present in the possession of this Government or in that of Mr. Louis Vernet; remonstrating also against his appointment as Civil and Military Governor of the Malvinas, Tierra del Fuego and other Islands in the Atlantic Ocean adjacent to Cape Horn, and claiming ample indemnity for all other property of American Citizens which may have been seized, sold or destroyed, by the said Vernet or any Persons acting under his orders; and full and ample immunity and reparation for all consequential losses and damages arising therefrom, together with full indemnity to all American Citizens for personal wrongs, whether resulting from detention, imprisonment, or personal indignities.

In reply, the Undersigned, in his Note of the 25th June, had the honor to make known to the Chargé d'Affaires of The United States, that the Government had resolved under that date to require from Mr. Louis Vernet, explanations on all and every subject of complaint against his public conduct, in the cases resting on his responsibility; and that when it should be enabled to form its opinion thereon, as well from what the said Vernet might set forth as from the grounds on which his Honor founded his remonstrances, His Excellency would then discharge his duty, without infringing the individual rights of the Citizens of North America who may prove to have been aggrieved or injured, and likewise without sacrificing to exorbitant pretentions the rights of Mr. Louis Vernet; and much less the public ones, which, by the common Law of Nations, belong to the Argentine Republic, as a sovereign and independent State.

After the Undersigned addressed to the Chargé d'Affaires the Communication alluded to, his Honor, in a Note of 26th of same month, endeavored to maintain that such explanations were unnecessary, inasmuch as Mr. Louis Vernet had publicly acknowledged under his own signature the fact of the capture of the American Vessels, as if this were the only charge and complaint brought forward by the Chargé d'Affaires; thus shewing his desire to vary the course of the Negotiation, since, without desisting from the charges he had adduced, or from the denial of the right of the Argentine Republic to the Malvina Islands, &c., he limited himself principally to exact (insisting on the same in his subsequent Note of 11th July) that this Government should declare, whether on its part it claimed to have any right or authority to detain or capture, or otherwise molest, interrupt or impede, the Vessels or the Citizens of The United States, employed in fishing in the waters on the Coasts of the Malvina Islands, and the other before-mentioned Places.

This want of stability, evinced in the first step taken by the Chargé d'Affaires, is, in the opinion of the Government, an indication of the violent efforts which his Honor makes to present as an incidental consequence of the principal point in discussion, the daring and cruel outrage committed in the said Islands by Mr. Duncan, Commander of the United States' Ship-of-War, *Lexington*, destroying in a time of profound peace, with rancorous fury, and in a manner alike perfidious and ferocious, a Settlement which had been formed publicly by this Government, without meeting at the time any opposition, and of which it had subsequently remained in full possession, in virtue of the indisputable right it had, and still has, to those Islands.

His Excellency believes that he should have been guilty of a breach of duty, had he dissembled, in a case of such marked incon-congruity, by listening to the pretensions of the Chargé d'Affaires. The barbarous act, committed by Mr. Duncan, in contempt of the established customs of Civilized Nations, and the courtesy which they invariably observe towards each other, is the point which should take precedence in the consideration of both Governments. It has attracted the public attention in every part where the news of that heinous outrage has reached—it has excited the disgust of all those who possess sentiments of justice and humanity—it has intensely wounded the honor and dignity of both Republics, by contemning and outraging the Argentine, and tarnishing and detracting from the credit and reputation which The United States have ever merited.

The truth is as ostensible, as it is easy to be felt. In order, however, to render it more palpable, the Undersigned will, for an instant, admit all his Honor has alleged, in support of his assertion, "that the Argentine Republic has no right whatever to the said Islands;" he will also admit that the Government of this Province, having acted under a mistaken belief, in conceding to Commandant Vernet the exclusive right to the Seal Fishery on those Coasts—which the latter claims and defends in behalf of himself and of his Colonists—that that right was null and void, and, consequently, that the capture of the *Harriet*, *Superior*, and *Breakwater*, was an unjust act. Even so: after these momentary gratuitous concessions—as Commandant

Vernet acted under the belief that he was merely exercising the same right by which he who considers himself robbed, apprehends the thief with the stolen property in his possession, and carries him before the nearest Authority to which he is subordinate, in order that he may receive justice at its hands—it is evident that the capture which the said Vernet made, can never be construed into an offence from Nation to Nation, or even as a formal act of injustice between man and man. The worst conclusion that could be drawn from it would be, that it was a fault committed in good faith, under a wrong impression, and for which the Captor was in nowise culpable.

In such a case, what ought to be done in conformity with the rights of Nations, and the established practice of all civilized People, who admit the principles of justice and moderation for the standard of their conduct? What course should be followed, in order to preserve peace and harmony among the general society of Nations, and to cause right to be respected by means of reason and conviction? Is it, perchance, that any Commander of a Vessel, belonging to the Nation of the captured Party, should take upon himself to destroy the place to which the Captor belonged, load the Inhabitants with irons, carry them captive to Foreign Lands, and despoil them of their property? Certainly not: such conduct would never have been resorted to towards powerful Nations, such as England and France; it could only take place by an ignoble abuse of strength against weakness, or between savage people, who know no other law than the dictates of their own passions, and who adopt no other method to obtain redress for their real or fancied injuries, but such as a blind and ferocious revenge instigate.

Every Sovereign Government has the exclusive right of judging its own Subjects within the limits of its own Dominions; and, in the exercise of this right, it should be considered sufficiently just to oblige them by legal means to make reparation for any loss or grievance they may cause to a Foreigner. In this respect, the presumptions are always in its favour, so long as there is no positive evidence to the contrary. Hence it is, that the rational and just measure which, in the supposed case, ought to have been adopted by the Captain of the *Harriet*, is the same which is admitted by all civilized Nations in the World, when a Privateer, through error, in fact, or in right, unjustly captures either a Merchant or Fishing Vessel, and carries her, with her Captain, before the competent Authority of the Country under whose Flag he cruizes. Captain Davison ought to have laid his complaint against Commandant Vernet before the Authorities of the Province, have justified his proceedings upon the same principles (or others,) which are at present adduced by the Chargé d'Affaires, and, consequently, demanded reparation for all losses and injuries which **Mr. Louis Vernet, as Commandant of Malvinas, had caused him.**

If the Authorities, admitting the justice of the claim, granted reparation, the affair would then have concluded in a rational and pacific manner; but, if on the contrary, redress were denied, that even would not form sufficient grounds for insulting the Argentine Flag, or justify the commission of such a violent and inhuman outrage, as that perpetrated by Captain Duncan. There still remained recourse to the pacific means of Negotiation—and if, by Negotiation, no redress could be obtained for notorious injustice, then, and not until then, should force be resorted to; not, however, by a Commander of a Vessel, rushing, as he did, by surprise and with deceit, like a Robber or a Pirate, upon a defenceless Settlement, unsuspicious of danger, in a time of profound peace, and relying on the good faith of all Nations: but, by adhering to all those previous forms and ceremonies as hitherto invariably observed, and which, in the present day, more than ever most scrupulously influence the councils and resolves of every civilized Nation, before declaring War against another. Vattel, whom the Chargé d'Affaires has quoted in one of his Notes, in support of his arguments, says, in Book the 2nd, Chap. 18th, Paragraph 354, " That those who have recourse to arms, without necessity, are a scourge to the human race, are barbarous enemies to Society, and rebels against the Law of Nature, or rather against the Laws of the common Father of Mankind."

Captain Davison and the Ex-Consul Slacum did not act in conformity to this doctrine. Both refused to adhere to a proper line of conduct. The former preferred to abscond from his Vessel, in the face of an official Communication from the then Minister of Foreign Relations, Dr. D. Tomas Manuel de Anchorena, addressed to the latter at the petition of Commandant Vernet; to the effect that he would intimate to the said Captain that if he absented himself from the Country, he should leave an Agent properly instructed in the cause under procedure, in relation to his capture, in which the before-mentioned Vernet was desirous he should answer to the charges he intended to bring against him. The Ex-Consul refused to convey that intimation; he engaged in opportune and extemporaneous questions infinitely beyond his official character, going to the extreme of adopting uncourteous language, inconsistent with that modest respect with which the Government of every Sovereign State ought to be addressed. At the same time Captain Duncan, interfering in the affair, had the audacity to write to the before-mentioned Minister in an uncivil and impolite manner.

All irregularity, injustice, insult and violence, have therefore been on the part of Messrs. Slacum and Duncan, but the more especially on that of the latter, for having carried to the last extremity his grossness and ferocity, destroying with unspeakable inhumanity and perfidy the Colony of Malvina Islands. Thus have they openly contemned, depressed and outraged the dignity of the Argentine People, with manifest dishonor to their own Nation and Government.

In the presence of such evident and scandalous aggressions, which do not admit of doubt or denial, it becomes the duty of the Government of this Province, acting for itself and as charged with the Foreign Affairs of the Republic, to demand, before all things, from the Government of the United States of America the most prompt and ample satisfaction for such outrages, and full redress and reparation to the Argentine Republic, to Commandant Vernet, and to the Colonists under his jurisdiction in the Malvina Islands, for all the damages and losses of whatever nature they may be, which they have suffered and are suffering in consequence of the aggressions committed by Captain Duncan.

In virtue of this, and seeing that the Chargé d'Affaires of The United States has declared that he is fully authorized to treat on the subject, the Undersigned has orders from his Government to demand from his Honor, as he now does in the most solemn and formal manner, the already expressed prompt and ample satisfaction, reparation and indemnity, for all damages and losses incurred.

The Government, notwithstanding its full confidence in the magnanimity and rectitude of principles which that of The United States has ever evinced; and although it is persuaded that the latter will not deny the absolute justice of this demand, or that it is bound in honor to accede to it; nevertheless, as the nature of the question requires this mode of proceeding; and as, on the other hand, it most deeply affects the honor and dignity of the Argentine Republic, it has not been able to avoid adopting the resolution just expressed.

The Undersigned has likewise received orders to state to the Chargé d'Affaires of the United States of America, that, until this Government shall have obtained its demands, it will not enter into the discussion of any of the other points comprised in the before-mentioned Notes of his Honor, inasmuch as this would be equivalent to passing over the acts of Captain Duncan, of which the Undersigned neither can or ought to lose sight for an instant. And on making this authorised declaration, he does not hesitate to assure the Chargé d'Affaires, that, in the mean time, his Government will exercise its rights in the manner it may deem proper.

The Undersigned, &c.

MANUEL VICENTE DE MAZA.
The Chargé d'Affaires of The United States.

(Enclosure)—Report of the Political, and Military Commandant of the Malvinas.　　　　　(Translation.)

EXCELLENT SIR,　　　　　　*Buenos Ayres,* 10th *August,* 1832.

YOUR Excellency has been pleased to furnish me with a Copy of a series of Charges which Mr. Baylies, Chargé d'Affaires of The

United States, in his Note of the 20th of June, has brought forward on the opening of the Negotiation relative to the Malvina Islands ; to the end, that, informing myself of its contents, *I may reply in a manner at once clear, frank and diffuse.* It is gratifying to me to find summed up all the Charges directed against me, and to have thus afforded me an opportunity to rebut them at one and the same time ; removing, perhaps, by this means, the principal obstacles the Government may have to encounter in the progress of the Negotiation now commenced. In the execution of this agreeable and delicate task, I shall not allow myself to be influenced by the example before me,—I shall not allow myself to be carried away by resentments, however just,—in fine, I shall not forget that I am addressing the Chief Authority of a civilized Country.

Long, indeed, is the list of accusations which the Chargé d'Affaires brings against me. To proceed distinctly, I shall compress them to what is essentially necessary, and present them in a reduced but correct point of view.

CHARGE 1.—" On the 30th day of July, 1831, the American Schooner *Harriet*, while engaged in lawful business, was captured by my orders, and the Captain and Crew, with the exception of the Mate, Cook and Steward, placed in confinement. I forcibly took the Vessel's Papers, and several articles of provisions, which I sold, without previous condemnation. I did the same on the 17th and 19th of August following, with the Schooner *Breakwater*, Capt. Carew, (with the difference that the Crew of this Vessel succeeded in escaping with her, and reaching their own Country,) and the Schooner *Superior*, Capt. Congar."

I could not have believed, that, after having so completely refuted all those points in the representation I presented to the Tribunal, which took cognizance of the seizure, and which has been printed, and must consequently have been read by the Chargé d'Affaires, that such futile and unjust accusations would have again been brought forward. I refer to that representation, and I will add, by way of *memorandum,* that I therein demonstrated,—1st, That in the year 1829, I found the *Harriet* loaded with Seal skins which had been taken in that jurisdiction. I generously permitted her to depart with her Cargo, warning her that in case of the recurrence of the offence, both Vessel and Cargo would be confiscated ; and, to make the notification more complete, as she returned again in 1830, I delivered the Captain a Circular containing the same general warning. 2d, That, in violation of this solemn prohibition, which I was expressly charged by the Government to promulgate and carry into effect, as Governor of that District, those 3 Vessels continued the same traffic, and were consequently detained, together with every thing belonging to them, to be arraigned before the competent Tribunal ; which voluntary violation has been confessed and admitted by the Captains of the *Harriet* and *Superior*, in the

Contract we afterwards entered into. 3d, That I received by inventory all that was on board the *Harriet*, but nothing was touched belonging to the *Superior*, as it was not necessary, nor of the *Breakwater*, as she made her escape. 4th, That a small part of the articles belonging to the *Harriet*, that is to say, provisions, were of necessity divided amongst the Colonists, in order to neutralize the effect of the presents Capt. Davison had clandestinely and prodigally distributed amongst some of them; as it was but just that such of the Colonists as remained faithful should not be deprived of that which the others enjoyed; and it being once necessary to make the distribution, it could only be done in the way I adopted; that is, by distributing the provisions by rations to such as were on duty, and by selling them to those who were not; the which could cause no injury to the Owners of the *Harriet*, for, if she should not ultimately be condemned, the value of these provisions, which would scarcely have amounted to 100 dollars, was secured to them by the inventory taken. 5th, That a great part of those articles still existed at the period of my departure from Malvinas, and another part still more considerable was distributed amongst the Crew of the *Harriet* and the Passengers who went in the *Elbe*, and served also to provision the *Superior* when she sailed afterwards to the southward. And I now add, that, with respect to the Papers, I not only had authority to seize them, but it was my duty so to do, as Captor of the Vessel, in order that they might be produced on the trial. 6th. That the restraint (not confinement, for he was not one instant imprisoned,) imposed on Davison by placing a guard to prevent his communicating with the Vessel or Crew, was a measure which his bad conduct rendered necessary,—one of those precautionary measures which every Government can legally adopt in times of extraordinary peril. Davison and his Crew were at liberty, and what was the result?—the seduction which he had begun to practice, and the formal preparations for a conspiracy, which would have caused blood to flow, and have annihilated a weak Colony. Then it was that the Crew were imprisoned, but only for the short space of time which elapsed prior to the voluntary departure of the Conspirators for Rio Janeiro.

All this and much more has been demonstrated in the representation of which I now accompany a printed Copy, in order that your Excellency may be pleased to transmit it to the Chargé d'Affaires. I therefore consider it unnecessary to enlarge more on these particulars, although in the reply to the other charges I may perhaps touch on some of them again. For the present I have only to remark : 1st. That the facts related have been all proved in the course of the trial, as may be seen by the Papers relative thereto, and the Chargé d'Affaires can call for certified Copies of them if he deem proper. 2nd, That the competent Tribunal has declared the said Vessels to be lawful Prizes and consequently has justified my proceedings.

But the Chargé d'Affaires has brought forward other Charges still more unfounded, so much so, that even the Ex-Consul Slacum, notwithstanding the levity and causticity, with which he conducted himself in this serious affair, was not bold enough to advance them. Let us proceed to examine them.

CHARGE 2.—" The Captain of the *Breakwater*, who remained in Malvinas with 4 men when that Vessel made her escape, desired to come to Buenos Ayres, but nevertheless I compelled him to go to Rio de Janeiro in a British Vessel."

All the individuals of the Crews of the 3 Schooners who sailed for Rio de Janeiro in this British Vessel (*Elbe*), which I had freighted, and which was the only one that then offered, went, because they chose to do so, with the express knowledge and consent of the Captain ; and not because they were compelled to it. This also will be found proved in the before-mentioned Papers. For the rest, this is the first time I have heard that the Captain of the *Breakwater* desired to come to this place in the *Harriet* in which I myself came ; and with the same frankness I will now say, that had I known it and even had he solicited me, I would not have consented to it. The *Harriet* brought only 4 men of my confidence. Captain Davison came in her, and it would have been a stupid imprudence, which might have been fatal to me, had I consented that Carew should have accompanied us, inasmuch as, even when I was in the very centre of my resources in the Colony, they had barefacedly set on foot a conspiracy. And was I to give them the opportunity of effecting it with more facility on board the *Harriet ?* I can prove that, at the time we sailed, Davison had formed the design of running away with the Vessel.

CHARGE 3.—" I forced the Captain and Crew of the *Superior*, with the Vessel, into my private service and for my personal interest. I induced them to enter into a mercantile Contract, in pursuance of which, they were to go to the South, beyond my jurisdiction, for the purpose of taking Seals on my account. In this written Agreement, they were induced to confess that their Vessels had been seized by me, as Civil and Military Governor, for having violated the Laws of the Republic, notwithstanding they had been previously warned not to do so. Regardless of the usages of Nations, I compelled these individuals, who were depressed by imprisonment and sufferings, to bind themselves by oaths to do nothing to compromise my interests ; and to agree that any infraction of this Contract should be considered as a breach of good faith, and that no Laws should liberate them from the penalties and forfeitures, which in that case I might deem proper ;—all for the purpose of securing my piratical interests. In this mode, instead of bringing the infractors to trial, I obliged them to enter into my service for my personal interest. I substituted myself in the place of the Owners of the Vessel. I degraded my Government in my official character, by transforming myself into a merchant, and by calling myself, in the Contract, Director of the Colony, instead of Civil and Military Governor."

How many facts, how many considerations, all equally striking, crowd here, Excellent Sir! Not the least important is, that a man requires a great command over his feelings to avoid steeping his pen in gall, when with such irritating and poignant injustice he finds himself represented, in a diplomatic Document, as a debased character, a high-sea robber, in short, Sir, as a *Pirate!* But I have determined to suppress my just resentments . I owe this sacrifice to the dignity of the Government I address, and to the respect which I sincerely profess for that of the great Nation, which the Chargé d'Affaires represents.

I will endeavor, therefore, to arrange and express my ideas, with order, on the various particulars embraced in this Charge.

After the escape of the *Breakwater*, the Captains of the *Harriet* and *Superior* waited on me one day and submitted to me certain proposals, which, after being duly considered, produced in result the Contract referred to, which is literally as follows :

" The Schooner *Harriet*, Captain R. Gilbert Davison, of Stonington, and the Schooner *Superior*, Captain Stephen Congar, of New York, having been seized for Sealing at the Falkland Islands and Staten-land, contrary to warning given them ; and being therefore about to be sent to Buenos Ayres to stand their trial; and said Captains considering the delays that often attend such trials, having suggested that it would be for the interest of all concerned, that only one Vessel be sent to Buenos Ayres, with the Papers and Documents respecting the seizure of both, and the other be permitted to go to a newly discovered, promising, Sealing ground, on the West Coast of South America; provided that satisfactory security could be given for the timely reappearance of such Sealing Vessels ; and Lewis Vernet, Esq., Director of the Colony of Port Louis, East Falkland Island, having taking upon himself the responsibility of said Vessels' re-appearance; has entered into the following Agreement with the aforesaid Captains, in the name of their respective Owners, viz :—

ART. 1.—It shall be left at the option of the said Lewis Vernet, Esq., to determine which of the 2 Vessels shall proceed on said Sealing voyage; which he shall determine within 24 hours after this Agreement has been signed, and state his choice in an Additional Article at the foot of this Agreement,—then the skins now belonging to such Vessel, shall be deposited in the hands of Mr. Vernet, and shall share the fate of the Vessel to which they belong, with respect to condemnation or liberation, in which latter case to be delivered to the Master of the Vessel to which they belonged, or to the persons authorised by him to receive them: after which such Vessel shall be fitted out with all convenient speed with the provisions, salt, stoves, and Sealing implements, of both Vessels, and be manned with such men as the Master of such Sealing Vessel shall consider best calculated for Sealing, and may be able to obtain; the whole Ship's Company signing for the purpose such Ship's Articles as the fulfilment of this Agreement shall require:

2.—The Vessel thus equipped and ready for sea, shall proceed from hence direct through the Straits of Magellan to the Sealing ground, on the West Coast of South America, where, according to information obtained from Capt. Low of the Brig *Adeona*, and from part of his Crew left on this Island, great quantities of fur Seal were lately seen by them; and, for the better finding of which place it is mutually agreed upon by the Contracting Parties to employ —— Clarke as Pilot,—the same having lately belonged to the *Adeona*, and considering himself competent to find the place; and the Vessel, after having obtained the cargo of Seal skins, or done her best to obtain one, shall, at the end of the season, return direct to Port Louis (dangers of the seas only excepted) and anchor in the basin where she now lays; then the voyage shall be considered as ended, and the Vessel and Cargo to be delivered up to Mr. Vernet upon the condition stated in the following Article.

3.—It is understood by the 2 Contracting Parties, that the said intended Sealing voyage shall be for account of Mr. Vernet if the Vessels are condemned, and for the Owners in America if not condemned, viz.: one half for each Owner in America, and whether condemned, or not condemned, the skins shall be counted, and the Ship's Company shall then immediately receive in skins the share that, according to the ship's Articles are due to them; after which, Mr. Vernet obligates himself, according as the result of the trial, that is to take place in Buenos Ayres, may be; that is in case of liberation, to deliver the remaining skins (that is the whole, less the quantity delivered to the Ship's Company according to the Ship's Articles) to the Captain of the Vessel, as lawful agent of both Owners in America, and in case of condemnation, Mr. Vernet shall keep said remaining skins; and, in order to avoid differences and doubts arising from unforeseen events, as well as to secure more expeditiously the pay of the Ship's company at all events, (save dangers of the seas); it is also understood, that if, after a trial in Buenos Ayres, there should be a decision different from a full condemnation or a full liberation of both Vessels and Cargoes,—such as, that only one Vessel being condemned and the other liberated, or the Vessels liberated and the Cargoes condemned, or the Vessels condemned and the Cargoes liberated, or one or more parts being liberated, on the payment of a sum of money, being imposed by the Court that tried them in Buenos Ayres, or the like unforeseen events,—in that case the Sealing voyage shall be considered as having been made, one half for account of Mr. Vernet, and the other half for account of the Owners in America, and the skins to be divided accordingly, each paying previously, to the Ship's Company in Port Louis, the pay due according to the Ship's Articles, constituting thus a full pay.

4.—The Master of the Sealing Vessel shall obligate himself by a solemn oath, that he will neither by word or deed, in any manner or shape, do on this present voyage any thing that can compromise the interest of Mr. Vernet, in the responsibility that he has taken upon himself, by the delivery of the Vessel to said Master for the intended voyage; but rather to counteract any evil disposition that might perhaps be displayed or suspected in others under his command, which obligation he will act up to in good faith, without seeking excuses; in short, to be guided by the principle 'to do as he would be done by,' and for the easier fulfilling of this Article, the Master will endeavor as much as possible to avoid a communication with other Sealers on this present voyage, unless he should meet any in distress or be in distress himself, and he shall not be required by Mr. Vernet to do any thing on this voyage that is in any way unlawful.

5.—This Agreement shall not invalidate the right that the Owners in America might think they have to claim damages, which claim of damages shall, however, with respect to skins, not exceed 2500 prime fur Seal skins, for each of the 2 Vessels, in case the Sealing Vessel gets no skins at all; but if she gets any skins, then the above number shall be lessened, according to the number that she may have acquired on the present voyage.

6.—The Sealing Vessel, being then delivered into the hands of the Master, with a Crew of his own choice, without further security than his word, any wilful deviation from this Agreement (of which at present there is not the most distant idea,) shall be considered a breach of faith; and no Laws shall liberate him from the penalty and forfeitures incurred according to the following Article.

7.—For the true and faithful fulfilment of this Agreement, the Contracting Parties, Captain Stephen Congar and Captain Gilbert R. Davison, for themselves, and in the names of their Owners, on the one part, and Mr. Lewis Vernet on the other part, solemnly bind themselves in the penal sum of 5000 dollars, and the forfeiture of their respective shares in the voyage alluded to in this Document; which forfeitures shall be applicable in favor of the party that fulfils the Agreement.

Given under our Hands and Seals in Port Louis, East Falkland Island, this 8th day of September, 1831.

(L.S.)	GILBERT R. DAVISON.
(L.S.)	STEPHEN CONGAR.
(L.S.)	LEWIS VERNET.

Signed, sealed, and delivered in presence of
JOHN TRUMBULL,
MATTHEW BRISBANE.

ADDITIONAL ARTICLE, 1st.—I, Lewis Vernet, mentioned in the foregoing Document, have, in conformity to the 1st Article of said Agreement, determined, and do hereby determine, that the Schooner *Superior*, Captain Stephen Congar, shall be the Vessel that is to proceed upon the intended Sealing voyage. In Port Louis, the year, day, and date before mentioned. **LEWIS VERNET.**

ADDITIONAL ARTICLE, 2nd.—I, Stephen Congar, approve the choice made of my Vessel; and oblige myself to act according as is stipulated in the foregoing Agreement for the Master of the therein named Sealing Vessel to act, and hereby make the oath required in the 4th Article of said Agreement; and I, Gilbert R. Davison, also approve of the said choice, and do hereby obligate myself to act for, and in the cause of both Vessels in Buenos Ayres, according to the best of my judgment, by myself or by my power of Attorney. In truth whereof we have each signed the 2nd Additional Article, in Port Louis, this 8th day of September, 1831.

GILBERT R. DAVISON.

JOHN TRUMBULL, } Witnesses.   **STEPHEN CONGAR.**
MATTHEW BRISBANE, }

All the Clauses in this Contract manifest the entire and absolute liberty with which these Captains signed it. The idea did not emanate from me; it was a proposal made to me by them. They themselves selected the Crew from among those of both Vessels, and even took various individuals of the Colonists. And indeed, how would it have been possible for me to force them to such an act, as the Chargé d'Affaires asserts, and what were those sufferings and those imprisonments which could produce the moral co-action? However certain these supposed sufferings might have been, they never could have exceeded those which they would entail on themselves by becoming my Slaves;—yes, Slaves, for so it has pleased the Chargé d'Affaires to represent them—Slaves who were to be employed in painful labor solely for my personal advantage! To believe that the Contract was the effect of coercion, it is necessary to suppose that these Captains were either children or imbeciles! Above all, Excellent Sir, it is an absolute contradiction to suppose that I kept these persons imprisoned and oppressed, and that at the same time I induced and forced them to an Agreement, in virtue of which they were to cease to suffer, liberate themselves from my oppression, go to sea without any other guarantee than their own good faith, and, in short, become masters of themselves. It would appear that in politics, as well as in the business of private life, the bias of the heart banishes reflection from the mind, and produces striking inconsistencies.

The idea that, in the celebration of this Contract, coercion of any species whatsoever had been resorted to, being thus removed, I will now shew, first, that the Contract was at once useful to the Colony, to the Captains, and to the Crews; and secondly, that I could enter into it without either swerving from my duty or degrading my public character.

It was useful. The primary advantage resulting from this measure to the Colony, was that of removing from it persons who might be prejudicial to it, and changing their then hostile disposition into a friendly one, by attaching them to its interests. The Colony was not strong enough to enforce respect from the Crews of both Vessels, which, after the attempt previously made at revolt, necessarily required my utmost vigilance. Strictly speaking, I had at that time in all the Colony only 20 men, natives of the Country, in whom I could place confidence. It was not prudent to confide too much in the rest of my Colonists, since the greater part of them were easily open to seduction, in consequence not only of their speaking the same language as the Crews of the captured Vessels, but likewise because many of them were Countrymen. Thus it is, that during the detention of the Crews, those 20 Men had to mount guard over them at night, for which they were paid a silver dollar per night each. This continual and painful fatigue, in the snowy season, and during the excessively long nights of that latitude, produced in them weariness and want of vigor, and necessarily caused them to abandon the labors of the Colony during the day. It became, therefore, absolutely necessary to relieve it from such an unnatural and ruinous state of things. Happily it was, under these circumstances, that the Captains made their proposal, and this proposal presented to me the best opportunity to get rid of these presumed enemies, in the manner which they themselves desired and solicited. The second advantage consisted in the positive utility which this stipulation would produce to the Colony, if (as there was every reason to hope,) the *Superior* should faithfully fulfil her Agreement; and in truth, since it was undeniable that these Schooners had been engaged in a business from which they knew they were prohibited under pain of confiscation; since in the Contract the Captains themselves had confessed this most essential point, the following proposition became to me not a mere hope, but an absolute certainty. These Vessels, together with their Cargoes, must necessarily be declared lawful prizes in Buenos Ayres, (and experience has since proved it to be so,) consequently I had a right and ought to calculate upon the secure foundation that these Vessels, together with their Cargoes, would eventually become the property of the Colony; and I said to myself, a long time must elapse before the trial relative to the Captures be concluded in Buenos Ayres, (and experience has shown that neither in this was I deceived;) in this interval these Vessels and their Cargoes will be laid up and rot (as is the case at present with the *Harriet*,) in the roads of Buenos Ayres; it is therefore better that, in the mean time, one of the Vessels be employed in the Seal-fishery in the Pacific, and that the other go direct with me and one of the Captains to Buenos Ayres, for the purpose of bringing on and concluding the trial in question. This was done, and done at the request of the only persons who, under any other circumstances, might have had reason to complain of it; it was done, too, for their own benefit. Your Excellency will observe that, according to the Contract, the Cargo which the *Superior* might obtain would belong to the Colony, should the Vessels be declared lawful prizes, or to the Owners, should they not be condemned; and, in either case, the Crew were to receive their share. It is evident, therefore, that such a Contract, far from being prejudicial, in the slightest degree, was on the contrary highly beneficial to the Owners of the Vessels; because, if they were declared to have been illegally detained, they could lose nothing by this Voyage; and, in the contrary case, they would be considerable gainers. It was highly beneficial to these Captains and their Crews; for, instead of being detained in the Islands, they put to sea in perfect liberty; and instead of consuming in idleness the long space of time the trial might require, they would be earning a good salary. I believe that even the greatest idiot would form this conclusion, and that, on perusal of the Contract, the Chargé d'Affaires will be undeceived, as to my having compelled these men to work for my own private advantage—he will see that the *Superior* went on her Voyage for the benefit of whoever might prove to be the proper Owner, and under all circumstances, for the emolument of the Crew. To afford great and certain gain, and besides complete liberty to men who could not then, nor would, for a long time, be able to earn a single cent, and who are represented as having been imprisoned and barbarously oppressed on the Island, is an act which ought rather to have excited gratitude on the part of the Chargé d'Affaires.

But unfortunately he has not viewed the subject in this light. Far from reflecting on the impossibility of loss and the certainty of gain, which, in either case, must result to the Captain and Crew of the *Superior*, he sees nothing but seduction and violence in this Contract. He even believes he finds the same in the Clause which imposes penalties on the party who should infringe the Agreement—penalties which are customary in all such Contracts, although denominated by him *forfeitures at my discretion*. He likewise sees seduction and violence in the Clause which declares every infraction thereof an inexcusable violation of good faith. How different amongst men are the conceptions of the mind! It appears to me, that all must find in this Clause, and in the oath by which the Captain bound himself to the due fulfilment thereof, the customary form of all Agreements, and which was absolutely indispensable in that which we entered into in the Malvinas. I had absolutely no guarantee whatever that the *Superior* would fulfil the Contract, and return. Its execution depended entirely on the good faith, on the word, on the honor, of the Captain; consequently it was not strange nor was it prejudicial to him that this should be expressed in the Contract. In what, then, is this oath opposed to the customs or usages of Nations? I think likewise that every impartial person, on viewing the unbounded confidence with which I allowed to go out of my possession, a Vessel which I considered as the future property of the Colony, and at the same time consented that the Captain should select for his Crew, Men in whom he could confide, with no other guarantee for his return than the mere oath of said Captain, far from criminating me, and of attributing to me depraved intentions, will discover just motives for approving my conduct. In fact, Excellent Sir, under the critical and extraordinary circumstances in which the Colony was placed at that period, this measure saved it from all risk, offered it a prospect of great gain, afforded the Crew profit and employment, and favorably inclined the Captain and Crew. Thus it was, that, scarcely had the Contract been signed, when all was joy and satisfaction among these men. I have in my possession Letters from various individuals of the said Crew, in which after treating on other matters, they manifest their content, and return me thanks for my kind conduct towards them. Some of these Letters, and others that the same individuals addressed to their comrades in Staten Land, were written when they were on board of the *Superior* and out of my power. I have also a Letter from the Captain, written under the same circumstances, in which he again requests my commands. Can this be reconciled with the idea that they were forced to make this voyage?

I could legally make this Contract. Perhaps the opposite opinion of the Chargé d' Affaires arises from his complete want of knowledge on the subject, although on the other hand, it must always appear strange, that, without either privately or officially calling for information, he should have opened the Negotiation, by thundering a tremendous accusation, which although directed against me personally, falls indirectly on the Government with whom he is negotiating.

Be this as it may, it is essential to establish the facts. By a Decree bearing date the 5th of January, 1828, the property of the waste lands on the Island of Soledad was granted to me, on condition that I should establish a Colony within the term of 3 years: to the Colony was granted an exemption of Taxes and Imposts for 20 years, with the enjoyment of the Fishery in all the Malvina Islands and on the Coasts of the Continent to the South of the Rio Negro. By this it appears that the character of my undertaking to colonize the Malvinas was exclusively and essentially mercantile; and thus it was that I, with my own capital, and without any assistance whatever from the Government, had established the Colony and maintained it in the same manner, under the title of Director, which was conferred on me by the before-mentioned Decree. The Colony commenced various labors, and entered on the enjoyment of the rights and privileges so granted. The depredations of Foreigners on the Coasts still went on, and there was no force in the Colony capable of restraining them, nor was there any public Officer to protest against them. This state of disorder obliged me to require the Government to adopt some measures. Accordingly, by Decree of the 10th of June, 1829, it ordered that a Civil and Military Governor of those Islands, and their adjacencies up to Cape Horn, should be appointed, imposing on him the duty of carrying into effect the regulations relative to the Seal-fishery. The nomination of this charge might have fallen on any other person than the *Director*. But the Government, either believing me to be the most proper person, or to save the expense of a salary, which, in any other case, would have been necessary, thought it expedient that the *Director* of the Colony should also be Civil and Military Governor ; and, by another distinct Decree, although of the same date, it nominated me to fill this office.

The Decree which ordered that a Governor should be named was published by the press; but the other under the same date, in which I was appointed Governor, was not published. This circumstance has doubtless given rise to the idea that I had appropriated to myself this title; if not, how is it possible that the Chargé d'Affaires should in his Note write as he has done, in the belief that my character as Governor was fictitious? It is therefore necessary that he should be convinced that I am so in reality, and your Excellency can give him official knowledge of the fact by transmitting him a Copy of the Decree by which I was appointed.

It is self-evident that the title of Governor, which relates to public business, did not divest me of that of Director of the Colony, which is relative to my private and mercantile undertaking, but rather was intended to secure the interests of the enterprize; it did not divest me of that mercantile character, since it was precisely for mercantile objects, which were at the same time highly beneficial to the Country, that I had established the Colony, and from the moment I should be deprived of the power of acting as Director and undertaker of it, and of performing acts of commercial speculation, the Colony would fall to the ground, and the burthensome charge of Governor of the Islands would be of no utility to me. What therefore is the deduction? That I could legally perform private acts of commerce for the benefit of my Colony, in the same manner as if I had never been invested with the title of Governor: that the enjoyment of this title solely imposed upon me the obligation of carrying into effect within my jurisdiction the Laws peculiar to the Province of Buenos Ayres, as well as those relating to the Fishery; that I could enter into the Contract referred to, inasmuch as it was a private speculation, and that consequently the Chargé d'Affaires has been egregiously mistaken in believing that I degraded both my Government and my public character by entering into mercantile enterprizes, since I could consistently do so. He is likewise mistaken when he believes that I had some concealed intention, when in the Contract I styled myself *Director* and not *Governor*, as I made that Contract precisely as *Director* and not as *Governor*.

Your Excellency is now enabled to judge whether there exists even the semblance of justice in all that Mr. Baylies has advanced in this Charge—whether he is entitled to accuse me of any act really reprehensible, or, still less, to insult me—and whether, with regard to my person, he is not bound in duty to alter his opinions, as well as the language which he has unfortunately adopted to express them.

CHARGE 4.—" I sent to Rio de Janeiro all the Crew of the *Harriet*, with the exception of 5 men, who entered into my service."

I have already spoken on this point; I have shewn the necessity which existed for the removal of these men, which was effected with their own free will, and with the consent of their Captains.—There only remains for me to add, that these 5 men were at complete liberty: they were already on board the *Elbe*, under the British Flag, and on the eve of sailing for Rio de Janeiro: their names were inscribed in the Passport. Under these circumstances, they returned on shore, and solicited permission to enter into the service of the Colony: I consented to it, and contracted with them: they commenced their labors, and requested some advances, which I made them; when suddenly they entered into the service of an English Ship, bound for the Pacific, leaving me unpaid and with the loss of all I had supplied them with.

CHARGE 5.—" The *Superior* had left 7 men on Staten Land with provisions for only 6 months, and, owing to her detention in the Malvinas, they were exposed to perish on that desolate Island, as the *Superior* was bound, in this Contract, to go and return direct, to avoid all communication with other Vessels, and to take no step to succor these men."

In the first place, your Excellency will be pleased to remark, that the Island of Staten Land, is within the jurisdiction of my Government, and your Excellency will perceive that it is for this reason, that the Chargé d'Affaires has remained silent as to the object for which these men were left there. The *Superior* left them previously to her detention, that they might employ themselves in killing Seals, and storing up the skins; that is to say, for a prohibited and clandestine occupation. Your Excellency, who has before you the Contract, will judge of the correctness of the assertion that the *Superior* was prohibited from succoring them; when the only prohibition existing was,

" that she should not communicate with other Sealing Vessels," and even to this she was not bound, in case of accident or distress. So far was I from wishing to prevent these men from receiving assistance, that, after the *Superior* had sailed to the South, I sent the *Harriet* to succor them, as well as to collect various articles which were scattered about the Island ; all with the express consent of Captain Davison, with whom, on the 16th of September, I signed an Agreement to that effect. According to this Agreement, the *Harriet*, which was to sail under the command of Captain Brisbane, accompanied by Davison, should, at the same time, bring from different parts, there designated, Seal-skins, Timber, &c. &c. on my account; but I was to pay Davison no less than 7½ per cent. on all he should bring, as also the wages of the Master, at the rate of 42 dollars per month, the Mate, 30, together with 7 Seamen and 8 Guards, at 15 hard dollars each. Such, Sir, were the Contracts with which I swindled these Captains, and made them labor for my benefit. Know then, your Excellency, that the cause which impeded the succoring of these 7 Americans (as appears in the process) was an American Schooner from New York, the *Elizabeth Jane*, which, although only a Fishing Vessel, was illegally armed with 6 guns; she, when she fell in with the *Harriet*, proposed to take her by force, and thus liberate her from the detention she was under. Davison opposed this, pointing out the probable consequence which might result therefrom, as Brisbane would resist by fighting to the last extremity. The *Elizabeth Jane*, notwithstanding, clearly appeared preparing to carry her project into execution, and thus obliged the Captain of the *Harriet* to return immediately to the Colony, in order to avoid a greater evil, without being able to accomplish the principal object of his voyage, viz., the succor of those men ; and thus I lost, in wages alone, 400 hard dollars. Since the Chargé d'Affaires has mentioned this affair, he ought not to have remained silent on the principal part of it, nor to have dissembled the criminal conduct of the *Elizabeth Jane* ;—yes, criminal ; and thus it is that, to evade the effects of the remonstrance your Excellency might make to the Government of The United States, scarcely had this Vessel arrived at New York, when she was advertised for sale in a Journal of that City, under date of the 7th March.

No less remarkable is the want of correctness with which he asserts that the *Superior* left provisions with those men for only 6 months ; when the Captain of that Vessel positively stated that he had provisioned them for 9 months : and that he did so, is clearly shewn by the Log-book of the Vessel, which is in my possession. This is also corroborated by the following incident : Captain Duncan, of the Ship-of-war, *Lexington*, committed the incivility of sailing from these Roads, for Malvinas, without waiting for a Reply from your Excellency ; which, I may be allowed to say, by the way, was really acting in contempt of the established usages of Nations. Mr. Slacum, then Consul, in a Note which he addressed to your Excellency, endeavored to excuse this want of courtesy in Duncan, under pretence of the urgent necessity which existed of rendering assistance to the men left on Staten Land. Any one would naturally conclude from this, that the first care of Duncan was to sail direct, and without losing an instant, to the succor of these men. But the fact is that he went to Port Louis, and occupied himself in the heroic achievement of destroying, in a vandalic manner, the Colony established there, and imprisoning and enchaining a few unarmed and unsuspecting Argentines. It was not till 20 days after his arrival at that place, that he recollected the urgent necessity which had obliged him to leave these Roads; he then sent the Schooner, *Dash*, to the assistance of the men, but not direct to Staten Land, as she had orders to touch first at various other Islands, on the mercantile business of some American Citizens. These Islands being to leeward, must necessarily have detained the *Dash* a long time; so that we are ignorant up to this day whether or not those 7 men ever received assistance. This fact shews how insignificant is the parade with which the Chargé d'Affaires wishes to represent the great danger to which those men were exposed.

Besides, had they perished, the blame would rest with the *Superior* only. She had left them there, knowing that the business in which she was engaged was illegal—that what has happened, might befall her; and that, in this event, they would be abandoned.

Above all, was it because these men might be exposed to danger, (which, as I have said, was not the case,) that I should abstain from detaining the *Superior* ? In this mode, any Vessel could elude all prohibitions and forfeitures, by merely leaving on some Island a part of her Crew, as she could not be detained under the pretence that in the mean time, they might perish for want. In fine, Sir, the fact is, that the urgency of the succor which Mr. Slacum represented in his Note, forms a striking contrast with the calmness and indifference with which the Captain of the *Lexington* viewed these men; and, hence, I infer, that either the latter rendered himself highly criminal by such apathy, or there was no truth in the urgent necessity of succor for want of provisions, which Mr. Slacum then deceitfully affirmed, and the Chargé d'Affaires now erroneously insinuates.

CHARGE 6.—"I endeavored to seduce American Seamen from their own Flag, and allure them to mine by the promise of extravagant gain."

This Charge is reduced to the assertion, that "I endeavored." But what are the deeds that the Chargé d'Affaires relates? Absolutely none—and, therefore, as this aereal charge does not rest upon any determined deed, it is not susceptible of a positive refutation. It will, consequently, suffice for me to affirm, that neither the Chargé d'Affaires, nor any other person, can reproach me with a deed of that nature. Constantly opposed to desertion, far from endeavoring to seduce any Seamen, whether Americans, or of any other Nation, I have invariably followed the system of not admitting any of the many who frequently presented themselves to me in the Malvinas, without the previous and express consent of the Captain of the Vessel to which they belonged. If I admitted the 5 men of the *Harriet*, alluded to, it was because they did not belong to any Vessel.

CHARGE 7.—" I imprisoned, without any consideration, the 4 Americans whom the Chargé d'Affaires mentions as forming a part of the Crew of the American Schooner, *Belville*, which had been wrecked on the Coast of Tierra del Fuego : I seized a large number of Seal-skins, which I sold to an English Vessel, and a quantity of Whalebone, which I transmitted to Buenos Ayres. By threatening these imprisoned and friendless Shipwrecked Men with sending them to Buenos Ayres, to be tried as Pirates, I obliged them to sign an Agreement on behalf of themselves, and other Shipmates of theirs, who were on Eagle Island, occupied in building a Shallop, in which it was stipulated, that as soon as the Shallop was completed, they should employ themselves with her, in the Seal-fishery, under the Argentine Flag. Not satisfied with seizing their property, and treating them as Slaves, I wished to reduce them to a degree of moral debasement as low as my own ; inasmuch as, in another Article, after ironically binding them to act as honest men, I would induce them to the commission of acts of violence and robbery on their own Countrymen, by promising to share with them the profits arising from the plunder of the Vessels. In this mode I compelled individuals belonging to the captured Vessels to engage in my service, and even to assist in the capture of their own Countrymen. On one occasion, I endeavored to subdue an American Seaman, of the name of Crawford, who resisted my persuasions, threats, and imprisonment, by depriving him of food, and he would have perished, had not Captain Davison secretly relieved him, in defiance of my orders."

I will remark, in the first place, that these men were 5, and not 4, as the Chargé d'Affaires says; only 2 belonged to the *Belville*, which was wrecked, the other 3 had belonged to different Crews, and had successively remained on the Islands. Consequently, it is incorrect that they were all shipwrecked Men, and it is no less so that they were abandoned ; inasmuch as all of them lived on the Islands of their own free will, and so much so, that, according as their Accusers affirmed, they had refused a passage for their own Country, which had been offered to them.

It is true that I arrested them. ⌐ it why does the Chargé d'Affaires conceal the motives ? I arrested these American Citizens because other American Citizens accused them as dangerous persons and of a piratical disposition: among these Accusers, Captains Congar and Davison, particularly the latter, distinguished themselves. I have in my possession their Affidavits. Therefore, if the imprisonment of these Americans was an injustice, it was owing to the calumny of other Americans.

But the Chargé d'Affaires calls me an oppressor, a robber, and a base being, for my conduct towards them. Your Excellency will judge: I did not harbor the least feeling of rancour, nor could I do so against men who had never offended me, and whom I then saw for the first time in my life; and thus it is, that one of them having requested me to allow him to depart in the *Elbe*, I immediately consented; and he went in her. So true is it, that I acted in consequence of those formal accusations, and not in virtue of threats, to which I had no occasion to resort; that my conduct towards them was not only just, but likewise generous. And in truth, it being a fact that they had been fishing within my jurisdiction; and it being equally certain that their own countrymen accused them as pirates, I could with justice confiscate their skins and their whalebone, and send them to this City to be tried. But I refused to augment their misfortunes; and the acts imputed to them not having been clearly proved, I resolved to set them at liberty, and thus to convert these then vagrants, but at the same time hardy and laborious men, into useful members of the Colony, by attaching them to it for their own interest. These men, weighing the advantages which might accrue to them from this measure, against the evils resulting from the wandering life they were leading, requested to be admitted as members of the Colony, and consequently under the Argentine Flag. We then entered into an Agreement, which to them was highly beneficial, and which, for that reason, I never suspected would draw down on me such bitter and painful insults as those now fulminated against me by the Chargé d'Affaires. By this Agreement I bound myself to render them every assistance, in the building of a small Schooner or Shallop, which they were constructing in a distant Island, called Eagle Island; and when finished, to allow them, as members of the Colony, to fish under the Argentine Flag, on shares. Such was the Agreement which is now so strongly declaimed against. Is there any thing in it usurious, compulsive or extraordinary? The fact is that when the Crew of the *Harriet* were already on board the *Elbe,* and on the eve of sailing for Rio Janeiro, one of these passengers requested to be admitted in the number of the supposed *unfortunate shipwrecked seamen,* and to participate in the advantages of the Agreement referred to: he was admitted; and signed it. Fulfilling on my part the stipulation, I gave them sails, rigging, provisions, and in short every thing requisite for finishing the construction of the Vessel, but as they had no one to become bound for their conduct, and guaranty to me the fulfilment of their part of the Agreement, they delivered to me, as security, 198 seal-skins, and 2744 pounds of whalebone, of which articles I could dispose freely, as I did. But the Chargé d'Affaires is mistaken, if he thinks that for this the men were deprived of these effects, or that I appropriated them to myself, as he asserts. They did not lose them—they had then no possibility of disposing of these articles —they were embarrassing to them rather than useful, and their preservation was expensive and difficult. They therefore ceded them to me; but I bound myself expressly to return them, in the same kind, and quantity, from the half which would belong to me of the product of the fishing which was to be undertaken by the Schooner. Is this robbing, Excellent Sir? Is this committing oppression or violence? Can the slightest trace of good faith be discovered in the persons who have so basely and deceitfully informed the Chargé d'Affaires on this head? Does my frank and generous conduct towards these individuals merit the infamous invectives which he lavishes so profusely against me? Sir, reason and the mutual respect which men owe to each other in Society, counsel the dissembling even of the most gross aberrations of the mind; but with respect to deeds, and to deeds which profoundly wound what man most appreciates, honor, it is necessary that he be conscious of his guilt to be able to tolerate them, in like manner as it is necessary to be deeply prejudiced in order to allege them without proofs.

Such was my conduct towards these individuals, which has brought on me the epithets of vile robber and oppressor. These men were contented and satisfied with their new state under the Flag of the Republic, and so well disposed to fulfil the obligations they had contracted, that, as soon as the Vessel was ready, they returned to the Port of the Colony to receive new outfits and provisions, which were furnished to them. They would have fulfilled them faithfully, but for the infamous aggression committed by the *Lexington.* Here it is not superfluous to state, that Capt. Duncan seized on the Shallop, obliged her to change her Flag, and thus deprived the Colony and the Republic of a Vessel which your Excellency has a right to demand the restitution of. Why is the Chargé d'Affaires silent with respect to this usurpation?

But he affirms that in this way I induced and obliged American Citizens to capture, and what he terms to plunder, the Vessels and persons of their Countrymen. This is not true. To effect the detention of the *Harriet, Superior* and *Breakwater,* no one was either induced or forced; nor had I occasion to resort to these means. All the individuals, as well Americans as of other Nations, who assisted in the taking of these Vessels, did so of their own accord, and because it suited their interests; they were all Members of the Colony, and, as such, participators in the prizes. Now the Fishery was a property of the Colony, and, if all who composed it had a right in the property sequestered, to make those Americans who were on the list of Colonists partakers in it, was not to induce them to rob their Countrymen, but to exercise an act of rigorous justice which could not be denied them from the time they became Members of the Colony.

For the rest, Sir, to detain myself in replying to the idle story relative to the seaman Crawford, whom it is said I attempted to starve to death, were almost to insult your Excellency's understanding—as though, had I harbored so ferocious a design, means or pretexts would be wanting to me for carrying it into effect more decorously in my character of Governor! And from what motive? Because he resisted the promises, threats, and imprisonment by which I endeavored to compel him to assist in the capture of the Vessels. Less wonderful would have been the supposed heroism of Crawford, than my stupidity in endeavoring to force into my service a man for whom I had no necessity, and in whom, from his reluctance to serve, I could have no confidence, but must always have considered dangerous. It is fit that your Excellency should know that the supposed hero assisted, like the rest, in the capture of the *Harriet*—he would not afterwards assist to capture the other Vessels, and, not only did not the least injury result to him therefrom, but he was preferred to go to the Pacific in the *Superior*. This is not all: he not only remained in and went freely from the Islands, but the debts he had there contracted were paid by me out of my pocket. What a contrast does this conduct form with that which is ascribed to me!

But an observation occurs to me here which I must not omit. If, in consequence of this entirely disproved and utterly false assertion, the Chargé d'Affaires thinks it his duty to grossly insult me, with how much justice can your Excellency answer him, with the completely proved fact of the ferocious brutality with which the Captain of the *Lexington* treated the innocent Colonists, destroying their little property, dragging them from their homes, and carrying them with him in chains for entire months, like infamous robbers. Oh! the Chargé d'Affaires says nothing about this. Is it that in Vernet every thing is crime, and in Duncan all heroism? To deeds of that magnitude and certainty, the Chargé d'Affaires should have confined himself in his accusations, instead of letting himself be diverted by silly tales, such as the supposed design of killing Crawford. But enough of this. There are insignificancies that are not, even in the trivial transactions of life, deserving the notice of men of sense; and much less in an affair with which are intimately connected the high interests of 2 Nations.

CHARGE 8.—" According to declarations which I have made as a Public Functionary, if they are to be viewed as the sentiments of my Government, there is reason to believe that a project is in contemplation, involving one of the most valuable interests of The United States —the Whale Fishery—for, according to the Report made by Captain Davison, I had determined to capture all American Vessels, including Whale Ships as well as those engaged in taking Seals, upon the arrival of an armed Schooner, for which I had contracted. I also declared that my special victims would be Citizens of The United States, and not of other Nations, inasmuch as when I was told that the English Vessel *Adeona* was taking Seals within my jurisdiction, I replied that I could not capture an English Vessel with the same propriety that I could an American."

If there were the least truth in this Charge, the complaint would be founded, and the pertinent remarks which the Chargé d'Affaires subjoins, on the injustice and dangers of odious preferences among Nations, would be well applied. But happily there is nothing but utter falsehood in all the information that has been given to the Chargé d'Affaires. I have never made such absurd declarations, for I have never been out of my senses.

The Vessel for which I had contracted was not intended for this purpose, although Davison assured Captain Duncan in the Malvinas that she was. To convince Duncan of the falsehood of Davison's assertion, Captain Brisbane, the Director of the Fishery, showed the Contract which I had made with an American house in this Capital, upon which Duncan became silent. It would appear that the Chargé d'Affaires was unaware of this circumstance. But why does he conceal the place from whence this Vessel was to come? Why does he not say that it was New York? Was it to make the refutation of this Charge more difficult? He is deceived. I refer to the testimony of the American house with whom I contracted ; for, although it may be now unfriendly to me, on account of the responsibility which it has incurred for the non-fulfilment of the Contract, nevertheless, I am confident that it will not fail to declare the truth, that is, that the Vessel was to come out equipped for the Seal-fishery, on account of the Colony, and not armed.

It is untrue that the *Adeona* had fished within my jurisdiction. She did so before my appointment as Governor, but after that period she abstained therefrom, as I can prove by written vouchers which I have in my possession, as well as the Log-books of the *Breakwater*, *Harriet*, and *Superior*, by which it appears that there was not then fishing in the Islands, any English Vessel, or Vessels of any other Nation. Consequently, although I might have wished to exercise foolish preferences, I had not the opportunity of so doing.

For the rest, the Chargé d'Affaires is aware that the Government with whom he is treating, knows its own rights and those of others— that it is not so foolish as to attempt to hinder any Nation from the Whale-fishery on the High Seas—that therefore there exists no such

project, nor the intention of limiting to the Americans alone the prohibition of fishing within the established bounds; but that this prohibition is extended to all Nations, saving the right of the Republic
to make to any of them special concessions, if it should at any time
think it expedient. In consequence, as the Charge is reduced in this
part merely to unfounded apprehensions, I consider that the Chargé
d'Affaires will dismiss them after a declaration to this effect.

CHARGE 9TH and LAST.—" The Decree of my Appointment as
Governor bears the date of the 10th of June, 1829, and it remained
as a dead letter to the North Americans until the 30th July, 1831.
The Chargé d'Affaires of The United States in this City, Mr. Forbes,
died here on the 14th June, 1831, and the acts of violence and depredation on American property commenced at the Malvinas immediately
on the arrival there of the news of his decease. I was convinced that
if I committed such atrocities while Mr. Forbes was alive, they would
have roused him from the apathy with which he beheld that Decree,
which had entailed so many injuries on his Fellow-Citizens, and of
which his Government, till this day has not been officially informed.
Had I confined myself to the capture of the Vessels, and to the institution of processes before the competent Tribunal, with the view of
ascertaining whether the Laws and Sovereignty of this Country had
been violated or not, I would have acted within the limits of the authority which had been entrusted to me; yet, in the view of the Government of The United States, even this would have been an essential
violation of its rights."

Your Excellency will have observed, that, in relation to several
charges, the Chargé d'Affaires, in the absence of *data*, or precise and
determinate facts, has recurred to conjectures and inferences, which,
for the reason that they are not supported by any proof, scarcely deserve
notice. Of this character are those which constitute this Charge ;
and in it, as in the rest, all that does not suit the purposes of the author, is kept silent. In effect, the Chargé d'Affaires adverts to the
wholly casual and accidental circumstance of the detention of the
Vessels in the Malvinas having commenced shortly after the death of
Mr. Forbes in this City; but he entirely overlooks the fact that in
November 1830, and in January and May 1831, that is to say, during
the life of Mr. Forbes, these very same Vessels were warned that if
they continued Fishing within my jurisdiction, they would be confiscated, together with their Cargoes. If the circumstance of the detention of the Vessels and the demise of Mr. Forbes having been coeta-
neous had not been a mere casualty,—if it were certain that the apprehension that these depredations might rouse him from his apathy, was
what kept me back from practising them during his life, it would also
have made me abstain from giving those warnings : for, if the act of
capturing those Vessels was unlawful, so was that of notifying them

that such capture would take place. I caused the Circular containing that notification to be published in the Journals of this City, entitled the *Gaceta Mercantil* and *British Packet*, in October 1830. He who dreads that his actions be known, never avows publicly and with anticipation his intention of performing them. Above all, it would have been a miserable puerility in me to wait, as the Chargé d'Affaires says, till there should be no Representative of The United States in Buenos Ayres, in order to commit my atrocities in the Malvinas; inasmuch as, although Mr. Forbes should be wanting, there would not fail to be some one to substitute him, and the Government of The United States would not fail to be acquainted with them and remonstrate thereon. The present accusations which are directed against me prove the correctness of this remark. But what is most singular and extraordinary, Excellent Sir, is that the Chargé d'Affaires should affirm that I intentionally captured the Vessels, at a time when there was no one in this City to remonstrate against it, when, in the next line, he asserts that I, as having resided in The United States, know that " no distance could smother the voice of just complaint of American Seamen,. . . . . that its echo would have traversed the wide expanse of the ocean-waters which roll between the two Hemispheres . . . . . that the Government of The United States will always cause its Flag to be respected, whether floating beneath the constellations of the North or the South," &c. &c. &c. How then could he imagine that I, being aware of all this, could commit the folly of endeavoring to conceal by such stupid means my depredations and my tyrannic acts?

Had I confined myself, he adds, to capturing the Vessels and bringing them to trial, I would have acted within the limits of my duty. And what else have I done, Excellent Sir? The imprisonment of various Individuals and the sending the *Superior* to the southward, were, as I have already stated, acts at once just, necessary, and even beneficial to the Americans themselves. But, if the Chargé means to say by this, that I ought to have limited myself to the mere capture of the Vessels, and that I ought not, as Governor, to adopt any measures of police and security, even when I saw the Colony in evident danger; that neither ought I, as Director of a Colony, to enter into mercantile speculations, he doubtless forgets the primary rights and duties of a Government, as he also forgets that, in my character of Director, I could undertake commercial operations. The imprisonment, contracts, and other measures resorted to, subsequently to the capture of the Vessels, were necessary consequences of the bad conduct of Davison, likewise subsequent to the said capture. But, with respect to the Vessels, I did no more than what the Chargé d'Affaires says I ought to have done. I did not confiscate them; I only captured and detained them, sending them for trial to Buenos Ayres, where an American Consul resided, who would take cognizance of the business; and, besides, I brought here Captain Davison, who, according to the Contract, was to answer, on the trial, for both Vessels. This is the way in which I acted. Unfortunately, Davison absconded during the trial, setting at nought the Laws of the Country, and violating his own word of honor; and the Consul, Mr. Slacum, allowing himself to be carried away inconsiderately, was wanting in respect towards your Excellency, exceeded his authority, and wished to give the character of a national insult to that which was no more than a strictly private affair—an affair of contraband— and, with exaggerated and false reports, he has precipitated his Government into very disagreeable discussions. The Chargé d'Affaires is greatly mistaken, when he affirms that my nomination was, during 2 years, a dead letter to the Americans. It was not so. When I returned to Malvinas, with the title of Governor, and with the special charge to cause the Laws, relative to the Fishery, to be respected, my first care was to make known the prohibition to all the Vessels, American or not American, accustomed to occupy themselves in Fishing. True it is that, prior to my appointment as Governor, and when I was only the private Director of a Colony, I made known to them the same prohibition: and that, consequently, without the necessity of repeating it, I could legally capture the *Harriet* and *Superior* in 1829. But I did not choose to do so. I determined to give them a second and a solemn warning in my character of Governor, and I suffered them to depart freely, taking with them the produce of their Fishery. And is it possible that this conduct, in every respect frank, generous, and beneficial to the North Americans, should now serve as a pretext for accusing me of having allowed my appointment to remain a dead letter? If, in the act of receiving it, and, without waiting for a second intimation, I had put in execution the duty imposed upon me, and had captured the Vessels, I should now be accused of injustice, precipitation, and an infraction of the *usages of Nations*. But, actuated by delicacy and scrupulosity, I declined exercising the powers I was invested with; and then, on accusing me for enforcing them, they very singularly accuse me for not having exercised them earlier. I do not understand this rare mode of appreciating the actions of men.

If there be any decisive fact in this memorable question—if there be any which evidently proves the justice with which I made that official intimation, and, consequently, the justice with which I carried it into effect, when the moment arrived for so doing, it is the tacit consent and constant deference which The Honorable Mr. Forbes paid to it, as well as to the Decree of my appointment. To attempt to cause it to be believed in Buenos Ayres that this conduct of his was the effect of apathy, is wantonly to throw discredit on a venerable tomb. Your Excellency, and all Buenos Ayres, know, from many years' experience, the integrity and zeal of that illustrious Diplomatist; you know, that, guided by principles of the strictest justice, he always supported the interests with which he was charged; and that in his copious official Correspondence, he never resorted to adulation, nor was he ever wanting in the respect due to the Government of this Country. It was not apathy—no, it was the firm conviction he felt of the needlessness of a Protest, and of the right which this Country had to the Malvinas, which caused him to view with respectful silence, not only the Decree of the 10th of June, and my Circular alluded to, but likewise many anterior acts of dominion exercised by this Republic over those Islands.

The Chargé d'Affaires says that the Decree in question was prejudicial to the interests of The United States. This may be, but Mr. Forbes well knew that utility, which may sometimes regulate the actions of an Individual, was never a just reason for not acknowledging the rights of others—he knew that, though the Decree might be prejudicial to particular interests, this did not prove the want of right to promulgate it. Prejudicial in the highest degree to the general commerce of Nations was the prohibition imposed by Spain of trading with her Colonies; but no Nation ever dared to call in question the right she had to impose it.

For the rest, if the Government of The United States was not officially informed of this Decree, I am ignorant of the reason why its Representative here should have omitted communicating it. Further on I will revert to this point: for the present, I will only remark, that, if this be said as a charge against the Government of this Country, the Chargé d'Affaires knows, or ought to know, that the Government cannot be taxed with having proceeded in this affair by surprise, or in the dark. To publish, by the press, the Decree establishing a Governor in the Malvinas, and that too in a City in which there reside the Representatives of several Nations, is undoubtedly to proceed in the most frank and public manner that is known. Besides, no principle of the Law of Nations obliged the Government of Buenos Ayres to officially inform any Nation of a measure essentially economical and administrative. The independence and dignity of States would be chimerical, if, for every Establishment they might propose forming on their Coasts, or in their Dominions, and for every prohibitory Law they might think proper to dictate thereon, it were necessary for them to give official notice, and wait for the consent of Foreign Governments. If England should resolve to adopt a similar measure, respecting any Establishment she may raise upon her desert Coasts of the Labrador, will she give previous official notice of it to the Government of The United States?

Such, Excellent Sir, are the Charges—such the Exculpations.—I have concluded the refutation of the accusations which are directed against me, and, notwithstanding your Excellency's injunction to ex-

express myself diffusely, I omit many observations and many details, because I am convinced that, in the discussion of arduous affairs, every trifle which is not absolutely necessary, only serves to complicate them still more, and to divert the attention from the only points to which it should be confined. Perhaps this has been the object of the Chargé d'Affaires, on opening the Negotiation, with a long list of Charges—that is, to divert your Excellency from those which with so much justice you might bring forward.

But I must not commit to silence certain observations which this affair, upon the whole, calls for, and which could not have a place in the simple and dry analysis of facts to which I have hitherto limited myself.

First—If the consciousness of perfect innocence is not fallacious, I think that every impartial person will form an opinion decidedly favorable and honorable to my person. To be fully convinced of the justice of my proceedings, it is necessary not to lose sight, for an instant, of one powerful consideration. In the common course of events there are actions, which, viewed in a false light, and shaded with a few cunning strokes of the pencil, appear criminal or faulty, but which, if presented with impartiality, and if sincerity at the same time show the special circumstances in which the Author of them was placed, lose their deformity, and appear what they really are—acts that are necessary, and, as such, just. This is now the case with respect to the loud accusation, founded on the voyage of the *Superior*, the confinement of certain men, &c. &c. These acts are brought forward with ostentation, but nothing is said as to who was the cause of them, or of the incidents which preceded and accompanied them. To depart, in difficult cases, from the rules of action adhered to in ordinary events, is fully justified by a sovereign law—necessity. This is an universal principle, and professed by the Chargé d'Affaires himself.

Your Excellency will be pleased to remark that part of his Note, in which, speaking incidentally and lightly of the criminal conduct of the Captain of the *Lexington*, instead of reprobating an aggression which will be an indelible stain on the American Flag, he expresses himself as follows: "A Naval Officer, of sufficient energy and patriotism to defend and protect those rights on his own responsibility." On his own responsibility! And why did he take it on himself? Doubtless, because he thought necessity authorized him to do so, and that the circumstances of the case would not allow him time to ask for, and receive, instructions from his Government, which, as is stated in the Message to Congress, had only ordered him to afford legal protection to the commerce of American Citizens. Hence it appears, that, according to the doctrine of the Chargé d'Affaires himself, circumstances authorize actions, which, in ordinary cases, would be very reprehensible; and even authorize a Subaltern not only to swerve from, but even openly to break the positive orders of his Government. How, then, can they deny to me this same right of acting according to circumstances? The Captain of the *Lexington* was not forced to this act by circumstances—the evil he wished to prevent was already done, neither could he repair it with an act of Piracy; he rather rendered the cause of his Fellow-Citizens worse. Notwithstanding all this, the Chargé d'Affaires approves, and even eulogizes a scandalous act, which none but the most extraordinary circumstances could in any way palliate. And when I, in circumstances really extraordinary and urgent, adopted measures a hundred times less ruinous, a hundred times less noisy, a hundred times less cruel, I am to be called a wretch, a pillager, an oppressor! Circumstances are to authorise the Commander of a Vessel, on his own responsibility, to resort to the most criminal and unnecessary measures for the protection of American Citizens; and shall they not authorize the Governor of a place, on his responsibility, to have recourse to measures customary in such cases, and absolutely necessary to the primary object of preserving order, and furthering the interests of the Establishment? It would appear that, in the Captain of the *Lexington*, that is *energy and patriotism* which all civilized People would denominate an act of Piracy:—and in the Governor of Malvinas, to put down conspiracies, to curb the authors of them, to remove them with their own free consent, and to attend to the commercial interests of a Colony, for the benefit, and to the satisfaction even of Countrymen of this same Commander, is to commit robbery, atrocity, oppression, and violence! If men are not to respect a principle common to all, and which regulates the actions of all, the examination of these actions will always be arbitrary, and the estimation of them uncertain; and that which is termed justice will be only a moveable shadow, which will appear under the divers forms which the interests or the passions of individuals may give to it.

Second—In the long series of incidents which the Chargé d'Affaires has agglomerated, not one is to be found which is not either curtailed or disfigured. In like manner, he relates them without deigning to bring forward the proofs which have induced him to give credence to them. Who has supplied him with intelligence relative to them? The desire to convince, by which (if, by no consideration, of a higher order,) he ought to be animated, should induce him to manifest it. If the Delinquents themselves, (and it is not possible it could be any others,) or those persons who are interested in this business, he can hardly be possessed of that moral conviction which could alone justify the positive manner in which he comes forward. On the contrary, as far as I am concerned, besides having proved, in the Papers referred to, a great part of the facts here stated, with indestructible Documents, and by individuals of all Nations, even Americans, individuals who have nothing either to hope or fear from me; I am moreover ready, Excellent Sir, to prove in the same manner all the other particulars I have now added. But even waiving all this, your Excellency can proceed in this business on a sure basis; which is, that, in the whole history of this affair, the Chargé d'Affaires cannot bring forward a single act, as transcendental as it is criminal, and as criminal as it is undeniable, whilst your Excellency can, with the greatest security, cite a fact of this nature—the outrage committed by the *Lexington*. Yes, this scandalous aggression, the Chargé d'Affaires, who is so extremely zealous of the *usages of Nations* as to consider as an infraction of them, an oath administered in a Contract, strangely denominates an act of energy and patriotism.

Third—That a Diplomatic Envoy, yielding to the imperious voice of duty, sustains with energy the interests of his Nation—that he, in the excess of his zeal, so far forgets himself as to use offensive expressions, which the customs of Nations have justly proscribed; in all this there is, doubtless, nothing uncommon. But that, when a private individual is one of the principal objects of a Negotiation, the Representative of a prudent and just Nation, should descend so low as unnecessarily to heap unmerited insults on that individual, which extend even to the Government of the Country in which he resides; this, although not new in the history of Diplomacy, is truly reprehensible, and fraught with evil consequences. The Chargé d'Affaires, occupying a position unassailable to me, and to which I cannot ascend to demand from him a legal satisfaction, borne away by his zeal, has thought himself authorised to term me a robber, a wretch, an oppressor, and a pirate. If it be possible, I demand a formal trial, where my Adversaries may produce their proofs, and bring forward the Affidavits which I am aware they have taken from the Crew of the *Elbe*, the fugitive Davison, and others; but without concealing any of them. This ought to be done; and if my Adversaries will not accede to it, they owe me a solemn reparation. I detained these Vessels, Excellent Sir, in fulfilment of the duty which had been imposed on me. I am a Public Officer of the State, if I am insulted for my official conduct, the insult falls likewise on the Government which prescribed it. As a Public Officer, as a Citizen, as a Man, I have a right to preserve my honor, and if I am deprived of demanding personally the reparation due to it, I consider that your Excellency is bound to do so, and to demand from the Government of The United States full satisfaction for the insults heaped on me by its Representative. Your Excellency and the dignity of the Country over which you preside, are compromised in this. When the Chargé d'Affaires was still in The United States, he might, from a want of information on the subject, think that my title of Governor was usurped or apocryphal; but, after his arrival in this Capital, he knew, or he ought to have ascertained, that it was real; and that the stage of the business was, that the Vessels had been declared good Prizes by the competent Tribunal of this Country: he therefore knew that in speaking of me, he spoke likewise of the Authorities of the Country who directed my acts, or who authorized them. Consequently, if I am a pillager and a pirate, so also is the Tribunal—so also is the Government itself.

Fourth—In my individual opinion, Excellent Sir, it is evident that the Chargé d'Affaires wanders from the primary and essential object of his Mission. Not having read his Instructions, I judge from other data, &c. It is well known that His Excellency, the President of The United States, in his Message to Congress, dated 6th of last December, in treating of the affair of the Malvinas, expresses himself in the following terms:—" I will, without delay, send a Minister, charged to investigate the nature of the occurrences, and of the claim, if there be any, of the Argentine Government to those Islands." This was just and rational; this was decorous, and worthy of a discreet Government. The President, informed of what had taken place, says to the Legislative Body :—prior to coming to a definite resolution, it is necessary to be fully informed, as well with regard to what has occurred, as to the foundation of the right which the Argentine Government claims to those Islands; and for this precise object, a Chargé d'Affaires shall be sent there. As there is not the least motive for supposing that the Government wished to deceive the Congress, and infringe public faith, we must conclude that the only, or at least the primary object of the Mission of Mr. Baylies, was to enquire into those particulars. Consequently it was to be expected that his first step in Buenos Ayres would be to demand from your Excellency a detailed account of the occurrences at the Malvinas; and an exposition of the grounds on which this Government founded its right to these Islands. Should it result from this enquiry that The United States had cause for remonstrance or complaint relative to either of the two points, then was he to remonstrate or complain. This is what was to be expected from the tenor of the Message; and, although it had not announced it, this is the course which reason should have dictated.

Who can doubt that, prior to remonstrating or complaining against an action, or a right, it is indispensable to enquire into, and obtain the necessary information relative to it? With what astonishment then, must the very opposite conduct of the Chargé d'Affaires be viewed ! Instead of investigating and examining into the business, he opens the Negotiation with demands and accusations. If he assert that prior to doing so he had acquired the necessary knowledge; this will prove more clearly the necessity he is under of naming the persons from whom he received his information.—But be they who they may, it appears to me that his Government has not sent him to Buenos Ayres to obtain this intelligence from simple individuals. If this was the only object, the sending a Minister was unnecessary; as prior to the arrival here of Mr. Baylies, the American Government was already in possession of these same accounts, given by persons under the influence of resentment. It sent him in order that, proceeding according to the practice of Nations, he should require *from the Government of Buenos Ayres* information respecting the 2 points in question. But he, giving full credit to accounts, the major part of which are probably got up here by persons of the character before expressed, without any previous investigation, without calling for any explanation from Your Excellency, as it was natural and expedient he should do, commences the Negotiation by laying down, as a fact, what he was sent here to investigate, and fulminating an accusation, in which, as I have already remarked, he comprehends the Authorities of the Country. My astonishment is increased when I hear (as has been publicly stated for some days past in this City,) that, after the Note of the 20th of June, he has addressed another to Your Excellency, in which he states that the Report called for from me will be useless, as I have already confessed I detained the said Vessels, and it is notorious that the *Harriet* is still in this Port. This is to wish every thing to be believed which suits his purposes, setting aside the enquiry whether or not the detention was just. If the Chargé d'Affaires does not require the information contained in my Report, Your Excellency may have occasion for it. Nevertheless, it is the Chargé d'Affaires who stands most in need of it, since he has come here *to enquire into the nature of that affair*, and consequently the Report is comformable to the object of his Mission. Above all,—I am the party accused, and it would be the first time, that, even in private affairs, the strange doctrine was advanced that it was useless to hear the accused party. How many errors are here committed at the very opening of the Negotiation ! Can the just Government of The United States approve this conduct, and these strange principles? I doubt it. And must I not believe that the Chargé d'Affaires has entirely mistaken the true object of his Mission ?—

Fifth,—An anticipated declaration, which I read in the Chargé d'Affaires' Note, confirms me in my opinion. The United States have no acknowledged right to the Malvinas. Thus it is that the President alleges none in the Message, nor does Mr. Baylies allege any, in his Note, but limits himself to lay down as a fact that the Fishing business in the Malvinas is lawful, and that this Republic cannot prohibit it ; that is, to lay down as a fact, the very same thing which he comes to enquire into. But to return to the Message—to this paramount Document which the Chargé d'Affaires cannot deny. I will send a Minister, it says, to enquire into the nature of the claims of Buenos Ayres to these Islands. This is not the language of one who is conscious of being possessed of a right—it is that of the prudent man who doubts, and wishes to be informed, in order to determine afterwards.

Now, then, the Chargé d'Affaires from the first Communication which he addressed to your Excellency, solemnly affirms, that he is authorized to declare that his Government utterly denies the existence of any right in this Republic to interrupt, molest, detain, or capture any Vessels belonging to Citizens of the United States of America, or any Persons, being Citizens of those States, engaged in taking Seals or Whales, or any species of Fish or marine animal, on any of the shores or lands of the Malvinas, Tierra del Fuego, Cape Horn, or any of the adjacent Islands in the Atlantic Ocean." The Chargé d'Affaires does not adduce one single reason to justify such an extraordinary declaration. Now I, for the reason that I am, as Mr. Baylies says, perfectly acquainted with the Institutions of The United States, and know the character which their Government sustains for its justness, cannot bring myself to believe that, without a previous examination of that right, a premature and absolute denial thereof is really the expression of its sentiments. It is true that its Envoy so avers; but it is no less true, that the President stated no such thing in his Message, but that he would send out a Minister—not for the purpose of roundly denying the right of this Republic, without giving any reason therefor— but solely for the purpose of examining into the right alleged; and there is a great difference between the examination of a doubtful fact, and the adoption of a determination regarding it. My reason revolts, Excellent Sir, at the terrible idea that such should be the sentiments of a Government I venerate; for indeed, if the decided resolution of that Government were to *utterly deny* the incontrovertible rights of this Republic, to what end was the *enquiry* of which the Message spoke?—to what end was the useless expense of sending a Minister to pronounce a simple *niego*, which might sooner and more easily have been said in the Note? But if, as it is to be inferred from the Message, all that the Government of The United States wished, was to inform itself thoroughly, how can it be believed that, before doing this, before instituting an enquiry, before giving a hearing, it should authoritatively pronounce an absolute and unjustified negative? Does it not know that in so doing it would be committing an injustice? Sir, if unfortunately this were true—if this extravagant language were really that of the President, all civilized Nations would immediately recognize in it the despotic language of Force,—they would look for and no longer find the principles of strict justice, which always regulated the resolves of the American Cabinet; for that language, translated into the idiom of reason, signifies—" I will not examine the rights adduced by a Nation, as independent as my own: however sacred they may be, I deny them: I disregard the prohibitions which it may dictate in exercise of its Sovereignty: my disregard proceeds from the knowledge of my strength, which I proclaim as the supreme regulator of international acts and rights.'' It would be insulting the public reason to believe the Government of The United States possessed of ideas so destructive of the most solemn principles, and of the independence of Nations. Nevertheless the Chargé d'Affaires affirms the existence of such sentiments. And am I not to believe, I repeat, that he has entirely mistaken the objects of his Mission?

These are, Sir, in compendium, the observations which rush upon the mind on view of this singular Negotiation—a Negotiation opened with unbecoming insults—devoid of every kind of proof—diverted from its primitive object—commenced where it ought to conclude, and in which it is impossible to distinguish the beginning from the *ultimatum* pronounced upon it.

But, having concluded my Report in the part which was enjoined me, may I be allowed, as a Citizen of the Republic, and as directly interested in the results of this important Controversy, to manifest my opinion and the foundation whereon it rests, with respect to the great question which is about to be submitted to the imposing Tribunal of the Civilized Nations? I speak of the question of the right of the Argentine Republic to the Malvina Islands and their Adjacencies, and to the Coasts of the Continent as far as Cape Horn. If the Government of The United States, or any other, deny the existence of that right, on your Excellency devolves the easy duty of demonstrating it to the World. Your Excellency will doubtless do so, and perhaps will find of some use the information which I proceed to communicate, moved principally by the strange denial which the Chargé d'Affaires had made of the aforesaid right.

Let us first establish general principles and ideas, which, applied afterwards to facts, will give us the solution of the difficulty it is endeavored to raise.

Certainly if we were only to attend to the practices observed by covetous Europe, in former hapless Ages, in arrogating to herself the Sovereignty of Countries whether inhabited or desert, it would be impossible to fix a universal rule respecting the means by which Nations acquire dominion. Those practices have varied according to circumstances; and the shameful history of the Ultramarine Establishments of Europe, both in the Eastern and Western Regions, presents no other authority for her rights than the voluble one of predominant interests in combination with the power of sustaining them. Nor has the odious right of conquest justified the appropriation of a great part of the most valuable Countries; for, in justice, there is no real conquest of a Country without previous war with its inhabitants—a war at once just and duly waged; but the Europeans have never hesitated to claim, by right of conquest, immense inhabited and inoffensive Countries, from the moment they set their feet on them, or raised a Cross or hoisted a Flag. What right had the Portuguese, in a time of Peace, to make themselves Masters of the East Indies? What the Dutch to eject them from these Possessions? What right had France and the Nations of the Baltic to divide amongst themselves the spoils of their ancient grandeur? What right had England to make herself almost exclusive mistress of those Dominions? Interest and force—nothing else; and at a time when the Civilized World was reduced to the very Nations which broke the Law of Nations, the general silence, or the applause of cupidity, succeeded almost in legitimating those means of acquiring dominion, which in process of time will perhaps inspire horror.

Europe did not follow any other measure in the usurpation, (which she gilded with the name of Colonization,) of the spacious Regions of the New World. In the complete subversion which the eternal principles of the Law of Nations had undergone, by the substitution of will and power for justice and reason, the European States rushed successively upon the pacific neighboring Territories. The first who arrived called himself Master—but his title was nominal, whilst he did not write it with his sword, or another did not erase it with his. Spain, Portugal and England were those who shared the most in the partition of a World. Their own interest taught them the necessity of mutually respecting their Acquisitions. Hence arose certain rules which they termed general, and which were successively established, either in a tacit manner, or by Conventions which they celebrated between themselves, or by Declarations of each Government, made as the cases occurred. Forgetting entirely the origin and the mode of the Acquisition, the Acquisition was only considered as a fact, and this fact as a right. But notwithstanding the Conventions and the rights which they mutually recognize, restless covetousness was burning in all of them, with the additional force which was communicated to it by the sight of what others possessed, and the unquenchable desire of possessing more. Hence so many aggressions, so many partial usurpations. An enterprising Nation possessed itself of a great part of Brazil; and this usurpation from Portugal, was viewed by Europe as a right, which in its turn disappeared by force, leaving scarcely the vestige which is now perceptible in Guayana. The English, French, and Dutch, either avowedly or under pretexts, endeavored at various times to establish themselves in, and make themselves Masters of, many Points, more or less important, belonging to the extensive possessions of Castile, especially in the Islands and Eastern Coasts of the Continent. The rich West India Islands presented an abridged representation of the conduct and system of acquiring pursued by Europe. He who seized on an Island was its owner, till he was in his turn ejected, in order to become again possessor; and that important Archipelago, was throughout, the theatre of a multitude of Sovereignties, many of

which were as varied and as moveable as the waters which surround
them.

And in the uncertain legislation which this tumultuous series of
reciprocal usurpations formed, can we perchance find the true rules
of the modes by which Nations acquire Dominion? No: we must
look for them in the immutable principles of the Law of Nations.—
This Law was infringed by those appropriations; but it had preceded
them, and therefore condemned them. It existed at the time of their
execution, and in despite of them; and it now exists—now that the
Nations, without repenting of their former acts, wish at least, from
respect to public opinion, to appear as regulating by it their present
conduct.

According to this universal Code, I unhesitatingly believe—

1st,—That the mere casual discovery of an uninhabited Country,
or of one inhabited by People whom it is easy to subject or destroy,
does not confer Dominion over it.

2nd,—That a discovery intentionally made in virtue of a determinate project or enterprize, confers it, provided this enterprize is
carried into effect by the actual settlement of the Discoverers in the
Country and their remaining therein; but not by their contenting themselves with a momentary possession, nor with leaving signs, which, after
the possession is concluded, are of no avail—such as flags, plates, inscriptions, coins, &c.

3rd,—That the means of acquiring, which Puffendorf calls origi-
nary, that is, the discovery and the occupation, or actual and permanent possession, with intention to retain,—are not the only ones. A
Nation can besides acquire over a Territory a Dominion which belonged to another, either by inheritance, by cession, by sale, by exchange, or by Treaty.

4th,—That the strongest and clearest of these rights, is that which
proceeds from the existence of another, as in the cases of cession,
exchange, &c., in which the right of one Nation passes to another,
whether this right may have originated in possession, or in any other
manner.

5th,—That this most valid title may, by being united to others,
become still stronger, as in the case of a Nation making the first discovery of a Country, and taking actual possession of it; and another,
which has pretentions to it, ceding the rights it may have, in favor of
the former.

6th,—That the Nation which, in any manner, acquires Dominion
over a District, and abandons it with the intention to return, manifested
by facts, such as leaving a part of its Establishment, letting the Settlements remain standing, or leaving other things of which it stood in
need, and might have taken away, &c. &c., still preserves that
Dominion.

7th,—That when a Nation acquires, by any of the aforesaid means, a Territory washed by the sea, it acquires, *ipso facto,* the Dominion over the Coasts, Ports, Islands, Gulfs, Fisheries, and all their Adjacencies.

8th,—That the Territory or jurisdiction of a State is all that space over which the action of its Government extends.

The effects of Dominion, considered, not on the whole, but only in that part which is applicable to the present question, are :

1st,—The power of enjoying and disposing of all the advantages which can be derived from its jurisdiction.

2nd,—The power of withholding or conceding this enjoyment.

3rd,—The power of punishing the infringers of the regulations which may be adopted with regard to this enjoyment, which power is inherent to every prohibitive right, as, without it, the right would be illusory.

This Dominion once acquired, is lost :

1st,—By the prevalence of Foreign Force, or by conquest.

2nd,—By exchange, sale, or express and definite cession, but not by the simple non-use of this or that District, or of this or that advantage ; nor by the toleration or tacit permission to a Nation of (for example,) the use of a Fishery ; for in these cases it is always presumed that the Nation to which the Dominion belongs, reserves its right.

3rd.—By dereliction or complete abandonment of the Territory with the intention of not returning to it, or when the intention of returning does not go beyond a mental resolve, or is not evinced by deeds ; in which cases it passes, *pro derelicto,* to the first who may occupy it ; but this does not take place when the abandonment is made in consequence of some extraordinary cause, or from necessity, or if it only consists in leaving uncultivated, deserted, or undefended, some Place for a short or long period of time.

The known wisdom of the Chargé d'Affaires will not fail to agree in the correctness of these principles, which, founded in reason uniformly admitted and generally observed, constitute an essential part of the common Code of Nations.

To apply them more clearly and suitably, we will enter on the irksome but necessary task of sketching the principal outlines of the history of the Malvinas, and the Eastern Coast of this Continent to the South of the River Plate.

We will first treat of the Coast, as being the part which offers the least difficulties.

It is entirely beyond dispute, that since the year 1519, and prior to the discovery of the River Plate, the Portuguese Magellan, in the service of Spain, and under the Reign of Charles V., discovered, nearly at the farthest point of the Continent, the Strait which now bears his name. It is equally indisputable that 8 years afterwards, Loaiza, likewise in the service of Spain, was the first who traversed that Strait; also, that to them succeeded other Spanish Navigators; among them, Alcozaba in 1535, Villalobos in 1549, &c.; it is equally so, that these anterior discoveries and labors of the Spaniards were what excited and aided the later undertakings of other Navigators, both Foreigners and Natives; counting among the former, the Englishmen Drake, Cavendish and Hawkins, in 1577, 1592, and 1593; and the Dutchmen Noort in 1599, Spilbert in 1615, Moore in 1619, &c.; and among the latter, Valdez in 1581, Nadal in 1618, &c. The English Nation pretends to attribute to Drake the discovery of Cape Horn in 1578, and Holland to the Dutchman Lemaire in 1616. The latter appears the most natural, as well from the etymology of the word Hornos (from Hoorn, a Town in Holland,) as from the fact that the celebrated English Navigator Cook, even with the knowledge possessed in his time, that is 150 years afterwards, could form no exact idea of the Cape. But be this as it may; that which appears beyond doubt, is, that the first who doubled the Cape was not an Englishman, but Lemaire. It is equally certain that no other Nation than Spain ever formed Establishments on any part of this extensive Coast: nor was there, in the beginning, any motive or interest for going to inhabit those misty and inclement Regions.

On the contrary, from the moment that Spain took possession of the River Plate, she had not only a motive, an interest—she was under the absolute necessity of taking and securing the whole extent of the Coast; as the primary object of her financial and colonial policy was always to keep the Foreigner aloof from her Dominions, in order to avoid a clandestine commerce. She, in effect, took possession of the Coast; but I shall not dilate much on this, nor on the large iron crosses which it is notorious she caused to be fixed on the whole line of Coast of Patagonia and Tierra del Fuego; I shall not, I repeat, dilate on this, as her Dominion was supported in actual, uninterrupted and expensive occupation, which was respected by Foreign Nations. On examining the public Archives of this Capital, it is found that the whole Coast was divided into 3 Districts: the first, from Cape San Antonio to Santa Elena; the 2nd, from thence to the Strait; and from the Strait onwards, including the Island of Los Estados, and Adjacencies, belonging to the District of the Malvinas, which constituted the third. It will likewise be seen that she formed Settlements in the Rio Negro, Puerto Deseado, San Julian, San José, and Santa Cruz, the first of which still exists.

The ever watchful Cabinet of Spain paid particular attention to these Establishments. On the 12th of March, 1780, she notified the remission of various Castilian, Gallician and Asturian Families, as Settlers. On the 9th of September, 1781, she concentrated the Government of the Coast in D. Francisco Viedma, naming him Superintendant of the Establishments from Cape San Antonio to Santa Elena, placing under his dependence those of San José, San Julian and Puerto Deseado; and marking out as the jurisdiction of the Superintendant of San Julian, all the space comprised from Santa Elena to the Strait of Magellan. On all these points she constructed and preserved depôts for Convicts and Military Detachments, the maintenance of which cost many dollars to the Treasury of Buenos Ayres. By a Royal Order of the 28th of September, 1781, 6 Vessels were permanently destined to these Establishments, for which Vessels the said Treasury had to pay the sum of 83,509 dollars; and such was the constant care for the preservation of these Settlements, notwithstanding the great expense they occasioned, that, San José having been abandoned by the greater part of its Inhabitants, owing to a scarcity of provisions, a Royal Order was signed at Pardo, on the 4th of March, 1780, conceding a premium to the few Soldiers who had not abandoned the Place, and pardoning the Convicts who remained. By another, dated at San Lorenzo, on the 22nd of November, 1795, the King approved all the measures which had been successively proposed to him by 2 Vice-Roys, the object of which was to preserve, foment, and add to the Establishments on the Coast, *in order that the English might not establish themselves there.*

Spain did not content herself with the mere permanent occupation of all the Coasts; she caused her Subjects to enter into the enjoyment of the advantages accruing therefrom. With this view, she in 1790 established a grand Maritime Company, the direction of which should be in Madrid, and the principal factory in Puerto Deseado. Its object was the settlement and improvement of the Coast, the curing of Fish, and the Whale and Seal Fisheries. Twelve months afterwards, various privileges were conceded to the Company. By a Royal Order of the 15th September, 1792, a further concession was made to it, allowing it to extend its Fishery to the Malvinas, and ordering the Convicts who were there to be employed in this occupation. By another of the 6th of February, 1791, it was already ordained that the Treasury of Buenos Ayres should lend assistance to D. Juan Muñoz, for sustaining the Establishment of Puerto Deseado, as the King was determined, even should the state of the Company not permit it to incur the expense, that the Establishment be supported at all costs, were it only as a Depôt for Convicts. By another of the 17th of April, 1798, it was ordered that the Treasury of Buenos Ayres assist the Company with 20,000 dollars annually. Finally, by another of the 13th November, 1799, it was ordained, among other things, that the 20,000 dollars be furnished every year without discount or delay; that the exclusive right to the Fisheries should belong to the Company; and that the Company should from that time be considered as a private property of the Royal patrimony.

It is unnecessary to state that this Company, though apparently it did not succeed, entered on the full and undisputed enjoyment of its rights and privileges, without any Nation calling them in question. On the contrary, all Countries respected them ; and on the few occasions on which Foreign Vessels touched at their Establishments, they acknowledged the jurisdiction of the Company, and acceded without repugnance to its Regulations. On the 2nd of June, 1793, the Commandant of Puerto Deseado, D. Miguel Recio, gave notice of the arrival at that place of the 2 American Vessels *Ark* and *Governor Brown,* for the purpose of fishing. They were ordered to abstain from doing so, and to set sail immediately ; when they excused themselves, under pretext that they only wished to re-establish the health of their Crews, attacked by scurvy, and not to fish in that Port, or in its neighborhood ; adding that they well knew they were not authorized to do so, on account of the Agreement entered into between Spain and England. In like manner, in 1803, an English Brig appeared off Puerto Deseado, and after standing off and on several times, she was not only reprimanded for navigating in those Seas, but was likewise deprived of some Seal skins she had taken on the Coast. On the 4th of April, 1802, a Shallop belonging to the American Ship *Diana*, Captain Smith, entered Rio Negro for the purpose of taking in water, when the Viceroy reprimanded the Commander of that place for not having ordered her to retire from those Seas. The Shallop having returned on the 21st of June in the same year, in quest of assistance for careening the Vessel, she was then ordered off, which order she obeyed immediately, and set sail, abandoning her Second Mate and 6 Seamen.

Thus the dominion of Spain over the whole extent of the Coast is founded on its discovery, on the first and exclusive permanent occupation of it, and on continual and repeated acts of Sovereignty, exercised under the eye of all Nations, without any having called it in question ; all, on the contrary, having acknowledged it.

Let us now turn to the Malvina Islands. Who was the first Discoverer of these Islands, is a question the solution of which has never been universally agreed to. There are many widely different opinions with regard to it. This enquiry, however, according to the principles here laid down, is not of itself sufficient to decide on the Sovereignty of these Islands. But he is deceived who may think that Spain has no pretensions to the discovery of them. It is true that the discovery was casual, and that not even a name was then given to the Islands ; but of this kind was likewise the discovery which the English attribute to Davies in 1592. To justify this pretension of Spain, I will not cite, as I might do, the assertions of Spanish Authors ; but rather that of a Frenchman, whose testimony cannot therefore be objected to by other Nations ; of a Frenchman, who, as the first Settler on the

Malvinas, had a special motive for enquiring into the matter. Bougainville, in the account of his second voyage to the Malvinas, thus expresses himself. "I am of opinion that the first discovery of them can only be attributed to the celebrated Navigator, Américo Vespucio, who, in the third voyage which he made for the discovery of America in 1502, run down the North Coast of them. It is certain that he did not know whether they formed part of an Island, or of the Continent; but from the route he followed, from the latitude to which he arrived, and even from the description he gives of the Island, it can easily be perceived that it was one of the Malvinas." The *British Naval Chronicle*, of 1809, written by various literary Characters, says, that, although the first discovery of the Malvinas has been attributed to Davies, it is very probable they were seen by Magellan, and by Others who followed him. Spain may therefore lay claim to the discovery.

Not so to the first occupation or settlement. It is not stated by any Writer that the Islands were colonized before the year 1764. There had been, it is true, projects in contemplation and wishes evinced to take possession of them; but they were never realized. What is said in this respect by an English Author, Miller, *(History of the Reign of George III.)* is worthy of notice. "It was first remarked by Lord Anson, on his return from his famous voyage round the Globe in 1744, that the possession of a Port to the southward of the Brazils would be of signal service to future navigators for refitting their Ships, and providing them with necessaries, previous to their passage through the Straits of Magellan, or the doubling Cape Horn; and among other places eligible for this purpose, he specified Falkland Islands. About 10 years after, on his Lordship's advancement to the head of the Admiralty, a plan in conformity to his ideas was on the point of being carried into execution; but strong remonstrances being made against it by the King of Spain under the old pretence of his exclusive right to all the Magellanic Regions, the Project, though not expressly given up, was suffered to lie dormant."

Some years afterwards, France formed a similar scheme and carried it into execution. According to Pernety's account, on the 8th September 1763, the Ship *Aigle*, carrying 20 guns and 100 men, under the command of M. Guyot, Captain of a Fireship, and the Corvette *Sphynx*, with 14 guns and 40 men, commanded by M. Clenart, set sail from St. Maloes for the Malvina Islands. On the 4th of February 1764 they entered the great Bay of La Soledad, which the English afterwards called Berkeley Sound; having disembarked, they ascended a hill, on the summit of which they erected a large wooden Cross, (a part of which exists to this day,) and on 17th of February they established themselves by constructing a Fort. After having brought cannons on shore and taken possession with a salute of 21 guns, in the name of His Most Christian Majesty, M. Nerville was appointed Governor.

In Bougainville's Work may be seen the sequel of this event—the labors undertaken—the entire absence of traces of former inhabitants, to the degree that the birds appeared to be entirely domesticated—the voyage which he made to France—his return to the Colony on the 5th of January 1765—the content in which the Colonists lived, &c. &c.

Thus it is evident that the French were the first settlers of those Islands, to which 60 years before, when they saw them for the first time and considered themselves the Discoverers, they gave the name of *Malouines*, a name which has prevailed more generally than those of Pepis, Falkland, and others which were likewise given them.

But as soon as Spain received intelligence of this occupation of the Islands, she asserted her right to them and they were restored to her. "In February, 1764," says Bougainville, "France had commenced an Establishment in the Malvinas. Spain claimed them as a Dependency of the Continent of South America. The King (of France) acknowledged her right, and I received orders to go and deliver our Establishment to the Spaniards."

In virtue of that acknowledgment, by a Royal Order of the 4th of October, 1766, D. Felipe Ruiz Puente was appointed Governor of the Malvinas; he repaired thither from Montevideo in company with Bougainville, who had arrived at that Port. In April of the following year, Bougainville made to Puente a formal and absolute delivery of the Establishment, Vessels, Effects, Arms, Provisions, &c., the value of which was reimbursed to the French, part in Spain and France, and the rest in Buenos Ayres.

In the meantime the English, (according to *Byron's Voyage round the World*,) under the command of Admiral Byron, visited these Islands on the 13th of January 1765, and on the 23rd took possession of them, under the name of Falkland, after a long time had elapsed, since they had borne that of Malouines, and after they had been colonized by the French since the preceding year. Byron declared that all of them belonged to His Britannic Majesty, and sailed from thence on the 27th, without leaving a hut or a single man. The harbour at which Byron had arrived, had not only been discovered by the French, but it had received from them the name of Port de la Croisade; the English gave it the appellation of Port Egmont.

In 1766, England, forgetting that 22 years before she had acknowledged the exclusive dominion of Spain over the Malvinas by desisting from the project of Lord Anson, sent an Expedition under the command of Capt. Macbride, who formed an Establishment in Port Egmont. So far from finding those Islands desert, and from being able to ground thereon a right, the English found the French established there since the 2 preceding years, and had it in contemplation to make use of force. "Capt. Macbride, Commander of the Frigate *Jason*," says

Bougainville, "came to my Establishment about the beginning of December of the same year (1766); he pretended that those Islands belonged to His Britannic Majesty, and threatened to disembark by force, were any resistance offered; he made a visit to the Commandant, and set sail the same day."

I must not omit here an observation which Bougainville makes immediately afterwards, as it proves that France acknowledged Spain to be possessed of a right to these Islands anterior to the French occupation of them, and consequently anterior to occupation of them by Macbride. "Such was," he says, "the state of the Malvina Islands when I gave them up to the Spaniards, whose *primitive right* was thus rendered stronger by that which we had undoubtedly acquired by the first occupation."

The Governor of the Malvinas, Puente, notified to the Viceroy, and he to his Court, the establishment of the English in Port Egmont. In the interim, he gave Instructions to the Commander of the Frigate *Santa Rosa*, in which, in virtue of the orders he had received from the Viceroy, he advised him that if he found there an English Settlement, or any English Vessels, he should warn them "*that they were violating the existing Treaties, by being in those Dominions without the express consent of His Catholic Majesty.*" These Treaties doubtless relate to the acknowledgment of the Spanish Dominion, even by the English themselves, in the time of Lord Anson.

Some time afterwards, a Force, under the Command of D. Juan Ignacio Madariaga, sailed from Buenos Ayres against the English. On the 3rd of July, 1770, accounts were received from Puente, including the Despatch of Madariaga, by which it appeared that on the 10th of June he had defeated and taken the English in the Port of La Croisade, or Egmont, of which George Tamer was Governor; and by the Capitulation entered into, the English were to give up all they had there, and were to be permitted to keep their Flag hoisted on board the Frigate and at the Garrison, until they had embarked, which was done.

This news produced an extraordinary excitement in England, and great preparations were made for war with Spain, which cost the Nation more than £3,000,000 sterling. But, on the 2nd of January, 1771, the dispute was settled by a Convention, which was signed in London, by Lord Rochfort, and the Spanish Ambassador, Prince Masserano, in which was stipulated the complete restitution of the Establishment to the English, *in statu quo;* but leaving pending the question as to the right claimed by Spain. We shall afterwards see whether or not this apparently trivial reservation was acted upon by that Power.

Spain honestly fulfilled her part of the Treaty. The Treasury of Buenos Ayres received orders to defray the expense of replacing every thing in Port Egmont, to which the English returned in 1771.

But 3 years afterwards, the English suddenly and silently abandoned the Settlement which had cost them so much. According to the principles laid down, it is of no importance whether or not they left inscriptions there. The fact is, they abandoned the place—they never returned to it; and neither to the Court of Spain, to the Government of Buenos Ayres, nor to the Governor of Malvinas, did they intimate their intention of returning, as it was easy and natural for them to do, had such intention existed; neither did they even inform those Authorities of the motives. But what is more extraordinary, not even the English Nation was ever informed of them. The Chargé d'Affaires cannot cite a single Document in contradiction of any of these assertions.

The mysterious abandonment of Port Egmont, Excellent Sir, is the most remarkable and the most curious incident in the history of the Malvinas; and, before going farther, it is highly important to examine into the nature and causes of this event. The result of the enquiry will be the conviction that this abandonment completely annihilated the rights, however valid they may have been, which Great Britain had to that part of the Islands; and that from that time they reverted to their first origin—the Crown of Castile.

What could have caused this extraordinary abandonment?—Could it be fear? No: for the English could have nothing to apprehend after the solemn restitution which had been made to them; neither could England, in the year 1774, stand in awe of Spain. Could it be the inutility of the Settlement? No: for the advantages laid down 30 years before by Lord Anson, were even greater at that time, on account of the increase, and greater activity which had been given, as well to her mercantile Shipping in general as to her lucrative commerce with the East Indies. Was it from economy? So says the Chargé d'Affaires of His Britannic Majesty, Mr. Parish, doubtless because he had no other motive to adduce in the Protest, which, by order of his Court, he presented to the Government of Buenos Ayres, on the 19th November, 1829, on occasion of the Decree of the 10th of June, 1829, appointing a Governor of the Islands.

But, Sir, to explain that phenomenon in the way in which Mr. Parish explains it, it is necessary to forget the character of the English Nation, and entirely to lose sight of her mercantile history. A Nation accustomed to make the greatest sacrifices for obtaining and securing every thing that can be of interest to her trade—a Government which never resists that which is called for by a majority of its Subjects, and whose policy tends principally to the aggrandizement of its commerce—a Nation which had shewn itself irritated to an extraordinary degree on being despoiled of Port Egmont, and which had not hesitated to expend, in a few months, nearly 20,000,000 of dollars in warlike preparations on that account—an opulent and enterprising mercantile Nation, which had so much occasion for that Place, as is proved by the numerous Vessels belonging to her, which, from that time, up to the present, have frequented the Islands, either to take in provisions, or for objects connected with the Fisheries—such a Nation, having just obtained pacifically, and without expense, the enjoyment of those advantages for ever, suddenly to abandon her Possessions, solely for the miserable saving of the expense of their support, when merely the produce of the Fisheries would more than repay the expenses of the Establishment—abandon them from motives of economy, without leaving even a Vessel, or a few men, notwithstanding her riches, her numerous Navy, and her excessive Population—abandon them in silence when she might have spoken openly, and it was so much her interest to do so! This, Excellent Sir, I can say, with confidence, is impossible. To render it credible, it would be necessary they should bring forward proofs and deeds as irrefragable as is this fact, that the English did entirely abandon the Malvinas.

There must, therefore, have existed some other cause; and the fact of concealing it plainly proves that it was not favorable to the pretensions of England. In effect, she agreed to an express Treaty— at least there are grounds for believing this, without referring to the Archives, a thousand times stronger than any that exist for stating as Mr. Parish did, that the abandonment was only *in consequence of the system of economy at that time adopted by the Government of His Britannic Majesty.*

The Treaty to which I allude had its origin in the year 1771, and by it Port Egmont was restored to the English, with reservation as to the right of Spain. To prove it, I will present the positive assertions of respectable Writers; purposely setting aside all those who might be objected to by England, and selecting only English Writers. The result of this labor will shew:

1st.—That the abandonment of Port Egmont was complete and absolute, and not, as Mr. Parish asserts, with an intention to return to it—an intention, which under all circumstances, would have been merely mental, and as secret as the abandonment was public.

2nd.—That the following is what gave rise to this abandonment. While treating for the restitution of Port Egmont, England did not disavow the exclusive right of Spain to the Islands; as neither had she disavowed it in the time of Lord Anson. But as she could not cede them at that time, without augmenting the irritation which existed in the minds of the People, and deeply wounding the national pride, it was agreed to make the restitution on conditions, which should not be expressed; for which purpose was inserted the Clause—"*that that Act should not affect the question of prior right of Sovereignty over the Malvinas.* In this way the English People were satisfied, and the Negotiation was left open, so as afterwards to agree to the total evacuation of Port Egmont.

3rd.—That, consequently, Spain recovered the full enjoyment of her rights over all the Archipelago of the Malvinas.

Miller, in the before-cited Work, after relating the excitement produced by the news of the expulsion of the English from Port Egmont, and the Agreement by which it was restored, adds, that Parliament voted an Address of Thanks to His Majesty's Government, for having obtained that accommodation, and to justify it, it was said that " the atonement made by Spain was as ample as could be justly required; and that Ministers would have been in the highest degree reprehensible, had they involved the Nation in a War for the sake of so insignificant an object as the reserved pretensions of Spain to 1 or 2 barren spots under a stormy sky in a distant quarter of the Globe." This Extract, I will remark by the way, shows that the Nation attacked the Ministry for having consented to that reservation, either because it apprehended the results thereof, or penetrated into what was kept concealed from it. The Protest which 19 Peers of the Realm entered, on this occasion, may be referred to on the subject. From these attacks arose that pompous and contradictory justification of the Treaty. An Address of Thanks to the Government is voted for having obtained something great; and at the same time an endeavor is made to underrate it by representing the Islands as barren, useless, &c. Wherefore was the contradiction? Because it was necessary to prepare the public mind for what was to take place afterwards.

Miller continues: " the possibility of a similar dispute (between England and Spain,) was precluded by the *total evacuation* of that Settlement about 3 years after."

The celebrated oracle of the Opposition, under the assumed name of JUNIUS, did not allow himself to be deceived; he bitterly criticised the Ministry for having admitted that reservation, and penetrating, or knowing the real state of the case, he said the restoration was *temporary,* and announced as certain to the Nation the future cession of the rights of England to the Malvinas. In the Edition of his famous Letters which I have before me, the English Editor remarks on this occasion, that the Spaniards fulfilled their engagement by restoring the Establishment, and the English *fulfilled* theirs by abandoning it after such surrender.

Brookes's *General Gazetteer*, published in London, says: " In 1770 the Spaniards dislodged the English from Port Egmont—this affair was settled by a Convention, and the English regained possession; but in 1774 the Settlement was abandoned, and the *Islands ceded to Spain."*

Chapter 39, of the *Anecdotes of the Life of the Right Honorable William Pitt, &c.*, contains the following: " While Lord Rochford was negotiating with Prince Masserano, Mr. Stuart Mac-Kenzie was negotiating with Monsieur François. At length, about an hour before

the Meeting of Parliament, on the 22nd of January, 1771, a Declaration was signed by the Spanish Ambassador, under French Orders
and a French indemnification, for the restitution of Falkland Islands
to His Britannic Majesty ; *but the important addition, upon which this
Declaration was obtained, was not mentioned in the Declaration.* This
condition was, *that the British Forces should evacuate Falkland Islands
as soon as convenient after they were put in possession of Port and
Fort Egmont.* And the British Ministry engaged, *as a pledge of
their sincerity* to keep that promise, that they would be the first to
disarm.

" During the month of February, 1771, the Spanish Minister at
Madrid hinted to Mr. Harris the intention of the Spanish Court to
require of the British Ministry *a perfection of engagements, as they
were mutually understood.* Mr. Harris's Despatch, containing this
hint, was received by the Ministry on the 4th of March. 3 days afterwards, a Spanish Messenger arrived, with Orders to Prince Masserano,
*to make a positive demand of the cession of Falkland Islands, to the King
of Spain.* The Spanish Ambassador first communicated his information of these Orders to the French Ambassador, with a view of
knowing whether he would concur with him in making the demand.
On the 14th, they held a Conference with Lord Rochford on the subject. *His Lordship's Answer was consonant to the spirit he had uniformly shewn* In consequence of this Answer, Messengers were sent to
Paris and Madrid. The Reply from France was civil, but mentioned
the Family Compact. The Answer from Spain did not reach London
till the 20th of April. In the mean time the Ministers held several
Conferences with Mr. Stuart M'Kenzie—the result of the whole was,
the English set the example to disarm : and Falkland Islands *were totally evacuated and abandoned in a short time afterwards; and have
ever since been in the possession of the Spaniards.* The British Arma-
ment cost the Nation between 3 and 4 millions of money, besides the
expense and inconvenience to Individuals."

All these facts are confirmed by the testimony of Gumes, in his
Memorial against Fort, Roger, and Delpech, who had accused him of
jobbing in the Public Funds.

The before-mentioned *British Naval Chronicle,* after relating that
in 1774, the English Government ordered Capt. Clayton to evacuate
Port Egmont, and take away the effects, and that he, on his departure,
fixed a leaden Plate, with an Inscription, saying, that the Islands belonged to His Britannic Majesty, concludes: " but these Islands so
pertinaciously claimed by the English, *were ceded to Spain.*"

The *British Encyclopedia* contains the following: " Port Egmont
was restored to the English, who again took possession of it, but a
short time after, *it was abandoned in consequence of a private agreement between the Ministry and the Court of Spain.*"

These unimpeachable testimonies are sufficient to acquaint us with the nature and motives of that strange, sudden and silent abandonment. We may, therefore, assert, as an unquestionable fact, that in 1774, in virtue of a Convention, all the rights which England might have had to the Malvinas were surrendered and transferred to the Kings of Spain. Here I may repeat the remark, that Bougainville makes on the occasion of the former cession by France : " Thus was rendered more secure the *primitive right* of Spain,"—a right, I may add, recognized by England since the time of Lord Anson. Let us now continue the sketch of the History of the Malvinas.

From 1774 onward, Spain was the exclusive Mistress of all the Islands—no Nation disputed her rights—none dared to establish itself in the Archipelago—she legislated over it, and exercised without interruption, Acts of Sovereignty, which were respected by Foreign Countries. I will enumerate some of them. In 1774, she appointed Don Francisco Gil, Governor of the Malvinas; in February, 1777, Don Ramon Clairac; in 1784, Don Agustin Figueroa ; in June 1790, Don Juan José Elizalde ; in February, 1793, Don Pedro Pablo San Gineto ; in 1799, Don Ramon J. Villegas; and in 1805, Don Antonio de la Barra, &c.

Since 1767, she constantly supported, with great sacrifices, the Establishment of La Soledad, in which, and in the Garrison, Vessels, &c., she expended 150,000 dollars per Annum, which sum was supplied mostly by the Treasury of Buenos Ayres ; but she did not confine herself to an insignificant Settlement; she endeavored to promote agriculture, and for this purpose transported thither Convicts, Cattle, &c., so that, in 1784, according to the returns of Governor Figueroa, the buildings amounted to 34, the population to 82 persons, including 28 Convicts, and the Cattle of all kinds to 7,774 head.

In the beginning of 1776, Captain Juan P. Callejas formally reconnoitred Port Egmont and the adjacent Bays; he found the roads covered with grass, the doors of the Houses and Stores open, the roofs almost entirely fallen in, and some effects scattered on the shore.

Under date of 7th February, 1776, the Court sent word that the Prince of Masserano had complained to the Cabinet of London, of several English Vessels having been seen in Port Egmont, *in opposition to the solemn and repeated protestations with which Spain had been assured of the total abandonment of that place.* The British Minister again assured him of the abandonment, adding that he had reason to suspect that Vessels belonging to the revolted Colonies of North America often went to the Islands to fish for Whales ; on which account the Court of London had it in contemplation to send 1 or 2 Frigates to expel them. On this occasion, the Government of Buenos Ayres was desired to cause the Governor of the Malvinas to again reconnoitre the Islands, and if he found any individuals there to order them off immediately.

On the 9th of August of the same year, 1776, the Court ordained, that, England having already evacuated the Establishment she had formed in the Malvinas, the Government of Buenos Ayres should destine 2 Frigates to cruize in those parts; and on the 26th of September, it gave orders to warn the Vessels of the English Colonies to abstain from frequenting those Seas and Coasts, as they belonged to the King of Spain.

On the 1st of April, 1777, the head Pilot of the Royal Squadron, Don Pablo Sisur was commissioned to make a new survey of Port Egmont. In his Instructions he was ordered, if he found there any American Vessels, to make to them the before-mentioned intimation, as it was no longer under British dominion; and in case he should find there any English Vessels, he should make the same intimation to them, and further accuse them of a want of good faith.

In 1777, the Governor of Malvinas received Orders from the King to entirely demolish the Establishment of Port Egmont, and not to leave a vestige of it remaining. This was afterwards done, and the Spanish Government, under date of the 8th of February, 1781, acknowledged the receipt of the Despatch acquainting it with the fulfilment of its Instructions.

Spain declared War against Great Britain on the 8th of July, 1779, and in the year following the Viceroy of Buenos Ayres received Orders to make every sacrifice for sustaining the Malvinas, in order that England might never claim them, *pro derelicto.* This was done, and happily, in January 1783, Preliminaries of Peace between the 2 Nations were agreed on; and the Convention celebrated in virtue thereof was communicated to Buenos Ayres.

In March, 1787, by order of the Viceroy, the Marquis of Loreta, Don Pedro Meza reconnoitred the whole of the Malvinas, and did not find there a single British Subject, or a Foreigner of any other Nation.

By a Royal Order, dated in Aranjuez on the 28th of April, 1788, Instructions were given to foment the Fisheries in the Islands, and to reconnoitre their Establishments, in order not to allow any English to remain, either on Falkland or any other part.

On the 28th of October, 1790, a Treaty or Convention was entered into at San Lorenzo, between the Governments of Spain and England, for settling various disputed points relative to Fishing, Navigation, and Commerce in the Pacific and South Seas; and at the same place the Ratifications were exchanged on the 22nd November following. By this Treaty, after regulating various other points, it was agreed in Article IV, that British Subjects should not fish or navigate in the South Seas, within the distance of 10 maritime leagues of any part of the Coasts then occupied by Spain. In Article VI, it was stipulated that in future the Subjects of both Nations' should be prohibited from forming any Establishment to the south of those parts of the Coasts and Islands adjacent, which were then occupied by Spain, but that they should be allowed to erect temporary huts for the object of the Fisheries.

On the 22nd November, 1791, Elizalde, Governor of the Malvinas, with a Frigate and a Brig, was commissioned to reconnoitre those parts in the vicinity of Cape Horn and Tierra del Fuego, in which the English might have established themselves, and to oblige them to fulfil the Treaty of 1790. In the Instructions he is told, among other things, that, " according to the literal tenor of Article VI, the English should not be allowed to fish or to construct huts on Coasts which, although desert, may be situated to the north of Territories occupied by Spain, such as the Coasts of Puerto Deseado, those of San José, and even the Bay of San Julian, and other places in which we may have had occupation or settlements, or which may be accessory to Districts actually occupied."

With respect to the constant and strict prohibition from fishing, or even navigating the Malvinas, imposed by Spain on Foreigners, many examples can be adduced. To avoid prolixity, I shall only notice a few, of different epochs.

On the 7th of February, 1790, the American Schooner, *Peregrine*, Captain Palmer, arrived at the western Bay. The Governor caused her to be taken to La Soledad; and the Captain, on being reprimanded for touching there, replied that he had no other object than to procure an anchor. He was ordered to leave the Islands, and immediately obeyed.

In 2 cruizes made by Don Ramon Clairac in 1787, he found in different parts of the Islands, the Ship *Hudibras*, the Shallop *Audaz*, and the Brig *Malplaquet*, all English Vessels. They made divers excuses for being there, and were all likewise ordered off.

On the 29th of July, 1793, the Governor Sangineto learned that, in the Islands, and the neighborhood of them, were various foreign fishing Vessels; he called a Council of his Officers, in which it was resolved that Lieut. Don Juan Latre, in the Brig *Galvez*, should go in quest of these Vessels, and expel them. The *Galvez* sailed on the 11th of September, and found in the Isla Quemada the American Brig *Nancy*, Captain Gardener, to whom he addressed the following Note: —" In consequence of the recent Treaties between the Spanish and British Governments, and of the Orders I have received from the Commander and Governor of these Islands of Malvina, it is my duty to inform you that you have no right either to fish or to anchor in the neighborhood of Spanish Settlements; as solely the English Royalists are allowed to fish at a distance of 10 leagues from the said Establishments; nor are they permitted in this part of America to construct huts in any place not situated to the south of them : therefore, the Anglo-Americans not being comprehended in the privilege enjoyed by the Royalists ; and even were they, this privilege not allowing them to anchor in the Ports of the said Islands ; you will set sail so soon as the weather shall permit, and go to some other part where it is allowed to do it. God preserve you," &c. &c. (Latre afterwards relates the destructive method resorted to by these Vessels for taking Seals ; burning the rushes to force them out, and destroying them without distinction of age or sex.) A short time after receiving this intimation the American Vessel set sail.

On the 14th, in the Port of Los Desvelos, Latre found 6 American Vessels, all from New York, and 1 French Vessel, viz.—Ship *Josefa,* Captain Hewitt ; and Brigs *Nancy,* Captain Green ; *Maria,* Captain MacCall ; and *Mercury,* Captain Bernard. These Vessels were employed in fishing. Not only was the same intimation made to them, but their huts and gardens were destroyed ; the Crews of the Vessels assisting in the demolition. All of them successively obeyed the orders ; and on setting sail, duly saluted the Spanish Flag, by lowering their own.

On the 31st of January, 1802, the Governor, Villegas, notified the arrival of the American Ship *Juno,* Captain Kendrick, for the sole purpose of taking in water, and stated that she was the bearer of a recommendation from the Spanish Consul resident in The United States, which had been given her in case of her being forced to touch at the Malvinas. The Viceroy replied to him, under date of 4th May, that, notwithstanding such recommendation, he should fulfil the orders he had received with respect to any Foreign Vessel arriving there.

I think I have now cited sufficient facts of this nature.

We have now arrived at the epoch of the great blow struck by America, against the Power and Dominion of the Kings of Spain.— Here let us pause a moment. The long series of accredited facts I have brought forward clearly proves that Spain possessed and exercised an exclusive Sovereignty over all the Archipelago of the Malvinas. Notwithstanding this, it may not be superfluous to note down here a few of the many observations which present themselves.

It can no longer be denied that, prior to any Nation taking possession of the Islands, Spain called them hers. This pretension may have been founded on a first discovery made by Americo Vespucio, by Magellan, or by others ; but no matter on what it be founded, or who may have really been the first Discoverer; the fact is, the claim existed and was acknowledged. This is proved by England having desisted from the plan of Lord Anson. If England had possessed any right over the Islands, the demand of the Spanish Minister, relative to the object of the Expedition, would have been ridiculous and insulting. Why question the owner of a thing, as to what he is about to do with that which belongs to him? Above all, had such right been inherent in England and not in Spain, England would not have desisted: therefore up to that time England possessed no right.

France was the first Nation which, long after this, took possession of the Malvinas: Spain claimed them as Adjacencies of the Continent: her Dominion over them was acknowledged, and they were given up to her.

More than 12 months subsequently to the French, England took possession and was dislodged; and hardly had a restitution of her rights been made to her, when she ceded them to Spain by a Treaty. Thus Spain, by these acts, reassumed all the rights which may have appertained to France or England. From that time Spain continued in the full enjoyment of an acknowledged Sovereignty; in the exercise of which she, in 1790, granted to the English permission to Fish at a distance of 10 leagues from the Coast. Long posterior to that date, and since then, not content with written titles, she exercised a positive Dominion over them; formed and supported permanent Establishments, and her orders were obeyed by all the Foreign Vessels which touched at her Possessions. Thus, then, if we make the application of the principles laid down, we shall find that the right of Spain was founded: 1st.—In the Discovery: at least it cannot be proved that it was not due to her Navigators. 2nd.—In the first Occupation: for the rights which France had acquired thereby, were transferred to Spain. 3rd.—In the Possession, not ideal and nominal, but a permanent, real, positive and expensive Possession. 4th.—In the Cession made by the only 2 Nations, England and France, who could lay any claim to the Islands; Cessions which obviate any doubt or dispute which could be brought forward relative to the first discovery or the first occupation: of which Cessions, that of England is proved by the Treaty of the year 1790; for if, as Mr. Parish maintains, England had not lost her rights by the abandonment of the Islands, she would not, in 1790, have contented herself with the limited and trivial right of Fishing at a distance of 10 leagues from them. I mean therefore to say, that the right of Spain is founded on the most respectable and universal principle acknowledged by the Law of Nations; and which has been before laid down.

In conformity with these same principles, it is evident that Spain possessed the right to prohibit Foreigners from the enjoyment of the advantages afforded by these Islands, and of punishing, discretionally, those who might infringe her regulations.

It is clear, then, that all these rights passed to the Nation which had succeeded to Spain in the Sovereignty over those Regions.

It would be both useless and ridiculous to lose time in demonstrating that, from the moment the Argentine Republic became an Independent Nation, it acquired and legally appropriated to itself all those rights formerly possessed and exercised over its Territory by Spain. But there has not been wanting a Foreign Newspaper to advance the singular idea that, the former Viceroyalty of Buenos Ayres having been subdivided into various Sovereign States, it could not be known to which of them belonged the right which Spain had over the Coasts up to Cape Horn, and the adjacent Islands.

To which could it belong, if not to that to which they are indissolubly bound by nature? The Territory which formerly composed the United Provinces of the River Plate having been subdivided into various States, each has remained mistress of the advantages which the locality of her Territory presented. This is both natural and just; as it is conformable to the principle of the Law of Nations, and to the primordial objects of the institution of Governments. Paraguay, the Oriental State, or Bolivia, governing our Coasts and the Islands adjacent to them; and the Argentine Republic legislating, with similar right, in the Ports of Assumption and Maldonado, or relative to the mines of Potosi; would present an inextricable labyrinth, whose only outlet would be war, and the consequent misfortunes of the Regions so governed. This consideration has uniformly operated in all the States raised on the ruins of the old Spanish Dominion. There is not one of them, from Mexico to Buenos Ayres, but, on separating from Spain, adopted the principle, that to each State, whether large or small, belongs the whole extent of Territory which appertained to the Viceroyalty, or Captain Generalship, to which it has succeeded (except in cases of special agreement), as also the exclusive enjoyment of all the rights and advantages inherent to the said Territory. It cannot, therefore, be denied that the Argentine Nation succeeded to Spain in the Dominion over the Malvina Islands, on separating herself from that Country in 1810.

Let us now trace the last period of the History of the Malvinas, which commences in 1810.

From that year, up to 1820, no Establishment (at least, no permanent one), was formed by any Nation, either in the Malvinas, or on the Coasts of the Continent; and this, notwithstanding that the Argentine Republic was not then in a situation to attend to the defence of them; and, notwithstanding that, in this interval, Foreign Nations continued to frequent those Seas, either for the purposes of Navigation, or for the Fisheries, and that, therefore, it was of importance to them to form permanent Establishments there. This plainly proves that Foreign Nations continued to consider those Regions as appertaining to a Dominion which has since devolved on this Republic.

In 1820, the Government of Buenos Ayres took formal and solemn possession of the Malvinas, in the person of the Colonel of its Navy, Mr. Daniel Jewitt.

When Jewitt arrived at La Soledad, he found disseminated in the Islands, more than 50 Foreign Vessels. I will name some of them :— ENGLISH—Ship, *Indian*, Capt. Spiller, from Liverpool; Brig, *June*, Weddle, from Leith; do., *Hette*, Bond, from London; do., *George*, Richardson, from Liverpool; Cutter, *Eliza*, Powell, Liverpool; do., *Sprightly*, Frazier, from London. AMERICAN—Ships, *General Knox*, *Eucane*, *Newhaven*, and *Governor Hawkins*; Brigs, *Fanning* and *Harmony*; Schooners, *Wasp*, *Free Gift*, and *Hero*—from New York and Stonington.

All these Vessels were engaged in the Seal-fishery, and they even killed on the Islands the Cattle which had been carried there from Buenos Ayres by the Spaniards. In the presence of these Vessels anchored in the Port of La Soledad, Jewitt took possession, firing a salute of 21 guns, with the artillery which he landed. He treated them all with urbanity, and notified to them in writing the fact of the Republic having taken possession, and the prohibition to Fish on the Islands, or kill Cattle thereon, under the penalty of detention, and the remission of the Infringers to Buenos Ayres to be tried.

In 1823, the Government appointed Don Pablo Areguati, Commandant of the Malvinas. In the same year Don Jorge Pacheco and myself, convinced of the right of this Republic, and seeing it recognized by the tacit and general consent of all Nations during the 3 preceding years, solicited and obtained from the Government the use of the Fishery, and of the Cattle on the Eastern Malvina Island, and likewise tracts of lands thereon, in order to provide for the subsistence of the Settlement we should establish there. An Expedition was, in effect, fitted out, composed of the Brigs, *Fenwick* and *Antelope*, which carried out, among other things, a quantity of horses— and of the Schooner, *Rafaela* (which was armed,) for the Seal-fishery; all under the direction of Mr. Robert Schofield. The difficulties attendant on every new undertaking, were in this instance so great, as to discourage the Director, Schofield, who abandoned it the following year, losing more than 30,000 dollars and ruining himself, so that, dying shortly afterwards in Buenos Ayres, he left his widow and small children in a state of indigence.

But I was not disheartened on this account. The year following, with the assistance of some of my friends, I prepared an Expedition, which sailed in January, 1826, under my direction, in the Brig, *Alerta*. After many sacrifices, I was enabled to surmount great obstacles; but still, that which we expected to effect in 1 year, was not realized before the expiration of 5. My partners lost all hope, and sold me their shares. I bought successively 3 Vessels, and lost them; I chartered 5, one of which was lost. Each blow produced dismay in the Colonists who several times resolved to leave that ungrateful Region, but were restrained by their affection for me, which I had known how to win, and by the example of constancy and patience which my family and myself held out to them.

Fully aware of the great advantages which the Republic would derive from Establishments in the South; and some experiments which I had made in agriculture having been attended with success; I resolved to employ all my resources, and avail myself of all my connections, in order to undertake a formal Colonization, which should secure those advantages and lay the foundation of a National Fishery, which has been at all times, and in all Countries, the origin and nursery of the Navy, and of the mercantile Marine. But wishing, as was natural, not to hazard my own labor and money, as well as that of the Colonists and of those who had assisted me, I solicited from the Government not only a grant of Land, but also the exclusive right to the Fishery, for the benefit of the Colony. The Government, convinced of this necessity,—of the utility which would accrue to the Republic from the enterprise, although it were nothing more than having a Port to the Southward for maritime operations, in case of a war like that which was then being carried on; and of the expenses which the undertaking required; issued a Decree on the 5th January, 1828,* whereby, in conformity with the spirit of the Law enacted by

---

* Decree. *Buenos Ayres, 5th January,* 1828.   (Translation.)

The Government,—taking into consideration the great benefit the Country will derive by populating the Island, the ownership of which is solicited, and that, besides the increase of commerce, which naturally must result, with other Nations, new channels will be opened to national prosperity by encouraging the important branch of Fishery, the benefit of which would flow to the Inhabitants of the Republic, which hitherto have fallen into the hands of Foreigners;—that, in the present War with the Emperor of the Brazils, and in any other in which the Republic may some future day see itself engaged, nothing can be more convenient than to find among those Islands a point of support for maritime operations, which will furnish to the Privateers safe Harbours to convey their prizes to ;—that towards the settling and extension of Territory on the Southern Coasts the settlement on these Islands is a great step ;—and lastly, that the great expenses required to put into execution a scheme of this nature, can by no means be compensated, but by the ownership of lands, which, if not granted, an opportunity of doing a great national good would be lost, and even the right of Sovereignty over them ;—doth, in conformity to the spirit of the Law of 22nd October, 1821, cede to Mr. Lewis Vernet, Resident and Merchant of this place, the Island of Statenland, and all the lands of the Island of Soledad, excepting those that were ceded to Dn. Jorge Pacheco, by a Decree dated 13th December 1823, and which has been ratified by a Decree of this day ; and excepting moreover an extent of 10 square leagues in the Bay of San Carlos, which the Government reserves for itself; with the object, and under the express condition, that, within 3 years of the date hereof, a Colony shall be established, and that at the end of that time the Government shall be informed of its state, in order to determine what it may consider convenient for the interior or exterior administration of the same.

And further, the Government, wishing to contribute as much as possible to the encouragement and prosperity of the Colony, has further determined:

First, That the Colony shall be free from every description of contribution, excepting what may be necessary for the maintenance of the local Authorities that may be established, from excise, tolls, and export duties, as also free from import duties on such merchandize as shall be introduced for the use of the Colony, which privileges are granted for 20 years, exclusive of the 3 years fixed for the establishment of the Colony.

the Honorable House of Representatives, on the 22nd October, 1821,*
it granted to me the right of property to the waste land on the Island,
(after deducting the Tracts conceded in 1823 to Don Jorge Pacheco,
and 10 square leagues which the Government reserved to itself in the
Bay of San Carlos,) and likewise to Staten Land. It also conceded
to the Colony exemption from taxation for 20 years, and for the same
period the exclusive right to the Fishery in all the Malvinas, and on
the Coast of the Continent, to the southward of the Rio Negro; under
the condition that within 3 years I should have established the Colony.

In consequence of this, I put all my connections in requisition and
exhausted all my resources, to the degree that I was in want of the
necessaries for the decent maintenance of my family, for several years.
I made Contracts in The United States, and in various Countries in

---

Secondly, That, for the same term of 20 years, the Colony shall be at liberty
to carry on the Fishery, free of duties at the 2 Islands whose property is ceded,
in all the Islands of Malvinas, and on the Coast of the Continent south of Rio
Negro of Patagonia.

Thirdly, That, in case of the population extending to the other Islands,
within the period of the 3 years allowed for the establishment of the Colony, the
Director of the same shall be under the obligation of informing the Government
of such further Population, in order to determine what may be convenient.

The Notary of Government is hereby authorized to furnish the Petitioner
with as many Copies hereof as he may require.

BALCARCE, (Minister.)

---

* DECREE. *Buenos Ayres,* 22nd October, 1821.   (Translation.)

Fishery on the Patagonian Coast.

THE Honorable Junta, having taken into consideration the Project of Law
concerning the Fishery on the Coast of Patagonia, and the encouragement of
that Establishment, which Project Your Excellency in your Note of the 1st
instant advises them to approve, have, in their Sitting of the 20th instant, sanctioned the Articles contained in that Project in manner following:

Art. 1. It shall be lawful for the Natives and Inhabitants of the Province to
export from, and to import into, any point of it, as well as to re-export, free of
all Duties, the produce of the Fishery, as well as that of the chase of amphibious
animals, of the Patagonian Coast, in National Vessels;—if they employ in it
Foreign Vessels they shall pay one dollar per ton, on their departure from that
Coast.

II. Foreigners resorting thither, periodically, to exercise the fishery and
chase, shall pay 6 dollars per ton.

III. Foreigners forming a Settlement, with 6 families at the least, and bringing
the latter along with them for such purpose, and providing them with a dwelling, furniture, and implements of husbandry, on the lands which shall be gra-
tuitously granted to them by the Government, shall pay 1 dollar per ton, and
shall enjoy such privilege at the rate of 1 year for every 2 families.

IV. Foreigners who shall provide and erect a building, with the view of ex-
tracting oil from, and preparing the skins of, amphibious animals, shall pay 3
dollars per ton.

V. Foreigners forming a fixed settlement for salting Fish, shall enjoy complete
liberty to export the same, during 8 years.

VI. The duty per ton shall be collected on the whole admeasurement or
tonnage of the Vessel, whether her Cargo be complete or not.

And this is communicated by the honorable Junta to Your Excellency for
your information and the proper purposes.

God preserve Your Excellency many years.

Hall of the Sittings at Buenos Ayres, 22nd October, 1821.

SANTIAGO RIVADAVIA, President.
PEDRO ANDRES GARCIA, <i>Secretary, ad interim.</i></div>

H. E. the Governor and Captain-General of the Province.

Europe, for bringing out families and acquiring vessels, which would become the property of the Colony, without any disbursement, by paying for them with the product of the Fishery—so that, in a short time, the Republic would possess a Fishing Marine. When the aggression of the *Lexington* happened, one of these Vessels had sailed from The United States; others were about to depart but were stopped by the intelligence of that event. I have in my possession the Letters in which this information is communicated to me.

In the mean time, prior and subsequently to the Decree of 5th January, 1828, Merchant Vessels of all Nations frequented the Colony in their voyages to the Pacific, and on their return from thence. They there took in fresh provisions, refitted themselves and recruited their sick. So content were they with the treatment they received, that they viewed the Establishment of the Colony, as a great benefit to commerce in general, as it saved them from deviating from their route to call at Rio de Janeiro or St. Catherine's, as they used to do before. This is sufficiently proved by the great number of Merchant Vessels, which repeatedly visited the Colony. The Fishing Vessels, on the contrary, which trafficked among the Islands, began to avoid coming in contact with it: they seldom called at the Port, confining themselves to the Bay of San Salvador, distant by water 14 leagues from the Colony. Whenever they did visit it, they received the best treatment. I have not spoken with any of them, that was not aware of the prior dominion of the Spaniards, of the prohibition imposed by them to frequent those Seas, and of the Act of Sovereignty exercised by this Republic in 1820.* Warned not to continue fishing there, they all promised to obey, but none of them ever did so; and the Colony, without any repressive force, beheld its prerogatives rendered sterile and contemned.

The damage which these depredations occasioned the Colony was not trifling, since it was rapidly hurrying it to complete dissolution. It is evident that the Seal Fishery in those Islands, is exhaustible,— for in the time of the Spaniards it was so abundant, that only large Vessels were engaged in it, and now only small Vessels are employed.

---

* Captain Orne, who arrived here on Tuesday last from the Falkland Islands, has furnished us with the following *Act of Sovereignty*, for publication.
                                              Salem Gazette, 8th June, 1821.
(Circular.)   " *National Frigate*, Heroina, *Port Soledad, 9th Nov.,* 1820."
    " SIR,—I have the honor to inform you of my arrival at this Port, to take possession of these Islands, in the name of the **Supreme Government of The United Provinces** of South America.
    " This ceremony was publicly performed on the 6th day of this present November, and the National Standard hoisted at the Fort, under a Salute from this Frigate, in the presence of several Citizens of The United States, and Subjects of Great Britain.   " I am, &c.
                                                        " D. JEWETT,
        " *Colonel of the Marine of the United Provinces of South America,*
                            " *Commander of the Frigate* Heroina.
" *Capt. W. B. Orne, Ship* General Knox, *of Salem.*"

Foreigners who only seek present and immediate utility, without considering the future, effect the slaughter in a pernicious manner. They set fire to the fields and slaughter indiscriminately, and in all seasons, even in that of bringing forth young. In consequence of this, and of the constant and great concourse, has ensued the present diminution of Seals, of which there are now scarcely the twentieth part of what there were in 1820. It is not impossible that this valuable species may return to its former abundance, by means of a well regulated slaughter, and some years of respite. But whilst Foreigners continue to slaughter, it is impossible, and the species will become extinct. If this take place, the Colony is undone, for this slaughter is the great allurement which it presents. Who would go and remain in that cold and desolate Region merely for agricultural pursuits, when the Province of Buenos Ayres offers, with a temperate climate, so many means of following them with facility, and without the heavy expenses attendant on a residence in the Malvinas? I perceived the danger to which this disorder exposed the Colony; and did not venture to bring out new Settlers without having an effectual guarantee for their fully enjoying their privileges.

For this reason I requested the Government to furnish me with a Vessel of War, to enable me to cause the rights of the Colony to be respected. The Government was aware of the necessity of the measure; but not then being able to place a Vessel at my disposal, it resolved to invest me with a public and official Character; and for that purpose issued the 2 Decrees of the 10th of June, 1829; the one, establishing the Governorship of the Malvinas and Tierra del Fuego; and the other, nominating me to fulfil that Office.

In virtue of this nomination, on the 30th of August, 1829, the Governorship and Commandantcy of the Island was formally reinstalled, under salutes of artillery. Without deviating in the least from the urbanity which had before characterized my proceedings, I wrote to the Commanders of the Fishing Vessels, to inform them of the new Character with which I was invested; and acquainting them with the Resolutions of the Government of Buenos Ayres; and of the necessity there was for their desisting from Fishing, under the penalty of being detained and sent to Buenos Ayres for trial. I made this notification to the American Schooners *Superior* and *Harriet*, permitting them, nevertheless, to carry off the Cargo they had collected on the Islands; and I candidly declare that I fully believed in the sincerity of their promises.

By this time the Colonists had become accustomed to the climate; they had commenced various labors, and counted on a certain and decent subsistence; they had become, particularly, very much attached to the Colony; and they considered themselves happy, and I likewise considered them so.

I then no longer doubted of the fortunate result of my undertaking; and I felt convinced that it would, in a short time, begin to reimburse my immense outlay, and to recompense me for the incessant labor it had cost me.

But these Schooners repeated the offence, and they were detained: --Your Excellency and the public know the rest;--know that, for thus defending the rights of the Colony, and causing the Resolutions of my Government to be respected, I brought upon myself the vengeance of a Vessel of War belonging to a friendly Nation, which, in violation of the most sacred principles, took pleasure in oppressing innocent People, and in destroying in one hour what had cost me an immense sum, and many years of industry, of labor, and of perseverance.

I have now arrived, Sir, at the point from which I set out in the commencement of this Report; thus completing the sketch of the history of the Malvina Islands.

But this interesting subject appears to be inexhaustible; and I must not omit some remarks to which the latter period of the history gave rise.

The apparent indifference of the Republic with respect to the Malvina Islands, during the first 10 years of its political existence, may perhaps be adduced as an argument against its right of sovereignty over them; but such objection would be entirely void of good faith; for according to the principles laid down, the abandonment of a Territory does not annul the right to it, unless it be spontaneous, and without any intention of returning to it. Then only is there a real *abandonment*; in the opposite case there is only a *non use*, but the right still exists. This *non use* by the Republic during those 10 years did not arise from a want of will to occupy, but from another most powerful and extraordinary motive, well known to all Nations :--the necessity of securing its independence by supporting expensive wars. Not a single fact, not a single Document, can be cited to prove that during that interval the Republic had really abandoned the Malvinas, or that it had no intention to establish itself there. Thus, then, even adopting the opinion of those Writers on the Laws of Nations which are most contrary to the interests of the Republic, that is to say, that there exists prescription among Nations; even then, this could not be brought against her, as all the requisites demanded by prescription have been absolutely wanting. The first and most urgent duty of the Republic was to secure its political existence, but no sooner had the war with Spain subsided, than her first care was to resume formal possession of the Islands, which she did in 1820.

This Act was public and solemn; it was effected in the presence of a number of Vessels, which were, besides, informed of it in writing; and which carried and spread the intelligence among all Maritime

Nations. Those Nations were silent on the subject; and the Republic continued peacefully and publicly to exercise those acts of dominion which have been before stated; and during which, repeating the warning, she declared to the World her resolution and her rights.

The Sovereignty of the Argentine Republic over the Malvinas is therefore unquestionable, if we consult the principles of the Laws of Nations, and the undoubted facts to which we have applied those principles.

According to these same principles, she had a right to prohibit Fishing within her jurisdiction, and to detain and bring to trial any Vessel which might, by infringing the prohibition, voluntarily submit itself to the results. She could do it, because she is mistress of the Isles—she ought to do it, because her interests required it—and as it was her interest to do it, she did it.

The Seal Fishery will produce great profits to the State if it be properly organized; and it will, besides, produce them without any expense to the Treasury. These revenues are more required by us than by the opulent Nation of The United States. We should be fools indeed, if, in the infancy of our progress, we consented to allow Foreigners to reap all the advantages which nature has bestowed on our Isles and Coasts; advantages which will in time draw to us foreign capital and foreign population. If the North Americans had shewn a ruinous indifference for lucrative undertakings, would they now see populous and flourishing Cities where before were nothing but woods and deserts? The immense Fisheries of New-foundland, which produce yearly many millions of dollars, and contribute to supply excellent Sailors for the 3 greatest Maritime Powers in the World, were raised from nothing by a private individual; and with the assiduous care and protection of enlightened Governments, have arrived at an astonishing state of prosperity. Why should not the Fisheries of the South become in the course of time proportionally as valuable to us as are those of the North to the English?

The celebrated Ulloa says, very justly; speaking of the exclusive Fishery of England in Newfoundland:—"It would be ridiculous for her to allow others to partake of what to her is of the greatest value, (the Fishery), as being the only advantage produced by that Island, and which other Nations have vied with each other to acquire, by asserting Dominion over a Country which yields no other riches to its possessor than its Fishery, and to obtain which, it is necessary to support the inconveniences of a Climate, which, from its excessive rigor, is hardly inhabitable during the greater part of the year." It would seem that Ulloa was thinking of the Malvinas when he wrote this.

Not only is it right that Nations should appropriate to themselves the exclusive enjoyment of these advantages, but it is what is always done. We have a striking example of this in Newfoundland. Why have other Nations required express and especial concessions from England, ere they could undertake this Fishery? Why have the Banks of that Island been the subject of so many Treaties?—Why has England been able to allow, prohibit, or restrict, Fishing there, and to trace the limits in which it might be carried on? Because she is the owner, and because it suited her interests.

The Spaniards were the first who discovered and peopled that Island. This is proved by the Spanish names given to its Capital, Placentia, and to other places, such as Cabo de Buena Vista, Punta Rica, &c. Abandoned by them, it was afterwards taken possession of and abandoned by the Englishman, Gerber; but, in 1622, another Englishman, named George Calvert, succeeded in establishing himself there, permanently, carrying with him every thing that was necessary. He then privately commenced the famous Cod-Fishery, which has since become of such immense importance, as to excite the desires of all Nations. Spain, (perhaps on the ground of the first discovery and occupation,) claimed a right to this Fishery, as may be seen by the XIIIth Article of the Treaty of Utrecht, made in 1713;* which claim she only recently gave up, in 1763, by the XVIIIth Article of the Treaty of Paris,† made in that year; notwithstanding that Spanish

---

* *Treaty of Peace between Great Britain and France.* Utrecht, $\frac{\text{31st March,}}{\text{11th April,}}$ 1713.

ART. XIII. The Island called Newfoundland, with the adjacent Islands, shall, from this time forward, belong of right wholly to Britain; and to that end the Town and Fortress of Placentia, and whatever other places in the said Island, are in the possession of the French, shall be yielded and given up, within 7 months from the exchange of the Ratifications of this Treaty, or sooner, if possible, by the Most Christian King, to those who have a Commission from the Queen of Great Britain for that purpose. Nor shall the Most Christian King, his Heirs and Successors, or any of their Subjects, at any time hereafter, lay claim to any right to the said Island and Islands, or to any part of it or them. Moreover, it shall not be lawful for the Subjects of France to fortify any place in the said Island of Newfoundland, or to erect any buildings there, besides stages made of boards, and huts necessary and usual for the drying of Fish; or to resort to the said Island, beyond the time necessary for Fishing, and drying of Fish. But it shall be allowed to the Subjects of France to catch Fish, and to dry them on land, in that part only, and in no other besides that of the said Island of Newfoundland, which stretches from the place called Cape Bonavista, to the Northern point of the said Island, and from thence running down by the Western side, reaches as far as the place called Point Riche. But the Island called Cape Breton, as also all others, both in the mouth of the River of St. Lawrence, and in the Gulf of the same name, shall hereafter belong of right to the French; and the Most Christian King shall have all manner of liberty to fortify any place or places there.

---

† *Treaty of Peace between Great Britain, France, and Spain.*

Paris, 10th *February*, 1763.

ART. XVIII. His Catholic Majesty desists, as well for himself, as for his Successors, from all pretension, which he may have formed, in favour of the Guipuscoans, and other his Subjects, to the right of Fishing in the Neighbourhood of the Island of Newfoundland.

Subjects, especially the Guipuscoans, had been in the tranquil enjoyment of that right.

By the same Treaty of Utrecht, the French were prohibited from establishing themselves on the Island, or even remaining on it a longer time than was necessary for taking and drying the Fish; which they could only do between Cape Breton and Punta Rica; and the Islands of the River and Gulf of St. Lawrence, were declared to belong to them. Perhaps this concession was made to them on account of the French being then Masters of Placentia, which they ceded to the English, and of Canada, to which Continent the River St. Lawrence belonged. Thus it was that they lost it by the Vth Article of the Treaty of 1763;* by which they were only permitted to fish in the Gulf, at the distance of 3 leagues from the English Coasts, and without Cape Breton, at the distance of 15: all which was confirmed, with some variations, by the IVth, Vth, and VIth Articles of the Treaty of Versailles, in 1783.†

---

* *Treaty of Peace between Great Britain, France and Spain.*
Paris, 10th February, 1763.

ART. V. The Subjects of France shall have the liberty of Fishing and drying, on a part of the Coasts of the Island of Newfoundland, such as it is specified in the XIIIth Article of the Treaty of Utrecht; which Article is renewed and confirmed by the present Treaty, (except what relates to the Island of Cape Breton, as well as to the other Islands and Coasts, in the mouth and in the Gulf of St. Lawrence.) And His Britannic Majesty consents to leave to the Subjects of the Most Christian King the liberty of Fishing in the Gulf of St. Lawrence, on condition that the Subjects of France do not exercise the said Fishery, but at the distance of 3 leagues from all the Coasts belonging to Great Britain, as well those of the Continent, as those of the Islands situated in the said Gulf of St. Lawrence: and as to what relates to the Fishery on the Coasts of the Island of Cape Breton out of the said Gulf, the Subjects of the Most Christian King shall not be permitted to exercise the said Fishery, but at the distance of 15 leagues from the Coasts of the Island of Cape Breton; and the Fishery on the Coasts of Nova Scotia or Acadia, and every where else out of the said Gulf shall remain on the footing of former Treaties.

---

† *Treaty of Peace between Great Britain and France. Versailles,* 3rd *Sept.* 1783.

ART. IV. His Majesty, the King of Great Britain, is maintained in his right to the Island of Newfoundland, and to the adjacent Islands, as the whole were assured to him by the XIIIth Article of the Treaty of Utrecht; excepting the Islands of St. Pierre and Miquelon, which are ceded in full right, by the present Treaty, to His Most Christian Majesty.

V. His Majesty, the Most Christian King, in order to prevent the quarrels which have hitherto arisen between the two Nations of England and France, consents to renounce the right of Fishing, which belongs to him in virtue of the aforesaid Article of the Treaty of Utrecht, from Cape Bonavista to Cape St. John, situated on the Eastern Coast of Newfoundland, in 50 degrees North Latitude; and His Majesty, the King of Great Britain consents on his part, that the Fishery assigned to the Subjects of His Most Christian Majesty, beginning at the said Cape St. John, passing to the North, and descending by the Western Coast of the Island of Newfoundland, shall extend to the place called Cape Raye, situated in 47 degrees, 50 minutes, Latitude. The French Fishermen shall enjoy the Fishery which is assigned to them by the present Article, as they had the right to enjoy that which was assigned to them by the Treaty of Utrecht.

VI. With regard to the Fishery in the Gulf of St. Lawrence, the French shall continue to exercise it conformably to the Vth Article of the Treaty of Paris.

In like manner, by the Treaty concluded on the 20th of October, 1818,* between Great Britain and The United States, the latter were allowed to fish in Newfoundland, within certain limits which were minutely detailed, and at a distance of 3 Maritime miles.

It will be seen from this, and many other Acts, that England appropriated to itself the exclusive enjoyment of the Cod-fisheries; interdicted other Nations from the use of them, and pointed out the limits which they should respect. We likewise see here an instance of Sovereignty acknowledged and exercised over an Island whose Coasts were either uninhabited, or peopled by Esquimaux Indians, who, as in Labrador and Hudson, do not acknowledge the British Dominion, and live independent.

But in order to shew more fully the mode in which England exercised her right over the Bank of Newfoundland—of the precautions she has taken—of the penalties she has imposed, and the rigor she has displayed in this respect, we will here copy 2 Acts of Parliament relative to the Fishery, during the Reigns of George III. and George IV.

[Extract. Act 26 Geo. III. Cap. 26. § 20.]

" It shall and may be lawful for all and every Officer, or Officers,

---

* *Convention between Great Britain and the United States of America.—London, 20th October,* 1818.

Art. I. Whereas differences have arisen respecting the liberty claimed by The United States, for the Inhabitants thereof, to take, dry, and cure fish, on certain Coasts, Bays, Harbours, and Creeks, of His Britannic Majesty's Dominions in America; it is agreed between the High Contracting Parties, that the Inhabitants of the said United States shall have, for ever, in common with the Subjects of His Britannic Majesty, the liberty to take Fish of every kind, on that part of the southern Coast of Newfoundland, which extends from Cape Raye to the Rameau Islands, on the western and northern Coast of Newfoundland, from the said Cape Raye to the Quirpon Islands, on the Shores of the Magdalen Islands, and also on the Coasts, Bays, Harbours, and Creeks, from Mount Joly, on the southern Coast of Labrador, to and through the Streights of Belleisle, and thence northwardly indefinitely along the Coast, without prejudice, however, to any of the exclusive rights of the Hudson's Bay Company. And that the American Fishermen shall also have liberty, for ever, to dry and cure fish in any of the unsettled Bays, Harbours, and Creeks, of the southern part of the Coast of Newfoundland hereabove described, and of the Coast of Labrador; but so soon as the same, or any portion thereof, shall be settled, it shall not be lawful for the said Fishermen to dry or cure Fish at such portion so settled, without previous Agreement for such purpose, with the Inhabitants, Proprietors, or Possessors of the ground. And The United States hereby renounce for ever, any liberty heretofore enjoyed or claimed by the Inhabitants thereof, to take, dry, or cure Fish, on or within 3 marine miles of any of the Coasts, Bays, Creeks, or Harbours, of His Britannic Majesty's Dominions in America, not included within the above-mentioned limits: provided, however, that the American Fishermen shall be admitted to enter such Bays or Harbours, for the purpose of shelter and of repairing damages therein, of purchasing wood, and of obtaining water, and for no other purpose whatever. But they shall be under such restrictions as may be necessary to prevent their taking, drying, or curing Fish therein, or in any other manner whatever abusing the privileges hereby reserved to them.

having the command of any of His Majesty's Ships stationed at the Island of Newfoundland, to stop and detain all and every Ship, Vessel, or Boat, of what nature or description soever, coming to, or going from the said Island, and belonging to, or in the service or occupation of any of His Majesty's Subjects residing in, trafficking with, or carrying on Fishery in, the Island of Newfoundland, Parts adjacent, or on the Banks of the said Island of Newfoundland, which he shall have reason to suspect to be going to, or coming from, the Islands of St. Pierre or Miquelon, for the purposes before-mentioned, in any place within the limits of their Station, and to detain, search, and examine such Ship, Vessel, or Boat; and that if, upon such search or examination, it shall appear to such Officer or Officers, that there is reasonanle ground to believe that such Ship, Vessel, or Boat, or any tackle, apparel, or furniture, used, or which may be used, by any Ship, Vessel, or Boat, or any implements or utensils, used, or which may be used, in the catching or curing of Fish, or any fish, oil, blubber, seal-skins, fuel, wood, or timber, then on board of such Ship, Vessel, or Boat, was or were intended to be sold, bartered for, or exchanged, to the Subjects of any Foreign State, or shall be discovered to have been so sold, bartered for, or exchanged; or if any goods, or commodities whatsoever, shall be found on board such Ship, Vessel, or Boat, or shall be discovered to have been on board, having been purchased, or taken in barter or exchange, from the Subjects of any Foreign State; then and in every such case, to seize and send back such Ship, Vessel, or Boat, to the Island of Newfoundland; and that such Ship, Vessel, or Boat, shall, upon due condemnation, be forfeited and lost; and shall and may be prosecuted for that purpose by the Officer or Officers so seizing the same, in the Vice-Admiralty Court of the said Island of Newfoundland; such forfeiture to be given, one moiety to the said Officer or Officers, and the other moiety to the Governor of Newfoundland for the time being; to be applied, under the direction of such Governor, in defraying the passages home of such Person or Persons, as by this or any former Act, are directed to be sent back to the Country to which they belong."

[Extract. Act 5 Geo. IV. Cap. 21. § 2.]

" No Alien or Stranger whatsoever shall at any time hereafter take bait, or use any sort of Fishing whatsoever in Newfoundland, or the Coasts, Bays, or Rivers thereof, or on the Coast of Labrador, or in any of the Islands or Places within or dependant upon the Government of the said Colony, always excepting the rights and privileges granted by Treaty to the Subjects or Citizens of any Foreign State or Power in amity with His Majesty."

In view of these strong regulations, by which the fact of finding in a Vessel, a few fish, a little wood, &c., is sufficient to detain, search, bring to trial and confiscate her, can it rationally be a matter of complaint and surprise, that this Republic, by prohibiting the Fishery within its jurisdiction and punishing the Infringers, should exercise the same rights, although not in a manner so inquisitorial, vexatious and rigorous? The impartial of all Nations will decide.

But as often as I have hitherto employed the word *Fishery*, I have done so to accommodate myself to common usage. I think that this word is not the most proper to express the act which is meant to be designated by it. What Foreigners do in the Malvinas is not *fish*, but *slaughter*, which is performed by ball, clubs, &c., and always on the Shore. The real Fishery is only in the High Seas.—The use of this word, when treating only of slaughter, has given rise abroad to mistaken ideas with respect to the pretensions of this Republic; it being probably believed that she prohibits fishing in the Seas. The first intelligence which reached The United States of the detention of the Schooners, was given by the Mate of the *Breakwater*, and he represented it with that character. The United States Gazette announced it in this distorted manner:

" Arrived at Stonington, on Monday, Schooner *Breakwater*, from the Falkland Islands, whither she went on a Sealing voyage. The *Breakwater* put in at Port Louis, where she was forcibly taken possession of by Vernet the Governor, acting, as he said, under the Decree of the Buenos Ayrean Government, *forbidding all fishing in those Seas*......Schooner *Harriet* has also been seized *under similar circumstances*."

On this account it was, Excellent Sir, that a Friend of mine, a Native of The United States, having written to the Secretary of State upon this affair, received for answer that " measures were taken to *ascertain* (and this is another proof that such is the object of Mr. Baylies' Mission,) on what foundation the claim of jurisdiction over the Islands rested, but the sickness and death of Mr. Forbes had for the time interrupted the investigation : our right of Fishery, however, *in those Seas*, is one that the Government considers indisputable, and it will be given in charge to the Minister about to be sent there, to make representations against, and demand satisfaction for all interruptions of the exercise of that right," (the Fishery in the Seas.) It is also on this account that the President only speaks in his Message of *those Seas*. The Owners and Parties interested in the captured Vessels endeavored, in this manner, to deceive, in order that, the capture being then declared illegal, they might claim their Insurance from the Underwriters; and the Government and the Nation candidly believed that the question was relative to a Fishery, not on the shores of a Foreign Jurisdiction, but on the High Seas, such as the Whale Fishery. The Consul, Slacum, quoted in one of his Notes a *part* of the Instructions given to Mr. Forbes, to protest against any restriction of the right of The United States, but if he had quoted the *whole* of them, perhaps we should see that the *right in question* (as Mr. Slacum expresses himself,) related to the Fishery *in the Seas;* and that Mr. Forbes, seeing that this Republic set up no pretensiou in this respect, deemed it unnecessary to make any remonstrance.

I have already said that this Republic, in order to establish the prohibition against Fishing on the Coasts belonging to it, within the distance it might think necessary for the purpose of securing that enjoyment, was not under the obligation of giving previous notice to any Nation; I now add that it was unnecessary. With what justice, can it be said, that the want of official notice respecting this prohibition injured any Nation? How—in what manner? If any one considered it had reason to complain of this appropriation, why wait to do so till it should receive official information? But it is useless to expatiate on this. No Nation can say that it was not aware of the exclusive right of Spain, and that this right had devolved on the Argentine State; which, strictly speaking, did not establish any new prohibition, but continued that which Spain had imposed, though not with the same extent or with the same rigor.—On the other hand, the taking possession of the Islands in 1820 was quite public: the subsequent Acts of the Government were so, likewise, and the Decree of June 10th, 1829, and my Circular, had been printed. How is it that the English Government did not wait for official intimation, to make, through Mr. Parish, the Protest which it conceived itself entitled to make? Besides, in 1829, my appointment as Governor of the Malvinas and of the Tierra del Fuego as far as the Cape, was published in The United States; and the year following, several Journals inserted various notices, among others one in which Settlers were invited, and, to entice them, it was expressly stated that the Colony enjoyed the exclusive right to the Fishery. But, above all, did not Mr. Slacum say that Mr. Forbes had received orders to remonstrate against that Decree? Therefore the Government of The United States did not await, nor did it require, official notice to take the steps it considered it its duty to adopt.

Although there had been (which there was not,) any obligation incumbent on this Government to acquaint another with its resolutious, an omission of this kind does not give room for complaint or remonstrance, nor can any right be founded on it, except when it entails injury on another Nation. The injury which may ensue to a Nation in such cases, can only arise from a want of knowledge of the measures adopted by another, and from being thereby precluded from taking steps on its part, or from sustaining its rights.—But, in the present case, there was no want of knowledge in other Nations, nor have they consequently failed to act as they have deemed proper.

Thus far I have confined myself, Excellent Sir, to justifying the right of this Republic to the Islands, and the resolutions of the Government with respect to Nations in general. I now wish to limit myself specially to the United States of America, whose Government is, of all others, that which most distinguishes itself in the untenable pretension of questioning or denying that right; but, of all others, it is certainly that which can do so with the least justice.

That England or France should do so, although without grounds, would not be surprising. But it is really so that The United States should attempt it; and if it be true that Mr. Baylies' Mission is, to *deny*, and not to *ascertain* the right, it may be said to them: " He who denies the right of another should produce his own titles.'' And what can The United States shew? Absolutely none: at least, as yet I have never heard of any.

But not to leave any thing unanswered, I will call to recollection that some Journals of The United States have affirmed that that supposed right was inherited. No such inheritance, however, does exist or has existed; 1st. because England, from which alone they could have derived it, is destitute of it, as has been shewn; 2nd, because when Spain conceded to England the Fishery at the distance of 10 leagues, she did not concede it to The United States, which already formed another Nation; 3rd, because even did the Malvinas belong to His Britannic Majesty, The United States, by the Treaty of October 20th 1818, engaged not to fish within 3 miles of the Coasts, Ports, &c., of His Britannic Majesty in *America;* 4th, because, although there had been nothing of this, it is inconceivable how this right should descend to The United States, and remain at the same time with England, who claims it, according to Mr. Parish's Protest; 5th, because it is a political absurdity to pretend that a Colony which emancipates itself, inherits the other Territories which the Metropolis may possess. We inherited the Malvinas because they formed a part of the Spanish Government of Buenos Ayres at the time of the Revolution. If that singular doctrine were to be found in the Code of Nations, the Low Countries, for example, on their independence being acknowledged in 1648, would have succeeded to Spain in her rights to America, and in the same manner The United States would have appropriated to themselves the British Possessions in the East Indies. Inheritance, indeed! The United States did not inherit the rights of England in Newfoundland notwithstanding its contiguity, and are they to inherit those which she may have to the Malvinas, at the southern extremity of the Continent, and in the opposite Hemisphere?

But let us pass on to another argument of a more elevated origin, and the only one of any weight. "One of our Vessels engaged in a traffic which we have always enjoyed, without molestation, has been

captured," says the President of The United States, in his Message.—
Behold here, Excellent Sir, the whole title which they allege—"we have
fished freely, therefore we have a right to continue doing so."

The fact is not correct, nor if it were, would the inference be so.
In the time of the Spaniards, as we have seen, not even the Navigation
of those Seas was allowed, much less the Fishery at the Malvinas. In
1820, and in the subsequent years, the Republic again enjoined,
through Jewitt and me, the prohibition as far as regarded the Fishery.
Your Excellency will have remarked, in the historical sketch of the
Malvinas, that, with very few exceptions, the Fishing Vessels there,
and on the Coast of the Continent, have been English and American, and the greater number of the latter Nation. How, then, can
it be sustained that the United States have *always* enjoyed the right
of Fishery, and that, too, *without molestation?* The only time they
may have freely enjoyed the Fishery, is the period elapsed between 1810 and 1820. But this enjoyment does not authorize that
inference. It was temporary, and owing to the serious attentions
of the Republic; and, according to the principles laid down, the
non-use of a right, produced by an extraordinary circumstance or
event, does not entail a forfeiture thereof, in like manner as the
tacit toleration of the enjoyment of it by another Country does not
occasion it; for, when there is no express cession or abandonment
proved by facts, the presumption is that the enjoyment tolerated to
the other Nation, is without prejudice to the owner's right. The
United States, cannot, therefore, found any right on the fact of having
fished freely during those 10 years; for, to do so, it would be necessary
that that of the Republic had become extinct. Therefore, the
United States have absolutely no right to carry on the Fishery in
defiance of this Republic, either in the Malvinas, or on the Coasts
of the Continent. There are, besides, special circumstances, which
render it imperative that The United States should be the last Nation of the Universe to deny the Sovereignty of this Republic in
those Regions, if, as I firmly believe, they intend to adhere to good
faith and to the principles which the civilized world respects.

In 1816, the Representatives of the Nation declared the Independence of the United Provinces of the Rio de la Plata, comprised
within the limits of the ancient Vice-royalty of this name. The Commissioner of their Government resident in The United States, Don
Manuel H. Aguirre, was directed to solicit the acknowledgment of
that Declaration. He commenced his Negotiations with the Secretary
of State, Mr. John Quincy Adams, immediate Predecessor of General
Jackson in the Presidency. The Minister asked Mr. Aguirre, in a
Note dated 27th of August, 1817, whether the Provinces occupied by
the Spaniards, Monte Video in possession of the Portuguese, and the
Banda Oriental governed by Artigas, and at war with the National
Government, were comprised in the Territory of the Republic. Mr.

Aguirre answered in the affirmative; and without further doubts respecting the Territory of the Republic, The United States Government, under date of 25th of March, 1818, transmitted a Message to Congress on this subject, stating among other things the following:—" The Commissioner has manifested that the Government, the acknowledgment of whose Independence he solicits, is that of the Territory, which, prior to the Revolution, formed the Vice-royalty of La Plata. He being then asked whether it (the Territory) comprised that occupied by the Portuguese, (it being besides known that the Banda Oriental was under the rule of General Artigas, and several Provinces in quiet possession of Spain) he replied in the affirmative. He observed that Artigas, although in hostility with the Government of Buenos Ayres, sustained nevertheless the cause of the Independence of these Provinces."

Hence it is evident, First—that The United States knew ⸱⸱⸱⸱ the Territory of the Republic was that of the Vice-royalty; Second—that their doubts respecting the Territory were limited to the Provinces occupied by Spain, Portugal, and Artigas; but that they harbored none relative to the other Possessions which were formerly comprised in the Vice-royalty; and they cannot now say that they did not know that the Malvinas and the Coasts of the Continent entered into the number of those Possessions.

But it was not solely through the Envoy of this Government that they knew it; they were likewise informed of it through their own.

In 1818, the Government of The United States sent Commissioners to this Capital, for the express purpose of obtaining the information which it deemed expedient. Mr. Rodney, who, some years after, died here whilst exercising the functions of Minister Plenipotentiary, and who was one of the Commissioners, stated, among other things, in the Report which, in fulfilment of his Mission, he addressed to Mr. Adams, the following:—" In 1778, a new Vice-royalty was established at Buenos Ayres, comprehending all the Spanish Possessions to the East of the Western Cordilleras, and to the south of the River Marañon" * * * * * * * * " extending in a direct line, from its north to its south boundary, a distance of more than 2,000 miles; and from its eastern to its western not less than 1,100." * * * * * * * * The Report of Mr. Graham, also one of the Commissioners, contains the same; these are his words:—" The Country formerly known as the Vice-royalty of Buenos Ayres, extending from the north-western sources of the River La Plata to the *Southern Cape of America,* and from the Confines of Brasil and the Ocean to the ridge of the Andes, may be considered that which is called ' the United Provinces of South America.'" * * * * * * * * Therefore the Territory of the Republic is that of the Vice-royalty, (in which were included the Malvinas) extending to the most southern Cape of this part of America, which is Cape Horn.

To these Reports of the Commissioners the greatest publicity was given. The President submitted them to Congress—the Congress ordered them to be printed, and they were even republished in London a short time afterwards.

Being thus fully informed—being in possession of all these antecedents—knowing that the Territory of this Republic was that of the Vice-royalty, which comprised the Malvinas—knowing that it extended itself towards the Pole, as far as the most Southern Cape of South America—without the slightest doubt, objection, or difficulty, having occurred thereon, as had occurred with respect to the dissident Provinces, or those occupied by Foreign Powers, the Congress of The United States of North America, adopting the proposal made by the President in March, 1822, and in contempt of the remonstrances of the Spanish resident Minister, in 1823, proclaimed in the face of the Universe that it acknowledged the Argentine Republic as a sovereign and independent Nation. Can it be possible that that same Government, as well as the English, which, with equal information on the subject, imitated it 3 years afterwards, now, better informed, deny to the Republic the essential right of legislating over its own Territory, and exercising a Sovereignty which they spontaneously acknowledged? No; it is impossible! Such a phenomenon would convert the gentle feelings of gratitude into the most rancorous animosity.

It is therefore indisputable, that, besides the decisive facts which justify the right of the Republic with respect to Nations in general, there are other special and powerful motives which oblige The United States in particular now not to disavow it.

Yet, solely for having supported this right, I am now grossly reviled. Justice demands the reparation of these outrages. I again say, Sir, that if my conduct has been criminal, if I am a pirate, a thief, and an oppressor, the duty and the honor of Your Excellency require that I be punished; but if my conduct has been just—if I have been no more than a public Servant, fulfilling the Instructions of my Government, and if, for so doing, I find my fortune destroyed, and my name dishonored—if I have been no more than a good Citizen, who, with my labor and my capital, endeavored to gain an honorable subsistence, rendering at the same time a great service to the State, the duty and the honor of Your Excellency require that the reparation and the satisfaction shall immediately succeed the injury and the insult.

In like manner, if we consider the positive proofs on which the right of the Republic to the Malvinas are decidedly founded, and the facts which most especially bind the North Americans to the acknowledgment of this right, how dark must appear the picture presented to the World by the action of Captain Duncan in the Malvinas! If the Chargé d'Affaires can only see in it pleasing traits of patriotism, enlightened People will discover in it nothing but the fierce characteristics of oppressive power—a power which Duncan would have been very careful not to exercise towards England, France, or any other Maritime Nation. I think, Sir, that the criminal humiliation of the Flag of the Republic, and the great insult then offered to the reputation and rights of this Nation, loudly call for the most solemn satisfaction and atonement, prior to entering into any Negotiation. Even admitting that my conduct had been that of a noted Pirate, in the Country existed the Government on which I depended, and before which I ought to have been accused. This ought to have been done, since Duncan uncourteously refused the offer I made, of calling on him personally and giving him any explanation he might require. Granting even that the Malvinas do not belong to the Republic; yet The United States cannot deny that the Republic was in actual possession of them. Therefore, the insulting, inhuman, violent and unnecessary spoliation she suffered, ought, before all to be repaired and atoned for. There is nothing uncommon in a Nation arrogating to itself rights which do not belong to it, or giving, in her actions, plausible motives of complaint. Let us suppose for an instant that this is the case with the Republic. But what will become of the dignity of Nations, the order of society, and the peace of the Universe, if a single Individual, who, whether justly or not, may consider his Country offended, shall *take on himself the responsibility* of vandalically avenging her. For Duncan to be in this Port; myself in this City; this affair under discussion, and for him to absent himself under a feigned pretext; and when he was only empowered to afford *legal protection*, to rush unnecessarily, without formality, treacherously, and in time of profound peace, to a formidable act of war; destroying an Establishment, usurping its property, and keeping innocent and defenceless men during 3 months in chains, is an atrocious and barbarous action—a horrible crime, the cruelty of which the Government of The United States cannot deny without for ever tarnishing the spotless glory of its name.

But I must here close this long Report. I do so, Sir, with the regret produced by the consciousness of one's own incapacity, when interests of the first importance are under discussion. If I have not been so fortunate as to bring conviction to the mind, in the part which relates to me personally, I shall feel it the less if these lines serve at least to assist in restoring to their immunity the incontrovertible and trampled rights of the soil which has adopted me.

H.E. Don M. V. de Maza.   **LEWIS VERNET.**

(26.)—*The American Chargé d'Affaires to the Buenos Ayres Minister.*
Buenos Ayres, 18th *August,* 1832.

THE Undersigned has the honour to acknowledge the receipt of the Note of His Excellency the Provisional Minister of Foreign Affairs, dated the 14th instant.

A Communication addressed to His Excellency which accompanied the Note, appearing to be a Memorial of Lewis Vernet, is returned.

Having no authority to stipulate that reparation shall be made to Lewis Vernet or to the Argentine Republic, for the acts of the Commander of the *Lexington* at the Falkland Islands; and being expressly directed by his own Government to justify those acts,—the Undersigned must yield to that alternative which His Excellency has made imperative; and, as his continuance here would be useless to his Country, he asks Passports for himself and his family.

He relies on His Excellency for the necessary and usual facilities for embarking his personal effects and the Library and Archives of the Legation.

In closing his Correspondence, the Undersigned tenders, &c.

H.E. Don M. V. de Maza.   FRANCIS BAYLIES.

(27.)—*Protocol of Conference between the Buenos Ayres Minister and the American Chargé d'Affaires, of the* 27th *August,* 1832.

(Translation.)

THE Conference was opened in the Government House, by the Minister charged with the Foreign Relations stating to the Chargé d'Affaires of North America, that the Government had been much surprised by the return of the Copy of the Report which accompanied its Note of the 14th August, and by His Honor stating that he was not authorised for what was therein asked, and therefore demanding his Passport; that the Government, considering this act as the result of some misunderstanding, had desired its Minister of Foreign Relations to invite His Honor to this Conference, for the purpose of obtaining the necessary explanations relative to the return of the said Report, to which the Government could not agree.

The Chargé d'Affaires replied, that he should have much pleasure in corresponding, in his diplomatic character, with His Excellency the Minister of Foreign Relations, but that he could receive no Communication from Mr. Lewis Vernet.

The Minister then explained to the Chargé d'Affaires of the Republic of The United States, that Mr. Lewis Vernet had not sent any Communication to His Honor,—that the Copy which had been joined to the Note was a Document in answer to the series of Charges which formed nearly the whole subject of the first Note with which the Chargé d'Affaires opened the Negotiation—that, as such, it was a component part of the Correspondence—that the having transmitted the Answers to the Charges, as they were given by Mr. Lewis Vernet, did not import the remission to His Honor, in his official character, of any other Notes than those of the Minister of Foreign Relations.

The Chargé d'Affaires was not satisfied with this convincing answer, and replied, that as Chargé d'Affaires of his Government, he had not come here to act as a party in a litigated affair, or as accuser of Mr. Lewis Vernet before the Government of Buenos Ayres.

To which was answered: that the having remitted a Copy of the Report of Vernet, neither was, nor could be considered as done with a view to give to the Chargé d'Affaires the character of an accuser, or of a party in a suit; that on the contrary, inasmuch as the Government of Buenos Ayres did not consider the Chargé d'Affaires as being a special advocate of the Citizens of North America, merely because he had presented a remonstrance in support of the rights of those Citizens; so neither could it be imputed to this Government that it had made a private individual a party in the Negotiation, merely because it had adopted the contents of the returned Copy as an Answer to the Charges preferred; that Vernet was a Public Officer of the Government, which had confided to his charge the Civil and Military command of the Malvinas; that, criminated as he was in the Communication of the 20th of June, the Government could not but hear him in reply to the Charges brought against him, as was officially stated to the Chargé d'Affaires of North America. Vernet having cleared himself from these Charges, and it being necessary to reply to the Chargé d'Affaires on this head, a Copy of the Report itself appeared the most proper, as it sufficiently illustrated the matter; the Report becoming from that moment a part of the Note of the 14th of August, in answer to the part relating to the Charges.

His Honor the Chargé d'Affaires still insisted on his former declaration, adding that, as the Government of the Argentine Republic, by means of the said Official Note of the 14th August, asked for indemnification for the losses sustained in the destruction of the Establishment at the Malvinas, by the Commander of The United States' Ship of War, *Lexington*, and reparation for the insult thereby offered to the Argentine Republic, without which it would not enter into the discussion of the other points; and as he had not received any Instructions on this head, he considered his continuance near this Government as unnecessary, and was therefore under the necessity of asking for his Passport.

The Minister then observed to the Chargé d'Affaires, that he had stated himself to be fully authorised; and that therefore the Government never anticipated the breaking off of the Negotiation for want of authority or Instruction; but, at the same time that it could see no reason that could justify the return of the explanations given by the Civil and Military Commander of the Malvinas, so neither did there exist any reason for the Chargé d'Affaires asking his Passport, even though his Honor should not consider himself sufficiently authorised, on account of his having been sent expressly to justify the acts of Duncan; 1st, because, if the line of conduct adopted by the latter had not been marked out for him, it is inconceivable how it can be approved and justified by the Government of The United States. 2nd, because *it is* no less difficult to comprehend, that that Government should propose that the Negotiation for which Mr. Baylies was sent here, should be solely for what might interest itself, without any reference to what might be required from it; and 3d, because, with respect to the extreme measure adopted by the Chargé d'Affaires of asking his Passport, the Minister took the liberty to consider it inopportune, as it was not uncommon in this kind of Negotiation, especially between 2 Republics of congenial principles, in order to avoid the appearance of a want of good understanding, to ask for fresh Instructions; that the Government could not so far lose sight of an event which compromised the honor and the dearest interests of a sovereign and independent State, as not to give it exclusively the first place in the Negotiation; and that if unfortunately, when the Chargé d'Affaires should have received the Instructions of his Government, the affair could not be concluded here; then the 2 Governments would treat by means of a Minister from this Republic being sent to The United States; and should they not be able to conclude the business there, then a Neutral Power should intervene.

The Chargé d'Affaires immediately asked, what were the questions which should be submitted to a Neutral Power, and who that Neutral Power should be?

He was answered, that the Minister had ventured to throw out that indication, with a sincere desire to prove to his Honor the Chargé d'Affaires, that his not being provided with sufficient Instructions did not render it necessary for him to ask for his Passport; and not that he considered it an affair of the moment, but one for the discussion of which time would present the proper opportunity: that the principal questions were two; one of fact, the other of right: that the first comprised the conduct of Captain Duncan in the Island of La Soledad; and the Minister repeated that, until satisfaction was given for the insult, and reparation and indemnification were made, he could not pass to the discussion of any other point: that he likewise repeated, that it was an offence against the Argentine Government to announce the justification of the conduct of an Officer of The United States' Navy, when that Officer had no farther powers for acting than the General Instructions given to the Commanders of its Naval Force, relative to the protection of the commerce and Citizens of The United States.

In this state the Conference was ended; the Chargé d'Affaires stating that he still adhered to the request he had made for his Passport, and recommending the Government to decide promptly.

The Minister stated to him that it was necessary to commit the Conference to writing, and to insert it in the Book or Protocol of Conferences.

His Honor would not agree to this: the difference of language on the one part, and it not being customary to do so in The United States, prevented him from acceding to the wish of the Minister, notwithstanding all that he could urge in support of it.

MANUEL VICENTE DE MAZA.

(28.)—*The Buenos Ayres Minister to the American Chargé d'Affaires.*
(Translation.) *Buenos Ayres, 3rd September,* 1832.

THE Government, surprised no less by His Honor the Chargé d'Affaires having on the 18th ult. returned the Copy of the Report of Don Lewis Vernet, than by the statement that he has been sent here to justify the acts of Captain Silas Duncan at the Malvinas, and that, not having therefore any authority to stipulate reparation for them, his continuance here would be useless to his Country, directed the Undersigned, previously to answering His Honor's Communication, to invite him to a Conference, as the most easy and expeditious means to clear up any misunderstanding that might have occasioned the aforesaid return, and perhaps influenced the Chargé d'Affaires's resolution to ask his Passport. That Conference having taken place on the 27th instant, and His Honor having objected to the proposal of the Undersigned to resume it next day, and likewise to the recording of Minutes of what had occurred therein, the Undersigned informed his Government thereof; and has received orders to state to the Chargé d'Affaires, that, it being impossible under such circumstances to proceed in a secure manner towards the happy termination of this affair, His Excellency the Governor conceives it expedient to suspend all further Negotiation; and, in consequence, the Undersigned herewith remits the Passport which the Chargé d'Affaires has asked, regretting not having been able to gratify such a distinguished Guest of a Sister Republic; but cherishing the sanguine hope that the Government of Washington, convinced of the insult and outrage committed on the dignity and honor of an independent and friendly Nation, will feel the duty imposed upon it by justice and its own dignity, of speedily granting redress and indemnification for the grievances and injuries occasioned by one of its Naval Officers.

On making this Communication, the Undersigned has the honor to inform the Chargé d'Affaires, that the directions which he requests, for embarking his personal effects, have been issued, and takes the opportunity, &c.

MANUEL VICENTE DE MAZA.
The Chargé d'Affaires of The United States.

(29.)—*The American Chargé d'Affaires to the Buenos Ayres Minister.*
Buenos Ayres, 6th September, 1832.

THE Undersigned, Chargé d'Affaires from the United States of America, near this Government, has the honor to inform His Excellency the Minister of Grace and Justice, charged provisionally with the Department of Foreign Affairs, that he has appointed and commissioned George Washington Slacum, Esqr., Private Secretary to the American Mission, and that he is a Member of his Diplomatic Family.

The Undersigned tenders, &c.

FRANCIS BAYLIES.

H. E. Don Manuel Vicente de Maza.

(30.)—*The Buenos Ayres Minister to the American Chargé d'Affaires.*

(Translation.)   *Buenos Ayres, 7th September,* 1832.

THE Undersigned, Minister of Grace and Justice, charged provisionally with the Department of Foreign Relations of the Argentine Republic, has had the honour of laying before his Government the Note under date of yesterday, addressed to him by the Honorable Francis Baylies, Chargé d'Affaires of the United States of America, informing him that he has appointed and commissioned Mr. George W. Slacum, Private Secretary to the American Legation, and that he is a Member of his Diplomatic Family; and although His Excellency does not see in this nomination one of those official Appointments which should be announced to him, yet he has not been able to dissemble the astonishment which such an election has produced in him.

The Chargé d'Affaires cannot but be aware that Mr. Slacum, prosecuted by the Magistrates of the Country for a crime which the Laws of the Republic punish even with the last penalty, succeeded in eluding the search of the Police, by seeking asylum in His Honor's house, where he has remained accessible to his connections.

After this event, the Government of Buenos Ayres, who was not ignorant of the extent of its authority in the case of Mr. Slacum, nor of the immunity of the residence of a Foreign Public Minister, flattered itself that it should merit from the Chargé d'Affaires of The United States, the respect which its excessively liberal conduct was calculated to inspire, and that he would have comprehended, that, notwithstanding the serious nature of the complaints against Mr. Slacum, the Government was uniformly actuated by principles of moderation and circumspection. But if the Chargé d'Affaires be not sensible of the circumstances which yet unfortunately surround Mr. Slacum, the Undersigned is directed by his Government to declare to His Honor, that its own dignity forbids it at present to consider that Gentleman in any other light than that of a Violator of the Laws of the Republic, who has taken refuge in the house of the public Minister of a friendly Nation.

The Undersigned has the honor, &c.

MANUEL VICENTE DE MAZA.

The Chargé d'Affaires of The United States.

MESSAGE of the Government, on t..e Opening of the Legislature of the Province of Buenos Ayres.—31st May, 1833.

———

(Translation.)

GENTLEMEN REPRESENTATIVES,

IT is highly satisfactory to the Government to see assembled this day, the 11th Legislative Assembly of the Province; and it felicitates you sincerely upon so pleasing an event. In rendering you an account of the state of public affairs entrusted to its charge, it congratulates itself in being able to state to you, that, since the triumph obtained by the defenders of the Laws, the experience of the great evils caused by their disturbers, has inspired among all classes of society a horror of anarchy, and a firm determination to support order. The Government entertains well founded hopes, that that order will be unalterably preserved, and that its efforts for the prosperity of the People over whom it presides, will not be fruitless, when it finds in this august Body, so many Citizens distinguished for patriotism, wisdom, and probity; and it counts upon their efficacious co-operation in furtherance of this important object.

The Government continues charged with the Foreign Relations of the Republic, and preserves with all friendly Powers the good understanding and harmony which the honour and dignity of the Country require.

The Minister sent by the Government of Washington, whose expected arrival was announced to you in the preceding year, and whom it was resolved to await, in order to come to an explanation with him, relative to the destruction, by an armed force, of the Settlement in the Island of Soledad, one of the Malvinas, (Falkland Islands) by the Commander of The United States' Sloop of War *Lexington*, did, in fact, arrive here, and was received in the character of Chargé d'Affaires. You are, already, Gentlemen, aware of the state of that negotiation. The Government, in order to resume it, has named a Minister, and has notified his appointment to the Government of Washington: he will shortly be despatched thither, with Instructions calculated to obtain satisfaction and reparation for so serious an injury.

The renewal of the Settlement at the Falkland Islands was immediately resolved upon, to such an extent as the other necessary claims upon the attention of the Province permitted; but shortly afterwards an event, as unexpected as unpleasant, occurred. The Government has already informed you, that the Commander of His Britannic Majesty's Sloop of War *Clio*, supported by a superior force, and favoured by circumstances of which you are aware, took possession of those Islands in the name of his Sovereign. The Government, at the time, acquainted you with the course it intended to pursue. It has accordingly instructed its Minister in London, energetically to protest against this violation of the most sacred principles of the Law of Nations, to demand the restitution of those Islands, and to require such satisfaction as shall correspond with the justice and honour of both Governments, by those means which probity, good faith, and sound reason recommend.

Previous to an event so rare in the history of political occurrences, a British Consul had been admitted here, and a Secretary of Legation acknowledged, in the character of Chargé d'Affaires, *ad interim*, of His Britannic Majesty, until the arrival of the Minister Plenipotentiary, who should be named to succeed the one of that rank who had before resided with this Government.

Previous also to the affair of the *Clio* at the Falkland Islands, our Chargé d'Affaires residing with the British Government was elevated to the rank of Minister Plenipotentiary.

The Commission assembled there to liquidate the claims of certain British Subjects, for losses sustained from the acts of our Privateers during the last foreign war, has not as yet terminated its labours. Some of the claims have already been liquidated, and in cases where undue demands have been put forward, our Minister has conducted himself in the manner most conformable with justice and the National honour.

It is painful to the Government to see itself surrounded by difficulties, which it has not been able to overcome, during the course of the year that has expired since the opening of the 10th Assembly of the Legislature to the present time, and to be still unable to direct its attention to the payment of the Dividends upon the Loan which various Individuals of the British Nation advanced to this Government. The payment of the Dividends still remains suspended; although the Government is anxious to occupy itself preferably with a question which so much affects its credit.

His Majesty the King of the French had nominated a *Chargé d'Affaires* to reside in this Republic; but the Government, considering the intimate understanding which ought to subsist between the 2 States, and availing itself of an inherent right, has not thought it fit to receive him; it has, however, explained to His Majesty, in a friendly manner, the grounds of this determination.

The Preliminary Convention of amity and commerce, which the Consul-General of France is empowered to negotiate, has not been entered upon; the Government considering that the time had not yet arrived for accepting the honourable invitation of His Majesty the King of the French. A Consul-General has been subsequently appointed to France.

It is satisfactory to announce to you that the American Republics of Chile, Colombia, and Mexico, maintain with the Argentine Republic, friendly and fraternal relations; and that, with respect to the other States of America, formerly Spanish, no obstacle exists on the part of this Government to the maintenance of the same with them.

The Legation which the Government sent to the Republic of Bolivia is already, however, on its return, in conformity with the orders it has received. You will be particularly informed, through the Department of Foreign Affairs, of such circumstances relating to this matter, as it is proper that you should be acquainted with: in the mean time, the Government can assure you, that it has reason to hope that what has occurred, up to the present time, is not likely to disturb the peace subsisting between the 2 Republics.

The Empire of Brazil and this Republic preserve the best harmony and good understanding. A Minister Plenipotentiary has been named for the adjustment of the Definitive Treaty of Peace, which, in conformity with the XVIIth Article of the Preliminary Convention of the 27th August, 1828, is to be concluded between the Government of this Republic and that Empire. He will set out for the Court of Rio de Janeiro, so soon as the Government shall have drawn up instructions for his guidance.

Our relations with the Oriental State of the Uruguay have been sustained in a frank and friendly manner by the Government. The Chargé d'Affaires whom the Government of the Oriental Republic announced as having been named to reside here, has not been received; because, even had the Government allowed itself to overlook the political position of that State, it has not as yet obtained either satisfaction for its complaints, or a guarantee against the recurrence of similar injuries to those which gave rise to them. Nevertheless, it is to be hoped that the means of an approximation, upon terms advantageous to both Governments, will be easily attainable; for which important object, the Government has shewn itself disposed to receive a Commissioner for that express purpose.

It is most satisfactory to the Government to announce to you the happy termination of the Representative Commission of the Governments of the Littoral Provinces of the Argentine Republic, which was assembled in the Capital of Santa Fé. The public peace, and the invitation held out by the XVIth Article of the Treaty of the 4th January, 1831, were the last results of its labours, the exact fulfilment of which, has given it a claim to the gratitude and particular consideration of all good Citizens.

All the Provinces of the Republic enjoy tranquillity, and as their respective Legislatures assemble, their Governments, with the competent authorization, manifest their adhesion to the said Treaty of the 4th of January. It is gratifying to the Government to acquaint you that, in all of them, there prevails a spirit of order, which has been produced by experience, and the perfecting of which is the work of peace, of constancy, and of great efforts.

The hostile Indians, emboldened by the opportunities afforded for their incursions, during the unfortunate period of the convulsions which the Republic has endured, kept the Frontier Provinces of the South in continual alarm, and subjected them to considerable depredations. By one of those vigorous efforts, produced by the state of harmony which prevails throughout the Argentine Provinces, they have organized a combined expedition, which is already in motion, and has begun to operate with good success. The Republic of Chile has been invited to co-operate, and the Government has the satisfaction of announcing to you, that its reply leads to the expectation that it will concur in an enterprize so important to the Territories of both States.

The Government has perceived that the want of a distinct regulation, touching the ceremonial to be observed upon occasions of etiquette, with respect to the Diplomatic Body, and certain informalities which have been introduced, under circumstances entirely differing from the present, have originated doubts and discussions which it is desirable to avoid. Conforming itself, in this particular, to the received usages of the Governments and Republics of Europe and America, it has duly regulated, by a Decree, the ceremonial to be observed by the Diplomatic Body towards the Government, upon public occasions.

Gentlemen, you will now be pleased to direct your attention to the internal affairs of the Province.

In the Administration of Justice, there has been no other alteration, than that the Government has determined that the Presidency of the Tribunal of the Chamber of Appeal, should, from the beginning of the present year, be filled by that Member of it, whom the Government shall annually name, until a General Law be passed upon this subject; in pursuance of the reform which is in progress of the administration of this Branch. The Offices of Fiscal in the Civil and Criminal Courts, and in the Department of the Treasury, have been provisionally united in one person: and, in the same manner, the Fiscal Agencies have been incorporated in the person of one Advocate.

The Project of a reform in the important branch of the Administration of Justice, which was announced to you in the preceding year, although retarded by the illness of some of the Members of the Tribunal, has been lately received by the Government, and will be presented to you by the Minister of Justice, with the observations which may be deemed necessary upon the occasion. This Project is the result of the wisdom and experience of the most distinguished Members of the Chamber of Justice; but as this subject has ever been a matter of difficulty to eminent Men, it will require to be weighed with all the wisdom of your Counsels, and will be sanctioned in the form which you may be pleased to recommend.

The Commission, appointed in compliance with the Law of the 17th

October, 1831, to draw up the Commercial Code, has far advanced in that work; and it will be submitted to you, so soon as it shall have been received and examined by the Government.

The Government has not neglected to attend to the Resolution of the Honourable House of the 11th July last, relative to Appeals in Ecclesiastical Suits, and it is at present occupied with the preliminary deliberations which the subject demands.

The attention of the Government has been directed to the state of the Public Prison; and, in order to combine security with the accommodation and decent maintenance of the unfortunate beings confined therein, provisional regulations are in preparation, which are calculated to attain those objects, and in which the Ladies of the Society of Beneficence take a most important part, with respect to the Female Prisoners.

The Government, desiring to give to Religious Worship the respectability which is fitting, and to cause it to be performed with due splendour, has filled up the vacant stalls in the Ecclesiastical Senate. Persuaded also, that it is a duty incumbent upon the Country, and one imposed by Religion, to offer up to the Supreme Being the prayers of the Church, for the prosperity of the Republic, and for the wisdom of its Governors,—a custom which had been unfortunately suspended,—the illustrious Bishop and Vicar Apostolic of this Diocese has been invited to renew it; and it is gratifying to announce to you, that the Ecclesiastical Prelate has fulfilled the desire of the Government: In the same manner, that Prelate has acceded to the wishes already expressed, with regard to the suppression of many of the holidays, whose excessive number was injurious to commerce, to industry, and to the morals of the Country.

The service of the Posts, which the infliction of the drought had very sensibly deranged, in the direction of the interior Provinces, is in process of being re-established; and it is gratifying to inform you that, in this Province, this mode of communication has been considerably augmented towards the South, so as to reach, in some directions, even to the Deserts.

The Department of Police has particularly engaged the attention of the Government: convinced of the necessity of leaving its action unrestrained, in order that it may confine itself to the important objects of its establishment, and also of the utility and advantage which will result to the Revenue, by reforming the system of its Accounts in the manner prescribed by the existing regulations, the Accountant's Office of the Department has been suppressed, and a Commission appointed to carry on its operations in future. Regulations are also in preparation, calculated to introduce other improvements of importance into this branch.

The labours of the Topographical and Engineer Departments have been approved by the Government. The works of the Canal of

San Fernando are far advanced; and those of San Nicolas de los Arroyos are also in progress. The public works in the City have been confined merely to repairs, excepting those of the " Casa de Exercicios," (House of Religious Seclusion,) which have been defrayed by the funds of the Establishment, and by some small assistance from the Government, but, principally, by the subscriptions of the Pious. In the Country Towns, the construction of the Churches, the commencement of which the Government had announced to you, is carrying on; the Church of the Fort " Federacion" is already finished, and that of Guilmes will be so shortly.

The Government is desirous that the Education of Youth, in a Country which is rapidly advancing in civilization, should be as complete as possible, and has apportioned funds for the promotion of this important object; deeply convinced, that it is that which most contributes to the morality and intelligence of a Nation, and that the individuals adorned with these valuable qualities, are ever the most zealous defenders of their Country, and the best supporters of the Law. The University is gradually improving in its system of studies. Its Rector has submitted a new regulation, to which the Government will give a preferable consideration, and it is occupied with the complete organization of this useful establishment: in it have been educated, in their several branches, various Professors of Medicine and the Law, who do honour to the Country of their birth.

· The Primary Schools, for the youth of both sexes, fulfil the wish of the Government; the number of the scholars daily encreases, and their progress is remarkable. The Province must acknowledge a debt of gratitude to the Superintendant, with respect to that for boys, which, owing to his efforts and personal contributions, has efficaciously advanced the object in view.

In the City and Country, Vaccination is generally employed, and the period of infancy is thus preserved from that fatal scourge, which still afflicts some other parts of America. The Foundling Hospital continues to be well regulated; the College of Orphans is in the best condition, as are all the other Establishments which are under the care of the Society of Beneficence. In the Hospital for Women, important improvements have been effected; and the Superintendant has answered the expectations of the Government. In the Hospital for Men, the part of the building which was inhabited had suffered some injury, owing to the decayed state of that part which was uninhabited, and the Government ordered its immediate repair; the sick, according to the Reports of the Inspectors, are well provided for.

Measures have been taken to extend the Population as far as the new Forts; and the ground which is to be considered as attached to the respective Fort, and the sites best adapted for the location of the Settlements and the distribution of the Settlers, have been marked out. The means adopted by the Government to check the theft of Cattle, and for the security of the property of the inhabitants of the Country Districts, have produced very favourable results; and the evils which were experienced in this respect have been considerably lessened.

The important Establishment at Bahia Blanca continues to make considerable progress; the Government has adopted the measures conducive to that object, and, among them has considered it necessary to raise a regiment of " Blandengues," availing itself, for that purpose, of the remains of the 2nd regiment of Cavalry of the Line, which was cantoned in that quarter.

The Establishment at Patagonia, which has suffered great injuries from various incursions of the Indians, has been particularly attended to. All necessary aid has been provided for its security, and a company of Infantry, and another of Cavalry have been formed there.

The Establishment at the Falkland Islands had also particularly occupied the attention of the Government, and it had sent thither a Political and Military Commandant, with a detachment of Troops to form a Garrison, and a Vessel of War for its support; but the beneficial objects of their mission were frustrated by the disagreeable incident which the Government has communicated to you.

The Indians established on our frontier, and many of those beyond it, have continued to give constant proofs of fidelity to the Government. Nevertheless, some hostile Chiefs have made various incursions, in which they have been completely vanquished by our brave divisions who garrison the Frontiers; and it is very satisfactory that, in these operations, many of the friendly Indians have taken part with us. Some of them come frequently to the Capital to barter their commodities, and they observe the utmost regularity of conduct. But, while the hostile Indians invaded our Country Settlements, the plains of the Sister Provinces were devastated,—properties were destroyed, and even many families became the victims of their ferocity. In such a state of things, it was useless to employ pacific measures with them, and it became indispensable to put in motion a Division of the Army, to operate in conjunction with the Forces which the other Provinces have destined to exterminate them. It is already on its march, under the command of an illustrious Citizen, who has rendered great services to his Country, and under whose skilful direction a prosperous result may be expected. On the other hand, the brave soldiers who accompany him, have displayed an unexampled enthusiasm and ardour, which will lead them to resign themselves to the hardships and fatigues which they must encounter, in order to attain the important end proposed,—that of subduing the proud insolence of the common enemy of the Republic.

The permanent Army of the Province improves daily in subordination and discipline; the soldiers in the interior who have been engaged with the Indians who invaded some points of our frontier, have given satisfactory proofs of their courage; the Corps of Country Militia are in the best order, and perform with exactness the service to which they are destined; the Militia of the Capital satisfactorily fulfil their duties. The Government being desirous of calling back to the Country a considerable number of Individuals who had abandoned it, in order to elude the fatigues of service, by deserting from the Regiments of the Line, has issued a Decree of Pardon, dated the 21st of December, 1832.

The Public Revenue, that important branch which constitutes the most vital part of States, would now afford us a flattering picture, had not extraordinary exigencies arisen to increase the demands upon the Treasury. In the preceding year, the Receipts of the Customs, and other resources of which the Government was enabled to avail itself to provide funds, were sufficient to cover all the ordinary and extraordinary Expences; and the Debt which existed at the close of the year 1831, so far from being augmented, was somewhat diminished. It now, however, becomes the duty of the Government, in order to escape that responsibility which is imposed upon it, to suggest to you, that it would be very hazardous to rely with confidence, solely upon the means which the Customs' Duties afford, as sufficing to meet all demands which may be made upon it; more especially as, in the present year, such large sums have been expended in the equipment of the Troops employed, in concert with the other Provinces, against the hostile Indians.

The Government has not been unmindful of the immense sums required for the equipment of this Corps of the Army, and for its maintenance in the different positions where it is to act; but, nevertheless, its duty to be faithful to its engagements with the Governments of the other Provinces of the Republic, to whose sufferings it could not remain indifferent, and its persuasion that the results of the present important Expedition will be prosperous, and will give permanent security to the principal source of wealth of this Country, the grazing-farms of our fertile and beautiful plains, have compelled it to make efforts very far exceeding its scanty resources. Unfortunately even these have diminished, in consequence of the non-realization of the 1,500,000 dollars, for the raising of which by a Loan, you granted authority to the Government, by the Law of the 5th of February of the present year. The proposals sent in to the Minister of Finance were totally inadmissible, and the Government is so circumstanced, as to be obliged to request that the Honourable House, in compliance with Article III. of the said Law, will determine upon such measures as their wisdom may suggest, to replace the deficit which will otherwise exist in the Revenue of the present year, unless that sum be opportunely provided. For which purpose, it most especially recommends this matter to your consideration, and hopes that you will give it every preference. Meanwhile, it is gratifying to state to you, that the regularity with whicn the Government Bills, those of the Custom House, and those of the Sinking Fund, have been paid, has raised the credit of the Treasury to the highest degree. The holders of them delay to receive their money for many days after they become due, from the confidence they feel in the punctuality of the payments. The Government will continue this system without alteration; regretting that it cannot attend to all the urgencies of the State with equal exactness.

The Government has carried into execution what it announced to you, with regard to reforms in the regulation of the Corps of Revenue Officers. Its good effects have already been felt in the diminution of that fatal system of contraband, the destruction of u orality in commerce, and of the resources of the Treasury. The Government will direct its particular attention to the strict observance of the Law in this respect, in order to secure the permanency of such inestimable advantages.

The situation of the Bank has not improved; on the contrary, from the last Statement presented by the Directors, the urgent necessity is demonstrated, that the Legislative Body should turn its attention to the state of that Establishment. The Government has already declared its sentiments upon this subject, in its last Message, and to them it will continue to adhere.

The Revenues of the State have been established upon the system of Accounts formerly adopted, concentrating their direct collection in one point, in order to simplify their management, and to render more clear and easy the operations of the Receiver and Treasurer General's Offices, and thus to avoid the complicated and laborious system upon which many of the subordinate Offices were conducted. The Commission appointed to draw up the plan of this useful measure, will shortly present their labours to the Government.

In the midst of the pecuniary difficulties felt by the Government, in liquidating the Debt of the Province, contracted in the year 1829, on account of the supplies furnished to the restoring Army, it was under the necessity of adopting some measure to indemnify in a certain degree the creditors. It in consequence ordered, that the Bills acknowledged by the Receiver-General's Office should be received in payment of the rent of the lands of the State.

The Minister of Finance will submit to you the Estimates for the approaching year 1834, and the Accounts of the past year.

Buenos Ayres, 31st May, 1833.

JUAN RAMON BALCARCE.
VICTORIO GARCIA DE ZUNIGA.
MANUEL VICENTE DE MAZA.
ENRIQUE MARTINEZ

MESSAGE of the Government to the House of Representatives of the Province of Buenos Ayres, relative to the occupation of the Malvinas (Falkland Islands) by Great Britain.—24th January, 1833.

TO THE HONOURABLE HOUSE OF REPRESENTATIVES.

Buenos Ayres, 24th January, 1833.

(Translation.)   *24th year of Liberty, and 18th of Independence.*

IF great has been the pain which the Government has felt on receiving the news of the violent abuse of power exercised in the Malvinas by a Vessel of War belonging to His Britannic Majesty, in dishonour of the Argentine Flag, in violation of the integrity of the Territory of the Republic, of its rights, of justice, and of the faith due to the relations of friendship and good understanding, cultivated without interruption with the Court of St. James; it feels no less pain in acquainting the Honourable Representatives with the new and scandalous aggression, which has been committed in the Malvinas by an Officer of the English Navy; an aggression rendered the more remarkable from the reciprocal relations and Treaties of Friendship and Commerce subsisting between the 2 Countries, than that which was last year committed by the Officer of another friendly Nation—the United States of North America.

The Schooner-of-War, *Sarandi,* anchored in the outer roads on the 15th instant, on her return from Port Louis de la Soledad, in the

Malvina Islands. Her Commander, Don Jose Maria de Pinedo, reports that he has returned from thence, prior to receiving orders for so doing, in consequence of His Britannic Majesty's Vessel of War *Clio*, having, on the 2nd of this month, arrived at the Island of Soledad, at a time when, owing to the insubordination of a few Soldiers of the Garrison, the Chief of the Establishment had been killed, and good order disturbed (in the restoration of which the Naval Commander was occupied when the *Clio* arrived;) that having sent 2 of his Officers on board the *Clio*, to make the corresponding offers of attention and friendship, they returned, and informed him that Mr. Onslow, the Commander of His Britannic Majesty's Sloop, intended to go on board the *Sarandi*; which he did, on the same day, about 3 in the afternoon, accompanied by 2 of his Officers; and entering into conversation with the Commander of the *Sarandi*, he informed him that he came to take possession of the Malvinas, as belonging to His Britannic Majesty; that he had positive orders to hoist the British Flag thereon within 24 hours, as he had already done in other Ports of the said Islands; to give a passage in one of his Vessels to the Officer and Troops stationed there, and to the other Inhabitants; and to cause every thing belonging to Buenos Ayres to be embarked and sent away; in consequence whereof, he requested that the Argentine Flag which was then flying on shore, might be struck the following day, as he was bound to fulfil the orders he had received.

The surprize of Commandant Pinedo, under such circumstances, was as natural as the aggression and violent intrusion which caused it was unexpected, considering that this gross outrage was committed by a friendly and powerful Nation, which had always boasted of its good faith and moderation, and which had lost no opportunity of manifesting the cordiality of its kind feelings towards the Argentine Republic.

After having made to Captain Onslow the corresponding Protest, and remarking to him that, as the 2 Governments were in peace and friendship, this proceeding was most extraordinary, he told him that his duty would not allow him to consent to this unjust pretention without receiving express Orders to that effect from his Government. Mr. Onslow then took his leave, telling Commandant Pinedo that he would reply to him in writing.

Accordingly, about 4 o'clock in the afternoon of the same day (the 2nd), the said Commandant received the Note, of which the subjoined No. 1, is a Copy; when, on viewing the intimation therein contained, he wished to resist at all hazards; but he met with difficulties which he considered insurmountable: nevertheless he resolved to send a Deputation which, in the name of the Government, should repeat to Mr. Onslow the former Protest, and inform him that, if he contemplated the execution of his project by force, he should consider himself bound to resist it, and he therefore hoped that Captain Onslow would prefer waiting until the Government should have marked out to him (Pinedo) the line of conduct he ought to pursue.

It was after 10 o'clock at night, when the Deputation returned on board the *Sarandi*, without having been able to obtain an interview with Captain Onslow.

In this state of affairs, after having endeavoured in vain to surmount the difficulties which, in his opinion, would render the most desperate resistance unavailing, he became thoroughly convinced of it; and at 6 o'clock on the morning of the 3rd, he went personally on board the Sloop *Clio*, and, for the last time, protested to her Commander against the violation he was about to commit. Captain Onslow replied to him in the sense of the latter part of the subjoined Note, assuring him that he could not defer the execution of the Orders he had received to take possession of the Malvinas; that he could see what Force he had, and that he was in momentary expectation of more; and that he, Commandant Pinedo, could therefore act as he might think fit. Commandant Pinedo immediately withdrew, declaring that Great Britain was responsible for the insult, and violation of the dignity and rights of the Republic, which were thus inconsistently and disrespectfully trampled upon, by force: that it was his intention to depart, but that he would not strike the Flag on shore.

Commandant Pinedo, accordingly, returned to his Vessel; and adopted, among other measures, prior to setting sail, that of prohibiting the People on the Island from lowering the Argentine Flag, and of conferring the command of the Establishment, in writing, on the Superintendant of the Establishment, Don Juan Simon, who was to remain, with some others.

At 9 o'clock in the morning of the 3rd, 3 boats manned with Seamen and Marines, from the English Sloop, landed at the point of Port Louis, and, placing a Flag-staff at the house of an Englishman, about 4 squares distant from the Commandantcy, they hoisted thereon the British Flag, and then proceeded to strike that of the Republic, which was still flying on shore; and which was immediately delivered up to the *Sarandi* by an Officer sent for that purpose. Captain Pinedo was ready, on that day, to remove from the scene of the insult; but the weather compelled him to remain the whole of the 4th, and up to 5 o'clock on the evening of the 5th, when he set sail.

These facts, as now transmitted by the Government to the Honourable Representatives, in conformity with the Official Report of the Commander of the Schooner *Sarandi*, exhibit a most flagrant abuse of power, and belie the friendly protestations it has been accustomed to receive from a Nation with which it had hoped to maintain the best understanding, by scrupulously fulfilling the duties imposed upon it by the subsisting Treaties, and exercising a generous liberality, in proof of the most sincere friendship.

By Documents Nos. 2, 3, and 4, the Honourable Representatives will learn what steps have been taken by the Government in this serious and delicate affair; and likewise its firm resolution to maintain the rights of the Argentine Republic, and not to come to any accommodation inconsistent with reason and the national honour; taking every measure which justice and prudence may dictate, for the purpose of obtaining from the Cabinet of His Britannic Majesty, full reparation, the acknowledgment of our right to the Malvinas, and the exercise of our dominion over that Territory; and should this not suffice, then to adopt such measures as may be most conducive to obtaining a declaration of the opinion of the World upon the matter, to which a Government like that of England, which wishes to be considered as ranking amongst the most free and enlightened of Europe, cannot be indifferent.

God preserve the Honourable Representatives many years.

JUAN RAMON BALCARCE.
MANUEL VICENTE DE MAZA.

(1.)—*The British to the Buenos Ayres Commander.*
His Majesty's Sloop, Clio,

SIR,   *Berkeley Sound, 2nd January,* 1833.

I HAVE to acquaint you that I have received directions from His Excellency the Commander-in-Chief of His Britannic Majesty's Ships and Vessels of War, on the South American Station, to exercise the rights of Sovereignty over these Islands, in the name of His Britannic Majesty.

It is my intention to hoist, to-morrow morning, the National Flag of Great Britain on shore; when I request you will be pleased to haul down your Flag, and to withdraw your Forces, taking with you all the stores, &c., belonging to your Government.

I am, &c.

J. J. ONSLOW, *Commander.*
H. E. the Commander of the Buenos Ayrean Forces at Port Louis, Berkeley Sound.

(2.) *The Buenos Ayres Minister to the British Chargé d'Affaires.*
Department of Foreign Relations,

(Translation.)   *Buenos Ayres, 16th January,* 1833.

THE Undersigned, Minister of Grace and Justice, charged provisionally with the Department of Foreign Relations of the Argentine Republic, has the honour to address the Chargé d'Affaires, *ad interim,* of His Britannic Majesty in this City, to acquaint him, that the Government has just learned that the Commander of His Britannic Majesty's Sloop-of-War *Clio,* has taken possession of the Island of La Soledad, in the Malvinas, and has hoisted the British Flag where that of the Argentine Republic had waved. This unexpected event has sensibly affected the feelings of the Government of Buenos Ayres; and although it cannot discover any thing to justify such a proceeding, nevertheless, presuming that the Chargé d'Affaires, whom the Under-signed addresses, is informed upon a measure which openly compro-mises the dignity and rights of the Argentine Republic, it has directed the Undersigned to request of the Chargé d'Affaires of His Britannic Majesty, the competent explanations.

God preserve the Chargé d'Affaires many years.

MANUEL VICENTE DE MAZA.

The Chargé d'Affaires of His Britannic Majesty.

(3.)—*The British Chargé d'Affaires to the Buenos Ayres Minister.*

Buenos Ayres, 17*th January,* 1833.

THE Undersigned, His Britannic Majesty's Chargé d'Affaires, in acknowledging the receipt of the Note, dated yesterday, of his Excel-lency Señor Don Manuel Vicente de Maza, the Minister charged with the Department of Foreign Relations of the Argentine Republic, has the honour to inform his Excellency that he has received no Instructions from his Court to make any communication to the Government of Buenos Ayres, upon the subject to which his Excellency's Note refers.

The Undersigned will hasten to submit the same to His Majesty's Government, and he avails himself, &c.

PHILIP G. GORE.

H. E. Señor Don Manuel Vicente de Maza.

(4.)—*The Buenos Ayres Minister to the British Chargé d'Affaires.*

Department of Foreign Relations,

(Translation.) *Buenos Ayres,* 22*nd January,* 1833.

THE Undersigned, Minister of Grace and Justice, charged provi-sionally with the Department of Foreign Relations of the Argentine Republic, is directed by his Government to address the Chargé d'Af-faires, *ad interim,* of His Britannic Majesty in this City, and to inform him, that, on the 2nd instant, His Britannic Majesty's Sloop of War *Clio,* anchored in the Port of San Luis, in the Island of La Soled/d, one of the Malvinas, for the purpose of taking possession of them as belonging to His Britannic Majesty;—Captain Onslow of the said Vessel stating that he had positive orders to hoist the British Flag on shore, within 24 hours. He had already done so in other Ports of the Islands, and finally did the same in that of La Soledad, in defiance of the Protest of the Commander of the Schooner-of-War *Sarandi;* who was there in fulfilment of the Orders of his Government, but which, through a fatality of unforeseen circumstances, he could not strictly perform, by forcibly resisting the occupation of the Islands.

The Undersigned abstains, for the present, from expatiating on the inconsistency of such a violent and rude proceeding in a time of profound Peace, when the close and friendly relations between the 2 Governments on the one hand, and on the other the moderation, cordiality and purity of intentions, of which England has made ostentation, gave no reason to expect that the confidence in which the Argentine Republic reposed would be so unceremoniously violated. Nevertheless, in fulfilment of the Orders of his Government, and in its name, and in consideration of what we owe to our own dignity, to posterity, and to the deposit which the United Provinces have entrusted to the Government of Buenos Ayres, and in short, to the whole World, whose eyes are fixed upon us,—the Undersigned protests, in the most formal manner, against the pretensions of the Government of Great Britain to the Malvina Islands, and its occupation of them; as likewise against the insult offered to the Flag of the Republic, and against the damages which the latter has received and may receive in consequence of the aforesaid proceedings, and whatever may hereafter take place on the part of the British Government in this respect.

The Chargé d'Affaires, whom the Undersigned addresses, will be pleased to transmit this Protest to his Government, and manifest the decided resolution of this Republic to sustain its rights; at the same time that it desires to maintain inviolate the friendly relations which it has hitherto cultivated with Great Britain, and that Peace may prosper and be perpetual between the Two States.

God preserve the Chargé d'Affaires many years.

MANUEL VICENTE DE MAZA.

The British Chargé d'Affaires.

(5.)—*The British Chargé d'Affaires to the Buenos Ayres Minister.*

Buenos Ayres, 24th January, 1833.

THE Undersigned, His Britannic Majesty's Chargé d'Affaires, has the honour to acknowledge the receipt of the Note, which His Excellency Señor Don Manuel Vicente de Maza, Minister of Grace and Justice, charged with the Department of Foreign Relations of the Argentine Republic, has addressed to him, dated the 22nd instant.

The Undersigned will lose no time in transmitting His Excellency's Note to His Majesty's Government.

He avails himself of this opportunity, &c.

PHILIP G. GORE.

H. E. Senor Don Manuel Vicente de Maza.

[For Protest of M. Moreno of the 17th June, 1833, and Answer of Viscount Palmerston of the 8th January, 1834. See Vol. 1833, 1834.]

PROTESTATION

DU

GOUVERNEMENT DES PROVINCES UNIES

DU

RIO DE LA PLATA,

PAR SON

MINISTRE PLENIPOTENTIAIRE À LONDRES,

SUR L' ARROGATION DE SOUVERAINETÉ DANS LES

ILES MALVINES, OR FALKLAND, PAR LA GRANDE BRETAGNE,

ET L' EJECTION DE L' ETABLISSEMENT DE

BUENOS AYRES À PORT LOUIS.

À LONDRES :

CHEZ CUNNINGHAM ET SALMON, CROWN COURT, FLEET STREET.

1833.

PROTEST.

&c. &c. &c.

THE Undersigned Minister Plenipotentiary of the United Provinces of Rio de la Plata, has the honor of addressing to His Excellency Viscount Palmerston, Principal Secretary of State for Foreign Affairs, the present Memoir and Protest upon the proceedings of His Britannic Majesty's Government, in assuming the sovereignty and possession of the Malvinas, otherwise called the Falkland Islands, and in forcibly stripping the said United Provinces of a part of their territory and dominion.

But previously to resorting to this mode of upholding the sovereign rights of his government, the undersigned had, on the 24th of April last, the honor of requesting that His Majesty's Government would be pleased to inform him if they had really given orders to eject the Buenos-Ayrean garrison from the Malvinas, as pretended, by Captain Onslow of His Majesty's corvette, CLIO; and also whether they did authorize and would recognize the declaration, also alleged to have been made, respecting the right of dominion to those islands, because on the arrival here of the correspondence from Buenos Ayres, dated the 14th of January, it was made known, from private intelligence which found its way into the London newspapers, that the Buenos-Ayrean garrison and colony in the Malvinas, together with a ship of war, the SARANDI, stationed in that part of the Argentine republic, had been forcibly constrained to withdraw upon an intimation from the said Captain Onslow, who declared that he was going to take, and did take, possession of the islands in the name of His Britannic Majesty, notwithstanding a pending discussion thereupon.

LE Soussigné, Ministre Plénipotentiaire des Provinces Unies de Rio du la Plata, a l'honneur d'adresser à Son Excellence le Vicomte Palmerston, Principal Sécretaire d'état des Affaires étrangères, le present Mémoire et la Présente protestation contre les actes du gouvernement Britannique, qui s'est emparé de la posséssion et souveraineté des Malvines, autrement appelées Iles Falkland, et a dépouillé, par la force, les Provinces Unies d'une partie de leur territoire.

Mais avant d'avoir recours aux moyens de défense des droits souverains de son gouvernement, le Sousigné a eu l'honneur, le 24 Avril dernier, de prier que le gouvernement de Sa Majesté voulut bien l'informer s'il avait réellement donné des ordres pour qu'on expulsat des Malvines la garnison Buenos-Ayrienne, ainsi que l'a prétendu Monsieur Onslow, Capitaine de la corvette de Sa Majesté la CLIO ; comme aussi, s'il a autorisé et voudrait reconnaître la déclaration, supposée avoir été faite, relativement au droit de possession de ces Iles. Parceque, à l'arrivée de la correspondance de Buenos Ayres, datée du 14 Janvier, on avait appris par des lettres particulières qui furent insérrées dans les journaux de Londres, que la garnison Buenos-Ayrienne et les colons des Malvines, ainsi qu'un vaisseau de guerre le SARANDI stationé dans cette partie de la République Argentine, avaient été forcés et contraints de se retirer, sur un ordre du dit Capitaine Onslow ; lequel a déclaré qu'il allait prendre, et prit en effet, possession des Iles, au nom de Sa Majesté Britannique, malgré la discussion pendante.

B

6

An explanation of this sort was the more called for from the circumstance of the Argentine Government not having, up to that period, received any notification of the fact, excepting what was incidentally afforded to them by the arrival at Buenos Ayres, on the fifteenth of the same month of January, of their garrison and colonists who had been expelled in a manner so surprizing; nor had their legation at this court any other notion of His Majesty's Government's intentions than what fell verbally from a chief person in the department for foreign affairs, signifying to the undersigned that instructions, relative to the discussion, were about to be given to the newly-appointed Minister to Buenos Ayres, Mr. Hamilton, but who has not yet quitted Paris.

His Excellency Lord Palmerston replied on the 27th of the same month of April " that the proceedings of the Commander of the CLIO took place in consequence of instructions given by His Majesty's government to Admiral Baker, the late Commander-in-Chief of the South American station; that this admiral had orders to send a ship of war to the Malvina Islands, there to exercise the ancient and undoubted rights of sovereignty which," according to His Excellency, "are vested in His Majesty, and to act in that quarter as in a possession belonging to the crown of Great Britain, and, of course, in case of meeting in those islands, any foreign persons or military force, not acknowledging the sovereignty of His Majesty, the commander of the ship-of-war was to request such persons and such military force to withdraw, and he was to assist them with the means of doing so."

The note of His Excellency Lord Palmerston, concludes with stating that " the said instructions were made known by Admiral Baker to His Majesty's Legation at Buenos Ayres."

If, however, this information, so transmitted to His Majesty's Legation, was truly intended to come to the knowledge of the Argentine government, in order that they might not be taken by surprize at the meditated deprivation, as may be supposed from the existing amity between the two countries and the courtesies usually observed between governments, it is very painful to remark that the British Legation did not comprehend it in this manner, since they gave no information, nay more, they absolutely forgot, or denied, that they had any thing to communicate on the subject. By the correspondence received in the month of May last, it appears that on the 16th of January, two days after

Une explication de cette espèce était d'autant plus nécessaire, que le gouvernement de la République Argentine n'avait reçu, jusqu'à cette époque, aucune notification de ce fait; excepté ce qu'il avait appris, par hazard, à l'arrivée à Buenos Ayres le 15 du même mois de Janvier par la garnison et les colons qui avaient été chassés d'une manière si surprenante; et la légation à cette cour n'ayant aussi eu d'autre information des intentions du gouvernement de Sa Majesté que ce que fut dit verbalement par une des personnes principales du département des affaires étrangères, qui déclara au soussigné que des instructions relatives à la discussion étaient sur le point d'être données au ministre nouvellement nommé à Buenos-Ayres, Mr. Hamilton; le quel n'a pas encore quitté Paris.

Son Excellence Lord Palmerston répondit, le 27 du même mois d'Avril, " que le commandant de la CLIO n'avait qu'exécuté les instructions données par le gouvernement de Sa Majesté à l'Amiral Baker, qui dernièrement commandait en chef la station de l'Amérique du Sud; que cet Amiral avait des ordres d'envoyer un vaisseau de guerre aux Iles Malvines, pour y exercer les droits de souveraineté anciens et incontestables qui, (d'après son Excellence) appartiennent à Sa Majesté, et d'agir sur les lieux comme étant une possession de la couronne de la Grande Bretagne; et que par suite de ces mêmes ordres, dans le cas où il se rencontrat dans ces Iles des personnes étrangères ou des forces militaires qui ne reconnussent pas la souveraineté de Sa Majesté, le commandant du vaisseau de guerre devait requérir ces personnes et ces forces militaires de se retirer; il devait aussi leur procurer les moyens de le faire."

La note de son Excellence Lord Palmerston se termine en disant " que les instructions cy-dessus furent communiquées par l'Amiral Baker à la légation de Sa Majesté à Buenos Ayres."

Si cependant cette information transmise à la légation de Sa Majesté eut dû être communiquée au gouvernement de la République Argentine, pour éviter qu'il ne fut dépouillé à l'improviste, comme on devait le supposer d'après l'amitié existante entre les deux nations et les déférences ordinairement observées entre les pouvoirs souverains, il est très pénible de remarquer que la légation Britannique ne l'ait pas compris de cette manière; puis qu'elle n'a point donné d'information; et de plus qu'elle ait entièrement négligé, ou nié qu'elle eut rien à communiquer sur ce sujet. Par la correspondance reçue dans le mois de Mai dernier, il paraît que le 16 Janvier, deux jours après le retour de la garnison

Documents • 303

7

the return of the garrison to the roadsted of the capital the Minister for Foreign Affairs of the Republic officially communicated to His Majesty's chargé d'affaires " that he had just learned that the commander of the corvette of war CLIO had occupied the site of La Soledad in the Malvinas, and hoisted the English flag, where that of the Argentine Republic was before flying; that this unexpected event had deeply affected the feelings of the Buenos-Ayrean government, and although nothing colorable could be found to warrant it, yet considering that the chargé d'affaires, to whom he addressed himself, must be possessed of information on a procedure that compromized the rights of the Republic, he requested from him the necessary explanations."

The answer of His Majesty's chargé d'affaires was expressly, in his note of the 17th of January 1833, that " he had not received instructions from his court to make any communication to the government of Buenos Ayres upon that subject." (See letters A and B in the appendix).

In the absence of all explanation, anterior or subsequent to the act of deprivation, the Buenos-Ayrean government proceeded to verify the fact by the depositions of their expelled officers from whose testimony it appeared that, on the 4th of January 1833, there anchored in Port Luis de la Soledad de Malvinas, His Majesty's corvette CLIO, J. J. Onslow, Commander, who, at three in the afternoon of that day, went on board the ship of war SARANDI, and intimated to her commander that he came to take possession of the Malvinas as belonging to His Majesty's crown; that he had positive orders to hoist there the English flag, within twenty-four hours, as he had already done in other ports of the islands, and peremptorily demanded that, on the following day, the flag of the Republic should be lowered also on shore; that the commander of the SARANDI refused to comply with that demand, protesting against the insult and the violation of the rights of the Republic; that, determined not to yield, excepting to superior force, he forbade the inhabitants ashore from striking the Argentine flag there; that at nine in the morning, however, of the following day, three armed boats with marines and seamen landed from the CLIO in Port Luis, and, fixing a staff on the dwelling of an Englishman at some distance from the house of the Commandancy, hoisted the English flag, and then proceeded to lower, with their own hands, the flag of the Republic which was then flying.

dans la rade de la capitale, le ministre des affaires étrangères de la République communiqua officiellement au chargé d'affaires de Sa Majesté "qu'il venait d'apprendre que le commandant de la corvette de guerre la CLIO avait pris possession du port de la SOLEDAD, dans les Malvines; et qu'il avait arboré le drapeau Anglais où celui de la République Argentine flottait auparavant; que cet évènement inattendu avait profondément affecté le gouvernement de Buenos Ayres; et quoiqu'il n'y eut aucun prétexte pour justifier cette conduite, cependant il était persuadé que le chargé d'affaires, à qui il s'adressait, devait avoir connoissance du motif qui avait occasionné un acte qui compromettait les droits de la République; il le priait de lui en donner les explications nécessaires."

Par sa réponse •le Chargé d'affaires exprimait clairement, dans sa note du 17 Janvier 1833, que " il n'avait aucune instruction de sa cour pour donner des communications sur ce sujet au gouvernement de Buenos Ayres." (Voyez les lettres A et B de l'appendice.)

En l'absence de toute explication antérieure et subséquente sur l'acte de dépouillement, le gouvernement de Buenos Ayres s'est occupé de vérifier le fait par les dépositions des officiers renvoyés; des témoignages desquels il résulte que, le 4 de Janvier 1833, la corvette de Sa Majesté la CLIO était à l'ancre dans le port Louis de la Soledad des Malvines, J. J. Onslow le commandant, à trois heures après midi du même jour, alla à bord du vaisseau de guerre le SARANDI et signifia au commandant qu'il venait prendre possession des Malvines, comme appartenant à la couronne de Sa Majesté; qu'il avait des ordres positifs d'arborer le drapeau Anglais dans l'espace de vingt quatre heures, ainsi qu'il l'avait déjà fait dans les autres ports des Iles, et demanda péremptoirement que, le lendemain, le drapeau de la République fut retiré; que le commandant du SARANDI refusa de se rendre à cette demande, protestant contre cette insulte et la violation des droits de la République; que déterminé, à ne céder qu'à une force supérieure, il défendit aux habitants de l'Ile de retirer le drapeau de la République Argentine; et qu'enfin, le jour suivant à neuf heures du matin, trois chaloupes armées, montées par des soldats et des matelots, débarquèrent de la CLIO dans le Port Louis; et après avoir fixé un bâton de pavillon sur l'habitation d'un Anglais à quelque distance de l'hotel du gouvernement, y arborèrent le drapeau Anglais et descendirent ensuite de leurs propres mains celui de la République qui flottait alors.

8

It is essential to a right view of the question, thus untowardly renewed, as to the sovereignty of the Malvinas, to divide their history into three distinct parts.

1st. The discovery originally, or simultaneously, made by different European nations.

2nd. The formal occupation of them, from 1764 to 1774; and the consequent dispute between Spain and England.

3rd. Their state from the ending of that dispute; and under what uncontroverted sovereignty they have existed down to the present day, that is, for the last sixty years.

This naturally leads to the question of—whether the sovereignty of the Malvinas has been, and is still vested, in the crown of Great Britain?—or—whether it has been, and is still, vested in the United Provinces of the Rio de la Plata?

The history of the Malvinas is one of the simplest and best authenticated upon record; and yet,—either because it relates to times when there existed a mania for discovering remote and unpeopled lands; or because new dominions were acquired on very lax principles, and in a manner very indefinite when the law of nations was still imperfect; or because the lively, though ephemeral, interest, taken in an ancient dispute, may have given rise to some erroneous traditions or national prejudices,—the matter has sometimes been confounded in a very extraordinary manner, wholly contrary to what might have been expected from the evidence of public documents of sufficient solemnity, and of easy access. Even geographical errors have arisen: *Puerto de la Cruzada, or Port Egmont,* has been spoken of as comprehending *Port Luis,* or *Port de la Soledad,* &c.; and, by another error, a part, and not the greatest part, of the Malvinas has been strangely mistaken for the whole of them.

It has been sometimes pretended that the first glimpse, whether accidental or otherwise, of an until then unknown country, by a *civilized and christian people,* gave a title of seignory over the newly-seen land in favor of that nation to which the navigators, or persons figuratively styling themselves discoverers belonged.

This mode of appropriation of a territory, in virtue of a casual view thereof, was so vague; so far from reasonable; so liable to interminable disputes; and it was almost always so nearly impossible to decide upon the jarring pretensions of dif-

Pour avoir une idée juste de la question ainsi renouvellée relativement à la souveraineté des Malvines, il est essentiel d'en diviser l'histoire en trois parties distinctes.

1°. Leur découverte primitive faite, simultanément ou non par différentes nations Européennes.

2°. Leur occupation éffective depuis 1764 jusqu'à 1774; et la dispute qui s'en suivit entre l'Espagne et l'Angleterre.

3°. Leur état depuis la fin de cette dispute, et sous quelle souveraineté incontestée elles sont restées jusqu'à ce jour; c'est à dire depuis soixante ans.

Ce qui conduit naturellement à cette question: la couronne de la Grande Bretagne à-t-elle été, et est elle encore investie du droit de souveraineté sur les Malvines; ou bien est-ce le gouvernement des provinces Unies du Rio de la Plata qui a été et est encore investi de ce droit de souveraineté?

L'histoire des Malvines est une des plus simples et des plus authentiques que l'on connoisse; et cependant, soit parcequ'elle se reporte à des tems où la manie des découvertes de pays éloignés et non peuplés prévalait; soit que les nouvelles possessions fussent acquises sur des principes faibles et sans règle à une époque à laquelle les lois des nations étaient encore si imparfaites; ou soit enfin que l'interêt vif, quoiqu'éphémère, provenant d'une ancienne dispute, ait pu donner lieu à des traditions érronées ou des préjugés nationaux, la question a été quelques fois interpretée d'une manière fort extraordinaire, et entièrement opposée à ce qu'on devait attendre de l'évidence de documens publics d'une authenticité suffisante et faciles à se procurer. Des érreurs géographiques même ont eu lieu: *Porto de la Cruzada ou Port Egmont* a été cité comme comprenant *le Port Luis ou le Port de la Soledad,* &c.; et par un outre erreur on a pris une portion des Malvines, et non la plus grande portion, pour leur totalité.

On a quelques fois prétendu que la première découverte d'un pays inconnu jusqu'alors, faite par des *hommes civilisés et chrétiens,* qu'elle fut due au hazard ou autrement, donnoit un droit de souveraineté sur la terre nouvellement vue à la nation à la quelle appartenoient les navigateurs, ou les personnes qui se donnoient pour les avoir découvertes les premiers.

Ce mode d'appropriation d'un territoire, en vertu d'une première vue accidentelle, était si vague et si contraire à la raison; si sujet à d'interminables disputes; parcequ'il etait presque toujours impossible dé décider sur les prétentions de diffé-

9

ferent European nations, that it has very properly ceased to be accounted a good title to dominion; and although attempts have been made to remove uncertainties, by the observance of certain forms on taking possession, such as the military ceremonial of landing under salutes—hoisting the national colors —erecting crosses—or leaving other memorials,— the same inconveniences and uncertainties continued until, at length, by an understanding, which may be called universal, and more conformable to the principles of reason and philosophy, it was agreed or admitted that—to establish a right to dominion, the fortuitous act of discovery, or a momentary possession, is not sufficient:—it must be a formal and tranquil settlement, which includes habitation and culture.

With reference to this principle, a modern Publicist says "the simple fact of having been the first to discover, or to visit, an island, &c., abandoning it afterwards, appears to be an insufficient title when no permanent vestige of possession, and will, remains; and it is not without reason that frequent disputes have arisen between nations, as among philosophers, as to whether crosses, flag-staffs, inscriptions, &c. be sufficient to give, or preserve, the exclusive dominion to a country not in culture." (De Martens Précis du droit des gens modernes de l'Europe).

It is not, therefore, of much importance, in the present day, to ascertain which was the nation that first caught sight of the Malvinas, as they are called by the French and Spaniards—Falkland Isles, by the English—Sabal, and Gibbel de Wert, by the Dutch—and Pepys by others,—because neither the discovery alone, nor the name, can be taken as deciding, or proving, any thing touching the sovereignty and possession of those islands.

But if this point were in any way interesting, and if there be some data to clear it from obscurity, all the probabilities concur in awarding to Spaniards the claim of being the earliest discoverers.

It is undeniable that Fernando Magallanes, in the service of Spain,—who gave his name to the Straits which terminate the southern continent, and divide it from TIERRA DEL FUEGO—was the first navigator who visited those regions, which he did in October 1520, long before the Rio de la Plata was discovered, and when scarcely twenty-seven years had elapsed since the grand discovery of the New World by Columbus. MAGALLANES must have seen the Malvinas, and would hardly neglect the proper forms according to the usages of his time, and so generally practised by his cotempora-

rentes nations Européennes, que c'est avec raison qu'il a cessé d'être considéré comme un juste titre à la domination; et quoique l'on ait essayé de remédier aux incertitudes, en observant certaines formes à la prise de possession, telles que le cérémonial militaire de débarquer sous le salut du cannon; arborant les couleurs nationales, érigeant des croix, ou laissant d'autres souvenirs; les mêmes inconvénients et incertitudes se représentèrent, jusqu'à ce qu'enfin, par un arrangement qu'on peut dire universel et plus conforme aux principes de la raison et de la philosophie, il fut convenu que, pour établir un droit de domination, le fait accidentel d'une découverte, ou d'une possession momentannée n'étoit pas suffisant. Ce doit être un établissement formel et tranquille, habité et cultivé.

Relativement à ce principe, un publiciste moderne dit: "Le simple fait d'avoir été le premier à decouvrir ou à visiter une isle, &c, abandonnée ensuite, semble insuffisant, même de l'aveu des nations, tant qu'on n'a point laissé de traces permanentes de possession et de volonté; et ce n'est pas sans raison qu'on a souvent disputé entre les nations, comme entre les philosophes, si des croix, des poteaux, des inscriptions, &c., suffisent pour acquerir ou pour conserver la proprété exclusive d'un pays qu'on ne cultive pas." (De Martens Précis du droit des gens modernes de l'Europe.)

Ainsi il n'est pas d'une grande importance aujourd'hui de savoir quelle fut la nation qui, la première, découvrit les *Malvines*, ainsi qu'elles sont appelées par les Français et les Espagnols, et *Falkland* par les Anglais; *Sabal* et *Gibbel de Wert* par les Hollandais et *Pepeys* par d'autres: parceque, ni la découverte seule, ni le nom, ne peut servir à décider ou à prouver rien de ce qui a rapport à la souveraineté et à la possession de ces Iles.

Mais, si ce point était du moindre intérêt, et s'il y avait quelques données pour l'éclairer, toutes les probabilités concourrent à accorder aux Espagnols le droit de les avoir découvertes les premiers.

Il est reconnu que Fernando Magallanes, qui était au service d'Espagne et qui donna son nom au détroit qui est à l'extremité de l'Amérique du Sud et la sépare de la TERRE DE FEU, a été le premier navigateur qui ait visité ces régions; ce qu'il fit en Octobre 1520, long tems avant la découverte du Rio de la Plata, et vingt sept ans seulement après la grande découverte du Nouveau Monde par Colombus. MAGALLANES doit avoir vu les Malvines, et n'aurait certainement pas voulu négliger les formes usitées de son tems et si généralement observées par ses contemporains dans des entreprises de

10

ries in enterprizes of this nature to caracterize them as fruits of their own exertions in honor of their sovereign. Eight years afterwards the Straits were passed by the Spaniard LOIZA, who was followed by navigators of the same nation—ALCOZABA in 1535—VILLALOBOS in 1549, and others. For more than a century the navigation to the Pacific was by way of Magellan's Straits, and this navigation, which was entirely in the power of Spain, then exclusive mistress of Chili and Peru, must have given frequent opportunities to her mariners for exploring the islands referred to, and which were situated on their route.

SIR FRANCIS DRAKE, in the service of England, entered the Straits in 1578. To him has been ascribed the discovery of Cape Horn, and he might also have seen the Malvinas. His observations, however, left all in so much uncertainty that, 196 years afterwards, the celebrated Captain Cook on his second voyage of discovery, in the year 1774, was still without any accurate idea of the configuration of the Cape, nor did he know whether it formed a part of Tierra del Fuego. The general opinion has pronounced that Jacob le Maire, in the service of the Dutch republic, was the first discoverer of Cape Horn: his voyage took place in 1616.

If English writers have wished to fix upon Davis, the companion of Cavendish, the fortuitous discovery of the Malvinas in 1592, in the reign of Queen Elizabeth, and remark that two years afterwards they were visited by Sir Richard Hawkins, who gave them the name of MAIDENLAND in honor of his sovereign, still it cannot be denied that this was an act so transient that in 1598 the States of Holland believed that they had discovered them anew, and denominated them the ISLES OF SABAL DE WERT, in compliment to the admiral of that expedition.

France has also contended for the honor of the first discovery by means of vessels sent expressly from St. Malo, between 1700 and 1708. These voyages acquired for the islands the name of Malouines, or Malvinas, which has been generally preserved to them on all charts that are not English; and no doubt exists that it was the French who first took formal possession of them; who established the first settlement in them; and who first ~~established~~ inhabited them.

Respecting the original discovery, there remains to be noticed two opinions not devoid of force: the first is that of Monsieur de Bougainville, chief of the French colony in the Malvinas, who, in the

cette nature pour les caractériser comme fruit de leurs travaux en l'honneur de leur souverain. Huit ans après l'Espagnol LOIZA passa le détroit et fut suivi par des navigateurs de la même nation—ALCOZABA en 1535—VILLALOBUS 1549, et autres. Car pendant plus d'un siecle le voyage à la mer Pacifique se faisait par le détroit de Magellan ; et cette navigation, qui était entièrement au pouvoir de l'Espagne, alors maîtresse exclusive du Chili et du Pérou, doit avoir offert à ses marins de fréquentes occasions d'explorer les iles dont il est question, et qui étaient situées sur leur passage.

SIR FRANCIS DRAKE, au service d'Angleterre, entra dans le détroit en 1578. C'est à lui qu'on attribue la découverte du Cape Horn, et il pourroit aussi avoir vu les Malvines. Aureste ces observations laissent le tout dans une si grande incertitude que, 196 ans après, le célèbre capitaine COOK, pendant son second voyage, de découverte en l'année 1774, n'avait point encore une idée éxacte de la configuration du Cap, et ne savoit même pas s'il faisoit partie de la Terre de Feu. L'opinion générale a établi que Jacob Lemaire, au service de la République Hollandaise, a été le premier qui ait découvert le Cap Horn. Son voyage eu lieu ent 1616.

Si des écrivains Anglais ont cherché à faire attribuer à Davis, le compagnon de Cavendish, la découverte accidentelle des Malvines en 1592, sous le règne de la Reine Elizabeth, et font remarquer que, deux ans après, elles furent visitées par Sir Richard Hawkins, qui leur donna le nom de MAIDENLAND, en honneur de sa Souveraine : il n'en est pas moins incontestable que ce fut un acte tellement transitoire, qu'en 1598 les états de Hollande pensèrent les avoir découvertes de nouveau, et les appellerènt les ILES DE SABALDE WERT, par compliment à l'amiral de cette expédition.

La France a aussi disputé l'honneur de la première découverte, au moyen de vaisseaux envoyés à cet effet de St. Malo depuis 1700 jusqu'au 1708. Ces voyages firent donner aux iles le nom de Malouines ou Malvines, qui leur a généralement été conservé dans toutes les cartes marines qui ne sont pas Anglaises; et il ne peut y avoir le moindre doute que ce furent les Français qui les premiers en prirent possession en forme ; qui firent, les premiers établissemens, et que les Français ont été les premiers qui les aient habitées.

Quant à la découverte primitive, il reste à developper deux opinions qui ne sont pas sans force. La première est celle de Monsieur de Bougainville, chef de la colonie Française dans les Malvines, qui,

11

printed account of his second voyage to them, observes "I believe that the first discovery can be attributed solely to the famous navigator AMERIGO VESPUCCI who, in the third voyage that he made for the discovery of America, explored the northern coast of them in 1502. He certainly did not know whether they formed part of an island, or of the continent, but from the route that he followed; from the latitude to which he attained; and even the description which he gives of the island, there is no difficulty in deciding that it was that of the Malvinas."

The other opinion is that broached by the British Naval Chronicle, of 1809, which states that "although the discovery of the Malvinas has been attributed to Davis, they were very probably seen by Magellan, and others who followed him."

To finish, here, the controversy, namely, if no nation whatever could produce other titles to the Malvinas than—first discovery, unsupported by actual possession—it is clear that Spain, during the period now under consideration, is the only one who could justify any species of right to what may be deemed accessory, points, or outworks of the continent, and immediately conducive to its security; and it was more reasonable for Spain to keep the points adjacent to her American coasts, than to forego her claims, in favor of another power separated by three thousand leagues of ocean. At least the Malvinas, until then, might be looked upon as being without an owner, *res nullius.*

It may be further inferred, from the foregoing, that there exists no positive, or satisfactory, proof that English navigators were the first who discovered those islands.

Having settled the first point of this enquiry,— namely, *the primitive discovery of the Malvinas, unfollowed by occupation,*—we now come to the second, that is to say, their formal occupation from 1764 to 1774, and the consequent dispute between Spain and England. From a doubtful and questionable title, that of—*the first discovery*—we pass on to a real title, firm and manifest, that of—*first possession ;*—and here occurs, in an authentic manner, the proof that *the people by whom the first European settlement was made, and possession first taken, were the French.*

Monsieur de Bougainville, Colonel of Infantry and Captain in the French navy, was the first founder of a colony, in those islands, with the leave

dans l'histoire imprimée du second voyage qu'il y fit, fait cette observation. "Je crois que la première découverte ne doit être attribuée qu'au fameux navigateur AMERIC VESPUCE, qui, dans le troisième voyage qu'il fit pour découvrir l'Amérique, *visita leurs côtes septentrionales en 1502.* Certainement il ne sut pas si elles faisaient partie d'une ile ou du continent; mais par la route qu'il a suivie, par la latitude à laquelle il est parvenu, et même par la *description qu'il donne de l'ile,* il n'est pas difficile de décider que c'étoit une des Malvines."

La seconde opinion est celle prononcée par *The British Naval Chronicle* de 1809, qui prétend que : "quoique la découverte des Malvines ait été attribuée à *Davis,* elles avoient probablement été vues par *Magallanes* et les autres qui l'ont suivi."

Pour terminer ici la controverse, c'est à dire, si aucun gouvernement pourroit produire d'autres titres aux Malvines que la *première découverte, non appuyée de possession actuelle,* il est évident que l'Espagne, pendant l'espace de temps dont il s'agit, est la seule puissance qui puisse justifier d'une sorte de droits à ce qu'on peut considérer comme points accessoires au continent, et par conséquent importants à sa sureté ; car il étoit plus raisonnable pour l'Espagne de conserver des points contigus à ses côtes Américaines, que de céder ses droits à une autre puissance séparée par trois mille lieues de mer. Au moins les Malvines jusque là pourroient être considerées comme sans possesseur, *res nullius.*

Et de plus, on peut conclure de ce qui vient d'être dit qu'il n'existe vraiment pas de preuve positive, ni même conjecturale, que les navigateurs Anglais aient été les premiers qui aient découvert ces Iles.

Après avoir terminé le premier point de ces recherches : c'est à dire *la découverte primitive des Malvines non suivie d'occupation,* nous passons maintenant au second point : *leur possession formelle, depuis 1764 à 1774, et la dispute qui en a été la conséquence entre l'Espagne et l'Angleterre.* D'un titre. douteux et incertain, celui de la *première découverte,* nous arrivons à un titre réel, solide et manifeste, celui *de première possession ;* et ici il est prouvé d' une maniere authentique que *ceux par qui le premier établissement Européen fut formé, et la première prise de possession opérée, furent les Français.*

M. de Bougainville, colonel d'infanterie et capitaine dans la marine Française, a été le premier fondateur d'une colonie dans les iles avec permis-

12

and under the sanction of Louis XV. He sailed from St. Malo on the 15th of September 1763 and arrived at the islands on the 3rd of February 1764, when he found them totally destitute of inhabitants and without any traces of ever having been cultivated. Having caused houses to be built for his colonists, together with a warehouse and a small fort on the easternmost island, which was afterwards called *Port Louis*, or the *Port de la Soledad de Malvinas*, he, on the 17th of March, erected an obelisk, under which was deposited a medallion of his Sovereign, bearing an inscription commemorative of the event. (See C). He returned to France in quest of further aids for the enterprise thus begun : and early in 1765 re-visited that colony which thrived unmolested, but at length he had orders from his court to deliver it to Spain, which orders he complied with on his third voyage to the Malvinas in 1767. The details of all these circumstances are extant in the work of that officer, entitled " *Voyage autour du Monde, par la Frégate du Roi, la Boudeuse, et la Flûte l'Etoile en* 1766, 1767, 1768, et 1769.—Paris 1771."

Spain who had complained of the establishment in the Malvinas, and who regarded it as intrusive, did nevertheless respect the possession, and the title of first occupant *(favor possessionis)* vested in the French government, nor was the cession of the colony negotiated without stipulating for a considerable sum, as an indemnification, the payment of which is certified in a receipt signed by Monsieur de Bougainville on the 4th of October 1766, as will be found in appendix (E).

By this instrument Monsieur de Bougainville acknowledged to have received from Spain six hundred and eighteen thousand one hundred and eight livres, thirteen sous, and eleven deniers, to re-imburse the St. Malo company their expences in forming their settlements in the Malvinas, and it is worthy of passing remark that more than half that sum, or 62,625 dollars, was received in bills paid by the treasury of Buenos-Ayres.

Meanwhile in England where, it would appear, nothing was known of that French colony, Commodore *Byron* was sent, in 1765, a year after the settlement of Port Louis, to take the islands in the name of His Britannic Majesty, but this officer did no more than enact some pretensive ceremonies in *Port Egmont*. In 1766 he was succeeded by

sion et autorisation de Louis XV Il fit voile de St Malo, le 15 Septembre 1763, et arriva aux iles le 3 Février 1764. Il les trouva alors entièrement inhabitées et sans la moindre trace qui put indiquer que jamais elles eussent été cultivées. Ayant fait construire des habitations pour les colons, ainsi qu'un magasin et un petit fort sur l'ile le plus à l'est, laquelle fut ensuite appellée *Port Louis* ou *Port de la Soledad des Malvines*, il fit ériger, le 17 de Mars, un obélisque sous le pied duquel fut déposée une médaille de son Souverain, portant une inscription commémorative de cet évènement. (Voyez appendice C.) Il retourna en France solliciter de nouveaux secours pour l'entreprise ainsi commencée ; et, dans les premiers mois de 1765, il visita de nouveau la colonie, qui continua à prospérer sans être inquiétée, jusqu'à ce qu'enfin il reçut des ordres de sa cour d'en faire la remise à l'Espagne ; et ce fut à son troisieme voyage aux Malvines, en 1767, qu'il obéit à ces ordres. Les détails de toutes ces circonstances sont développés dans l'ouvrage de cet officier, intitulé : " *Voyage autour du monde par la Frégate du Roi la Boudeuse, et la Flûte l'Etoile, en* 1766, 1767, 1768 et 1769. Paris, 1771.

L'Espagne, qui avait fait des plaintes sur l'établissement Français dans les Malvines, ce qu'elle considéroit comme une usurpation, n'en montra pas moins son respect pour le principe de possession,— et le titre de premier occupant, *(favor possessionis)* dont étoit investi le Gouvernement Français ; et la cession de la colonie ne fut pas négociée, sans qu'une somme considérable n'eut été stipulée comme indémnité. Le payement s'en trouve constaté dans un reçu signé par M. de Bougainville et daté du 4 Octobre 1766, comme on le vera dans l'appendice. (E)

Par cette pièce M. de Bougainville reconnoit avoir reçu de l'Espagne six cent dix huit mille soix. ante huit livres treize sous et onze deniers, pour rembourser à la compagnie de St. Malo ses dépenses de la formation de ses établissemens dans les Malvines ; et il est important de remarquer que plus de la moitié de cette somme, ou 65,625 gourdes — fut reçue en lettres de change payées par la trésorerie de Buenos-Ayres.

En même temps on envoya d'Angleterre, où l'on vouloit paroitre n'avoir aucune connoissance de la colonie Française, le commodore *Byron*, en 1765 : un an après l'établissement du *Port Louis*, pour s'emparer des iles, au nom de Sa Majesté Britannique ; mais cet officier se borna à répéter quelques cérémonies de peu d'importance, pour établir des

13

Captain *Macbride* who, with a military force, landed at that place, and built a fort. Now it is quite clear that the arrival of this expedition, under Captain *Macbride* at one of the Malvinas, is the epoch at which British occupancy began, and that this was subsequent to the occupancy of the French. In other words, the French had anticipated, by two years, the English settlement,—not with flags and salutes but,—with inhabitants, habitations, and actual culture. The fact, then,—supported by historical evidence, of the most authentic character, and even by English authorities,—is that the first occupancy belongs indisputably to the French.

In what manner the concurrent parties (the English and the French) behaved towards each other is apparent from the testimony of Monsieur de Bougainville in his before-cited work, chap. 3, pag. 52 to 53 where he says, "Yet, as we have just observed, Commodore *Byron* had come, in the month of January 1765, to reconnoitre the Malvinas islands. He had touched at the west of our settlement in a harbour which we had already denominated *Puerto de la Cruzada*, and had taken possession of those islands for the crown of England, without leaving, there, any inhabitant. It was not until 1766 that the English sent a colony to settle in the Puerto de la Cruzada, which they had named *Port Egmont*; and Captain *Macbride* commandant of the frigate, *Jason*, came to our settlement in the beginning of December of the same year. His pretension was that these lands belonged to the King of Great Britain; he threatened to make a forcible landing if continued resistance was opposed to him; paid a visit to the commandant; and, on the same day, put to sea."

"Such was," he adds, "the state of the Malvina Islands when we delivered them up to the Spaniards, *whose original right was thus corroborated by that which we incontestably derived from the fact of our being the first occupants.*"

The court of Spain appointed Don *Felipe Ruiz Puente* to receive the Malvinas from the French authorities, in virtue of the before-named convention, and in virtue of orders to the same effect from His Most Christian Majesty. Puente announced his arrival, to the Governor of Buenos-Ayres, Don *Francisco Buccarelli*, in a despatch of the 25th of April 1767, stating that on the 27th of March, the forms of the cession had been fulfilled.

prétentions sur le *Port Egmont*. En 1766 il fut remplacé par le Capitaine *Macbride*, qui débarqua sur ce point avec une force militaire et y bâtit un fort. Ainsi il est tout à fait évident que l'arrivée de cette expédition, sous les ordres du Capitaine *Macbride*, à l'une des Malvines, est l'époque à laquelle commença l'occupation par les Anglais; et que cette époque étoit postérieure à la prise de possession par les Français. En d'autres termes les Français avoient devancé de deux ans l'établissement des Anglais, non seulement en plantant des drapeaux et par des salves d'artillerie; mais par des habitans, des résidences et la culture de l'île. Ainsi le fait, appuyé par la preuve historique la plus complette, la plus précise, et même par les autorités Anglaises, est que la première possession appartient incontestablement aux Français.

La manière dont les parties prétendantes (l'Angleterre et la France) se conduisirent, est indiquée par le témoignage de M. de Bougainville, dans son ouvrage déjà cité, chap. 3, pag. 52 et 53, dans lequel il dit: "Cependant, comme nous venons de le dire, le Commodore Byron étoit venu au mois de Janvier 1765 reconnoitre les iles Malouines, il y avoit abordé à l'ouest de notre établissement, dans un port nommé déjà par nous *Port de la Croisade*, et il avoit pris possession de ces îles pour la couronne d'Angleterre, sans y laisser aucun habitant. Ce ne fut qu'en 1766, que les Anglais envoyèrent une colonie s'établir au Port de la Croisade, qu'ils avoient nommé *Port d'Egmont*; et le Capitaine Macbride, commandant la frégate *le Jason*, vint à notre établissement au commencement de Décembre de la même année. Il prétendit que ces terres appartenoient au Roi de la Grande Bretagne, menaça de forcer la descente, si l'on s'obstinoit à la lui refuser; fit une visite au commandant, et remit à la voile le même jour."

"Tel étoit," ajoute-t-il, "l'état des îles Malouines, lorsque nous les remîmes aux Espagnols, dont le droit primitif se trouvoit ainsi étayé encore par celui que nous donnoit incontestablement la première habitation."

La cour d'Espagne nomma *Don Philippe Ruiz Puente* pour recevoir des autorités Françaises les Malvines, en vertu de la convention cy dessus mentionnée, et en vertu d'ordres donnés à cet effet par Sa Majesté très Chrétienne. *Puente* annonça son arrivée au gouverneur de Buenos-Ayres *Don Francisco Buccarelli*, dans une dépêche du 25 d'Avril 1767. Prévenant aussi que le 27 Mars, la cession s'étoit faite dans les formes voulues.

14

After the Spaniards had been installed in the dominion, and possession, of this heretofore French colony, with the sanction of its founders, and by the payment of a price, which gave to this transaction all the character of a perfect contract,—they were nevertheless disquieted by an intimation, brought in a ship from the English colony of *Port Egmont,* that these islands belonged to the crown of Great Britain. This intimation was answered, by the Spaniards, with an expression of their surprise at a proceeding which disallowed their rights; and said, that they were within the dominions of their own sovereign, therefore, it was for the English to go away. This answer appears to have been natural, since the Spaniards had long been accustomed to observe that England did not deny their prior claim, to those islands. An English author (Miller, History of the Reign of George III.) says,—that in 1744 the English projected an establishment in the Malvinas, on the re-commendation of Lord *Anson,* after his voyage round the globe, as the best place for establishing a port of refreshment before doubling Cape Horn. Preparations were made, about ten years after-wards,—when the same Admiral *Anson* was placed at the head of the Admiralty,—for carrying his plan into effect, but it was *opposed by the King of Spain, as the islands belonged to him.* The Spanish ministry declared that if the object of the voyage were to form an establishment in the islands, it would be an act of hostility towards Spain, the mistress of them; but that if it was merely curiosity he would give whatever information was desired without the necessity of incurring the expense of expeditions for its gratification. On perceiving this, (adds the author) the English desisted from that enterprize.

Nor did the Spaniards confine themselves to answering in the terms observable above, for they made remonstrance directly with the settlement at *Port Egmont,* giving instructions to their cruizers to protest, to the English officers, that it was contrary to the faith of treaties for them to come into those dominions without the express consent of His Catholic Majesty. This is apparent from the official correspondence of Don *Felipe Ruiz Puente* in the archives of Buenos-Ayres.

At length this altercation acquired a new interest from the expedition sent from Buenos Ayres in the beginning of 1770 by the governor *Buccarelli,* under the commandant of the Royal Marine, Don *Juan Ignacio Madariaga,* to expel the colony from

Après que les Espagnols eurent été installés dans la souveraineté et la possession de cette colonie, Française jusqu'alors, avec la sanction des fonda-teurs et sur le payement d'un prix qui avoit donné à cette transaction tout le caractère d'un contrat parfait, ils n'en furent pas moins troublés et inquié-tés par la signification apportée par un vaisseau de la colonie Anglaise du *Port Egmont,* que ces iles appartenoient à la couronne de la Grande Bretagne. Les Espagnols répondirent à cette signification par l'expression de leur surprise d'un procédé qui an-nulloit leurs droits; ils soutinrent qu'ils étoient dans les possessions de leur propre souverain, et que c'etoit aux Anglais à se retirer. Cette réponse parait avoir été d'autant plus naturelle, que les Es-pagnols s'étoient accoutumés, depuis long tems, à observer que l'Angleterre n'avait jamais contesté leurs droits antérieurs sur ces iles. Un auteur An-glais (Miller, Histoire du Règne de George III.) dit qu'en 1744 les Anglais projetèrent un établisse-ment dans les Malvines, par la suggestion de Lord *Anson,* après son voyage autour du monde, comme étant le point le mieux calculé pour établir un port de rafraichissement avant de doubler le Cape Horn. Dix ans plus tard, lorsque le même amiral *Anson* fut placé à la tête de l'amirauté, on fit des prépara-tifs pour executer son projet; mais le Roi d'Espagne s'y opposa comme possesseur des iles. Le minis-tère Espagnol déclara que, si le sujet du voyage était de former un établissement dans l'ile, ce serait un acte d'hostilité envers l'Espagne qui en était maîtresse; mais que, si ce n'était que par sim-ple curiosité, il donnerait toutes les informations qu'on pourrait desirer, sans la nécessité d'encourir la dépense d'une expédition pour satisfaire cette curiosité. En voyant cela, ajoute cet auteur, les Anglais abandonnèrent cette entreprise.

Les Espagnols ne se bornèrent point à répondre dans les termes qu'on observe cy dessus; car ils firent immédiatement des remontrances à l'établis-sement du *Port Egmont,* donnant des instructions à leurs envoyés de protester auprès des officiers An-glais qu'il étoit contraire à la foi des traités de venir dans ces possessions sans le consentement ex-près de Sa Majésté Catholique. Ceci se prouve par la correspondance officielle de Don *Philippe Ruiz Puente,* restée dans les archives de Buenos-Ayres.

Enfin l'altercation prit un nouveau dégré d'inté-rêt par l'expédition envoyée de Buenos Ayres, au commencement de l'année 1770, par le Gouverneur *Buccarelli,* sous les ordres du commandant de la marine royale Don *Juan Ignacio Madariaga,* pour

15

Port Egmont; and on the 10th of June in that year was signed a capitulation by which the British forces and subjects were to retire from the island within a specified period, and which they did, it being allowed that, until their departure, the English flag should remain hoisted at their barracks on shore; but that the artillery and other warlike stores should be left behind.

In order to establish the circumstances and details of this incident, the most extraordinary that occurs in the history of the Malvinas, and to obviate repetitions, the Undersigned may be permitted to refer to the *State Papers*, published in the *Annual Register* of 1771, (Vol. XIV, seventh edition, London, 1817.) in which occurs the correspondence of the commandant *Madariaga*; the capitulation of the British forces in *Port Egmont*; the dispute that subsequently arose out of it, between England and Spain; and the adjustment thereof, on the 22nd of January 1771, by the Prince of *Masserano*, ambassador from Spain to London, and accepted by the Earl of *Rochford*, secretary of state for foreign affairs to His Britannic Majesty.

The British government, resenting the insult which had been offered to them, by the expulsion of their colony in Port Egmont, made an urgent claim on the cabinet of Madrid for ample satisfaction. Negotiations to this effect began on the 12th of September of the same year 1770, but, in consequence of the studied procrastinations of the Spanish government, great military preparations were made in England, and Mr. *Harris* (afterwards Lord Malmsbury) was ordered to leave Madrid where he was pressing the demand for satisfaction. The vicissitudes of this affair are well known; the intervention of France by means of the Count de Guines, her ambassador in London; the letters of recall despatched to Mr. *Harris*, and afterwards revoked; the recall, and continuance, of the Prince of Masserano; the alternate appearances of rupture and accommodation; and the excitement of the English nation, but it is essential to keep in mind that the dispute maintained was rather on account of the ejectment by arms and with violence, than on account of the sovereignty of the islands, as is proved by the tenor of the convention, by which it was terminated.

In point of fact, this dispute was set at rest by the *Declaration*, made in the name of the Court of Spain, dated London, 22nd January 1771, by their ambassador, the Prince of Masserano, in which he notifies, that His Britannic Majesty *having com-*

E

expulser la colonie Anglaise du Port Egmont; et le 10 Juin de cette année, on signa une capitulation aux termes de laquelle les forces Anglaises, ainsi que les sujets, devoient se retirer de l'ile dans un temps indiqué; ce qui fut éxécuté. Il leur fut accordé que, jusqu'à leur départ, le drapeau Anglais resteroit hissé à leurs casernes sur terre; mais l'artillerie et le matériel de guerre devoient être laissés.

Pour établir les circonstances et les détails de cet évènement, le plus extraordinaire qui se trouve dans l'histoire des Malvines, et pour éviter les répetitions, qu'il soit permis au Sousigné de renvoyer aux *State Papers*, publiés dans le Régistre annuel de 1771(Vol. XIV, 7eme. édition, à Londres 1817), dans lequel se trouve la correspondance du commandant *Madariaga*; la capitulation des troupes Anglaises dans le *Port Egmont*; la discussion à laquelle elle donna lieu entre l'Angleterre et l'Espagne; et enfin l'arrangement fait le 22 Janvier 1771, par le Prince de *Masserano*, ambassadeur d'Espagne à Londres, et accepté par le Comte du *Rochford*, sécretaire d'état aux affaires étrangères de Sa Majesté Britannique.

Le gouvernement Anglais, ressentant l'insulte qui lui avait été faite par l'expulsion de sa colonie du Port Egmont, adressa au cabinet de Madrid une pressante demande de complette satisfaction. Des négociations à cet effet furent entammées le 12 Septembre de la même année 1770; mais, par suite de délais médités de la part du gouvernement Espagnol, de grands préparatifs militaires furent faits en Angleterre, et Mr. Harris (plus tard Lord Malmsbury) reçut l'ordre de quitter Madrid, où il insistoit pour la satisfaction demandée. Les diverses vicissitudes de cette affaire sont connues; l'intervention de la France, par l'entremise de M. le Comte de Guines, son ambassadeur à Londres; les lettres de rappel expediées à Mr. Harris, et ensuite révoquées; le rappel et ensuite la continuation du Prince de Masserano; les apparences alternatives de rupture et d'arrangement; et sur tout, l'irritation de la nation Anglaise. Mais il est essentiel de se rappeler que la véritable source de la dispute existante étoit plutot dans l'expulsion par les armes et la violence, que dans la souveraineté des iles; ainsi qu'on en trouve la preuve par le contenu de la convention qui y mit fin.

Le fait est que cette dispute fut terminée par la *Déclaration* faite, au nom de l'Espagne, par son ambassadeur le Prince de Masserano, et datée de Londres le 22 Janvier 1771, dans laquelle il notifie que Sa Majesté Britannique *s'étant plainte de la*

16

plained of the violence committed on the 10th of June 1770, he had received instructions to declare, and did declare, that His Catholic Majesty had seen with displeasure that expedition capable of disturbing the peace, and disavowed that violent enterprise, promising to give immediate orders that things should be restored to the same state in which they were on the 10th of June, for which purpose His Catholic Majesty would give orders *to restore the Port and Fort called Egmont*, with the artillery, munitions of war, and effects of His Britannic Majesty, and of his subjects, that were there at the time the objects and effects were verified by inventory.

But this declaration also adds: "*the Prince of Masserano declares at the same time, in the name of the King his master, that the promise, of His Catholic Majesty to restore to His Britannic Majesty the Port and Fort called Egmont, neither can nor ought in any manner to effect the question of anterior right of sovereignty over the Malvinas, otherwise called the Falkland Islands.*"

On the same day this declaration was accepted by the government of His Britannic Majesty, under the signature of the Earl of Rochford, notifying that His Britannic Majesty would consider the said declaration of the Prince of Masserano, with the entire fulfilment of the convention on the part of His Catholic Majesty, as a satisfaction for the injury done to the crown of Great Britain. (See State Papers, in the Annual Register of 1771, and also De Martens, Recueil de Traités, vol. II. Declarations Reciproques de l'Espagne, et de l'Angleterre, au suject des Iles de Falkland 1771 to 1774.)

The court of Spain in consequence sent, through their Minister Don Julian Arriaga to the commandant of the Malvinas, Don Philip Ruiz Puente, the following Royal Order, dated 7th February 1771.

"It being agreed between the King and His Britannic Majesty—by a convention, signed in London on the 22nd of January last, by the Prince of Masserano and the Earl of Rochford,—that the great Malvina, called by the English Falkland Island, shall be immediately restored to the state in which it was before it was evacuated by them on the 10th of June in the year preceding, I notify to you, by command of the King, that, as soon as the person commissioned by the court of London appear before you with this, you will arrange for the delivering up of Port la Cruzada, or Egmont, and of its fort and dependencies, as well as of all

violence commise le 10 *Juin* 1770, il avoit reçu instruction de déclarer, et déclaroit en effet, que Sa Majesté Catholique avoit vu avec déplaisir cette expédition qui auroit pû détruire la paix entre les deux nations, et désavouoit cette entreprise faite de violence; promettant de prendre des mesures immédiates pour que les choses fussent remises dans le même état où elles étoient le 10 Juin; et qu'à cet effet, Sa Majesté Catholique donneroit l'ordre de *restituer le Port et le Fort Egmont* avec l'artillerie, les munitions de guerre et les différens effets trouvés dans le temps sur les lieux, et reconnus par inventaires, appartenant tant à Sa Majesté Britannique qu'à ses sujets.

Mais cette déclaration portoit aussi "*le Prince de Masserano déclare, en même temps, au nom du Roi son maître, que l'engagement de Sa Majesté Catholique de restituer à Sa Majesté Britannique le Port et Fort appelé Egmont, ne pouvoit ni ne devoit, en aucune manière, affecter la question de droit antérieur de souveraineté sur les Malvines, autrement appelées les Iles Falkland.*"

Le même jour cette déclaration fut acceptée par le gouvernement de Sa Majesté Britannique, sous la signature du Comte de Rochford, spécifiant que Sa Majesté Britannique considéreroit la dite déclaration du Prince de Masserano, avec l'entière exécution de la convention de la part de Sa Majesté Catholique, comme une satisfaction de l'offense faite à la couronne de la Grande Bretagne, (voyez les *State Papers* dans le Registre annuel de 1771; et aussi De Martens, Recueil de Traités vol. II., Déclarations réciproques de l'Espagne et de l'Angleterre au sujet des Iles de Falkland 1771 à 1774.)

En conséquence, la cour d'Espagne envoya, par l'entremise de son Ministre Don Julian Arriaga, au commandant des Malvines Don Philippe Ruiz Puente, l'ordre royal suivant, en date du 7 Février 1771.

"Attendu qu'il a été convenu entre le Roi et Sa Majesté Britannique, par un acte signé à Londres le 22 Janvier dernier par le Prince de Masserano et le Comte de Rochford, que la Grande Malvine, appelée par les Anglais Ile Falkland, sera immédiatement remise dans l'état où elle étoit avant qu'elle en fut évacuée par eux le 10 de Juin de l'année dernière, je vous signifie, par ordre du Roi, que, aussitôt que la personne commissionnée par la cour de Londres vous présentera cet ordre, vous ayez à prendre les mesures nécessaires pour la remise du Port de la Cruzada, ou Egmont, et de son fort et dépendances; aussi bien que de toute l'artillerie,

17

the artillery, munitions, and effects found there, belonging to His Britannic Majesty, and to his subjects, according to the inventories signed by George Farmer and William Maltby, Esquires, on the 11th of July in the said year, on departing therefrom, and of which I transmit to you the annexed copies, authenticated by my hand; and that as soon as both shall have been effectuated in due form, you will cause the officer and other subjects of the King, who may be there, to withdraw immediately."

By this order,—which was placed in the hands of the British government,—England was, in the same year, reinstated in possession of the colony of Port Egmont, the Treasury of Buenos Ayres replacing the effects ordered to be restored.

Thus terminated the dispute between England and Spain respecting the Malvinas, or rather respecting Port Egmont. Henceforward, that is to say from 1771, there occurs no complaint, or quarrel; no compulsion, or violence; and if Great Britain, reinstated in possession of the disputed point, abandons it three years afterwards, (in May 1774) it must have been because she was either impelled to do it of her own free-will, or, as we shall soon see, at the dictation of her own honour, and by her engagement contracted in the convention of the 22nd of January.

By this treaty we see the English re-possessed of Port Egmont, and satisfied. We see the Spaniards also continuing in possession of Port Luis, in the same group of islands, and in immediate vicinage. Both possessors are in front of each other; they observe each other near at hand; and they respect each other. The islands are very small, to be an appendage of two crowns. One of the two possessors must preponderate as the more ancient and, therefore, the more true.

The first glance at the convention of the 22nd of January 1771, suggests peculiar reflections. The Spanish government protest, in this solemn instrument, that the restitution of Port Egmont is not to operate to their prejudice, and *reserve to themselves their rights to the sovereignty of the islands.* His Britannic Majesty's government, in the precise act of answering this instrument and of accepting it, do not advert to that clause. Is not this admitting the reservation with which Spain invested herself? At least this silence was not the way to resist or invalidate her claim; and it really appears that the opportunity, or perhaps the necessity, of answering

munitions et effets qui y avoient été trouvés appartenant à Sa Majesté Britannique et à ses sujets, suivant les inventaires signés par Messieurs George Farmer et William Maltby le 12 Juillet de la dite année, lors de leur départ de ce port; desquels je vous transmets, cy joint, des copies conformes aux originaux et certifiées par moi; et qu'aussitot que ces deux remises, auront été exécutées dans les formes voulues, vous ayez à faire revenir immédiatement l'officier et les autre sujets du Roi qui pourroient se trouver dans le pays."

En vertu de cet ordre, qui fut remis au gouvernement Britannique, l'Angleterre reprit possession de la colonie du Port Egmont dans la même année. La trésorerie de Buenos-Ayres restant chargée de remplacer les effets qu'on avoit ordonné de restituer.

Ainsi se terminèrent les discussions entre l'Angleterre et l'Espagne au sujet des Malvines, ou pour mieux dire, du Port Egmont. Depuis cette époque, c'est à dire depuis 1771, il ne survient ni plainte, ni querelle, ni contrainte, ni violence; et, si la Grande Bretagne, réinstalée dans la possession du point disputé, l'abandonna trois ans après (en Mai 1774) ce dut être ou par sa propre volonté; ou, comme nous allons le voir bientôt, parce que son honneur le lui dictait, en raison de son engagement contracté dans la convention du 22 de Janvier.

Par ce traité nous voyons les Anglais en possession de nouveau du Port Egmont, et plainement satisfaits; et nous voyons aussi les Espagnols posseder de leur coté le Port Louis dans le même groupe d'iles et dans un voisinage immédiate. Les deux possesseurs sont en face l'un de l'autre, ils s'observent de près et se respectent mutuellement. Les iles sont trop petites pour être l'apanage de deux couronnes: l'un des deux doit l'emporter, comme étant le plus ancien possesseur et, par cette raison, le mieux fondé.

Un coup d'oeil jeté sur la convention du 22 Janvier 1771, suffit pour suggérer des reflexions singulieres. Dans cet acte solennel, le gouvernement Espagnol proteste que la restitution du Port Egmont ne doit avoir aucune conséquence à son préjudice, *et fait toutes réserves pour ses droits à la souveraineté des iles.* Le Gouvernement de Sa Majesté Britannique, dans sa réponse et son adhésion à cet acte, ne s'oppose point à cette clause. N'est ce donc pas là admettre et consentir à la réserve que s'étoit faite l'Espagne? Ou du moins, ce silence n'étoit surement pas le moyen de s'opposer ou d'infirmer ses droits; et véritablement il est

18

it by a counter-reservation, could not be more natural, or more obvious, considering all the circumstances of the case. This gives birth to a very strong suspicion that, below the surface of this transaction, there was something mysterious, but withal of so much importance, that it affected, and decided, the nature of the convention. Hence it was that it had scarcely seen the light, when it excited the astonishment of a no less wary, and accomplished, statesman than the illustrious Earl of Chatham, when, on the 6th of February in that year, he made a motion for laying before the twelve judges, the following questions:—

" 1st. Whether, in consideration of law, the Imperial Crown of this realm can hold any territories or possessions thereunto belonging, otherwise than in sovereignty?"

" 2dly. Whether the declaration or instrument, for the restitution of the port and fort called Egmont, to be made by the Catholic King to His Majesty, under a reservation of disputed right of sovereignty, expressed in the declaration or instrument stipulating such restitution, can be accepted or carried into execution, without derogating from the maxim of law, before referred to, touching the inherent and essential dignity of the Crown of Great Britain?"

On the other hand, could it have been credible that a convention which apparently left two rival jurisdictions on the same spot, was formed, or was ever intended to be permanent?

Whence could have originated the persuasion common to English historians, geographers, and other writers of the time, who agree uniformly, and with express reference to the convention of the 22nd of January 1771, *that Great Britain ceded the Malvina Islands to Spain?* Can they all be in error? Is it possible that national historians treating, *ex professo*, of the restitution of Port Egmont to Great Britain, would call it neither more nor less *a cession of all the Falkland Islands to Spain on the part of England*, if such had not been really the case?

The Undersigned might, here, make numerous citations from those authorities which afford evidence of the cession; but he will confine himself to the mention of one production of that period, also English, which pointedly clears up the mystery attending the convention of the 22nd of January. "Anecdotes of the Right Honorable William Pitt, Earl of Chatham, Vol. III., chap. 39." states:—

évident que l'occasion, et peut être même la nécessité d'y répondre par une contre réserve, ne pouvoit être plus naturelle et plus facile à concevoir, si l'on considère toutes les circonstances du cas dont il s'agit. Ceci laisse fortement soupçonner qu'au fond de cette transaction il y avoit quelque chose de mystérieux, mais en même temps de si grande importance, que cela influença et décida la nature de la convention. De là vint qu'à peine eut elle été mis au jour qu'elle excita la surprise et l'étonnement d'un homme d'état aussi prévoyant et distingué que le célèbre Comte de Chatham qui, le 6 de Février de la même année, fit la motion de placer sous les yeux des douze juges les questions suivantes:—

" 1 °. Si, en point de loi, la couronne impériale de ce royaume pouvoit conserver aucun territoire ou possessions lui appartenant, autrement qu'en souveraineté?"

" 2 °. Si la déclaration ou l'acte, relatif à la restitution à faire du port et fort appelé Egmont par le Roi Catholique à Sa Majesté, sous une réserve d'un droit de souveraineté disputé, exprimée dans la déclaration ou l'acte stipulant cette restitution, peut être acceptée, ou mise à exécution, sans déroger au principe de loi cy dessus invoqué relatif à l'inhérente dignité de la couronne de la Grande Bretagne?"

D'un autre coté eut-il été probable qu'une convention, qui évidemment laissoit deux jurisdictions opposées sur les même lieux, ait jamais été faite, ou du moins déstinée à être durable?

D'où pourroit donc venir la persuasion uniforme des historiens géographes Anglais et d'autres écrivains de ce temps là, qui s'accordent tous à dire, en s'appuyant éxprèssement de la convention du 22 Janvier 1771, *que la Grande Bretagne céda les Iles Malvines à l'Espagne?* Peuvent-ils donc être tous dans l'erreur? Est-il admissible que des historiens nationaux, traitant *ex professo* de la restitution du Port Egmont à la Grande Bretagne, l'eussent appelée précisément une cession de la part de l'Angleterre, si ce n'eut pas été véritablement le fait?

Le Soussigné pourroit faire ici de nombreuses citations des autorités qui donnent la preuve de la cession; mais il se bornera à mentionner une production de cette époque, aussi d'un auteur Anglais, qui fort apropos jette un grand jour sur le mystère qui accompagnoit la convention du 22 Janvier, (Anecdotes du très Honorable William Pitt, Comte de Chatham, Vol. III., chap. 39.)—

19

" While Lord Rochford was negociating with Prince Masserano, Mr. Stuart M'Kenzie was negociating with Monsieur François, Secretary to the Embassy of France at the court of London. At length,—about an hour before the meeting of parliament on the 22nd January 1771,—a declaration was signed by the Spanish ambassador, under French orders, and a French indemnification, for the restitution of Falkland's Islands to his Britannic Majesty, *but the important condition upon which the declaration was obtained, was not mentioned in the declaration. This condition was that the British forces should evacuate Falkland's Islands as soon as convenient after they were put in possession of Port and Fort Egmont.* And the British ministry engaged, as a pledge of their sincerity to keep that promise, that they would be the first to disarm.

" Two days after the Spanish ambassador had signed the declaration, he received orders of recall ; but his fate was like that of Mr. Harris ; in a short time afterwards he received orders to remain.

" In the month of February 1771, the Spanish minister at Madrid hinted to Mr. Harris, the intention of the Spanish court, to require, of the British ministry, *a perfection of engagements as they were understood.* Mr. Harris's dispatch, containing this hint, was received by the minister on the 4th of March. Three days afterwards, the Spanish messenger arrived, with orders to Prince Masserano to make a positive demand of the cession of Falkland Islands, to the King of Spain. The Spanish ambassador first communicated his information of these orders to the French ambassador, with a view of knowing if he could concur with him in making the demand. On the 14th they held a conference with Lord Rochford on the subject. His Lordship's answer was consonant to the spirit he had uniformly shewn. The reply from France was civil, but mentioned the family compact. The answer from Spain did not reach London until the 20th of April. In the mean time, the ministers held several conferences with Mr. Stuart Mackenzie. The result of the whole was, the English set the example to disarm ; and *Falkland's Islands were totally evacuated and abandoned in a short time afterwards, and have ever since been in the possession of the Spaniards.*"

This disclosure which,—by the rules of impartial criticism,—cannot but be allowed to have considerable weight, is confirmed,—with respect to the cession or relinquishment of the Malvinas on the part of England,—by two dispatches from the Spanish

" Pendant que Lord Rochford négocioit avec le Prince Masserano, Mr. Stuart M'Kenzie négocioit avec Mr. François Secrétaire, de l'Ambassade de France à la cour de Londres. Enfin, à peu près une heure avant que le parlement fut assemblé, le 22 Janvier 1771, une déclaration fut signée par l'Ambassadeur Espagnol, sous les ordres de la France, à qui une indemnité fut accordée, pour la restitution des Iles Falklands à Sa Majesté Britannique ; *mais la condition importante, sur laquelle cette déclaration fut obtenue, n'étoit pas mentionnée dans la déclaration. Cette condition était que les forces Britanniques devroient évacuer les Iles Falkland aussitôt que possible, après qu'elles auroient été mises en possession du Port et Fort Egmont.* Et le ministère Britannique s'engagea, comme une preuve de sa sincérité à tenir cette promesse, qu'il seroit le premier à effectuer le désarmement.

" Trois jours après que l'Ambassadeur eut signé la déclaration, il fut rappelé ; mais son sort fut le même que celui de Mr. Harris ; très peu de temps après il reçut ordre de rester.

" Dans le mois de Février 1771, le ministère Espagnol à Madrid donna à entendre à Mr. Harris l'intention de la cour d'Espagne de requérir du ministère Britannique *l'exécution des engagemens tels qu'ils avoient été convenus.* La dépêche de Mr. Harris, contenant cet avis, fut reçue par le ministère le 4 Mars. Trois jours après, le messager Espagnol arriva, portant des ordres au Prince Masserano de faire la demande positive de la cession des Iles Falklands au Roi d'Espagne. L'Ambassadeur Espagnol donna d'abord communication de ces ordres à l'ambassadeur Français, dans l'intention de savoir s'il voudroit l'aider de son concours dans cette demande. Le 14 ils eurent une conférence sur ce sujet avec Lord Rochford, dont la réponse fut en harmonie avec le caractère qu'il avoit uniformement montré. La réponse de la France fut civile, mais mentionnoit le pact de famille ; et la réponse d'Espagne n'arriva à Londres que le 20 Avril. Pendant ce temps là, les ministres eurent différentes conférences avec Mr. Stuart Mackenzie. Le résultat de tout cela fut que les Anglais donnerent l'exemple de désarmement ; que les iles Falklands furent totalement évacuées et abandonnées peu de temps après ; et qu'elles ont été en la possession des Espagnols depuis cette époque."

Cette révélation, que, suivant un jugement impartiale, on ne peut nier être d'un très grand poids, se trouve confirmée, relativement à la cession ou l'abandon des Malvines par l'Angleterre, par deux dépêches du ministre Espagnol Arriaga qui, le 7

20

Minister Arriaga, who signed the order of the 7th February 1771, for the restitution of Port Egmont, and who, on the 9th of April 1774, told the viceroy of Buenos-Ayres, and the governor of the Malvinas, that *the Court of London had* OFFERED *to abandon the establishment in the great Malvina,* which was the same with Port Egmont. Authentic copies of these dispatches, taken from the archives of Buenos Ayres, where the originals exist, are in the possession of the Undersigned, who believes them to be of sufficient importance to require that he should cite them literally :

" By the annexed copy of a dispatch, you will be acquainted with the information this day given to the Governor of the Malvinas, relative to *the* OFFER *of the Court of London to abandon the establishment which they made in the great Malvina,* of which, by order of the King, I apprise you that you may, on your part, make dispositions for its fulfilment. God preserve you many years.
Aranjuez, 9th of April 1774."
(Signed)　　Don Julian de Arriaga.
Sr. Don Juan José Vertiz.

" OFFERS *being made, as they are, by the Court of London, to relinquish* the settlement made by them in the great Malvina, withdrawing thence the few troops and inhabitants who were there, the King desires that you be made acquainted with this matter, in order that you may consequently observe, with due prudence and caution, whether the English do, in fact, abandon the said settlement, without undertaking to form any other in the immediate vicinity; and that, having ascertained that they have done that in the terms set forth, you will, from time to time, renew your exertions to make sure that they do not return to that quarter, informing me most precisely of whatever may occur at present, or at any future time : which instruction I communicate to you by His Majesty's order, to be exactly complied with, until, on a future opportunity, a more complete idea be given of all that pertains to this subject. God preserve you many years. Aranjuez, 9th April 1774."
(Signed)　　Don Julian de Arriaga.

" P. S. Until farther advices, which I shall address to you, you are not to deviate from the letter of the instructions I now give you : nor allow any one to proceed to the said relinquished settlement, except those whom you send for the purpose on which they are ordered.
To the Governor of the Malvinas."

Février 1771, signa l'ordre pour la restitution du Port Egmont, et qui, le 9 Avril 1774, dit au vice-roi de Buenos-Ayres et au gouverneur des Malvines que *la cour de Londres avoit offert d'abandonner l'établissement dans la grande Malvine ;* ce qui étoit la même chose que Port Egmont. Des copies authentiques de ces dépêches, prises des archives de Buenos-Ayres où sont déposés les originaux, sont dans les mains du Soussigné, que les croit d'une importance assez grande pour qu'il les cite ici littéralement :—

" Par la copie d'une dépêche cy-jointe, vous apprendrez l'information donnée aujourd'hui au Gouverneur des Malvines relativement à l'offre faite par la cour de Londres *de céder l'établissement qu'elle a fait dans la grande Malvine,* ce dont je vous préviens par ordre du Roi ; afin qu'en ce qui vous regarde, vous fassiez les dispositions nécessaires pour son exécution. Dieu vous conserve de longues années. Aranjuez, 9 Avril 1774."
(Signée)　　Don Julian de Arriaga.
A Sr. Du. Juan José Vertiz.

" Des offres étant faites, comme elles le sont, par la cour de Londres, *d'abandonner* l'établissement formé par elle dans la grande Malvine, en en retirant le peu de troupes et les habitans qui y sont, le Roi veut que vous soyez instruit des détails de cette transaction, afin que vous puissiez observer avec attention et prudence si en effet, les Anglais abandonnent le dit établissement, sans chercher à en former aucun autre dans l'immédiate voisinage ; et, qu'après vous être assuré qu'ils l'ont exécuté dans les termes indiqués, vous renouvelliez de temps en temps vos efforts pour savoir positivement s'ils ne retournent pas dans ces parages : en m'informant avec la plus grande précision de tout cequi pourroit arriver dans le moment, ou à telle époque que ce puisse être. Ces instructions vous sont transmises par ordre de Sa Majesté, pour que vous les exécutiez ponctuellement, jusqu'à ceque, par une future occasion, il vous soit donné une idée plus complette de tout ce qui se rattache à ce point. Dieu vous conserve de longues années. Aranjuez, 9 Avril 1774."
(Signée)　　Don Julian de Arriaga.

" P. S. Jusque aux nouveaux ordres que je vous adresserai, vous devez vous conformer, *à la lettre,* aux instructions que je vous donne maintenant ; et vous ne permettrez à qui que ce soit de se rendre au dit établissement cédé, excepté ceux que vous enverez pour exécuter les ordres que vous aurez donnés.
Au Gouverneur des Malvines."

21

In fact, on the 22nd of May 1774, three years after the restitution, we see England peacefully withdrawing her settlement from Port Egmont without any one having compelled her to this step, and without the occurrence of any new altercation, or violence. The former dispute was terminated; and it would be an anachronism to confound this voluntary egress, with the ejection in 1770 by the expedition of Buccarelli. The fact, then, of this pacific abandonment comes singularly in support of the reality of the *cession*, or, as some English writers explain it, the fulfilment of the contract by each party, for *"the Spaniards fulfilled their engagement by restoring Port Egmont, and the English fulfilled theirs by abandoning it after such surrender."*

Lieutenant Clayton who commanded in Port Egmont in the name of His Britannic, Majesty left an inscription, on a leaden plate, bearing date the 22nd of May 1774, in which he declared that the *Falkland Islands*, as well as the fort of Port Egmont, and its warehouses, stores, &c. belonged, of right, solely to His Majesty George III.; in further proof of which he also left hoisted the British flag.

But, in the first place, if an inscription were sufficient to preserve a dominion, that of Lieutenant Clayton's was long subsequent to the French inscription of 1764, and, for that reason, is of no validity. In the second place, it is over-done, for it seeks to invalidate the Spanish dominion of *Port Luis*, acknowledged in the convention of the 22nd of January 1771. Lastly, it was illegal if, as there is reason to believe, the relinquishment of Port Egmont was in consequence of an agreement on the part of the government to which he belonged; an agreement not the less binding because it was secret.

It has been said that this inscription, and this flag, thus left behind, were intimative of an intention of returning to occupy the territory at a more convenient opportunity; which, by the way, does not appear to have occurred until after the lapse of sixty years.

Notwithstanding, it is requisite to observe that if this *intention* was effective, it cannot be reconciled with the faith that was pledged; and the question would resolve itself into,—whether Great Britain had offered to withdraw from those islands. Then, to prove that intention, it was requisite to leave other more permanent vestiges of possession and will. It is clear, that if neither exterior signs of that nature, nor even the priority of discovery sufficed for a title of dominion, conformably to es-

Au fait, le 22 Mai 1774, trois ans après la restitution, nous voyons l'Angleterre se retirant paisiblement son établissement de Port Egmont, sans que personne l'ait obligée à cette démarche, et sans l'occurence d'aucune nouvelle altercation, ou violence. L'ancienne dispute était terminée; et confondre cette sortie volontaire avec l'éjection, en 1770, par l'expédition de Buccarelli, serait un anachronisme. Ainsi le fait de cet abandon paisible vient précisement à l'appui de la réalité de la *cession ;* ou, comme l'expliquent certains écrivains Anglais, chacune des parties remplit son engagement. " Les Espagnols acquittèrent leur promesse, en restituant Port Egmont; et les Anglais remplirent la leur, en l'abandonnant après cette réddition."

Le Lieutenant Clayton, qui commandoit dans Port Egmont au nom de Sa Majesté Britannique, laissa une inscription gravée sur une plaque de plomb, portant la date du 22 de Mai 1774, dans laquelle il déclare que les Iles Falkland et le Port et Fort Egmont, ainsi que les magasins, provisions de guerre, &c. appartenaient de droit, seulement à Sa Majesté George III.; en preuve de quoi il y laissoit aussi le drapeau Anglais hissé.

Mais, d'abord, si une inscription suffisait pour garantir une domination, celle du Lieutenant Clayton fut postérieure de beaucoup à l'inscription Française de 1764; et par, cette raison, n'est d'aucune validité. En second lieu, elle va trop loin, car elle tend à invalider les droits de la souveraineté Espagnole sur *Port Louis*, reconnus par la convention du 22 Janvier 1771. Enfin, elle étoit illégale si, comme il y a toute raison de le penser, l'abandon de Port Egmont étoit fait par suite d'un traité de la part du gouvernement auquel il appartenait; traité qui, pour être secret, n'en était par moins obligatoire.

On a prétendu que cette inscription et le drapeau, ainsi laissés en arrière, étoient l'indication d'une intention de revenir occuper le territoire dans un temps plus opportun; lequel, soit dit en passant, ne paroit être arrivé qu'après un laps de soixante années.

Cependant, on doit remarquer que, si cette intention étoit réelle, on ne sauroit la concilier avec la foi qui avait été engagée; et la question pourroit se résoudre à savoir, si la Grande Bretagne a offert de se retirer de ces Iles? Alors, pour preuve de cette intention, il auroit fallu laisser des traces plus durables de possession comme de volonté. Il est clair que si, ni des signes extérieurs de cette nature, ni même la priorité de la découverte, ne pouvaient suffir pour donner un droit à la souveraineté confor-

22

tablished opinions, as little could they suffice for its preservation, and transmission.

Property merely intentional must yield to formal and physical property. It may also be observed, as singularly strange, that the very act of the evacuation which puts an end to the possession, should have the effect of extending the *ideal* dominion, to points which England never obtained, to *all the Malvina Islands,* and specially to *Port Luis,* or *Puerto de la Soledad,* called, by the English, *Berkeley Sound.* It might be asked whether Lieutenant Clayton, on completely abandoning Port Egmont, could impose a *veto* to all nations of the globe, that they should never inhabit the islands which he left desert, nor make use of them for cultivation, as of an abode which the *hand, and the will, of the Creator* had destined for man. In especial manner it may be remarked that, this interdict could not be extended to Spain, whom England had admitted, and treated with, as sovereign of the isle, to the eastward, in which is situated Port Luis.

From what has been stated, it results that the claims of Spain to the Malvinas, were—her *formal occupation* of them; the purchase of them from France, at a price agreed on; and the cession, or relinquishment, of them by England *(derivative occupation.)* This closes the period of the ten years, just passed in review, or the dispute between the two crowns from 1764 to 1774.

" Property is acquired *de jure* by an occupation without defect; it is preserved by a *continual possession.*" (Günther's Völkerrecht.)

This Spanish occupation then continued without disturbance on the part of any other power; and it is worthy of remark that, in the public treaties that subsequently took place between England and Spain, no allusion, or reference, is made to those islands, the inference being, that the ancient question was considered as definitively settled. Here might be given a list of Spanish Governors who held command in the islands, and resided constantly in Port Luis, in immediate dependance on, and at the expense of the vice-regal government of Buenos Ayres.

It is well known to all the World that, by the Revolution which took place on the 25th of May 1810, and the solemn Declaration of Independence on the 9th of July 1816, a political Community was constituted, in the jurisdiction of Buenos Ayres, under the

mement aux opinions établies, encore moins pouvaient ils suffir pour conserver et transmettre ce droit.

La proprieté purement intentionnelle doit céder à la proprieté formelle et phisique. On doit observer encore, comme singulièrement étrange, que ce même fait de l'évacuation qui, réellement met fin à la possession, aurait au contraire pour effet d'étendre la domination idéale sur des points que l'Angleterre n'obtint jamais; sur toutes les Iles Malvines et particulièrement sur *Port Louis,* ou *Puerto de la Soledad,* appelé par les Anglais *Berkeley Sound.* On pourroit demander encore, si le Lieutenant Clayton, en abandonnant entièrement Port Egmont, pouvoit imposer un *veto* à toutes les nations du globe pour qu'elles n'habitassent jamais les iles qu'il avoit laissé désertes; ou qu'elles ne les cultivassent jamais, comme un séjour que la main et *la volonté du Créateur* avaient *destiné à l'homme.* On devrait particulièrement remarquer que cette prohibition ne pouvoit s'étendre à l'Espagne, que l'Angleterre avait reconnue et avec laquelle elle avait traité comme souveraine de l'île à l'est, dans laquelle se trouve Port Louis.

Il résulte de ce qui a été établi, que les droits de l'Espagne sur les Malvines étaient son *occupation formelle;* l'achat de ces droits de la France à un prix convenu; et la cession ou abandon que l'Angleterre lui en a fait *(occupation dérivative.)* Ceci termine le période des dix années que nous venons de passer en revue, ou la dispute entre les deux couronnes depuis 1764 jusqu'à 1774.

" La propriété est acquise *de droit* par une occupation sans défaut; elle est conservée par une possession continue." (Günther's Völkerrecht.)

Depuis cette époque cette occupation de la part de l'Espagne se continua sans qu'aucun autre pouvoir vint l'inquiéter. Et il est à remarquer que dans les traités qui eurent lieu par la suite entre l'Angleterre et l'Espagne, il n'est fait aucune allusion, aucune mention relatives à ces iles; l'induction doit être que l'ancienne question étoit considérée comme définitivement terminée. Nous pourrions citer ici la liste des gouverneurs Espagnols qui ont eu le commandement des iles, et qui ont constamment résidé à *Port Louis* sous la dépendance immédiate et aux frais du Gouvernement de la vice-royauté de Buenos-Ayres.

Il est connu du monde entier que par suite de la Révolution qui eut lieu le 25 Mai 1810, et la solemnelle Déclaration d'Indépendance du 9 Juillet 1816, une Communauté politique a été constituée dans la jurisdiction de Buenos-Ayres, sous les nom, style et

23

name, style, and title of "THE UNITED PROVINCES OF THE RIO DE LA PLATA,"—which has been recognized by Great Britain, and other principal nations. This political Community could not exist without territory, as where there is no independence of territory there can be no sovereign state, and thus as the community acquired the right of treaties, and that of competency to negociate with foreign powers, it also acquired the right of state property *(jus in patrimonium republicæ.)* The United Provinces, consequently succeeded Spain in the rights which that nation, from whom they separated, had possessed in that jurisdiction. The Malvinas had always been a part of that country, or of that district, and, as such, they formed part of the dominion, or public property, of the new state, *(patrimonium reipublicæ publicum;)* and were claimed, inhabited, and garrisoned by its subjects. The sovereignty of the islands which ceased, in the Spanish government, on the Independence of America, could not pass in succession to England, nor revive a question, and claims that were extinct.

Supported by so great, and so solid, a basis;—strong in the justice of their cause, and in the consciousness of their rights,—The Government of the Republic protested, on the 22nd of January 1833, to the British Legation in Buenos Ayres, against the expulsion of their garrison and settlement from the Malvinas, and against the assumption of sovereignty which has been made in them, in the name of Great Britain, &c., giving orders to the Undersigned to reiterate this Protest to the Government of His Britannic Majesty.

Therefore, the Undersigned,—in fulfilment of his orders and instructions,—PROTESTS FORMALLY in the name of the United Provinces of the Rio de la Plata, against the sovereignty lately assumed in the Malvina Islands by the crown of Great Britain, and against the espoliation and ejection, of the Republic's settlement in Port Luis, otherwise called *Puerto de la Soledad*, by His Britannic Majesty's corvette CLIO, with demand for reparation claimable in such cases for *lesion* inflicted, as well as for every act consequent on that proceeding.

THE UNITED PROVINCES make this just demand to the honour of His Britannic Majesty's Government, and to the opinion of an impartial World.

London, June 17th 1833. Year the twenty-fourth

G

titre de "Provinces Unies du Rio de la Plata;" laquelle a été reconnue par la Grande Bretagne et les autres nations principales. Cette Communauté politique ne pourrait exister sans territoire, puisqu'où il n'y a pas d'indépendance de territoire, il ne peut y avoir d'état souverain; et ainsi, comme la communauté avoit acquis le droit de traités et celui de compétance pour négocier avec les puissances étrangères, elle avoit aussi acquis le droit de propriété d'état *(jus in patrimonium reipublicæ.)* Les Provinces Unies, par conséquent, succédèrent à l'Espagne dans les droits que cette nation, de laquelle elles s'étaient séparées, possaidait dans cette jurisdiction. Les Malvines avaient toujours fait partie de cette contrée, ou de ce district; et, comme telles, elles formaient une portion du domaine, ou de la propriété publique du nouvel état *(patrimonium reipublicæ publicum.)* Et elles furent réclamées et habitées par ses sujets, qui y établirent garnison. La souveraineté des iles qui cessa d'appartenir au gouvernement d'Espagne, par l'Indépendance de l'Amérique, ne put passer en succession à l'Angleterre; ni renouveller une question et des prétentions qui étaient éteintes.

Appuyé sur une si grande et si solide base, fort de la justice de sa cause et de la conscience de ses droits, le Gouvernement de la République protesta le 22 Janvier 1833, à la Légation Britannique à Buenos-Ayres, contre l'expulsion de sa garnison et de son établissement des Malvines, et contre l'appropriation de souveraineté qui s'y étoit faite au nom de la Grande Bretagne, &c. donnant, en même temps, ordre au Soussigné de réitérer cette protestation au Gouvernement de Sa Majesté Britannique.

En conséquence, le Soussigné, en exécution de ses ordres et de ses instructions, proteste formellement au nom des Provinces Unies de Rio de la Plata, contre la souveraineté dont s'est dernièrement emparée la couronne de la Grande Bretagne dans les Iles Malvines; et contre la spoliation et l'expulsion, de l'établissement de la République dans *Port Louis*, autrement appelé *Puerto de la Soledad*, par la corvette de Sa Majesté Britannique *la Clio*; demandant toute réparation exigible en pareil cas pour lésion soufferte, aussi bien que pour tous faits qui pourraient être la conséquence de cette action.

Les Provinces Unies font cette juste demande à l'honneur du Gouvernement de Sa Majesté Britannique, et la soumettent à l'opinion des hommes impartiaux.

Londres le 17 Juin 1833. L'an 24eme. de la

24

of the liberty, and eighteenth of the Independence of the United Provinces of the Rio de la Plata.

(Signed)   MANUEL MORENO.

His Excellency,
The Right Honorable Viscount Palmerston, G.C.B.
&c. &c. &c.

APPENDIX.

A.

(Translation.)

Department of Foreign Relations. Buenos Ayres, January 16, 1833, 24th Year of the Liberty, and 18th of the Independence of the Republic.

The Undersigned, Minister of Justice, charged provisionally with the Department of Foreign Relations of the Argentine Republic, has the honour to address the Chargé d'Affaires *ad interim* of H. B. M. in this city, to acquaint him that the government has just learned that the commander of His Britanic Majesty's corvette of war CLIO has taken possession of the island of La Soledad, in the Malvinas, hoisting the British flag where that of the Argentine Republic waved. This unexpected event has sensibly affected the feelings of the Government of Buenos Ayres; and although it cannot discover any thing to justify such a proceeding, nevertheless, presuming that the Chargé d'Affaires whom the undersigned addresses himself, is informed upon a measure which openly compromises the dignity and rights of the Argentine Republic, it has directed the undersigned to request of the Chargé d'Affaires, of H. B. M, the competent explanation.

God preserve the Chargé d'Affaires many years.

(Signed) MANUEL VICENTE DE MAZA.

To the Chargé d'Affaires, *ad interim*,
of His Britanic Majesty, &c. &c.

B.

(Copy.)

Buenos Ayres, January 17, 1833.

The Undersigned, His Britannic Majesty's Chargé d'Affaires, in acknowledging the receipt of the note, dated yesterday, of His Excellency

25

Señor Don Manuel Vicente de Maza, Minister charged with the Department of Foreign Relations of the Argentine Republic, has the honour to inform His Excellency, that he has received no instructions from his Court to make any communication to the Government of Buenos Ayres, upon the subject to which his Excellency's note refers.

The Undersigned will hasten to submit it to His Majesty's Government, and he avails himself of this opportunity, to repeat to His Excellency Señor de Maza the assurance of his high and distinguished consideration.

(Signed)   PHILIP G. GORE.

To His Excellency Don Manuel Vicente de Maza, &c. &c. &c.

Manuel Vicente de Maza, Ministre, chargé du Département des Relations extérieures de la République Argentine, a l'honneur d'informer Son Excellence, qu'il n'a reçu de sa Cour aucune instruction de donner communication au Gouvernement de Buenos Ayres du sujet qui fait le motif de la note de Son Excellence.

Le Soussigné s'empressera de la soumettre, au Gouvernement de sa Majesté, et il saisit cette occasion pour renouveller à Son Excellence, Señor de Maza, l'assurance de sa considération haute et distinguée.

(Signé)   PHILIP G. GORE.

A Son Excellence Don Manuel Vicente de Maza, &c. &c. &c.

C.

INSCRIPTION FRANÇAISE.

"Etablissement des Iles Malouines, situées au 51 deg. 30 min. de lat. aust., et 60 deg. 50 min. de long. occid. merid. de Paris, par la Frégate l'Aigle, Capitaine P. Duclos Guyot, Capitaine de Brulot, et la Corvette Le Sphinx, Capitaine F. Chénard de la Girandais, Lieut. de Frégate, armées par Louis Antoine de Bougainville, Colonel d'Infanterie, Capitaine de Vaisseau, Chef de l'Expédition, G. de Nerville, Capitaine d'Infanterie, et P. D'Arboulin, Administrateur Général des Postes de France.

Construction d'un Obélisque décoré d'un Medaillon de Sa Majesté Louis XIV., sur les plans d'A. l'Huillier, Eng. Géogr. des Camps et Armées, servant dans l'Expédition ; sous le Ministère d'E. de Choiseul, Duc de Stainville, *en Février*, 1764.

Avec ces mots pour exergue :   *Conamur tenues grandia.*"

D.

(*Translation.*)

Instrument executed by Mons. Louis de Bougainville for the delivering up of the Malvinas.

"I, Louis de Bougainville, Colonel of His Most Christian Majesty's army, have received six hundred and eighteen thousand one hundred and eight livres, thirteen sous and eleven deniers, being the amount of an estimate, that I have given in, of the expenses incurred by the St. Malo Company in equipments for founding their intrusive establishments in the Malvina Islands, belonging to His Catholic Majesty, in the following manner :—

Forty thousand livres, delivered, on account, to me in Paris, by His Excellency the Count

(*Traduction.*)

Acte signé par Monsieur Louis de Bougainville pour la remise des Malvines.

Moi, Louis de Bougainville, Colonel des armées de Sa Majesté très Chrétienne, ai reçu *six cent dixhuit mille cent huit livres, treize sols et onze deniers*, montant de l'estimation que j'ai donnée des dépenses faites par la Compagnie de St. Malo, pour équipements et fondation de ses établissemens illegitimes dans les Iles Malvines, appartenant à Sa Majesté Catholique, savoir :

Quarante mille livres, payées, en à compte, à Paris, par Son Excellence le Comte de Fuentes,

26

de Fuentes, Ambassador of His Catholic Majesty to that court, for which I gave the proper receipt.

Two hundred thousand livres, which are to be delivered to me at the same court of Paris, according to bills drawn in my favor by the Marquess Zambrano, Treasurer-General of His Catholic Majesty, upon Don Francisco Ventura Llorena, Treasurer-Extraordinary of the same; and *sixty-five thousand six hundred* and *twenty-five* hard dollars, and three fourths parts of another, which are equivalent to the three hundred and seventy-eight thousand one hundred and eight livres, three sous, and eleven deniers, that are due, at the rate of five livres per dollar, which I have to receive in *Buenos Ayres* on account of bills which have been delivered to me, drawn by His Excellency the Baylio Fray, Don Julian Arriaga, Secretary of State for the general department of the Indies and Navy of His Catholic Majesty.

In consideration of these payments, as well as in obedience to His Most Christian Majesty's orders, I am bound to deliver up, in due formality, to the Court of Spain, those establishments, along with the families, houses, works, timber, and shipping built there, and employed in the expedition; and, finally, every thing therein belonging to the St. Malo Company, as included in the accounts which are so settled, and to His Most Christian Majesty, by this *voluntary cession*, making void for ever all claims that the Company, or any person interested therein, may have, or might produce, upon the Treasury of His Catholic Majesty; nor can they, henceforth, demand more pecuniary, or any other compensation whatsoever. In testimony whereof, I set my name to this present instrument, and voucher, as one principally interested, as well as authorised, to receive the whole of this sum, agreeably to a registry in the department of the State in St. Ildephonso, 4th October, 1766.

(Signed) **LOUIS DE BOUGAINVILLE.**

Ambassadeur de Sa Majesté Catholique, pour les quelles j'ai donné quittance.

Deux cent mille livres, qui doivent m'être comptées à la même Cour de Paris, suivant des traites souscrites en ma faveur par le Marquis Zambrano, Trésorier Général de Sa Majesté Catholique, sur Don Francisco Ventura Llorena, Trésorier Extraordinaire de Sa Majesté.

Et soixante-cinq mille six cent soixante et quinze gourdes trois quart, équivalant aux trois cent soixante dixhuit mille cent huit livres trois sous, onze deniers dus, au taux de cinq livres par dollars que j'ai à recevoir à *Buenos Ayres*, en à compte de lettres de change qui m'ont été delivrées, tirées par Son Excellence le Baylio Fray Don Julian Arriaga, Secrétaire d'Etat du départment général des Indes et de la Marine de Sa Majesté Catholique.

En considération de ces payemens, aussi bien que par soumission aux ordres de Sa Majesté très Chrétienne, je m'oblige à remettre, en due forme à la Cour d'Espagne ces établissemens, ainsi que les familles, maisons, travaux, bois de construction, vaisseaux en chantier ou employés à l'expédition; et, enfin, tout ce qui, sur les lieux appartient à la Compagnie de St. Malo, tel que porté sur l'inventaire, ainsi que ce qui appartient à Sa Majesté très Chrétienne, *qui en fait la cession volontaire* renonçant pour toujours à tous droits que la Compagnie, ou tout autre intéressé, ait pu ou pourrait produire sur la Trésorerie de Sa Majesté Catholique, sans qu'ils puissent à l'avenir faire aucune demande d'argent, ou compensation quelconque. En foi de quoi, je signe le présent acte et le garantis, comme étant un des principaux intéressés, aussi bien qu'autorisé à recevoir le montant de toute la somme, conformement au Registre minute du département de l'état. A St Ildefonse, le 4 Octobre, 1766.

(Signé) **LOUIS DE BOUGAINVILLE.**

No. 2.—Viscount Palmerston to Don Manuel Moreno.

Foreign Office, January 8, 1834.

THE Undersigned, &c. has the honour to acknowledge the receipt of the Note of M. Moreno, &c., dated the 17th of June last, in which he formerly protests, in the name of his Government, " against the Sovereignty lately assumed in the Malvina (or Falkland) Islands, by the Crown of Great Britain."

Before the Undersigned proceeds to reply to the allegations advanced in M. Moreno's Note, upon which his Protest against this act on the part of His Majesty is founded, the Undersigned deems it proper to draw M. Moreno's attention to the contents of the Protest which Mr. Parish, the British Chargé d'Affaires at Buenos-Ayres, addressed, in the name of his Court, to the Minister for Foreign Affairs of the Republic, on the 19th of November, 1829, in consequence of the British Government having been informed that the President of The United Provinces of the Rio de la Plata had issued Decrees, and had made Grants of Land, in the nature of Acts of Sovereignty over the Islands in question.

That Protest made known to the Government of The United Provinces of the Rio de la Plata:—

1st. That the Authority which that Government had thus assumed, was considered by the British Government as incompatible with the Sovereign Rights of Great Britain over the Falkland Islands.

2dly. That those Sovereign Rights, which were founded upon the original Discovery and subsequent Occupation of those Islands, had acquired an additional sanction from the fact, that His Catholic Majesty had restored the British Settlement, which had been forcibly taken possession of by a Spanish Force, in the year 1771.

3rdly. That the withdrawal of His Majesty's Forces from the Falkland Islands, in 1774, could not invalidate the just rights of Great Britain, because that withdrawal took place only in pursuance of the system of retrenchment adopted at that time by His Majesty's Government.

4thly. That the Marks and Signals of Possession, and of Property, left upon the Islands, the British Flag still flying, and all the other formalities observed upon the occasion of the departure of the Governor, were calculated not only to assert the rights of Ownership, but to indicate the intention of resuming the Occupation of the Territory at some future period.

Upon these grounds, Mr. Parish protested against the pretensions set up on the part of the Argentine Republic, and against all acts done to the prejudice of the just rights of Sovereignty theretofore exercised by the Crown of Great Britain.

The Minister for Foreign Affairs of the Republic acknowledged the receipt of the British Protest, and acquainted Mr. Parish that his Government would give it their particular consideration, and that he would communicate to him their decision upon the subject, so soon as he should receive directions to that effect.

No Answer was, however, at any time returned, nor was any objection raised, on the part of the Government of The United Provinces of the Rio de la Plata, to the rights of Great Britain, as asserted in that Protest; but the Buenos-Ayrean Government persisted, notwithstanding the receipt of that Protest, in exercising those acts of Sovereignty against which the Protest was specially directed.

The Government of The United Provinces of the Rio de la Plata could not have expected, after the explicit Declaration which had been so formally made of the right of the Crown of Great Britain to the Islands in question, that His Majesty would silently submit to such a course of proceeding; nor could that Government have been surprised at the step which His Majesty thought proper to take, in order to the resumption of rights which had never been abandoned, and which had only been permitted to lie dormant, under circumstances which had been explained to the Buenos-Ayrean Government.

The Claim of Great Britain to the Sovereignty of the Falkland Islands having been unequivocally asserted and maintained, during the Discussions with Spain, in 1770 and 1771, which had nearly led to a War between the 2 Countries, and Spain having deemed it proper to put an end to those Discussions, by restoring to His Majesty the Places from which British Subjects had been expelled; the Government of the

United Provinces could not reasonably have anticipated that the British Government would permit any other State to exercise a right, as derived from Spain, which Great Britain had denied to Spain herself; and this consideration alone would fully justify His Majesty's Government in declining to enter into any further explanation upon a question which, upwards of half a century ago, was so notoriously and decisively adjusted with another Government more immediately concerned.

But M. Moreno, in the Note which he has addressed to the Undersigned, has endeavoured to shew that, at the termination of the memorable Discussions referred to between Great Britain and Spain, a Secret Understanding existed between the 2 Courts, in virtue of which Great Britain was pledged to restore the Islands to Spain at a subsequent period, and that the evacuation of them, in 1774, by His Majesty, was the fulfilment of that pledge.

The existence of such a Secret Understanding is alleged to be proved; 1st. By the reservation, as to the former right of Sovereignty over the Islands, which was contained in the Spanish Declaration, delivered at the time of the restoration of Port Egmont and its Dependencies to His Majesty; and, 2ndly. By the concurrent description of the Transaction, as it took place between the Parties, given in certain Documents and Historical Works.

Although the reservation referred to, cannot be deemed to possess any substantial weight, inasmuch as no notice whatever is taken of it in the British Counter-Declaration, which was exchanged against it; and although the evidence adduced from unauthentic Historical Publications cannot be regarded as entitled to any weight whatever, with a view to a just decision upon a point of International Rights; yet, as the Allegations above-mentioned involve an imputation against the good faith of Great Britain, to which His Majesty's Government cannot but feel sensibly alive, the Undersigned has been honoured with the King's Commands to cause the Official Correspondence with the Court of Madrid, at the period alluded to, to be carefully inspected, in order that the circumstances which really took place upon the occasion might be accurately ascertained.

That inspection has accordingly been made; and the Undersigned has the honour to communicate to M. Moreno the following Extracts, which contain all the material information that can be gathered from that Correspondence relative to the Transaction in question:—

The Earl of Rochford to James Harris, Esq.
"*St. James's, January* 25, 1771.
"I inclose to you a Copy of the Declaration signed on Tuesday last by Prince Masserano, with that of my acceptance of it in His Majesty's name."

Spanish Declaration.—London, 22nd January, 1771.

"Sᴀ Majesté Britannique s'étant plainte de la violence qui avoit été commise le 10 Juin de l'année 1770, à l'Ile communément appelée la Grande Maloüine, et par les Anglais dite Falkland, en obligeant par la force le Commandant, et les Sujets de Sa Majesté Britannique, à évacuer le Port par eux appelé Egmont, démarche offensante à l'honneur de sa Couronne, le Prince de Masseran, Ambassadeur Extra-ordinaire de Sa Majesté Catholique, a reçu ordre de déclarer, et déclare, que Sa Majesté Catholique, considérant l'amour dont elle est animée pour la paix, et pour le maintien de la bonne harmonie avec Sa Majesté Britannique, et réfléchissant que cet évènement pourroit l'interrompre, a vu avec déplaisir cette expédition capable de la troubler; et dans la persuasion où elle est de la réciprocité de ses sentimens, et de son éloignement pour autoriser tout ce qui pourroit troubler la bonne intelligence entre les 2 Cours, Sa Majesté Catholique désavoue la susdite entreprise violente; et, en conséquence, le Prince de Masseran déclare, que Sa Majesté Catholique s'engage à donner des ordres immédiats pour qu'on remette les choses dans la Grande Maloüine, au Port dit Egmont, précisément dans l'état où elles étoient avant le 10 Juin, 1770, auquel effet Sa Majesté Catholique donnera ordre à un de ses Officiers, de remettre à l'Officier autorisé par Sa Majesté Britannique, le Fort et Port Egmont, avec toute l'artillerie, les munitions, et effets de Sa Majesté Britannique et de ses Sujets, qui s'y sort trouvés le jour ci-dessus nommé, conformément à l'Inventaire qui e a été dressé.

"Le Prince de Masseran déclare en même tems, au nom du Roi son Maitre, que l'engagement de Sa dite Majesté Catholique, de restituer à Sa Majesté Britannique la Possession du Port et Fort dit Egmont, ne peut ni ne doit nullement affecter *la question du Droit antérieur de Souveraineté* des Iles Maloüines, autrement dites Falk-land.

"En foi de quoi, moi, le susdit Ambassadeur Extraordinaire, ai signé la présente Déclaration de ma Signature ordinaire, et à icelle fait apposer le Cachet de mes Armes. A Londres, le 22 Janvier, 1771.

(L.S.)   "LE PRINCE DE MASSERAN."

British Counter-Declaration.—London, 22nd January, 1771.

"Sᴀ Majesté Catholique ayant autorisé son Excellence le Prince de Masserano, son Ambassadeur Extraordinaire, à offrir, en son Nom Royal, au Roi de la Grande Bretagne, une satisfaction pour l'injure faite à Sa Majesté Britannique, en la dépossédant du Port et Fort du Port Egmont; et le dit Ambassadeur ayant aujourd'hui signé une Déclaration, qu'il vient de me remettre, y exprimant, que Sa Majesté Catholique, ayant le désir de rétablir la bonne harmonie et amitié qui subsistoient ci-devant entre les 2 Couronnes, désavoue l'expédition contre le Port Egmont, dans laquelle la force a été employé, *contre les Possessions, Commandant, et Sujets* de Sa Majesté Britannique, et s'engage aussi que toutes choses seront immédiatement remises dans la situation précise dans laquelle elles étoient avant le 10 Juin, 1770; et que Sa Majesté Catholique donnera des ordres en conséquence à un de ses Officiers de remettre à l'Officier, autorisé par Sa Majesté Britannique, le Port et Fort du Port Egmont, comme aussi toute l'artillerie, les munitions, et effets de Sa Majesté Britannique, et de ses Sujets, selon l'Inventaire qui en a été dressé; et le dit Ambassadeur s'étant de plus engagé, au nom de Sa Majesté Catholique, que le contenu de la dite Déclaration sera effectué par Sa Majesté Catholique, et que des duplicatas des Ordres de Sa dite Majesté Catholique à ses Officiers seront remis entre les mains d'un des Principaux Secrétaires d'Etat de Sa Majesté Britannique, dans l'espace de 6 semaines; Sa dite Majesté Britannique, afin de faire voir les mêmes dispositions amicales de Sa part, m'a autorisé à déclarer, qu'elle regardera la dite Déclaration du Prince de Masserano, avec l'accomplissement entier du dit Engagement de la part de Sa Majesté Catholique, comme une satisfaction de l'injure faite à la Couronne de la Grande Bretagne. En foi de quoi, moi, Soussigné, un des Principaux Secrétaires d'Etat de Sa Majesté Britannique, ai signé la présente de ma Signature ordinaire, et à icelle fait apposer le Cachet de mes Armes. A Londres, ce 22 Janvier, 1771.

(L.S.) "ROCHFORD."

James Harris, Esq. to the Earl of Rochford.

"*Madrid, February* 14, 1771.

" THEY keep the Declaration here as secret as possible. I do not find any to whom they have shewn it, except those to whom they are obliged to communicate it. They also report that we have given a verbal assurance to evacuate Falkland's Islands, *in the space of 2 months.*"

The Earl of Rochford. JAMES HARRIS.

The Earl of Rochford to James Harris, Esq.

"*St. James's, March* 8, 1771.

" HIS Majesty has been pleased to order the *Juno* Frigate of 32 guns, the *Hound* Sloop, and *Florida* Store-Ship, to be prepared to go to Port Egmont, in order to receive the Possession from the Spanish Commander there; and as I have spoken so fully to Prince Masserano on the manner of its being executed, it is needless for me to say any more to you upon it.

"I think it right to acquaint you, that the Spanish Ambassador pressed me to have some hopes given him of our agreeing to *a mutual abandoning of Falkland's Islands*, to which I replied, that it was impossible for me to enter on that subject with him, as the restitution must precede every discourse relating to those Islands.

"You will endeavour, on all occasions, to inculcate the absurdity of Spain having any apprehensions, from the state in which Port Egmont was before its capture, or the Force now sent out, of His Majesty's intending to make use of it for the annoyance of their Settlements in the South Sea, than which nothing can be farther from the King's inclination, who sincerely desires to preserve Peace between the 2 Nations."

James Harris, Esq.   ROCHFORD.

———

The Earl of Rochford to the Lords of the Admiralty.

"*St. James's, March 15, 1771.*

"YOUR Lordships having acquainted me that, in consequence of His Majesty's pleasure, signified in my Letter of 22nd last, you had ordered the *Juno* Frigate, the *Hound* Sloop, and *Florida* Store-Ship, to be prepared to proceed to Falkland's Islands, I am commanded to signify to your Lordships His Majesty's pleasure, that you order the Commander of the said Frigate, as soon as those Ships are ready for Sea, to repair directly with them to Port Egmont, and, presenting to Don Felipe Ruiz Puente, or any other Spanish Officer he finds there, the Duplicates of His Catholic Majesty's Orders sent herewith, to receive, in proper form, the restitution of possession, and of the Artillery, Stores, and Effects, agreeably to the said Orders, and to the Inventories signed by the Captains Farmer and Maltby, (Copies of which are annexed,) and that you direct him to take an exact account of any deficiency which there may be of the things mentioned in the said Inventories, in order that the same may be made good by His Catholic Majesty; giving a Copy of the said Account, signed by himself, to the Spanish Officer, and desiring an acknowledgment under his hand of the same being a true Account.

"After the said restitution shall have been completed, it is the King's pleasure that Captain Stott should return immediately to England with the *Juno* Frigate and the *Florida* Store-Ship, unless he find it necessary to leave the latter behind; and that the *Hound* Sloop should remain stationed in the Harbour till His Majesty's farther Orders.

"Your Lordships will direct Captain Stott to behave with the greatest prudence and civility towards the Spanish Commander and the Subjects of His Catholic Majesty, carefully avoiding anything that might give occasion to disputes or animosity, and strictly restraining the Crews of the Ships under his command in this respect; but if, at or after the Restitution to be made, the Spanish Commander should make any Protest against His Majesty's right to Port Egmont, or Falkland's Islands, it is His Majesty's pleasure that the Commander of his Ships should answer the same by a Counter-protest, in proper terms, of His Majesty's right to the whole of the said Islands, and against the right of His Catholic Majesty to any part of the same.

"In case, from any accident or otherwise, Captain Stott should not, on his arrival at Port Egmont, find any Officer there on the part of the King of Spain, your Lordships will direct him (supposing he shall find it necessary to put any of his Men on Shore) to avoid setting up any Marks of Possession, or letting His Majesty's Colours fly on Shore, as it is for the King's honour that the Possession should be formally restored by an Officer of His Catholic Majesty; and for that reason it will be proper that the King's Commanding Officer should keep a good look-out, and, upon perceiving the approach of any Vessel of His Catholic Majesty, should re-embark any of his Men who may at that time be on Shore, that the Possession may be indisputably vacant.

"If it should happen that after the King's Ships shall have remained as late as all October, no Spanish Officer should yet appear, your Lordships will direct Captain Stott, in such case, either to proceed himself, or send an Officer to Soledad, to deliver His Catholic Majesty's Orders to the Spanish Commander there, taking care not to salute the Fort as a Spanish Garrison, and making a Protest, in civil terms, against that Settlement of His Catholic Majesty's Subjects in an Island belonging to His Majesty.

"If, within a reasonable time after the delivery of the said Order to the Spanish Commander, at Soledad, there still shall not arrive at Port Egmont any Officer of His Catholic Majesty to make the Restitution, it is the King's pleasure that the Commanding Officer of his Ships should then draw up a Protest of the inexecution of His Catholic Majesty's late Declaration, and should take formal possession, in His Majesty's name; hoisting His Majesty's Colours on Shore; and that, leaving there the *Hound* Sloop, and *Florida* Store-ship (if the latter is necessary), and sending a Duplicate of his Protest to the Spanish Officer at Soledad, he should proceed to England to lay before your Lordships, for His Majesty's information, his Report of the manner in which he has executed his Commission.

"Your Lordships will take care that a sufficient quantity of Provisions and Necessaries of all kinds may be sent out in the said 3 Vessels; and will, at a convenient distance of time, despatch another Store-ship for a further supply.   ROCHFORD.

"P.S. I also inclose to your Lordships the Copy of His Catholic Majesty's Order to Don Felipe Ruiz Puente, with its Translation."
The Lords Commissioners of the Admiralty.

Order of The King of Spain.—(Translation.)

"*Pardo, February* 17, 1771.

"IT being agreed between the King and His Britannic Majesty, by a Convention signed in London on the 22nd of January last past, by the Prince of Masserano and the Earl of Rochford, that the Great Malouine, called by the English Falkland, should be immediately replaced in the precise situation in which it was before it was evacuated by them on the 10th of June last year; I signify to you, by the King's order, that, as soon as the Person commissioned by the Court of London shall present himself to you with this, you order the delivery of the Port de la Cruzada or Egmont, and its Fort and Dependencies, to be effected, as also of all the Artillery, Ammunition, and effects, that were found there, belonging to His Britannic Majesty and his Subjects, according to the Inventories signed by George Farmer and William Maltby, Esqrs., on the 11th July of the said year, at the time of their quitting the same, of which I send you the inclosed Copies, authenticated under my hand; and that, as soon as the one and the other shall be effected with the due formalities, you cause to retire immediately the Officer and other Subjects of the King which may be there.

God preserve you many years.

"The BALIO FRAY, DON JULIAN DE ARRIAGA.
"*To Don Felipe Ruiz Puente.*"

———

Captain Stott to the Lords of the Admiralty.

"*Juno, Plymouth, December* 9, 1771.

"I MUST beg leave to refer their Lordships to the Letter I had the honour of writing you from Rio de Janeiro, the 30th of July last, for the occurrences of my Voyage to that time; from whence I sailed with His Majesty's Ships under my command, the next day, and arrived at Port Egmont the evening of the 13th of September following.

The next morning, seeing Spanish Colours flying, and Troops on shore, at the Settlement formerly held by the English, I sent a Lieutenant to know if any Officer was there on behalf of His Catholic Majesty, empowered to make restitution of possession to me, agreeably to the Orders of his Court for that purpose, Duplicates of which I had to deliver him: I was answered, that the Commanding Officer, Don Francisco de Orduna, a Lieutenant of the Royal Artillery of Spain, was furnished with Full Powers, and ready to effect the restitution. He soon after came on board the *Juno* to me, when I delivered him His Catholic Majesty's Orders.

We then examined into the situation of the Settlement and Stores, adjusted the form of the restitution and reception of the Possession,—Instruments for which were settled, executed, and reciprocally delivered.

That which I received from the Spanish Officer, and a Copy of what I gave him, are here inclosed.

On Monday, the 16th of September, I landed, followed by a party of Marines, and was received by the Spanish Officer, who formally restored me the Possession; on which I caused His Majesty's Colours to be hoisted and the Marines to fire 3 Volleys, and the *Juno* 5 Guns, and was congratulated, as were the Officers with me, by the Spanish Officer, with great cordiality on the occasion. The next day Don Francisco, with all the Troops and Subjects of the King of Spain, departed in a Schooner which they had with them. I have only to add, that this transaction was effected with the greatest appearance of good faith, without the least claim or reserve being made by the Spanish Officer in behalf of his Court."

The Lords Commissioners of the Admiralty.

Lord Grantham to the Earl of Rochford.

" *Madrid, January* 2, 1772.

" I HAVE received the honour of your Lordship's Despatch, containing the agreeable intelligence of the Restitution of Port Egmont and its Dependencies, with the due formalities. On receiving this notice I waited on the Marquis de Grimaldi, to assure him of His Majesty's satisfaction at the good faith and punctuality observed in this transaction. M. de Grimaldi seemed aware of the intention of my visit, and was almost beforehand with me in communicating notice of this event being known in England. He seemed well pleased at the conclusion of this affair, but entered no further into conversation upon it."

The Lords Commissioners of the Admiralty.   GRANTHAM.

The Lords of the Admiralty to the Earl of Rochford.

" *Admiralty Office, February* 15, 1772.

" HAVING received by the *Florida* Store-ship, lately arrived at Spithead, a Letter from Captain Burr, of His Majesty's Sloop the *Hound*, dated at Port Egmont, in Falkland Islands, the 10th of November last, giving an account that, in the preceding month, 2 Spanish Vessels had arrived there with the Artillery, Provisions, and Stores, which had been taken from thence by the Spaniards, and that he had received the same from a Commissary appointed by Don Felipe Ruiz Puente, to deliver them up to him; we send your Lordship herewith a Copy of Captain Burr's said Letter, together with a Copy of the Inventory of the Artillery, Provisions, and Stores, which he had received as aforesaid, for His Majesty's information.

The Earl of Rochford.

The Earl of Rochford to Lord Grantham.

"*St. James's, March* 6, 1772.

" IT may be of use to inform your Excellency, that His Majesty has determined to reduce the Force employed at Falkland Islands to a small sloop with about 50 Men, and 25 Marines on shore, which will answer the end of keeping the Possession: and, at the same time, ought to make the Court of Spain very easy as to our having any intention of making it a settlement of annoyance to them.

Lord Grantham. ROCHFORD.

The Earl of Rochford to Lord Grantham.

"*St. James's, February* 11, 1774.

"I THINK it proper to acquaint your Excellency that Lord North, in a Speech some days ago in the House of Commons, on the subject of the Naval Establishment for this year, mentioned the intention of reducing the Naval Forces in the East Indies, as a material object of diminishing the number of Seamen; and at the same time hinted, as a matter of small consequence, that, in order to avoid the expense of keeping any Seamen or Marines at Falkland Islands, they would be brought away, after leaving there the proper marks or signals of possession, and of its belonging to the Crown of Great Britain. As this measure was publicly declared in Parliament, it will naturally be reported to the Court of Spain; and though there is no necessity of your Excellency's communicating this Notice officially to the Spanish Ministers, since it is only a private regulation with regard to our own convenience; yet, as I am inclined to think, from what passed formerly upon this subject, that they will rather be pleased at this event, your Excellency may, if they mention it to you, freely avow it, without entering into any other reasonings thereon. It must strike your Excellency that this is likely to discourage them from suspecting designs, which they must now plainly see never entered into our minds. I hope they will not suspect, or suffer themselves to be made believe, that this was done at the request, or to gratify the most distant wish, of the French Court; for the truth is, that it is neither more nor less than a small part of an economical Naval regulation."

Lord Grantham. ROCHFORD.

M. Moreno will perceive that the above authentic Papers, which have been faithfully extracted from the Volumes of Correspondence with Spain, deposited in the State Paper Office, contain no allusion whatever to any Secret Understanding between the 2 Governments, at the period of the restoration of Port Egmont and its Dependencies to Great Britain, in 1771; nor to the evacuation of Falkland Islands, in 1774, as having taken place for the purpose of fulfilling any such

Understanding. On the contrary, it will be evident to M. Moreno, that their contents afford conclusive inference that no such Secret Understanding could have existed.

The Undersigned need scarcely assure M. Moreno, that the Correspondence which has been referred to, does not contain the least particle of evidence in support of the contrary supposition, entertained by the Government of the United Provinces of the Rio de la Plata, nor any confirmation of the several particulars related in M. Moreno's Note.

The Undersigned trusts, that a perusal of these details will satisfy M. Moreno, that the Protest which he has been directed to deliver to the Undersigned, against the re-assumption of the Sovereignty of the Falkland Islands by His Majesty, has been drawn up under an erroneous impression, as well of the understanding under which the Declaration and Counter-Declaration relative to the restoration of Port Egmont and its Dependencies were signed and exchanged between the 2 Courts, as of the motives which led to the temporary relinquishment of those Islands by the British Government; and the Undersigned cannot entertain a doubt but that, when the true circumstances of the case shall have been communicated to the knowledge of the Government of The United Provinces of the Rio de la Plata, that Government will no longer call in question the right of Sovereignty which has been exercised by His Majesty, as undoubtedly belonging to the Crown of Great Britain.

The Undersigned requests, &c.

M. Moreno.   PALMERSTON.

CHARLES L. WILLIAMS *vs.* THE SUFFOLK INSURANCE COMPANY.

The government of the United States having insisted, and continuing to insist, through its regular executive authority, that the Falkland islands do not constitute any part of the dominions within the sovereignty of Buenos Ayres, and that the seal fishery at those islands is a trade free and lawful to the citizens of the United States, and beyond the competency of the Buenos Ayres government to regulate, prohibit, or punish; it is not competent for a Circuit Court of the United States to inquire into, and ascertain by other evidence the title of the government of Buenos Ayres to the sovereignty of the Falkland islands.

When the executive branch of the government, which is charged with the foreign relations of the United States, shall, in its correspondence with a foreign nation, assume a fact in regard to the sovereignty of any island or country, it is conclusive on the judicial department.

Where a vessel, insured on a sealing voyage, was ordered by the government of Buenos Ayres not to catch seal off the Falkland islands, and having continued to take seal there the vessel was seized and condemned, under the authority of the government of Buenos Ayres; the government of the United States not having acknowledged, but having denied the right of Buenos Ayres to the Falkland islands; the insurers were liable to pay for the loss of the vessel and cargo: the master, in refusing to obey the orders to leave the island, having acted under a belief that he was bound so to do as a matter of duty to the owners, and all interested in the voyage, and in vindication of the right claimed by the American government. The master was not bound to abandon the voyage under a threat or warning of such illegal capture.

ON a certificate of division from the Circuit Court of the United States for the district of Massachusetts.

This was an action brought by the plaintiff, a citizen of the state of Connecticut, against the Suffolk Insurance Company of Boston, Massachusetts, to recover a loss, on part of the schooner Harriet, and part of her cargo, they having been insured by the defendants. There was a similar action against the defendants to recover losses sustained on the schooner Breakwater and her cargo. Both the cases were brought from the Circuit Court of Massachusetts, on certificates of division of opinion of the judges of the Circuit Court.

The cases were stated in the record as follows:—

" These were actions of assumpsit on policies of insurance, dated the 19th of August, 1830, whereby the plaintiff caused to be insured by the defendants for nine per cent. per annum premium, warranting twelve per cent. 'lost or not lost,' forty-nine hundred and nineteen dollars on fifteen sixteenths of schooner Harriet, and eighteen hundred and seventy-five dollars on board said vessel, at and from Stonington, Connecticut, commencing the risk on the 12th day of August, instant at noon, to the southern hemisphere, with liberty to stop for salt at the Cape de Verd islands, and to go round Cape Horn, and to touch at all islands, ports, and places for the purpose of taking seals, and for information and refreshments, with liberty to put his skins on board of any other vessel or vessels until she returns to her port of discharge in the United States; it being understood that the value of the interest hereby insured, as it relates to this insurance, is not to be diminished thereby. It is understood and agreed, that if the Harriet should not proceed south-easterly of

[Williams *vs.* The Suffolk Insurance Company.]

Cape Horn on a voyage towards the south Shetland islands, and there be no loss, then the premium is to be six per centum per annum, the assured warranting only nine. per cent.: vessel valued at five thousand dollars; outfits valued at two thousand dollars.

" There was a similar policy underwritten by the defendants for the plaintiff on the same day, for the like voyage in all respects, of thirty-five hundred dollars, on the schooner Breakwater, and two thousand dollars on outfits on board, at the same premium; the vessel being valued at thirty-five hundred dollars, and the outfits at two thousand dollars, upon which, also, an action was brought.

" The declaration upon each policy averred a total loss, by the seizure and detention of one Lewis Vernet and other persons, pretending to act by the authority of the government of Buenos Ayres, with force and arms.

" The causes came on to be heard together, by the Court, upon certain facts and statements agreed by the parties; the parties agreeing that the verdict should be rendered by the jury for the plaintiff, and for the defendants; according to the opinion of the Court upon the matters of law arising upon those facts and statements; and the cause was argued by C. G. Loring for the plaintiff, and by Theophilus Parsons for the defendants. It appeared from these facts and statements, that both of the vessels insured were bound on a sealing voyage, and proceeded to the Falkland islands in pursuance thereof; and were there both seized by one Lewis Vernet, acting as governor of those islands, under the appointment and authority of the government of Buenos Ayres. The Harriet was seized on the 30th of July, 1831, and was subsequently carried by the captors to Buenos Ayres; where certain proceedings were had against her in the tribunals, and under the sanction of the government of Buenos Ayres. She has never been restored to the defendants, but has been condemned for being engaged in the seal trade at the Falkland islands.

" The Breakwater was seized at the islands, on or about the 18th day of August, 1831, and was afterwards re-captured by the mate and crew, who remained on board; and was by them brought home to the United States; and after her arrival was libelled for salvage in the district Court of Connecticut district, and salvage was awarded of one-third part of the proceeds of vessel and property.

" Copies of the orders and decrees of the Courts of Buenos Ayres respecting the seal fisheries, of the appointment of Vernet as governor of the Falkland islands, of the proceedings against the Harriet, of the correspondence of the American government with the Buenos Ayrean government, relative to the jurisdiction of the Falkland islands; were produced and read, de bene esse, in the case."

The following points and questions occurred in the case, on which the judges of the Circuit Court were divided in opinion; and they were stated and ordered to be certified to the Supreme Court to be finally decided :—

[Williams *vs.* The Suffolk Insurance Company.]

1. Whether, inasmuch as the American government has insisted and does still insist, through its regular executive authority, that the Falkland islands do not constitute any part of the dominions within the sovereignty of the government of Buenos Ayres, and that the seal fishery at those islands is a trade free and lawful to the citizens of the United States, and beyond the competency of the Buenos Ayrean government to regulate, prohibit, or punish; it is competent for the Circuit Court in this cause, to inquire into and ascertain by other evidence, the title of said government of Buenos Ayres to the sovereignty of the said Falkland islands; and if such evidence satisfies the Court, to decide against the doctrines and claims set up and supported by the American government on this subject; or whether the action of the American government on this subject is binding and conclusive on this Court, as to whom the sovereignty of those islands belongs.

2. Whether, if the seizure of the Harriet, by the authority of the Buenos Ayrean government, for carrying on the seal fishery at the Falkland islands, was illegal and contrary to the law of nations, on account of the said islands not being within the territorial sovereignty of the said Buenos Ayrean government, and the master of the Harriet had warning from the government of the said islands under the government of Buenos Ayres, that he should seize the said Harriet if she should engage in the seal fishery, and after such warning, the master of the Harriet engaged in such seal fishery, and the Harriet was illegally seized and condemned therefor, the loss by such seizure and condemnation was a loss for which the plaintiff is entitled to recover in this case; if the master of the Harriet acted, in engaging in such seal fishery bona fide, and with a sound and reasonable discretion, and under a belief that he was bound so to do, as a matter of duty to his owners, and all others interested in the voyage, and in the vindication of the rights recognised and claimed by the American government; or whether he was bound by law to abandon the voyage under such a threat and warning of such illegal seizure.

The case was submitted to the Court by Messrs. C. G. Loring and E. G. Loring for the plaintiff; and by Mr. Parsons for the defendants.

The printed argument for the plaintiff contained a full statement of the case.

Mr. Parsons, for the defendants, contended,—

1. That the Malvinas are rightfully in possession of Buenos Ayres; and that historical evidence, and established principles of the law of nations show this to be so.

2. That however this may be, the Courts of this country will not decide this question against Buenos Ayres, unless authorised to do so by a formal act of our government: Buenos Ayres being a nation friendly to us, claiming the Malvinas, certainly under colour of right, and claiming and exercising that dominion for many years.

[Williams *vs.* The Suffolk Insurance Company.]

3. That there is no such act of our government. An American sloop of war, (the Lexington, captain Duncan,) arriving at Buenos Ayres, soon after the seizure of the Harriet and Breakwater, proceeded to the Falklands, and broke up the establishment by violence. The government of Buenos Ayres complained urgently of this, and a correspondence ensued, wherein our Consul, and our Charge d'Affaires at Buenos Ayres, and our Secretary of State, took a part; but the question remains unsettled between the countries;—and,

4. By the constitution of this country, it is of vital importance that our Courts call nothing an act of the government but one which passes through the forms of the Constitution, and has the force and sanction of regular enactment. No analogies drawn from European nations (if any there be) can apply; because the Judiciary holds no such place, and is intrusted with no such duties in other nations.

It would seem difficult to doubt, from the historical evidence, and the plain principles of territorial and international law, that the ancient government of Spain, and the government of Buenos Ayres as their successor, had a right, as owners of the islands and the coast, to regulate the fisheries thereon, and within a reasonable distance of their shores, and that the decrees actually passed are therefore justifiable by the laws of nations; and, consequently, fishing in violation of those decrees is an illicit and prohibited trading within the policy. It follows inevitably that a seizure for that cause is not protected by the policy, though the condemnation may be informal.

If it be said, that the trespassers upon these islands and their fisheries appear to have been notified and threatened before, and then permitted to transgress with impunity, and that punishment for the offence was therefore unlawful; there is surely an obvious and sufficient answer to this. It is, that after mild means had been carried so far as to prove them ineffectual, more positive measures were resorted to. This is a plain and fair statement of the whole case upon this point; and if the whole testimony were examined, and the indisputable facts of the case considered, they would fully confirm this view. Will the Court then say that forgiveness, with renewed prohibition and caution, implies perpetual forgiveness? That if the first offence, or any single offence, be pardoned by a nation, or one of its authorities, it shall never be lawful again to punish the offence; how often soever it be repeated, or howsoever aggravated the circumstances by which it is attended? It can hardly be expected that such a principle as this can receive the sanction of this Court; for it seems not more repugnant to law and justice, than to mere humanity.

Mr. Justice M'LEAN delivered the opinion of the Court:—

Two actions were commenced by the plaintiffs against the defendant, in the Circuit Court of the United States for the state of Massachusetts, on policies of insurance dated 19th August, 1830; whereby the plaintiffs caused to be insured by the defendants, for nine per centum per annum premium, warranting twelve per centum lost or not lost, forty-nine hundred and nineteen dollars on fifteen-sixteenths of schooner Harriet; and eighteen hundred and seventy-five dollars on board said vessel, at and from Stonington, Connecticut, commencing the risk on the 12th August instant at noon, to the southern hemisphere; with liberty to stop for salt at the Cape de Verd islands, and to go round Cape Horn, and to touch at all islands, ports and places, for the purpose of taking seals, and for information and refreshments; with liberty to put his skins on board of any other vessel or vessels, until she returns to her port of discharge in the United States: it being understood that the value of the interest hereby insured, as it relates to this insurance, is not to be diminished thereby, &c.

On the same day there was a similar policy of thirty-five hundred dollars on the schooner Breakwater; and two thousand dollars on outfits on board, at the same premium, &c.

And on the trial the following points were raised in the case, on which the opinions of the judges were opposed, and on which the case is certified to this Court.

1. Whether, inasmuch as the American government has insisted, and does still insist, through its regular executive authority, that the Falkland islands do not constitute any part of the dominions within the sovereignty of the government of Buenos Ayres; and that the seal fishery at those islands is a trade free and lawful to the citizens of the United States, and beyond the competency of the Buenos Ayres government to regulate, prohibit, or punish; it is competent for the Circuit Court in this cause, to inquire into, and ascertain by other evidence, the title of said government of Buenos Ayres to the sovereignty of the said Falkland islands; and if such evidence satisfies the Court, to decide against the doctrines and claims set up and supported by the American government on this subject: or whether the action of the American government on this subject is binding and conclusive on this Court, as to whom the sovereignty of those islands belongs.

2. Whether, if the seizure of the Harriet by the authority of the Buenos Ayrean government, for carrying on the seal fishery at the Falkland islands, was illegal and contrary to the law of nations, on account of the said islands not being within the territorial sovereignty of the said Buenos Ayrean government; and the master of the Harriet had warning from the governor of the said islands under the government of Buenos Ayres, that he should seize the said Harriet if she should engage in the seal fishery; and after such warning the master of the Harriet engaged in the seal fishery, and the Harriet was illegally seized and condemned therefor; the loss by such seizure and condemnation was a loss for which the plaintiff is entitled to recover in this case, if the master of the Harriet acted in engaging in such seal fishery bona fide, and with a sound and reasonable discretion, and under a belief that he was bound so to do as a matter of duty to his owners and all others interested in

[Williams *vs.* The Suffolk Insurance Company.]

the voyage; and in the vindication of the rights recognised and claimed by the American government: or whether he was bound by law to abandon the voyage under such a threat and warning of such illegal seizure.

As the fact is stated in the first point certified, that there is a controversy between this government and that of Buenos Ayres, whether the jurisdiction is rightful, which is assumed to be exercised over the Falkland islands by the latter; and that this right is asserted on the one side and denied by the other, it will not be necessary to look into the correspondence between the two governments on the subject.

To what sovereignty any island or country belongs, is a question which often arises before Courts in the exercise of a maritime jurisdiction; and also in actions on policies of insurance.

Prior to the revolution in South America, it is known that the Malvinas, or Falkland islands, were attached to the vice-royalty of La Plata, which included Buenos Ayres. And if this were an open question, we might inquire whether the jurisdiction over these islands did not belong to some other part, over which this ancient vice-royalty extended, and not to the government of Buenos Ayres: but we are saved from this inquiry by the attitude of our own government, as stated in the point certified.

And can there be any doubt, that when the executive branch of the government, which is charged with our foreign relations, shall in its correspondence with a foreign nation assume a fact in regard to the sovereignty of any island or country, it is conclusive on the judicial department? And in this view it is not material to inquire, nor is it the province of the Court to determine, whether the executive be right or wrong. It is enough to know, that in the exercise of his constitutional functions, he has decided the question. Having done this under the responsibilities which belong to him, it is obligatory on the people and government of the Union.

If this were not the rule, cases might often arise in which, on the most important questions of foreign jurisdiction, there would be an irreconcilable difference between the executive and judicial departments. By one of these departments, a foreign island or country might be considered as at peace with the United States; whilst the other would consider it in a state of war. No well regulated government has ever sanctioned a principle so unwise, and so destructive of national character.

In the cases of Foster *vs.* Neilson, 2 Peters, 253. 307, and Garcia *vs.* Lee, 12 Peters, 511, this Court have laid down the rule, that the action of the political branches of the government in a matter that belongs to them, is conclusive.

And we think in the present case, as the executive, in his message, and in his correspondence with the government of Buenos Ayres, has denied the jurisdiction which it has assumed to exercise over the Falkland islands; the fact must be taken and acted on by this Court as thus asserted and maintained.

[Williams *vs.* The Suffolk Insurance Company.]

The decision of the first point materially affects the second, which turns upon the conduct of the master.

If these islands are not within the jurisdiction of the Buenos Ayrean government, the power assumed and exercised by Governor Vernet was unauthorized, and the master was not bound to regard it. He was not necessarily to be diverted from the objects of his voyage, and the exercise of rights which belonged in common to the citizens of the United States by an unauthorized threat of the seizure of his vessel. He might well consider the prohibition of Vernet as influenced by personal and sinister motives, and would not be enforced. If the principle were admitted, that the assured were bound to regard every idle threat of any individual who might assume to exercise power, as in this case, it would be most injurious, and in many cases destructive, to commercial rights.

The inquiry is, whether the master, under all the circumstances of the case, acted in good faith, and with ordinary prudence.

If he acted fraudulently, he was guilty of barratry; and the underwriters are discharged.

In 4 Taunton, 858, Mr. Justice Gibbs, in giving the opinion of the Court, lays down the true rule. " The master," says he, " being asked why he had not British colours and British papers, said, I cannot have them, because I have not a British register. He stands on his strict rights. He says, I will do nothing to endanger my owners; I am a neutral, and I have a right to enter your port. The master really communicated the true facts of the case when she was searched; and says, I cannot go off, because of my charter-party. The other says: Then I will seize you. We think, then, each party stands on his strict rights; and we are now to consider the strict point of law, not the question whether it would have been more prudent for him to go to Tercera, but whether he acted bona fide."

And so in the present case, the question is not whether the master of the Harriet would not have acted with more prudence had he yielded to the inhibition of Vernet; but whether, in placing himself upon his strict rights, he did not exercise a proper discretion.

He violated no regulation which he was bound to respect. In touching at the Falkland islands, for the purpose of taking seal, he acted strictly within the limits of his commercial enterprise; and did not voluntarily incur a risk which should exonerate the insurers.

It was the duty of the master to prosecute his voyage, and attain the objects of it, for the benefit of his owners: and, in doing this, he was not bound to abandon the voyage by any threat of illegal seizure. We think, therefore, that the underwriters are not discharged from liability, by the conduct of the master, as stated in the second point.

The other case depending upon the same principles, the same certificate will be affixed to that case.

This cause came on to be heard on the transcript of the record from the Circuit Court of the United States, for the district of Mas-

[Williams *vs.* The Suffolk Insurance Company.]

sachusetts, and on the points and questions on which the judges of
the said Circuit Court were opposed in opinion, and which were
certified to this Court for its opinion, agreeably to the act of Congress in such case made and provided, and was argued by counsel.
On consideration whereof, it is the opinion of this Court, 1st, That,
inasmuch as the American government has insisted and still does
insist, through its regular executive authority, that the Falkland islands do not constitute any part of the dominions within the sovereignty of the government of Buenos Ayres, the action of the American government on this subject is binding on the said Circuit Court,
as to whom the sovereignty of those islands belongs. And, secondly:
That the seizure and condemnation of the Harriet was a loss for
which the plaintiff is entitled to recover in this case, under the circumstances as stated in the second point certified. Whereupon, it
is ordered and adjudged by this Court, that it be so certified to the
said Circuit Court, accordingly.

Case No. 3,661.

DAVISON v. SEAL-SKINS.

[2 Paine, 324.][1]

Circuit Court, D. Connecticut. 1835.

SALVAGE — PROPERTY RESCUED FROM PIRATES — "PIRACY" DEFINED — ADMIRALTY JURISDICTION — SEIZURE BY UNITED STATES OFFICER IN FOREIGN TERRITORY — ADMIRALTY APPEALS.

1. Salvage is demandable, of right, upon property taken from pirates. But to entitle a party to salvage in such case, the taking must have been lawful and meritorious.

2. A pirate is one who acts solely on his own authority, without any commission or authority, from a sovereign state, seizing by force, and appropriating to himself without discrimination, every vessel he meets with.

[Cited in Dole v. New England Mut. Marine Ins. Co., Case No. 3,966; The Ambrose Light, 25 Fed. 423.]

3. Robbery on the high seas is piracy. But to constitute the offence the taking must be felonious; and the quo animo may be inquired into.

[Cited in The Ambrose Light, 25 Fed. 426.]

4. If a court of admiralty has cognizance of the principal thing, it has also of the incident, though that incident would not, of itself and if it stood alone, be within the admiralty jurisdiction. Therefore, in the case of a piratical taking, the court may have jurisdiction, although the retaking was upon land. And for the same reason, goods taken by pirates and sold upon land, may be recovered from the vendee, by suit in the admiralty.

5. An officer of the United States has no right, without express directions from his government, to enter the territorial jurisdiction of a country at peace with the United States, and forcibly seize upon property found there, and claimed by citizens of the United States. Application for redress should be made to the judicial tribunals of the country.

6. Where D., an officer of the United States, without the direction of his government, seized property at the Falkland Islands, claimed by citizens of the United States, and which it was alleged had been piratically taken by one V., who pretended to be governor of the Falkland Islands under the government of Buenos Ayres, and it was proved that V. was not acting on his own authority but under a commission from the government of Buenos Ayres, it was *held* that the seizure of the property by D. being unlawful, a claim for salvage by A. for personal services bestowed upon the property after it was delivered over to him by D., could not be sustained.

7. Where the evidence is conflicting, and it is doubtful on which side it preponderates, the decree of the court below will not be disturbed on the ground that it is against evidence.

[Cited in The Maggie P., 25 Fed. 206.]

THOMPSON, Circuit Justice. This case comes up on appeal from a decree of the district court of the United States for the dis-

[1] [Reported by Elijah Paine, Jr., Esq.]

trict of Connecticut. This libel filed in the case is for salvage upon a quantity of seal-skins, alleged to have been saved and rescued from the unlawful and piratical capture of Lewis Vernet, at Port St. Lewis, in the Eastern Falkland Island, on the 19th of August, in the year 1831. The libel alleges the skins to have been taken from on board the schooner Superior, Congdon, master, by the said Vernet; who was wrongfully and unlawfully pretending and claiming to be governor of the Falkland Islands, under the government of Buenos Ayres, and landed and put into a store-house. Salvage is also claimed upon a quantity of seal-skins, alleged to have been taken in like manner from a boat's crew, commanded by Isaac P. Waldron, and put into the same store. The libellant [Gilbert R. Davison] states that he was carried a prisoner on board the schooner Harriet, to Buenos Ayres, where he arrived on the 20th of November, when he was liberated; and on the 1st of December he shipped as second sailing-master on board the Lexington, a sloop-of-war of the United States, commanded by Captain Duncan, and sailed for Port Lewis, and arrived there on the 27th of December, and sent a boat on shore and took the skins from the store-house, and broke up Vernet's establishment there: that he obtained a discharge as sailing-master, for the sole purpose of saving the skins for the rightful owner. The skins having been delivered by Captain Duncan to him, were put on board the schooner Dash, on the 5th day of January, 1832, and were afterwards transhipped to the schooner Carrier, of Stonington, John S. Barnum, master; who signed a bill of lading for 790 prime fur, and 401 pup-skins, consigned to Thomas Davison. The Carrier arrived at Stonington on the 15th of April, 1833. And the salvage claimed is for the personal services of the libellant, bestowed upon the skins after they were delivered over to him by Captain Duncan. The skins by order of the district court, were sold by the marshal of the district, and the money brought into court, and a claim for the proceeds was filed by Silas E. Burrows, as owner of the schooner Superior, and her cargo.

Isaac P. Waldron, in behalf of the boat's crew mentioned in the libel, or under the right of purchase made from them, filed a claim for a portion of the skins. The freight of the skins having been ordered to be paid out of the proceeds, the court decreed against the claim of the libellant for salvage; and after deducting the costs, that $704.52 should be paid to Isaac P. Waldron on his claim, and the remainder of the proceeds to be paid to Silas E. Burrows on his claim. From this decree the libellant and Burrows have severally filed an appeal; and the questions which arise under this appeal, relate, in the first place, to the claim for salvage, and, in the next place, to the respective proportions of Burrows and Waldron to these proceeds.

The right to salvage in this case has been placed on the ground that the taking was piratical,[2] and gave a legal right to any person to retake, and claim a compensation for all meritorious and beneficial services rendered in saving the property. There can be no doubt that salvage is demandable of right upon property taken from pirates; and if the taking, in this case, by Vernet, is to be deemed piratical, the claim for salvage may be maintained; but to entitle a party to salvage, two circumstances must concur. The service rendered must be in a lawful taking of the property, and must be meritorious and useful. The taking must be lawful; for no claim can be maintained in a court of justice, founded on an act in itself tortious. It has, accordingly, been held, that as a recapture made by a neutral power, no claim for salvage can arise, although the beneficial service rendered may be the same as if the recapture had been by a belligerent; but the act of taking by the neutral being unlawful, no right can arise from an act in itself unlawful. [Talbot v. Seeman] 1 Cranch [5 U. S.] 28. Robbery on the high seas is understood to be piracy by our law. The taking must be felonious. A commissioned cruiser, by exceeding his authority, is not thereby to be considered a pirate. It may be a marine trespass, but not an act of piracy, if the vessel is taken as a prize, unless taken feloniously, and with intent to commit a robbery; the quo animo may be inquired into. [U. S. v. Pirates] 5 Wheat. [18 U. S.] 184; U. S. v. Jones [Case No. 15,494]. A pirate is one who acts solely on his own authority, without any commission or authority from a sovereign state, seizing by force, and appropriating to himself, without discrimination, every vessel

---

[2] By article 1, § 8, of the constitution of the United States, congress have power to define and punish piracies and felonies committed on the high seas, and offences against the law of nations. If any person commit, upon the high seas, or in any river, haven, basin or bay, out of the jurisdiction of any particular state, murder or robbery, or any other offence, which, if committed within the body of a county, would, by the laws of the United States, be punishable with death; or if any captain or mariner of any vessel, shall piratically and feloniously run away with such vessel, or any goods or merchandise to the value of fifty dollars, or yield up such vessel voluntarily to a pirate; or if any seaman shall lay violent hands upon his commander, thereby to hinder and prevent his fighting in defence of his ship, or goods committed to his trust, or shall make a revolt in the ship, every such offender shall be deemed, taken, and adjudged to be a pirate and felon, and being thereof convicted shall suffer death; and the trial of crimes committed on the high seas, or in any place out of the jurisdiction of any particular state, shall be in the district where the offender is apprehended, or into which he may be brought. Act 30th April, 1790, § 8 [1 Stat. 113]. If any citizen shall commit any piracy or robbery aforesaid, or any act of hostility against the United States, or any citizen thereof, upon the high sea, under color of any commission from any foreign prince or state, or on pretence of authority from any person, such offender shall, notwithstanding the pretence of any such authority, be deemed, adjudged and taken to be a pirate, felon, and robber, and on being convicted thereof, shall suffer death. Id. § 9.

Every person who shall, either upon the land or the seas, knowingly and willingly aid and assist, procure, command, counsel, or advise any person to do or commit any murder or robbery, or other piracy aforesaid, upon the seas, which shall affect the life of such person, and such person shall thereupon do or commit any such piracy or robbery, then every such person so as aforesaid aiding, assisting, procuring, commanding, counselling, or advising the same, either upon the land or the seas, shall be, and they are hereby declared, deemed and adjudged to be accessory to such piracies, before the fact, and every such person, being thereof convicted, shall suffer death. Act 30th April, 1790, § 10. After any murder, felony, robbery, or other piracy whatsoever aforesaid, is or shall be committed by any pirate or robber, every person who, knowing that such pirate or robber has done or committed any such piracy or robbery, shall, on the land or at sea, receive, entertain, or conceal any such pirate or robber, or receive or take into his custody any vessel, goods or chattels, which have been by any such pirate or robber piratically and feloniously taken, shall be, and are hereby declared, deemed and adjudged to be accessory to such piracy or robbery after the fact, and on conviction thereof, shall be imprisoned not exceeding three years, and fined, not exceeding five hundred dollars. Id. § 11. If any person shall, upon the high seas, or in any open roadstead, or in any haven, basin or bay, or in any river where the sea ebbs and flows, commit the crime of robbery, in or upon any vessel, or upon any of the ship's company of any vessel, or the lading thereof, such person shall be adjudged to be a pirate; and being thereof convicted before a circuit court of the United States for the district into which he shall be brought, or in which he shall be found, shall suffer death. Act 15th May, 1820, § 3 [3 Stat. 600]. And if any person engaged in any piratical cruise or enterprise, or being of the crew or ship's company of any piratical vessel, shall land from such vessel, and on shore shall commit robbery, such person shall be adjudged a pirate, and on conviction thereof before a circuit court of the United States for the district into which he shall be brought, or in which he shall be found, shall suffer death. Provided, that nothing in this section contained shall be construed to deprive any particular state of its jurisdiction over such offences, when committed within the body of a county, or authorize the courts of the United States to try any such offenders, after conviction or acquittance, for the same offense in a state court. Id. § 3. If any citizen of the United States, being of the crew or ship's company of any foreign vessel engaged in the slave trade, or any person whatever, being of the crew or ship's company of any vessel owned in whole or in part, or navigated for, or in behalf of any citizen or citizens of the United States, shall land from any such vessel, and on any foreign shore seize any negro or mulatto, not held to service or labor by the laws of either of the states or territories of the United States, with intent to make such negro or mulatto a slave, or shall decoy, or forcibly bring or carry, or shall receive such negro or mulatto on board any such vessel, with intent as aforesaid, such citizen or person shall be adjudged a pirate, and on conviction thereof before the circuit court of the United States for the district wherein he may be brought or found, shall suffer death. Id. § 4. If any citizen of the United States, being of the crew or ship's company of any foreign vessel engaged in the slave trade, or any person whatever, being of the crew or ship's company

he meets with; and hence pirates have always been compared to robbers. The only difference between them is, that the sea is the theatre of action for the one, and the land for the other. 2 Arun. 351. Although the retaking in this case was upon land, yet if it was a piratical taking, the court might have had jurisdiction; for if the admiralty has cognizance of the principal thing, it has also of the incident, though that incident would not, of itself, and if it stood for a principal thing, be within the admiralty jurisdiction: and upon this principle it is, that goods taken by pirates and sold upon land, may be recovered from the vendee by suit in the admiralty. 1 Kent, Comm. 353. In this view of the case, it becomes proper to inquire into the situation and capacity in which Vernet was acting, and as connected therewith, the territorial government and jurisdiction of the Falkland Islands; and

it is very clear, from the evidence in the case, that he was not then acting on his own authority, but under a commission from the government of Buenos Ayres, claiming to exercise jurisdiction over the Falkland Islands.

Mr. Slocum, in his letter to the minister of foreign affairs, dated 21st November, 1831, complaining of the conduct of Vernet, asks whether the government of Buenos Ayres intends to avow and sustain the capture. The minister of foreign affairs, in his reply of November 25, informs him that the subject was under the consideration of the government, which would adopt such decision as the laws of the country required; which Mr. Slocum, by his letter of the 26th of November, informs the minister that he cannot consider the answer in any other light than as an express admission, on the part of his government, of the right to capture American vessels fishing for seals at the Falkland Is-

---

of any vessel, owned wholly or in part, or navigated for or in behalf of any citizen or citizens of the United States, shall forcibly confine, or detain, or aid and abet in forcibly confining or detaining on board such vessel, any negro or mulatto, not held to service by the laws of either of the states or territories of the United States, with intent to make such negro or mulatto a slave, or shall, on board any such vessel, offer or attempt to sell as a slave, any negro or mulatto, not held in service as aforesaid, or shall, on the high seas, or anywhere on tide-water, transfer or deliver over to any other vessel, any negro or mulatto, not held to service as aforesaid, with intent to make such negro or mulatto a slave, or shall land or deliver on shore from on board any such vessel, any such negro or mulatto, with intent to make sale of, or having previously sold, such negro or mulatto as a slave, such citizen or person shall be adjudged a pirate, and on conviction thereof, before the circuit court of the United States for the district wherein he shall be brought or found, shall suffer death. Id. § 5.

The president of the United States is authorized and requested to employ so many of the public armed vessels as in his judgment the service may require, with suitable instructions to the commanders thereof, in protecting the merchant vessels of the United States, and their crews from piratical aggressions and depredations. The president of the United States is authorized to instruct the commanders of the public armed vessels of the United States, to subdue, seize, take, and send into any port of the United States, any armed vessel or boat, or any vessel or boat, the crew whereof shall be armed, and which shall have attempted or committed any piratical aggression, search, restraint, depredation, or seizure, upon any vessel of the United States, or of the citizens thereof, or upon any other vessel: and also to retake any vessel of the United States, or its citizens, which may have been unlawfully captured upon the high seas. Act 3d March, 1819, § 1 [3 Stat. 511]. The commander and crew of any merchant vessel of the United States, owned wholly or in part by a citizen thereof, may oppose and defend against any aggression, search, restraint, depredation or seizure, which shall be attempted upon such vessel, or upon any other vessel owned as aforesaid by the commander or crew of any armed vessel whatsoever, not being a public armed vessel of some nation in amity with the United States; and may subdue and capture the same; and may also retake any vessel owned as aforesaid, which may have been captured by the commander or crew of any such armed vessel, and send the same into any port

of the United States. Id. § 3. Whenever any vessel or boat, from which any piratical aggression, search, restraint, depredation or seizure, shall have been first attempted or made, shall be captured and brought into any port of the United States, the same shall and may be adjudged and condemned to their use, and that of the captors, after due process and trial, in any court having admiralty jurisdiction, and which shall be holden for the district into which such captured vessel shall be brought; and the same court shall thereupon order a sale and distribution thereof accordingly, and at their discretion. Id. § 4. If any seaman or other person shall commit manslaughter upon the high seas, or confederate, or attempt or endeavor to corrupt any commander, master, officer or mariner, to yield up or to run away with any vessel, or with any goods, or turn pirate, or to go over to or confederate with pirates, or in anywise trade with any pirate, knowing him to be such, or shall furnish such pirate with any ammunition, stores or provisions of any kind, or shall fit out any vessel knowingly and with a design to trade with or supply or correspond with any pirate or robber upon the seas; or if any person shall any ways consult, combine, confederate or correspond with any pirate or robber on the seas, knowing him to be guilty of any such piracy or robbery; or if any seaman shall confine the master of any vessel, or endeavor to make a revolt in such vessel: such person so offending, and being thereof convicted, shall be imprisoned not exceeding three years, and fined not exceeding one thousand dollars. Act 30th April, 1790, § 12. By the common law, piracy consists in committing upon the high seas, or elsewhere within the jurisdiction of the admiralty, such acts of robbery and depredation, as if committed on land, would have amounted to felony there. The admiralty jurisdiction does not extend in general to any offence done infra corpus comitatus. All rivers in England till they flow past the furthest point of land next the sea, are infra corpus comitatus. As to havens, creeks and arms of the sea, where the sea flows in between two points, a straight imaginary line being drawn from one point to the other, the courts of common law have jurisdiction of all offences committed within that line, as being infra corpus comitatus. It would seem, however, to be infra corpus comitatus, one must be able to see with the naked eye from one side of the creek, &c., to the other. The admiralty has exclusive jurisdiction on the coasts beyond low-water mark. And between low and high-water mark, the admiralty has jurisdiction if the offence be done upon the high water when the tide is in, and the courts of

lands, and then proceeds to deny in toto the right of Buenos Ayres to prohibit the Americans from taking seals, and protests against all acts which have been adopted by the government for that purpose, including the decree of the 10th of June, 1829, by which the said islands and coasts, and their fisheries, are declared to belong to that government; and protests against all acts of the government asserting any such right. And Capt. Duncan, in his letter of the 1st of December, admits that the captures or services by Vernet were made under the authority of that government. He, therefore, before he sailed on the expedition against the Falkland Islands, understood that Vernet was acting under the authority of the government of Buenos Ayres; and the proclamation of the 14th of February, 1832, shows the light in which the conduct of Capt. Duncan was considered. It charges him with having

invaded that rising colony, and destroying the public property, and carrying away goods legally deposited there for judicial inquiry: and Capt. Duncan, after he had broken up the establishment, and taken as prisoners all the persons found there, writes to the minister of foreign affairs that he would deliver up and set at liberty the prisoners on board the Lexington, on assurance being given by the Buenos Ayrean government that they had been acting under its authority; and the minister, in his answer of the 15th of February, 1832, expressly declares, that Vernet was appointed political and military governor of the Falkland Islands, in consequence of the decree of the 1st of June, 1829, published on the 10th of the same month; and that Vernet, and the individuals acting under his authority, could only be judged of by their own government. Here was a full and complete sanction, by the government of Buenos

---

common law, if done on the strand when the tide is out. In cases purely dependent on the locality of the act done, the admiralty jurisdiction is limited to the sea, and to the tide-water as far as the tide flows. See Lewis, Cr. Law, p. 461, and cases there cited.

In England, in a case at the admiralty session, of a murder committed in a part of Milford Haven, where it was about three miles over, about seven or eight miles from the mouth of the river, or open sea, and about sixteen miles below any bridges over the river, a question was made whether the place where the murder was committed, was to be considered as within the limits to which commission granted under St. 28 Hen. VIII. c. 15, do by law extend. Upon reference to the judges, they were unanimously of opinion that the trial was properly had. And it is said that during the discussion of the point, the construction of this statute by Lord Hale (2 Hale, P. C. 16, 17) was much preferred to the doctrine of Lord Coke (3 Inst. 111); and that most, if not all of the judges, seem to think that the common law has a concurrent jurisdiction with the admiralty in this haven, and in all other havens, creeks and rivers in this realm. Brace's Case, 2 Leach, 1093. It appeared to them that 28 Hen. VIII. applied to all great waters frequented by ships; that in such waters the admiral, in the time of Henry VIII., pretended jurisdiction; that by havens, &c., havens in England were meant to be included, though they are all within the body of some county; and that the mischief from the witnesses being seafaring men was likely to apply to all places frequented by ships. MS. Bayley, J. If a robbery be committed in creeks, harbors, ports, &c., in foreign countries, the court of admiralty indisputably has jurisdiction of it, and such offence is, consequently, piracy. Rex v. Jemot, Old Bailey, 28th Feb. 1812. It is clear that upon the open sea-shore the common law and the admiralty have alternate jurisdiction between high and low-water mark (3 Inst. 113); but it is sometimes a matter of difficulty to fix the line of demarcation between the county and the high sea in harbors, or below the bridges in great rivers. The question is often more a matter of fact than of law, and determinable by local evidence; but some general rules upon the point are collected by Mr. East. He says, that "in general it is said that such parts of the rivers, arms or creeks, are deemed to be within the bodies of counties, where persons can see from one side to the other. Lord Hale, in his treatise De Jure Maris, says, that the arm or branch of the sea which lies within the fauces terrae, where a man may reasonably discern between shore and shore, is, or at least may be,

within the body of a county. Hawkins, however, considers the line more accurately confined, by other authorities, to such parts of the sea where a man, standing on the one side of the land, may see what is done on the other: and the reason assigned by Lord Coke in the admiralty case (13 Coke, 52), in support of the county coroner's jurisdiction, where a man is killed in such places, because that the county may well know it, seems rather to support the more limited construction. But at least, where there is any doubt, the jurisdiction of the common law ought to be preferred." 2 East, P. C. c. 17, § 10, pp. 803, 804.

The question, whether the act was committed on the sea, or within the body of a county, is of main importance. For if it turn out that the goods were taken anywhere within the body of a county, the commissioners under St. Hen. VIII., can have no jurisdiction to inquire of it; and if it should appear that the goods were taken at sea and afterwards brought on shore, the offender cannot be indicted as for a larceny in that county into which they were carried, because the original felony was not a taking of which the common law takes cognizance. 2 East, P. C. c. 17, § 12, p. 805. And St. 39, Geo. III. c. 37, relates only to offences committed on the high seas, and out of the body of any county. Where a man was indicted for stealing three chests of tea out of the Aurora, of London, on the high seas, and it was proved that the larceny was committed while the vessel lay off Wampa, in the river, twenty or thirty miles from the sea, but there was no evidence as to the tide flowing, or otherwise, at the place where the vessel lay, it was held, from the circumstance, that the tea was stolen on board the vessel, which had crossed the ocean, that there was sufficient evidence that the larceny was committed on the high seas. Rex v. Allen, R. & M. C. C. R. 494. It was decided that where A., standing on the shore of a harbor, fired a loaded musket at a revenue cutter, which had struck upon a sand-bank in the sea, about one hundred yards from the shore, by which firing a person was maliciously killed on board the vessel, it was piracy; for the offence was committed where the death happened, and not at the place from whence the cause of death proceeded. 1 Hawk. P. C. c. 37, § 17. And if a man be struck upon the high sea, and die upon the shore after the reflux of the water, the admiral by virtue of his commission, has no cognizance of the offence. 2 Hale, P. C. 17, 20. And as it was doubtful whether it could be tried at common law, it was provided by statute that the offender may be tried in the county where the death stroke, poisoning, or hurt happened.

Ayres, of the acts of Vernet: and Commodore Rodgers, in his letter of the 24th of April, 1832, to the minister of foreign affairs, on the subject of Capt. Duncan's conduct, says that he, (Capt. Duncan,) previous to his departure, wished to ascertain whether the persons alluded to acted under the authority of the government of Buenos Ayres; but not being able to obtain any official declaration upon the subject, he believed that he was justified in considering them as acting without authority, and in treating them as pirates; but that as the government had since officially declared, that the establishment at the Falkland Islands was under its special protection, and that the individuals in charge of it acted under its special authority, he considered the government responsible for the improper conduct of its agents, and that the persons arrested by Capt. Duncan were no longer responsible (except to their own government) for their outrages. He should, accordingly, set them at liberty; and he declares that he acts in this measure without instructions from his government; that it is not his intention to discuss the question pending between the two governments. This he should leave to the agent duly authorized to treat upon that matter, and who, it is expected, would shortly arrive at Buenos Ayres. From this correspondence thus far, it is evident that Capt. Duncan, when he went to the Falkland Islands, and broke up Vernet's establishment, was under the impression that they were a nest of pirates; and that Commodore Rodgers, as soon as he found this to be a mistake, but that they were acting under the authority of the Buenos Ayrean government, discharged the prisoners, disclaiming to hold them as pirates: and there is no pretence, in any of this correspondence, that Capt. Duncan, in this particular act, was pursuing any special order of the government of the United States; but he was, no doubt, acting in good faith, under what he considered his duty, in protecting the rights of American citizens.

I do not mean to enter into the question whether or not American citizens had a right to take seals upon the Falkland Islands: that was a disputed question between our government and that of Buenos Ayres. But if these islands were held in the possession and under the jurisdiction of the Buenos Ayrean government, and Vernet's establishment then was under the authority and protection of that government, as it clearly was, and even admitting that Vernet had abused his power, Captain Duncan could have no right, without express directions from his government, to enter into the territorial jurisdiction of a country at peace with the United States, and forcibly seize upon property found there and claimed by citizens of the United States. Such a principle would be too hazardous to the peace of nations to be admitted in practice. If the seizure of these skins by Vernet was wrongful, and a violation of the rights of American citizens, the presumption is. that on application to the judicial tribunals of Buenos Ayres, there would have been a restoration of the property; and if that, and all appeal to the government, should fail of redress it might become a case for the interference of the government of the injured party, and might ultimately lead to a just war. Such, according to the law of nations, would be the course to be adopted toward the citizens or subjects and the government of every sovereign power; and the weakness or strength of such power does not alter the principle. And this would seem to have been the understanding of the libellant himself, by the contract he entered into with Vernet, relative to the appeal to the tribunals of Buenos Ayres, for the trial of the right of seizure by Vernet, of the Harriet and Superior; and the employment of the Superior in sealing, until the determination and result of such trial should be known. This was an arrangement beneficial to all parties, and is not at all consistent with the charge that it was a piratical capture. I can discover nothing in the evidence to warrant the conclusion that this contract was forced upon the libellant and Captain Congar, by Vernet. It purports to have been entered into at the instance of these captains; and I see no reason to conclude that the trial would not have been proceeded in had not the property been retaken, and the whole establishment broken up by Captain Duncan, which the government of Buenos Ayres considered a gross violation of their rights. This right of taking seals (or fishery as it is called, though, perhaps, not strictly proper, as the seals are taken on shore) at the Falkland Islands, was then under discussion between our government and that of Buenos Ayres, as would appear by the letter of the secretary of state to Mr. Forbes, of the date of 10th of February, 1831, in which he says it is the wish of the president that you should address an earnest remonstrance to that government against any measures that may have been taken by it, including the decree and circular letter referred to, if they be genuine, which are calculated in the remotest degree to impose any restraint whatever upon the enterprise of our citizens engaged in the fisheries in question (the taking seal at the Falkland Islands), or to impair their undoubted right to the freest use of them. But notwithstanding this strong language on the part of our government, it did not undertake to pronounce this a piratical establishment, or to direct our public vessels to proceed there and break it up; but was negotiating on the question. Our government must have been fully apprized of the course pursued by the government of Buenos Ayres; for the decree referred to in this letter was undoubtedly the decree under which Vernet was acting. And that decree, which bears date on the 10th of June, 1829, in terms declares, that the Falkland Islands shall be governed by a military and civil governor, to be appointed by the government of the republic, and whose residence should be on the island of Solidad, and that he should see to the regulations of the fisheries on that coast. And our secretary of state, in a letter of 29th of October, 1836, in answer to the inquiry whether our government had formally declared that it did not recognize the claims of the republic of Buenos Ayres to the jurisdiction of the Falkland Islands, says: "Measures were taken by my predecessor to ascertain on what foundation the claim of jurisdiction to these islands rested; but the sickness and death of Mr. Forbes, our charge d'affaires at Buenos Ayres, had for a time interrupted the investigation. Our right of fishery, however, in those seas, is one that the government considers indisputable, and it will be given in charge to the minister about to be sent there, to make representations against and demand satisfaction for all interruptions of the exercise of that right." Thus our government, four years after the seizure of the Superior, and, as must be presumed, with full knowledge of the fact, treated this right as a subject for negotiation between the two governments, and does not undertake to affirm such seizure to be a piratical act. And under this view of the case, I cannot consider the retaking by Captain Duncan a lawful act; and unless it was so, the claim of the libellant to compensation as for salvage services, in a court of admiralty, cannot be sustained. I do not, therefore, enter into the inquiry whether any meritorious and beneficial services have been rendered by the libellant. If any have been rendered, which in law entitles him to compensation, his redress must be sought in a court of common law, and not in a court of admiralty. The appeal of the libellant must, therefore, be dismissed.

I have not been able to arrive at so satisfactory a conclusion in relation to the distribution of the proceeds of the skins, as between Mr. Burrows and Captain Waldron. It is not denied but that all the skins taken on board the Superior belonged to Mr. Burrows; nor is it denied but that Captain Waldron was the owner of the skins taken from the boat's crew of the Belville, he having purchased the rights of the other part owners; and it is very satisfactorily established that all these skins were put into the same storehouse at Port Lewis. But the doubt arises from the difficulty of ascertaining whether the whole of the skins taken from the boat's crew were shipped on board the Thomas Lowry and sent to London, or whether a part remained, and were taken away by Captain Duncan.

The evidence upon this part of the case is certainly very contradictory in several respects, and cannot be reconciled. Vernet swears that the skins taken from the boat's crew were put separately in the store-house, and were all put on board the Thomas Lowry. In this he is contradicted by several witnesses, who swear that these skins were stored promiscuously in the store-house with the skins of the Harriet and Superior, and that the skins shipped on board the Lowry were selected from the aggregate quantity. Under this view of the case, it cannot with any satisfactory certainty be said on which side the evidence preponderates, so as at all events to justify an appellate court on this ground to disturb the decree of the court below. I am, accordingly, of opinion that the decree of the district court be affirmed.

1514 (XV). Declaration on the granting of independence to colonial countries and peoples

The General Assembly,

Mindful of the determination proclaimed by the peoples of the world in the Charter of the United Nations to reaffirm faith in fundamental human rights, in the dignity and worth of the human person, in the equal rights of men and women and of nations large and small and to promote social progress and better standards of life in larger freedom,

Conscious of the need for the creation of conditions of stability and well-being and peaceful and friendly relations based on respect for the principles of equal rights and self-determination of all peoples, and of universal respect for, and observance of, human rights and fundamental freedoms for all without distinction as to race, sex, language or religion,

Recognizing the passionate yearning for freedom in all dependent peoples and the decisive role of such peoples in the attainment of their independence,

Aware of the increasing conflicts resulting from the denial of or impediments in the way of the freedom of such peoples, which constitute a serious threat to world peace,

Considering the important role of the United Nations in assisting the movement for independence in Trust and Non-Self-Governing Territories,

Recognizing that the peoples of the world ardently desire the end of colonialism in all its manifestations,

Convinced that the continued existence of colonialism prevents the development of international economic co-operation, impedes the social, cultural and economic development of dependent peoples and militates against the United Nations ideal of universal peace,

Affirming that peoples may, for their own ends, freely dispose of their natural wealth and resources without prejudice to any obligations arising out of international economic co-operation, based upon the principle of mutual benefit, and international law,

Believing that the process of liberation is irresistible and irreversible and that, in order to avoid serious crises, an end must be put to colonialism and all practices of segregation and discrimination associated therewith,

Welcoming the emergence in recent years of a large number of dependent territories into freedom and independence, and recognizing the increasingly powerful trends towards freedom in such territories which have not yet attained independence,

Convinced that all peoples have an inalienable right to complete freedom, the exercise of their sovereignty and the integrity of their national territory,

Solemnly proclaims the necessity of bringing to a speedy and unconditional end colonialism in all its forms and manifestations;

And to this end

Declares that:

1. The subjection of peoples to alien subjugation, domination and exploitation constitutes a denial of fundamental human rights, is contrary to the Charter of the United Nations and is an impediment to the promotion of world peace and co-operation.

2. All peoples have the right to self-determination; by virtue of that right they freely determine their political status and freely pursue their economic, social and cultural development.

3. Inadequacy of political, economic, social or educational preparedness should never serve as a pretext for delaying independence.

4. All armed action or repressive measures of all kinds directed against dependent peoples shall cease in order to enable them to exercise peacefully and freely their right to complete independence, and the integrity of their national territory shall be respected.

5. Immediate steps shall be taken, in Trust and Non-Self-Governing Territories or all other territories which have not yet attained independence, to transfer all powers to the peoples of those territories, without any conditions or reservations, in accordance with their freely expressed will and desire, without any distinction as to race, creed or colour, in order to enable them to enjoy complete independence and freedom.

6. Any attempt aimed at the partial or total disruption of the national unity and the territorial integrity of a country is incompatible with the purposes and principles of the Charter of the United Nations.

7. All States shall observe faithfully and strictly the provisions of the Charter of the United Nations, the Universal Declaration of Human Rights and the present Declaration on the basis of equality, non-interference in the internal affairs of all States, and respect for the sovereign rights of all peoples and their territorial integrity.

947th plenary meeting,
14 December 1960.

---

[36] *Official Records of the General Assembly, Fifteenth Session, Supplement No. 2* (A/4494).

MALVIÑAS ISLANDS

STATEMENT BY THE REPRESENTATIVE OF ARGENTINA,

H. E. Dr. JOSE MARIA RUDA,

BEFORE THE SUBCOMMITTEE III OF THE SPECIAL COMMITTEE
ON THE SITUATION WITH REGARD TO THE IMPLEMENTATION
OF THE DECLARATION ON THE GRANTING OF INDEPENDENCE
TO COLONIAL COUNTRIES AND PEOPLES

New York, September 9, 1964

Mr. President:

The Argentine Delegation must first thank the members of this Sub-Committee III for vouchsafing us the opportunity of making known our position regarding the problem of the Malvinas Islands.

We come to this Sub-Committee to reaffirm again the irrenounceable and imprescriptible rights of the Argentine Republic, to the Malvinas Islands. The Malvinas are a part of the Territory of Argentina, illegally occupied by Great Britain since 1833, following upon an act of force which deprived our country of the possession of the Archipelago. Thereupon, Great Britain then imposed a colonial regime on the area.

Since that time, since 1833, the Argentine Republic has required redress for this outrage suffered, from Great Britain. In the course of these 131 years, we have never consented -and will never conse to have part of our national territory wrested from us by an illegal and untenable act.

We come to this Sub-Committee to restate our rights to th Malvinas to the International Community, strengthened as we are by the will and the unanimous feelings of the Argentine people, and by a sound an unbroken position of protest at the outrage maintained by all Argentine Governments that have succeeded one another since 1833.

Our intention is to persuade the Internacional community that the islands in question are an integral part of Argentine territory and that Great Britain's moral and legal duty is to restore them to their true owner, thereby setting the principle of the sovereignty and territorial integrity of states on a sure footing of peaceful international relations. Th will fulfil the generous purposes implicit in Resolution 1514 (XV), and thu a long-awaited act of justice will have been rendered.

England is today the possessor of the Malvinas Islands, solely thanks to an arbitrary and unilateral acts of force. The Argentine authorities settled in the Island were expelled by the British Fleet. Legal speaking, this act of force cannot generate nor create any right, and, politically speaking, the events of 1833 were only another aspect of the imperialist policies that the European powers developed for America, Africa and Asia during the XIXth Century. The Malvinas may, perhaps, be considered one of the most outstanding symbols of this fortunately outmode

- - - -

- - - -

policy. . Under the threats of its guns, the British fleet evicted a peaceful
and active Argentine population that was exercising the legitimate rights
that the Argentine Republic possessed as the Heir of Spain.

Prior to 1833, the English had never effectively possessed
the totality of the Malvinas Archipelago. In 1766, they merely founded a
fort of Port Egmont on one islet called Saunders Isle. In 1774, they
voluntarily abandoned it and only 59 years later they appeared, in order to
oust violently the Argentine population and thus set up their sole claim.

But the history of the Malvinas does not begin in 1833 -nor
even in 1765. Quite the contrary, these islands were the concern of the
Chancelleries of Europe many years earlier, and a number of diplomatic
incidents had taken place in the XVIIIth Century that touched upon them.

In order to gauge the illegality of the British act of 1833,
the previous events have to be examined -events that are not recounted in
document A/AC. 109/L. 98/Add. 2, which this Sub-Committee had before it,
but which surely prove the wantonness of the act committed in 1833.

We shall not go into a study of the question of the discoverer
of the Malvinas Islands. Documentation published at the time shows
conclusively that the Islands were discovered by Spanish navigators. In
Spanish maps and charts of the beginning of the XVIth Century, the Islands
already appeared. The first map is that of Pedro Reinel (1522-23) which
shows an archipelago situated on the parallel 53º 55' latitude South. Then
there is the work of Diego Rivero, Principal Cartographer to Charles V
who inserted the islands in the Castiglione (1526-27), Salviati (1526-27) and
Rivero (1527) maps and also in two charts of 1529. Then come the Maps
of Yslario de Santa Cruz of 1541, the Planisphere of Sebastian Gaboto of
1544, the Map of Diego Gutierrez of 1561 and that of Bartolome Olives of
1562 among others. It is to Esteban Gomez, of the Expedition of Magallanes in 1520, that the discovery of the archipelago must be attributed. The
area was also sailed by Simon de Alcazaba in 1534 and Alonso de Camargo
in 1540. All these were pilots of Spanish ships, sailing towards the Straits
of Magellan, also discovered by Spain and one of the bases for its claims
over the islands as being adjacent to the said straits. Sarmiento de Gamboa,
in 1580, took symbolic possession of the Straits in keeping with the usage
of the times, and in 1584, founded a settlement.

- - - -

-- - -

The Dutch navigator, Sebald de Weert, in his log book for 24 January 1600, stated that he had sighted the Islands. The British contend that in 1592 John Davis, and in 1594 Richard Hawkins had discovered the Archipelago, but the truth of the matter is that the English cartography of the period does not show the islands, nor does there exist any proof that will substantiate the hypothetical discoveries.

Basically, until the middle of the XVIIIth Century, knowledge of the existence of the Islands was not certain in London, and at times they were confused with some imaginary Islands called The Pepys, which shows the degree of ignorance of the period. It was then, in 1748, that on the suggestion of Admiral Anson, England decided to send an expedition to "discover" and settle the Malvinas and Pepys Islands. Great Britain consulted Spain and in view of the latter's objections, desisted from the plan. I should like to quote here the instructions received by the British Representative regarding the communication to be made to the Spanish Court in Madrid: "Since there is no intention of making settlement in any of the afore-mentioned islands and since His Majesty's corvettes wish neither to make nor touch any part of the Spanish coast, His Majesty fails to understand how this project can in any way cause objections from Madrid". The first matter that was aired in this original diplomatic skirmish over the islands was whether the British had any right to enter the regions.

The acts of consultation of 1749, addressed to the Spanish Court, are a clear proof of England's recognition of the rights of Spain over the islands and the coasts of South America, in areas where British ships could neither sail nor trade, much less give themselves to occupation.

We shall not mention the rights granted to Spain by virtue of the Papal Bulls Inter Coetera and Dudum si Quidem or of their validity erga omnes, nor of the Treaty of Tordesillas between Spain and Portugal, in our defence of the position that we have stated, but we shall speak of the treaties between England and Spain.

The Peace Treaty of 1604 between Spain and England, returned matters and rights to the Status quo ante bellum, nullifying anything that might have been obtained prior to the signature, including the so-called English discovery. Later, in the Treaty of Madrid of 1670, it was agreed that Great Britain would retain all the lands, islands, colonies and dominions she possessed in America; but this recognition of British

- - - -

sovereignty in North America was accompanied by a counter-recognition, whereby in another clause it was stated that "the subjects of Great Britain would not direct their trade to, nor sail in, ports or places which His Catholic Majesty possesses in the above-mentioned Indies, nor will they trade with them". Furthermore, the Treaty of Madrid of 1713 established that "His Britannic Majesty has agreed to issue the most stringent prohibitions and threatened with the most strict penalties, so that no subject or ship of the English Nation shall dare to sail to the Southern Sea nor traffic in any other part of the Spanish Indies". This provision which prohibited sailing and trading by Great Britain in areas not open to traffic at the end of the XVIIth Century was again ratified in 1713 in the Treaty of Utrecht.

Therefore, in 1749, when Great Britain tried to send the first expedition, she could not have considered the Malvinas Islands res nulius, and therefore open to appropriation.

In February 1764 there occurred the first essay at colonisation and then it was by a French sailor, Louis Antoine de Bougainville, who founded Port Louis in the Eastern Malvina in the name of the King of France.

Spain considered this settlement an encroachment of her rights and started negotiations with Paris to obtain handing-over of the French settlement. England then dispatched a clandestine expedition which in 1766 founded Port Egmont on Saunders Island, which is near Western Malvina, close to a place that Bougainville had christened Port de la Croisade.

In the meantime, Spain formally protested to the French Government and her rights of dominion were recognized. King Louis XV ordered Bougainville to hand over Port Louis on the compensatory payment of all expenses incurred in. The transfer was solemnly performed in a ceremony held on 1 April 1767 in Port Louis itself, thus recognizing the legal rights of the Spanish Crown to these Islands. Previously, the Government had issued a Royal Bill dated 4 October 1766 which declared the Islands to be dependencies of the Captaincy General of Buenos Aires, and Don Felipe Ruiz Puente was designated Governor. The Spanish were thus left in possession of the Port, whose name was changed to Port Soledad with Spanish settlers about and a military establishment located.

- - - -

- - - -

On Saunders Isle, however, there was still the small British garrison of Port Egmont which had been set up in 1766. At the time of the transfer of Port Louis by France to Spain, the British had been silent and made no reservations regarding their presumed sovereignty. Once her difficulties with France were solved, Spain turned her attention to Port Egmont, and the British garrison was evicted from Saunders Isle by the Spanish forces of the Rio de la Plata Fleet under the command of the Governor of Buenos Aires, Buccarelli, on 10 June 1770. Spain had thus reacted clearly and categorically in the face of both intruders and ensured respect for her sovereign rights, since the French had withdrawn after diplomatic pressure and the British after force had been exercised. Britain, however, felt that her honour had been impugned by the use of force against Port Egmont and presented a claim at the Court of Madrid.

The diplomatic negotiations -in which France also participated;. were long and involved and a solution was finally arrived at on 22 January 1771. Spain's ambassador to London, Prince de Masserano, declared that his Sovereign "disapproves the aforementioned violent enterprise and binds himself to reestablish matters as they were prior to the episode", adding that "the restoration to His BritannicMajesty of the Port and Fort called Egmont, cannot and must not in any way affect the question of prior sovereign rights over the Malvinas Islands". This declaration was accepted by the Government of His Britannic Majesty on the same day, and under Lord Rochfort's signature, it was stated that His Britannic Majesty would consider the declaration of the Prince of Masserano, with the entire fulfilment of the agreement by His Catholic Majesty as adequate redress for the affront done to the Crown of Great Britain. From this diplomatic act, there stands out, first and outmost, the <u>acceptance</u> of the Spanish declaration, an acceptance which does not contain any rejection of the express reservation on the part of Spain, regarding sovereignty over the Islands. Great Britain's silence in the light of such an express, and written, reservation, can only be interpreted in its true form, namely, as an acceptance which, furthermore, is borne out by the original title of the British document, which is not called a "Counter-Declaration", as Lord Palmerston called it in 1834, but "Acceptance", according to the Official Edition of the State Papers of 1771.

We must also point out that in all the documentation covering these diplomatic negotiations, and in all the final papers, mention is only made of the restoration of Port Egmont to the <u>status quo ante</u>, but

- - - -

▲ - - -

nbt of the Malvinas Islands in general, which latter area, however, was
clearly included in the express declaration regarding Spanish sovereignty.
Furthermore, while the negotiations were taking place, and uninterruptedly
after it was restored by France, Port Soledad was occupied by the Spanish
without Great Britain's making the slightest move nor reservation. What
is more, as can be seen in the papers covering the restoration of Port
Egmont, it is specified that the United Kingdom receives it from hands of
the "Commissioner General of His Catholic Majesty in Port Soledad". Both
owners found themselves face to face and respected one another for three
years, but those whose rights were more legitimate had to prevail.

On 22 May 1774, the English voluntarily abandoned Saunders
Isle, which at the time the British called Falkland Island (in the singular).
The English, on leaving the Island, left behind a metal plate reading:-
"BE IT KNOWN TO ALL NATIONS THAT FALKLAND's ISLAND WITH
THIS PORT...". And we must point out that Falkland's Island is mentioned
in the possessive singular, which, linked to the British acceptance of the
fact of the Spanish possession of Puerto Soledad, proves that the English
claims were limited -during their stay in Port Egmont- exclusively to this
settlement and not to the entire archipelago.

Fifty-nine years were to elapse before the English returned
to the Malvinas and the only title they were able to show in 1833 was this
metal plate which had been removed by the Spanish and taken to Buenos
Aires. Great Britain's astounding claim in 1833 was based on a presumed
possession in the form of a metal plate, which was contrary to international
law of the period which required, as proof and condition of dominion,
effective possession.

We do not wish to go into the discussion that has lured so
many scholars, namely the existence of a secret pact between the British
and Spanish Crowns regarding the honourable redress in the form of the restoration of Port Egmont, and its subsequent abandonment by the British,
but the English silence on the Spanish reservation regarding the Malvinas
Islands is significant, as is also the fact that the British quitted these
Islands almost immediately on the Spanish transfer. The truth of the matter
Mr. Chairman, what we can be sure of, is that the British only stayed in
the island for three years after the return of Port Egmont and that they did
not go back until 1833. Fifty-nine years elapsed, during which, with no
protest whatever from Great Britain, the islands remained in the possession

- - - -

- - - -

of Spain first, and then of Argentina, which Governments exercised all prerogatives not only in Port-Soledad, but in the entire Archipelago and the neighbouring seas, with the consent of the British Crown.

Spain exercised all sorts of acts of dominion over the Malvinas Islands until the Revolution of May 1810, which was the beginning of Argentine independence.

In 1776 she created the Vice-Royalty of the Rio de la Plata, including the above-mentioned islands which belonged to the Governorship of Buenos Aires -and England said nothing.

In 1777, all buildings and installations of Port Egmont were razed in order to avoid awakening the cupidity of ships flying other flags -and England still said nothing.

The Spanish Government named numerous and successive Governors of the Islands between 1774 and 1811 who exercised uninterrupted authority over them and their neighbouring seas -and still England said nothing.

England's silence over the Malvinas between 1774 and 1829 confirms her recognition of Spanish rights and her desire not to return to the Archipelago.

Not only did Spain exercise effective possession between 1774 and 1811, but Great Britain did not bring to bear any rights over Port Egmont in the different instruments dated around the end of the XVIIIth Century and dealing with territorial questions, although she had complete and public knowledge of the sovereign occupation of the Archipelago by Spain. Thus, in the 1783 Peace Treaty of Versailles, at the end of the North American War of Independence, there was a ratification of the previous stipulations of 1670, 1713 and others that prohibited the English from sailing in the Southern Seas. Even further, the conflict that was motivated by England's trying to found a settlement on Nootka Sound, on the West Coast of Canada, led to the signing of the Saint Lawrence Convention of 1790. This agreement granted freedom of navigation to the British in the Pacific on three conditions: The First, that this navigation would not be a pretext for illegal trading with Spanish dominions, it being prohibited within "ten maritime leagues from any coasts already occupied by Spain"; the second, that there be free trade between the settlements founded in

- - - -

the North Pacific since 1789 and those subsequently to be set up, and finally, article 7 of the convention established that "It has also been agreed, regarding both the Eastern and Western coasts of South America, and its adjacent Islands, that the respective subjects shall in the future make no settlements in those parts of the coasts situated South of the said coasts and of the adjacent islands already occupied by Spain".

This agreement did away with the contention that there were closed seas on the East or West coasts of America. But the British right to establish colonies was only recognized regarding the coasts of North America; with regard to other areas, the Spanish Crown only acknowledged mere fishing rights, and the parties bound themselves not to establish new colonies in the South Atlantic or Pacific, and what existed would remain in status quo. This was precisely the interpretation given by Great Britain to the Nootka Sound Convention signed after the incident on the Canadian frontier in 1826 between Great Britain and the United States.

When, in the 1790 Convention, Great Britain recognized the status quo existing in the South of America, she was thereby giving the definitive legal proof of her lack of grounds upon which to base her claims to set up settlements of any permanence in the Malvinas. It is, by the same token, one of the grounds for the Argentine claims over the Islands of the South. The English had no right to people the South of the coasts or Islands already occupied by Spain, that is to say, including the South of the Malvinas and of Puerto Deseado in the Patagonia. Regarding the Malvinas themselves, there had been a renunciation of any rights England might have contended, for the commitment was not to settle any place already occupied by Spain, aside from not sailing within 10 leagues of the coast.

In one word, gentlemen, after Great Britain's voluntary abandonment of Port Egmont in 1774, Spain was left as unchallenged and unchallengeable Mistress of the Malvinas Islands, and as such, she exercised absolute sovereignty over them, she occupied them, she designated authorities for them, without the slightest protest on the part of Great Britain. International instruments of the nature of those I have just cited were signed, which even reaffirmed Spain's rights, and these were the rights that the Argentine Republic inherited in 1810.

The process of Argentine independence was a long and painful one. Its armies travelled over half of America, helping in the

- - --

independence of the sister countries; and this struggle was carried on without outside help and at the cost of great sacrifices. Yet, in 1820, the Government of the Argentine Republic sent the frigate "Heroina" to the Malvinas. Don David Jewett, commanding the ship, notified vessels in Malvinas waters of the Argentine laws regulating sealing and fishing in the area and informed them that trespassers would be sent to Buenos Aires to stand trial. Furthermore, in a solemn ceremony, he took formal possession of the islands that belonged to Argentina as the Heir of Spain. There was no opposition to the statement of Argentine rights over the archipelago, nor was any claim raised against it, despite the fact that the communication was published in newspapers in the United States and elsewhere.

In 1823 the Government of Buenos Aires designated Don Pablo Areguati Governor of the Malvinas Islands.

That same year, the government granted lands and also the rights of exploitation of wild cattle on the islands and of fishing on the Western Malvina, to Don Jorge Pacheco and Don Luis Vernet. An expedition took out the supplies needed for the new settlement, but it only prospered partially, due to climactic conditions which were unfavourable. In January 1826, the concessionaries again sent groups of families and these managed to remain.

The colonizing enterprise in the archipelago gained ground in the course of subsequent expeditions which took men, supplies and animals to Port Soledad.

In 1828, a decree was signed granting Vernet concessions in Eastern Malvina and, in its desires to encourage the economic development of the archipelago, the Government of Buenos Aires declared the settlement exempt from all taxes excepting those required to ensure the upkeep of the local authorities.

At no time did England object to the Argentine settlement of the Malvinas, despite the fact that extremely important legal acts had taken place between the two countries, such as the signing of the Treaty of Friendship, Trade and Navigation of February 1825. This instrument does not contain any British reservation whatever on Malvinas Islands, and despite the action of the Commander of the "Heroina" in 1820 and other acts that the Government had carried out and authorized touching the Islands.

- - - -

- - - -

The settlement established under the protection of laws of the Government of Bueños Airés häd prospered and was in good condition in 1829.

This being the case, in 10 June of that same year, 1829, the Government of Buenos Aires created the Political and Military Commandancy of the Malvinas Islands, located in Port Soledad, and whose competence included all the islands adjacent to Cape Horn on the Atlantic side. The same Mr. Luis Vernet was named Commandant.

It was then, in the heyday of the expansionist eagerness of Great Britain, that the English interest in the Archipelago was awakened, an interest that was nothing but the renewal of its old aspirations of possessing lands in the South Atlantic. That had been the intention that had led Great Britain to invade Buenos Aires in both 1806 and 1807, being violently repulsed by the population both times. She had also occupied the Cape of Good Hope on the southernmost tip of Africa in 1806 and which served as a spearhead for later expansion. In 1815 she took Saint Helena and in 1816 the Isle of Tristan da Cunha.

The expansionist ambitions in the South Atlantic were again resumed by the British Admiralty, which hungered for a naval station on the strategic route, via Cape Horn, to Australia and the South Pacific, where Britain's aspirations had to compete with another European power.

Commercial interests linked with the fishing wealth also moved her and these were all tied in with her strategic desires to own a base in the South Atlantic.

Impelled by these interests, Great Britain decided to protest against the establishment of the Political and Military Commandanc On 10 November 1829 she made her claim, stating that the Argentine Gover ment had assumed "an authority that is incompatible with the Sovereign Rights of His Britannic Majesty over the Islands".

Here, a brief parenthesis should be made in order to recal some of the salient facts. In 1766, England had clandestinely founded a fort and a port of Egmont on the Isle of Sounders. In 1770, the English were forced out by the Spanish fleet. In 1771 they again occupied Port Egmont, following upon reparation offered by Spain, with the corresponding

- - - - -

- - - -

reservation of sovereignty. In 1774, three years after the transfer, the British voluntarily abandoned Port-Egmont and from then on, from 1772 until 1829, for over half a century, they made neither protest nor claims on the Spanish and later Argentine occupations. The truth of the matter is that during all that time, Great Britain was not interested in the Malvinas and she only became so and turned her eyes to them when they played a part in her plans of imperial expansion. The archipelago assumed great importance for colonial navigation.

There are, in point of fact, two situations, that are independent of one another, namely a) The XVIIIth Century incident that ended for Great Britain with her withdrawal from the Islands, and b) a totally new situation, in 1829, determined by strategic factors connected with her access to her possessions in the Pacific which were threatened at the time and her fishing and sealing interests.

But it was not only the British ambitions and interests that came into play. The United States also showed an interest in protecting the sealing activities of her nationals, off the Malvinas coasts. When Vernet endeavoured to implement Argentine legislation relating to fishing, and held up three North American vessels, another powerful country came into the picture.

On May 31 1831 the North American Corvette Lexington appeared before Port Soledad - she flew the French flag and carried signal asking for pilots and headed for the wharf. Thus the American sailors managed to land, destroyed the settlement and committed other acts of violence. The reason for this act was the rejection by the Argentine Government of a claim by the North American Consul whereby he sought the immediate return of one of the still detained fishing vessels. He also wanted the Politico-Military Commandant of the Malvinas to stop any intervention in the activities of the United States citizens in the area. The Lexington incident provoked a diplomatic clash between Argentina and the United States, which wound up with a virtual breaking off of diplomatic relations between the two countries.

During his stay in Buenos Aires, the representative of the United States established close relationship with the Chargé d'Affaires of Great Britain and their talks, which are documented in the correspondence published by their respective countries, shows that at a given moment, the

- - - -

- - -

...terests of these two powerful states united in order to oust a young and ...eak country from the Malvinas Islands.

In 1832, for the third time, Argentina returned to settle in ...uerto Soledad, and a new Civil and Military Governor was designated.

But the British die was cast: the British Admiralty instruct-...d Captain Onslow to set sail for the Malvinas, and on January 3, 1833, the ...orvette Clio appeared off Puerto Soledad. A small Argentine vessel, the ...arandí was riding at anchor. The English captain insisted that the Argen-...ine detachment withdraw. The difference in numbers allowed of no possible ...ight and added to that was the element of surprise.

The Argentine leader replied to the order by saying that ...he held Great Britain responsible for the outrage and the violation of the ...espect due to the Republic, and its rights that were being assaulted by ...force --as blind as it was irresponsible" and added that "he was withdrawing, but that he refused to lower his flag".

The British thereupon lowered the Argentine flag and by force, occupied Port Soledad. Thus, by plunder, another chapter of colonial history was written. Almost all the Argentine inhabitants of the islands were then evicted.

On January 3, 1833, almost 60 years after the voluntary withdrawal of 1774, the British committed the act of force in Port Soledad in the Island of Eastern Malvina. In a place where they had never been. And by the next year, they had occupied the entire archipelago.

What I have just described is an act that is simple and easy to understand. In 1833, Great Britain, having no right on her side, could only resort to force in order to occupy the Islands. And the situation has not changed since that time: Force is still the cornerstone of Britain's presence in the Archipelago.

At the beginning of this statement we said that this act of force, this arbitrary and unilateral act was never and shall never be con-sented to by the Argentine Republic; and we added that it cannot generate nor create any rights for Great Britain.

- - - -

- - - -

But the Argentine reaction was not long in coming. The population of Buenos Aires gave vent to its indignation at the incident and in the Islands themselves, the rest of the settlers who resisted the invade were taken and sent to London for trial under different pretexts and never returned. On January 15, the Government protested to the British Charg d'Affairs in Buenos Aires, who replied that he lacked instructions. On th 22nd January the protest was reiterated and the English Minister renewed his passive stand. In the meantime, the Minister Manuel V. Maza notifie the American Foreign Offices of the events in a circular. The reply of Brazil is worthy of mention, for that country instructed its Minister in Great Britain to offer to his Argentine colleague in London "the most fran and diligent cooperation to ensure success to his endeavours". Bolivia also replied that she would be among the first countries "to seek reparati for such a dire outrage".

On 24 April 1833, the Argentine representative in London Don Manuel Moreno, on instructions from Buenos Aires, presented a note of protest to His Britannic Majesty's Government, which he reiterated on June 17, in a lengthy and documented protest memorandum. Viscount Palmerston replied on 8 January 1834 contending that the rights of Great Britain "were based on the original discovery and subsequent occupation o the said Islands", arguments which Moreno rejected on 29 December 1834

Since then, whenever possible, the Argentine Republic ha repeated its protests at the act of force and illegal occupation.

Gentlemen: The Argentine Republic was a recently indepe ent country, lacking in the material means of the great powers of the per yet it reacted with determination at the outrage suffered. Protests were raised a few days after the plunder of Port Soledad. Taking into account the distances and the difficulties through which the country was going, more speed could not have been expected. The outrage caused a wave of indignation all over the country and that feeling of protest still imbues the Argentines today.

Mr. Chairman, in the course of the last 131 years, we have never ceased to clamour to the deaf ears of Great Britain for the restoration of the Islands which are ours. Today, a new hope is offered the Argentine Republic, a hope that we may find the understanding and the support of the United Nations, one of whose noblest purposes is to end the colonial era all over the world.

- - - -

- - -

The colonialist policies of that period have an outstanding example in the case of the Malvinas Islands.

At that time, advantage was taken of a country that was in the throes of organization and struggling, as are many new countries in Africa and Asia today, to achieve political and economic progress.

We defended ourselves on the strength of our dignity and of law, but we had no means to offer resistance. Our friends, the new nations of Latin America, also in the midst of their own formation, could only render us their moral support for they shared our material weakness. Now was there, then, an international forum to which we might carry our complaint and the European Concert was apportioning the world and its spheres of influence according to its own interests. It was not the age of justice - it was the age when the Great Powers used force and Great Britain acted in the Malvinas in keeping with the habits of the day.

According to Lord Palmerston's note, Great Britain contended in 1834 that "the discovery and subsequent occupation" constituted the source of her rights, and added that these rights were given an additional sanction by the fact that Spain had restored the Port of Egmont to Great Britain in 1771.

As far as the discovery is concerned, we have seen that if anyone first sighted the Malvinas, it was the Spanish navigators. Apart from the historical facts, the legal problem must be examined in the light of the moment when the problem was born and we must bear in mind the fact that since the end of the XVIth Century, international law provided that for the acquisition of res nulius territories, occupation was necessary, and it prevailed over discovery which only offers preliminary and precarious rights and titles. This title -called inchoate title- had to be affirmed by means of effective occupation; in the XVIIIth Century neither discovery nor fictitious or symbolic occupation sufficed.

Regarding occupation, it can in no way be termed, firstly, "subsequent" to discovery since the first English sailor who is supposed to have sighted the Islands, according to the British themselves was Davis in 1592, and it was only 174 years later, that is, in 1766 that the English settled in Port Egmont. The presence of the English, challenged by the Spanish, was only in a location called Port Egmont, and lasted between 1766 and 1774, with the protests of Spain and the resulting events and voluntary abandonment. The first effective occupation was that of France

- - - -

- - - -

in 1764, which recognized the rights of Spain, restoring the settlement to her, whereby the effective Spanish occupation antedates the British presence. The latter continued during the eight years when the English were in Port Egmont and afterwards. It has been correctly stated that the English occupation only showed negative facets: it was illegal -since it violated existing treaties; it was clandestine, that is, it was kept secret until the Spanish found out about it; it was belated, because it took place after the effective occupation of the French who handed it over to Spain; was challenged, because Spain resisted it and made an express reservati in its regard; it was partial, because it only applied to Port Egmont whil Spain possessed Port Soledad and the entire Archipelago; it was fleeting, for it only lasted eight years; it was precarious, for after 1774 it was no more. On the other hand, while the Spanish occupation preceded the English, it coexisted with it without disturbance and outlasted the abando .ment by England. The 1833 British arguments only serve to cloak a clea fact: the use of arms against a new nation that possessed the Islands by virtue of its rights as the Heir to Spain, rights which were unchallengeab

Gentlemen, In one hundred and thirty three years, we h been unable to evict Great Britain from the position into which she entre ed herself by force. But times have changed and today we are witnessing the twilight of colonialism, which is why British presence in the islands an anachronism and must be eliminated. The days are gone forever whe a young nation lacks voice and decision in international affairs. In the course of its entire history, my country has opposed this way of handling international relations, and we have constantly given proof of our sense responsibility and our willingness to settle our international disputes peacefully. Almost the entire length of the Argentine frontiers were established by arbitration, without our even having resorted to violence t settle territorial problems.

Furthermore, in 1933, in the VIIth American Internation Conference in Montevideo, the American States set forth a fundamental doctrine of American law when they stated that "The Contracting States set forth as a definitive norm of conduct their specific obligation not to recognize territorial acquisitions or special advantages obtained by force whether this be by the use of arms, by threatening diplomatic representa tions or by any other coercive measures. The territory of States is inviolable and cannot be the object of military occupation or of other measures of force imposed by another State, whether it be directly or indirectly, for any reason or even of a temporary nature".

- - - -

Convinced of this, we signed the Charter of the United
tions in 1945 not only as a peace-keeping machinery and to ensure inter-
tional peace and security, but also as a system whereby to find just
lutions to international problems, and especially those that emanated from
e colonial system. Even at the San Francisco Conference, the Argentine
ade an express reservation regarding our country's rights over the
alvinas Islands.

From the inception of this Organization, Argentina was well
vare of the importance of Art. 73 e of the Charter. As soon as ever Great
ritain began to supply information on the Malvinas, the Argentine Republic
formed the United Nations -as it had so often in the past- of its rights of
overeignty over the territory. And thus, through the General Assembly,
rgentina yearly reminded the organization of its rights, and stated that the
formation supplied by the United Kingdom on the Malvinas Islands, the
eorgias and the South Sandwich in no way affected Argentine sovereignty
ver these territories, that the occupation by Britain was due to an act of
orce, never accepted by the Argentine Government and that it reaffirms its
nprescriptible and inalienable rights. At the same time, in the Organizatio:
American States, my country has advocated an end to colonial situations in
merica.

The Xth Inter-American Conference of Caracas in 1954
dopted Resolution 96 on Colonies and Territories occupied in America, and
eclared "that it is the will of the peoples of America that an end be put to
olonialism maintained against the will of the peoples and also the occupation
f territories". It proclaimed also "the solidarity of the American Repu-
lics with the just claims of the Peoples of America regarding territories
ccupied by extra-continental countries", and, finally, it repudiated "the
se of force in the perpetuation of colonial systems and the occupation of
erritories in America".

After 1955, the United Nations was renewed by the admis-
ion of new Members, especially of those that emerged from the process
f de-colonization imposed on the European powers by the new political
tructure of the world. Thus, a new perspective was created in our over
ne-hundred-year-old claim for the Islands.

When in 1960, with our support, there was adopted the now
istoric Resolution 1514 (XV), "Declaration on the Granting of Independence
Colonial Countries and Peoples", the process of decolonization all over
he world took on a new impetus.

- - - -

        Clearly, calmly and constructively, our country supporte
and will support this process of decolonization which is taking place today
with the help of the United Nations. We ourselves being a product of a
similar process of independence -which we achieved by our own means-
we are consistent with our historical tradition and determined supporters
the elimination of the colonial system. Thus, we wholeheartedly voted in
favour of the additional resolutions to 1514(XV), that is, Resolutions 1654
(XVI), 1810(XVII) and 1956(XVIII).

        Today, this Sub-Committee III of the Committee of 24 is
to take up the question of the Malvinas Islands.

        The Malvinas Islands are in a different situation from tha
of the classical colonial case. De facto and de jure, they belonged to the
Argentine Republic in 1833 and were governed by Argentine authorities an
occupied by Argentine settlers. These authorities and these settlers wer
evicted by violence and not allowed to remain in the territory. On the
contrary, they were replaced, during those 131 years of usurpation, by a
colonial administration and a population of British origin. Today the
population amounts to 2172 souls, and it is periodically renewed to a larg
extent by means of a constant turn-over: thus in 1962, 411 persons left an
268 arrived; in 1961, 326 left and 244 arrived; in 1960, it was 292 that
left and 224 who arrived. This shows that it is basically a temporary pop
lation that occupies the land and one that cannot be used by the colonial
power in order to claim the right to appl he principle of self-determination.

        Our Government holds, and has thus stated it to successi
General Assemblies, that this principle of self-determination of peoples,
as set forth in Article 1, paragraph 2 of the Charter, must, in these excep
tional cases, be taken in the light of the circumstances which condition its
exercise.

        Therefore, we consider that the principle of self-determi
nation would be ill-applied in cases where part of the territory of an independent state has been wrested -against the will of its inhabitants- by an
act of force, by a third State, as is the case in the Malvinas Islands, with
out there being any subsequent international agreement to validate the de
facto situation and where, on the contrary, the aggrieved state has consta
ly protested the situation. These facts are specifically aggravated when t

-- - -

- - -

xisting population has been ousted by this act of force and fluctuating
roups of nationals of the occupying power supplanted them.

Furthermore, the indiscriminate application of the
rinciple of self-determination to a territory so sparsely populated by
ationals of the colonial power, would place the fate of this territory in the
ands of the power that has settled there by force, thus violating the most
lementary rules of international law and morality.

The basic principle of self-determination should not be
used in order to transform an illegal possession into full sovereignty under
the mantle of protection which would be given by the United Nations.

This strict interpretation of the principle of self-determination is specifically based upon Resolution 1514(XV), whose main aim
should not be forgotten, namely: to end colonialism in all its forms.

After recognizing the principle of self-determination, the
Preamble of that Resolution states that the peoples of the world "ardently
desire the end of colonialism in all its manifestations". It also adds that
"all peoples have an inalienable right to complete freedom, the exercise of
their sovereignty and the integrity of their national territory".

Article 2 of the Declaration reaffirms the principle
whereby "All peoples have the right to self-determination; by virtue of that
right they freely determine their political status and freely pursue their
economic, social and cultural development".

But this article is conditioned by article 6, for it clearly
states that "Any attempt aimed at the partial or total disruption of the
national unity and the territorial integrity of a country is incompatible with
the purposes and principles of the Charter of the United Nations". In its
article 7, while reaffirming the above, it goes on to state that "All States
shall observe faithfully and strictly the provisions of the Charter of the
United Nations, the Universal Declaration of Human Rights and the present
Declaration on the basis of equality, non-interference in the internal
affairs of all States, and respect for the sovereign rights of all peoples and
their territorial integrity".

The purposes of the Resolution -as its wording makes
manifest- is quite in keeping with the true interpretation of the principle
of self-determination insofar as the Malvinas Islands are concerned.

- - - -

- - - -

Colonialism in all its manifestations.must be brought to an end; national unity and territorial integrity must be respected in the implementation of the Declaration. It shall not be used to justify the outrages perpetrated in the past against newly independent countries.

Resolution 1654 (XVI), pursuant to which this Special Committe was established, stresses this fact when in its Preamble it states the deep concern on the part of the Assembly that "contrary to the provisions of paragraph 6 of the Declaration, acts aimed at the partial or total disruption of national unity and territorial integrity are still being carried out in certain countries in the process of decolonization".

The American Regional Organization adopted a resolution at its Xth Foreign Ministers'Conference setting forth "the need for extra-continental countries having colonies in the territories of America, speedily to conclude the measures defined according to the terms of the Charter of the United Nations in order to allow the respective peoples fully to exercise their right to self-determination, in order once and for all to eliminate colonialism from America". But bearing particularly in mind the situation of states whose territorial unity and integrity are affected by foreign occupation, this same resolution went on to state that it "does not refer to territories under litigation or the subject of claims between extra-continental countries and some countries of the hemisphere". This resolution was also transmitted to the United Nations.

The future of these islands, separated from the Argentine Republic, would be both illogical and unreal. Geographically they are close to our Patagonian coasts, they enjoy the same climate and have a similar economy to our own south-lands. They are part of our own continental shelf, which, by International Law and since the Geneva Conventions of 1958, belongs in all rights to the coastal State.

Their economic development on stable basis is linked to that of the Argentine Republic with which they at present have neither communication nor direct maritime trade because of the prevailing situation.

Furthermore, if we carefully analyze the same document submitted by the Secretariat of the United Nations on the strength exclusively of the information supplied by the British, we note how the colonial system manifests itself in the economic side of the life of the Islands. Ownership of the land is virtually in the hands of the Falkland Islands Company Limited, among whose Board of Directors -located in London-

- - - -

- - - -

figure members of the British Parliament. This Company -which we have no compunction in labelling monopolistic- owns 1,230,000 acres of the best land, in outright freehold, and on them three hundred thousand sheep graze. The next largest land-owner is the British Crown with 56,500, acres. The company, and its subsidiaries, control all the export and import trade. It also holds the wool monopoly which is the main source of wealth of the Islands.

British domination of the Malvinas Islands is not only contrary to the Charter of the United Nations, but it also creates a sterile situation in a territory which could enjoy a greater economic boom if linked to its natural and legal owners. Proof positive of this is the fact that the statistics for 1912 show that there were 2295 inhabitants in the Malvinas Islands and that since that time the population has remained stagnant. According to a census taken on 18 March 1962, 2172 souls live in the Islands. It is the only human family in America that instead of increasing, shrinks.

Gentlemen: the United Kingdom has no right to continue in the Islands, nor does the spirit of our day allow of it.

In concluding this statement, may I sum up the view of the Argentine Government, which reflects the feelings of its entire people:

1. The Argentine Republic decidedly claims the restoration of its territorial integrity by means of the return of the Malvinas, South Georgias and South Sandwich Islands which were wrested from her by force by the United Kingdom. This is the only solution that justice prescribes. Respectful of fundamental human rights and of the obligations flowing from the Charter of the United Nations, the Argentine Republic will bear well in mind the welfare and the material interests of the present inhabitants of the Malvinas Islands. Together with men of all races and creeds the world over, under the protection of the guarantees granted by our constitution, they will be able to integrate themselves in the life of the Nation.

2. The Argentine Republic, however, will not agree to having the principle of self-determination vitiated by seeing it applied in order to consolidate situations flowing from colonial anachronisms, to the detriment of its legitimate rights of sovereignty over the Islands.

- - - -

- - - -

The outrage of 1833 entitles us to require the United Kingdom to consider this dispute realistically and with the required far-sightedness; thus will Great Britain have again applied its undisputed political wisdom.

In the Atlantic Charter, on 14 August 1941, Churchill an Roosevelt both declared that they wished to see restored to nations their sovereign rights and their independence to the peoples who had lost their rights by force.

I can assure you, gentlemen, that Latin America is determinedly united in its decision to wipe out the last vestiges of colonialism that still exist in the Hemisphere.

Thank you, Mr. Chairman.

2065 (XX). Question of the Falkland Islands (Malvinas)

The General Assembly,

Having examined the question of the Falkland Islands (Malvinas),

Taking into account the chapters of the reports of the Special Committee on the Situation with regard to the Implementation of the Declaration on the Granting of Independence to Colonial Countries and Peoples relating to the Falkland Islands (Malvinas),[15] and in particular the conclusions and recommendations adopted by the Committee with reference to that Territory,

Considering that its resolution 1514 (XV) of 14 December 1960 was prompted by the cherished aim of bringing to an end everywhere colonialism in all its

---

[13] *Ibid., Twentieth Session, Annexes,* agenda items 23 and 24, document A/5962.

[14] *Ibid.,* document A/5961.

[15] *Ibid., Nineteenth Session, Annexes,* annex No. 8 (part I) (A/5800/Rev.1), chapter XXIII; *ibid., Twentieth Session, Annexes,* addendum to agenda item 23 (A/6000/Rev.1), chapter XXII.

forms, one of which covers the case of the Falkland Islands (Malvinas),

Noting the existence of a dispute between the Governments of Argentina and the United Kingdom of Great Britain and Northern Ireland concerning sovereignty over the said Islands,

1. *Invites* the Governments of Argentina and the United Kingdom of Great Britain and Northern Ireland to proceed without delay with the negotiations recommended by the Special Committee on the Situation with regard to the Implementation of the Declaration on the Granting of Independence to Colonial Countries and Peoples with a view to finding a peaceful solution to the problem, bearing in mind the provisions and objectives of the Charter of the United Nations and of General Assembly resolution 1514 (XV) and the interests of the population of the Falkland Islands (Malvinas);

2. *Requests* the two Governments to report to the Special Committee and to the General Assembly at its twenty-first session on the results of the negotiations.

1398th plenary meeting,
16 December 1965.

REPORT
OF THE SPECIAL COMMITTEE ON THE SITUATION
WITH REGARD TO THE IMPLEMENTATION
OF THE DECLARATION
ON THE GRANTING OF INDEPENDENCE
TO COLONIAL COUNTRIES AND PEOPLES

VOLUME V

GENERAL ASSEMBLY

OFFICIAL RECORDS: TWENTY-EIGHTH SESSION

SUPPLEMENT No. 23 (A/9023/Rev.1)

UNITED NATIONS
New York, 1975

CHAPTER XXVII

FALKLAND ISLANDS (MALVINAS)

A. CONSIDERATION BY THE SPECIAL COMMITTEE

1.   The Special Committee considered the question of the Falkland Islands (Malvinas) at its 939th to 941st meetings, between 17 and 21 August.

2.   In its consideration of the item, the Special Committee took into account the provisions of the relevant General Assembly resolutions, including in particular resolution 2908 (XXVII) of 2 November 1972 on the implementation of the Declaration on the Granting of Independence to Colonial Countries and Peoples, by paragraph 11 of which the Assembly requested the Special Committee "to continue to seek suitable means for the immediate and full implementation of General Assembly resolutions 1514 (XV) and 2621 (XXV) in all Territories which have not yet attained independence and, in particular, to formulate specific proposals for the elimination of the remaining manifestations of colonialism and report thereon to the General Assembly at its twenty-eighth session". The Committee also took into account the decision taken by the General Assembly on 18 December 1972 on the question of the Falkland Islands (Malvinas). 1/

3.   During its consideration of the item, the Special Committee had before it a working paper prepared by the Secretariat (see annex to the present chapter) containing information on action previously taken by the Committee and the General Assembly, as well as on the latest developments concerning the Territory.

4.   The Special Committee also had before it: (a) a letter dated 15 August 1973 from the Permanent Representative of Argentina to the United Nations addressed to the Secretary-General regarding the item (A/9121) and (b) a written petition dated 14 May 1973 from Mr. José Ramón Cornejo concerning the Territory (A/AC.109/PET.1250).

5.   The administering Power did not participate in the work of the Special Committee during its consideration of the item.

6.   At the 939th meeting, on 17 August, the Chairman informed the Special Committee that the representative of Argentina had indicated his wish to make a statement in connexion with the Committee's consideration of the item. The Committee decided to accede to the request. The representative of Argentina made a statement (A/AC.109/PV.939 and Corr.1). Subsequently, the Chairman made a statement (A/AC.109/PV.939 and Corr.1).

7.   At the 940th meeting, on 20 August, the representative of Venezuela introduced a draft resolution (A/AC.109/L.905) on the item.

1/ Official Records of the General Assembly, Twenty-seventh Session, Supplement No. 30 (A/8730), p. 90.

8.   The Special Committee considered the draft resolution at its 940th and 941st meetings, on 20 and 21 August. Statements were made at the 940th meeting by the representatives of Chile and the Syrian Arab Republic (A/AC.109/PV.940), and at the 941st meeting by the representatives of Iraq and the United Republic of Tanzania (A/AC.109/PV.941).

9.   At its 941st meeting, on 21 August, the Special Committee adopted the draft resolution (A/AC.109/L.905) without objection (see paragraph 13 below).

10.   At the same meeting, the representative of Argentina made a statement (A/AC.109/PV.941).

11.   On 27 August, the text of the resolution was transmitted to the Permanent Representatives of Argentina and of the United Kingdom of Great Britain and Northern Ireland to the United Nations for the attention of their respective Governments.

B.   DECISION OF THE SPECIAL COMMITTEE

12.   The text of the resolution (A/AC.109/436) adopted by the Special Committee at its 941st meeting, on 21 August, to which reference is made in paragraph 10 above, is reproduced below:

Having examined the question of the Falkland Islands (Malvinas),

Recalling General Assembly resolution 1514 (XV) of 14 December 1960, containing the Declaration on the Granting of Independence to Colonial Countries and Peoples,

Recalling also General Assembly resolution 2065 (XX) of 16 December 1965, which invites the Governments of Argentina and the United Kingdom of Great Britain and Northern Ireland to proceed without delay with the negotiations recommended by the Special Committee with a view to finding a peaceful solution to the problem of the Falkland Islands (Malvinas), bearing in mind the provisions and objectives of the Charter of the United Nations and of resolution 1514 (XV) and the interests of the population of the Falkland Islands (Malvinas),

Gravely concerned at the fact that eight years have elapsed since the adoption of resolution 2065 (XX) without any substantial progress having been made in the negotiations,

Considering that resolution 2065 (XX) indicates that the way to put an end to this colonial situation is the peaceful solution of the conflict of sovereignty between the Governments of Argentina and the United Kingdom with regard to the aforementioned islands,

Taking note of the letter 2/ from the Permanent Representative of Argentina in which he reports on the present state of the negotiations between the two parties and on the position of his Government concerning the need to resume such negotiations in an appropriate manner,

Expressing its gratitude for the continuous efforts made by the Government of Argentina, in accordance with the relevant decisions of the General Assembly, to facilitate the process of decolonization and to promote the well-being of the population of the islands,

1.   Declares the need to accelerate the negotiations between the Governments of Argentina and the United Kingdom of Great Britain and Northern Ireland called for in General Assembly resolution 2065 (XX) in order to arrive at a peaceful solution of the conflict of sovereignty between them concerning the Falkland Islands (Malvinas);

2.   Urges the Governments of Argentina and the United Kingdom, therefore, to proceed without delay with the negotiations in order to put an end to the colonial situation;

3.   Requests both Governments to report to the Secretary-General and to the General Assembly as soon as possible and not later than at its twenty-ninth session on the results of the negotiations.

2/ A/9121.

ANNEX*

WORKING PAPER PREPARED BY THE SECRETARIAT

CONTENTS

---

* Previously issued under the symbol A/AC.109/L.898.

3160 (XXVIII). Question of the Falkland Islands (Malvinas)

The General Assembly,

Having considered the question of the Falkland Islands (Malvinas),

Recalling its resolution 1514 (XV) of 14 December 1960 containing the Declaration on the Granting of Independence to Colonial Countries and Peoples,

Recalling also its resolution 2065 (XX) of 16 December 1965, in which it invited the Governments of Argentina and the United Kingdom of Great Britain and Northern Ireland to proceed without delay with the negotiations recommended by the Special Committee on the Situation with regard to the Implementation of the Declaration on the Granting of Independence to Colonial Countries and Peoples with a view to finding a peaceful solution to the problem of the Falkland Islands (Malvinas), bearing in mind the provisions and objectives of the Charter of the United Nations and of resolution 1514 (XV) and the interests of the population of the Falkland Islands (Malvinas),

Gravely concerned at the fact that eight years have elapsed since the adoption of resolution 2065 (XX) without any substantial progress having been made in the negotiations,

Mindful that resolution 2065 (XX) indicates that the way to put an end to this colonial situation is the peaceful solution of the conflict of sovereignty between the Governments of Argentina and the United Kingdom with regard to the aforementioned islands,

Expressing its gratitude for the continuous efforts made by the Government of Argentina, in accordance with the relevant decisions of the General Assembly, to facilitate the process of decolonization and to promote the well-being of the population of the islands,

1. *Approves* the chapters of the report of the Special Committee on the Situation with regard to the Implementation of the Declaration on the Granting of Independence to Colonial Countries and Peoples relating to the Falkland Islands (Malvinas)[60] and, in particular, the resolution adopted by the Special Committee on 21 August 1973 concerning the Territory;[61]

2. *Declares* the need to accelerate the negotiations between the Governments of Argentina and the United Kingdom of Great Britain and Northern Ireland called for in General Assembly resolution 2065 (XX) in order to arrive at a peaceful solution of the conflict of sovereignty between them concerning the Falkland Islands (Malvinas);

3. *Urges* the Governments of Argentina and the United Kingdom, therefore, to proceed without delay with the negotiations, in accordance with the provisions of the relevant resolutions of the General Assembly, in order to put an end to the colonial situation;

4. *Requests* both Governments to report to the Secretary-General and to the General Assembly as soon as possible, and not later than at its twenty-ninth session, on the results of the recommended negotiations.

2202nd plenary meeting
14 December 1973

ORGANIZATION OF AMERICAN STATES

INTER-AMERICAN JURIDICAL COMMITTEE
Rio de Janeiro

OEA/Ser.Q/IV.12
CJI-27

WORK ACCOMPLISHED BY
THE INTER-AMERICAN JURIDICAL COMMITTEE
DURING ITS
REGULAR MEETING
Held from January 12 to February 13, 1976

General Secretariat of the Organization of American States

Washington, D. C.

May 1976

INTER-AMERICAN JURIDICAL COMMITTEE

Rio de Janeiro, January 22, 1976

CJI/1

Excellency:

I have the honor to transmit to Your Excellency the Declaration of the Inter-American Juridical Committee on the Problem of the Malvinas Islands, approved on January 16, 1976.

Accept, Excellency, the renewed assurances of my highest consideration.

(s) Reynaldo Galindo Pohl
Chairman
Inter-American Juridical Committee

His Excellency Alejandro Orfila
Secretary General of the
Organization of American States
Washington, D. C. 20006
USA

DECLARATION OF THE INTER-AMERICAN
JURIDICAL COMMITTEE ON THE
PROBLEMS OF THE MALVINAS
ISLANDS

THE INTER-AMERICAN JURIDICAL COMMITTEE

Recalling its resolution of February 18, 1974, in which it expressed its concern "because territories occupied by foreign powers still remain in American lands, despite the repeated claims of Latin American states calling for their return since they constitute an integral part of their national territories";

Recalling its declaration of February 1, 1972, with respect to the presence of British warships in the Caribbean Sea, stating that "Naval or air maneuvers conducted in or over territorial waters of American states or waters adjacent to such waters, without prior consent, by warships or military aircraft of foreign states constitute threats to the peace and security of the continent as well as flagrant violations of the international standards on nonintervention";

Recalling the just title the Republic of Argentina possesses to sovereignty over the Malvinas Islands, based on the international rules in force at the time the dispute began; that the archipelàgo appears in the nautical charts of the South Atlantic prepared by the cartographers of the Casa de Contratación of Seville (1522-23), in connection with the voyage of Magellan; that the first efective occupation of the aforementioned islands, made by a group of French colonists, concluded with the agreement of 1767 by which they handed over those islands to the Spanish authorities under the Government and Captaincy General (Capitanía General, of Buenos Aires; that the occupation of the Malvinas Islands by the English was only partial, since it was confined to Puerto Egmont, and temporary, since after eight years (1766-74) it was abandoned; that by decree of June 10, 1829, the Government of the United Provinces of the River Plate (Provincias Unidas del Río de la Plata) established a political and military government in the Malvinas Islands, under the Civil and Military Commandant Luis Vernet; that on January 3, 1833, the English corvette Clio violently dislodged the Argentine authorities there established and proceeded to illegitimate occupation by the United Kingdom; that the Argentine Government has constantly maintained its claim to its rights since the first moment of the dispute (note from the Argentine Minister in London dated June 17, 1823) and during all the time since;

Recalling Resolution 2065 of the United Nations, adopted at the Twentieth Session of the General Assembly, in 1965, in which it invited the governments of Argentina and of the United Kingdom of Great Britain and Northern Ireland to proceed without delay with the negotiations aimed at settling the dispute regarding sovereignty over the Malvinas Islands, bearing in mind the interests of the population of the islands; and Resolution 3160 of the United Nations, approved at the Twenty-eighth Session of the General Assembly in 1973, in which, after expressing its gratitude to the Government of Argentina for its continuous efforts to promote the well-being of the population of the islands, it declared the need to accelerate the negotiations between the two governments in order to arrive at a peaceful solution of the conflict of sovereignty between them concerning those islands;

Recalling that, in compliance with those resolutions, the Argentine Government signed with the Government of the United Kingdom of Great Britain and Northern Ireland various agreements on cooperation and took measures concerning communications, supplies, social welfare service, and maintenance of infrastructure works on behalf of the interests of the people of the islands, which earned the praise of the United Nations General Assembly (RES. 3160-XXVIII);

Considering the recent sending, supported and encouraged by the Government of the United Kingdom of Great Britain and Northern Ireland, of the so-called "Shackleton Mission" to the Malvinas Islands with the declared purpose of making an "economic and fiscal evaluation" of the archipelago and surrounding areas;

Considering that the opposition by the Government of the United Kingdom of Great Britain and Northern Ireland to continuing the bilateral negotiations to settle the dispute regarding sovereignty over those islands, because it considers them "sterile" negotiations, and the proposal to limit them to an agenda on "economic cooperation," amounts to taking the question back to the old thesis, sustained by that government in its diplomatic note of 1887, in which it stated to the Argentine Government that it considered the discussion closed;

Considering that the withdrawal of the Chiefs of Mission of the two governments is causing a state of tension in the relations between the two countries;

Noting that the scope of Resolutions 2065 (XX) and 3160 (XXVIII) of the United Nations involves a commitment accepted by the governments of Argentina and the United Kingdom of Great Britain and Northern Ireland to speed up the process directed at reestablishing legitimate sovereignty over the territory of the Malvinas Islands, a legal framework within which the two governments are obligated to act, for which reason the unilateral breaking off of the negotiations by the United Kingdom of Great Britain and North Ireland constitutes a violation both of the resolutions cited and of the spirit of compromise assumed; and

Reaffirming that the authentic ideals of our republics make it necessary to put an end to every occupation, usurpation, enclave, and every other form of persistence of colonial domination in the Americas,

DECLARES:

1. That the Republic of Argentina has an undeniable right of sovereignty over the Malvinas Islands, for which reason the basic question to be resolved is that of the procedure to be followed for restoring its territory to it;

2. That the "Shackleton Mission," sponsored by the Government of the United Kingdom of Great Britain and Northern Ireland amount to making a change unilaterally, and therefore is in contradiction to resolutions 2065 (XX) and 3160 (XXVIII of the United Nations;

3. That the presence of foreign warships in waters adjacent to American states and the intimidatory announcement by British authorities of the sending of other ships constitute threats to the peace and security of the continent, as well as flagrant violations of the international rules on nonintervention;

4.   That all of that amounts to hostile conduct intended to silence the claims of the Government of Argentina and to obstruct the course of the negotiations recommended by the General Assembly of the United Nations.

(s)   Reynaldo Galindo Pohl
Jorge A. Aja Espil
José Joaquín Caicedo Castilla
Antonio Gómez Robledo
José Eduardo do Prado Kelly
Américo Pablo Ricaldoni
Alberto Ruiz Eldredge

Rio de Janeiro, February 13, 1976

CJI/7

Excellency:

I have the honor to transmit to Your Excellency the Annual Report of the Inter-American Juridical Committee for the regular meeting held in January-February, 1976, drawn up in accordance with the provisions of Article 13 of its Rules of Procedure, and approved on February 13, 1976.

I respectfully request that this report be presented to the sixth regular session of the General Assembly.

Accept, Excellency, the renewed assurances of my highest consideration.

(s)   Reynaldo Galindo Pohl
           Chairman
           Inter-American Juridical Committee

Ambassador Alejandro Orfila
Secretary General of the
Organization of American States
Washington, D. C. 20006

REPORT OF THE INTER-AMERICAN JURIDICAL COMMITTEE
TO THE GENERAL ASSEMBLY OF THE
ORGANIZATION OF AMERICAN STATES ON THE
REGULAR MEETING HELD IN JANUARY-FEBRUARY 1976

Members of the Committee

The following members of the Committee attended this regular
meeting: Dr. Reynaldo Galindo Pohl (El Salvador), Dr. Jorge A.
Aja Espil (Argentina), Dr. José Joaquín Caicedo Castilla (Colombia),
Dr. Antonio Gómez Robledo (Mexico), Dr. José Eduardo do Prado
Kelly (Brazil), Dr. Américo Pablo Ricaldoni (Uruguay), Dr. Seymour
J. Rubin (U.S.A.), Dr. Alberto Ruiz-Eldredge (Peru) and Dr. Edmundo
Vargas Carreño (Chile).

Chairman and Vice Chairman

Drs. Reynaldo Galindo Pohl and Jorge A. Aja Espil served as
chairman and vice-chairman respectively.

Secretariat

Drs. Renato Ribeiro and Renzo Minut were secretaries to the
Committee.

Organization of American States

Dr. Isidoro Zanotti, Chief of the Codification Division of the
Department of Legal Affairs of the OAS also attended this meeting as
the representative of the Secretary General.

Visit of the Secretary General of the OAS
Dr. Alejandro Orfila

At the opening session of the meeting held on January 12, the
Committee was pleased and honored to receive a visit from the Secretary General of the OAS, Dr. Alejandro Orfila.

The Chairman, Dr. Galindo Pohl, welcomed Dr. Orfila and
stressed the importance of this official visit of the Secretary General
to the organ charged with serving the Organization as an advisory body
on juridical matters, and with promoting the progressive development
and the codification of international law.

13.   Administrative and budgetary matters,

14.   Course of international law,

15.   Cooperation of the Department of Legal Affairs of the General Secretariat with the Inter-American Juridical Committee, and

16.   Secretariat of the Inter-American Juridical Committee.

<u>The Problem of the Malvinas Islands</u>

With regard to this subject, the Inter-American Juridical Committee unanimously approved the following statement:

THE INTER-AMERICAN JURIDICAL COMMITTEE

<u>Recalling</u> its resolution of February 18, 1974, in which it expressed its concern "because territories occupied by foreign powers still remain in American lands, despite the repeated claims of Latin American states calling for their return since they constitute an integral part of their national territories";

<u>Recalling</u> its declaration of February 1, 1972, with respect to the presence of British warships in the Caribbean Sea, stating that "Naval or air maneuvers conducted in or over territorial waters of American states or waters adjacent to such waters, without prior consent, by warships or military aircraft of foreign states constitute threats to the peace and security of the continent as well as flagrant violations of the international standards on nonintervention";

<u>Recalling</u> the just title the Republic of Argentina possesses to sovereignty over the Malvinas Islands, based on the international rules in force at the time the dispute began; that the archipelago appears in the nautical charts of the South Atlantic prepared by the cartographers of the Casa de Contratación of Seville (1522-23), in connection with the voyage of Magellan; that the first efective occupation of the aforementioned islands, made by a group of French colonists, concluded with the agreement of 1767 by which they handed over those islands to the Spanish authorities under the Government and Captaincy General (Capitanía General) of Buenos Aires; that the occupation of the Malvinas Islands by the English was only partial, since it was confined to Puerto Egmont, and temporary, since after eight years (1766-74) it

was abandoned; that by decree of June 10, 1829, the Government
of the United Provinces of the River Plate (Provincias Unidas del
Río de la Plata) established a political and military government
in the Malvinas Islands, under the Civil and Military Commandant
Luis Vernet; that on January 3, 1833, the English corvette Clio
violently dislodged the Argentine authorities there established
and proceeded to illegitimate occupation by the United Kingdom;
that the Argentine Government has constantly maintained its
claim to its rights since the first moment of the dispute (note
from the Argentine Minister in London dated June 17, 1823) and
during all the time since;

Recalling Resolution 2065 of the United Nations, adopted at
the Twentieth Session of the General Assembly, in 1965, in which
it invited the governments of Argentina and of the United Kingdom
of Great Britain and Northern Ireland to proceed without delay
with the negotiations aimed at settling the dispute regarding
sovereignty over the Malvinas Islands, bearing in mind the interests of the population of the islands; and Resolution 3160 of the
United Nations, approved at the Twenty-eighth Session of the
General Assembly in 1973, in which, after expressing its gratitude to the Government of Argentina for its continuous efforts to
promote the well-being of the population of the islands, it declared
the need to accelerate the negotiations between the two governments
in order to arrive at a peaceful solution of the conflict of sover-
ignty between them concerning those islands;

Recalling that, in compliance with those resolutions, the
Argentine Government signed with the Government of the United
Kingdom of Great Britain and Northern Ireland various agreements on cooperation and took measures concerning communications, supplies, social welfare service, and maintenance of
infrastructure works on behalf of the interests of the people of
the islands, which earned the praise of the United Nations General
Assembly (RES. 3160-XXVIII);

Considering the recent sending, supported and encouraged
by the Government of the United Kingdom of Great Britain and
Northern Ireland, of the so-called "Shackleton Mission" to the
Malvinas Islands with the declared purpose of making an "economic and fiscal evaluation" of the archipelago and surrounding
areas;

Considering that the opposition by the Government of the
United Kingdom of Great Britain and Northern Ireland to

continuing the bilateral negotiations to settle the dispute regarding sovereignty over those islands, because it considers them "sterile" negotiations, and the proposal to limit them to an agenda on "economic cooperation," amounts to taking the question back to the old thesis, sustained by that government in its diplomatic note of 1887, in which it stated to the Argentine Government that it considered the discussion closed;

Considering that the withdrawal of the Chiefs of Mission of the two governments is causing a state of tension in the relations between the two countries;

Noting that the scope of Resolutions 2065 (XX) and 3160 (XXVIII) of the United Nations involves a commitment accepted by the governments of Argentina and the United Kingdom of Great Britain and Northern Ireland to speed up the process directed at reestablishing legitimate sovereignty over the territory of the Malvinas Islands, a legal framework within which the two governments are obligated to act, for which reason the unilateral breaking off of the negotiations by the United Kingdom of Great Britan and North Ireland constitutes a violation both of the resolutions cited and of the spirit of compromise assumed; and

Reaffirming that the authentic ideals of our republics make it necessary to put an end to every occupation, usurpation, enclave, and every other form of persistence of colonial domination in the Americas,

DECLARES:

1. That the Republic of Argentina has an undeniable right of sovereignty over the Malvinas Islands, for which reason the basic question to be resolved is that of the procedure to be followed for restoring its territory to it;

2. That the "Shackleton Mission," sponsored by the Government of the United Kingdom of Great Britain and Northern Ireland amount to making a change unilaterally, and therefore is in contradiction to resolutions 2065 (XX) and 3160 (XXVIII of the United Nations;

3. That the presence of foreign warships in waters adjacent to American states and the intimidatory announcement by British authorities of the sending of other ships constitute threats to the peace and security of the continent, as well as flagrant violations of the international rules on nonintervention;

4. That all of that amounts to hostile conduct intended to silence the claims of the Government of Argentina and to obstruct the course of the negotiations recommended by the General Assembly of the United Nations.

Telegram from the Minister of Foreign Affairs and Worship of the Republic of Argentina

With respect to the declaration above transcribed, the Minister of Foreign Affairs of the Republic of Argentina sent the following telegram to the Committee:

In view of declaration by the Inter-American Juridical Committee on the Malvinas Islands, I convey to you the profound satisfaction of the Argentine Government at this clear and serene statement that is framed within the most genuine principles that form and that guide our America. The Committee, in defending once again the legal values that prevail in the international community of our times, has confirmed the deservedness of its high prestige. I congratulate the Chairman. My highest consideration. Raúl Quijano, Minister of Foreign Affairs and Worship of the Republic of Argentina.

Course of International Law

In view of the excellent results obtained in the first and second courses, and in accordance with the provisions of Resolution AG/RES. 185 (V-O/75) approved by the General Assembly of the OAS in May 1975, the Inter-American Juridical Committee will hold the third course on international law in Rio de Janeiro, in cooperation with the General Secretariat of the OAS and the Getúlio Vargas Foundation.

The course will last for four weeks, from Monday to Friday, from 9:30 a. m. to 1 p. m. It will begin on July 19, 1976.

In accordance with suggestions made and approved in the CJI meetings held January 21 and 26, and February 5, 1976, plans have been made for a series of lectures which will be, in the main, the responsibility of members of the CJI. The director of the course will arrange into the timetable some seminars and round-tables for the purpose of extended debate on topics relating to the course curriculum. The participants will also have the opportunity to attend some of the meetings of the CJI, depending on the plans which are made.

NITED NATIONS

ENERAL

SSEMBLY

~~ ꜱᴛᴀᴛᴇ ᴅᴇᴘᴛ

Distr.
GENERAL

A/AC.109/520
7 May 1976
ENGLISH
ORIGINAL: SPANISH

ECIAL COMMITTEE ON THE SITUATION
WITH REGARD TO THE IMPLEMENTATION
OF THE DECLARATION ON THE GRANTING
OF INDEPENDENCE TO COLONIAL COUNTRIES
AND PEOPLES

QUESTION OF THE FALKLAND ISLANDS (MALVINAS)

Letter dated 6 May 1976 from the Permanent Representative of
Argentina to the United Nations addressed to the Chairman of
the Special Committee

In accordance with instructions received from my Government, I have the honour
refer to the letter of 3 March 1976 from the representative of the United
ngdom of Great Britain and Northern Ireland (A/AC.109/518), in which he takes
ception to the conclusions contained in the Declaration of 16 January 1976 of
e Inter-American Juridical Committee concerning the present status of the question
the Malvinas, the text of which was circulated to members of the Special
mmittee as document A/AC.109/511.

In expressing our agreement with the well-founded arguments and correct
nclusions contained in the Declaration, which have not been invalidated by the
ited Kingdom note, I wish to set out our position concerning certain statements
the United Kingdom document, which my Government rejects for the following
asons.

First of all, we strongly reaffirm the legitimate sovereign rights of the
rgentine Republic over the Malvinas. The existence of a dispute with the United
ngdom Government concerning sovereignty over the islands was recognized by the
ecial Committee and, subsequently, by the United Nations General Assembly in its
solutions 2065 (XX) of 16 December 1965 and 3160 (XXVIII) of 14 December 1973, in
ich the parties are invited and urged to proceed with bilateral negotiations with
view to finding a peaceful solution to the problem, bearing in mind the
ovisions and objectives of the Charter of the United Nations and of resolution
514 (XV) of 14 December 1960 and the interests of the population of the islands.
e General Assembly adopted both resolutions by very large majorities: the first
94 votes to none, with 14 abstentions, and the second by 116 votes to none,
ith 14 abstentions.

5-09467

4.   Both the purpose and the spirit of these resolutions and of the repeated consensuses adopted along the same lines were disregarded by the United Kingdom Government, which repeatedly refused to proceed with the negotiations, as my Government pointed out in the plenary General Assembly on 8 December 1975. 1/ Furthermore, as this Committee is also aware, the United Kingdom Government took unilateral initiative in the Malvinas question by dispatching a mission, headed by Lord Shackleton, to carry out an "economic and fiscal evaluation" of the archipelago and surrounding areas in order to assess the possibility of economic exploitation of its natural resources. The mission was carried out in spite of the express opposition of my Government, which stated publicly that it would not be welcome.

5.   This unfriendly act on the part of the United Kingdom was the subject of a statement in the House of Commons on 14 January 1976 by James Callaghan, then Foreign Secretary of the United Kingdom and today Prime Minister. Replying to a question by John Gilmour, a Member of Parliament, as to what safeguards were being provided for the Shackleton mission, Mr. Callaghan noted that the HMS Endurance of the Royal Navy was in the vicinity of the archipelago and that two other vessels were ready to proceed there, thus making it quite clear that the vessels in question were on an operational mission.

6.   This is referred to by the Inter-American Juridical Committee when it states that "the presence of foreign warships in waters adjacent to the American States and the intimidating announcement by the British authorities of the sending of other ships constitute threats to the peace and security of the continent and flagrant violations of the international rules on non-intervention".

7.   We must also characterize as hostile a course of conduct which has consisted not only in persistent refusal to proceed with the negotiations repeatedly recommended by the United Nations - disregarding the mandate of the Organization instead of pursuing the path of peaceful settlement of disputes - but also in the creation of dangerous situations through unilateral activities undertaken in disregard of repeated statements by the Argentine Government.

8.   When the question of the Malvinas was taken up in Sub-committee III of the Special Committee, the representative of Argentina, José María Ruda, in a statement on 9 September 1964, 2/ clearly outlined the manner in which possession of the Malvinas had been usurped by the United Kingdom on 3 January 1833 - a fact now disputed by the United Kingdom note. I shall briefly recall that when the British corvette Clio appeared in Puerto Soledad, a town with an established, permanent Argentine population where the schooner Sarandí was lying at anchor, the commanding officer, Captain John Onslow, ordered the Argentine detachment to withdraw so that he could take possession of the islands in the name of the King. Facing superior forces, the Argentine commandant, José María Pinedo, replied that he would withdraw "holding Great Britain responsible for the insult and the violation of the respect

---

1/ A/PV.2431.

2/ A/AC.109/SC.4/SR.25.

e to the Republic and to its rights, which were being trampled upon by force in high-handed manner and without regard for the consequences".

. When Commandant Pinedo refused to lower the national flag, the British forces id so, proceeding to expel almost all the Argentine inhabitants of the islands.

). On 15 January 1833, as soon as it learned of these events, the Argentine overnment filed a protest with the British chargé d'affaires in Buenos Aires, ailip G. Gore. It would take too long to enumerate here the series of protests, aims and reservations of rights which have been made on a continuing basis by rgentine Governments and have been disregarded by the United Kingdom Government, it it must be stated that, in the light of the illegitimate act of force that was ommitted, it is indeed audacious to declare that the events in 1833 represented a peaceable reassertion of British sovereignty". The British usurpation of 1833 annot serve as the basis for a prescriptive title in favour of the United Kingdom, lose possession of the islands is illicit, disputed and not peaceful in nature.

L. The United Kingdom document gives 1765 as the date when "British sovereignty" is "first established" in the islands. In order to set the historical record craight, we wish to state that it was in February 1764 that France established the irst group of settlers in Saint-Louis (East Malvina), which was ceded to Spain id the latter's rights recognized. The date 1765 can only refer to the stop made a the islands by the expedition of Commodore John Byron, who continued on his way the straits of Magellan without establishing a colony or occupying the islands.

2. In presenting its case, the United Kingdom also persists in citing esolutions 2065 (XX) and 3160 (XXVIII) in such a way as to suggest that the uestion of the Malvinas is one involving self-determination. Both of these esolutions clearly refer to the "interests" of the population of the islands and ot to its "wishes". When it is considered that Argentina was deprived of the slands by an illegitimate act of force, it becomes clear that the governing rinciple here is that of the territorial integrity of a country, which is nunciated in paragraph 6 of resolution 1514 (XV). To take any other view would ean accepting this act of force, which also entailed the expulsion of the ndigenous Argentine population and its replacement by subjects of the colonial ower.

3. At the present time, approximately 40 per cent of the population consists of ritish civil servants and employees of a private company which owns nearly 50 per ent of all property in the islands.

4. Notwithstanding the assertion made in the United Kingdom note, this population as remained virtually stationary, since, although it increased during the ineteenth century, in keeping with a world-wide demographic trend, it has declined nstead of increasing during the past 60 years.

15. Proof of this is the fact that British statistics for 1912 show the Malvinas as having had 2,295 inhabitants and that the present population is 1,840. As someone once expressed it, the Malvinas are the only family in the Americas which is declining in size rather than growing.

16. The measures taken by Argentina for the benefit of the island population hav won recognition from the General Assembly, as expressed in resolution 3160 (XXVII The measures taken under the 1971 Communications Agreement have clearly favoured the islanders' interests, to which my Government is fully prepared to continue to attach the necessary importance, as it has repeatedly informed the United Kingdom Government.

17. The Argentine Government also regrets that the attitude of the United Kingdo Government in refusing to renew the negotiations, which it has described as "sterile", and the sending of the Shackleton mission, which constituted a unilateral initiative in the matter, have compelled the Argentine Government to keep its Ambassador to the United Kingdom away from his post and to call upon the Government of Her Britannic Majesty to take similar action with regard to its Ambassador in Argentina.

18. With regard to this problem, my Government is fully prepared to seek areas o agreement which will make normalization possible in this aspect of Argentine- United Kingdom relations, bearing in mind the mandate contained in General Assemb resolutions 2065 (XX) and 3160 (XXVIII) to arrive, through bilateral negotiations at a peaceful and definitive solution of the dispute concerning sovereignty over the Malvinas.

19. I should be grateful if you would have this letter circulated as an official document of the Special Committee.

(Signed) Carlos ORTIZ DE ROZAS
Ambassador
Permanent Representative

NITED NATIONS

ENERAL

SSEMBLY

Distr.
GENERAL

A/AC.109/670
5 August 1981

ORIGINAL: ENGLISH

PECIAL COMMITTEE ON THE SITUATION WITH
REGARD TO THE IMPLEMENTATION OF THE
DECLARATION OF THE GRANTING OF
INDEPENDENCE TO COLONIAL COUNTRIES
AND PEOPLES

FALKLAND ISLANDS (MALVINAS)

Working paper prepared by the Secretariat

CONTENTS

FALKLAND ISLANDS (MALVINAS) 1/

1. GENERAL

1.   The Falkland Islands (Malvinas) lie in the South Atlantic, some 772 kilometres
north-east of Cape Horn. They comprise 200 islands and cover a total area of
11,961 square kilometres. There are two large islands, East Falkland and West
Falkland. Apart from a number of small islands, the Dependencies consist of
South Georgia, 1,287 kilometres east-south-east of the Falkland Islands (Malvinas
and the uninhabited South Sandwich Islands, some 756 kilometres south-east of
South Georgia.

2.   At the last census, held in 1972, the population of the Territory, excluding
the Dependencies, numbered 1,957, almost all of whom were of European descent,
mainly of British origin. Of this total, 1,079 lived in Stanley, the capital.
The preliminary results of the December 1980 census showed a total of 1,812
resident civilians in the Territory.

2. CONSTITUTIONAL AND POLITICAL DEVELOPMENTS

A. Constitution

3.   The constitutional arrangements for the Territory, introduced in 1949 and
amended in 1955, 1964 and 1977, are outlined in earlier reports of the Special
Committee. 2/ Briefly, the governmental structure consists of: (a) the Governor
appointed by the Queen (currently Mr. Rex Masterman Hunt); (b) an Executive
Council consisting of two ex officio members (the Chief Secretary and the
Financial Secretary), two unofficial members appointed by the Governor and two
elected members of the Legislative Council, elected by the members of that Counci
(c) a Legislative Council consisting of the Governor who presides, two ex officio
members (the Chief Secretary and the Financial Secretary) and six members elected
on the basis of universal adult suffrage; and (d) a Court of Appeals set up in
July 1965 to hear and determine appeals from the courts of the Territory.

4.   Elections under the amended constitutional arrangements were held in
October 1977, and the newly elected Legislative Council was sworn in on

---

1/ The information contained in this paper has been derived from published
reports and from information transmitted to the Secretary-General by the Governme
of the United Kingdom of Great Britain and Northern Ireland under article 73 e
of the Charter of the United Nations on 22 October 1980 for the year 1979.

2/ Official Records of the General Assembly, Twenty-fifth Session, Supplemen
No. 23 (A/8023/Rev.1), vol. IV, chap. XIX, annex, paras. 4-7; and ibid.,
Thirty-third Session, Supplement No. 23 (A/33/23/Rev.1), vol. IV, chap. XXVIII,
annex I, paras. 4-7.

November 1977. There remains one nominated member of the Legislative Council owing to the fact that one of the elected seats was not contested.

It will be recalled 3/ that, in a speech to the newly elected Legislative Council in June 1978, the Governor suggested that the Council might consider from time to time how the newly instituted constitutional and legislative arrangements were working. He said that readjustments might be possible in one or two respects, and invited the members to submit their views on the matter. At a meeting of the Legislative Council in June 1980, Mr. W. H. Goss, one of the members, stated that with the prospect of elections in 1981, the Council should consider revising the Constitution. In his opinion, the community was too small to have two councils, which had led to considerable duplication of work and documentation. He felt that there should be only four elected members of the Legislative Council, all of whom would serve on the Executive Council.

B. Public service

According to information provided to the United Kingdom House of Commons, 4/ the territorial Government employs 315 persons, including those employed on a contract basis. The policy of the Government is to give all members of the public service every opportunity to enhance their capabilities through further training, thereby reducing the need to recruit officers from abroad. In a speech in June 1978, the Governor stated that proposals would be submitted to the Legislative Council for expanding the training scheme for nurses and introducing in-service secretarial and clerical training in the public service for school leavers. Efforts were also being made to encourage training overseas, not only in academic institutions but through individually arranged working attachments.

A review of the salary structure of the public service was expected to be made in December 1980 by Mr. H. P. Ritchie, a Salaries Commissioner from the United Kingdom. The Falkland Islands Civil Service Association, in a circular dated 9 September 1980, urged the full participation of all its members in the review, stating that one of the most important problems facing the Association was the reduction of "the immense emoluments gap" between locally recruited officers and those recruited abroad. The Association also felt that the review should cover the loss of free medical and dental treatment and the need for periodic adjustments to the cost-of-living bonus.

C. Relations between the Governments of Argentina and the United Kingdom

Detailed information concerning relations between the Governments of Argentina

---

3/ Ibid., Thirty-fourth Session, Supplement No. 23 (A/34/23/Rev.1), vol. IV, chap. XXVIII, annex, para. 5.

4/ Parliamentary Debates, House of Commons, 17 December 1980, col. 313.

and the United Kingdom on the question of the Falkland Islands (Malvinas) prior to 1980 is contained in earlier reports of the Special Committee. 5/

9. On 28 and 29 April 1980, a ministerial meeting was held at New York on the question of the Falkland Islands (Malvinas) and related issues in the South Atlantic. The delegations were led by Commodore Carlos Cavándoli, Under-Secretary for External Relations and Worship of Argentina, and Mr. Nicholas Ridley, Minister of State at the United Kingdom Foreign and Commonwealth Office. Mr. Adrian Monk, a member of the Falkland Islands Legislative Council, was part of the United Kingdom delegation.

10. Reporting to the United Kingdom House of Commons on the meeting, Mr. Ridley stated that "the exchanges were conducted in a cordial and positive spirit. Each side was able to reach a better understanding of the other's position. No decisions were taken, though it was agreed that contacts on day-to-day matters between the islands and Argentina should be expanded ...". 6/ Subsequently, in response to questions in Parliament, Mr. Ridley said that arrangements had been set in hand to institutionalize contacts between the islanders and the Argentines in Government and the private sector with whom there was co-operation on economic and supply matters. 7/

11. On 25 September 1980, during the thirty-fifth session of the General Assembly Brigadier Carlos W. Pastor, Minister for External Relations and Worship of Argentina, and Lord Carrington, United Kingdom Secretary of State for Foreign and Commonwealth Affairs, held a meeting at New York.

12. On 11 November, by its decision 35/412, the General Assembly, on the recommendation of the Fourth Committee, decided to defer consideration of the question of the Falkland Islands (Malvinas) until its thirty-sixth session and requested the Special Committee to keep the situation in the Territory under review.

13. In November 1980, Mr. Ridley paid his second visit to the Territory, and on 2 December, reported to Parliament about it as follows:

> "We have no doubt about our sovereignty over the islands. The Argentines however, continue to press their claim. This dispute is causing continuing uncertainty, emigration and economic stagnation in the islands. Following my exploratory talks with the Argentines in April, the Government has been considering possible ways of achieving a solution which would be acceptable to all the parties. In this, the essential is that we should be guided by the wishes of the islanders themselves.

5/ For the most recent, see Official Records of the General Assembly, Thirty-fourth Session, Supplement No. 23 (A/34/23/Rev.1), vol. IV, chap. XXVIII, annex, paras. 7-17; and A/AC.109/615, paras. 6-14.

6/ Parliamentary Debates, House of Commons, 8 May 1980, col. 224.

7/ Ibid., 14 May 1980, col. 1478.

"I therefore visited the islands between 22 and 29 November in order to consult island councillors and subsequently, at their express request, all islanders, on how we should proceed. Various possible bases for seeking a negotiated settlement were discussed. These included both a way of freezing the dispute for a period or exchanging the title of sovereignty against a long lease of the islands back to Her Majesty's Government.

"The essential elements of any solution would be that it should preserve British administration, law and way of life for the islanders, while releasing the potential of the islands' economy and of their maritime resources, at present blighted by the dispute. It is for the islanders to advise on which, if any, option should be explored in negotiations with the Argentines. I have asked them to let me have their views in due course. Any eventual settlement would have to be endorsed by the islanders, and by this House." 8/

n response to a question on the wisdom of placing the lease-back proposal on the negotiating table, Mr. Ridley stressed that none of the options had been put to the Argentine Government for negotiation. They were for discussion among the islanders, who would decide whether they wished any of them to be pursued.

4. According to The Times (London) of 27 November, the options put to the islanders, in addition to those mentioned by Mr. Ridley, included: (a) the outright transfer of sovereignty to Argentina; (b) the institution of a condominium arrangement similar to that which existed in the New Hebrides under France and the United Kingdom; and (c) the breaking off of negotiations.

5. On 28 November, The Times reported that during a meeting of the Sheepowners' Association in the Territory, Mr. Ridley had stated that under the lease-back proposal "your life style would not be changed, and there would be new financial benefits from fishing, tourism, and oil, which would commence as soon as possible after the change".

6. According to the January 1981 issue of The Falkland Island Times (a local newspaper), Mr. Monk and another member of the Legislative Council visited their constituents in order to ascertain their views on the options open to them. Mr. Monk also addressed the entire community in radio broadcasts on 1 and 2 January 1981. He urged the islanders not to cede their sovereignty and to maintain the position that they were British and wished to remain so.

7. On 7 January, the Legislative Council of the Territory, by a vote of 7 to 1, adopted a motion asking the United Kingdom Government to continue discussions with the Argentine Government with a view to reaching an agreement which would freeze the dispute over sovereignty for a determined period of time. Mr. Monk, who cast the vote against the motion, expressed the view that there should be no further discussion of the question between Argentina and the United Kingdom.

8/ Ibid., 2 December 1980, cols. 195-196.

18. On 23 and 24 February, a further round of talks was held at New York. The Argentine delegation was headed by Commodore Cavándoli and included the Argentine Ambassador to the United Kingdom. The United Kingdom delegation, led by Mr. Ridley, included the United Kingdom Ambassador to Argentina as well as Mr. Mor and Stuart B. Wallace, both members of the territorial Legislative Council.

19. According to press reports, although the Argentine delegation rejected the proposal that there be a "freeze" on the question of sovereignty, as the islanders had requested, the talks were considered to have been cordial. No date was set for the resumption of negotiations which, it appeared, would not take place until after a general election was held in the Territory.

20. On their return to the Territory after the talks, Messrs. Monk and Wallace met with the other members of the Legislative Council. Subsequently, in a press conference, it was reported that the Argentine delegation, in a direct appeal to the councillors, had offered to make the islands a "most pampered region" and to maintain the democratic, legal, social and educational systems of the Territory, if the inhabitants gave up United Kingdom sovereignty in favour of Argentine sovereignty.

21. Since elections are scheduled to be held in the Territory before November 1981, the present Council believes that any decision on the future of the negotiations should be left to the new Legislative Council.

3. ECONOMIC CONDITIONS

A. Shackleton report

22. It will be recalled 9/ that a report entitled Economic Survey of the Falkland Islands, 10/ prepared by Lord Shackleton, was issued by the United Kingdom Government in 1976. In the introduction to the report, it was stated that the terms of reference were very wide since it was intended to provide an over-all survey of the economic prospects of the Territory in all sectors. In order to assess fully the development potential of the Territory, account had to be taken of the social dimensions of the situation. The terms of reference excluded any political consideration, however, and the report was thus based on the premise that the political status of the Territory would remain as it had been over the past 150 years. It was none the less stated that in certain proposed areas of development, particularly those related to the exploitation of offshore resources, "co-operation with Argentina - even participation - should, if possible, be secured".

23. As reported above (see para. 13), Mr. Ridley indicated in December 1980 that, until there was a solution to the political problem, there could be no development

---

9/ Official Records of the General Assembly, Thirty-third Session, Supplement No. 23 (A/33/23/Rev.1), vol. IV, chap. XXVIII, annex I, paras. 17-21.

10/ London, H.M. Stationery Office, 1976.

the Territory's economy or its maritime resources. Later that month, in response
a question in the House of Commons on the implementation of the Shackleton
port, Mr. Ridley expanded on this theme, stating:

"We desperately want to develop the economy of the islands. My honourable
friend mentioned improved farming and markets for farming produce. A great
deal of credit is needed to open up those possibilities, and we must get
commercial banks to perform their functions in the islands. There is also
the question of revenue from the rich harvest of fish and the possibility -
there can be no certainty - of finding oil. He wanted us to exert our undoubted
rights over the fishing zones and the economic zones that surround not only
the islands, but our dependencies. My honourable friend mentioned the vexed
question of Magellanes Este, the oil block that straddles the median line.
Nothing would give us more pleasure than to be able to say that we had agreed
the median line, and that we and the Argentine respected that median line, so
that oil exploration and exploitation could go ahead.

. . .

"We also believe that there is a need for good communications. The
airport, the supply of fuel, the air and sea services, education and advanced
health services are all adequate at present, but they depend on Argentina for
their provision.

"The difference of interpretation between my honourable friend and myself
is over how we achieve these aims. That must be made more particular by
asking the effect of the long-run dispute with Argentina on these questions.
At present, the relationship between Great Britain and Argentina is good and
friendly. We are still negotiating in a series of talks with the Argentine
Government, as we were for many years before this Government took over. In
spite of that, it is still not possible to declare those 200-mile fishery
zones, to get the licence fees from foreign fishing in those zones, to explore
or exploit oil, or to legalize the position of Southern Thule. Even the
commercial banks are unwilling to set up the islands, because of the political
risks.

"These hazards are real. It must be recognized that solving these problems
requires an over-all political settlement. The economy of the islands, even
at this time of relative peace, co-operation and good relations, is still in
decline. The population declined last year from about 1,800 to about 1,700.
It must be apparent to my honourable friend that even with the status quo,
these problems cannot be solved and they are leading to a worsening economic
condition in the islands.

. . .

"My honourable friend seemed to believe that, in spite of these political
difficulties, which I can assure him are very real, there was a solution which
consisted of pumping more money into the islands. My honourable friend

quoted the Shackleton report. I can tell him that a very large number of th recommendations have been implemented - 49 out of 90. Of the remainder, 14 have been rejected, 20 are in train and 7 are undecided. I concede that the bulk of the recommendations in terms of money have not been implemented because we come immediately to the question of the runway, and the vast proportion of the work that has not been done is the new runway to the airport.

"There are two reasons why it has not been done, both of which seem equally valid to me now. The first is that a runway to take large jets woul require the existence of some commercial demand. With 1,700 people in the islands, it is unsurprising that that demand is very small. No commercial airline has expressed any interest in running long-haul jet services there because they frankly and rightly believe that the traffic would not be available." 11/

B. General

24. The economy of the Territory continues to be overwhelmingly dependent on sheep farming for wool production. The grasslands are generally poor, owing to difficult climatic and soil conditions, and the resulting yield per hectare is low Research into the improvement of pastures and related aspects of sheep farming is being conducted by the Grasslands Trial Unit (GTU), established in 1975 and entirely financed by the United Kingdom Government. In July 1979, the staff of GT was increased from 4 to 6. GTU has also been providing assistance to the territorial Government on agricultural matters pending the recruitment of an agricultural officer.

25. In 1978/79, the latest year for which figures are available, there were 659,012 sheep in the Territory, an increase of 10,646 over the record figure of th previous year. The distribution was as follows: East Falkland, 377,237; West Falkland, 213,743; and other islands, 68,032.

26. The economy is closely tied to the price of wool on the world market, which has tended to remain static in the past few years while production costs have continued to rise. None the less, in 1979, exports of wool amounted to 2,133 metr tons, bringing earnings of £2,463,615, 12/ compared to 1978 earnings of £2.0 million. Exports of hides and skins totalled 48 metric tons in 1979, with a value of £38,636 (£3,457 in 1978). It will be recalled that, in November 1977, an expert in the tanning and processing of sheepskins and hides paid a visit to th Territory to advise on the development of this activity. 13/

11/ Parliamentary Debates, House of Commons, 18 December 1980, cols. 996-998.

12/ The local currency is the pound sterling.

13/ Official Records of the General Assembly, Thirty-third Session, Supplemen No. 23 (A/33/23/Rev.1), vol. IV, chap. XXVIII, annex I, para. 23.

. During the period under review, sheepowners in the Territory sought sistance in the preparation of wool clip for marketing. A member of the w Zealand Wool Board spent some time in the Territory demonstrating techniques of oper evaluation and classification of the wool clip and ways in which the clip uld be made more attractive to buyers.

. The Falkland Islands Company (FIC), registered in the United Kingdom in 1851, the major contributor to the economy, and the development of the Territory is osely tied to the growth of the company. As the owner of almost half the sheep the Territory and an equivalent proportion of the land, FIC is the largest oducer of wool and controls much of the local banking, commerce and shipping.

. Other potential areas of economic development include tourism, fisheries and e processing of kelp into alginates. At one time, Alginate Industries, Ltd., s making plans for the production of alginate in the Territory, but discontinued em in 1977. In the past years, new approaches have been made to commercial mpanies. The Taiyo Fishing Company of Japan and, more recently, the White Fish thority of the United Kingdom have been carrying out research into the fishing sources of the Territory. There are stocks of king crab and of krill, a small awn high in protein; several countries are interested in the exploitation of e latter.

. Tourism, which is based on the abundance of marine and bird-life in the rritory, including breeding colonies of albatross, seals and geese, was the bject of a recent study in which the Government invested some £25,000. Recent ports indicate that Mr. Julian Fitter, the tourism expert who made the study, has t up an organization called Falkland Wildlife to take tourists by ship to visit e wild-life areas of the Territory.

. The possibility that large oil deposits exist in the Territory and its f-shore areas has aroused the interest of several major oil companies. In 1978, e United Kingdom Government reported that two private companies had completed ismic surveys in the waters surrounding the islands, one of which had been made behalf of the Argentine and United Kingdom Governments. The results of the rvey, according to reports in the press, were "more encouraging than discouraging". l companies and consultants feel that oil exploration in the area is now an onomic proposition, and according to The Times (London), several large companies ve projected expenditures totalling some £130 million for exploration in the ters between Tierra del Fuego and the Territory.

. In mid-February 1981 it was announced that the largest Argentine off-shore oil rike had been made near the Patagonian coast. The well, discovered by the Shell mpany, is reported to have a flow rate of approximately 2,000 barrels per day. is located in an area adjacent to Magellanes Este, a concessionary licensing ock for which tenders are now being sought and which is within 154 kilometres of e Falkland Islands (Malvinas). The block also straddles what the United Kingdom gards as the "putative" median line between Argentina and the Territory (see also ra. 23 above).

. As noted above, the Territory specializes in the production of wool for export nd depends heavily on imported goods for the satisfaction of local requirements.

In 1979, imports totalled £2,502,251. The United Kingdom continues to absorb mos of the Territory's exports and to provide most of its imports. Recently, attempt have been made to increase trade relations between the Territory and the Argentin mainland, and also with Chile.

34. According to the approved budget estimates for 1980/81, ordinary revenue wou amount to £2,213,201 (compared with the revised estimates of £2,338,530 for 1979/80), while expenditure would amount to £2,284,320, leaving a deficit of £71,119. The principal items of revenue were customs duties, internal revenue, posts and telecommunications and municipal services, which were estimated at £1,321,150. The principal items of expenditure were public health (£257,381), public works (£254,256), education (£223,640), posts and telecommunications (£191,500) and civil aviation (£302,289). Capital expenditure for 1980/81 was estimated at £891,605, of which £520,770 was to come from United Kingdom aid. Th major projects to be financed by United Kingdom aid were the school hostel projec (£250,000) and the roads project (£180,090). The major items of development expenditure from local funds were housing (£100,000) and roads (£45,160).

35. In 1971, the Governments of Argentina, the Falkland Islands (Malvinas) and the United Kingdom signed a Communications Agreement at Buenos Aires, designed to improve economic, social and cultural co-operation between the Falkland Islands (Malvinas) and Argentina. Air communications between Argentina and Stanley are operated on a weekly basis by Líneas Aéreas del Estado (LADE), a State-owned Argentine airline. The permanent airport at Stanley, constructed with United Kingdom aid at a cost of £6 million and by Argentine technicians, was opened to traffic on 1 May 1979. The airport was designed to take aircraft up to the size of the Hawker Siddeley HS-748 or other medium-haul aircraft.

36. Following the publication of the Shackleton report, the United Kingdom Government agreed to carry out a survey of the internal transport service (road, sea and air) in the Territory. This led to the initiation of a road development programme, the first stage of which is the construction of an all-weather road from Stanley to Darwin. The internal air service run by the territorial Governmen was expanded in 1979 by the addition of a twin-engine land-plane to the fleet of sea-planes which make unscheduled flights between the settlements and Stanley.

4. SOCIAL AND EDUCATIONAL CONDITIONS

37. During the period under review, the labour situation in the Territory continu to decline due to emigration. Vacancies continue to exist in the agricultural industry of the islands, mainly for skilled mechanics. The development projects currently under way are reported to have put a strain on available labour, and in some cases, their completion has been delayed. According to The Observer (London) of 18 January 1981, a proposal to counteract the decline in the population of the Territory by encouraging the immigration of people from St. Helena, another United Kingdom colony in the South Atlantic, attracted hundreds of applicants, including persons from the United Kingdom. The territorial Government, however, had intended to start with a pilot scheme of four families, in which the men would be suitably qualified tradesmen whose wives could be employed in clerical position in the Governm t.

8. The Government maintains a 17-bed general hospital at Stanley, providing edical, surgical, obstetric and geriatric care. Of the original 27 beds, 0 have been converted to provide hostel accommodations. The Medical Department s responsible for public health and sanitation in the Territory and employs one enior medical officer, two medical officers and other staff. A general ractitioner is available in the town, while a flying-doctor service reaches the utlying farm settlements.

9. The installation at the hospital of new X-ray equipment, acquired at a cost f £32,000 with funds from the United Kingdom, was to have been completed late n 1980. Expenditure on public health for the year 1980/81 was estimated at 257,381.

0. According to information submitted by the administering Power, there were 13 pupils attending the 11 government schools, which are staffed by 32 teachers. ducation is free and attendance compulsory in Stanley for children between the ges of 5 and 15 years, and outside Stanley, for those between the ages of 7 and 5 years. Education is provided mainly at the primary level, except at the enior School at Stanley, which offers secondary education in a limited range of ubjects up to the ordinary level of the General Certificate of Education. n 1978, scholarships for secondary education abroad were discontinued and in 1979, it was announced that overseas education allowances would also be discontinued nce the current beneficiaries had completed their studies. The Argentine overnment provides an unlimited number of scholarships for secondary education f students from the Territory, as well as two teachers of Spanish for the schools t Stanley. Estimated expenditure on education for the year 1980/81 amounted to £223,640.

NITED NATIONS

ENERAL

SSEMBLY

Distr.
GENERAL

A/36/23 (Part V)*
29 September 1981

ORIGINAL: ENGLISH

irty-sixth session
enda items 19 and 93

REPORT OF THE SPECIAL COMMITTEE ON THE SITUATION WITH REGARD
TO THE IMPLEMENTATION OF THE DECLARATION ON THE GRANTING OF
INDEPENDENCE TO COLONIAL COUNTRIES AND PEOPLES

(covering its work during 1981)

Rapporteur: Mr. Moh. Farouk ADHAMI (Syrian Arab Republic)

CHAPTERS IX-XXVI

WESTERN SAHARA, EAST TIMOR, GIBRALTAR, BRUNEI, COCOS (KEELING)
ISLANDS, PITCAIRN, ST. HELENA, GUAM, TRUST TERRITORY OF THE
PACIFIC ISLANDS, BERMUDA, BRITISH VIRGIN ISLANDS, MONTSERRAT,
CAYMAN ISLANDS, TURKS AND CAICOS ISLANDS, UNITED STATES VIRGIN
ISLAND AND FALKLAND ISLANDS (MALVINAS)

CONTENTS

* This document contains chapters IX-XXVI of the Special Committee's report
the General Assembly. The general introductory chapter will be issued under the
mbol A/36/23 (Part I). Other chapters of the report will be issued under the
mbol A/36/23 (Parts II-IV, VI and VII). The complete report will be issued
bsequently as Official Records of the General Assembly, Thirty-sixth Session
pplement No. 23 (A/36/23/Rev.1).

-24679

CHAPTER XXIV

FALKLAND ISLANDS (MALVINAS)

A. Consideration by the Special Committee

1.   At its 1184th meeting, on 21 January 1981, by adopting the suggestions relating to the organization of its work put forward by the Chairman (A/AC.109/L.1385 and Corr.1), the Special Committee decided, inter alia, to take the question of the Falkland Islands (Malvinas) as a separate item and to conside it at its plenary meetings.

2.   The Special Committee considered the Territory at its 1200th meeting, on 19 August 1981.

3.   In its consideration of the item, the Special Committee took into account th provisions of the relevant General Assembly resolutions, including in particular resolution 35/119 of 11 December 1980 on the implementation of the Declaration on the Granting of Independence to Colonial Countries and Peoples. By paragraph 12 that resolution, the Assembly requested the Committee "to continue to seek suitab means for the immediate and full implementation of General Assembly resolution 15 (XV) in all Territories which have not yet attained independence and, in particular: ... to formulate specific proposals for the elimination of the remaining manifestations of colonialism and to report thereon to the General Assembly at its thirty-sixth session". The Committee also took into account General Assembly decision 35/412 of 11 November 1980 concerning the Territory. Further, the Committee took into account the relevant provisions of General Assembly resolution 35/118 of 11 December 1980 containing the Plan of Action for the Full Implementation of the Declaration on the Granting of Independence to Colonial Countries and Peoples.

4.   During its consideration of the item, the Special Committee had before it a working paper prepared by the Secretariat containing information on developments concerning the Territory (A/AC.109/670) and the following communications addresse to the Secretary-General:

     (a) Letter dated 23 March 1981 from the Permanent Representative of Argenti to the United Nations (A/36/155);

     (b) Letter dated 23 March 1981 from the Chargé d'Affaires a.i. of the Permanent Mission of the United Kingdom of Great Britain and Northern Ireland to the United Nations (A/36/156);

     (c) Letter dated 29 July 1981 from the Permanent Representative of Argentin to the United Nations (A/36/412).

B. Decision of the Special Committee

5.   At its 1200th meeting, on 19 August 1981, taking into account the relevant resolutions of the General Assembly and its own and on the basis of the related

consultations, the Special Committee decided, without objection, to continue its consideration of the item at its next session, subject to any directives which the General Assembly might give in that connexion at its thirty-sixth session and, in order to facilitate consideration of the item by the Fourth Committee, to transmit the relevant documentation to the Assembly, including in particular the communications referred to in paragraph 4 above.

S

NITED
ATIONS

Security Council

Distr.
GENERAL

S/RES/502 (1982)
3 April 1982

RESOLUTION 502 (1982)

Adopted by the Security Council at its 2350th meeting,
on 3 April 1982

The Security Council,

Recalling the statement made by the President of the Security Council at the 2345th meeting of the Security Council on 1 April 1982 (S/14944) calling on the Governments of Argentina and the United Kingdom of Great Britain and Northern Ireland to refrain from the use or threat of force in the region of the Falkland Islands (Islas Malvinas),

Deeply disturbed at reports of an invasion on 2 April 1982 by armed forces of Argentina,

Determining that there exists a breach of the peace in the region of the Falkland Islands (Islas Malvinas),

1. Demands an immediate cessation of hostilities;

2. Demands an immediate withdrawal of all Argentine forces from the Falkland Islands (Islas Malvinas);

3. Calls on the Governments of Argentina and the United Kingdom to seek a diplomatic solution to their differences and to respect fully the purposes and principles of the Charter of the United Nations.

Reference Services
Central Office of Information, London

The Falkland Islands and Dependencies

The Falkland Islands and its Dependencies were illegally invaded and occupied by Argentine military forces in early April. The British Government has no doubt of its sovereignty over the Islands, which have been continuously, peacefully and effectively occupied by Britain since 1833; and, in seeking a solution to the dispute, Britain has emphasised that it will not support any transfer of sovereignty against the wishes of the Falkland Islanders. This paper provides background information on the Falkland Islands and Dependencies together with a brief history of the dispute with Argentina.

THE FALKLAND ISLANDS
Situated in the South Atlantic, the Falkland Islands lie about 772 km (480 miles) north-east of Cape Horn. They consist of about 200 islands, the largest being East Falkland and West Falkland, and their total land area is some 12,173 sq km (4,700 sq miles).

The People
The 1980 census showed a population of 1,813 of which 1,360 were born in the Islands and 302 in Britain. Most can trace their origins in the territory back to the nineteenth century. Although rising to a peak of 2,392 in 1931, population has declined ever since. The birth rate per 1,000 in 1980 was 17·25 and the death rate was 4·85 per 1,000. Stanley, the capital, with a population of 1,050 in 1980, is the only town: elsewhere the largest settlement is Goose Green (95 people) on East Falkland. English is the language of the Islanders. There are Anglican, Roman Catholic and Non-conformist churches.

Physical Features
The coastline is deeply indented and affords many good anchorages. There are no inland waters. The surface is generally hilly except in Lafonia, the southern half of East Falkland; the highest points are Mount Usborne (705 m − 2,312 ft) in East Falkland and Mount Adam (700 m − 2,297 ft) in West Falkland. Much of the upland is comparatively bare of vegetation and consists of eroded peat, scree and stone runs − 'rivers' of angular quartzite boulders. Because of the climate there are few trees, the natural vegetation being grassland with some species of heath and dwarf shrubs. Bird and marine mammal life − geese, penguins, seabirds and seals − is diverse and relatively unspoiled. There are no native land mammals.

Climate
The climate is characterised by a narrow temperature range, strong winds, a fairly low rainfall evenly distributed throughout the year and frequent cloud cover. Snow has been recorded in every month of the year except February, but seldom lies for long. Climatic figures for Stanley are:

Mean annual temperature	5·6°C (42° F)
Mean annual wind speed	17 knots
Mean annual rainfall	635 mm (25 inches)
Annual maximum temperature around	21·1°C (70° F)
Annual minimum temperature around	−5·6°C (22° F)
Average annual sunshine	1,640 hours

History

The Falkland Islands were probably first sighted by the English captain John Davis in 1592: other sightings were by Sir John Hawkins in 1594 and the Dutch sailor Sebald de Weert in 1600. The first known landing was in 1690 by Captain John Strong, who gave the Islands their English name after Viscount Falkland, then Treasurer of the Navy. French seal-hunters, who were frequent visitors to the area in the eighteenth century, called the islands 'les Iles Malouines', from the port of St Malo, hence the Spanish designation, las Islas Malvinas.

In 1764 a small French colony, Port Louis, was established by de Bougainville in East Falkland. Three years later the settlement was handed over to Spain on payment of a sum then equal to about £24,000. The Spaniards renamed the settlement Puerto de la Soledad. Meanwhile a British captain, John Byron, had made a comprehensive survey of West Falkland in 1765 and noted the fine anchorage in Saunders Island, which he named Port Egmont. In the following year Byron's subordinate, Captain Macbride, established a British settlement of about a hundred people at Port Egmont. When in 1770 a Spanish force compelled the British settlers to leave, this brought Spain and Britain to the verge of war, but in 1771, after protracted negotiations, the Spaniards handed back Port Egmont to Britain, which re-established the settlement but withdrew it again in 1774 on grounds of economy. The British claim to sovereignty was, however, maintained and, as was then customary, a leaden plaque left, declaring the Falkland Islands to be 'sole right and property' of King George III. The Spanish settlement on East Falkland was withdrawn in 1811.

In 1820 the Buenos Aires Government, which had formally declared its independence of Spain in 1816, sent a ship to the Falkland Islands to proclaim its sovereignty. A settlement was established at Puerto de la Soledad in 1826 under the leadership of Luis Vernet, whom the Buenos Aires Government appointed Governor, despite British protests. Five years later, however, a United States warship, the *Lexington*, destroyed the fort at Soledad as a reprisal for the arrest of three American vessels by Vernet, who was attempting to establish control over sealing in the islands. Captain Silas Duncan, the commander of the *Lexington*, declared the Falklands free of all government and they remained once again without visible authority. In January 1833 a British warship visited the settlement and the British occupation of the Islands was resumed. The Islands were at first put in charge of a naval officer, but in 1841 a civil Lieutenant-Governor was appointed, and in 1843 an Act of the British Parliament put the civil administration on a permanent footing. The Lieutenant-Governor's title was changed to Governor and the first Executive and Legislative Councils were set up in 1845. Although there was a majority of official members in the Legislative Council until 1951, nominated unofficial members played an increasingly important part, and in 1949 members elected by universal adult suffrage were introduced to the Council.

A grant in aid to the settlement was approved in 1841 and continued until 1880. A grant in aid for a mail service continued until 1884-5, since when the territory has been self-supporting. The development of the islands has been closely linked with the growth of the Falklands Islands Company, founded in 1851, which is now the largest landowner and trading company.

Government

The present constitution of the Falkland Islands came into force on 21 November 1977. The government is administered by a Governor assisted by an Executive Council composed of two *ex officio* members, two unofficial members appointed by the Governor and two elected members of the Legislative Council nominated by that Council, and a Legislative Council composed of two *ex officio* members and six elected members.

Elections are by universal adult suffrage, Stanley being represented by three elected members, East and West Falkland by one each, and the other member representing all country districts. In 1977 the voting age was lowered from 21 to 18 years. The last general election took place in 1981.

The Judiciary
The judicial system is administered by a Supreme Court (there is a non-resident Chief Justice), a Magistrates' Court presided over by the senior magistrate, and a court of summary jurisdiction, presided over by a bench of magistrates composed of two or more Justices of the Peace. A Court of Appeal for the territory sits in London.

Defence
The Ministry of Defence maintains a Royal Marine detachment which trains the Falkland Islands Defence Force, a voluntary and part-time local force.

The Economy
The Falklands economy is based almost entirely on sheep farming (about 650,000 sheep). Studies are in hand to improve pastures and methods of sheep farming. Over the past few years the Islands have received substantial aid from Britain for economic development and to build up the dependency's infrastructure.

In 1975 the British Government commissioned an economic study by Lord Shackleton (see p 7) in order to determine the prospects for, and the best means to achieve, the development and diversification of the Islands' economy. The survey team included experts on fisheries, oil and wool, which were regarded as the main areas of potential development. Published in 1976, Lord Shackleton's report recommended a number of major capital projects including the establishment of a tourist industry, the enlargement of the airport, and the development of a fishing industry and offshore oil and gas production.

It is hoped to develop a specialised tourist industry centred around the abundant wild-life. Research has also been carried out into the fishing resources of the territory, for there are stocks of king crab and krill (a small prawn high in protein). Britain recognises that without a political settlement it will be difficult to persuade private enterprise to invest in the Falklands' economy, to declare a 200-mile fishing zone or to explore for or exploit oil.

All land is freehold, except for some 11,370 hectares (28,100 acres) of Crown reserves which can be rented. Most land is divided into a few large farms, and nearly half is owned by the Falkland Islands Company. The Falkland Islands Government has concluded that some of the Islands' large farms can be made more profitable by sub-dividing them and selling the smaller farms to the Islanders and expatriates. One farm is already operating this way and appears to be successful and another is now available for sub-division. No field crops are grown except for a small quantity of oats grown for hay. Most householders grow their own vegetables.

Labour
About half the workforce is employed in sheep farming. In Stanley the largest sources of employment are government and public services, trading and shipping.

The only trade union, the Falkland Islands General Employees Union, has some 500 members. Legislation is in force concerning minimum wages, working conditions, compensation for accidents at work, and providing for arbitration in the unusual event of a labour dispute which cannot be settled by direct negotiation.

Trade
Exports consist almost entirely of wool, hides and skins. The main imports are foodstuffs, manufactured goods, timber and machinery. Most of the external trade of the Falkland Islands is with the United Kingdom; recent trade figures are as follows:

Year	Imports from Britain (£000)	Exports to Britain (£000)
1977	2,387	1,524
1978	2,765	1,499
1979	3,319	2,359
1980	2,846	2,083

Public Finance

Total estimated revenue for 1981-82 is nearly £2·5 million, its main sources being internal revenue (£597,110), posts and telecommunications (£572,942), municipal services (£248,000), investments (£222,010), harbour (£182,800), customs (£180,800) and aviation (£98,244); other revenue amounted to £377,205. Estimated ordinary expenditure was just over £2·4 million, the main items being public works (£598,007 – recurrent and other), aviation (£283,763), posts and telecommunications (£280,316), medical (£269,772), and education (£256,274).

Taxation

Individuals pay a graduated income tax ranging from 22½p in every £ of the first £500 of taxable income to 50p in every £ exceeding £4,500. Companies pay a flat rate of 52p in the £. Import duties are payable on liquor, beer and tobacco.

Agreements are in force with Britain, Denmark, Norway, Switzerland, and the United States under which double taxation is avoided.

Currency and Banking

The currency is local coinage and local £10, £5, £1 and 50p notes which are interchangeable with sterling. Some banking facilities are provided by the Falkland Islands Company, the Stanley Co-operative Society, and the Government Savings Bank. Plans are being made to establish a commercial bank.

Development

In the period from 1976 to 1980 the total amount of British aid was £6·6 million, an average of £735 per head per annum. Several important projects have been financed, notably the electricity power station and the permanent airport at Stanley, opened in 1979. Grants have also been provided towards the costs of constructing a road from Stanley to Darwin, building a secondary school hostel in Stanley, purchasing a land plane and hangar for the internal air service, and rehabilitating plant and establishing storage facilities for the Public Works Department. In 1981 there were 46 professionally or technically qualified people working in the Falkland Islands under the British aid programme, mainly in the education and health services.

Social Welfare

Education

Education is free and compulsory for children between the ages of 5 and 15 years. There is a senior school at Stanley offering secondary education in a limited range of subjects up to the ordinary level of the General Certificate of Education. Because of a recent decision by the Falkland Islands Government to centralise education in Stanley a residential hostel has been built to accommodate pupils from other parts of the territory: the costs are being met from British aid funds. For children wanting to take the advanced level of the General Certificate of Education, the British Government's aid programme finances them in a boarding school in Britain. The few students undertaking higher education courses abroad are also assisted under the British Government's aid programme.

Health

The Government Medical Department is responsible for public health and sanitation in the territory and employs a senior medical officer, two medical officers, a dental officer and ten nursing staff. A flying doctor service is available for outlying farm settlements. The Falkland Islands Government maintains a general hospital at Stanley providing medical, surgical, obstetric and geriatric care; new X-ray equipment recently installed in the hospital was purchased through funds from Britain.

The commoner ailments in the colony are the common cold, nasopharyngitis, bronchitis, gastro-enteritis and rheumatism in its chronic form.

Social Security
There is a system of family allowances, and two old age pension schemes, one contributory and the other non-contributory, which cover all persons reaching the age of 65.

Libraries
There is a public lending library in Stanley and also a lending library operated by the Education Department. A Camp library scheme provides a postal service designed to bring library facilities to residents outside Stanley.

Communications and Services
A weekly air service links Stanley with southern Argentina. The permanent airfield at Stanley, constructed with the help of British aid funds, opened in 1979 and is designed to take medium-haul aircraft. A small government-owned internal air service (two Beaver float planes and one Islander aircraft) provides the main internal passenger link between Stanley and the rest of the territory, priority being given to medical cases. Other internal transport arrangements are maintained by sea, a commercially owned ship carrying heavy freight and sea mail to the outlying districts and collecting the wool crop. A ship on charter to the Falkland Islands Company makes the round trip to Britain four or five times a year transporting the islands' wool and hide exports, and calls at Mar del Plata in Argentina to pick up freight.

There are about 14 km (8½ miles) of roads in and around Stanley of which almost 9·6 km (6 miles) are macadamised while the remainder consist of rock rubble. Britain is financing the construction of a road between Stanley and Darwin. Unsurfaced tracks connect most settlements on the east and west islands where travellers generally use Land-Rovers, motorcycles or horses, depending on weather conditions. There are about 1,000 motor vehicles in the territory. There are no railways or inland waterways.

Telecommunications
Internal telecommunications and broadcasting are the responsibility of the Posts and Telecommunications Department, whereas external communications are the responsibility of the Cable and Wireless Company. Stanley has a telephone system to which most East Falkland farms are connected, and there is a similar service on West Falkland, centred on Fox Bay. Traffic between the main islands and contact with farms on the smaller islands is by radio telephone. Britain has provided funds to help purchase new and improved transceiver sets. Telephone calls can be made between the territory and Britain, Argentina and most other countries.

Broadcasting and the Press
The Falkland Islands Government runs a broadcasting station at Stanley and there are over 550 radio licence holders. There is also a government-operated wired broadcasting service in Stanley. Periodicals published in the territory, other than the official gazette, are *The Falkland Islands Times* (published monthly), *Penguin News* (monthly) and the *Falkland Islands Journal* (published annually).

Public Utilities
A new electricity power station was completed in the 1970s and supplies power to Stanley. Most farms and settlements have their own private generating plant. A water purification and filtration plant supplies clean water for Stanley. There is scope for wind power generation, hydro-electric and tidal power.

Meteorological Services
Meteorological services for the Falkland Islands are provided by a Government Meteorological Department which has its headquarters in Stanley. The service provides forecasts for shipping and aircraft and undertakes some research into the meteorology of the area.

THE FALKLAND ISLANDS DEPENDENCIES
The Falkland Islands have as dependencies South Georgia, the South Sandwich Islands, the Shag Rocks and Clerke Rocks. South Georgia lies 1,290 km (800 miles) east-south-east of the Falklands, and the South Sandwich Islands some 760 km (470 miles) south-east of South Georgia.

The Dependencies are British dependent territories, but for convenience they are administered by the Falkland Islands Government, which is empowered to legislate for them. A magistrate, who is also the Base Commander of the British Antarctic Survey Station, resides at King Edward Point in South Georgia where there has been a government station since 1909.

The population of South Georgia comprises the staff of the British Antarctic Survey Station at King Edward Point and in 1980 numbered about 20. Sea communications with the island are dependent on Royal Research Ships *Bransfield* and *John Biscoe*. All food is imported and there are no exports.

Those territories south of latitude 60° south which were formerly part of the Falkland Islands Dependencies (the South Orkney Islands, the South Shetland Islands, and the Antarctic Peninsula) together with the sector of the Antarctic continent lying between longitudes 20° and 80° west, were constituted a separate territory in 1962 under the name of British Antarctic Territory. This covers all British territories lying in the area affected by the Antarctic Treaty, which was signed in 1959 and came into force in 1961.

The island of South Georgia has an area of 3,755 sq km (1,450 sq miles) and is some 160 km (100 miles) long with a maximum breadth of 32 km (20 miles). The land is very mountainous, rising to 2,793 m (9,625 ft), the valleys being filled with glaciers, many of which descend to the sea. The climate is not entirely Antarctic, but is very severe, the mountains being largely ice- and snow-covered throughout the year. The only indigenous mammals are seals, but there is a large herd of wild reindeer which were first introduced in 1911.

The South Sandwich Islands consist of a chain of uninhabited, actively volcanic islands some 240 km (150 miles) long. The climate is wholly Antarctic. In the late winter the islands may be surrounded by pack ice. The prevalent westerly storms always make landing difficult.

History
South Georgia was sighted at least twice between 1675 and 1756, but the first landing was that of Captain James Cook in 1775. The South Sandwich Islands were discovered during the same voyage. Thereafter, South Georgia was much visited by sealers of many nationalities, who reaped a rich harvest from the immense number of fur seals and elephant seals which frequented these shores. By 1815, the slaughter of seals had reached such proportions that sealers were beginning to look elsewhere for them.

Whaling began in the twentieth century and grew into a highly specialised industry. The principal development took place in 1903, when C. A. Larsen became the first modern whaling company to establish a shore factory in South Georgia. The industry immediately prospered and continued to expand quickly up to and during the first world war. From the beginning, South Georgia was the most important centre of the industry and shore factories were operated at Grytviken, Leith Harbour, Stromness, Husvik, Godthul and Prince Olaf Harbour. Since the late 1920s increasing use has been made of pelagic factory ships which operate in open ocean throughout the whaling season. After the second world war three shore stations were worked at South Georgia but all shore stations had ceased operations by December 1965. Since then the main economic activity in the Dependencies has been fishing by distant water fishing fleets.

THE DISPUTE WITH ARGENTINA
There is no pressure for independence since the Islanders are united in their wish to remain British despite a claim to sovereignty by Argentina on the grounds that it has succeeded to rights claimed by Spain in the eighteenth century. Successive British Governments have had no

doubt about British sovereignty over the Islands, which have been continuously, peacefully and effectively occupied by Britain since 1833.

The Falkland Islands' position as a non-self-governing territory has been debated by the United Nations. The Islanders' elected representatives have explained the population's wish to retain its association with Britain and not to become independent or associated with any other country. Britain has pointed out that in these circumstances the Argentine claim is contrary to the principle of self-determination.

In 1965 the UN General Assembly approved a resolution inviting Britain and Argentina to hold discussions with a view to finding a peaceful solution to the problem, bearing in mind the interests of the Islanders. Subsequent discussions were pursued between the two Governments through diplomatic channels. In 1969 Argentina offered to discuss a lifting of the ban on direct communications between the mainland and the Islands, and in 1970 special talks opened in London between Argentine and British delegations, the latter including participants from the Falkland Islands. As a result of further talks in 1971 in Buenos Aires, agreements were reached covering air and sea communications, postal services, educational and medical facilities for Falkland Islanders in Buenos Aires, and customs measures.

In 1974 Britain and Argentina signed two further agreements relating to the Falkland Islands: one to facilitate trade and the carriage of goods between the Islands and the mainland, and the other to allow the Argentine state petroleum company to supply the Islands with petroleum products.

The findings of an economic survey of the Islands conducted in 1976 by Lord Shackleton underlined the need for closer co-operation with Argentina. In 1977 the British Government concluded that the time had come to consider whether a new framework of economic and political co-operation with Argentina should be established. After detailed consultation with the Islanders and with Argentina, terms of reference were agreed for British-Argentine negotiations on political relations, including sovereignty, and on economic co-operation in the Falkland Islands, their Dependencies and the south-west Atlantic in general. Parallel working groups were subsequently established to study these two themes in depth, but no progress was made.

A round of wide-ranging but exploratory talks was held with Argentina in April 1980. In February 1981 further talks took place in New York between Argentina and Britain whose delegation included two Falkland Islands' Councillors. Argentina rejected the British proposal for a 'freeze' on the dispute for an agreed period of time during which both sides could co-operate to develop the Islands' resources.

In February 1982 another round of formal talks took place in New York between Argentina and Britain whose delegation again included two Falkland Islands' Councillors. The two sides reaffirmed their resolve to find a solution to the sovereignty dispute and considered in detail an Argentine proposal for procedures to make better progress.

Argentina also claims the Falkland Islands Dependencies. These claims have at different times been based on proximity to Argentina and alleged inheritance of title from Spain. Argentina first claimed South Georgia in 1927 and the South Sandwich Islands in 1948. Britain rejects these claims as being without legal or historical foundation. In 1947, and subsequently, Britain offered to submit the dispute on the Dependencies to the International Court of Justice, and in 1955 the British Government applied unilaterally to the Court for redress against encroachments on British sovereignty in the Dependencies by Argentina and also by Chile. Both countries, however, declined to submit to the Court's jurisdiction in this matter.

FURTHER READING

Information about the Falkland Islands is contained in the annual *Yearbook of the Commonwealth*, published by Her Majesty's Stationery Office (HMSO). The Shackleton Report, *Economic Survey of the Falkland Islands*, was published in two volumes (South America Department, Foreign and Commonwealth Office — £14·50 including postage and packing) in 1976. The second edition of a book by Ian Strange (*The Falkland Islands*, ISBN 0 7153 8133 4, David and Charles, 1981, £8·50) provides an account of the territory's people, geography, history, administration, agriculture and fisheries, communications and natural history.

(Spanish in preparation)

This paper is one of a series of reference publications prepared for the Foreign and Commonwealth Office. Although the text is Crown Copyright, it may be freely reproduced outside Britain, with or without acknowledgment. Similar publications on other subjects may be obtained from British Embassies, High Commissions or Consulates.

HE FALKLAND ISLANDS AND DEPENDENCIES

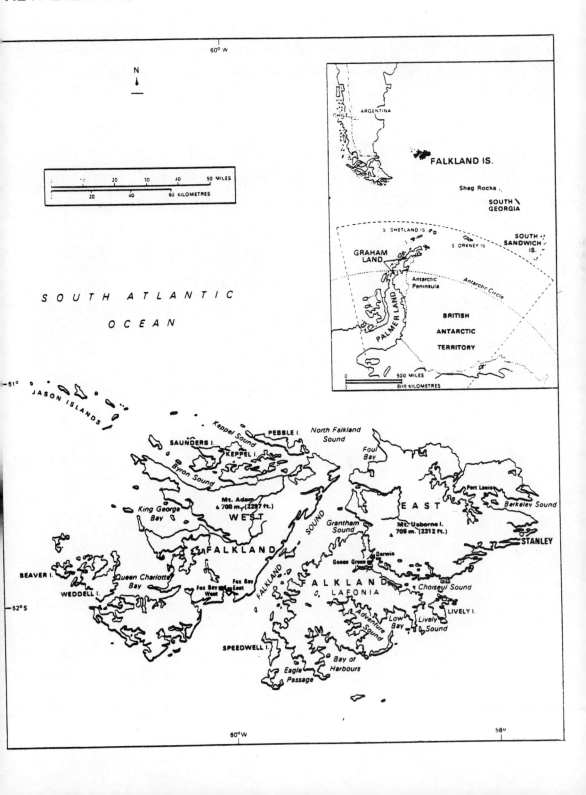

PROVISIONAL

S/PV.2350
3 April 1982

ENGLISH

UNITED NATIONS

SECURITY

COUNCIL

PROVISIONAL VERBATIM RECORD OF THE TWO THOUSAND
THREE HUNDRED AND FIFTIETH MEETING

Held at Headquarters, New York,
on Saturday, 3 April 1982, at 11 a.m.

President:	Mr. KAMANDA wa KAMANDA	(Zaire)
Members:	China	Mr. LING Qing
	France	Mr. LOUET
	Guyana	Mr. KARRAN
	Ireland	Mr. DORR
	Japan	Mr. NISIBORI
	Jordan	Mr. NUSEIBEH
	Panama	Mr. ILLUECA
	Poland	Mr. WYZNER
	Spain	Mr. PINIES
	Togo	Mr. ADJOYI
	Uganda	Mr. OTUNNU
	Union of Soviet Socialist Republics	Mr. TROYANOVSKY
	United Kingdom of Great Britain and Northern Ireland	Sir Anthony PARSONS
	United States of America	Mr. LICHENSTEIN

This record contains the original text of speeches delivered in English and interpretations of speeches in the other languages. The final text will be printed in the Official Records of the Security Council.

Corrections should be submitted to the original speeches only. They should be sent under the signature of a member of the delegation concerned, within one week, to the Chief of the Official Records Editing Section, Department of Conference Services, room A-3550, 866 United Nations Plaza, and incorporated in a copy of the record.

82-60458/A

UNITED NATIONS

SECURITY

COUNCIL

PROVISIONAL

S/PV.2350

3 April 1982

ENGLISH

PROVISIONAL VERBATIM RECORD OF THE TWO THOUSAND
THREE HUNDRED AND FIFTIETH MEETING

Held at Headquarters, New York,
on Saturday, 3 April 1982, at 11 a.m.

President: Mr. KAMANDA wa KAMANDA   (Zaire)

Members:	
China	Mr. LING Qing
France	Mr. LOUET
Guyana	Mr. KARRAN
Ireland	Mr. DORR
Japan	Mr. NISIBORI
Jordan	Mr. NUSEIBEH
Panama	Mr. ILLUECA
Poland	Mr. WYZNER
Spain	Mr. PINIES
Togo	Mr. ADJOYI
Uganda	Mr. OTUNNU
Union of Soviet Socialist Republics	Mr. TROYANOVSKY
United Kingdom of Great Britain and Northern Ireland	Sir Anthony PARSONS
United States of America	Mr. LICHENSTEIN

This record contains the original text of speeches delivered in English and interpretations of speeches in the other languages. The final text will be printed in the Official Records of the Security Council.

Corrections should be submitted to the original speeches only. They should be sent under the signature of a member of the delegation concerned, within one week, to the Chief of the Official Records Editing Section, Department of Conference Services, room A-3550, 866 United Nations Plaza, and incorporated in a copy of the record.

82-60458/A

The PRESIDENT (interpretation from French): The Security Council will
w resume its consideration of the item on its agenda.

The first speaker is the Minister for Foreign Affairs of Argentina,
.s Excellency Mr. Nicanor Costa Mendez. I welcome him and invite him to make his
:atement.

Mr. COSTA MENDEZ (Argentina) (interpretation from Spanish): Perhaps the
:ginning of my statement may be considered repetitive, but I consider it none the
:ss useful to state that the reason for the calling of these meetings lies in the
lvinas Islands, which is part of Argentine territory and which was illegally
:cupied by the United Kingdom in 1833 by an act of force which deprived our
untry of that archipelago.

The British fleet in 1833 displaced by force the Argentine population and the
thorities which were exercising the legitimate rights that belonged to the
public at that time as the heir to Spain.

Legally speaking, that act of force cannot give rise to any right at all,
nd politically the events of 1833 were one more reflection of the imperialist
licy which the European States carried out in the nineteenth century at the
xpense of America, Africa and Asia. Hence, we can say today that this is a
lonial problem in the most traditional sense of that political and economic
henomenon.

Since 1833, the Republic of Argentina has been claiming reparation from the
nited Kingdom for the great wrong done. The Republic of Argentina has never
onsented to that act of usurpation of its national territory, usurpation carried
ut by unacceptable and illegal means. All the successive Governments of
rgentina, regardless of party or faction, have remained united and steadfast in
heir position during those 149 years of strongly protesting against that arbitrary
ccupation.

(Mr. Costa Mendez, Argentina)

No one can have the slightest doubt as to the historic role of the United Nations in the decolonization process. This is perhaps the area in which the United Nations has proved most fruitful, a task that it has carried out most effectively, one that has changed the course of international relations. Proof of this is that the original membership of 54 has increased to 157. Many of the young nations represented here in the Council have been freed from the colonial yoke, and their contribution to the organized international community is of such magnitude that I do not need to mention it - far less to emphasize it.

Of the 54 original Members 20 belong to the Latin American Group, and their decisive influence in the early days of the Organization must be recognized. That group of nations was very active in giving impetus to the decolonization process. The Latin American Group was, if we may say so, a champion of that caus because it had suffered from the effects of colonization. We too had been colonies: we too had fought the hard struggles for national independence.

One of the last vestiges of colonialism on Latin American territory ended yesterday. The claims that my country has been making repeatedly since 1833 have enjoyed the support of the decisions of the world Organization, and of the individual assistance of these new nations just emerging from the colonial era.

Despite the Organization's efforts and my country's arduous and careful work time passed and brought with it only continued frustration, resulting from the evasive tactics and time-wasting manoeuvres of Great Britain - and all that despite the many alternatives put forward by Argentina and despite the imagination and flexibility with which we approached negotiations.

Two days ago the Permanent Representative of my country made reference here to the willingness and readiness on our part demonstrated by the facilities offered in 1971 in terms of communications and other concessions to the inhabitant of the islands. Those 1,800 inhabitants, as the United Kingdom representative

(Mr. Costa Mendez, Argentina)

aid yesterday, would fit without difficulty into this chamber. They
ave been and are the subject of constant concern in Argentina, which has
given them attention that I venture to say, with all due respect, they have
not received from their "homeland". The Government of Argentina is always
careful to respect individual rights and physical integrity.

Yesterday Argentina stated that its position did not represent any kind
of aggression against the present inhabitants of the islands, whose rights
and way of life - and I stress this - will be respected in the same way as
those of the countries freed by our liberators'. Troops will be used
only when absolutely necessary and they will not in any way disturb the
inhabitants of the islands; quite the contrary, they will protect the
institutions and inhabitants, since they are part of us. This is a most solemn
commitment by the Government of Argentina to the international community.

The United Kingdom has invoked the presence of the inhabitants of
the Malvinas Islands as an excuse for its colonial presence in those islands.
But I ask members: What, then, is the pretext for that presence in the South
Sandwich or South Georgia Islands? I here, as the _Times_ of London said in
an editorial of 29 March last, the only natives, according to the
Commonwealth and Foreign Offices, were seals - and in the present state of
international law seals do not enjoy the right to self-determination?

In view of the fact that my country opened up communications, the
British Government did not seem too concerned over the physical and
historical isolation in which the inhabitants of the islands lived.

I shall not go into details about the change in the standard of
living brought about by the facilities offered by Argentina. As the
President of my country has said, we are ready to guarantee all the
individual rights of the inhabitants. But we cannot allow anyone to
use those 1,800 persons as something enshrined in international law
as a "population".

(<u>Mr. Costa Mendez</u>, Argentina)

In previous statements the characteristics of that group of persons have been dealt with, but I must say again here that, to a large extent, those persons are officials of the British Government and a large number of them are employees of the Falkland Islands Company, a typical colonial firm - a complete anachronism a colonial corporation of those who had letters patent from the eighteenth centur the trade branch of colonialism and imperialism: history offers various examples of this.

Those foreigners with interests there, with no right other than trade and colonial ones, are those who most strongly and systematically have prevented the British Government from taking action.

Of necessity, the recalcitrant attitude of the British Government that I hav mentioned brought about tension and difficulties. More than once peace and security in the region were threatened by the persistent colonial presence.

We have already mentioned in another statement the <u>Shackleton</u> incident of 1976, an episode - and I wish to emphasize this although I am sorry to have to cite this - that supplies a fine example of the Inter-American Committee's resolution, which states:

"Threats to peace and security in the region, together with flagrant violations of international rules on non-interference, are constituted by the presence of foreign war ships in American waters, and also by the announcements made by the British Government concerning their dispatch of other vessels."

It would seem that this would apply equally well today.

The foregoing episode and the episode I have mentioned which was the immediate origin of the present situation are both covered in the statement made by the Permanent Representative of my country and the letter dated 1 April 1982 from my Government to the Security Council which has been circulated as document S/14940

(Mr. Costa Mendez, Argentina)

That incident was serious, but was made even more serious by the United
gdom because it sent warships to the region in a clear attempt at
imidation, which constituted a real threat to my country and to the continent.
ce the statement I have just read out about the Shackleton episode from the
er-American Committee is still fully valid in 1982.

The military preparations and the despatch of warships to the region by
United Kingdom, to which I have already referred, explain and justify the
ions taken of necessity by the Government of Argentina in defence of its rights.

Some delegations here have stated that my Government acted hastily.
eave it to the Council to judge, but I must point out that it seems difficult
describe my country as acting hastily when, with the greatest respect for
ceful solutions, it has borne with a situation of continued usurpation of
territory by a colonial Power for 150 years. Argentina has wisely,
iently and imaginatively negotiated on its long-standing claim
the United Kingdom has not given the slightest indication of being flexible
made a single just proposal. Furthermore, we have been accused in this chamber
violating Article 2 (3) and (4) of the United Nations Charter. No provision
the Charter can be taken to mean the legitimization of situations which have
ir origin in wrongful acts, in acts carried out before the Charter was adopted
which subsisted during its prevailing force. Today, in 1982, the purposes
the Organization cannot be invoked to justify acts carried out in the last
tury in flagrant violation of principles that are today embodied in international
.

Throughout the years we have celebrated the excellent results of the
reversible march of history typified by decolonization and at the same time,
ile we were celebrating and taking part in that process, our frustration was
owing because of the conviction that the United Kingdom was not ready to
ve up the territory it had usurped from Argentina. The accession of emerging
oples to international politics and the change in international society are a
sult of the historic process I mentioned at the beginning of my statement.
is is a real force, and this real force in the world order was reflected in the

(Mr. Costa Mendez, Argentina)

establishment of the Non-Aligned Movement, which my country joined in 1973 and in which it takes part as an active member. That Movement promotes the eradicating of historical injustices, whether they be political or economic. Members of the Non-Aligned Movement, as our Permanent Representative has already said, have repeatedly recognized and acknowledged the justice of the Argentine claim and our country's sovereignty over the Malvinas Islands, the South Georgia and Sandwich Islands, they have already stated that the principle of self-determination does not apply in this case for special historical reasons I have already explained.

The representative of the United Kingdom said that he had doubts about being able to arrive at an agreement with the representative of my country as to the historical vicissitudes. That is possible, but it would seem difficult for us not to agree on the facts of history which are absolutely indisputable.

The Government of Argentina has not invaded any foreign territory, as the United Kingdom claims. As was stated very simply by the President of my country,

> "Safeguarding our national honour and without rancour or bitterness, but with all the strength that comes from being in the right, we have recovered a part of our national heritage".

The same cannot be said of the United Kingdom Government vis-à-vis our country.

Apart from the case which concerns us today, in 1806 and 1807 British expeditionary forces attacked and temporarily occupied the city of Buenos Aires and its suburbs, a historical fact that may not be well known to everybody. On both occasions the British troops were repelled by the Argentine people. In 1840 and in 1848 the Government of Great Britain organized naval blockades against the Republic of Argentina, and, to abide by historical facts, it is rather strange to notice that another colonial power, France, whose representative was so quick to rally to the colonial position yesterday, was already associated in 1848 with these colonial ventures since it took part in the blockade that year that I have mentioned.

(Mr. Costa Mendez, Argentina)

All that is by way of providing the Council with the background. None
e less, I want to mention something familiar to all members of the Council.

Yesterday France made reference to the Malvinas Islands and even mentioned
em by their English name, ignoring the General Assembly decision which provides
at in referring to the islands they shall be called the Malvinas Islands and
e Falkland Islands - always using both names. The representative of France
d all representatives of the French-speaking nations in the Organization
nnot be unaware that the name Malvinas has its origin in the famous trip
de by Bougainville from Saint Malo to the Archipelago; it became "Malouines",
ich was hispanized to "Malvinas".

(<u>Mr. Costa Mendez, Argentina</u>)

I dare not think that there may be ideological or political subtleties underlying this historical error of language, but I mention it because it is surprising.

I have made reference to something of which everyone is aware: the spirit of conciliation and the firm resolution of successive Governments of Argentina to seek by peaceful means a solution to our dispute with Great Britain. Furthermore, everyone is aware that on several occasions our Government has had to discourage sectors of the Argentine community that considered that the total lack of response from the British community made imperative the use of other means. Recent events have affirmed our presence in the islands, and we have offered every guarantee and safeguard so that the new state of peace may be maintained. We have again here told the British Government that we are ready and willing to negotiate and to hear its position. But we must make it absolutely clear in this chamber that any change or disturbance in the peace that may come about from now on in the area of the islands will be the sole responsibility of the United Kingdom.

There is something of which members may not be so aware. The Government of Argentina, after very lengthy negotiations, all fruitless in view of the reluctance of Great Britain, finally proposed a written paper to institutionalize the meetings and to structure the talks so that we could move forward to a peaceful, honourable and just solution. We thus handed the British Embassy a document before a meeting that was to be held on 4 February 1982 with the express, formal and pressing request that it should be answered on the occasion of the meeting. The British delegation, always cordial in matters of form, agreed to the meeting but gave no response to our presentation despite our urgent request. We called upon the meeting to set a date for the response. No date was agreed to. We asked that it should be before the end of March. We were told that they would think about it, but that it was not possible to give any date at that time.

I want to tell members that Argentina felt great discouragement, sadness, and frustration at hearing all that non-news. And yet, despite that recalcitrance, despite that inexplicable reluctance, the Government of Argentina offered a press release that we believed to be extremely important. I shall now read it out:

(<u>Mr. Costa Mendez, Argentina</u>)

"The representatives of Argentina and the United Kingdom, at a
meeting in New York in February, have considered an Argentine proposal
for the establishment of a system of monthly meetings with a pre-established
agenda, the venue to be established beforehand, presided over by officials
from the highest echelons. Such meetings will have the purpose of speeding
up to the utmost the on-going negotiations to arrive at recognition of
Argentine sovereignty over the islands and of thus obtaining substantial
results within a time-limit which at this stage of the talks must of
necessity be short.

"Argentina has negotiated with Great Britain with patience, honesty and
good faith for more than 15 years within the framework mentioned in the
relevant resolutions of the United Nations to arrive at a solution to the
dispute over the sovereignty of the islands. The new system is an effective
measure to arrive at a prompt solution.

"However, if this does not come about, if there is no response
from the British side, Argentina reserves the right to put an end to the
operation of such a mechanism and freely to choose the procedure it deems
most fit in accordance with its interests."

This forewarning was given to the representative of Great Britain. There was
not, and there has not been as yet, any reply except the presence of
HMS <u>Endurance</u> in the Georgias and a note from Lord Carrington the terms of
which I shall refrain from mentioning for various reasons.

I now wish to make reference to the draft resolution submitted by the
United Kingdom. It speaks volumes that the terms are absolutely identical to
those put forward more than 22 years ago in this same chamber in the case of
Goa, when Portugal was hanging on to its colonial power, which consumed it and
gave rise to a new Portugal. That resolution sought to deny India its territorial
rights, just as an attempt is being made here to deny my country its proper rights.
That draft resolution was thrown out by the Council because it was merely a
defence, an expression of continuing colonialism.

(Mr. Costa Mendez, Argentina)

The United Kingdom is the only other party to this dispute. It is the only sponsor of the single draft resolution before the Council. This also is strange. In trying to deny us our territorial integrity and our right to it, the United Kingdom calls for the withdrawal of the Argentine troops which recovered the Malvinas for national sovereignty. If the United Kingdom took those islands through an illegitimate act of force, why has it not withdrawn in the last 149 years on the basis of the same principles that it is today invoking in order to avoid this conflict, which now seems to be of such deep concern to it?

Obviously I am at variance with the draft resolution submitted by the United Kingdom, but I wish to say that I am in agreement on one point. The Republic of Argentina is threatening nobody, the Republic of Argentina is not carrying out acts of aggression or hostility against anyone. It is of no interest to us to have any armed confrontation with anybody at all. We are ready to negotiate through diplomatic channels. I would say that again: we are willing to negotiate through diplomatic channels any differences we have with the United Kingdom except our sovereignty, which is not open to negotiation.

(Mr. Costa Mendez, Argentina)

We have a clear conscience about our rights, and we shall maintain them
th firmness and prudence until we arrive at a proper and peaceful settlement.
is useless to whip up emotions when there is clear justice, as in our case.
r policy, the policy of Argentina has, at all time been lofty, conciliatory
d prudent - and there is no evidence to the contrary. I am sure that it
ll lose none of those attributes here.

The PRESIDENT (interpretation from French): The next speaker is
e representative of Brazil. I invite him to take a place at the Council table
d to make his statement.

Mr. BUENO (Brazil) (interpretation from Spanish): Sir, I should like
rst of all to thank you and, through you, the other members of the Council
r giving me this opportunity to participate, on behalf of my delegation,
the Council's debate. I should also like to express my Government's
tisfaction at seeing you, a worthy representative of a friendly African
untry, presiding over the Security Council. Your diplomatic qualities are
ll known to all, and we have no doubt that you will succeed in guiding
th your customary skill, the proceedings of the Council at this turbulent
ment in history. Similarly, my delegation would like to congratulate
mbassador Kirkpatrick for the impartial and excellent way in which she presided
ver the work of the Council during the month of March.

On instructions from my Government, I am making this statement before the
ecurity Council on a subject which is of considerable concern to us in Brazil.

As everyone knows, and as the Ambassador of the sister Republic of
rgentina mentioned in his statement a few days ago, the Government of Brazil
as always supported the Argentine Government in the territorial dispute over the
alvinas Islands in which it has been engaged for more than a century with the
nited Kingdom of Great Britain and Northern Ireland. This support and the
osition of principle of the sister Republic of Argentina dates from 1833,
hen our two countries had only recently freed themselves from colonial status.

The PRESIDENT (interpretation from French): The representative of the United Kingdom has asked to speak in exercise of the right of reply and I call on him.

Sir Anthony PARSONS (United Kingdom): I have no intention of speaking polemically vis-à-vis the representative of Argentina any more than he did so in his own statement, and any more than my Government has any intention or desire of disturbing the peace in the South Atlantic. I should simply like to make a number of points at this stage in the discussion.

First, I should like to go back to the reason why I called for an immediate meeting of the Council two days ago. This was not - I repeat: not - in any sense to discuss the rights or wrongs of the very-long-standing issue betw Britain and the Republic of Argentina over the islands in the South Atlantic. This was not in any sense my intention. I was summoned two or three days ago by the Secretary-General, acting on his own initiative and on press reports that had come to his notice, and he extended to me a call for my Government to exercis restraint in what appeared to him to be an incipiently serious situation. Shortly after my conversation with the Secretary-General I received information from my Government that an armed attack by Argentina on the Falkland Islands was imminent. I therefore took the step - exceptional for the British Government - of asking the President of the Security Council for an immediate meeting. My only intention in calling for a meeting of the Council was that the Council shoul act in such a way as to pre-empt, to deter, any threat of armed force and to conduct itself in its finest role: defusing a growingly dangerous situation. That was my only objective in calling for a meeting of the Council.

As has been said many times round this table, you, Mr. President, issued an appeal on behalf of the same Council the same evening, unanimously, calling on both sides to exercise restraint and to refrain from the threat or use of forc

The following morning my delegation learnt, to its very great distress, that that appeal had not been heeded by one party and that Argentine armed forces had invaded the Falkland Islands.

(Sir Anthony Parsons, United Kingdom)

My object in calling for a second meeting of the Council again had nothing
atsoever to do with the rights or wrongs of the long-standing issue between my
untry and the Republic of Argentina. It was not in any sense concerned with the
rits; it was entirely in response to this armed invasion. That is why I called
r a second meeting of the Council.

I should like to go on to make one or two observations on certain points
ich the Foreign Minister of Argentina raised in his statement.

I think I am right in saying that he suggested that the immediate origin of
e present crisis was the incident which had taken place in South Georgia some
ys, or even two or three weeks, previously.

I find that contention impossible to accept. This was an incident of relative
iviality. It was a question of the resolution of what we, the United Kingdom
vernment, considered to be the illegal presence of 10 scrap-metal dealers on
e island of South Georgia. We had no intention of resolving that incident by
e use of force. It would have been bizarre, ludicrous, for the Government of
e United Kingdom to bring an incident of that dimension to the Security Council.
had no doubt that we would be able to resolve it peacefully with the Government
the Republic of Argentina. And I cannot see how this very small dispute could
nceivably justify the armed invasion of a group of inhabited islands located
0 miles away from the point at which the 10 scrap-metal dealers were located.

The Foreign Minister of Argentina also stated that his Government had not
ted hastily in using force to assert its claim over the Falkland Islands and he
ferred to the state of negotiations between his Government and mine. Earlier in
s statement he referred to our manoeuvres, our evasive tactics, our procrastination
er the years. Of course, I cannot accept these charges.

At the risk of wearying the Council, I wish to give our side of the state of
gotiations as they were before this very grave crisis exploded.

There was a meeting in New York, at ministerial level, between the British
d Argentine Governments in late February this year, at which were present also
ected representatives of the people of the Falkland Islands. At the end of that
eting a joint communiqué was agreed between the two Ministers who were conducting
e negotiations. The communiqué read as follows:

(Sir Anthony Parsons, United Kingdom)

"The British and Argentine Governments held a meeting at ministerial level in New York on 26 and 27 February 1982 to discuss the Falkland Islands question within the negotiating framework referred to in the relevant resolutions of the United Nations General Assembly.
The British and Argentine delegations were led respectively by Mr. Richard Luce, Member of Parliament, Minister of State at the Foreign and Commonwealth Office in London, and Ambassador Enrique Ross, Under-Secretary of State at the Ministry of Foreign Affairs and Worship in Buenos Aires. The meeting took place in a cordial and positive spirit. The two sides reaffirmed their resolve to find a solution to the sovereignty dispute and considered in detail an Argentine proposal for procedures to make better progress in this sense. They agreed to inform their Governments accordingly."

The next thing that happened was that the Government of the Republic of Argentina unilaterally published the statement to which the Foreign Minister referred and which, indeed, he quoted in extenso in his statement.

(Sir Anthony Parsons, United Kingdom)

That statement by the Government of Argentina differed from the joint
communiqué which we thought had been agreed at ministerial level in New York.
contained a final sentence quoted by the Foreign Minister of Argentina,
ch read as follows:

"However, should this not occur" - that is, the early solution of the dispute
"Argentina reserves the right to terminate the working of this negotiating
mechanism and to choose freely the procedure which best accords
with her interests."

The fact that the Government of Argentina unilaterally published its
statement when we believed that there would be a joint publication of an
eed communiqué, and the presence in the statement of that final sentence,
sed great alarm to the people of the Falkland Islands and, indeed, it
sed a certain controversy within the British Parliament and apprehension in
British Government.

We have since been trying to reconcile this issue and to get back to an
eed statement which would enable a negotiating process to begin. Unfortunately,
now find ourselves in the situation which we are today debating.

I would like to refer to another proposition which, if the interpretation
correct, I understood the Foreign Minister of Argentina to include in his
tement. I understood him to say that the principles in the Charter
ating to the settlement of international disputes by peaceful means - I refer
course to Article 2, paragraphs 3 and 4 - were not necessarily applicable
situations which arose before the Charter was adopted.

If my understanding of the Foreign Minister's meaning is correct, I submit
the members of the Council that this is an extremely dangerous doctrine. The
ld is distressingly full of crisis situations, which have from time to time
ploded into hostility in every continent on the globe. A large number of
se situations have their origins years, decades, centuries before the United

(Sir Anthony Parsons, United Kingdom)

Nations Charter was adopted in 1945. If the proposition were to be accepted that the use of force was valid for situations which originated before the Charter was adopted, by heaven I believe the world would be an infinitely more dangerous and flammable place than it already is.

I said at the outset of my statement that I had not come here to enter into the rights and wrongs of the problem of sovereignty between the Republic of Argentina and my own country. It has been very widely aired by other speakers this morning, and I would just like to say one or two words which relate to it.

The Foreign Minister of Argentina argued that the people of the Falkland Islands are not a population in international law. Those 1,800 or 1,900 people are not recent arrivals in the Islands. The vast majority of them were born there to families which had been settled there for four, five, six generations since the first half of the nineteenth century. In the judgement of my Government, whether they are 1,800 or 18,000 or 18 million, they are still entitled to the protection of international law and they are entitled to have their freely expressed wishes respected.

These have been the only objectives of my Government in that area for a very long time. I cannot believe that the international community takes the view that Britain in the 1980s has a "colonialist" or "imperialist" ambition in the South Atlantic. The proposition is self-evidently ludicrous. We threaten nobody; we have simply concerned ourselves with the protection of the interests and respect for the wishes of the small population of the Islands.

Finally, it has also been argued that this was not an invasion because the Islands belong to Argentina, a proposition which of course my Government contests. But the fact is that the United Kingdom has been accepted by the United Nations - by the General Assembly, by the Committee of 24 - as the Administering Authority. It therefore flies in the face of the facts and in the face of reason to suggest that this was not an armed invasion.

S

JITED
ATIONS

Security Council

Distr.
GENERAL

S/15001
26 April 1982
ENGLISH
ORIGINAL: SPANISH

TELEGRAM DATED 21 APRIL 1982 FROM THE SECRETARY-GENERAL
OF THE ORGANIZATION OF AMERICAN STATES ADDRESSED TO THE
SECRETARY-GENERAL OF THE UNITED NATIONS

In accordance with Article 54 of the United Nations Charter, I have the honour
transmit to you herewith the text of resolution CP/RES. 360 (493/82) adopted
day by the Permanent Council of the Organization, in which it convenes the
entieth Meeting of Consultation of Ministers of Foreign Affairs:

"CP/RES. 360 (493/82)

"CONVOCATION OF THE TWENTIETH MEETING OF CONSULTATION
OF MINISTERS OF FOREIGN AFFAIRS

"WHEREAS:

"In its note dated April 19, 1982, the Government of Argentina requested
convocation of the Organ of Consultation, pursuant to Article 6 of the
Inter-American Treaty of Reciprocal Assistance, to consider the measures that
it would be advisable to take for the maintenance of the peace and security of
the hemisphere, and

"The Permanent Council of the Organization of American States has heard
the statement by the Permanent Representative of Argentina denouncing a grave
situation that threatens the peace and security of the hemisphere and that
affects the sovereignty and territorial integrity of his country, and
describing the measures that the Argentine Government has adopted in exercise
of the right of legitimate self-defense,

"THE PERMANENT COUNCIL OF THE ORGANIZATION OF AMERICAN STATES

"RESOLVES:

"1. To convene the Organ of Consultation under the provisions of the
Inter-American Treaty of Reciprocal Assistance, and in accordance with
Article 70 of the Rules of Procedure of this Permanent Council, to consider
the grave situation that has arisen in the South Atlantic.

"2.   To decide that the Organ of Consultation shall meet at the headquarters of the General Secretariat of the Organization on April 26, 1982, at 10 a.m.

"3.   To constitute itself and to act provisionally as Organ of Consultation, pursuant to Article 12 of the Inter-American Treaty of Reciprocal Assistance."

Alejandro ORFILA
Secretary-General
Organization of American States

ORGANIZATION OF AMERICAN STATES

MEETING OF CONSULTATION OF MINISTERS OF FOREIGN AFFAIRS

TWENTIETH MEETING OF CONSULTATION
OF MINISTERS OF FOREIGN AFFAIRS
April 26, 1982
Washington, D.C.

OEA/Ser.F/II.20
Doc.74/82
28 May 1982
Original: English

TEXTS OF THE PROPOSALS FOR AGREEMENT MADE BY THE GOVERNMENT
OF THE UNITED STATES TO THE GOVERNMENTS OF ARGENTINA
AND OF THE UNITED KINGDOM OF GREAT BRITAIN
AND NORTHERN IRELAND

GENERAL SECRETARIAT OF THE ORGANIZATION OF AMERICAN STATES, WASHINGTON, D.C. 20006

United States Department of State

United States Permanent Mission to the
Organization of American States

Washington, D. C. 20520

His Excellency
Estanislao Valdes Otero
President of the Twentieth Meeting
of Consultation of Ministers of
Foreign Affairs
Washington, D.C.

Excellency:

In light of interest expressed by proposals made
to the Government of Argentina and Great Britain on
April 27, 1982, by the United States Government, I
would like to ask that you circulate the enclosed
document containing those proposals among the delegations
accredited to the Twentieth Meeting of Consultation
of Ministers of Foreign Affairs. Both English and
Spanish texts are included.

Accept, Excellency, the assurances of my highest
consideration.

J. William Middendorf
Ambassador
Special Delegate

MEMORANDUM OF AGREEMENT

Preamble:

On the basis of United Nations Security Council Resolution 502, and the will of the Argentine Republic and of the United Kingdom to resolve the controversy which has arisen between them, renouncing the use of force, both Governments agree on the following steps, which form an integrated whole:

PARAGRAPH 1

1. Effective on the signature of this Agreement by both Governments, there shall be an immediate cessation of hostilities.

PARAGRAPH 2

    2. Beginning at 0000 hours local time of tne day after the day on which this Agreement is signed, and pending a definitive settlement, the Republic of Argentina and the United Kingdom shall not introduce or deploy forces into the zones (hereinafter, "zones"), defined by circles of 150 nautical miles' radius from the following coordinate points (hereinafter, "coordinate points"):

        A) LAT. 51° 40' S
          LONG. 59° 30' W

        B) LAT. 54° 20' S
          LONG. 36° 40' W

        C) LAT. 57° 40' S
          LONG. 26° 30' W

    2.1. Within 24 hours of the date of this Agreement, the United Kingdom will suspend enforcement of its "zone of exclusion" and Argentina will suspend operations in the same area.

    2.2. With 24 hours of the date of this Agreement, Argentina and the United Kingdom will commence the withdrawal of their forces in accordance with the following details:

        2.2.1. Within seven aays from the date of this Agreement, Argentina and the United Kingdom shall each have withdrawn one-half of their military and security forces present in the zones on the date of this Agreement, including related equipment and armaments. Within the same time period, the United Kingdom naval task force will stand off at a distance equivalent to seven days' sailing time (at 12 knots) from any of the coordinate points, and Argentine forces that have been withdrawn shall be placed in a condition such that they could not be reinserted with their equipment and armament in less than seven days.

2.2.2. Within fifteen days from the date of this Agreement, Argentina shall remove all of its remaining forces from the zones and redeploy them to their usual operating areas or normal duties. Within the same period, the United Kingdom shall likewise remove all of its remaining forces from the zones and shall redeploy such forces and the naval task force and submarines to their usual operating areas or normal duties.

2.3. In accordance with its letter of acceptance of even date, the United States shall verify compliance with the provisions of this paragraph, and the two Governments agree to cooperate fully with the United States in facilitating this verification.

PARAGRAPH 3

    3. From the date of this Agreement, the two
Governments will initiate the necessary procedures
to terminate simultaneously, and without delay, the
economic and financial measures adopted in connection
with the current controversy, including restrictions
relating to travel, transporation, communications,
and transfers of funds between the two countries.
The United Kingdom at the same time shall request
the European Community and third countries that have
adopted similar measures to terminate them.

PARAGRAPH 4

4. The United Kingdom and Argentina shall each appoint, and the United States has indicated its agreement to appoint, a representative to constitute a Special Interim Authority (hereinafter "the Authority") which shall verify compliance with the obligations in this Agreement (with the exception of paragraph 2), and undertake such other responsibilities as are assigned to it under this Agreement or the separate Protocol regarding the Authority signed this date. Each representative may be supported by a staff of not more than ten persons on the islands.

PARAGRAPH 5

5.1 Pending a definitive settlement, all decisions,
laws and regulations hereafter adopted by the local administration on the islands shall be submitted to and expeditiously
ratified by the Authority, except in the event that the
Authority deems such decisions, laws or regulations to
be inconsistent with the purposes and provisions of this
agreement or its implementation. The traditional local
administration shall continue, except that the Executive
and Legislative Councils shall be enlarged to include:

(A) two representatives appointed by the Argentine
Government to serve in the Executive Council; and
(B) representatives in each Council of the Argentine
population whose period of residence on the islands
is equal to that required of others entitled to representation, in proportion to their population, subject
to there being at least one such representative in
each Council. Such representatives of the resident
Argentine population shall be -nominated by the Authority.

The flags of each of the constituent members of the Authority
shall be flown at its headquarters.

5.2 Pending a definitive settlement, neither Government shall take any action that would be inconsistent with the purposes and provisions of this Agreement or its implementation.

PARAGRAPH 6

6.1 Pending a definitive settlement, travel, transportation, movement of persons and, as may be related thereto,
residence and ownership and disposition of property, communications and commerce between the mainland and the islands
shall, on a non-discriminatory basis, be promoted and facilitated. The Authority shall propose to the two Governments
for adoption appropriate measures on such matters. Such
proposals shall simultaneously be transmitted to the Executive
and Legislative Councils for their views. The two Governments
undertake to respond promptly to such proposals. The Authority
shall monitor the implementation of all such proposals
adopted.

6.2 The provisions of paragraph 6.1 shall in no way
prejudice the rights and guarantees which have heretofore
been enjoyed by the inhabitants on the islands, in particular
rights relating to freedom of opinion, religion, expression,
teaching, movement, property, employment, family, customs,
and cultural ties with countries of origin.

Paragraph 7

7. December 31, 1982 will conclude the interim period
during which the two Governments shall complete negotiations
on removal of the islands from the list of Non-Self-Governing
Territories under Chapter XI of the United Nations Charter
and on mutually agreed conditions for their definitive
status, including due regard for the rights of the inhabitants
and for the principle of territorial integrity, in accordance
with the purposes and principles of the United Nations
Charter, and in light of the relevant Resolutions of the
United Nations General Assembly. The negotiations hereabove
referred to shall begin within fifteen days of the signature
of the present Agreement.

PARAGRAPH 8

    8. In order to assist them in bringing their negotia-
tions to a mutually satisfactory settlement by the date
stipulated in the preceding paragraph, the Authority shall,
after consultation with the Executive Council, make specific
proposals and recommendations as early as practicable to
the two Governments, including proposals and recommendations
on:

    8.1 The manner of taking into account the wishes
and interests of the islanders, insofar as islands
with a settled population are concerned, based on
the results of a sounding of the opinion of the inhabitants,
with respect to such issues relating to the negotiations,
and conducted in such manner, as the Authority may
determine;

    8.2 Issues relating to the development of the resources
of the islands, including opportunities for joint
cooperation and the role of the Falkland Islands Company;
and

    8.3 Such other matters as the two Governments may
request, including possible arrangements for compensation
of islanders, or matters on which the Authority may
wish to comment in light of its experience in discharging
its responsibilities under this Agreement.

    8.4 The Governments have agreed on the procedure
in sub-paragraph 8.1 without prejudice to their respective
positions on the legal weight to be accorded such opinion
in reaching a definitive settlement.

PARAGRAPH 9

9. Should the Governments nonetheless be unable to
conclude the negotiations by December 31, 1982, the United
States has indicated that, on the request of both Governments,
it would be prepared at such time to seek to resolve the
dispute within six months of the date of the request by
making specific proposals for a settlement and by directly
conducting negotiations between the Governments on the
basis of procedures that it shall formulate. The two Governments
agree to respond within one month to any formal proposals
or recommendations submitted to them by the United States.

PARAGRAPH 10

    10. This Agreement shall enter into force on the date of signature.

Ministro de Relaciones Exteriores y Culto

Washington,D.C., 29 de abril de 1982

Estimado Señor Secretario de Estado:

Hemos examinado cuidadosa
mente el documento que Ud. nos hizo llegar, comparándolo con
nuestras anteriores propuestas y con los puntos de vista que
hemos mantenido en nuestros diversos encuentros. De ese aná
lisis han surgido diferencias significativas, algunas de las
cuales suscitan dificultades que es indispensable superar.

Como ya ha manifestado mi
Gobierno al Sr.Secretario, el objetivo que la Argentina se ha
fijado es el reconocimiento de su soberanía sobre las Islas
Malvinas. Ese elemento central de nuestras discusiones es el
último justificativo de las acciones emprendidas por mi país
y, como ya he tenido ocasión de expresarles muchas veces, cons
tituye para nosotros un fin irrenunciable.

Paralelamente a la cuestión
de la soberanía, la crisis actual suscita, en lo inmediato, la
necesidad de establecer un régimen provisorio para la adminis
tración de las Islas, como paso indispensable del proceso de
separación de las dos fuerzas militares y como pausa razonable
frente a la imposibilidad lógica de formalizar ahora su desti
no final.

Sobre esas dos cuestiones
-reconocimiento de soberanía y régimen de administración pro
visoria- se han basado fundamentalmente las conversaciones
que hemos mantenido. Los restantes problemas tienen más sen
cilla solución si hay acuerdo sobre los dos puntos que acabo
de mencionar.

///

Su Excelencia
Alexander Haig, Jr.
Secretario de Estado
Washington,D.C.

. Ministro de Relaciones Exteriores y Culto

///

Lo cierto es que ambos
están intimamente relacionados. En la medida en que resul
tan imprecisas las disposiciones relativas al reconocimien
to a nuestro favor de la soberanía, se hace necesario para
nosotros -si no queremos volver a la frustrante situación
anterior al 2 de abril- el establecimiento de mecanismos
que nos den mayores facultades para la administración de
las Islas.

A la inversa, si quedara clar
que se reconocerá en última instancia la soberanía argentina,
aumenta nuestra flexibilidad en materia de administración
provisoria.

El documento enviado
por el Sr.Secretario de Estado, cae más acá de las demandas
argentinas y no dá satisfacción a sus aspiraciones mínimas
en ninguno de los dos puntos. Por el contrario, en ambos
se han introducido modificaciones desfavorables. En materia
de administración de las Islas, se ha disminuido el número
de representantes argentinos, y se ha anulado la posibilidad
de aumentar el control por parte de mi país en el caso en
que las negociaciones sobre la cuestión de fondo se eterni
zaran sin hallar solución. Nos encontramos así ante la po
sibilidad cierta de que se establezca una administración
predominantemente británica sin término fijo de expiración.

En lo que toca a la
cuestión de soberanía, se ha quitado toda precisión al con
cepto de integridad territorial y se ha introducido el ele
mento nuevo de un virtual referendum para consultar los
"deseos" de los habitantes, en abierta oposición a la Reso
lución 2065 de las Naciones Unidas y a la posición invaria
blemente sostenida por la Argentina.

///

Ministro de Relaciones Exteriores y Culto

///

Sabe el Sr.Secretario que estas modificaciones no pueden ser aceptadas por nosotros. En mi opinión, se hace necesario encontrar otras fórmulas, tarea para la cual estaremos siempre a disposición del Sr.Secretario. Ellas deberían contemplar el equilibrio a que me he referido más arriba para balancear adecuadamente los datos relativos a la cuestión de soberanía con las disposiciones que organizan la administración provisoria de las Islas, dándole a éstas término fijo y progresiva participación argentina o, en su defecto, asignando a aquéllas una precisión tal que dé seguridad acerca del reconocimiento de los derechos de la Argentina en un plazo determinado.

Si esta posición argentina fuera comprendida quedaría enormemente facilitado el acuerdo, y la redacción final del documento no ofrecería dificultades insalvables.

Al agradecerle una vez más sus arduas y difíciles gestiones, saludo al Señor Secretario con mi más alta consideración.

Nicanor Costa Mendez

ORGANIZATION OF AMERICAN STATES

MEETING OF CONSULTATION OF MINISTERS OF FOREIGN AFFAIRS

TWENTIETH MEETING OF CONSULTATION
OF MINISTERS OF FOREIGN AFFAIRS
April 26, 1982
Washington, D.C.

OEA/Ser.F/II.20
Doc. 78/82
28 May 1982
Original: Spanish

NOTE OF THE ARGENTINE DELEGATION TRANSMITTING THE TEXT OF A LETTER
FROM THE MINISTER OF FOREIGN AFFAIRS OF ARGENTINA TO THE SECRETARY OF
STATE OF THE UNITED STATES ON THE PROPOSALS FOR AGREEMENT
MADE BY THE UNITED STATES

GENERAL SECRETARIAT OF THE ORGANIZATION OF AMERICAN STATES, WASHINGTON, D.C. 20006

PERMANENT MISSION OF THE ARGENTINE REPUBLIC
TO THE ORGANIZATION OF AMERICAN STATES

Washington, D.C. May 28, 1982

VS No. 37 (2.1.41)/82

Mr. President of the
Twentieth Meeting of Consultation
of Ministers of Foreign Affairs
D. ESTANISLAO VALDES OTERO

Mr. President:

I have the honor to address Your Excellency with respect to the document of this Meeting of Consultation bearing the title "Texts of the Proposals for Agreement Made by the Government of the United States to the Governments of Argentina and of the United Kingdom of Great Britain and Northern Ireland" (doc.74/82), to present a copy of the letter that, in my capacity as Minister of Foreign Affairs and Worship of the Argentine Republic, I sent on April 29, 1982, to Secretary of State Alexander Haig, Jr., informing him of the Argentine Government's views on the proposals for agreement made by the Government of the United States.

In making known this reply, the Argentine Government wishes to state, as the attached letter shows, that at no time did it term unacceptable the proposals of the United States Secretary of State. Instead its objection was directed primarily at certain specific points, including some changes that had been made in the document compared to previous drafts, and it suggested that other formulas be sought. It added that if "Argentina's position were encompassed, agreement would be facilitated enormously and the final text of the document would not pose any insurmountable problems."

The Argentine Government wishes this important point to be made clear, in view of the statements that have been made in the sessions of the General Committee of this Meeting of Consultation, which were ratified by circulation of the document cited.

I request that this note with its attachment be distributed immediately as an official document of the Twentieth Meeting of Consultation of Ministers of Foreign Affairs.

Accept, Excellency, the renewed assurances of my highest consideration.

Nicanor Costa Méndez
Minister of Foreign Affairs and Worship
of the Argentine Republic

Attached: copy of the letter from
the Minister of Foreign Affairs and
Worship of the Argentine Republic
Dr. Nicanor Costa Méndez

number of Argentine representatives involved in administration of the islands has been decreased, and the opportunity of expanding my country's control in the event that negotiations on the basic issue go on endlessly without a solution has been barred. Thus we are faced with the real possibility of establishing a predominantly British administration with no fixed expiration date.

As concerns the matter of sovereignty, the concept of territorial integrity has been stripped of all meaning. Further, the new element of a virtual referendum to determine the "wishes" of the inhabitants has been introduced in open opposition to United Nations Resolution 2065 and the unwavering position sustained by Argentina.

The Secretary knows that we cannot accept these changes. In my opinion, other formulas must be found. For this effort, we will always be at the disposal of the Secretary. These formulas should provide for the balance that I referred to above in order to weigh properly the data relating to the matter of sovereignty against the provisions regulating temporary administration of the islands. These provisions should have a fixed term and include gradually larger Argentine participation or, in lieu of this, the provisions should be made precise enough to offer security for recognition of Argentina's rights within a specific period.

If Argentina's position were encompassed, agreement would be facilitated enormously and the final text of the document would not pose any insurmountable problems.

Thank you once again for your ardous and difficult negotiations.

Accept, Mr. Secretary, the renewed assurances of my highest consideration.

(Signed)

Nicanor Costa Méndez

95-I/6528B

Embassy
of the
Argentine Republic

The Malvinas Islands and its dependencies (South
Georgia Islands and South Sandwich Islands) are part of the
territory of the Argentine Republic, which the United Kingdom
illegally occupied by an act of force in 1833.   That year, a
British force attacked the Malvinas, imprisoned the Argentine
Governor, expelled the Argentine population settled on the
islands and dismantled the Argentine administration. This action
was typical of the colonialistic policies implemented by the
European powers in America, Asia and Africa during the XIX
century.   This British behavior was only an example in a
pattern of naked agression as shown by the earlier British
invasions and occupation of Buenos Aires in 1806 and 1807 and
the naval blockades of Argentina in 1840 and 1848.

Thus, under the threat of its guns and without
regard to the principle of self-determination, a British naval
force evicted a peaceful population that was exercising the
legitimate rights which Argentina, as heir to Spain since 1810,
enjoyed on these territories located 300 miles off its coast.

Prior to 1833, England's silence confirmed her
recognition of Argentina's sovereignty.   In contrast, since
1833 Argentina has persistently and firmly protested British
illegal occupation of the islands.

// /

/ / /

Nearly 150 years of constant British rebuff and
16 years of sterile and frustrating bilateral negotiations
held under U.N. auspices bear witness to Argentina's good will
and readiness to solve the dispute through peaceful means.
This positive attitude was recognized by the U.N.General
Assembly in 1973 through Resolution 3160 (XXVIII) approved by
116 votes in favor and none against. That resolution, after
stating that the General Assembly was "Gravely concerned at
the fact that eight years have elapsed since the adoption of
Resolution 2065 (XX) without any substantial progress having
been made in the negotiations", expressed "its gratitude for
the continuous efforts made by the Government of Argentina,
in accordance with the relevant decisions of the General Assembly
to facilitate the process of decolonization and to promote the
well-being of the population of the islands." The same recog
nition was repeated in 1976 in Resolution 31/49.

During the last round of bilateral negotiations,
the Argentine Government put forward a series of written
proposals to the British Government in order to find a peace
ful solution to the sovereignty dispute. No answer whatsoever
was received thus demonstrating that the long process of
negotiations had not served for anything or taken us anywhere.

Recently Argentina was dismayed to see the
pattern of British dilatory tactics and evasiveness turn
again to outright intimidation attempts. Despite the fact
that the Joint Declaration on Communications, signed in

/ / /

///

1971 by both countries, established a "temporary card" as
the only document required for Argentine citizens to travel
to the islands, the British Government not only denied its
validity in the case of a group of Argentine workers who
went to the South Georgia Islands to dismantle an old whaling
station, but declared them illegal aliens and announced its
decision to oust them from the island by force. This was
coupled with the dispatch of warships and a nuclear submarine
to the area, a move worthy of the best colonialist tradition.

This threat of imminent use of force constituted
an act of aggression and conclusive proof of the United
Kingdom's lack of good will to carry out serious and fruitful
negotiations on sovereignty, the core of the dispute.

The need to counter this new threat, designed
to perpetuate British hold on the islands, left Argentina
with no choice but to protect its menaced workers and
sovereign rights by regaining the lands that legitimately
form part of its national territory.

Having purposely accomplished this without
shedding a single drop of British blood, while several
Argentine soldiers died as a result of this one-sided
restraint, the Argentine Embassy feels compelled to acquaint
American public opinion with the following:

///

///

1) The recovery of the islands by Argentina entails no threat whatsoever to the present inhabitants of the islands, whose security, property and rights will be respected and guaran teed.

2) The British Ambassador to the U.S. has stated openly and repeatedly that the inhabitants of the Malvinas are "hostages". Such intemperate allegations on the part of a high-ranking diplomat who cannot fail to be aware of the deep emotional charge which the term holds for the American public, are appalling. It must be made quite clear, as stated by the Argentine Minister of Foreing Affairs that "the islanders are free to leave and any who do will be compensated for any damages."

3) In contrast with the empty declarations of the British Government's interest for the well-being of the islanders, Argentina can show concrete proof of the efforts it has made to improve their access to facilities and services, tied as they are inextricably to the mainland, by provid ing maritime transportation, regular flights, airport facilities, postal services, fellowships for students, medical care, supply of subsidized oil, etc.

4) The principle of self-determination of the islanders -which the United Kingdom so ardently defends now after

///

///

having trampled it in 1833 -cannot possibly apply to the
question of the Malvinas.

De facto and de jure, the islands belonged to
Argentine Republic in 1833 and were governed by Argentine
authorities and occupied by Argentine settlers. These
authorities and these settlers were evicted by violence
and not allowed to return to the territory. On the contrary,
they were replaced, during those 149 years of usurpation,
by a colonial administration and a population of British
origin, now numbering some 1800 inhabitants. It is basi
cally a temporary population that occupies the land and
one that cannot be used by the colonial power in order
to claim the right to apply the principle of self-determi
nation.
Therefore, this principle would be ill-applied in cases
like this, where part of the territory of an independent
state has been wrested -against the will of its inhabitants-
by an act of force, by a third State, without there being
any subsequent international agreement to validate the
de facto situation and where, on the contrary, the aggrieved
state has constantly protested the situation.

5) The recovery of part of its national territory was an
   Argentine decision fully backed by the whole Nation.

///

/ / /

For 150 years it has been a matter beyond any partisan considerations, as shown by the widespread support received from all political parties, trade unions and every segment of Argentine society.

6) No State can possibly pretend to perpetuate today the statu quo of a colonial situation and at the same time feel affronted when the victim of this injustice reacts to redress it. No humiliation could be so profound as the one Argentina endured for 150 years during which part of its land was governed by a metropolis 8000 miles away, with complete disregard for its sovereign rights and with force as the only basis for the occupation.

7) The Argentine Republic is ready to explore all appropriate peaceful channels to solve its dispute with the United Kingdom.
Justice and reason are on Argentina's side. All aspects of the question -except sovereignty- are subject to discussion. But it stands just as ready to defend its rights and meet any aggression by every means at its disposal.

United Nations
Press Release

Department of Public information
Press Section
United Nations, New York

SC/4401
5 May 1982

STATEMENT BY SECURITY COUNCIL PRESIDENT ON SITUATION
IN FALKLAND ISLANDS (ISLAS MALVINAS) REGION

The following statement was made tonight by the President of the Security
Council, Ling Qing (China), on behalf of the members of the Council:

The members of the Security Council express deep concern at the
deterioration of the situation in the region of the Falkland Islands (Islas
Malvinas) and the loss of lives.

The members of the Security Council also express strong support for the
efforts of the Secretary-General with regard to his contacts with the two
parties.

The members of the Security Council have agreed to meet for further
consultations tomorrow, Thursday, 6 May 1982.

* *** *

4059B

Peru-U.S. Proposal Dated May 5

Draft Interim Agreement on the Falkland/Malvinas Islands

An immediate ceasefire, concurrent with:

Mutual withdrawal and non-reintroduction of forces, according
a schedule to be established by the Contact Group.

The immediate introduction of a Contact Group composed of
azil, Peru, The Federal Republic of Germany and the United
ates into the Falkland Islands, on a temporary basis pending
reement on a definitive settlement. The Contact Group will
sume responsibility for:

(A) Verification of the withdrawal;

(B) Ensuring that no actions are taken in the Islands, by the
cal administration, which would contravene this interim
reement; and

(C) Ensuring that all other provisions of the agreement are
spected.

. Britain and Argentina acknowledge the existence of differing
d conflicting views regarding the status of the Falkland Islands.

. The two Governments acknowledge that the aspirations and
terests of the Islanders will be included in the definitive
ttlement of the status of the Islands.

. The Contact Group will have responsibility for ensuring that
e two Governments reach a definitive agreement prior to April
, 1983.

ource: U.S. Department of State

Propuesta De Acuerdo Interino Sobre Las Islas Malvinas/Falklands Islands

1. Cesacion inmediata de hostilidades simultanea con:

2. Retiro mutuo y no redespliegue de todas las fuerzas, de conformidad con un programa que establecera el Grupo de Contacto.

3. La inmediata introduccion de un Grupo de Contacto compuesto por Brasil, Peru, La Republica Federal de Alemania y Los Estados Unidos en las Islas Malvinas, a titulo provisional, hasta que se llegue a una solucion definitiva. El Grupo de Contacto tendra la responsibilidad de:

   (A) Verificar el retiro;

   (B) Administrar el gobierno de las Islas en el periodo interino consultando con los representantes elegidos de la poblacion de las Islas, y asegurar que no emprenda accion alguna en las Islas que contravenga este acuerdo interino; y

   (C) Asegurar que se respeten todas las demas disposiciones del acuerdo.

4. Gran Bretana y la Republica Argentina reconocen la existencia de reclamaciones discrepantes y conflictivas con respecto a la condicion de las Islas Malvinas.

5. Los dos Gobiernos reconocen que los anhelos e intereses de los islenos se incluiran en la solucion definitiva de la condicion de Las Islas.

6. El Grupo de Contacto tendra la responsibilidad de velar por que los dos Gobiernos lleguen a un acuerdo definitivo antes del 30 de abril de 1983.

Source: U.S. Department of State

took South Georgia. In the ensuing weeks she has shown no sign of complying with the Security Council Resolution: on the contrary, she has continued a massive build up of the occupying forces on the Falkland Islands. There could hardly be a clearer demonstration of disregard for international law and for the United Nations itself.

The British Response

3. Britain need have done nothing more than rest on the mandatory Resolution of the Security Council. Indeed, Britain's inherent right of self-defence under Article 51 of the United Nations Charter would have justified the Government in adopting a purely military policy for ending the crisis. But, in pursuit of a peaceful settlement, Britain adopted a policy, frequently explained by the Government in Parliament, of building up pressure on Argentina.

Military pressure was exerted by the rapid assembly and despatch of the British Naval Task Force. Diplomatic pressure, first expressed in Security Council Resolution 502, was built up by the clear statements of condemnation of Argentine aggression which were made by many countries across the world. It was widely recognised that aggres-

sion could not be allowed to stand, since otherwise international peace and order would be dangerously prejudiced in many regions. The members of the European Community, Australia, New Zealand, Canada and Norway joined Britain in rapidly imposing economic measures against Argentina.

Efforts for a Negotiated Settlement

4. Britain dedicated her maximum diplomatic efforts to the search for a negotiated solution, and the Government kept Parliament as fully informed as the confidentiality of difficult negotiations would allow. Efforts for an interim agreement to end the crisis were first undertaken by the United States Secretary of State, Mr Alexander Haig. His ideas for an interim agreement were discussed repeatedly with Argentina and Britain. The Government expressed their willingness to consider Mr Haig's final proposals, although they presented certain real difficulties. Argentina rejected them. The next stage of negotiations was based on proposals originally advanced by President Belaunde of Peru and modified in consultations between him and the United States Secretary of State. As the Foreign and Commonwealth Secretary informed

SH GOVERNMENT DOCUMENT.
1, 1982

AND ISLANDS: NEGOTIATIONS
PEACEFUL SETTLEMENT

ne Aggression

now almost seven weeks since Argen-
aded the Falkland Islands. This un-
se of force in unprovoked aggression
ned not only to destroy the democratic
life freely chosen by the Falkland
rs but also the basis on which interna-
rder rests. The invasion was also a
r act of bad faith: it took place when
and Argentina were engaged in ne-
ons in accordance with requests from
ited Nations.
On 1 April the President of the United
Security Council had formally ap-
to Argentina not to invade the Falklands. Yet on 2 April Argentina invad-
3 April the United Nations Security
l passed its mandatory Resolution 502,
ding a cessation of hostilities and an
iate withdrawal of all Argentine forces
he Islands. The same day, Argentina

WESTERN HEMISPHERE

Parliament on 7 May, Britain was willing to accept the final version of these proposals for an interim agreement. But Argentina rejected it.

5. Since then, the Secretary-General of the United Nations, Senor Perez de Cuellar, has been conducting negotiations with Britain, represented by our Permanent Representative at the United Nations, Sir Anthony Parsons, and Argentina, represented by the Deputy Foreign Minister, Senor Ros. In these negotiations, as in earlier ones, Britain made repeated efforts to establish whether Argentina was willing to be sufficiently flexible to make a reasonable interim agreement possible. But it became increasingly clear that Argentina was not seeking an agreement but was playing for time in the negotiation in the hope of holding on to the fruits of aggression, with all that this would imply for the international rule of law. There was an important meeting of British Ministers, attended by Sir Anthony Parsons and the British Ambassador in Washington, Sir Nicholas Henderson on Sunday 16 May. On the following day, Sir Anthony Parsons returned to New York and handed to the United Nations Secretary-General two documents:

• A draft interim agreement between Britain and Argentina which set out the British position in full,
• A letter to the Secretary-General making clear the British position that the Falkland Islands dependencies were not covered by the draft interim agreement.

6. Sir Anthony Parsons made clear to the Secretary-General that the draft agreement represented the furthest that Britain could go in the negotiations. He requested that the Secretary-General should give the draft to the Argentine Deputy Foreign Minister. The Secretary-General did this, and asked for a response within two days. Argentina's first response to the Secretary-General, late on 18 May, was equivocal and contained points known to be unacceptable to the United Kingdom. Early on 19 May, Sir Anthony Parsons pointed this out to the Secretary-General and requested that Argentina's final position should be conveyed within the two day period originally set for a reply to the British draft agreement.

7. Argentina's response, which HMG received late on 19 May, represented a hardening of the Argentine position and amounted to a rejection of the British proposals.

Britain's Fundamental Principles in Negotiations

8. The Government's approach in all the negotiations has been based on important principles, which ministers have set out repeatedly in Parliament:

A. International Law: Argentina's unlawful aggression must end and Security Council Resolution 502 must be implemented. Aggression must not be rewarded, or small countries across the world would feel threatened by neighbours with territorial ambitions.

B. Freedom: The Falkland Islanders are used to enjoying free institutions. The executive and legislative councils were established with their agreement and functioned with their participation. Britain insisted that any interim administration in the Falkland Islands must involve democratically elected representatives of the Islanders, so as to enable the latter to continue to participate in the administration of their affairs and to ensure that they could express freely their wishes about the future of the Islands, in accordance with the principle of self-determination.

C. Sovereignty: Britain has no doubt of her sovereignty over the Falkland Islands, having administered them peacefully since 1833. Nevertheless, successive British Governments have been willing, without prejudice, to include the question of sovereignty in negotiations with Argentina about the future of the Falkland Islands. In the recent negotiations, the Government have been willing that an interim agreement should provide for new negotiations about the future of the Islands, which likewise could discuss sovereignty in good faith, so long as there was no prejudgement as to the outcome of negotiations. Although Argentina seemed, at one point in the United Nations Secretary-General's negotiations, to be accepting a formula about not pre-judging the outcome of future negotiations, she continued to insist on other provisions running counter to this, thus casting grave doubt on the seriousness of this acceptance. This doubt was reinforced by repeated public statements by Argentine leaders.

9. Britain upheld these principles in the draft agreement which we presented on 17 May to the United Nations Secretary-General:

• The agreement provided for complete Argentine withdrawal from the Falkland Islands within 14 days, thus terminating the aggression and upholding international law.
• It provided that the legislative and executive councils representing the Falkland Islanders would continue in existence and be consulted by the UN interim administrator, thus maintaining the democratic structure of the administration.
• It provided explicitly that the outcome of negotiations about the future of the Islands was not prejudged, thus safeguarding the British position on sovereignty. Britain, in participating in those negotiations, would have been guided by the wishes of the Islanders.

10. In the Secretary-General's negotiations, Britain has insisted that the Falkland Islands dependencies should not be covered by an interim agreement to end the crisis. South Georgia and the South Sandwich Islands are geographically distant from the Falkland Islands themselves. They have no settled population. The British title to them, of which the Government have no doubt, does not derive from the Falkland Islands, and these territories have been treated as dependencies of the Falkland Islands only for reasons of administrative convenience.

11. Throughout the negotiations has been firm on the essential princi willing to negotiate on matters wher principles were not breached. In par

A. In return for Argentine witho from the Falkland Islands, Britain w ing (Article 2(3)) [see following anne withdraw her task force to a distance nautical miles. She was also willing t international verification (Article 6(4 mutual withdrawal, in which the Uni tions might have made use of surveil craft from third countries.

B. Britain was willing that the e zones (Article 3) declared by herself Argentina, and the economic measur cle 5) introduced during the present should be lifted from the moment of fire, although these actions would giv comfort to Argentina than to Britain.

C. Britain was prepared to accep pointment of a UN Administrator (A 6(3)) to administer the government o Falkland Islands. Britain wanted him charge his functions in consultation w representative institutions in the isla legislative and executive councils—wh have been developed in accordance w terms of Article 73 of the UN Charte makes clear that the interests of the tants of non-self-governing territories paramount and refers to the need to account of the political aspirations of peoples.) It is inconceivable that Brit any other democratic country, could a that her people should be deprived of democratic rights. Britain was nevert willing to accept that one representati the Argentine population of the Islan 30 people out of 1800) should be adde each of the councils.

Additionally, Britain was willing t the presence of up to 3 Argentine obs on the Islands in the interim period.

D. Britain was willing (Article 7) to re-establishment of communications travel, transport, postage, etc, betwee Falkland Islands and the Argentine m on the basis existing before the invasi

E. Britain was willing to enter int negotiations (Article 8) under the ausp the UN Secretary-General for a peace tlement of the dispute with Argentina the Falkland Islands and to seek the c tion of these negotiations by the targe of 31 December 1982. Our position wa no outcome to the negotiations should either excluded or predetermined.

12. Argentina's final position in th negotiations speaks for itself. In partic

A. Argentina insisted that South G and the South Sandwich Islands be cov by the interim agreement. One effect o would be that British forces would hav withdraw from the British territory of Georgia.

B. Argentina wanted thirty days f completion of the withdrawal of forces wanted all forces to return to their nor bases and areas of operation, thus requ British forces to be enormously furthe than Argentine ones.

WESTERN HEMISPHERE

gentina wanted the administration
ands to be exclusively the responsi-
he United Nations. There would
n Argentine and British observers.
inistration would have been free to
dvisers from the population of the
n equal numbers from the Argentine
n and from the population of British
he flags of Britain and Argentina
ve flown together with that of the
ations.

rgentina wanted free access for her
to the Islands, with respect inter
sidence, work and property. Argen-
opposed a provision in the British
eement (end of Article 6(3)) but the
inistrator exercising his powers in
ty with the laws and practices tradi-
bserved in the Islands. It was evi-
: Argentina hoped to change the
: Falklands society and its demo-
ake-up in the interim period, and
udge the future.

rgentina proposed a formula about
ons on the future of the Islands
ated that they should be 'initiated'
prejudice to the rights and claims
ions of the two parties. Argentina
t accept an additional phrase stating
the outcome would not be pre-
Argentine leaders continued in public
at Argentina insisted on having sov-
In the negotiations Argentina also
a provision in the British draft (be-
of Article 9) which would have en-
at the interim arrangements should
lace until a definitive agreement
e future of the Islands could be im-
ed. Argentina's evident aim in resist-
was that, if no definitive agreement
reached by the target date of 31
er 1982, the interim administration
ase to exist and a vacuum be created
rgentina could hope to fill.

he present crisis was brought about
ntina's unlawful act of aggression. In
osequent attitude the Argentine
ent showed that they had no respect
r democratic principles or for the
aw. Britain stands firmly for both.

X—FALKLAND ISLANDS: INTERIM AGREEMENT

ernment of the Republic of Argen-
the Government of the United
n of Great Britain and Northern
responding to Security Council
on 502 (1982) adopted on 3 April
der Article 40 of the Charter of the
Nations,

ng entered into negotiations through
offices of the Secretary-General of
ed Nations for an interim agreement
ng the Falkland Islands (Islas
s), hereinafter referred to as 'The

ing in mind the obligations with
o non-self governing territories set
rticle 73 of the Charter of the United
the text of which is annexed hereto.
e agreed on the following:

Article 1
1. No provision of this Interim Agreement shall in any way prejudice the rights, claims and positions of either party in the ultimate peaceful settlement of their dispute over the Islands.

2. No acts or activities taking place whilst this Interim Agreement is in force shall constitute a basis for asserting, supporting or denying a claim to territorial sovereignty over the Islands or create any rights of sovereignty over them.

Article 2
1. With·effect from a specified time, 24 hours after signature of this Agreement (hereinafter referred to as Time 'T'), each party undertakes to cease and thereafter to refrain from all firing and other hostile actions.

2. Argentina undertakes:

(A) To commence withdrawal of its armed forces from the Islands with effect from Time 'T';

(B) To withdraw half of its armed forces to at least 150 nautical miles away from any point in the Islands by Time 'T' plus seven days; and

(C) To complete its withdrawal to at least 150 nautical miles away by Time 'T' plus fourteen days.

3. The United Kingdom undertakes:

(A) To commence withdrawal of its armed forces from the Islands with effect from Time 'T';

(B) To withdraw half of its armed forces to at least 150 nautical miles away from any point in the Islands by Time 'T' plus seven days; and

(C) To complete its withdrawal to at least 150 nautical miles away by Time 'T' plus fourteen days.

Article 3
With effect from Time 'T', each party undertakes to lift the exclusion zones, warnings and similar measures which have been imposed.

Article 4
On the completion of the steps for withdrawal specified in Article 2, each party undertakes to refrain from reintroducing any armed forces into the Islands or within 150 nautical miles thereof.

Article 5
Each party undertakes to lift with effect from Time 'T' the economic measures it has taken against the other and to seek the lifting of similar measures taken by third parties.

Article 6
1. Immediately after the signature of the present Agreement, Argentina and the United Kingdom shall jointly sponsor a draft resolution in the United Nations under the terms of which the Security Council would take note of the present Agreement, acknowledge the role conferred upon the Secretary-General of the United Nations

therein, and authorise him to carry out the tasks entrusted to him therein.

2. Immediately after the adoption of the resolution referred to in paragraph 1 of this Article, a United Nations administrator, being a person acceptable to Argentina and the United Kingdom, shall be appointed by the Secretary-General and will be the officer administering the government of the Islands.

3. The United Nations administrator shall have the authority under the direction of the Secretary-General to ensure the continuing administration of the government of the Islands. He shall discharge his functions in consultation with the representative institutions in the Islands which have been developed in accordance with the terms of Article 73 of the Charter of the United Nations, with the exception that one representative from the Argentina population normally resident on the Islands shall be appointed by the administrator to each of the two institutions. The administrator shall exercise his powers in accordance with the terms of this Agreement and in conformity with the laws and practices traditionally obtaining in the Islands.

4. The United Nations administrator shall verify the withdrawal of all armed forces from the Islands, and shall devise an effective method of ensuring their non-reintroduction.

5. The United Nations administrator shall have such staff as may be agreed by Argentina and the United Kingdom to be necessary for the performance of his functions under this Agreement.

6. Each party may have no more than three observers in the Islands.

Article 7
Except as may be otherwise agreed between them, the parties shall, during the currency of this Agreement, reactivate the Exchange of Notes of 5 August 1971, together with the Joint Statement on Communications between the Islands and the Argentine mainland referred to therein. The parties shall accordingly take appropriate steps to establish a special consultative committee to carry out the functions entrusted to the Special Consultative Committee referred to in the Joint Statement.

Article 8
The parties undertake to enter into negotiations in good faith under the auspices of the Secretary-General of the United Nations for the peaceful settlement of their dispute and to seek, with a sense of urgency, the completion of these negotiations by 31 December 1982. These negotiations shall be initiated without prejudice to the rights, claims or positions of the parties and without prejudgement of the outcome.

Article 9
This Interim Agreement shall enter into force on signature and shall remain in force until a definitive agreement about the future of the Islands has been reached and implemented by the parties. The Secretary-General will immediately communicate its text to the Securi-

ty Council and register it in accordance with Article 102 of the Charter of the United Nations.

ARGENTINE DIPLOMATIC NOTE TO DEPARTMENT OF STATE, MAY 26, 1982

The Embassy of the Argentine Republic presents its compliments to the Department of State and has the honor to inform, with regard to the proposal of the United Nations Secretary General referred to the conflict over the Islas Malvinas and its dependencies, the position of the Government of the Argentine Republic was clearly stated in the Proposed Agreement submitted in the course of the negotiations held at the United Nations, which text reads as follows:

"The Government of the Argentine Republic and the Government of the United Kingdom of Great Britain and Northern Ireland, hereinafter referred to as "the Parties",

In response to the provisions of Security Council Resolution 502 (1982) of April 3, 1982, and taking into account the Charter of the United Nations, Resolution 1514 (XV) 2065 and other Resolutions of the General Assembly on the question of the Malvinas (Falkland) Islands, have accepted, in accordance with Article 40 of the Charter of the United Nations, the assistance of the Secretary General of the United Nations and have engaged in negotiations and arrived at the following provisional agreement relating to the Malvinas, South Georgia and South Sandwich Islands, hereinafter referred to as "The Islands" for the purposes of this agreement.

I. 1. The geographical scope of the area within which the withdrawal of troops is to be carried out shall comprise the Malvinas, South Georgia and South Sandwich Islands.

2. The withdrawal of the forces of both parties shall be gradual and simultaneous. Within a maximum period of thirty days, all armed forces shall be in their normal bases and areas of operation.

II. With effect from the signature of this agreement, each party shall cease to apply the economic measures which it has adopted against the other and the United Kingdom shall call for the same action by those countries or groups of countries which, at its request, adopted similar measures.

III. 1. Supervision of the withdrawal of the forces of both countries shall be carried out by specialized personnel of the United Nations, whose composition shall be agreed with the parties.

2. The interim Administration of the Islands while the negotiations for final settlement of the dispute are in progress shall conform to the following provisions:

A) The Administration shall be exclusively the responsibility of the United Nations with an appropriate presence of observers of the parties.

B) The said Administration shall perform all functions (executive, legislative, judicial and security) through officials of different nationality from that of the parties.

C) Notwithstanding the provisions of 2(A) and (B), and in order not to cause unnecessary changes in the way of life of the population during the period of the interim Administration by the United Nations, local judicial functions may be exercised in accordance with the legislation in force on April 1, 1982 to the full extent compatible with this agreement. Similarly, the United Nations interim Administration may appoint as advisers persons who are members of the population of British origin and Argentines resident in the Islands, in equal numbers.

D) The flag of the parties shall fly together with that of the United Nations.

E) During the period of interim Administration, communications shall be kept open, without discriminatory restrictions of any kind for the parties, including freedom of movement and equality of access with respect to residence, work and property.

F) Freedom of communication shall also include the maintenance of freedom of transit for the state airline (Lade) and for merchant ships and scientific vessels, in addition, telephone, telegraph and telex communications, Argentine television transmissions and the state petroleum (YPF) and gas services shall continue to operate freely.

IV. The customs, traditions and way of life of the inhabitants of the Islands, and their social and cultural links with their countries of origin, shall be respected and safeguarded.

V. 1. The parties undertake to enter immediately into negotiations in good faith under the auspices of the Secretary General of the United Nations for the peaceful and final settlement of the dispute and, with a sense of urgency, to complete these negotiations by December 31, 1982, with a single option to extend until June 30, 1983, in order to comply with the Charter of the United Nations, Resolutions 1514 (XV), 2065 (XX) and other relevant resolutions of the General Assembly on the question of the Malvinas Islands. These negotiations shall be initiated without prejudice to the rights and claims or positions of the two parties and in recognition of the fact that they have divergent positions on the question of the Malvinas, South Georgia and South Sandwich Islands.

2. The negotiations shall be held in New York.

3. The Secretary General of the United Nations may be assisted in the negotiations by a contract group composed of representatives of four States members of the United Nations. To that end, each party shall nominate two States and shall have the right to a single veto of one of the States nominated by the other.

4. The Secretary General of the United Nations shall keep the Security Council assiduously informed of the progress of the negotiations.

VI. If the period specified in point V(1) above expires with out the attainement of a

final agreement, the Secretary Gene... draw up a report addressed to the G... Assembly of the United Nations, in o... that the latter may determine, as app... and with greater urgency, the lines t... the said final agreement should conf... order to achieve a speedy settlement question."

The Argentine Government, in th... of the position stated in the aforemer... proposed agreement, which reflects t... reasonableness which has continuousl... spired its negotiating behaviour, deep regrets that the peace efforts carried U.N. Secretary General, in which pur... and final success the Argentine Repu... trusted, have been frustrated as a res... the unilateral decision of the British ... ment announced on May 20th.

The real possibilities of reaching ... peaceful settlement to the conflict an... avoiding, with the responsibility that ... situation demanded, further bloodshe... imminent breaking of peace and secu... the hemisphere, finally proved to be disregarded by the intransigence and bornness with which the Government United Kingdom has tried to make th... force prevail over reason and peace.

The Government of the Argentine Republic, therefore, formally holds th... Government of the United Kingdom o... Britain and Northern Ireland responsi... the serious consequences which in the may stem from its denial to exhaust t... available means towards a peaceful se... ment, and expressly reserves its right... legitimate defense recognized by the ... Nations Charter.

The Embassy of the Argentine Re... avails itself of this opportunity to rene the Department of State the assurance highest consideration.

UNITED STATES MISSION TO THE UNITED NATIONS

'99 UNITED NATIONS PLAZA
NEW YORK, N. Y. 1001'

ESS RELEASE

RELEASE ON DELIVERY
CK TEXT AGAINST DELIVERY

Press Release USUN 37(82)
May 22, 1982

STATEMENT BY

AMBASSADOR JEANE J. KIRKPATRICK

UNITED STATES REPRESENTATIVE TO THE UNITED NATIONS

IN THE SECURITY COUNCIL

ON THE QUESTION CONCERNING THE SITUATION IN THE
REGION OF THE FALKLAND ISLANDS (ISLAS MALVINAS)

MAY 22, 1982

Mr. President, I should like to begin by expressing the appreciation of my government for your judicious and skillful leadership of the affairs of this Council in this deeply troubled time, as we seek a solution to the tragic conflict underway in the South Atlantic.

We desire to express in this public arena our gratitude to the Secretary General for his tireless and determined efforts to find a peaceful resolution to the conflict between the United Kingdom and Argentina. The Secretary General knows, as we should like the world as well to know, that he enjoyed the active support and cooperation of the United States in his search for a peaceful resolution of the conflict.

This conflict poses a particularly acute problem for persons and nations who love peace and also for this international body whose very raison d'etre is to promote and ensure the peaceful settlement of disputes.

The United States stands behind the principle that the use of force to settle disputes should not be allowed anywhere, and especially in this hemisphere where a significant number of territorial disputes remain to be solved diplomatically. For the United States, the Falkland crisis has been and still is a particularly agonizing, tragic event.

As the whole world knows, we have a longstanding alliance
and, beyond that, the closest relations of friendship with
Great Britain, the country from which our political
institutions, law and language derive. But we have not
forgotten for a moment our close geographical, economic and
political relations with our Latin neighbors. We do not only
care about this hemisphere, we are part of this hemisphere,
and we share many of the aspirations, goals and dreams of all
nations of the Americas. Our own culture and society are
deeply influenced by a growing Hispanic population. We can
never turn our backs on, or be insensitive to, hemispheric
goals and aspirations that we ourselves have promoted and
defended.

That is why the United States tried so hard to avoid
the conflict on the Falklands, why we are hoping so intensely
to reduce and isolate it, and why we are eager and ready
to back any realistic diplomatic initiative which will put
a just end to it. And we especially mean to stay in close
touch with our Latin neighbors while efforts are made to solve
this tragic conflict, in order to restore peace with honor
so, that once again we can concentrate our efforts on the
resolution of our problems. The quicker we put this tragic
conflict behind us, the quicker we can begin building our
future. And there, as always, Latin America will find how

deeply the U.S. is committed to the cause of peace and
prosperity in our hemisphere.

Mr. President, as the fighting intensifies and
the cost in lives mounts in the South Atlantic, I think we
all share a sense of anguish that it has not yet been
possible to prevent this tragic conflict.

We have all come to appreciate how deep the roots
of the conflict are. Britain, in peaceful possession of the
Falkland Islands for 150 years, has been passionately devoted
to the proposition that the rights of the inhabitants should
be respected in any future disposition of the Islands. No
one can say that this attitude, coming from a country that
has granted independence to more than 40 countries in a genera
tion and a half, is a simple reflex to retain possession.

Yet we know too how deep is the Argentine commitment
to recover islands they believe were taken from them by
illegal force. This is not some sudden passion, but a long-
sustained national concern that also stretches back 150
years, heightened by the sense of frustration at what Argentin
feels were nearly 20 years of fruitless negotiation.

From the start it has been widely recognized that the
conflict engages basic principles without which a peaceful
international order cannot stand. Unless the principle is
respected that force must not be used to settle disputes, the

entire international community will be exposed to chaos
and suffering. And unless the right of self-defense is
granted, only those countries that use force first will
have the protection of law.

The Security Council was profoundly right to reassert
those principles in Resolution 502, which forms the indispensable
framework in which a peaceful solution has been sought and will
ultimately be found. It is of fundamental importance that
both Argentina and Britain have accepted Resolution 502 in
its entirety.

For the United States, the conflict has a special
poignancy. We do not take -- have never taken -- any position
on the underlying claims. Britain is a country to which
we are bound by unique ties of friendship, values, and
alliance. And Argentina is also an old friend, a country of
immigrants and settlers like our own, a country with which we
share the enormous human and national potential of the New
World experience.

That a conflict of such dimensions should take place,
and that it should occur here, in the Western Hemisphere --
whose countries havelong shared a particular commitment to
each other, to their mutual welfare and to peace -- causes us
the deepest concern. This conflict, however urgent, cannot
be permitted to obscure the common engagement of all American
states to the rule of law and to the well-being of this
hemisphere.

So it was natural that the United States should make a particular effort to help Argentina and Britain find a solution.

That effort began before April 2nd, when we offered to the two sides our good offices to help find a solution to the South Georgia incident.

After April 2nd, both President Galtieri and Prime Minister Thatcher asked the United States to see whether it could be of assistance. At President Reagan's direction, Secretary of State Haig undertook two rounds of intense discussions in both capitals. Finally, on April 27th, as prospects for more intense hostilities arose, we put forward a proposal. It represented our best estimate of what the two parties could reasonably be expected to accept. It was founded squarely on Resolution 502 by providing for a cessation of hostilities, withdrawal of forces, and a political settlement of the dispute.

The British government indicated that it would seriously consider our proposal, although it presented certain real difficulties for it. However, the proposal was not acceptable to Argentina.

Immediately afterward, President Belaunde of Peru, after consultation with Secretary Haig, took the initiative to put forward a much simplified peace plan, also drawing on the fundamental elements of Resolution 502.

On May 5th a draft text was forwarded by Peru to
uenos Aires; we forwarded the same text to London.

Britain made clear that it could seriously consider
he proposal. Argentina chose not to consider it, asking
nstead that the Secretary General use his good offices as,
f course, it was its full privilege to do.

Mr. President, the tragic conflict before us also
as special poignancy for the United Nations. It is precisely
he kind of problem this organization was created to resolve.
he Charter commits us "... to bring about by peaceful means,
nd in conformity with the principles of justice and international
aw, adjustment or settlement of international disputes or
ituations which might lead to a breach of the peace." "To
evelop friendly relations among nations based on respect
or the principle of equal rights and self-determination of
eoples, and to take other appropriate measures to strengthen
niversal peace;
To achieve international cooperation in solving international
roblems...
To be a centre for harmonizing the actions of nations in
he attainment of these common ends."

The United Nations record in dealing with this conflict
s commendable. The Security Council responded rapidly to the
rgentine seizure of the Islands. The fact that both parties

accepted Resolution 502 proves that it was a constructive response.

The Secretary General's determined and imaginative efforts were, of course, fervently welcomed by all of us. Again the elements of settlement seemed to be present or nearl' present. Again peace eluded us. I believe the institutions of the United Nations have functioned in this crisis in the manner foreseen by its founders and its Charter. We can be proud of it; proud, especially, of the Secretary General.

We have already heard his account of his search for a formula that could resolve the conflict. I think all of us have been deeply impressed by the skill and sensitivity, by the judgment and fairness that the Secretary General brought to this task. That his effort has not so far succeeded does not mean that it has not realized important gains, notably in the establishment of a mutually acceptable concept of negotiations. The United States will wholeheartedly support any initiative that can help Argentina and Britain make peace with honor.

Despite all our efforts, the problem is not solved. Young men die in icy waters, on freezing beaches.

The dispute that appeared to many to be simple has nonetheless proved extraordinarily difficult to resolve. But we must not abandon the effort. Resolution 502, with its concept of linked and simultaneous cessation of hostilities,

withdrawal of forces, and negotiations, must remain the
framework of the search for peace. The problem is too
important -- for the rule of law, for the future of the
Americas, for many of us friends of Britain and Argentina --
not to make an all-out effort to settle this tragic conflict,
so costly in every way.

UNNOFFICIAL TRANSLATION

Embassy
of the
Argentine Republic

D.E.No. 526

              The Embassy of the Argentine Republic presents its compliments to the Department of State and has the honor to inform, with regard to the proposal of the United Nations Secretary General referred to the conflict over the Islas Malvinas and its dependencies, the position of the Government of the Argentine Republic was clearly stated.in the Proposed Agreement submitted in the course of the negotiations held at the United Nations, which text reads as follows:

> "The Government of the Argentine Republic and the Government of the United Kingdom of Great Britain and Northern Ireland, hereinafter referred to as "the Parties",
>
> In response to the provisions of Security Council Resolution 502 (1982) of April 3,1982, and taking into account the Charter of the United Nations, Resolution 1514 (XV) 2065 and other Resolutions of the General Assembly on the question of the Malvinas (Falkland) Islands, have accepted, in accordance with Article 40 of the Charter of the United Nations, the assistance of the Secretary General of the United Nations and have engaged in negotiations and arrived at the following provisional agreement relating to the Malvinas, South Georgia and South Sandwich Islands, hereinafter referred to as "The Islands" for the purposes of this agreement.
>
> I. 1. The geographical scope of the area within which the withdrawal of troops is to be carried out shall comprise the Malvinas, South Georgia and South Sandwich Islands.
>
>   2. The withdrawal of the forces of both parties shall be gradual and simultaneous. Within a maximum period of thirty days, all armed forces shall be in their normal bases and areas of operation.

                                     ///

TO THE DEPARTMENT OF STATE
Washington,D.C.

/ / /

II.   With effect from the signature of this agreement, each
        party shall cease to apply the economic measures which
        it has adopted against the other and the United Kingdom
        shall call for the same action by those countries or
        groups of countries which, at its request, adopted
        similar measures.

III.   1. Supervision of the withdrawal of the forces of both
           countries shall be carried out by specialized personnel
           of the United Nations, whose composition shall be agreed
           with the parties.

        2. The interim Administration of the Islands while the
           negotiations for final settlement of the dispute are in
           progress shall conform to the following provisions:

           A) The Administration shall be exclusively the responsa
              bility of the United Nations with an appropriate
              presence of observers of the parties.
           B) The said Administration shall perform all functions
              (executive, legislative, judicial and security)
              through officials of different nationality from that
              of the parties.
           C) Notwithstanding the provisions of 2 (A) and (B), and
              in order not to cause unnecessary changes in the way
              of life of the population during the period of the
              interim Administration by the United Nations, local
              judicial functions may be exercised in accordance
              with the legislation in force on April 1, 1982 to the
              full extent compatible with this agreement.
              Similarly, the United Nations interim Administration
              may appoint as advisers persons who are members of
              the population of British origin and argentines
              resident in the Islands, in equal numbers.
           D) The flag of the parties shall fly together with that
              of the United Nations.
           E) During the period of interim Administration, communica
              tions shall be kept open, without discriminatory
              restrictions of any kind for the parties, including
              freedom of movement and equality of access with respect
              to residence, work and property.
           F) Freedom of communication shall also include the main
              tenance of freedom of transit for the state airline
              (Lade) and for merchant ships and scientific vessels,
              in addition, telephone, telegraph and telex communi
              cations, Argentine television transmissions and the
              state petroleum (YPF) and gas services shall continue
              to operate freely.

IV.   The customs, traditions and way of life of the inhabitants
        of the Islands, and their social and cultural links with
        their countries of origin, shall be respected and safeguarded.

V.   1. The parties undertake to enter immediately into negotiations
           in good faith under the auspices of the Secretary General
           of the United Nations for the peaceful and final settlement
           of the dispute and, with a sense of urgency, to complete
           these negotiations by December 31, 1982, with a single
           option to extend until June 30, 1983, in order to comply
           with the Charter of the United Nations, Resolutions 1514
           (XV), 2065 (XX) and other relevant resolutions of the
           General Assembly on the question of the Malvinas Islands.

/ / /

///

These negotiations shall be initiated without prejudice
to the rights and claims or positions of the two parties
and in recognition of the fact that they have divergent
positions on the question of the Malvinas, South Georgia
and South Sandwich Islands.

2. The negotiations shall be held in New York.

3. The Secretary General of the United Nations may be
   assisted in the negotiations by a contact group composed
   of representatives of four States members of the United
   Nations. To that end, each party shall nominate two
   States and shall have the right to a single veto of one
   of the States nominated by the other.

4. The Secretary General of the United Nations shall keep
   the Security Council assiduously informed of the progress
   of the negotiations.

VI. If the period specified in point V (1) above expires with
    out the attainement of a final agreement, the Secretary
    General shall draw up a report addressed to the General
    Assembly of the United Nations, in order that the latter
    may determine, as appropriate and with greatest urgency,
    the lines to which the said final agreement should conform
    in order to achieve a speedy settlement of the question."

The Argentine Government, in the light of the
position stated in the aforementioned proposed agreement, which
reflects the reasonableness which has continously inspired its
negotiating behaviour, deepley regrets that the peace efforts
carried out by the U.N.Secretary General, in which pursuance
and final success the Argentine Republic trusted, have been
frustrated as a result of the unilateral decision of the
British Government announced on May 20th.

The real possibilities of reaching a peaceful
settlement to the conflict and of avoiding, with the responsi
bility that the situation demanded, further bloodshed and an
imminent breaking of peace and security in the hemisphere,
finally proved to be disregarded by the intransigence and
stubbornness with which the Government of the United Kingdom
has tried to make the use of force prevail over reason and peace.

The Government of the Argentine Republic,
therefore, formally holds the Government of the United Kingdom
of Great Britain and Northern Ireland responsible for the
serious consequences which in the future may stem from its
denial to exhaust the available means towards a peaceful
settlement, and expressly reserves its rights to a legitimate
defense recognized by the United Nations Charter.

The Embassy of the Argentine Republic avails

itself of this opportunity to renew to the Department of State

the assurances of its highest consideration.

Washington,D.C., May 26,1982

*Embajada
de la
República Argentina*

D.E.526

Washington, D.C.

26 de mayo de 1982

La Embajada de la República Argentina
presenta sus atentos saludos al Departamento de Estado,
y tiene el honor de llevar a su conocimiento que, con
relación a la propuesta del Secretario General de las
Naciones Unidas referida al conflicto sobre las Islas
Malvinas y sus dependencias, la posición del Gobierno de
la República Argentina fué claramente expuesta en el Pro
yecto de Acuerdo presentado en el curso de las negociacio
nes celebradas en las Naciones Unidas, cuyo texto expresa:

"El Gobierno de la República Argentina y el Gobierno del
"Reino Unido de la Gran Bretaña e Irlanda del Norte, en
"adelante denominados "las Partes",
"Respondiendo a lo dispuesto en la Resolución 502 (1982)
"del Consejo de Seguridad de fecha 3 de abril de 1982 y
"teniendo en cuenta la Carta de las Naciones Unidas, las
"Resoluciones 1514 (XV), 2065 (XX) y las demás Resolucio
"nes de la Asamblea General relativas a la cuestión de
"las Islas Malvinas (Falkland Islands), han aceptado, de
"conformidad con el artículo 40 de la Carta de las Nacio
"nes Unidas, la asistencia del Secretario General de la
"Organización de las Naciones Unidas y han llevado a cabo
"negociaciones y alcanzado el siguiente Acuerdo Provisio
"nal referente a las Islas Malvinas, Georgias del Sur y
"Sandwich del Sur, de aquí en adelante denominadas "las Islas"
"a los efectos del presente acuerdo.

"I. 1.El ámbito geográfico dentro del cual deberá cumplirse
"   el retiro de las tropas abarca las Islas Malvinas,
"   Georgias del Sur y Sandwich del Sur.
"   2.El retiro de las fuerzas de ambas partes deberá ser
"   gradual y simultáneo. En un plazo máximo de treinta
"   días todas las fuerzas armadas deberán hallarse en
"   sus bases y áreas normales de operación.
"II.   A partir de la firma del presente acuerdo cada parte
"   dejará sin efecto las medidas económicas que haya
"   adoptado en contra de la otra y el Reino Unido soli
"   citará igual conducta de los países o grupos de países
"   que, a su pedido, adoptaron medidas similares.

AL DEPARTAMENTO DE ESTADO
Washington,D.C.

" III. 1 - La supervisión del retiro de las fuerzas de ambos
"   países será llevado a cabo por personal especia-
"   lizado de las Naciones Unidas, integrado con la con-
"   formidad de las partes.

"   2 - La administración interina de las islas mientras se
"   realizan las negociaciones para la solución definiti-
"   va de la disputa, se ajustará a las siguientes dispo-
"   siciones:
"   A) La administración estará exclusivamente a cargo de
"   las Naciones Unidas con presencia adecuada de obser-
"   vadores de las partes.
"   B) Dicha administración desempeñará todas las funcion-
"   nes (ejecutivas, legislativas,judiciales y de se-
"   guridad) con funcionarios de nacionalidad distinta
"   de las partes.
"   C) No obstante lo manifestado en 2.A) y B) y a efectos
"   de no producir alteraciones innecesarias en el sis-
"   tema de vida de la población, durante el período de
"   administración interina por parte de las Naciones
"   Unidas, las funciones judiciales locales podrán ser
"   ejercidas de conformidad con la legislación vigente
"   al 1ro. de abril de 1982 en todo aquello que resulte
"   compatible con el presente acuerdo.
"   Del mismo modo la administración interina de las Na-
"   ciones Unidas podrá nombrar como asesores a perso-
"   nas integrantes de la población de origen británico
"   y a argentinos residentes en las islas, en igual nú-
"   mero.
"   D) Las banderas de las partes flamearán junto a la de
"   las Naciones Unidas.
"   E) Durante el período de administración interina las co-
"   municaciones se mantendrán abiertas, sin restricción
"   discriminatoria de naturaleza alguna, para las par-
"   tes, incluyendo la libre circulación, igualdad para
"   el acceso en materia de residencia, de trabajo y de
"   propiedad.
"   F) La facilidad de comunicaciones incluirá además el
"   mantenimiento de la libre operación de las comunica-
"   ciones telefónicas, telegráficas y telex, y transmi-
"   siones de televisión argentinas y la libre operación
"   de los servicios de YPF y de Gas del Estado.

" IV. Las costumbres, tradiciones, estilo de vida de los habitan-
"   tes de las islas, así como sus vínculos sociales y cultura-
"   les con sus países de origen serán respetados y salvaguarda-
"   dos.

" V. 1. Las partes se comprometen a emprender de inmediato negocia-
"   ciones de buena fe bajo los auspicios del Secretario Gene-
"   ral de las Naciones Unidas, para la solución pacífica y de-
"   finitiva de la disputa y con sentido de urgencia completar
"   estas negociaciones antes del 31 de diciembre de 1982, con
"   una única opción de prórroga hasta el 30 de junio de 1983
"   para cumplir con la Carta de las Naciones Unidas, las Reso-
"   luciones 1514 (XV), 2065 (XX) y las demás resoluciones per-
"   tinentes de la Asamblea General sobre la cuestión de las Is-
"   las Malvinas. Estas negociaciones se iniciarán sin perjui-
"   cio de los derechos y reclamaciones o las posiciones de am-
"   bas partes y reconociendo que ellas tienen posiciones dis-
"   crepantes en torno a la cuestión de las Islas Malvinas,
"   Georgias del Sur y Sandwich del Sur.

                                            ....

///

"   2.Las negociaciones se realizarán en la ciudad de Nueva
"   York.
"   3.El Secretario General de las Naciones Unidas podrá ser
"   asistido en las negociaciones por un grupo de contacto
"   formado por representantes de cuatro Estados miembros
"   de las Naciones Unidas. A tal efecto cada una de las
"   partes propondrá dos Estados y tendrá derecho a vetar
"   por única vez a uno de los Estados propuestos por la
"   otra.
"   4.El Secretario General de las Naciones Unidas mantendrá
"   asiduamente informado al Consejo de Seguridad sobre la
"   marcha de las negociaciones.
" VI.   Si expira el plazo fijado en el inciso 1) del punto V
"   supra sin que se haya alcanzado un arreglo definitivo,
"   el Secretario General elaborará un informe dirigido a
"   la Asamblea General de las Naciones Unidas, a fin de que
"   ésta determine, según corresponda y con la mayor urgencia,
"   las pautas a que deberá ajustarse dicho arreglo defini
"   tivo de manera de lograr una rápida solución de la cues_
"   tión.

El Gobierno Argentino, a la luz de la posición
expuesta en el mencionado Proyecto de Acuerdo, que refleja la
razonabilidad que inspiró en todo momento a su conducta nego_
ciadora, lamenta profundamente que, por decisión unilateral
del Gobierno Británico anunciada el día 20 de mayo, se hayan
visto frustradas las gestiones de paz conducidas hasta ese
momento por el Secretario General de las Naciones Unidas, en
cuya prosecución y éxito final confiaba la República Argentina.

Las posibilidades ciertas de hallar una solu_
ción pacífica al conflicto y de evitar, con la responsabili_
dad que la situación exigía, un mayor derramamiento de sangre
y un inminente quebrantamiento de la paz y la seguridad en
el hemisferio, resultaron en definitiva desatendidas por la
intransigencia y obstinación con que el Gobierno del Reino
Unido ha procurado imponer el uso de la fuerza en desmedro
de la razón y de la paz.

El Gobierno de la República Argentina, por lo
tanto, hace formalmente responsable al Gobierno del Reino
Unido de la Gran Bretaña e Irlanda del Norte por las graves
consecuencias que en lo sucesivo se deriven de su negativa
a agotar los medios de solución pacífica disponibles, y hace
expresa reserva de su derecho a la legítima defensa reconoci_
do por la Carta de las Naciones Unidas.

La Embajada de la República Argentina

reitera al Departamento de Estado las expresiones de su

más alta y distinguida consideración.

Falkland Islands

pril 2, 1982, the British-held
Islands (250 miles off the south-
ip of Argentina) and the South
and South Sandwich Islands
aded by several thousand Argen-
y, Navy, and Air Force troops.
lands have been a British colony
3 but since Argentina gained in-
ce in 1816, it has maintained
herited a Spanish claim to the
which the Argentines call the
lvinas.

wing are statements by
Haig; J. William Middendorf
Permanent Representative to the
White House; the Department
texts of U.N. and OAS resolu-
d a declaration of foreign
s of the OAS.

HOUSE STATEMENT,
1982[1]

ation report indicates the
e Government now claims to
upied the Falkland Islands and
ers as the South Georgia and
andwich Islands. The British
ment acknowledges that an inva-
taken place, but we have no in-
on other than conflicting reports
ing or casualties.
have made clear to the Govern-
Argentina that we deplore use
to resolve this dispute. We have
Argentina to cease, immediate-
lities and to withdraw its
forces from the Falkland

are continuing to work bilateral-
in multilateral forums such as
ted Nations—to obtain a cessa-
hostilities and a withdrawal.
ause of our concern over the ten-
tween Argentina and the United
m, the U.S. Government
es and strongly supports the
nt by the President of the U.N.
y Council, made yesterday on
f the Council. We fully endorse
ncil's call for the exercise of ut-
straint at this time, the
ce of the use or threat of force in
ion, and for the continuation of
rch for a diplomatic solution.

SECURITY COUNCIL RESOLUTION 502, APR. 3, 1982[2]

The Security Council

Recalling the statement made by the President of the Security Council at the 2345th meeting of the Security Council on 1 April 1982 (S/14944) calling on the Governments of Argentina and the United Kingdom of Great Britain and Northern Ireland to refrain from the use or threat of force in the region of the Falkland Islands (Islas Malvinas),

Deeply disturbed at reports of an invasion on 2 April 1982 by armed forces of Argentina,

Determining that there exists a breach of the peace in the region of the Falkland Islands (Islas Malvinas),

1. *Demands* an immediate cessation of hostilities;
2. *Demands* an immediate withdrawal of all Argentine forces from the Falkland Islands (Islas Malvinas);
3. *Calls* on the Governments of Argentina and the United Kingdom to seek a diplomatic solution to their differences and to respect fully the purposes and principles of the Charter of the United Nations.

WHITE HOUSE STATEMENT, APR. 7, 1982[3]

This morning the President met with his national security advisers to review the situation in the South Atlantic. After the meeting, the President is departing for Jamaica, where he will meet with Prime Minister Seaga to further the close working dialogue opened during the Prime Minister's visit last year. He then continues on to Barbados, where he will meet with leaders of eastern Caribbean countries to discuss regional issues of mutual concern.

In keeping with the initiatives the President has taken with both [British] Prime Minister Thatcher and [Argentine] President Galtieri and his offer of assistance, the President has directed Secretary of State Haig to continue consultations with the Governments of the United Kingdom and Argentina in the interest of assisting both parties in the search for a peaceful resolution of the dispute in the South Atlantic.

The President directed Secretary Haig to proceed to London and Buenos Aires at the invitation of both governments.

SECRETARY HAIG, ARRIVAL STATEMENT, LONDON, APR. 12, 1982[4]

As you know, I have just arrived from Buenos Aires. I am bringing here to the British Government—Mrs. Thatcher and her ministers—some ideas which have been developed on the basis of U.N. Security Council Resolution 502 and look forward to these discussions.

SECRETARY'S STATEMENT, LONDON, APR. 12, 1982[5]

You will recall that this morning—I think it was this morning—upon arrival I said I was bringing some ideas that we had developed in Buenos Aires. Today we had an opportunity to discuss these ideas with her senior cabinet. We made some progress in these discussions, but a number of substantial difficulties remain, so we will be returning this evening to Buenos Aires as time is slipping away from us on this subject.

Q. Can you tell us what the main sticking point was or is?

A. No, I'm not going to discuss any of the details of the negotiation; it only complicates the process.

Q. You talk about time slipping away—what sort of scale are you talking about, how long have you got?

A. But I think you are as able to assess that as am I.

Q. Is there a 72-hour truce?

A. No, there is no truce or no hesitation or pause in any of the military preparations, as I understand, that are underway.

Q. Are you more hopeful now than you were?

A. No, not at all.

OAS RESOLUTION 359, APR. 13, 1982[6]

THE SITUATION OBTAINING BETWEEN THE REPUBLIC OF ARGENTINA AND THE UNITED KINGDOM OF GREAT BRITAIN AND NORTHERN IRELAND IN RELATION TO THE MALVINAS (FALKLAND) ISLANDS

WHEREAS:

The dispute between the Republic of Argentina and the United Kingdom of Great Britain and Northern Ireland in relation to

WESTERN HEMISPHERE

the Malvinas (Falkland) Islands is endangering the peace of the hemisphere, and

The fundamental principles and purposes established in the Charter of the Organization of American States include those of strengthening the peace and security of the continent, preventing possible causes of difficulties and ensuring the peaceful settlement of disputes,

THE PERMANENT COUNCIL OF THE ORGANIZATION OF AMERICAN STATES, RESOLVES:

1. To express its profound concern over the serious situation that the Republic of Argentina and the United Kingdom of Great Britain and Northern Ireland now face.

2. To express its fervent hope that a rapid, peaceful solution can be found to the disagreement between the two nations within the context of the rules of international law.

3. To offer its friendly cooperation in the peace efforts already under way, in the hope of contributing in this way to a peaceful settlement of the dispute that will avert once and for all the danger of war between countries that deserve the respect of the international community.

SECRETARY'S STATEMENT, ANDREWS AIR FORCE BASE, APR. 13, 1982[7]

As you know, I've just returned from London and will report to the President on the status of our efforts to help in achieving a diplomatic solution to the crisis in the South Atlantic in conformance with U.N. Security Council Resolution 502. We left here early Thursday and had intensive discussions in London, Buenos Aires, and again in London. The parties have received some new ideas today which they are considering, and this will give me an opportunity to discuss the situation directly with President Reagan, to catch up on some other work here in Washington before proceeding on to Buenos Aires and the continuation of our efforts.

Q. [Inaudible].

A. I conferred with him in the morning and have been in touch with him continuously both telephonically and by message throughout this journey.

Q. How long before you go back?

A. It's too early to say. We want to look at these new ideas and it will be done very soon.

Q. Do you have any sense of optimism?

A. I don't want to describe my judgments on this at all. As you know, we are trying to assist the parties who have difficult problems to overcome.

SECRETARY'S STATEMENT, APR. 14, 1982[8]

I want to make a statement on the dispute between Argentina and the United Kingdom. It is an exceptionally difficult—and exceptionally dangerous—problem.

The positions that both countries hold are deeply felt and, in many cases, mutually contradictory. But the leaders of both countries have assured me and in turn the President, again today, that they are prepared to go on working with us to reach a peaceful solution. That will require flexibility on both sides—not abandonment of principle but responsible and defensible adjustments. As a result of my conversations in London, plus telephone conversations today, I have developed new ideas which I have described to the Argentine Government. Based on these new ideas, the Argentinians have invited me to return to Buenos Aires. I propose to do so tomorrow.

From the outset of this crisis, the United States has viewed its role as that of assisting the two sides in finding a peaceful solution. Our ability to do this is based on our longstanding relations with both the United Kingdom and Argentina. We have been careful to maintain these relationships in order to preserve our influence with both governments. Failure to live up to existing obligations—or going beyond them—would obviously jeopardize our ability to play the role both countries wish us to perform.

Since the onset of the crisis, the United States has, therefore, not acceded to requests that would go beyond the scope of customary patterns of cooperation based on existing bilateral agreements. That will continue to be our stand while our efforts are underway.

The exchanges of the last several days indicate that each government welcomes our role and recognizes the importance of preserving our ability to continue it.

WHITE HOUSE STATEMENT, APR. 15, 1982[9]

Late this afternoon, President Galtieri of Argentina called President Reagan to discuss the situation in the South Atlantic.

During the conversation, President Reagan said that he was wholeheartedly committed to a peaceful resolution the dispute. He said that a conflict the hemisphere between two Western nations would be a tragedy and would leave a bitter legacy. President Reagan also asked for flexibility and restraint all parties in the days ahead. With this he said, we should be able to get through this together. We still have ways to go, he added, but he is hopeful that we can find a just and peaceful solution to this very serious matter. President also said that Secretary [Haig] his personal representative, would be arriving in Buenos Aires in a few hours continue the efforts of the United States.

As he had in a previous conversation, President Galtieri reaffirmed President Reagan his personal desire for a peaceful resolution of the dispute.

SECRETARY HAIG, QUESTION-AND-ANSWER SESSION BUENOS AIRES, APR. 18, 1982[10]

Q. It's been about 24 hours since we've had any news. Could you give some idea of how the talks are going?

A. We're continuing to work on problem with all the effort that a situation of this seriousness demands.

Q. You've had some moments when you were going, and you're going now. What has caused you to these ups and downs in these negotiations?

A. I think it's typical of difficult problems of this kind and we're just continuing to work.

Q. Could you give us any idea where the issue of sovereignty stands right now?

A. I think it serves no purpose have this session here. I've been in close touch with the President, and we're going to continue to do our work.

Q. Do you feel that any progress has been made at all, any progress?

A. I'm not going to describe on the sessions—

Q. What do you feel about the members of the ruling junta being

WESTERN HEMISPHERE

Falkland Islands

ber of Islands: Two large (East West Falkland) and approximately maller islands and islets.
: 4,700 sq. mi. (slightly smaller than ecticut).
ain: East and West Falkland are ated by Falkland Sound. Their lines are extremely irregular with rous intricate inlets, many of which potential harbors. East Falkland is st cut in half by a pair of deep in-The northern portion of the island minated by a rugged east-west e of hills. The southern portion is a undulating plain. West Falkland is hilly.
ate: The only long-term climate ds available are the records of vations made in Stanley (East land), where the temperature has been known to exceed 79°F. or to elow 12°F. Rainfall averages 25 s a year and is spread fairly evenly ghout the year. No month is entire-st free; snow falls on about 50 days g the year and has been recorded ery month. It is light, however, and

soon melts. Calm conditions are more frequent than storms.
Population: About 1,825 (of which 1,075 live in Stanley; the remainder live in 30 or more settlements scattered throughout the islands). About 95% of the labor force of 1,100 are involved with agriculture, primarily sheep.
Telecommunications: Stanley and Fox Bay (West Falkland) have a telephone system to which most farms are connected. Contact with farms on the smaller islands is by radio telephone.
Economy: Main industry is sheep raising, and the entire economic organization of the islands is geared to the production of wool.
Transportation: There are no railroads. There are 317 miles of roads, only a small portion of which is paved. Stanley is the only developed port for oceangoing vessels. Inter-island boat traffic is important. The only permanent-surface airfield is near Stanley; about 35 unsurfaced landing strips are on the islands which are used by the inter-island air service.

Utilities: A diesel power station supplies power to Stanley. Elsewhere most of the settlements and farms have their own generating plants. A water purification and filtration plant provides clean water for Stanley.
Commerce: All consumer goods, construction materials, vehicles, spare parts—literally everything on the islands—arrive in Stanley from the United Kingdom by charter vessel four times a year. The same vessel takes the wool bales to the United Kingdom for sale. When the ships arrive, Stanley's general stores abound with such luxuries as ice cream, butter, frozen chickens, etc., which are generally sold out within the first few weeks. Except for the general stores, Stanley has no other commercial establishments (no shoe stores, laundries or drycleaners, barbershops, or taxi service). Few homes have refrigerators so fresh meat is kept outside in a cold storage box, and butchering is usually postponed during the warm months. ■

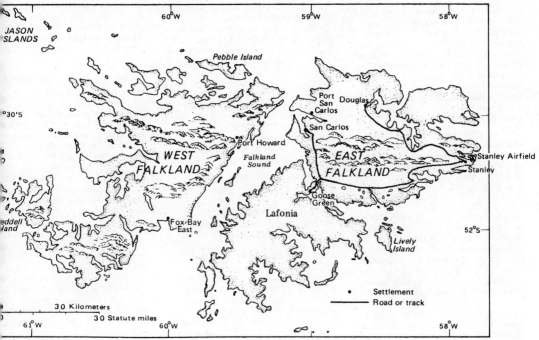

(lezlep, INR, Department of State)

WESTERN HEMISPHERE

brought into the negotiations? What's the significance of that?

A. I wouldn't apply any significance or any lack of significance.

Q. As a former military man?

A. Not at all.

SECRETARY HAIG,
QUESTION-AND-ANSWER SESSION
BUENOS AIRES,
APR. 18, 1982[11]

Q. What do you expect out the next stage of the negotiations here?

A. I think we are continuing to talk, we're continuing to work. More than that I can't say [inaudible].

Q. How long are you prepared to continue, the way you have been going?

A. I think all of us can be thankful that the effort is still underway and as long as it is underway—there is no other alternative [inaudible].

Q. How close are the Argentines to invoking the treaty of Rio. And second, do U.S. commitments to Great Britain take precedence over the treaty of Rio?

A. I think it's too early to say and I can't speak for the Argentine Government on the Rio treaty. There are a number of complications in that it would raise questions as to whether it was appropriate for [inaudible] to invoke the Rio treaty. I would not care to go beyond that in the context of our longstanding obligations to Great Britain which are well known and seriously taken [inaudible].

Q. Is there any indication that either the Argentines or the British are willing to compromise in any way over the question of sovereignty? And secondly, when you leave here do you plan to go to Washington or to London?

A. The question of sovereignty it seems to me is best not raised in the context of the current crisis. There are differing views on both sides, clearly. It's a subject for perhaps negotiation later. It's too early to say whether we are going to go from here to Washington to report to President Reagan. I've stayed in very close touch from the outset of this, received his instructions daily [inaudible]. It's still too early to say to answer that question; perhaps tomorrow or later [inaudible].

Q. You said that sovereignty is best discussed later. Does that mean that it is not being discussed now?

A. No, it clearly has an impact on the whole conduct of the discussion.

Q. Are the British conscious that the Argentinians intend to remain on the island dead or alive at any price?

A. I can't speak for the British on this subject and I can't speak for the Argentinians; they're capable of speaking for themselves.

SECRETARY'S STATEMENT,
BUENOS AIRES,
APR. 19, 1982[12]

Before leaving I have a brief formal departure statement to make.

On Thursday, when I returned to Buenos Aires, I brought with me new ideas which provided the basis for my very intensive meetings with the leadership of the Argentine Government. Others have been developed here. In these more than 3 days of very detailed talks, there has been a further identification and refinement of the Argentine position. We have now finished this stage of our work. I am making the results available to the British Government, and I am returning to Washington to report to the President.

We continue to believe firmly in the urgent necessity for a diplomatic solution to the South Atlantic crisis based on Security Council Resolution 502 and consistent with the principles and the purposes of the U.N. Charter. These are the guidelines we have followed since the outset of our effort. And I am more convinced than ever that war in the South Atlantic would be the greatest of tragedies and that time is, indeed, running out.

SECRETARY'S STATEMENT,
CARACAS, APR. 19, 1982[13]

Mr. Zambrano [Venezuela Foreign Minister Jose Alberto Zambrano Velasco] and I have just had a detailed exchange of views on the situation in the South Atlantic. I told the minister, on the question of Buenos Aires, that we went to Buenos Aires at the invitation of the Government of Argentina with some new idea with which to deal in accordance with U.N. Security Council Resolution 502. We had detailed exchanges there; we received some additional views and ideas from the Govern-

ment of Argentina which we ha transmitted to London. We're i process of having completed tha of the activity we've been involv and I will now return to Washir discuss the situation with Presic Reagan and to await further developments.

Q. Do you view a possible tine call for an OAS meeting a positive or negative sign?

A. I don't want to commen whether it is a positive or a neg sign. I think the Argentine Gov(has been considering such a ster considerable period. It remains seen.

Q. Why did you stop in Ca twice?

A. Clearly this is the place for refueling of the aircraft. It p me also a very convenient oppor exchange views with my colleag Zambrano on the situation. And say I noted with some interest t! speculation that followed our in! discussion here on my last leg. S the speculation was totally devoi basis in fact.

We had no discussions about anything at that time other than situation in the South Atlantic, » some other discussions about ou concerns about the situation in C America. So I am somewhat puz surprised to see that speculation

AMBASSADOR MIDDENDOR.
OAS, APR. 20, 1982[14]

The U.S. delegation is deeply dis by the implications of the propos tion that we are called upon to d today. In brief, we question whe such a proposal is either necessai appropriate and whether, therefc may contribute to a peaceful sett

We would have thought it un necessary to come before the OA day. Nevertheless, if a majority o members believes the time has cc build upon our work of last week Permanent Council, there is more ample basis for us to do so under OAS Charter.

As we all agreed last week, i resolution put forward by the distinguished representatives of C bia, Ecuador, and Costa Rica an proved by this body by consensus proper role for our organization i difficult situation is to be availabl

WESTERN HEMISPHERE

e ongoing efforts to reach a
settlement and to maintain our
ity as a valuable source of sup-
hese efforts.

cles 59 and 60 of the OAS
provide an entirely appropriate
or this organization to serve
. And Article 24 of the charter
y contemplates precisely the
mechanisms—such as good of-
ediation, conciliation, and in-
ion—that may be needed in this

ontrast, convocation under the
ty, as is proposed today, seems
appropriate for the present con-
a time when Secretary Haig is
in an ongoing effort to promote
ul settlement within the
ork of U.N. Resolution 502,
e are anxious not to prejudice, it
o my government particularly in-
iate to seek consideration of this
vithin the Rio treaty. Despite its
r peacekeeping purposes, the
ty is generally viewed as an in-
t for developing and implement-
ective security measures. While,
e, there has been no suggestion
ver that we consider adopting
asures, the mere fact of our
under the Rio treaty rubric
evitably cast the activities of
up in an unhelpful confronta-
ght.

could avoid such an unfortunate
our deliberations and achieve our
s equally well, if not better, by
under the OAS Charter. Ac-
y, it is the intention of my
on to abstain on the proposed
on under consideration.

ESOLUTION 360,
1, 1982[15]

s:

s note dated April 19, 1982, the
ent of Argentina requested convoca-
he Organ of Consultation, pursuant
e 6 of the Inter-American Treaty of
al Assistance, to consider the
s that it would be advisable to take
naintenance of the peace and security
emisphere, and

Permanent Council of the Organ-
f American States has heard the
nt by the Permanent Representative
ntina denouncing a grave situation
eatens the peace and security of the
ere and that affects the sovereignty
itorial integrity of his country, and
ng the measures that the Argentine
nent has adopted in exercise of the
legitimate self-defense,

THE PERMANENT COUNCIL OF THE
ORGANIZATION OF AMERICAN STATES
RESOLVES:

1. To convene the Organ of Consultation
under the provisions of the Inter-American
Treaty of Reciprocal Assistance, and in accordance with Article 70 of the Rules of Procedure of this Permanent Council, to consider
the grave situation that has arisen in the
South Atlantic.

2. To decide that the Organ of Consul-
tation shall meet at the headquarters of the
General Secretariat of the Organization on
April 26, 1982, at 10 a.m.

3. To constitute itself and to act provisionally as Organ of Consultation, pursuant
to Article 12 of the Inter-American Treaty of
Reciprocal Assistance.

DEPARTMENT STATEMENT,
APR. 25, 1982[16]

In light of events in South Georgia, the
Argentines have asked for a postpone-
ment of the meeting with Mr. Haig. The
Secretary had a lengthy conversation by
telephone with the Argentine Foreign
Minister this afternoon. He has also
been in continuous communication with
the President. During the Secretary's
conversations with the Argentine
Foreign Minister, the Secretary made it
clear that President Reagan believes
every effort should be made to find a
peaceful solution. The Secretary will
discuss the situation with the Foreign
Minister tomorrow morning.

SECRETARY'S STATEMENT,
OAS, APR. 26, 1982[17]

As we meet here in the Hall of the
Americas, we are reminded of the Western Hemisphere's tradition of
democracy, its record of achievement,
and its devotion to peace. The Organization of American States is the living
testimony that our cooperation can be a
force for international progress. Clearly,
a vigorous inter-American system is of
fundamental importance to the future of
the hemisphere.

These facts must be uppermost in
our minds as we consider how best to
advance toward a peaceful solution to
the South Atlantic controversy. All of us
know that we are dealing today with an
enormously difficult and sensitive problem. Both the Republic of Argentina and
the United Kingdom assert that their
rights to the islands have been denied.
Argentina is motivated by a deep national commitment to establish possession of the islands. It is frustrated by

South Georgia Islands

Number of Islands: One large and approximately 25 smaller islands and
rocks.
Area: 1,450 sq. mi. (slightly larger than
Long Island, New York).
Climate: Rain falls about 200 days of
the year. The islands are covered entirely by snow and glaciers much of the
year.
Population: A British scientific station
at Grytviken is the only existing permanent settlement. The last whaling station closed in the early 1960s. ■

years of what it considers to be fruitless
negotiation. Britain emphasizes its
longstanding possession of the islands
and asserts that the wishes of the inhabitants must be respected in any
lasting settlement.

To understand these competing
claims and the emotions on both sides
does not mean to pass judgment on their
validity. But this organization—and the
world community—long ago made the
judgment that force should not be used
to solve international disputes. We shall
all suffer if this fundamental principle of
both the international order and hemispheric order, which the Rio treaty was
designed to protect, is ignored. I think
all of us are well aware of how many
members of the OAS are involved in a
dispute over territory with one or more
neighbors.

In the current conflict, the surest
guide to a peaceful settlement is to be
found in U.N. Security Council Resolution 502. It requires an immediate cessation of hostilities, and immediate
withdrawal of Argentine forces on the
islands, and that the resolution of the
problem be sought through diplomacy.
These three points form the indispensable basis for a solution: They form an integrated whole. They have been accepted by both parties, or at least not
rejected by either of them.

In support of Resolution 502, the
United States has offered its assistance
to both Britain and Argentina. We have
acted in the spirit of friendship with
both countries, heartened by the confidence of both governments. For the
past 3 weeks, I have pursued the
possibilities of averting wider conflict
and a framework for a peaceful settlement, here, in Buenos Aires, and in Lon-

WESTERN HEMISPHERE

don. These discussion have been long and difficult. They could not have been otherwise in the context of this anguishing controversy. President Reagan believes that the United States has a perhaps unique ability to assist the parties. Under his direction, I have made myself available to both, accepting their invitations to sound out their views and suggesting avenues to approach a framework of peace.

Throughout this arduous period, we have been aware that the stakes for the international community, the Americas, and the two countries are very great. Continued military action will exact a heavy price. The enemies of the West could find fresh opportunities to seek that position of influence on the mainland of the Americas they have so long sought.

It is quite clear that the crisis has reached a critical point. New military action has taken place. Unless a settlement can be found in the next few days, more intensive fighting is likely to occur.

The conflict over the islands affects us all. As we consider what we can do to help the situation, let us recall these points.

• There has been a use of force by an American state, followed by a U.N. Security Council resolution which clearly sets forth the basis for a peaceful settlement. While we should take advantage of the peaceful settlement procedures available to us in this forum, it would be neither appropriate nor effective to treat this dispute within the collective security framework implied by the Rio treaty.

• Any resolution considered for adoption by the foreign ministers should be examined against the criteria of whether it contributes to the peace process, whether it impairs the peace efforts already endorsed by the OAS, and whether it strengthens the ability of this organization to contribute in the future to easing this crisis.

Our participation in the inter-American system pledges us to strengthen the peace and security of the hemisphere. In the search for a solution that both parties can accept with honor and responsibility, the United States remains at the disposition of the parties. At this critical hour, we are redoubling our peace efforts. With your help we may succeed.

DECLARATION OF FOREIGN MINISTERS, OAS, APR. 26, 1982

The Twentieth Meeting of Consultation Ministers of Foreign Affairs, taking in count Resolution 359 of the Permanent cil and the serious situation that has br about this meeting, urges that peace be tained in the hemisphere and that law as a basis for international relations.

OAS RESOLUTION I, APR. 28, 1982[18]

CONSIDERING:

The principles of inter-American so ty and cooperation and the need to find peaceful solution to any situation that dangers the peace of the Americas;

That a dangerous confrontation has arisen between the United Kingdom of Britain and Northern Ireland and the tine Republic, which was aggravated to the events that have arisen from the presence of the British navy in the Sou Atlantic, within the security region ref to in Article 4 of the Rio Treaty;

That the primary purpose of the In American Treaty of Reciprocal Assista the maintenance of the peace and secu the hemisphere, which, in the case that arisen, requires ensuring the peaceful s ment of the dispute;

That to facilitate peaceful settleme the dispute, it is urgent that hostilities since they disturb, the peace of the hem sphere and may reach unforeseeable pr tions;

That it is an unchanging principle c inter-American system that peace be pr served and that all the American states unanimously reject the intervention of continental or continental armed forces any of the nations of the hemisphere;

That Argentina's rights of sovereig over the Malvinas (Falkland) Islands, a stated in some important resolutions pa by various international forums, includi Declaration of Inter-American Juridical mittee on January 16, 1976, which stat "That the Republic of Argentina has an undeniable right of sovereignty over th Malvinas Islands," must be borne in mi and

That the peace efforts being made the consent of the parties must be empl sized, and that inter-American solidarit tributes to that objective, and

HAVING SEEN:

Resolution 502 (1982) of the United tions Security Council, all of whose terr must be fulfilled; Resolution 359 of Apr 1982, adopted by the Permanent Counc the Organization of American States, an Declaration adopted unanimously by the Ministers of Foreign Affairs at the open session of the Twentieth Meeting of Cor

FALKLAND ISLANDS AND VICINITY

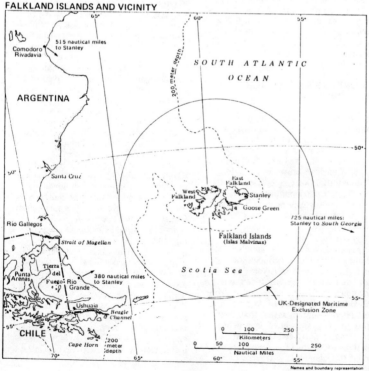

SOUTH ATLANTIC OCEAN

515 nautical miles to Stanley

Comodoro Rivadavia

ARGENTINA

Santa Cruz

Rio Gallegos

Strait of Magellan

Tierra del Fuego

Punta Arenas

380 nautical miles to Stanley

Rio Grande

Ushuaia

Beagle Channel

CHILE

Cape Horn

200 meter depth

West Falkland

East Falkland

Stanley

Goose Green

Falkland Islands (Islas Malvinas)

Scotia Sea

725 nautical miles: Stanley to South Georgia

UK-Designated Maritime Exclusion Zone

0   100   250
Kilometers
0   50   100   250
Nautical Miles

Names and boundary representation are not necessarily authoritative

(Bill Hezlep, INR, Department of State)

oc. 14/82), and in conformity with the
.merican Treaty of Reciprocal
.nce,

/ES:

To urge the Government of the United
.m of Great Britain and Northern
◀ immediately to cease the hostilities it
/ing on within the security region
◀ by Article 4 of the Inter-American
of Reciprocal Assistance, and also to
from any act that may affect inter-
:an peace and security.
To urge the Government of the
lic of Argentina likewise to refrain
iking any action that may exacerbate
uation.
To urge those governments im-
ely to call a truce that will make it
e to resume and proceed normally with
gotiation aimed at a peaceful settle-
·f the conflict, taking into account the
of sovereignty of the Republic of
:ina over the Malvinas (Falkland)
s and the interests of the islanders.
To express the willingness of the
of Consultation to lend support,
◀h whatever means it considers ad-
, to the new initiatives being advanced
regional or world level, with the con-
▪ the Parties, which are directed
◀ the just and peaceful settlement of
oblem.
To take note of the information re-
about the important negotiations of
:cretary of State of the United States of
:a and to express its wishes that they
an effective contribution to the
ul settlement of the conflict.
To deplore the adoption by members
European Economic Community and
states of coercive measures of an
nic and political nature, which are prej-
to the Argentine nation and to urge
:o lift those measures, indicating that
onstitute a serious precedent, inasmuch
y are not covered by Resolution 502
of the United Nations Security Council
e incompatible with the Charters of the
◀ Nations and of the OAS and the
al Agreement on Tariffs and Trade
").
To instruct the President of the Twen-
Meeting of Consultation to take im-
te steps to transmit the appeal con-
in operative paragraphs 1, 2 and 3 of
solution to the governments of the
d Kingdom of Great Britain and Nor-
Ireland and of the Republic of Argen-
.nd also to inform them, on behalf of
reign ministers of the Americas, that
ully confident that this appeal will be
ed for the sake of peace in the region
▪ the world.
To instruct the President of the Twen-
Meeting of Consultation immediately to
it this resolution formally to the Chair-
f the United Nations Security Council,
.t he may bring it to the attention of the
ers of the Council.
To keep the Twentieth Meeting of
ıltation open, especially to oversee

South Sandwich Islands

Number of Islands: Nine main and approximately 10 smaller islands and
islets.
Area: 120 sq. mi. From the Cook Island
in the south to Zavodovski Island in the
north, South Sandwich Islands span an
arc of approximately 200 nautical miles.
Climate: There are no long-term
meteorological records. However, the
islands are located well south of the approximate limits of pack ice for
September.
Population: Argentinian scientific base
on Southern Thule. ∎

faithful compliance with this resolution, and
to take such additional measures as are
deemed necessary to restore and preserve
peace and settle the conflict by peaceful
means.

AMBASSADOR MIDDENDORF,
OAS, APR. 28, 1982[19]

I will take only a moment to explain the
vote of my delegation on the resolution
just adopted.
We are gratified by the support expressed in operative Paragraph 5 for the
efforts of Secretary Haig to avert a
wider conflict and to obtain agreement
on a framework for peace.
It is precisely because of those efforts that my delegation has voted as it
did on the proposed resolution. The
resolution comes at a delicate moment in
Secretary Haig's efforts; at a moment
when the United States has redoubled
its peace efforts.
Given the Secretary's mission, the
United States is not in a position to express views on many of the issues addressed by the resolution and, therefore,
has abstained. In so doing, we reaffirm
the fervent hope, shared by each of us,
that all the actions of this distinguished
body will truly facilitate peace.

SECRETARY'S STATEMENT,
APR. 30, 1982[20]

The South Atlantic crisis is about to
enter a new and dangerous phase, in
which large-scale military action is likely. I would like to bring you up to date

on what we have done, why, and what
we must do now.
We have made a determined effort
to restore peace through implementation
of U.N. Security Council Resolution 502.
That resolution calls for an end to
hostilities, the withdrawal of Argentine
forces from the islands, and a diplomatic
settlement of the fundamental dispute.
The United States made this extraordinary effort because the stakes in
human lives and international order required it. From the outset, the United
States has been guided by the basic principle of the rule of law and the peaceful
settlement of disputes. The collapse of
that principle could only bring chaos and
suffering.
We also made this effort because the
crisis raised the vital issues of
hemispheric solidarity at a time when
the Communist adversaries seek positions of influence on the mainland of the
Americas, and latent territorial disputes
in much of the hemisphere called for unity and the resolute defense of principle.
We acted as well because the United
States has the confidence of the parties.
The United Kingdom is our closest ally,
and Prime Minister Thatcher's government looked to us to pursue a peaceful
solution. We have also recently
developed a better relationship with
Argentina as part of our success in
revitalizing the community of American
states. President Galtieri also requested
our involvement.
Under the direction of President
Reagan, I participated in many days of
intense discussions with the parties in
the search of a framework for implementing U.N. Security Council
Resolution 502. Our initial aim was to
clarify the position of the parties and to
offer suggestions on how those positions
might be reconciled. We took no position
on the merits of either the British or
Argentine claims to the islands. As the
prospects for more intense hostilities
arose, we set forth an American proposal. It represented our best estimate
of what the two parties could reasonably
be expected to accept and was based
squarely on our own principles and concern for the rule of law.
We regard this as a fair and a sound
proposal. It involves a cessation of
hostilities, withdrawal of both Argentine
and British forces, termination of sanctions, establishment of a U.S.-U.K.-
Argentine interim authority to maintain
the agreement, continuation of the traditional local administration with Argentine participation, procedures for encouraging cooperation in the develop-

WESTERN HEMISPHERE

ment of the islands, and a framework for negotiations on a final settlement, taking into account the interests of both sides and the wishes of the inhabitants.

We had reason to hope that the United Kingdom would consider a settlement along the lines of our proposal, but Argentina informed us yesterday that it could not accept it. Argentina's position remains that it must receive an assurance now of eventual sovereignty or an immediate *de facto* role in governing the islands which would lead to sovereignty.

For its part, the British Government had continued to affirm the need to respect the views of the inhabitants in any settlement.

The United States has thus far refrained from adopting measures in response to the seizure of the islands that could have interfered with our ability to work with both sides in the search for peace.

The British Government has shown complete understanding for this position. Now, however, in light of Argentina's failure to accept a compromise, we must take concrete steps to underscore that the United States cannot and will not condone the use of unlawful force to resolve disputes.

The President has, therefore, ordered the suspension of all military exports to Argentina, the withholding of certification of Argentine eligibility for military sales, and the suspension of new Export-Import Bank credits and guarantees.

The President has also directed that the United States will respond positively for requests to material support for British forces. There will, of course, be no direct U.S. military involvement.

American policy will continue to be guided by our concerns for the rule of law and our desire to facilitate an early and fair settlement. The United States remains ready to assist the parties in finding that settlement. A strictly military outcome cannot endure over time. In the end, there will have to be a negotiated outcome acceptable to the interested parties. Otherwise, we will all face unending hostility and insecurity in the South Atlantic.

[1]Made at the news briefing at the White House by Principal Deputy Press Secretary Larry Speakes (text from Weekly Compilation of Presidential Documents of Apr. 5, 1982).

[2]Adopted by a vote of 10 (U.S.)-1, with 4 abstentions.

[3]Text from Weekly Compilation of Presidential Documents of Apr. 12.
[4]Press release 124.
[5]Press release 125 of Apr. 13.
[6]Adopted by consensus by the Permanent Council of the OAS.
[7]Press release 126 of Apr. 14.
[8]Press release 131.
[9]Text from Weekly Compilation of Presidential Documents of Apr. 19.
[10]Press release 137 of Apr. 20.
[11]Press release 136 of Apr. 20.
[12]Press release 139 of Apr. 20.
[13]Press release 140 of Apr. 21.
[14]Made at the 20th meeting of the Consultation of Ministers of Foreign Affairs, OAS.

[15]Adopted by the convocation of the meeting of the Consultation of Minister Foreign Affairs, Permanent Council, O a vote of 18-0, with 3 abstentions (U.S.
[16]Made available to the press by De ment spokesman Dean Fischer.
[17]Made to the 20th meeting of the sultation of Ministers of Foreign Affair manent Council, OAS (press release 14 Apr. 27).
[18]Adopted by the 20th meeting of th Consultation of Ministers of Foreign Af Permanent Council, OAS, by a vote of with 4 abstentions (U.S.).
[19]Made at the 20th meeting of the C sultation of Ministers of Foreign Affair OAS.
[20]Press release 150. ■

Background on the Falkland Islands Crisis

by Neal H. Petersen
Office of the Historian

Summary

The Falkland Islands dispute dates to the era of early European exploration. Spain and England nearly went to war over control of the area in the 18th century, and the question of sovereignty has been a matter of keen significance to Argentina from its moment of independence in 1816. The United States was involved in events of the early 1830s. In 1833 the British established an enduring British presence. For the next 150 years, the British developed the islands as a colony supporting a whaling and a sheep industry protected by the Royal Navy. Argentina never allowed its sense of grievance to cool and in the post-1945 era raised the claim repeatedly. Sporadic U.K.-Argentine negotiations have occurred since 1966. The U.S. position has been to accept the fact of British presence without prejudice to the question of ultimate sovereignty and to avoid taking sides on the issue.

Early Claims

Contending claims to the Falkland/ Malvinas Islands date to the earliest phases of European exploration. The British maintain that the first confirmed voyage to the islands was undertaken in 1592 by the English sailor John Davis. The possibility of earlier voyages to the Falklands by various Spanish explorers, including Amerigo Vespucci in 1502, is generally discounted by scholars but continues to be advanced by some Argentine historians.

The first European settlement the Falklands was established in 17 the French who later sold their rig Spain. A British settlement took ho 1766. Britain and Spain nearly wen war over the islands in the 1770s. B ain withdrew in 1774 without the qu tion of sovereignty being resolved.

Until 1811, Spain enjoyed undis puted control of the Falklands but u them for little more than a penal co and withdrew entirely in 1811 durin Argentina's war for independence. new Argentine Government claimed vacant islands in 1820 and establishe colony in 1826.

U.S. Involvement
During the 19th Century

In 1831 the Argentine governor of t Falklands seized three American sea ships to demonstrate Argentine autl ty in the area. One escaped, one was released, but the third, the *Harriet*, taken to Buenos Aires as a prize. W Argentine rejected U.S. diplomatic p tests, the U.S.S. *Lexington*, an American warship, destroyed the Ar tina settlement in the Falklands and deported much of the population, including all responsible officials.

There ensued a 12-year break in U.S.-Argentine relations and a battle contending claims respecting the seiz of the *Harriet* and the destruction wrought by the *Lexington*. Argentina continued to demand reparations for decades. A U.S. reply of 1841 stated that the United States was suspendir judgment on the Argentine request because it did not want to commit its

Anglo-Argentine dispute over
eignty. In 1885 President
and defended the *Lexington's*
ction of the "piratical" Argentine
and publicly rejected the Argen-
aim as "wholly groundless."

Views of
ritish Colony

British occupied the islands in 1833
xercised control for the next cen-
.nd a half. The Falklands supported
fitable sheep-raising industry while
ng as a whaling station and naval
ing port. The victories achieved by
h warships operating out of and
the Falklands in both World Wars
-lined the islands' strategic value.
.S. policy on the issue of sovereign-
ns generally noncommittal and occa-
lly ambiguous and self-contra-
ry. The United States chose not to
der the British reoccupation of the
lands a violation of the Monroe Doc-
, basing its position on British
is antedating that pronouncement,
mbiguous state of the British/
ntine legal dispute, and the prac-
consideration that recognition of
ntine sovereignty would undercut
J.S. defense against Argentine
ns for damages.
The United States denied Britain's
t to proceed against U.S. whalers
fishermen as trespassers. Yet U.S.
mercial agents, and then consuls,
ed on the Falklands dealt with
ish authorities. The United States
listed the islands as a British
ession in a bilateral convention with
United Kingdom of 1902. The
ed States became a party to various
tilateral conventions to which the
ted Kingdom acceded on behalf of
Falkland Islands. The Falklands
e identified as British in a U.S. con-
r instruction of 1926 and listed as
ish in a press release of 1938 analyz-
a trade agreement with the United
gdom. On the other hand, apparently
ng to avoid implying U.S. acceptance
he British claim, the United States
ided mention of the Falkland Islands
he 1938 agreement itself.

The Issue Since 1945

Since the Second World War, successive
U.S. Administrations have hewed to a
course of strict neutrality on the
Falklands issue despite repeated Argentine requests for support. At inter-
American conferences of the 1945–55
period, the United States reiterated its
neutral position and called for a peaceful
settlement. With the Falklands in mind
it abstained or voted against resolutions
calling for a definitive end to colonialism
in the Americas, self-determination for
the colonies of extracontinental powers,
and the monitoring of dependent territories by the Organization of American
States.

In 1964 Argentina began a con-
certed international campaign for the
"return of the Malvinas," taking its case
to the United Nations and the Committee of 24 as a colonial issue. The United
States declined formal and informal
Argentine requests for support and abstained on a resolution calling for
bilateral U.K.-Argentine negotiations
and an end to "colonialism" in the
Falklands. In 1965 the United States
again abstained on an Argentine-
initiated resolution at the U.N. General
Assembly. The United Kingdom and
Argentina did begin negotiations in
January 1966, but a hijacking and symbolic "invasion" of the islands by a handful of Argentine nationalists occurred in
October, followed by anti-British
demonstrations in Argentina.

In November 1967 Prime Minister
Harold Wilson's Labor government appeared to accept the principle of eventual Argentine control of the islands,
dependent on the will of the inhabitants.
A visit to the Falklands by Lord
Chalfont, Minister of State, in
November 1968 raised the islanders'
fears of abandonment. An uproar in the
London press and Conservative Party
opposition in Parliament fueled senti-
ment to retain the islands. Rumors in
1969 of possible oil deposits added
another dimension to the controversy.

In July 1971 the two sides announced a series of agreements increasing commercial, communications, social,
and cultural links between the Falklands
and Argentina. However, following the

return of Juan Peron, the negotiations
collapsed in November 1973. The Argentine Government again asked for U.S.
support but was rebuffed by the familiar
stance of impartiality. A British
economic survey of the Falklands in
1976 met with a vigorous protest from
Argentina, and there occurred an incident at sea involving the Argentine
Navy and a British research vessel.
Probable oil deposits seemed to be a
cause for heightened tension. British
and Argentine negotiators resumed
discussions in 1977 and by December
1978 had agreed on scientific cooperation in research on the Falkland
dependencies. A new round of negotiations commenced in March 1981. In October the United Kingdom conducted
elections for a local legislative council.

Early in 1982, Argentina insisted
upon monthly bilateral negotiations with
a preestablished agenda and escalated
the level of its rhetoric on the issue.
Disagreement over the presence of
Argentines on the South Georgia Islands
to dismantle an abandoned whaling factory led to sharply rising tensions. There
followed the Argentine invasion of the
Falklands on April 2 and on South
Georgia on April 4.

Throughout the postwar period the
United States had not deviated from its
refusal to take a position on the issue of
sovereignty. ■

ASSEMBLY OF WESTERN EUROPEAN UNION

PROCEEDINGS

TWENTY-EIGHTH ORDINARY SESSION

FIRST PART

June 1982

I

Assembly Documents

WEU

PARIS

Document 907   20th April 1982

The Falklands crisis

DRAFT RECOMMENDATION [1]

submitted on behalf of the
Committee on Defence Questions and Armaments [2]
by Mr. Cavaliere, Chairman and Rapporteur

The Assembly,

(*i*)   Firmly condemning the armed invasion of the Falkland Islands by Argentina on 2nd April 1982 in flagrant violation of international law;

(*ii*)   Welcoming the rapid and effective operation of European political consultation leading to the statement issued by the Ten on 2nd April and the declaration of 10th April;

(*iii*)   Fully endorsing those declarations, but regretting that the Council did not meet in application of Article VIII.3 of the modified Brussels Treaty;

(*iv*)   Welcoming the initiative of the United States Secretary of State to seek accommodation between the two powers concerned;

(*v*)   Noting that the Soviet Union and certain of its allies have not hesitated to afford Argentina, after condemnation by the United Nations Security Council, certain assistance;

(*vi*)   Concerned at the weakening of allied forces in the North Atlantic following the necessary dispatch of large British forces outside the area,

RECOMMENDS THAT THE COUNCIL

Urge member governments:

1.   To implement fully the decision of the Ten to ban the export of arms and military equipment to Argentina and to ban all imports into the Community originating in Argentina;

2.   To concert their political, economic and diplomatic efforts in all countries and appropriate international bodies to secure the immediate withdrawal of Argentine forces from the Falklands in accordance with Security Council Resolution 502, the peaceful settlement of the dispute in full accord with the wishes of the inhabitants of the islands, and the widest support for the foregoing decision of the Ten;

3.   To study the lessons for European security which may be drawn from the crisis, including:

    (*a*) ways of ensuring that governments obtain earlier warning of impending military attack;

    (*b*) the need for the vital interests of the Alliance to be defended outside the area prescribed in Article 6 of the North Atlantic Treaty;

    (*c*) the compensatory measures to be taken by the allies within that area forthwith following the dispatch of large British forces outside the area;

4.   To draw the attention of the Council to Article VIII.3 of the modified Brussels Treaty.

---

1. Adopted in Committee by 15 votes to 1 with 0 abstentions.

2. *Members of the Committee:* Mr. *Cavaliere* (Chairman); MM. van den Bergh. Mayoud (Vice-Chairmen); Mr. Bahr, *Sir Frederic Bennett* MM. *Bernini.* Bizet, *Blaauw;* Bonnel (Alternate: *van der Elst*), *Cox,* Dejardin, Duraffour (Alternate: *Baumel*), *Edwards,* Fosson, *Grant. Kittelmann.* Lemmrich, Maravalle, Ménard (Alternate: *Louis Jung*), Pecchioli (Alternate: *Amadei*), Pignion, *Prussen.* Hermann Schmidt. Scholten, *Smith, Tanghe. Vohrer.*

N.B.   *The names of those taking part in the vote are printed in italics.*

Document 907 Revised

19th May 1982

The Falklands crisis

REPORT[1]

submitted on behalf of the
Committee on Defence Questions and Armaments[2]
by Mr. Cavaliere, Chairman and Rapporteur

TABLE OF CONTENTS

1. Adopted in Committee by 11 votes to 2 with 4 abstentions.

2. *Members of the Committee:* Mr. *Cavaliere* (Chairman); MM. van den Bergh. Mayoud (Vice-Chairmen); Mr. Bahr, Sir *Frederic Bennett*, MM. Bernini (Alternate: *Martino*), Bizet, *Blaauw*, Bonnel (Alternate: *De Decker*), Cox (Alternate: *Brown*), *Dejardin*, Duraffour, Edwards. Fosson (Alternate: *De Poi*), Grant (Alternate: *Hill*), *Kittelmann*, Lemmrich (Alternate: *Wittmann*), Maravalle (Alternate: *Della Briotta*), Ménard, Pecchioli, *Pignion*, *Prussen*, Hermann Schmidt, Scholten, *Smith*, *Steverlynck*, *Vohrer*.

N.B. *The names of those taking part in the vote are printed in italics*

Draft Recommendation
on the Falklands crisis

The Assembly,

(i)   Firmly condemning the armed invasion of the Falkland Islands by Argentina on 2nd April 1982 in flagrant violation of international law ;

(ii)   Welcoming the rapid and effective operation of European political consultation leading to the statement issued by the Ten on 2nd April and the declaration of 10th April ;

(iii)   Fully endorsing those declarations, but regretting that the Council did not meet in application of Article VIII.3 of the modified Brussels Treaty ;

(iv)   Regretting that the initiatives of the United States Secretary of State, the President of Peru and the Secretary-General of the United Nations to seek accommodation between the two powers concerned have not so far succeeded ;

(v)   Noting that the Soviet Union and certain of its allies have not hesitated to afford Argentina, after condemnation by the United Nations Security Council, certain assistance ;

(vi)   Concerned at the weakening of allied forces in the North Atlantic following the necessary dispatch of large British forces outside the area,

RECOMMENDS THAT THE COUNCIL

Urge member governments:

1.   To implement fully the decision of the Ten to ban the export of arms and military equipment to Argentina and to ban all imports into the Community originating in Argentina ;

2.   To concert their political, economic and diplomatic efforts in all countries and appropriate international bodies to secure the immediate withdrawal of Argentine forces from the Falklands in accordance with Security Council Resolution 502, the peaceful settlement of the dispute in full accord with the wishes of the inhabitants of the islands, and the widest support for the foregoing decision of the Ten ;

3.   To study the lessons for European security which may be drawn from the crisis, including:

(a) ways of ensuring that governments obtain earlier warning of impending military attack ;

(b) the need for the vital interests of the Alliance to be defended outside the area prescribed in Article 6 of the North Atlantic Treaty;

(c) the compensatory measures to be taken by the allies within that area forthwith following the dispatch of large British forces outside the area ;

4.   To draw the attention of the Council to Article VIII.3 of the modified Brussels Treaty.

Explanatory Memorandum
(submitted by Mr. Cavaliere, Chairman and Rapporteur)

1.　On 2nd April 1982 Argentine forces attacked and occupied the Falklands Islands.

2.　The Presidential Committee referred the matter to the Committee on Defence Questions and Armaments, requesting it to report to the Presidential Committee in time for it to be considered by that committee on 19th May.

3.　The committee adopted a draft recommendation on 20th April[1] and subsequently adopted the present report with revised draft recommendation on 19th May immediately prior to the meeting of the Presidential Committee on that day. In the revised draft recommendation now submitted – revised only in paragraph (*iv*) of the preamble to take account of mediation initiatives subsequent to 20th April – the committee first and foremost calls on the Assembly to condemn the unprovoked aggression committed by Argentina, in flagrant violation of international law. The use of force in pursuit of territorial claims must be universally condemned. Almost no corner of the world would be free of the threat of hostilities, and there would be a grave risk of world war, if nations could resort to force with impunity in such circumstances. The committee particularly deplores the fact that the Argentine attack on the Falklands took place on 2nd April in defiance of the agreed statement from the President of the United Nations Security Council on 1st April:

> " The Security Council accordingly calls on the Governments of Argentina and the United Kingdom to exercise the utmost restraint at this time and in particular to refrain from the use or threat of force in the region and to continue the search for a diplomatic solution. "[2]

4.　The committee's text welcomes the rapid and effective operation of European political co-operation, which *condemned* the armed intervention the same day that it occurred, and led to the European Communities agreeing on economic sanctions[3]; it calls for the widest support for that decision. It regrets, however, that the Council of WEU was not convened under Article VIII.3 of the modified Brussels Treaty which provides for consultation " with regard to any situation which may constitute a threat to peace, in whatever area this threat should arise... ".

5.　The committee notes that the position of the United States, and of NATO, was originally less clearly defined than that of the European Community. At the outset the United States sought to maintain an impartial status for its Secretary of State while Mr. Haig was acting as intermediary between the United Kingdom and Argentina, but the United States would also have preferred, if possible, to have secured a withdrawal of Argentine forces without impairing United States-Argentine relations, because of their importance to the present United States administration in its policy of resisting communist penetration of Latin America. With the failure of the Haig mission on 30th April, however, the United States finally took sides, offering " material " assistance to the United Kingdom, and denying military and economic assistance to Argentina, although not imposing economic sanctions.

6.　Comment by NATO has shifted similarly. At British request the North Atlantic Council held a special meeting on 2nd April after a statement issued by the Secretary General noted merely that " Members of the Council *expressed deep concern* at the dispute... ". The Defence Ministers of the eleven European NATO countries, members of Eurogroup, at their meeting on 5th May " *condemned* Argentina's armed invasion ", and the ministerial meeting of the NATO Defence Planning Committee on 7th May endorsed the Eurogroup statement[1].

7.　The basis for an end to hostilities is Security Council Resolution 502, adopted with only one vote against (Panama) and four abstentions (Soviet Union, China, Poland, Spain) on 3rd April. It " 1. Demands an immediate cessation of hostilities ; 2. Demands an immediate withdrawal of all Argentine forces from the Falkland Islands ; 3. Calls on the Governments of Argentina and the United Kingdom to seek a diplomatic solution to their differences and respect fully the purposes and principles of the Charter of the United Nations "[2]. This report does not examine subsequent attempts by various persons, alluded to in paragraph (*iv*) of the preamble, to secure the application of Resolution 502, which has not been accepted by Argentina, and a negotiated settlement of the crisis. While these efforts continue, any report on their progress would be out of date before it was distributed.

---

1. Text at Appendix I.
2. Full text at Appendix IV (*a*).
3. Texts at Appendix IV (*b*), (*c*) and (*f*).

1. Texts at Appendix IV (*c*), (*g*) and (*h*).
2. Full text at Appendix IV (*d*).

The recommendation calls simply for the withdrawal of Argentine forces in accordance with the resolution, and the peaceful settlement of the dispute in full accord with the wishes of the inhabitants.

8. While deploring the loss of human life that has so far resulted from the conflict, the committee is also aware that many conclusions can be drawn for European security, not least the need for early warning of impending military attack; the need to ensure that political authorities make proper use of warning when received and take proper measures to prevent a threat materialising; and the compensatory measures that need to be taken in the area covered by the Alliance when national forces are necessarily sent outside the area in the defence of vital interests. The committee calls for these and other lessons to be studied. It is too soon to attempt to draw such conclusions in the present report.

9. The present report does not examine the substance of the Argentine claim to the Falklands; there is a summary of the rival historical claims at Appendix I and of recent Anglo-Argentine negotiations at Appendix II. The committee merely notes that United Kingdom administration of the islands has been effective and uninterrupted since January 1833; that the population is of British stock and seeks no change in the status enjoyed by the islands prior to the Argentine invasion.

Opinion of the minority

10. The original draft recommendation of 20th April was adopted by 15 votes to 1 with 0 abstentions. The minority on that occasion, while supporting much of the recommendation, was opposed to the reference to the Soviet Union in paragraph (*v*) of the preamble, and to paragraph 3 of the operative text calling for the lessons for European security to be studied. The revised recommendation of 19th May was adopted by 11 votes to 2 with 4 abstentions. A proposal of the minority on this occasion was that the report should examine the history of the rights of the inhabitants of the Falklands. Some of those abstaining believed the report should have examined longer-term political solutions to problems raised by the crisis, including the improvement of relations between Europe and Latin America in general.

APPENDIX I

Document 907

20th April 1982

The Falklands crisis

<hr>

DRAFT RECOMMENDATION [1]

submitted on behalf of the
Committee on Defence Questions and Armaments [2]
by Mr. Cavaliere, Chairman and Rapporteur

<hr>

The Assembly,

(*i*)   Firmly condemning the armed invasion of the Falkland Islands by Argentina on 2nd April 1982 in flagrant violation of international law;

(*ii*)   Welcoming the rapid and effective operation of European political consultation leading to the statement issued by the Ten on 2nd April and the declaration of 10th April;

(*iii*)   Fully endorsing those declarations, but regretting that the Council did not meet in application of Article VIII.3 of the modified Brussels Treaty;

(*iv*)   Welcoming the initiative of the United States Secretary of State to seek accommodation between the two powers concerned;

(*v*)   Noting that the Soviet Union and certain of its allies have not hesitated to afford Argentina, after condemnation by the United Nations Security Council, certain assistance;

(*vi*)   Concerned at the weakening of allied forces in the North Atlantic following the necessary dispatch of large British forces outside the area,

RECOMMENDS THAT THE COUNCIL

Urge member governments:

1.   To implement fully the decision of the Ten to ban the export of arms and military equipment to Argentina and to ban all imports into the Community originating in Argentina;

2.   To concert their political, economic and diplomatic efforts in all countries and appropriate international bodies to secure the immediate withdrawal of Argentine forces from the Falklands in accordance with Security Council Resolution 502, the peaceful settlement of the dispute in full accord with the wishes of the inhabitants of the islands, and the widest support for the foregoing decision of the Ten;

3.   To study the lessons for European security which may be drawn from the crisis, including:

   (*a*) ways of ensuring that governments obtain earlier warning of impending military attack;

   (*b*) the need for the vital interests of the Alliance to be defended outside the area prescribed in Article 6 of the North Atlantic Treaty;

   (*c*) the compensatory measures to be taken by the allies within that area forthwith following the dispatch of large British forces outside the area;

4.   To draw the attention of the Council to Article VIII.3 of the modified Brussels Treaty.

<hr>

1. Adopted in Committee by 15 votes to 1 with 0 abstentions.

2. *Members of the Committee:* Mr. *Cavaliere* (Chairman); MM. van den Bergh, Mayoud (Vice-Chairmen); Mr. Bahr, *Sir Frederic Bennett,* MM. *Bernini,* Bizet, *Blaauw,* Bonnel (Alternate: *van der Elst), Cox,* Dejardin, Duraffour (Alter- nate: *Baumel),* *Edwards,* Fosson, *Grant, Kittelma──, Lemm-* rich, Maravalle, Ménard (Alternate: *Louis Jung,* Pecchioli (Alternate: *Amadei),* Pignion, *Prussen,* Herman, Schmidt, Scholten, *Smith, Tanghe, Vohrer.*

N.B. *The names of those taking part in the vote are printed in italics.*

APPENDIX II

History of the Falklands

(a) *British interpretation* [1]

14th August 1592

The islands are believed to have been first sighted by the English captain, John Davis, from the ship " Desire ". Two years later, in 1594, Sir Richard Hawkins sailed along their northern coast. In 1598, the Dutch sailor, Sebald van Weerdt, is said to have visited some of the islands of the archipelago (probably the Jason Islands).

27th January 1690

Captain John Strong of the British Royal Navy made the first known landing on the islands, which had never been inhabited, and named the sound between the western and eastern islands Falkland after Viscount Falkland, the Treasurer of the Royal Navy. French seal-hunters from St. Malo were frequent visitors to the islands in the eighteenth century, hence their French name of *Iles Malouines* and their Spanish name of *Islas Malvinas*.

31st January 1764

A French sailor-explorer, Bougainville, founded the first settlement on East Falkland in the name of France and at his own expense : Fort St. Louis on East Falkland.

12th January 1765

Commodore John Byron, sent by the British Admiralty to survey the islands, proclaimed that they were uninhabited and claimed them for Great Britain. In January 1766, after deciding that the occupation of the islands was " the key to the whole of the Pacific Ocean ", the Admiralty sent Captain John MacBride to complete the occupation with a settlement of about a hundred people at Port Egmont on Saunders Island off West Falkland and build a fort. He discovered the French settlement in December and told the settlers to leave.

1767

France relinquished its claim to the islands in return for the equivalent of a

1. *Sources:* United Kingdom Central Office of Information, Document 152/82, March 1982 : the Falkland Islands and their dependencies, article by David Cross in the *Times,* 15th April 1982.

£24,000 payment by Spain under a Franco-Spanish treaty of 1761: the *Pacto de familia*; Fort (now Port) Louis was renamed Puerto de Soledad.

4th June 1770

The Spaniards compelled the British to leave Port Egmont. The action brought Britain and Spain to the brink of war. In 1771, Port Egmont was returned to Britain and British settlers came back, before leaving voluntarily in 1774 for economic reasons. However, the British claim to sovereignty was maintained and a plaque was left on the islands.

Spain placed the islands under the jurisdiction of Buenos Aires, then a Spanish colony, and appointed nine successive governors. The last governor and the Spanish settlers left East Falkland in March 1811.

9th July 1816

The United Provinces of the Rio de la Plata, whose capital is Buenos Aires, declared their independence from Spain, claiming sovereignty over Spanish lands in the region. In 1816, the United Provinces consisted of Bolivia, Uruguay, Argentina and Buenos Aires (as a separate entity) but the first two territories seceded in 1825 and 1828. A Federal State of Argentina was proclaimed by the 1852 constitution but this was not ratified by Buenos Aires until 1880, thus conferring its present form on the country.

1820

The Buenos Aires government sent a ship under the command of Colonel Jewitt to take possession of the islands.

1826

Louis Vernet, a Hamburg merchant, was granted land and fishery rights by the Buenos Aires authorities and founded a settlement at Puerto de Soledad ; he was appointed governor by these authorities in 1828 in spite of British protests.

August 1831

An American warship, the Lexington, commanded by Captain Duncan, destroyed the fort of Soledad as a reprisal, Vernet having seized three American schooners in a dispute over fishery rights. The islands seem to have been under no apparent authority until September 1832, when a new governor was appointed by the Buenos Aires government.

January 1833

The British Government reasserted its sovereignty by sending out a warship, HMS Clio, under the command of Captain Onslow. On reaching Soledad, Captain Onslow ordered the some fifty inhabitants to leave the islands. Soledad then became Port Louis. Britain claims that the colony was established as of this date. Naval officers remained in charge until the formation of a civil administration in 1841.

Twentieth century

Buenos Aires did little about its claim to sovereignty over the Falklands in the nineteenth and early twentieth centuries.

The election of Juan Peron in 1946 led to a revival of Argentina's claims to the Falklands, their dependencies and the Antarctic continental shelf off Argentina. The matter was placed before the United Nations in 1965.

(b) Argentinian interpretation [1]

Argentina's claims to the Falklands are based on the following *de facto* and *de jure* circumstances:

1. " Priority of discovery ", although not sufficient to establish dominion, belongs to the Spanish or the Dutch but not to the British. The accounts of Captains Davis and Hawkins are too vague and circumstantial. Moreover, before their discovery by van Weerdt in 1598

---

1. *Source: La cuestion Malvinas* by R.S. Martinez Moreno, 1965.

there were maps of the Falklands (discovered and published in the 1960s) drawn up by Diego Ribeiro, a Portuguese mapmaker, in 1529 and by Bartolomé Olives in 1562, and therefore well before 1592 or 1594. Finally, according to the Argentinian historian Hector Rato, a Portuguese sailor in Magellan's expedition, Esteban Gomes, discovered the islands during his journey back to Spain in 1520.

2. The first effective occupation, in January 1764, the sole basis for dominion over territories which had never been inhabited, was by France, which ceded them to Spain, recognising the latter's sovereignty over the islands.

3. The Falkland Islands have belonged to Spain since America was discovered and were included in the domains assigned to Spain by the Papal Bull of Alexander VI in 1493 apportioning Spanish and Portuguese land, this domain being ratified with some changes by the Treaty of Tordesillas signed by the Portuguese and Spanish states.

It was under the *Pacto de Familia* of 1761 in which Spain and France gave each other mutual guarantees in respect of all the territories in their possession without reserve or exception that France returned the Falkland Islands to Spain.

4. Under the Treaty of Utrecht (1713), Britain recognised Spanish sovereignty over territories colonised by the latter.

5. Spain's devolution to Britain following the 1770 war concerned only Port Egmont with a secret verbal agreement that Britain would subsequently evacuate it, which it did in 1774, the agreement being intended to allay British susceptibility following the expulsion of British settlers in 1770.

6. Argentina inherited all Spain's rights by emancipation. It was dispossessed by force and its original rights remain intact.

APPENDIX III

Negotiations between Argentina and the United Kingdom
(1965-February 1982)

16th December 1965

The twentieth session of the United Nations General Assembly adopted Resolution 2065 (XX) which noted the existence of a dispute between Argentina and the United Kingdom about sovereignty over the Falkland Islands: it invited the two governments to negotiate and seek a peaceful solution. (This resolution is one of a series of resolutions on ending colonialism.) Argentina voted for the resolution and the United Kingdom abstained.

1966

On 18th July, the two countries started preliminary talks in London. For the British, there was no question of discussing the question of sovereignty.

On 28th September, there was a symbolic invasion of the Falklands by Argentinian commandos. The Argentinian Government dissociated itself from this invasion and from the anti-British demonstrations.

1967-71

On 19th December 1967, the twenty-first session of the United Nations General Assembly unanimously adopted a resolution urging the two countries to continue negotiations and find a peaceful solution as soon as possible.

The negotiations were continued in 1968 ; the British Secretary of State for Foreign and Commonwealth Affairs undertook, in the various parliamentary assemblies and during a visit to the Falklands (23rd-28th November), not to relinquish sovereignty over the islands to Argentina against the wishes of their inhabitants.

On 12th December, Argentina said it could not accept this position. The negotiations were continued in 1969 and 1970 with more particular attention being paid to the problem of communications since in 1969 Argentina said it was prepared to study ways of establishing and improving direct links between the continent and the islands.

On 1st July 1971, the two countries reached agreement on measures for establishing regular sea and air communications, improving postal, cable and telephone connections and

accepting inhabitants of the Falklands in schools and hospitals in Buenos Aires.

1973-77

The return to power of General Juan Peron revived the controversy between the two countries at the end of 1973. On 14th December 1973, the United Nations General Assembly adopted another resolution, No. 3160 (XXVIII), urging the two parties to find a solution in order to put an end to the colonial situation. Relations deteriorated seriously at the end of 1973 when the United Kingdom announced its intention of sending an economic delegation to the Falklands: the Argentinian Ambassador in London was recalled on 28th October 1975 and the British Ambassador in Buenos Aires on 19th January 1976. In December 1976, the United Nations General Assembly adopted another resolution which recalled earlier resolutions " and called upon the two parties to refrain from taking decisions which would imply introducing unilateral modifications in the situation while the islands were going through the process recommended in the abovementioned resolutions ". The United Kingdom voted against it.

The conclusions of the report of the economic delegation in 1976, which mentioned the need for closer relations with Argentina, led the United Kingdom to resume negotiations in 1977. After a series of consultations with the inhabitants of the Falklands and with Argentina in February, the two parties issued a memorandum preparing for Anglo-Argentinian negotiations on political relations, including the questions of sovereignty and economic co-operation in the archipelago, the dependencies and the South Atlantic as a whole. Two working groups were set up to this end, but with no concrete result (15th December 1977).

1978-82

Negotiations were resumed in February 1978 and again in April 1979 (inter alia with a representative of the islands' legislative council present) but without great success. It was not until 16th November 1979 that diplomatic relations were re-established at ambassadorial level.

In April 1980, a series of preparatory talks was organised on very varied subjects. On 26th and 27th February 1981, further talks were held in New York, two members of the islands' council being present. Argentina refused the British proposal to freeze the dispute for an agreed period, allowing the two countries to co-operate in exploiting the archipelago's resources. In the United Nations, Argentina warned the United Kingdom that it would not allow the Falklands to continue to exist as a British colony and asked for further serious negotiations.

In February 1982, a second series of official talks was held in New York. Argentina proposed measures for advancing the negotiations (creation of a standing committee). The United Kingdom refused. However, both parties asserted their determination to find a solution. The joint communiqué issued on 27th February declared that the talks had been held " in a cordial and positive spirit ".

APPENDIX IV

Official texts

(a) Agreed statement by the President of the United Nations Security Council, Mr. Kamanda wa Kamanda, Zaïre

1st April 1982

After holding consultations with members of the Council, I have been authorised to make the following statement on behalf of the Council:

" The Security Council has heard statements from the representatives of the United Kingdom and Argentina about the tension which has recently arisen between the two governments.

The Security Council has taken note of the statement issued by the Secretary-General of the United Nations, which reads as follows:

The Secretary-General, who has already seen the representatives of the United Kingdom and Argentina earlier today, renews his appeal for maximum restraint on both sides. He will, of course, return to headquarters at any time, if the situation demands it.

The Security Council, mindful of its primary responsibility under the Charter of the United Nations for the maintenance of international peace and security, expresses its concern about the tension in the region of the Falkland Islands (Islas Malvinas). The Security Council accordingly calls on the Governments of Argentina and the United Kingdom to exercise the utmost restraint at this time and in particular to refrain from the use or threat of force in the region and to continue the search for a diplomatic solution.

The Security Council will remain seized of the question. "

(b) European political co-operation – Communiqué issued by the ten Ministers for Foreign Affairs

2nd April 1982

The Foreign Affairs Ministers of the Ten condemn the armed intervention of the Argentinian Government in the Falkland Islands. violating the declaration made on 1st April by the President of the Security Council of the United Nations which is now dealing with the matter. They urgently call upon the Argentine Government to withdraw its forces immediately and to abide by the United Nations Security Council appeal asking it to refrain from the use of force and to continue efforts towards a diplomatic solution.

(c) Statement by the Secretary-General of NATO after the urgent meeting of the North Atlantic Council

2nd April 1982

Members of the Council expressed deep concern at the dispute between a member of the Alliance and a state with which all have friendly relations and reiterated the call made to the parties by the President of the Security Council yesterday to refrain from the use or threat of force and to continue the search for a diplomatic solution.

(d) United Nations Security Council Resolution 502

3rd April 1982

The Security Council,

Recalling the statement made by the President of the Security Council at the 2345th meeting of the Security Council on 1st April 1982 (S/14944) calling on the Governments of Argentina and the United Kingdom of Great Britain and Northern Ireland to refrain from the use or threat of force in the region of the Falkland Islands (Islas Malvinas),

Deeply disturbed at reports of an invasion on 2nd April 1982 by armed forces of Argentina,

Determining that there exists a breach of the peace in the region of the Falkland Islands (Islas Malvinas),

1. *Demands* an immediate cessation of hostilities,

2. *Demands* an immediate withdrawal of all Argentine forces from the Falkland Islands (Islas Malvinas),

3. *Calls* on the Governments of Argentina and the United Kingdom to seek a diplomatic solution to their differences and to respect fully the purposes and principles of the Charter of the United Nations.

(e) European political co-operation –
Declaration by the Ten
10th April 1982

1. Representatives of the Ten discussed the grave situation resulting from the invasion of the Falkland Islands by Argentina.

2. They recalled that in their declaration of 2nd April the Ten had already condemned the flagrant violation of international law which the Argentine military action constituted.

3. The Ten remain deeply concerned by the continuation of this crisis, which endangers international peace and security. They therefore attach the greatest importance to the immediate and effective implementation of Security Council Resolution 502 in all its aspects, namely an immediate cessation of hostilities, an immediate withdrawal of all Argentine forces from the Falkland Islands, and a search for a diplomatic solution by the Governments of Argentina and the United Kingdom.

4. To these ends, and in a spirit of solidarity among the member countries of the Community, the Ten decide to take a series of measures with respect to Argentina which should be put into operation as soon as possible. They will likewise take the measures necessary to ban all imports of Argentine origin into the Community. In this context the Ten noted that their governments have already decided to apply a complete embargo on the export of arms and military equipment to Argentina.

5. With respect to economic measures, these will be taken in accordance with the relevant provisions of the Community treaties.

6. Given that the situation resulting from the invasion of the Falkland Islands by the Argentine armed forces is a cause of grave concern for the entire international community, the Ten call on other governments to associate themselves with their decisions, so as to ensure the full implementation of Security Council Resolution 502 with the least possible delay.

(f) European Communities – Text of the regulation promulgated by the Council on economic sanctions against Argentina
14th April 1982

The Council of the European Communities.

Whereas the serious situation resulting from the invasion of the Falkland Islands by Argentina, which was the subject of Resolution 502 of the Security Council of the United Nations, has given rise to discussions in the context of European political co-operation which have led in particular to the decision that economic measures will be taken with regard to Argentina in accordance with the relevant provisions of the Community treaties;

Whereas following the measures already taken by the United Kingdom the member states have consulted one another pursuant to Article 224 of the treaty establishing the European Economic Community;

Whereas in the context of these consultations it has proved important to take urgent and uniform measures and whereas the member states have therefore decided to adopt a Council regulation pursant to the treaty;

Whereas in these circumstances the interests of the Community and the member states demand the temporary suspension of imports of all products originating in Argentina;

Whereas import documents issued and contracts concluded before the entry into force of this regulation should not be affected by it; whereas, however, transitional provisions should not be applied to imports into the United Kingdom which were the subject of United Kingdom measures with effect from 7th April;

Having regard to the treaty establishing the European Economic Community, and in particular Article 113 thereof;

Having regard to the proposal from the Commission,

Has adopted this regulation:

Article 1

Imports of all products originating in Argentina for the purpose of putting them into free circulation in the Community are hereby suspended.

Article 2

1. This regulation shall not preclude the putting into free circulation of products originating in Argentina

    – accompanied by import documents issued before the date of its entry into force which mention Argentina as the country of origin, or

    – to be imported in execution of contracts concluded before that date, or

    – in course of shipment to the Community at that date.

2. The provisions of paragraph 1 shall not apply to imports into the United Kingdom of products covered by this regulation which were

the subject of measures adopted by the United Kingdom with effect from 7th April.

Article 3

This regulation shall enter into force on the day of its publication in the Official Journal of the European Communities.

It shall apply until 17th May 1982.

Before that date, the Council, acting on a proposal from the Commission, shall examine whether it is appropriate to extend, amend, or, if necessary, repeal this regulation.

This regulation shall be binding in its entirety and directly applicable in all member states.

(g) *Eurogroup – Communiqué issued after the meeting of the eleven Defence Ministers*

5th May 1982

(*Extract*)

Ministers condemned Argentina's armed invasion of the Falkland Islands and the dependencies as well as her failure to comply with Security Council Resolution Number 502. Ministers noted the importance of maintaining the principle that aggression or occupation of territory by force should not be allowed to succeed, and urged the need to seek a negotiated solution acceptable to all parties concerned on the basis of the implementation of Security Council Resolution Number 502 in all its parts.

(h) *NATO Defence Planning Committee – Communiqué issued after the meeting of Defence Ministers*

7th May 1982

(*Extract*)

Ministers endorsed the statement by Eurogroup Ministers, in their communiqué of the previous day, in which they condemned Argentina's armed invasion of the Falkland Islands and the dependencies as well as her failure to comply with Security Council Resolution Number 502; noted the importance of maintaining the principle that aggression or occupation of territory by force should not be allowed to succeed; and urged the need to seek a negotiated solution acceptable to all parties concerned on the basis of the implementation of Security Council Resolution Number 502 in all its parts.

Document 907 Revised
Amendments 1 and 2

14th June 1982

The Falklands crisis

AMENDMENTS 1 and 2[1]
tabled by MM. Stoffelen and Miller

1.   Leave out paragraph (v) of the preamble to the draft recommendation.
2.   Leave out sub-paragraph 3 (b) of the draft recommendation proper.

Signed: Stoffelen, Miller

---

1. See 4th sitting. 16th June 1982 (report referred back to committee).

Document 907 Revised
Amendments 3, 4, 5, 6, 7, 8, 9 and 10

15th June 1982

The Falklands crisis

AMENDMENTS 3, 4, 5, 6, 7, 8, 9 and 10[1]
tabled by Mr. Cavaliere

3.   After paragraph (*iii*) of the preamble to the draft recommendation, insert a new paragraph as follows:

" Welcoming the position adopted by the United States after the failure of the attempted negotiations; ".

4.   After paragraph (*iv*) of the preamble to the draft recommendation, insert new paragraphs as follows:

" Expressing its solidarity with the United Kingdom concerning its decision to restore international order and to secure the application of Resolution 502 of the Security Council;

Expressing its solidarity with the United Kingdom concerning its decision to invoke Article 51 of the Charter of the United Nations; ".

5.   In paragraph (*v*) of the preamble to the draft recommendation, leave out " assistance " and insert " support ".

6.   After paragraph (*v*) of the preamble to the draft recommendation, add a new paragraph as follows:

" Concerned at the possible deterioration in relations between Western Europe and North America and Latin America; ".

7.   At the end of paragraph 1 of the draft recommendation proper, insert " in accordance with the decisions of the Council of the European Communities; ".

8.   In paragraph 2, line 2, of the draft recommendation proper, leave out " the immediate " and insert " after the ".

9.   In paragraph 2, lines 2 and 3, of the draft recommendation proper, leave out " in accordance with Security Council Resolution 502 ".

10.   In paragraph 2, line 4, of the draft recommendation proper, leave out from " islands " to the end of the paragraph and insert " and to safeguard relations with the countries of Latin America, so as to avoid any extension of Soviet influence in that continent; ".

Signed: Cavaliere

1   See 4th sitting, 16th June 1982 (report referred back to committee)

Document 907 Revised   **15th June 1982**
Amendment to Amendment 6

The Falklands crisis

AMENDMENT TO AMENDMENT 6[1]
tabled by Mr. Dejardin

In Amendment 6, line 1, leave out " the " and insert " a " and in lines 2 and 3 leave out " and North America ".

Signed: Dejardin

---

1. See 4th sitting, 16th June 1982 (report referred back to committee).

Document 907 Revised
Amendment 11

15th June 1982

The Falklands crisis

AMENDMENT 11[1]
tabled by Mr. Maravalle

11.   In paragraph 1 of the draft recommendation proper, leave out " and to ban all imports into the Community originating in Argentina ".

Signed: Maravalle

---

1 See 4th sitting, 16th June 1982 (report referred back to committee).

Document 907 Revised
Amendments 12 and 13

15th June 1982

The Falklands crisis

AMENDMENTS 12 and 13[1]
tabled by Mr. Dejardin

12.   After paragraph (*v*) of the preamble to the draft recommendation, add a new paragraph as follows:

" Expressing its relief at the announcement of the end of fighting and paying tribute to all the victims of the conflict; ".

13.   Leave out paragraph 2 of the draft recommendation proper and insert a new paragraph as follows:

" To concert their political, economic and diplomatic efforts in all countries and appropriate international bodies:

(*a*) with due respect for United Nations resolutions, to work out a solution which is fair for all the parties involved in the Falklands dispute, including, above all, the inhabitants of these islands, on the one hand to avoid the subsequent outbreak of further fighting and on the other hand to guarantee all the democratic rights of the inhabitants;

(*b*) to safeguard relations with the Latin American countries, inter alia with a view to promoting democratic ideals and avoiding any extension of Soviet influence; ".

Signed: Dejardin

---

1. See 4th sitting. 16th June 1982 (report referred back to committee).

GEOGRAPHICAL FACT SHEET ON:
The Falkland Islands,
South Georgia Island
and the
South Sandwich Islands

UNCLASSIFIED

.Office of The Geographer
U.S. Department of State

Prepared by:
Bill Hezlep
INR/GE/CA
Office of The Geographer
Tel: (202) 632-2156

Falkland Islands

Number of Islands:

Two large islands and approximately 200 smaller islands and islets; East Falkland is 145 km (90 mi.) long and 89 km (55 mi.) wide. West Falkland is 129 km (80 mi.) long and 72 km (45 mi.) wide.

Area:

East Falkland	6604 sq. km.	(2550 sq. statute mi.)
adjacent small islands	155 sq. km.	(60 sq. statute mi.)
West Falkland	4532 sq. km.	(1750 sq. statute mi.)
adjacent small islands	881 sq. km.	(340 sq. statute mi.)
Total Area	12173 sq. km.	(4700 sq. statute mi.)

In total area the Falklands are a little smaller than the state of Connecticut (5009 sq. miles.)

Highest Elevations:

East Falkland (Mt. Usborne)	705 m	(2312 ft.)
West Falkland (Mt. Adam)	700 m	(2297 ft.)

Terrain:

The two main islands, East and West Falkland, are separated by Falkland Sound, which ranges from 3 to 40 kilometers wide. The coastlines of the islands are extremely irregular with numerous intricate inlets, many of which form magnificent potential harbors.

East Falkland is almost cut in half by a pair of deep inlets. The northern portion of the island is dominated by a rugged east-west range of hills dominated by Mt. Usborne-- the highest peak in the islands. The southern portion,

known as Lafonia, is a low, undulating plain with elevations
rarely exceeding 30 meters above sea level. West Falkland is
more hilly than its neighbor. A range of hills occupies the
northern part of the island and another parallels Falkland
Sound. The hills and mountains are covered with thin layers
of soil broken by rocky outcrops, and many of the valleys are
characterized by stone "runs"--accumulations of closely packed
boulders that look like rivers of stone flowing to the sea.
The lowlands on both islands are boggy in many places.

Climate:

The only long-term climate records available for the Falklands
are the records of observations made in Stanley. There is
little precise information on how weather and climate vary
through the archipelago as a whole.

At Stanley the air temperature has never been known to exceed
26.1°C (79°F) or to fall below -11.1°C (12°F). There is little air pollution. Fog is rare except on the hills and dense
fog does not occur. Rainfall at Stanley averages 63.5cm
(25 inches) per year and is spread fairly evenly throughout
the year with an average of 16-21 days per month on which precipitation occurs. No month is entirely frost free. Snow
falls on about 50 days during the year and has been recorded
in every month. Snowfalls however are light and the snow soon
melts. The prevailing winds are westerly with three quarters
of the winds during the year coming from the southwest, west,
and northwest. The average wind speed is approximately 17 mph.
Although storms are recorded several times each month, gales
with winds in excess of 55-63 mph (a whole gale) are almost
unknown. Calm conditions are more frequent   than storms.

Climatic Averages for Stanley:

```
Mean annual windspeed          17 mph
Mean annual rainfall           63.5 cm (25 inches)
Average number of days per year with precipitation 250
Mean annual temperature        5.5°C (42°F)
```

Average Daily Temperatures;

```
January Max    13°C(55°F)    January Min    6°C(43°F)
April Max      10°C(50°F)    April Min      3°C(37°F)
July Max        4°C(39°F)    July Min      -1°C(30°F)
```

Average Monthly Rainfall

```
January    71mm    (2.8 in.)
April      62mm    (2.4 in.)
July       57mm    (2.2 in.)
```

Flora:

The plant community is similar to the moorland vegetation of
upland Britain: grasses, heath, small shrubs, virtualy no
trees. Low grade peat is available in abundance.

Fauna:

There are no known indigenous land mammals. Mice, rats,
rabbits, hares, cats and, on some islands, a species of
patagonian fox and guanaco occur, all were probably introduced by man. There are also sea lions, several species of
seals and a number of marine mammals.

Penguins are the most striking feature of the bird life in
the Falklands. There are three main species of penguin the
rockhopper penguin, the Magellan penguin and the Gentoo penguin. Two other species, the macaroni penguin and the king
penguin are found but both are rare. In addition to the
penguins, some 60 species of bird are known to breed in the
Falklands. Along the shore there are a wide variety of sea
birds, including the Black-Browed albatross. Inland, around
the freshwater ponds, there are two species of goose, several
varieties of duck and a number of other species includingsev-
eral starlings, finches, Cassin's Falcon and the red-backed
buzzard.

In addition to the wild life, there are an estimated 630,000
to 650,000 sheep which form the mainstay of the economy.
There are also a limited number of cattle and other domestic
animals.

Population:

Approximately 1,825 (of which 1,075 live in Stanley - the
rest live in 30 or more settlements scattered throughout the
islands). This has been a decline from the peak population of
2,400 in 1931. The labor force is about 1,100 of which over
95% are involved with agriculture, primarily sheep.

Telecommunications:

Stanley has a telephone system to which most East Falkland
farms are connected, and there is a similar service on West
Falkland, centered on Fox Bay. Traffic between the main
islands and contact with farms on the smaller islands is by
radio telephone.

Broadcasting and the Press:

The Government runs a broadcasting station at Stanley. In 1977 there were 591 ham radio operators in the territory. There is also a government-operated cable broadcasting service in Stanley, which had 274 subscribers in 1977. Periodicals published in the colony, other than the official gazette, are The Falkland Islands Times (published monthly) and the Falkland Islands Journal (published annually).

Economy:

The islands themselves are of little economic importance. The main industry on the islands is sheep raising and the entire economic organization of the islands is geared to the production of wool. The Falklands produce about two and one half million kilograms of wool each year at a value of about US $5 million. (By way of comparison, Argentina produces 155 million kilograms of wool per year and ex- ports 90 million kilograms.) Other economic endeavors--meat and kelp processing, canning, mink ranching--quickly met with failure.

Transportation:

There are no railroads. There are 510km (317 miles) of road, of which 30 km, in and around Stanley, are paved, 80km are gravel, and 400km are unimproved. An all-weather road running from Stanley to Darwin, at the head of Choiseul Sound, is under construction. Although many of the intricate inlets around the coast form magnificent natural potential harbors, Stanley is the only developed port for oceangoing vessels. In addition to Stanley there are four minor ports and many of the small settlements have jetties or landing places. Inter-island boat traffic is important, all heavy and/or bulky goods being shipped by boat. There is one permanent-surface airfield with a runway 1250 meters long, located approximately 8km from Stanley. There are approximately 35 small unsurfaced landing strips which are utilized by the inter-island air service, which also utilizes float planes. In 1969, 3,867 passengers plus a large volume of cargo were carried by air and the inter-island air service made over 2,000 landings outside of Stanley.

ıblic Utilities:

A government-owned diesel power station with a capacity of
1,280 kW generating at 3.3 kV, 50 Hertz, supplying power
to Stanley, was inaugurated in 1973. Elsewhere most of
the settlements and farms have their own private generating plants. A water purification and filtration plant
near Stanley provides a sufficient supply of clean water
for the town.

ɔmmerce:

All consumer goods, construction materials, vehicles, spare
parts--literally everything in the Islands--come to Stanley
from England by charter vessel four times a year. The same
vessel picks up the wool bales from Stanley warehouses for
sale in England. When the ships arrive, Stanley general
stores abound with such luxuries as ice cream, butter,
frozen chickens, fresh cookies, etc. which are generally
sold out within the first few weeks.

Except for the general stores, Stanley has no other commercial establishments: no taxi service, laundries or dry
cleaners, dressmakers, barbershops, shoe stores, or whatever.

Beef is relatively cheap but not always available. Since
homes rarely have refrigeraotrs and fresh meat is kept outside in a slat-sided cold storage box, butchering is usually
postponed during warm months to avoid spoilage. Mutton is
available year round and is free except for the delivery
charge.

South Georgia

Number of Islands:

One large and approximately 25 smaller islands and rocks; South Georgia Island is 161 km (100 mi.) long and 32 km (20 mi.) wide.

Area:

3755 sq. km.   (1450 sq. statute mi.)
Slightly larger than Long Island, New York.

Highest Elevation:

Mt. Paget   2934m   (9625 ft.)

Climate:

Average Daily Temperatures

January Max	9°C(49°F)	January Min	2°C(36°F)
April Max	6°C(43°F)	April Min	-1°C(31°F)
July Max	1°C(33°F)	July Min	-6°C(22°F)

Average Monthly Rainfall

January	74mm	(2.9 in.)
April	135mm	(5.3 in.)
July	137mm	(5.4 in.)

Average number of days/year with precipitation   200 (covered entirely by snow and glaciers much of the year).

Flora:

Approximately 20 species of hardy grasses and other flowering plants, lichens, and mosses

Fauna:

Birds (penguins, terns, skvas, tit-larks, ducks, petral and others); some reindeer which were introduced early in this century and now number about 2,000 head, and several species of seals.

Population:

A British scientific station at Grytviken is the only existing permanent settlement. The last whaling station closed in the early 1960's.

South Sandwich Islands

Number of Islands:

Nine main islands and approximately ten smaller islands
and islets.

Area:

311 sq. km.   (120 sq. statute mi.)

(From Cook Is. in the south to Zavodovski Is. in the north,
South Sandwich Islands span an arc of approximately
200 n.m.)

Highest Elevation:

Mt. Belinda (on Montagu Island) 1370m   (4500 ft.)

Climate:

There are no long-term meterological records for the South
Sandwich Islands. However, they are located well south of
the approximate limits of pack ice for September.

Flora:

Patches of vegetation

Fauna:

Birds and seals

Population:

Argentinian scientific base on Southern Thule

Transportation:

Few anchorages; most of which are subject to volcanic
activity

Distances:

Port Stanley, Falkland Islands
    to: Buenos Aires, Argentina   1030 nautical miles
         Mar Del Plata, Argentina   825   "   "
         Bahia Blanca, Argentina   805   "   "
         Comodoro Rivadavia, Argentina 505   "   "
         Puerto Descado, Argentina   390   "   "
         Rio Gallegos, Argentina   423   "   "
         Rio Grande, Argentina (on
           Tierra del Fuego)   380   "   "
         Punta Arenas, Chile   485   "   "
         Grytviken, South Georgia Island.
           Grytviken is the site of the
           British Antarctic Survey Team
           base.   785 nautical miles
         Thule Island, southernmost
           island in the South Sandwich
           Island chain and the island
           the Argentine research station
           is located on.   1195 nautical miles
         Tristan da Cunha, approximately 1940 nautical miles
         Ascension, approximately   3380 nautical miles
         Washington, D.C., approximately 5512 nautical miles
           (about the distance from
           Washington to Cairo)

Grytviken, South Georgia Island
    to: Zavodovski Island, the
           northernmost island
           in the South Sandwich
           Island chain   329 nautical miles
         Thule Island   428 nautical miles
         Tristan da Cunha, approximately 1300 nautical miles
         Ascension, approximately   2970 nautical miles

Zavodovski Island, South Sandwich Islands
    to: Thule Island, along the arc of
           the South Sandwich chain   203 nautical miles
         Tristan da Cunha, approximately 1160 nautical miles
         Ascension, approximately   2960 nautical miles

A PERSPECTIVE MAP OF THE WORLD
CENTERED ON THE FALKLAND ISLANDS

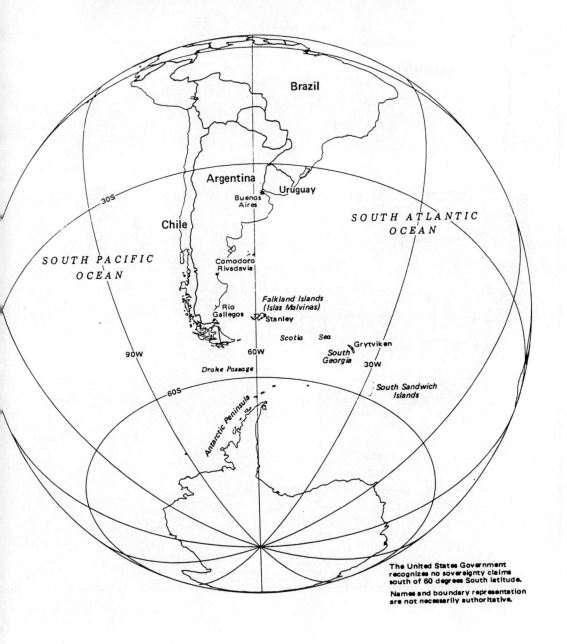

The United States Government recognizes no sovereignty claims south of 60 degrees South latitude.

Names and boundary representation are not necessarily authoritative.

The Falkland Islands

The Facts

Contents

Foreign and Commonwealth Office London May 1982

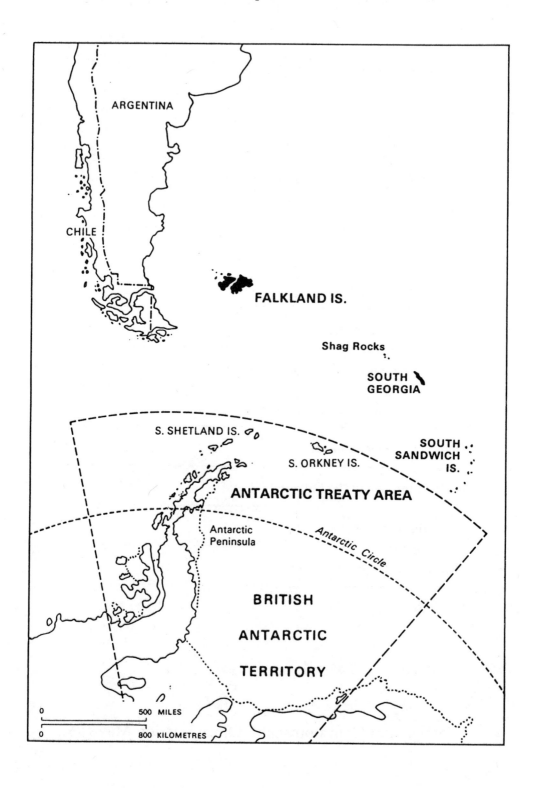

The Falkland Islands

The Facts

The invasion of the Falkland Islands by Argentine Armed Forces on 2 April, followed by the military occupation of South Georgia, was an act of unprovoked aggression – a clear violation of international law and of the fundamental principles of settlement of disputes by peaceful means and of the self-determination of peoples, both of which are enshrined in the UN Charter. On 3 April the UN Security Council adopted the mandatory resolution (SCR 502) calling for the immediate withdrawal of Argentine forces from the Islands.

Incident on South Georgia

Argentine allegations that the British reaction to events on South Georgia in March 1982 amounted to 'aggression' against Argentine citizens are spurious. A group of workmen hired by an Argentine entrepreneur, Constantino Davidoff, landed at Leith, a former whaling station in South Georgia, from an Argentine naval transport vessel on 19 March. Davidoff, who had a contract to dismantle the disused whaling station and sell it for scrap, had been told in advance of the need to comply with normal immigration procedures in South Georgia by first seeking permission to land from the British authorities there at Grytviken. His party deliberately chose to ignore these instructions, first by landing at Leith and then by continuing to refuse to seek the necessary authorisation even when requested to do so by the magistrate at Grytviken. At the same time, they hoisted the Argentine flag and, according to Argentine press reports, sang the Argentine national anthem as a further act of defiance. The Argentine ship subsequently departed, leaving a dozen workers behind. The British Government made clear to the Argentine Government that it regarded these men as being on British territory illegally and requested cooperation in arranging for their departure, pointing out, however, that the position could be

1

regularised if they were to seek proper authorisation. HMS *Endurance,* a naval ice-patrol vessel, was ordered to proceed to the area, to be available to assist as necessary.

Claims that the group had already been supplied with all necessary documentation in Buenos Aires under the terms of the 1971 Anglo-Argentine Communications Agreement are inaccurate. The 1971 agreement applies only to the Falkland Islands and not to the Dependencies. In any case, the possession of such documentation has never absolved either Argentines or Falkland Islanders from complying with normal immigration procedures. Like every other territory, the Falkland Islands and Dependencies have immigration rules governing visits and settlement by foreigners.

On 25 March an Argentine Antarctic supply ship which, the Argentine press stated, was capable of carrying marines, made further deliveries to the shore party. The Argentine Foreign Minister asserted that the Argentine party in South Georgia was on Argentine territory and would be given the full protection of the Argentine Government. Argentine naval vessels were in the area. Even when there were indications that the Argentine Government had decided to abandon the search for a diplomatic solution, the British Government continued to seek strenuously to defuse the situation, first by proposing the despatch of a British emissary to Buenos Aires to discuss a peaceful resolution of the incident and subsequently by representations to third parties.

As a result, messages were sent by the UN Secretary General to both parties, the President of the UN Security Council called for Argentine restraint and the American President telephoned the Argentine President with a similar urgent message. Nevertheless, Argentina proceeded with the invasion.

British Sovereignty

British Governments have never doubted the validity of the British claim to sovereignty over the Falkland Islands and Dependencies. In 1690 the British Captain Strong made the first recorded landing on the Falkland Islands, which had no indigenous population before the arrival of settlers in the second half of the eighteenth century. The first British settlement was established in 1766. But up to 1833 there was a period of some confusion, with France, Britain, Spain and the then Buenos Aires Government at various times establishing small, local settlements, none of which endured more than a few years. Apart from having had a small settlement and penal colony for a short period on the Islands before 1833 (the greater part of this was ejected for 'piracy' by the United States Navy in 1831) Argentina's claim to the Islands is based mainly on her having been the successor to the Spanish Viceroyalty of the River Plate, which also governed most of modern Uruguay, Paraguay, Bolivia and Chile. In 1833 the British took control of the Islands, and from that date have

2

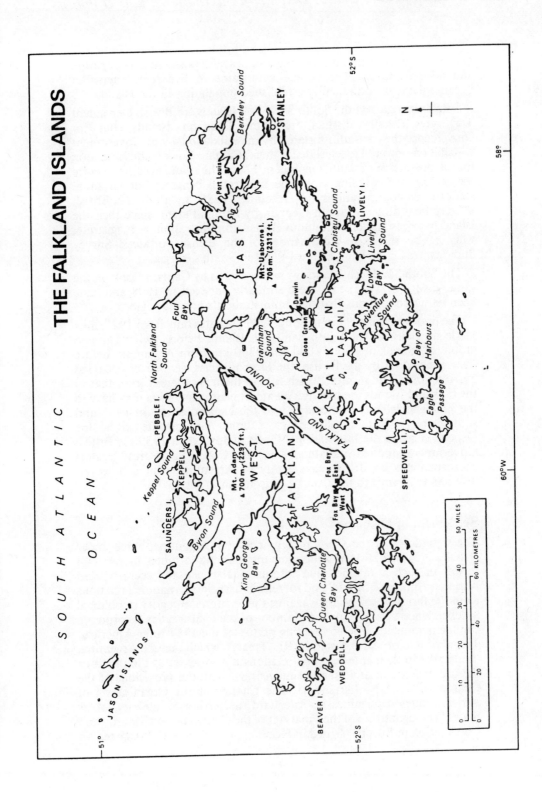

THE FALKLAND ISLANDS

been in open, continuous, effective and peaceful possession, occupation and administration. The people who came to live there thereafter became the first permanently established population in the Islands.

South Georgia and the South Sandwich Islands are British Dependent Territories, legally distinct from the Falkland Islands; but for convenience they are administered by the Falkland Islands Government which is empowered to legislate for them. Captain Cook landed and took formal possession of South Georgia in 1775. The Island became a centre for sealing and whaling from the nineteenth century; but all shore stations ceased operations by December 1965. In 1908 the British Government annexed South Georgia by Letters Patent; since then the Island has been under continuous British administration. A magistrate, who is also the Base Commander of the British Antarctic Survey Stations, resides at King Edward Point in South Georgia.

The South Sandwich Islands were discovered by Captain Cook on the same voyage in 1775; they were similarly annexed in 1908 and have been under continuous British administration since that date.

The first Argentine claim to South Georgia dates only from 1927; they made no claim to the South Sandwich Islands before 1948. The two groups of Islands lie about 1800 and 2300 km from Argentina. Before their annexation by the British, the Dependencies were never occupied by Argentina. The root of British title to them is different from that to the Falkland Islands themselves. Whatever claim Argentina may have to the Falkland Islands cannot apply to the Dependencies. In 1947 and subsequently, Britain offered to submit the dispute over the Dependencies to the International Court of Justice. In 1955 the British Government applied unilaterally to the Court for redress against encroachments on British sovereignty by Argentina, which, however, declined to submit to the Court's jurisdiction in the matter.

Settlement of Disputes

The signatories of the UN Charter, including Argentina, agree under Articles 2(3) and 2(4) to 'settle their international disputes by peaceful means in such a manner that international peace and security, and justice, are not endangered' and to 'refrain in their international relations from the threat or use of force against the territorial integrity or political independence of any State'. A number of regional treaties incorporate similar sentiments. The contracting parties of the 1947 Inter-American Treaty of Reciprocal Assistance (Rio Treaty), which include Argentina, 'undertake in their international relations not to resort to the threat or the use of force in any manner inconsistent with the provisions of the Charter of the UN' (Article 1). The Charter of the Organisation of African States determines 'to safeguard the territorial integrity' of its States. The signatories of the Final Act of the Conference on Security and Cooperation in Europe (signed in Helsinki on 1 August 1975) agreed, in the Declaration of Principles Guiding Relations between Participating States, to refrain from the threat or use of force against the territorial integrity or political independence of any State. Many States are subject to claims by neighbours, which are being pursued peaceably in accordance with the UN Charter. To condone Argentine aggression would be a bad precedent, serving only to encourage further similar acts, whether by the Argentine or others, with the most damaging implications for international law, world order and the peaceful resolution of disputes. Moreover, very few countries would be unaffected if boundaries were redrawn on the basis of claims dating back to 1833.

Decolonisation and Self-determination

Argentina's aggression cannot be said to have been a case of ending colonialism in the Islands; indeed, if allowed to persist, it would amount to colonialism in itself. Decolonisation, as it is normally understood, has consisted of the withdrawal of an alien administering power and the transition of a new State to independence or self-government, in accordance with the freely expressed wishes of its people. In this spirit Britain has brought over 40 countries to independence. Indeed, there is now no British dependent territory, except where their inhabitants wish to remain so.

Respect for the principle of self-determination remains a fundamental principle in international relations and in safeguarding international peace and security. The principle of self-determination is recognised in a number of international instruments, such as Article 1 of the UN Charter and the Declaration on Friendly Relations adopted by consensus by the UN General Assembly in 1970; this contains an entire section on 'the principle of equal rights and self-determination of peoples', stating, *inter alia,* that 'all peoples have the right freely to determine, without external interference, their political status and to pursue their economic, social and cultural development, and every State has the duty to respect this right in accordance with the provisions of the Charter'. The common Article 1 of the International Covenants on both Civil and Political Rights and on Economic, Social and Cultural Rights states that 'all peoples have the right to self-determination. By virtue of that right they freely determine their political status...'. The General Assembly resolution on decolonisation, Resolution 1514 (XV) of 1960, cites the wording of the Covenants on self-determination and calls upon States to transfer powers to the peoples of non-self-governing territories in accordance with their freely expressed will and desire. An essential element of this principle is therefore the free and genuine expression of the will of the people, such as has taken place regularly in the Falkland Islands.

5

The UN Charter itself contains important principles for the administration of dependent territories. Britain has always been recognised by the UN as the 'administering power' for the Falkland Islands and the Dependencies and has regularly submitted reports on them under Article 73(e). Article 73 imposes a positive obligation on Britain to treat the interests of the inhabitants as paramount, requiring Britain to accept 'as a sacred trust' the obligation to promote to the utmost their well-being. In particular, Article 73 obliges Britain

(a) to ensure, with due respect for the culture of the peoples concerned, their political, economic, social and educational advancement, their just treatment and their protection against abuses;

(b) to develop self-government, to take due account of the political aspirations of the peoples and to assist them in the progressive development of their free political institutions, according to the particular circumstances of each territory and its peoples and their varying stages of advancement.

It is therefore quite wrong to claim that the use of the term 'interests' in Article 73 allows the wishes of the inhabitants to be overridden. Nor is it for another country to lay down where a people's interests lie; the inhabitants of a country are the best judges of their own interests. Suggestions to the contrary can only encourage interference in the internal affairs of other States and the unprincipled use of force, and have been the classic argument used by those opposed to decolonisation, past and present.

An act of self-determination has come to be generally acknowledged as the correct preliminary to the introduction of changes (such as independence, incorporation into a neighbouring State or free association with the former administering power); and the UN has never countenanced the decolonisation of a territory by agreeing to hand over its people to alien rule in the face of their persistent opposition. Self-determination and decolonisation need not automatically lead to independence. The status of a territory after an act of self-determination is primarily a matter for the people of the territory itself to decide.

The community on the Falkland Islands, though small, is a permanent, not transient, population. The UN Committee of 24, set up by the General Assembly to supervise the implementation of Resolution 1514, has always maintained that factors such as the size of the population and geographical isolation should not militate against any people's right to self-determination in accordance with the Charter. The Falkland Islanders have no less right to be accepted internationally as a 'people' with rights of self-determination than the population of Argentina. They are not, as Argentina claims, mainly expatriate employees of a British company: 75 per cent were born on the Islands and most are from families established there for well over a century.

Military Dictatorship or Democracy

The current population of Argentina are descendants of settlers from Europe, the indigenous population having been largely eliminated during the opening up of the interior by the Army in the 'Indian Wars' of the late nineteenth century. The great majority of the population descend from immigrants who came to the country after 1870. Militarism has deep roots in Argentina. The military see themselves as 'creators of the nation, defenders of its culture' and guarantors of the cohesion of the State. They have not hesitated to intervene and suspend democratic processes in the face of what they considered an ineffectual civilian Government and a drift towards anarchy. This has occurred five times since 1930. The present regime is a Junta of the Army, Navy and Air Force Commanders-in-Chief, which seized power from Sra Isabelita Peron in 1976. It appointed General Galtieri President in December 1981.

The alternation between Peronism and military government during nearly the whole period since 1943 produced widespread frustration and a combination of right-wing and left-wing extremism, manifested in both urban and rural guerrilla movements. Under Señora Peron and then under their own authority the Armed Forces suppressed this terrorism with great ferocity. It is generally accepted that many who had no connections with terrorism at all must be numbered among those who 'disappeared', never to be seen again, during the course of what the Argentine Armed Forces themselves described as the 'dirty war'. A UN working group on enforced or involuntary disappearances estimated that the number might be as high as 9,000. Meanwhile emergency powers under the state of siege have been maintained, all elections suspended and Armed Forces' nominees placed in all elected offices.

In contrast the Falkland Islands, contrary to Argentine claims that the Islanders are second-class citizens, are free and democratic and have gradually moved towards a system of internal self-government. The population's reiterated desire to remain British, and not to become independent or part of Argentina, has been reinforced by the repressive and authoritarian nature of successive regimes in Argentina.

Falkland Islands Constitution

The Falkland Islands Legislative and Executive Councils were first formed during the nineteenth century. In 1949 and 1977 the Constitution was revised to increase the number of elected Councillors, elections being based on universal adult suffrage. The present (1977) Constitution lowered the voting age from 21 to 18. The Islands are administered by an appointed Governor, who is the personal representative of the Crown, advised by an Executive Council. This consists of two elected and two ex officio members of the Legislative Council and two nominated members. The Legislative Council, composed of six elected and two ex officio members, has the power 'to

7

make laws for the peace, order and good government' of the territory. It is concerned with the day-to-day running and administration of the Islands, their trade, general development, social services and education. Any member of the Council may introduce a bill or propose a motion; legislation is passed by a simple majority.

British Interest in the Falklands

Allegations that Britain has not shown interest in the welfare of the Islanders are ill-founded. Britain has given extensive aid—£6.6 million during 1976-80, an average of £735 per head per year. This has included several important projects, notably the electric power station, the permanent airport at Stanley, the road from Stanley to Darwin (the second largest settlement), a secondary school hostel in Stanley, aeroplane and hangar for the internal air service (the main internal link between Stanley and the rest of the territory), new X-ray equipment for the hospital and machinery and storage facilities for the Public Works Department. Education is free and compulsory for children aged 5 to 15; the Falkland Islands Government recently decided to centralise secondary education in Stanley (thus necessitating the building of the hostel) where education up to the ordinary level of the British Certificate of Education is available. Children wanting to take the advanced level of the General Certificate of Education and the few students undertaking higher education courses abroad are assisted under the British Government's aid programme. Most study in Britain, although a handful attend Anglo-Argentine schools. There are also two Argentine teachers, partly financed by the Falkland Islanders, who give Spanish lessons. The Falkland Islands Government maintains a general hospital at Stanley which provides medical, surgical, obstetric and geriatric care, and from time to time has offered emergency medical treatment to seamen and others in distress. There are full trades union rights under Falkland Islands law, legislation governing labour conditions and a full range of social services.

In 1975 the British Government commissioned an economic study by Lord Shackleton, to investigate the best means of developing and diversifying the Islands' economy. Published in 1976, the report recommended a number of major capital projects, including the establishment of a tourist industry centred on the abundant wild-life, the enlargement of the airport, the development of a fishing industry based on local stocks of king crab, krill and other fish, the harvesting of kelp (seaweed) and the possibility of offshore oil and gas production. Current assessments, however, suggest that the offshore oil and gas potential of the Islands and the Dependencies is unlikely, with present technology, to warrant the high costs which exploration and exploitation in the difficult local conditions would entail. Nor are there other mineral deposits worth exploiting. The development of the fishery potential is also uncertain; hake and Antarctic cod have been over-fished and require conservation,

8

southern blue whiting has only a small market for human consumption, and krill, while abundant at present, is of unproven commercial purpose. There are strong conservation reasons against uncontrolled exploitation.

Negotiations with Argentina

Lord Shackleton's report also advised closer cooperation with Argentina. In 1965 the UN General Assembly had approved a resolution inviting Britain and Argentina to hold discussions about a peaceful solution to their rival claims to the Islands, bearing in mind the Islanders' interests. Diplomatic discussions resulted in 1971 in a series of communications agreements. In 1974 a further agreement arranged for the Argentine State petroleum company to supply the Islands with petroleum products. The British Government were keen that such practical links between Argentina and the Islands should grow, as their future welfare and development would clearly be best assured with Argentine cooperation.

More talks took place in 1977 and 1980. Further exploratory talks were held in April 1980. In February 1981 talks took place in New York between Argentina and Britain, whose delegation included two of the Falkland Islands' elected Councillors. Argentina rejected the British proposal for a 'freeze' on the sovereignty dispute for an agreed period, during which both sides could cooperate to develop the Islands' resources.

At the end of February 1982 another round of formal talks took place in New York. The British delegation again included two Falkland Islands Councillors. The two sides reaffirmed their resolve to find a solution to the sovereignty dispute and considered in detail an Argentine proposal for procedures to make better progress. The joint communique issued on 1 March stated that the talks had been 'cordial and positive', yet on 2 April Argentina invaded the Islands. The invasion thus occurred while negotiations were still in progress.

Britain's Right of Self-defence

Argentina is in flagrant and open violation of the fundamental principles of the UN Charter by its unprovoked attack and subsequent military occupation of the Islands. Article 2 of the Definition of Aggression states that 'the first use of armed force by a State in contravention of theCharter shall constitute *prima facie* evidence of an act of aggression ...' (UN General Assembly Resolution 3314). These unlawful Argentine acts give Britain the right to use force in self-defence. This right, first exercised at the time of the invasion by the small detachment of Royal Marines on the Islands, extends to terminating the illegal occupation. It is expressly recognised by Article 51 of the UN Charter, which makes it clear that the right of self-defence is 'inherent' and that nothing in the Charter is intended to impair it. In compliance with its obligations under Article 51, the British Government has reported all measures of self-defence to the Security Council.

9

Security Council Resolution 502 recognises that Argentina was responsible for the breach of the peace; it does not seek to inhibit Britain from exercising her inherent right of self-defence. Article 51 preserves the right 'until the Security Council has taken measures to maintain international peace and security'. The Security Council decision has clearly so far not proved effective to achieve its stated objective, since Argentina during April, far from withdrawing her forces in accordance with the Resolution, sent reinforcements to the Islands. Agreement by Argentina to withdraw her forces, and to negotiate without preconditions for a diplomatic solution to the underlying dispute, as required by the Resolution, would remove the major obstacle to its complete implementation.

Britain remains fully committed to the search for a diplomatic solution to the crisis, which is obviously preferable to military confrontation. Nevertheless, failing such a solution, Britain is fully justified in exercising her inherent right. Her use of military force is governed by the principles of necessity and the use of force proportionate to the threat, as required by international law. British forces have been deployed with the sole limited objective of securing, with minimum casualties on both sides, the withdrawal of Argentine forces from the Islands, as called for by SCR 502. They form part of the graduated pressure—diplomatic, economic and military—to induce Argentina to return to the negotiating table.

Argentina claims that she does not wish to inflict injury or loss on the local inhabitants, nor to modify their way of life. She claims that she wishes to improve conditions for them. However, her recent actions have done nothing to promote her cause among the Islanders; far from winning their hearts and minds, which would have been a prerequisite for any peaceful change, the military occupation and the changes already enforced by the military governor have provided the Islanders with an all too vivid experience of what life can be like under a dictatorship which has scant respect for human rights.

The Argentine invasion is an act of unprovoked aggression. History provides many examples where the international community's failure to take action over such acts by aggressive powers led to much graver crises later.

Bulletin

OF THE EUROPEAN
COMMUNITIES

ECSC — EEC — EAEC
Commission of the European Communities
Secretariat-General
Brussels

1. Community solidarity in the Falklands conflict

1.1.1. The invasion of the Falkland Islands, a United Kingdom dependency which is also associated with the Community, by Argentine armed forces on 1 April was a subject of concern to the Community throughout the month.

The Foreign Ministers of the Ten, the Commission and Parliament urged Argentina to comply with United Nations Security Council Resolution 502, which demanded an immediate cessation of hostilities and an immediate withdrawal of all Argentine forces from the Falkland Islands and called on the governments of the two countries to seek a diplomatic solution to their differences.

To back up its various statements, the Community imposed an embargo on imports from Argentina,[1] and the governments of the Ten placed a total ban on exports of arms and military equipment to Argentina.[2]

Mr Davignon told Parliament on 21 April that Europe's display of solidarity was the expression of the Community's attachment to compliance with international law and its wish to safeguard peace. There could be no question of interpreting it as a move directed against Latin America or the developing nations or as a manifestation of protectionism.

Measures taken

1.1.2. On 16 April, following the statement made by the Ten on 10 April,[3] the Council adopted a Regulation suspending imports of all products originating in Argentina for the purpose of putting them into free circulation in the Community.[4] However, this Regulation did not apply to products accompanied by import documents issued before the date of its entry into force, products to be imported in execution of contracts concluded before that date, or products in course of shipment. The embargo was initially imposed for a month, by which time the Regulation would have to be extended, amended or repealed.

1.1.3. The governments of the Ten decided at the beginning of the month to apply a total ban on exports of arms and military equipment to Argentina.

Statements made

Declarations by the Foreign Ministers meeting in political cooperation

1.1.4. The following declaration was made on 2 April:

'The Foreign Ministers of the Ten condemn the armed intervention in the Falkland Islands by the Government of Argentina in defiance of the statement issued on 1 April by the President of the Security Council of the United Nations, which remains seized of the question.

They urgently appeal to the Government of Argentina to withdraw its forces immediately and to adhere to the appeal of the United Nations Security Council to refrain from the use of force and to continue the search for a diplomatic solution.'

1.1.5. The Ministers reaffirmed their position in the following statement put out by the Belgian Presidency on 10 April:

'The Ten discussed the serious situation resulting from Argentina's invasion of the Falkland Islands.

The Ten recall that, in their declaration of 2 April, they already condemned the flagrant violation of international law represented by Argentina's actions.

The Ten remain deeply concerned about the further development of this crisis, which jeopardizes international peace and security. They thus attach the greatest importance to effective and immediate application of all points of Security Council Resolution 502, i.e. the cessation of hostilities, the immediate withdrawal of all Argentine forces from the Falkland Islands and the search for a diplomatic solution by the Governments of Argentina and the United Kingdom.

With this in mind, and in a spirit of solidarity among the Member States of the Community, the Ten have decided to adopt a series of measures against Argentina which should be implemented as soon as possible.

[1] Point 1.1.2.
[2] Point 1.1.3.
[3] Point 1.1.5.
[4] OJ L 102, 16.4.1982.

Falklands: Community solidarity

The governments of the Ten have already decided to apply a total ban on exports of arms and military equipment to Argentina.

They will also take the measures needed to prohibit all imports into the Community from Argentina.

Since these are economic measures, they will be taken in accordance with the relevant provisions of the Community Treaties.

Since the situation resulting from the invasion of the Falkland Islands by Argentine armed forces is a matter of serious concern for the whole of the international community, the Ten call on other governments to support their decisions so that Security Council Resolution 502 can be fully implemented as soon as possible.'

1.1.6. At an informal meeting of the Foreign Ministers on 20 April the following statement was made to the press:

'The Ten reaffirm their full solidarity with the United Kingdom in the Falklands crisis. They confirm their desire for full implementation of Security Council Resolution 502.

Wishing for a peaceful settlement to this crisis in accordance with the Security Council resolution, they welcome and support the efforts made by Mr Haig, the American Secretary of State, to encourage a peaceful settlement.'

Statement by the Commission on 6 April

'The Commission of the European Communities condemns the armed intervention of Argentina against a British territory linked to the Community, an intervention committed in violation of international law and the rights of the inhabitants of the Falkland Islands. The Commission expresses its solidarity with the United Kingdom. It makes an urgent appeal to the Argentine Government to implement the resolution of the Security Council, calling on it to withdraw its troops from the Islands and to continue seeking a diplomatic solution. It expresses the hope that the Organization of American States will join its efforts to those of the United Nations in order to ensure, by diplomatic means, that a solution based on law prevails.'

Resolution by Parliament

1.1.7. In a resolution passed on 22 April following a debate,[1] the European Parliament:

'1. condemns unreservedly the invasion of the Falkland Islands;

2. notes and supports Resolution 502 of the Security Council of the United Nations on Argentina which demanded an immediate cessation of hostilities, and an immediate withdrawal of all Argentinian forces from the Falkland Islands and called on the Governments of Argentina and the United Kingdom to seek a diplomatic solution to their differences and to respect fully the purposes and principles of the Charter of the United Nations;

3. underlines the importance of Community solidarity which has been shown in the actions of the Council of Ministers;

4. records its agreement with the embargo on imports from Argentina and the ban on arms exports to Argentina and requires that these be maintained until the Security Council Resolution 502 has been implemented;

5. encourages the Commission and the Council to continue to review the possibility of taking further measures;

6. insists that in any solution it is necessary to take fully into account the wishes of the Falkland Islanders;

7. recognizes that Argentinian compliance with Resolution 502 by withdrawing its armed forces would lead to the halting of United Kingdom naval operations and so to the negotiation of a peaceful agreement...'.

---

[1] Point 2.4.5.

EUROPE 82

tep by step through a crisis that challenged the unity of the Ten

HE COMMUNITY AND THE FALKLANDS

PRIL Declaration of EEC foreign ministers condemning
ned intervention in Falkland Islands by Argentina. They
gently appeal to the Government of Argentina to withdraw its
ces and to comply with UN Security Council resolution 502
ling on it to withdraw its troops from the Islands and continue
search for a diplomatic solution.

PRIL Statement by Commission condemning the armed
ervention of Argentina against a territory linked to the
mmunity. The Commission expresses its solidarity with the
K and urges the Argentinian Government to implement
solution 502 of the Security Council.

APRIL EEC foreign ministers announce a complete embargo
arms and military equipment destined for Argentina. They also
nounce that necessary measures will be undertaken to ban all
EC imports coming from Argentina, this in conformity with
rticle 224 or 113 of the Treaty of Rome. A decision as to when the
nbargo would take place would be taken after Easter.

APRIL EEC foreign ministers make a unanimous decision to
spend imports of all products originating in Argentina. The
cision, which takes the form of a Regulation (Regulation 877/
), is effective from 16 April and valid until 17 May 1982. The
egulation does not apply in the following cases:

roducts accompanied by import documents issued before the
te of its entry into force which mention Argentina as a country of
igin;

roducts to be imported in execution of contracts concluded
fore that date;

roducts in course of shipment to the Community at that date.

similar decision is taken making sure that the embargo
mprises also products covered by ECSC Treaty and originating
Argentina.

APRIL Informal meeting of EEC foreign ministers in Brussels
Falklands crisis. The Ten agree on four conclusions:

eaffirmation of their solidarity with the UK in the Falklands
risis;

confirmation of the Community's desire for full implementation of
UN Security Council resolution 502 calling for withdrawal of the
Argentine forces;

a declaration calling for a peaceful solution to the crisis;

strong support for US Secretary of State Alexander Haig's
continuing efforts to encourage a settlement.

22 APRIL European Parliament approves by 203 votes to 28 a
resolution condemning the Argentine invasion of the islands and
backing the UN demand for the withdrawal of all Argentine
forces. It praises the quick action taken by the ten EEC member
states to impose an embargo on imports from Argentina and
recommends the EEC Commission and the Council of Ministers to
review the possibility of taking further measures.

12 MAY European Commission makes a formal proposal to EEC
foreign ministers to extend by another month until 17 June the
Community's ban on imports from Argentina if UN Security
Council Resolution 502 is not respected by the Argentine
Government.
European Parliament approves by 131 votes to 79 (11 abstentions)
a resolution asking EEC governments to agree to maintain
sanctions against Argentina if no peaceful solution to the conflict is
reached by 16 May, when current sanctions expire.

17 MAY EEC foreign ministers agree to renew trade sanctions
against Argentina for a week, i.e. till 24 May. Italy and Ireland
decide to opt out of the embargo but promise that they will do
nothing to undermine the agreement. Denmark argues that
sanctions should be left to national governments and promises to
pass legislation through its parliament to extend the ban.

24 MAY EEC foreign ministers decide to continue trade sanctions
against Argentina indefinitely although Ireland and Italy decide to
remain out of the arrangement. Denmark will operate the ban
independently because of domestic opposition to maintaining it
through a Community regulation.

12 JULY Acknowledgement by Argentinian Government of a
de facto cease-fire.

1 July: home from the
alklands. The
Canberra sails into
Southampton to a
apturous welcome.

PRESS ASSOCIATION

PREPARED STATEMENT OF
THOMAS O. ENDERS
ASSISTANT SECRETARY OF STATE
FOR INTER-AMERICAN AFFAIRS
BEFORE THE
SUBCOMMITTEE ON INTER-AMERICAN AFFAIRS
U.S. HOUSE OF REPRESENTATIVES
WASHINGTON, D.C.
August 5, 1982

1.

Mr. Chairman: I was delighted to receive your invitation to review with this Committee the impact of the Falklands/
Malvinas Islands conflict on the Inter-American System
and specifically on U.S. relations with Latin America.

The clash between Argentina and the United Kingdom
erupted suddenly, then as quickly disappeared from the
headlines. It left in its wake some haunting questions
-- about how to prevent war in the hemisphere, about the
future of Inter-American cooperation, even about regional
stability and progress.

This is not the first time that these islands have
vividly illustrated the risk of massive repercussions from
modest origins. These "few spots of earth which, in the
desert of the ocean, had almost escaped notice" once brought
"the whole system of European empire" to the point of convul-
sion. The remark is from <u>Thoughts on the Late Transactions</u>
<u>Respecting Falkland's Islands</u>, written by Samuel Johnson
in 1771.

This prepared statement addresses the disturbing consequences of the 1982 Falklands/Malvinas crisis beginning
in Part 6. Parts 2-5 record something of the origins and
course of the conflict itself.

2.

The territory immediately at issue consists of 2 main
islands and some 200 smaller ones located in the South
Atlantic 480 miles north-east of Cape Horn. The islands
cover a total area of 4,700 square miles. Their terrain
is alternately boggy and hilly, the environment wind-swept
and virtually treeless. Samuel Johnson described it as
"a bleak and barren spot in the Magellanick Ocean of which
no use could be made". But Johnson never went there to
see for himself. A U.S. Foreign Service Officer who did

so more than two centuries later in the course of her consular duties reported that "work is hard but life is simple
and not uncomfortable." According to the 1980 census,
the population was 1,813 -- down from the 1931 peak of
2,392. The predominant economic activity is the production
of fine wool.

It is their relationship to the outside world rather
than their marginal profitability that has made these islands
a source of seemingly endless contention. Even their name
reflects disagreement: though in English they are known
as the Falklands, in the Spanish-speaking world they are
invariably known as the Malvinas. There is even controversy
over which European first sighted the islands in the 16th
century.

But the central dispute has always been over sovereignty.
In 1770, England, France, and Spain almost went to war
over small outposts embodying competing claims to exclusive
dominion on the islands. That crisis was resolved pragmati-
cally when Spain restored to England the settlement of
Port Egmont on Saunders Island off West Falkland, founded
orginally by English settlers in 1766, then seized by Spain.
In turn, Spain kept Port Louis, which had originally been
founded by France in 1764 on East Falkland. Both Spain
and England maintained their broader sovereignty claims.

In 1774, apparently for reasons of economy, England
withdrew from Port Egmont, leaving behind a leaden plaque
declaring that "Falkland's Island" was the "sole right
and property" of King George III. From 1774 to 1811 the
islands were administered without challenge by a succession
of Spanish governors under the authority of the Viceroyalty
of La Plata in Buenos Aires.

In 1820, Argentina formally claimed sovereignty over
the then uninhabited islands as the successor to Spain.
In one of the many ironies of this history, the Frigate
<u>Heroina</u> sent to enforce Argentina's control was commanded
by David Jewett, one of the many British subjects who fought
in the Wars of Liberation in the service of the Argentine
Republic. In 1826, Argentina established a new capital
at the protected harbor of Stanley on East Falkland. In
1833, after a series of incidents over fishing rights,
one of which had led to action by the USS <u>Lexington</u> against
Argentine authorities, the corvette HMS <u>Clio</u> reasserted
Britain's claim.

For nearly a century and a half -- until an Argentine
naval force invaded Port Stanley last April 2 -- Britain
administered the islands, first as a Crown Colony, then
as a self-governing dependency. The royally chartered
Falklands Islands Company undertook the first large-scale

settlement of the islands, and provided ships that made
four or five round trips a year to Britain exchanging the
islands' wool and hides for everything from chocolates
to building materials.

3.

Argentina's commitment to recover territories Argentines
believe were illegally wrested from them by force is documented in countless pamphlets, articles, and books, some
of them distributed widely in Latin America. For the past
40 years or so, the claim to the "Malvinas" has been an
important component of Argentine nationalism, endorsed
by prominent civilian and military leaders across the political spectrum.

Immediately after World War II, Argentina moved its
claims beyond the bilateral exchanges that had marked its
efforts to recover the islands in the nineteenth and early
twentieth century. At inter-American conferences in Rio
in 1947, Bogota in 1948, Washington in 1953, and Caracas
in 1954, Argentine delegations introduced resolutions pressing Argentina's claims within a general framework of decolonization. In the arctic summer of 1947-48, an Argentine
task force of two cruisers and six destroyers conducted
maneuvers off the islands, but left when Britain dispatched
warships in response.

Argentine diplomacy registered a significant gain
in 1964. Since 1946, the United Nations had treated the
U.K. as the Administering Authority under Chapter XI of
the U.N. Charter. United Nations General Assembly resolution
2065(XX) called upon Argentina and the United Kingdom to
initiate talks with a view to resolving their conflicting
sovereignty claims peacefully. Confidential bilateral
talks began in 1966. With numerous ups and downs and occa-
sional interruptions, Argentine-U.K. negotiations continued
for sixteen years. Agreements were reached providing for
Argentine facilitation of air travel and communications,
postal and medical services, education and oil supply.
The two sides remained far apart, however, on the basic
issue of sovereignty and such related issues as land ownership and residence by Argentines. The last pre-crisis
round of talks took place in New York in February 1982,
ending barely six weeks before Argentina attempted to settle
the matter by force.

It has been said that Britain's approach reflected
a stubborn colonialist reflex. The fact that over the
last generation no fewer than nine members of the Organization of American States have received their independence
in peace and good will from Great Britain suggests that

the situation was rather more complex. The resident islanders, hardy individuals predominantly of Scottish and Welsh
extraction, proved to be satisfied with British rule and
adamantly united in opposing Argentine claims. Throughout
the negotiations, Britain stood by the proposition that
the rights and views of the inhabitants must be respected
in any future disposition of the islands.

The standoff became rooted in principle as well as
nationality: Britain arguing for self-determination, Argentina
for territorial integrity.

4.

The United States has at no time taken a legal position
on the merits of the competing sovereignty claims. In
the nineteenth century, U.S. officials made clear that
-- because the British claims antedated 1823 -- the United
States did not consider the reassertion of British control
a violation of the Monroe Doctrine. The U.S., however,
refused to become embroiled in the sovereignty issue, and
took no position on Argentine and British sovereignty claims.

Thirty-five years ago, at the signing of the Final
Act of the 1947 Rio Conference which created the Rio Treaty,
the United States delegation, headed by Secretary of State
George C. Marshall, made clear our view that the Rio Treaty
is without effect upon outstanding territorial disputes
between American and European states -- and explicitly
refused to endorse Argentina's claim.

U.S. neutrality on the question of sovereignty has
been confirmed repeatedly since then -- at the Organization
of American States and the United Nations as well as during
the recent fighting. I reassert it again today, before
this body: The United States takes no position on the
merits of the competing claims to sovereignty, nor on the
legal theories on which the parties rely.

For the record, I would like to add that although
we of course have an interest in peace there as elsewhere,
the United States has no direct interest in the islands.
Because some comments abroad have suggested otherwise,
I state explicitly that the United States has never had,
and does not now have, any interest in establishing a military base of any kind on these islands. The only occasion
on which any U.S. military presence has ever been contemplated was in April-May 1982 as a contribution to a peaceful
resolution had one been agreed to between Argentina and
the United Kingdom.

5.

Argentina's surprise military occupation of the islands beginning April 2 provoked dismay and apprehension throughout the international community. The next day, April 3, the United Nations Security Council adopted Resolution 502, demanding immediate cessation of hostilities and withdrawal of Argentine troops, and calling on Argentina and the U.K. to resolve their differences diplomatically. Invoking the right of self-defense under Article 51 of the UN Charter, the U.K. dispatched a war fleet toward the islands.

The looming military confrontation put the inter-American system under great stress. Some said that because war would pit an American republic against an outside power, the Rio Treaty required that all its members come to the assistance of the American republic.

Others said that the inter-American system -- which protects regional order based on law and the peaceful settlement of disputes -- could in no way be interpreted to support the resort to force to settle a dispute.

The United States' position was that because the unlawful resort to force did not come from outside the hemisphere, this was not a case of extra-continental aggression against which we were -- and are -- all committed to rally.

These different responses to a conflict for which the Inter-American system was not designed led to heated exchanges among Foreign Ministers at the meeting of the Rio Treaty Organ of Consultation that began April 26. Two days later, the Organ adopted by a vote of 17-0-4 (the United States abstaining) a resolution that urged an immediate truce, recognition of the "rights of sovereignty of the Republic of Argentina over the Malvinas (Falkland) Islands and the interests of the islanders," and called for "negotiation aimed at a peaceful settlement of the conflict."

Negotiation of a peaceful settlement of the conflict had in fact been the central objective of the United States' response to the crisis.

U.S. efforts to encourage a negotiated settlement began even before the initial use of force. In late March, we offered to the two sides our good offices to help find a peaceful solution to an incident on South Georgia Island on March 19 when an Argentine salvage team was threatened with expulsion for operating without British permission. On April 1, learning that Argentine military action appeared imminent, President Reagan called President Galtieri to urge that Argentina desist from the use of force.

After Argentina forcibly occupied the islands, both President Galtieri and Prime Minister Thatcher encouraged the United States to see whether it could be of assistance in finding a solution. At President Reagan's direction Secretary Haig undertook two rounds of intense discussions in each capital.

On April 27, as prospects for more intense hostilities increased, the United States put forward a proposal of its own. It represented our best estimate of what the two parties could reasonably be expected to accept. It was founded squarely on U.N. Security Council Resolution 502, which both sides asserted they accepted.

The U.S. proposal called for negotiations to remove the islands from the list of Non-Self-Governing Territories under Chapter XI of the U.N. Charter. It specified that the definitive status, of the islands must be mutually agreed, with due regard for the rights of the inhabitants and for the principle of territorial integrity. And it referred both to the purposes and principles of the U.N. Charter, and to the relevant resolutions of the U.N. General Assembly.

Those negotiations were to be completed by the end of the year. Pending their conclusion, an interim authority composed of Argentina, Britain, and the United States was to oversee the traditional local administration, to be sure that no decision was taken contrary to the agreement. Argentine residents of the islands were to participate in local councils for this purpose. During the interim period travel, transportation and movement of persons between the islands and the mainland were to be promoted and facilitated without prejudice to the rights and guarantees of the inhabitants.

The proposed interim authority of three countries was to make proposals to facilitate the negotiations, including recommendations on how to take into account the wishes and interests of the inhabitants, and on what the role of the Falkland Islands Company should be.

Should the negotiations not have been completed by year's end, the United States was to be asked to engage in a formal mediation/conciliation effort in order to resolve the dispute within six months.

The British government indicated that our proposal presented certain real difficulties but that it would seriously consider it. However, the proposal was not acceptable to the Argentine Government, which continued to insist that any solution must have a predetermined outcome.

On April 30, in light of Argentina's continued unwill-
ingness to compromise, we took concrete measures to underscore that the United States could not and would not condone
the unlawful use of force to resolve disputes. The President
ordered limited economic and military measures affecting
Argentina, and directed that we would respond positively
to requests for materiel support for British forces, but
without any direct U.S. military involvement. Secretary
Haig's statement announcing these measures emphasized our
belief that no strictly military outcome could endure,
that a negotiated settlement would be necessary in the
end, and that the United States remained ready to assist
the parties in finding that settlement.

On May 5, President Belaunde of Peru took the initiative
to put forward a new peace plan, drawing also on the fundamental elements of Resolution 502. We worked closely with
him. The simplified text forwarded by Peru to Buenos Aires
and London called for: an immediate cease-fire; concurrent
withdrawal and non-reintroduction of forces; administration
of the islands by a contact group pending definitive settlement, in consultation with the elected representatives
of the islanders; acknowledgement of conflicting claims;
acknowledgement in the final settlement of the aspirations
and interests of the islanders; and an undertaking by the
contact group to ensure that the two parties reached a
definitive agreement by April 30, 1983.

Britain made clear that it could seriously consider
the proposal. Argentina asked instead for the U.N. Secretary
General to use his good offices as, of course, it was its
full privilege to do.

By this time, however, the military tempo was rapidly
overtaking the negotiators. On May 2, two torpedoes from
a British submarine sank the General Belgrano, Argentina's
only cruiser. On May 4, a sea-skimming missile from an
Argentine jet devastated the HMS Sheffield, a modern British
destroyer. Despite intense new efforts by the U.N. Secretary-
General, the war we had worked so hard to avoid had come
in earnest.

By June 14, when the Union Jack was again raised over
Port Stanley, what Horace Walpole had in 1770 called "a
morsel of rock that lies somewhere at the very bottom of
America" had become the improbable scenario of bitter fighting. More than a thousand men and women were dead. Billions
of dollars had been expended. Emotions had surfaced in
both countries that promise to make this issue and others
even harder to resolve in the future.

6.

I said at the outset that the South Atlantic war faces us with several haunting questions.

Perhaps the most fundamental is how better to prevent war in the future in this hemisphere.

Many of us feared as soon as Argentina acted April 2 that the fighting would escalate. Argentina, it is true, did not cause casualties in its takeover. But that did little to diminish the shock. Any use of force invites further use of force. The shock in this case was increased because the two countries were both linked in friendship to us and to each other. It grew when brave men on both sides began to risk and lose their lives. But perhaps the deepest shock came because war between states had been virtually unknown in the Americas in our time.

In the world as a whole, some four million persons have lost their lives in armed action between states since the Second World War. Including the toll in the South Atlantic, fewer than four thousand of them have died in the Western Hemisphere. The countries of Latin America spend less of their national resources for arms than any other area in the world. Their military expenditures come to only 1.4 percent of GNP -- a quarter of the average in the Third World as a whole.

The South Atlantic war -- the fact of major fighting and the clear advantages demonstrated by modern weapons -- means that military institutions, throughout the hemisphere but especially in South America, have powerful new claims to resources. Because Latin America's military institutions and arsenals are relatively modest in size, demands for advanced weapons systems and for the expertise to maintain and employ them are likely to increase. Governments will also look for self-sufficiency in defense industries, for bigger stocks of weapons.

Budgetary limitations will of course constrain purchases, but we would be mistaken to expect arms modernization to be deferred as a result of the South Atlantic conflict. On the contrary. The duration and intensity of the fighting called into question the assumption that the Inter-American System guarantees that interstate conflicts in this hemisphere would be limited to a few days of actual fighting.

A new emphasis on military preparedness in a region long plagued by territorial disputes and military involvement in politics would undeniably challenge every member of the Inter-American System.

The hemisphere is laced with territorial questionmarks. The prevalence of territorial tensions (e.g., among Argentina-Chile-Peru-Bolivia-Ecuador, Colombia-Venezuela-Guyana, Nicaragua-Colombia, Guatemala-Belize) puts a premium on the peaceful settlement of disputes. To take just one example, tensions between Guatemala and Belize (the only place in the hemisphere other than the Falklands where the U.K. stations combat troops) will continue to fester if unresolved.

The challenge to regional peacekeeping is far from hopeless, however. The U.S. response to the crisis may serve to deter others from resorting to force. Moreover, the Inter-American System equips the New World with the means to prevent or control the conflicts that have kept other continents from realizing their potential.

Machinery exists to anticipate disputes and permit their peaceful and definitive settlement: various Inter-American arbitration and conciliation agreements, OAS peace-keeping mechanisms, the International Court of Justice, even the Treaty of Tlatelolco, which established the world's first nuclear free zone in a populated area. What appears lacking is the will to use this machinery to prevent and resolve contentious problems. The U.S. and other countries of the area have at one time or another been involved in calming or negotiating most of them. But this is a branch of hemispheric diplomacy that deserves fresh attention.

The interest of American states is clearly to avoid arms races. Even where competitive procurement cannot be avoided altogether, they will want to see that existing disputes are not needlessly exacerbated. U.S. arms sales as a proportion of South American purchases fell from 75 percent in 1960 to 25 percent in 1970, and 7 percent in 1980. The reduction in training and in-depth contacts between the U.S. and most South American militaries has been equally precipitous.

These patterns raise a question worth pondering in the wake of the Falklands/Malvinas episode. Can the United States maintain a degree of military access and communication with the states of South America so as to help maintain the regional balance of power with such limited personnel, doctrinal, and materiel relationships?

A related challenge is to prevent regional conflicts from having strategic consequences, changing the East-West balance. This is a real problem, for history shows the Soviet Union and its proxies are ready and eager to take advantage of instability. Should Moscow be willing to provide arms at bargain prices as it did to Peru in the

1970's, economic constraints on Latin American purchases
of military equipment from traditional Western sources
could give the Soviets a unique opportunity to forge closer
links with established governments in South America. Cuba
(and Nicaragua) rushed forward to exploit the Falklands
crisis. In Argentina some talked of playing the Cuban
card. We do not believe Argentina will turn to the country
that harbors in its capital the extremely violent Argentine
terrorist organization -- the Montoneros. But Cuba will
be working hard to use the crisis to lessen its current
isolation within the hemisphere.

7.

A second legacy of the conflict is the need to overcome
resentments of the United States that were triggered by
the crisis.

Although the immediate emotional strains of the crisis
are already receding, the perception of the U.S. as a reli-
able ally to Latin American nations in times of crisis
will take time to restore.

The commitment of the United States to the hemisphere
and its institutions has been called into question. I
have already noted the importance we attach to the OAS,
that we have taken no position on the question of sovereignty,
and that in our view no Rio Treaty action could apply to
this particular contingency. Nonetheless, U.S. support
for what on May 29 the second meeting of the Rio Treaty
Organ of Consultation condemned as an "unjustified and
disproportionate" U.K. military response was taken by some
to mean that the U.S. commitment to the Inter-American
System was superficial at best.

The fact that the conflict remained localized and
ended relatively rapidly helped mitigate damage to U.S.
interests. Nonetheless, our bilateral relationships with
certain countries have unquestionably been affected adversely.
The most severe impact is obviously on relations with Argentina.
But Venezuela, Panama, and Peru were also highly critical
of our support for the United Kingdom's military response,
and will be watching closely the future evolution of the
sovereignty issue. In contrast, U.S. relations with most
other South American countries, Mexico and the Caribbean
Basin appear less affected.

The lasting effects of this mood, which varies from
country to country, will depend on how the post-crisis
situation evolves and what posture we adopt. Reactions
may change as the position taken by the United States is
better understood. But the widespread view that the United

States does not take Latin America seriously could increase North-South and non-aligned rhetoric and inhibit cooperation in support of U.S. interests. The argument that the United States and United Kingdom acted as industrialized powers cooperating to keep a developing country "in its place" makes us once again a target for anti-colonialist and anti-imperialist emotions that will make it harder for us to accomplish our objectives.

It would be wrong to conclude from such reactions that the U.S. should not have acted as it did. There can be no position for the United States other than to oppose the unlawful use of force to settle disputes.

The first lesson for U.S. policy is that that this is a time for steadiness of purpose rather than for grandiose gestures, statements, or proposals. During the coming months, it will be especially important that we meet our commitments, protect our interests and respond to those of our neighbors in a meaningful and resourceful manner.

The Caribbean Basin Initiative is vitally important in this regard. Many Basin countries now wonder whether our contribution to the CBI will ever materialize. If Congress were not to act, the concerns these countries now express about their future and our commitment to them would deepen, widening opportunities for Soviet and Cuban adventurism. It is now up to the United States to deliver.

We must maintain our commitment in Central America, where democratic processes are vulnerable, and where fragile government institutions face a major challenge from Cuban supported guerrilla movements. Our political, economic and security assistance is essential to help them meet this challenge and make progress toward democracy, economic development, and the effective protection of human rights.

While we must continue to seek innovative solutions to the problems of our immediate neighborhood, we must understand what is happening in South America is also impor-tant to us. This was evident in the midst of the Falklands conflict -- for example, in the visit of President Figueiredo to Washington. The conflict between Argentina and the United Kingdom was a major topic of discussion. The exchange made clear that the positions of the U.S. and Brazil dif-fered, but that our basic interests and objectives were similar. For several years now, we have simply not given South America the attention its place in the world and our interests warrant.

8.

This brings me to a third challenge, the conundrum
of our relations with Argentina. Despite our many similarities, U.S.-Argentine relations have seldom been close.

The President's vision of region-wide cooperation
had led us to make efforts to improve ties to South America,
including Argentina. In the case of Argentina, however,
those efforts had not yet borne fruit by the time of the
crisis. We must continue to seek a dialogue that can develop
the bilateral and multilateral framework for more fully
cooperative relations.

During the South Atlantic crisis, our ties with Argentina
proved too weak to promote effective cooperation in support
of common interests. Repeated efforts were made by us
and by others -- before the Argentine landing on the islands,
again when the British fleet was approaching, and again
when the U.S. and Peruvian and UN peace plans were advanced
in turn -- to explain to Argentine leaders what would happen
if they did what they proposed to do. Although our predic-
tions consistently proved accurate, they were not believed.
Communication failed utterly.

Our objectives with Argentina today include encouraging
economic recovery, peaceful resolution of the dispute between
the U.K. and Argentina, and, of course, political comity.
Yet our ties to the government in Buenos Aires are now
more limited than previously. How long this will last
depends on several factors. But the fundamental point
is that we all share a compelling interest in an Argentina
that is true to hemispheric traditions and free of foreign
communist influence. We do not want the Soviets to be
their only alternative. Neither do they. We all should
be prepared to help Argentina maintain conditions in which
its people can realize their free world vocation.

So we must begin, in orderly fashion, to build the
solid, realistic relationship so evidently lacking until
now.

9.

Finally, the South Atlantic crisis has highlighted
economic problems in South America and throughout the hemisphere.

Even before the crisis, many of the region's countries were feeling the effects of the world recession on
their development. The problems vary. Virtually all depend
heavily on international trade and on access to international

financial markets. Some have contracted substantial debt.
The South Atlantic crisis could crystallize doubts about
stability and creditworthiness on a region-wide level,
particularly if arms procurement were to divert resources
from development priorities.

The major lesson here is the need for cooperation
in economic management -- not merely with Argentina, but
with Brazil, Venezuela and Mexico.

Many of the problems now associated with the South
Atlantic crisis have been developing for some time. The
growing assertiveness and needs of major developing countries
are not new. Let us hope that the crisis will strengthen
our ability to work more realistically together.

10.

Before the crisis erupted in the South Atlantic, we
had already begun to develop more sustained hemispheric
relationships.

-- We had started to achieve with Mexico a relationship that reflects its exceptional importance
   to the U.S. and its role in world affairs. Now
   comes the harshest test of that new relationship,
   as the economic slowdown in both countries threatens
   to aggravate all our joint accounts: trade, finance, immigration. We must be steadfast.

-- We had committed ourselves to help countries of
   the Caribbean Basin protect themselves against
   outside intervention, strengthen or develop democratic institutions, and overcome economic disas-
   ters. Now we must deliver.

-- We were beginning to respond to new realities
   in South America, rebuilding close bilateral relations with each country after a decade of drift,
   when the shadow of the South Atlantic crisis fell
   across our efforts. Now we must relaunch those
   efforts, joining others to maintain the network
   of constructive relationships that is essential
   to peace.

What this crisis may ultimately mean for the United
States is not that our recent decisions were wrong -- they
were right -- but that the accummulation from our past
decisions reveals a flaw in our outlook. We have pursued
an a la carte approach, ignoring our friends when it suited
us, yet demanding their help or agreement when it served
our interest. We took too much for granted, and invested

too little. When we needed close and effective dialogue on April 2, we didn't have it.

When a fight in distant islands reverberates around the world, the fundamental lesson is not how little we need each other but how closely connected we are. Our task is to make interdependence work, not against us, but for us. This requires long term commitments that will enhance our ability to influence events and protect our interests.

Legal Aspects of Falklands/Malvinas Crisis Negotiations

This paper addresses three aspects of the negotiations
which occurred during April and May of 1982 to avert the war in
the South Atlantic: the United States posture on the underlying
dispute over sovereignty of the Islands; the content of the
three most intensive settlement efforts, focusing on the two in
which the United States was most 'closely involved; and the consideration given to use of the International Court of Justice.

U.S. Position on Claims to the Islands

Throughout the more than 200-year history of this dispute,
the United States has maintained a legal neutrality on the competing United Kingdom and Argentine claims to the Falklands/
Malvinas, urging that their dispute be resolved through peaceful
means in accordance with international law. In the post-World
War II era, the United States has abstained on United Nations or
Organization of American States resolutions that implied a
position on the merits.

United States neutrality is also reflected in the United
States position on the non-applicability of the Monroe
Doctrine. Because the dispute over the Islands predated the
Monroe Doctrine, and because the United States took no position
on the dispute over sovereignty, the State Department long ago
expressed the view that the reinsertion of a British presence on
the Islands in 1833 was not a new attempt at colonization, and
that the Doctrine is thus inapplicable.

In addition to declining to take a position on the merits,
the United States has not taken a position on the underlying
legal theories on which the parties rely. Specifically, the
United States has taken no view on the relative weight to be
given to Britain's position on self-determination for the
Islanders, and Argentina's emphasis on the principle of
territorial integrity with the mainland. The application of
the principle of self-determination to the Falklands has raised
a number of legal questions in view of the size and origin of
the population, the existence of other legal principles which
may be applicable given the history and nature of the dispute,
and, in particular, the interpretation placed by Argentina on
the principle of territorial integrity contained in United
Nations General Assembly decolonization resolutions such as
Resolution 1514 (XV).

This United States position of neutrality was maintained
throughout, and facilitated our attempts to mediate, the crisis.

While remaining neutral on the merits of the dispute, the United States has acknowledged the fact of longstanding United Kingdom administration of the Islands. The United States has accordingly dealt with the United Kingdom on matters related to the Islands and has on occasion acquiesced in United Kingdom accession to bilateral agreements and international conventions on behalf of them. The United States position in such instances has been consistent with acknowledgment of the United Kingdom's de facto responsibility for the Islands' foreign relations as the administering authority in peaceful possession. This pragmatic policy of dealing with the administrator in de facto control is also that of the United Nations, which has accepted from the United Kingdom, as the administering authority, annual reports under Chapter XI of the United Nations Charter regarding Non-Self-Governing Territories.

April-May 1982 Negotiations

There were three intensive efforts after the Argentine occupation of the Islands to avert the coming military confrontation; each resulted in textual elaborations of the positions of both sides on acceptable outcomes on the range of issues involved in a package to promote a peaceful settlement. All of these efforts addressed four common elements:

--a cease-fire, linked to a mutual withdrawal of forces within a short period, and a commitment on non-reintroduction of forces, subject to third-party verification (this element was consistent with United Nations Security Council Resolution 502, operative paragraphs 1 and 2 of which called for an immediate cessation of hostilities and withdrawal of Argentine forces from the Islands);

--interim administrative arrangements for the Islands, based on some form of third-party supervision of local government, including provision for Argentine accesss to the Islands during this period;

--the composition and definition of the functions of the third-party mechanism to assist the parties in implementation of an agreement; and

--a framework for negotiations to reach a definitive settlement, including a deadline or target date, and the role in such negotiations for third-party assistance.

Each side, of course, approached these common elements from a different perspective, which in some cases shifted as the diplomatic and military situation changed over time. The United Kingdom was willing to consider variations on the form of

administration of the Islands, subject to certain basic
guarantees in respect of local rights and institutions. It was
prepared to accept third-party assistance in implementation of an
agreement, subject to inclusion of some role for the United
States. United Kingdom insistence on a cease-fire coupled with
immediate withdrawal of Argentine forces from the Islands
remained firm, consistent with its legal position based on
Article 51 of the United Nations Charter relating to self-
defense, and United Nations Security Council Resolution 502. The
United Kingdom also insisted that nothing in an agreement
prejudice the final outcome of the negotiations. This insistence
focused in particular on the drafting of a formula on future
negotiations that was neutral on the issue of sovereignty, and on
provisions to control Argentine intercourse with the Islands at
pre-war levels, consistent with a 1971 agreement between the two
countries.

Argentina, in turn, sought either effective interim control
of the Islands' administration, including freedom of access to
the Islands, or assurance that the formula on a definitive
settlement would automatically result in confirmation of
Argentine sovereignty over the Islands at some fixed future
time. While accepting the concept of a cease-fire linked to
mutual withdrawal of forces, Argentina sought an immediate United
Kingdom withdrawal of its units to home bases; the United Kingdom
viewed such a formula for the withdrawal period as imbalanced
(since Argentine forces would remain within close range of the
Islands) and as removing a necessary deterrent to Argentine
violation of the terms of an agreement. Argentina sought
drafting of the negotiation mandate to emphasize decolonization
and the principle of territorial integrity with the mainland, and
resisted references to a right of self-determination on the part
of the Islanders which were desired by the United Kingdom.
Argentina, in light of the long history of prior talks with the
United Kingdom, took the position that the mandate had to be
placed under a firm and short deadline date.

Both sides shared an evaluation that provisions on interim
arrangements and the framework for reaching a definitive
settlement were interlinked elements of the negotiation, each
prepared to be flexible in one area for gains in the other.

The three principal initiatives are discussed below, and the
resulting texts are attached.

United States Proposal of April 27. The first effort, that
of Secretary Haig, culminated in a fairly detailed set of
proposals to the two parties on April 27. It was based on the
three strenuous weeks of consultations he had held in London,

Buenos Aires and Washington, and our best perception of what might ultimately prove acceptable to each side. Its approach, and many of its elements, reappeared in subsequent proposals to and by the two parties.

The United States draft memorandum of agreement provided for an integral cease-fire and withdrawal linkage. The formula for providing for balanced withdrawals proved troublesome in each of the three negotiations, given the vastly different geographic perspectives of each side. The United States proposal resolved the problem by a formula based on parity in reinsertion time, rather than on conventional but more difficult geographic withdrawal distances. These commitments, and that of non-reintroduction of forces into the Islands and defined surrounding areas, were to be verified by the United States.

The proposal called for immediate steps to terminate simultaneously the various economic and financial measures each party had adopted, and for the United Kingdom to request termination of similar measures taken by its allies.

Local self-government on the Islands was to be restored. The office of Governor was to remain vacant, and its powers exercised by the next-ranking official, appointed by the United Kingdom. The local Executive and Legislative Councils were to be retained, but augmented by representation of the small local Argentine resident population by means of at least one representative in each Council, and by inclusion of two Argentine Government representatives in the upper, Executive Council. A Special Interim Authority was to be created, composed of a representative of each side and of the United States. The flags of each constituent country were to be flown at its headquarters. The Authority was to have supervision over Island administration, exercised by means of a veto power in the event the Authority, by majority vote, deemed an act of the local government to be inconsistent with the agreement. In all other cases, the Authority was called upon to ratify expeditiously all local decisions, laws and regulations.

The proposal called for decolonization of the Islands as the negotiation objective. This was framed in terms of removing the Islands from the list of Non-Self-Governing Territories under Chapter XI of the United Nations Charter. The potential means were not limited, but the conditions for their definitive status had to be mutually agreed. The negotiation mandate maintained neutrality on the competing legal positions of the two sides, noting that of each by short-hand references to due regard for the rights of the inhabitants and the principle of territorial integrity. Reference was made to relevant United Nations General Assembly

resolutions (which would include general decolonization
resolutions and specific resolutions on the subject of the
Falklands/Malvinas).

Foreshadowing the contact group concept utilized in later
proposals, the United States formulation provided a role for
the Special Interim Authority to catalyze the negotiations with
recommendations to the two sides, in particular on the sensitive issues of how to take into account the wishes of the
Islanders and the role of the Falkland Islands Company. If the
negotiations did not prosper by the deadline date (December 31,
1982), a second phase of negotiations, under a new six-month
target date, was to occur in which the United States would act
as a mediator/conciliator to press for an agreement.

With respect to contacts with the mainland, the draft
agreement stated a principle of promotion and facilitation of
non-discriminatory travel, commercial, communications, and
other links. The proposal provided for recommendation by the
Authority to the two Governments of specific measures on such
matters, and for securing the views of the local Councils on
the recommendations. These provisions were balanced by an
obligation to respect the traditional rights and guarantees of
the Islanders.

The United Kingdom, which had not yet landed on the
Falklands/Malvinas or suffered any serious combat losses, found
the proposal difficult, but was willing to give it "serious
consideration." This was the only time the United Kingdom
considered a proposal to cover the South Georgia and South
Sandwich Dependencies as well as the Falklands/Malvinas
(sensitivity to the implications of use of the English and
Spanish names for the Islands resulted in the United States
proposal defining the island groups by coordinates).

Despite many attractive features for the Argentines, the
Argentine Foreign Minister replied on April 29 that the
Government of Argentina could not accept the formulation since
it gave them neither effective interim control nor assurances
of obtaining sovereignty as a result of the negotiation process.

Peru-United States Proposal. At the initiative of the
President of Peru, and with our cooperation, another effort was
launched, culminating on May 5 with a more skeletal proposal,
limited in geographic scope to the Falklands/Malvinas. A
cease-fire and withdrawal of forces were inseparably linked,
but all implementing detail was to be deferred for decision by
a Contact Group composed of representatives of Brazil, Peru,
the Federal Republic of Germany and the United States.

The Contact Group was to verify the military provisions of an agreement. It would assume administration of the government of the Islands in consultation with the elected representatives of the Islanders, and ensure that no actions were taken inconsistent with the agreement. All details on implementation of administration--financial questions, applicable law, administrative, legal and appointive links to Britain, the role of the Councils, the exercise of powers of the office of Governor--were to be deferred for later decision by the Contact Group . The result conceivably might have paralleled the United States proposal once elaborated, but the door was open to other variations of third-party administration and the role to be played thereunder by the existing local institutions.

The existence of the parties' differing legal positions was noted; the proposal also included an acknowledgment that the "aspirations and interests" of the Islanders were to be "included" in a definitive settlement.

Finally, the Contact Group assumed a responsibility to attempt to ensure that the two governments reached a negotiated agreement on the future of the Islands by April 30, 1983. Again, the detail of modalities for the negotiation, and the role and procedures of the Contact Group in facilitating a result, were deferred for later decision. The negotiation formula was neutral, but included a deadline date as Argentina desired.

The United Kingdom indicated that it was willing to give this proposal serious consideration; Argentina, after the initiation of talks under the auspices of the United Nations Secretary-General, preferred to shift the focus of negotiations to New York.

United Nations Negotiations. With continued change in the military situation and, from the United Kingdom's perspective, in the wake of failure to secure agreement on the basis of substantial concessions reflected in the United States and Peruvian proposals, the positions of both sides hardened in a number of respects as evidenced by the texts each side publicly released at the breakdown of these talks in late May.

Both sides accepted the concept of a United Nations administration with generally defined authority. This formulation reflected a substantial concession by the United Kingdom on maintenance of administrative links to Britain in favor of local self-rule under United Nations supervision. Again, critical details would have had to be defined in implementing agreements or by United Nations Security Council resolution. United Nations verification of military disengagement provisions was also accepted by both sides in principle, as well as the auspices of the United Nations Secretary-General to conduct the negotiations.

The publicly-released positions permitted identification of very limited other common ground. The United Kingdom sought to subject a United Nations administration to local law and practices, "in consultation with" the Islands' representative institutions, which Argentina resisted. Argentina sought immediate, expanded access to the Islands, which the United Kingdom would not accept for fear that the population and character of the Islands might be unilaterally altered during the interim period. Argentina desired a firm deadline for negotiation to be followed, if necessary, by reference of the dispute to the United Nations General Assembly for decision; the United Kingdom rejected recourse to the General Assembly, and continued to consider a rigid timetable unrealistic. On these and other points (e.g., extent of geographical coverage; military withdrawal details; self-determination references), the two sides ended far apart.

The Secretary-General made last-minute proposals to the two sides before the talks unraveled. Prime Minister Thatcher, as events overtook these suggestions, simply noted that Argentina could not possibly have accepted them. We are unaware of any formal Argentine response. To our knowledge, the content of these suggestions was not publicly released.

Subsequent Developments. The United Kingdom and Argentine texts tabled at the conclusion of the Secretary-General's first round of negotiations remain the final textual elaboration of their views on settlement issues. There followed efforts in the Security Council to negotiate a resolution that would substitute for an agreement, notably involving a useful Brazilian draft text. None was the subject of intensive substantive negotiation. These efforts culminated in the Security Council's adoption, on May 26, of Resolution 505, which asked the Secretary-General to renew his good offices to secure a cease-fire; and in the United Kingdom-United States veto, on June 4, of a Spanish/Panamanian draft resolution that sought a cease-fire and implementation of the previous Security Council Resolutions, under verification of the Secretary-General, but with inadequate detail on withdrawal procedures and other elements to serve as a mutually agreeable vehicle for settlement of the conflict.

Possible Role for the International Court of Justice

The focus of United Nations General Assembly resolutions on the subject, the efforts of both countries over sixteen years, and of the peace-making efforts in the spring, was on a negotiated settlement of the dispute.

The United States Government is committed to the use of the International Court of Justice to resolve legal disputes, consistent with Article 36(3) of the United Nations Charter. The submission to a Chamber of the Court of our differences with Canada over delimitation of a maritime boundary in the Gulf of Maine is a concrete example. The dispute on sovereignty over the Falklands/Malvinas is an issue which the Court could appropriately decide. United States negotiators this spring raised this matter with both sides. Neither has ever indicated a willingness to have recourse to the Court over the Falklands/Malvinas. The case does not fall within the compulsory jurisdiction of the Court, and the agreement of both parties is thus necessary to submit the case for binding decision.

The United Kingdom on two occasions since World War II sought to submit to the Court the related dispute on sovereignty over the South Georgia and South Sandwich Island Dependencies, but Argentina did not agree to do so.

The United States continues to believe that a peaceful solution to this long-standing controversy is required, consistent with the United Nations Charter obligations of both parties, and it may be that possible use of the Court will be reconsidered among the other possible settlement options, including renewed negotiations, that would be consistent with Article 33 of the Charter.

UNITED
NATIONS

General Assembly

Distr.
GENERAL

A/AC.109/712
10 August 1982

ORIGINAL: ENGLISH

SPECIAL COMMITTEE ON THE SITUATION
 WITH REGARD TO THE IMPLEMENTATION
 OF THE DECLARATION ON THE GRANTING
 OF INDEPENDENCE TO COLONIAL
 COUNTRIES AND PEOPLES

FALKLAND ISLANDS (MALVINAS)

Working paper prepared by the Secretariat

CONTENTS

FALKLAND ISLANDS (MALVINAS) 1/

I. GENERAL

1.   The Falkland Islands (Malvinas) lie in the South Atlantic, some 772 kilometres north-east of Cape Horn. They comprise 200 islands and cover a total area of 11,961 square kilometres. There are two large islands, East Falkland and West Falkland. Apart from a number of small islands, the Dependencies consist of South Georgia, 1,287 kilometres east-south-east of the Falkland Islands (Malvinas), and the uninhabited South Sandwich Islands, some 756 kilometres east-south-east of South Georgia.

2.   At the last census, held in December 1980, the population of the Territory, excluding the Dependencies, numbered 1,813 (including 30 Argentine residents), almost all of whom were of European descent, mainly of British origin. Of this total, 1,000 lived in Stanley, the capital.

II.   CONSTITUTIONAL AND POLITICAL DEVELOPMENTS

A.   Constitution

3.   The constitutional arrangements for the Territory, introduced in 1949 and amended in 1951, 1955, 1964 and 1977, are outlined in earlier working papers prepared by the Secretariat. 2/ The latest amendment, the Falkland Islands (Legislative Council) (Amendment) Order 1977, had the effect of (a) increasing the number of elected members of the Legislative Council from four to six, thus giving that Council a majority of elected members; (b) retaining the two ex officio members and the Governor in the Legislative Council; and (c) lowering the voting age from 21 to 18 years. The governmental structure, therefore, consists of: (a) the Governor (Mr. Rex Masterman Hunt), appointed by the Queen; (b) an Executive Council consisting of two ex officio members (the Chief Secretary, Mr. Richard Baker; and the Financial Secretary, Mr. Harold Rowlands), two unofficial members appointed by the Governor and two elected members of the Legislative Council elected by the members of that Council; (c) a Legislative Council consisting of the Governor, who presides, two ex officio members (the Chief Secretary and the Financial Secretary) and six members elected on the basis of universal adult suffrage; and (d) a Court of Appeals set up in July 1965 to hear and determine appeals from the courts of the Territory. On 15 June 1982, the Office of Governor was suspended. A Civil Commissioner and Military Commissioner were appointed.

4.   At the most recent elections in the Territory, held on 15 October 1981, the following persons were elected to the Legislative Council: East Falkland: Mr. Ronald E. Binnie; West Falkland: Mr. Lionel G. Blake; East Stanley: Mr. William H. Goss, the only member of the previous Legislative Council to be re-elected; West Stanley: Mr. John E. Cheek; Stanley Division: Mr. Terrence J. Peck; Camp 3/ Division: Mr. Anthony T. Blake. The new Legislative Council was sworn in on 5 November for a four-year term of office, and the meeting was adjourned until the first regular meeting of the Council in January 1982.

/...

B.   Relations between the Governments of Argentina and the United Kingdom

5.   Detailed information concerning relations between the Governments of Argentina and the United Kingdom on the question of the Falkland Islands (Malvinas) prior to 1981 is contained in earlier working papers on the Territory. (For the most recent, see A/AC.109/615, paras. 6-14, and A/AC.109/670, paras. 8-21.)

6.   It will be recalled 4/ that on 15 December 1977, the two parties issued a joint communiqué (A/33/57, annex, and A/33/58, annex) in which they announced that, in accordance with the agreement reached in Rome in July, an Anglo-Argentine ministerial meeting had been held in New York from 13 to 15 December 1977 to continue negotiations on future political relations, including sovereignty, with regard to the Falkland Islands (Malvinas), South Georgia and the South Sandwich Islands and Anglo-Argentine economic co-operation with regard to the said territories in particular and the South West Atlantic in general.

7.   From 1977 onwards, meetings were held at ministerial level from time to time, with the participation of representatives of the islanders.

8.   As reported earlier (see A/AC.109/670, paras. 17-21), in February 1981, a round of talks was held in New York, at which the Argentine delegation rejected a proposal made by the United Kingdom, at the request of the territorial Legislative Council that a "freeze" be put on the discussions on sovereignty for a determined period of time. On their return to the Territory, the two members of the Legislative Council who had attended the talks reported in a press conference that the Argentine delegation had made a direct appeal to them, offering to make the islands a "most pampered region" and to maintain their democratic, legal, social and educational systems, if the inhabitants gave up United Kingdom sovereignty in favour of Argentine sovereignty.

9.   By a letter dated 29 July 1981 (A/36/412), the Permanent Representative of Argentina to the United Nations informed the Secretary-General of a declaration issued to the press by his Government on 27 July, concerning the Falkland Islands (Malvinas). In it, the Argentine Government invited the Government of the United Kingdom "to expedite resolutely the formal negotiating process" on the issue. The Government further stated that "no substantial progress has been made since negotiations were undertaken pursuant to resolution 2065 (XX)" and that the time had come for the negotiations to become effective.

10. On 25 November, by its decision 36/416, the General Assembly, on the recommendation of the Fourth Committee, decided to defer consideration of the question of the Falkland Islands (Malvinas) until its thirty-seventh session, and requested the Special Committee to keep the situation in the Territory under review.

11. On 14 December, it was announced that the round of negotiations scheduled to be held between the two parties at Geneva that month had been postponed to a date to be announced later.

12. On 26 and 27 February 1982, a meeting at ministerial level was held in New York. The Argentine delegation was headed by Mr. Enrique Ros, Under-Secretary

for External Relations and Worship and included Mr. Carlos Ortíz de Rozas, Ambassador to the United Kingdom. The United Kingdom delegation was led by Mr. Richard Luce, Minister of State at the Foreign and Commonwealth Office, and included Messrs. Anthony Williams, Ambassador to Argentina, and Anthony T. Blake and John E. Cheek, members of the Legislative Council of the Territory.

13. According to the press release issued after the talks, "the meeting took place in a cordial and positive spirit. The two sides reaffirmed their resolve to find a solution to the sovereignty dispute and considered in detail an Argentine proposal for procedures to make better progress in this sense".

14. Subsequently, the Argentine Government issued a further statement which was read out by the Minister of External Relations and Worship at the 2350th meeting of the Security Council, held on 3 April 1982. The statement read in part (S/PV.2350):

> "'Argentina has negotiated with Great Britain with patience, honesty and good faith for more than 15 years within the framework mentioned in the relevant resolutions of the United Nations to arrive at a solution to the dispute over the sovereignty of the islands. The new system is an effective measure to arrive at a prompt solution.
>
> 'However, if this does not come about, if there is no response from the British side, Argentina reserves the right to put an end to the operation of such a mechanism and freely to choose the procedure it deems most fit in accordance with its interests.'"

15. On 3 March, in response to a question about that statement in the House of Commons, Mr. Luce stated:

> "I can tell the honourable Gentleman that, without any shadow of a doubt, there will be no contemplation of any transfer of sovereignty without consulting the wishes of the islanders, or without the consent of the House. The statement reported to have been issued by the Argentine Government yesterday is not helpful to the process that we all wish to see, that will resolve this dispute." 5/

16. On 30 March, Mr. Luce made the following statement to the House of Commons:

> "A group of Argentines, employed by a commercial contractor, Mr. Davidoff, an Argentine citizen, landed at Leith Harbour on South Georgia on March 19 from an Argentine naval transport vessel.
>
> "Mr. Davidoff had been informed in advance of the need to seek the necessary permission from the British authorities at Grytviken to land and to carry out this salvage work.
>
> "He conveyed to the British Embassy in Buenos Aires his intention to begin work in South Georgia, but gave no indication that he would not follow the normal immigration procedures.

/...

"When the party arrived at Leith it did not seek the required documentation, and when requested by the base commander to proceed to Grytviken in order to do so, it failed to comply.

"Mr. Davidoff's commercial contract is straightforward, but it does not absolve him or his employees from complying with normal immigration procedures.

"Subsequently, the majority of the Argentine party and the Argentine ship departed, but about a dozen men remained on shore.

"We therefore made it clear to the Argentine Government that we regarded them as being present illegally on British territory, and sought their co-operation in arranging for their departure, pointing out however that their position could be regularised if they were to seek the necessary authorization.

"Meanwhile, HMS Endurance was ordered to proceed to the area to be available to assist as necessary. She has been standing by since March 24.

"On March 25, an Argentine vessel delivered further equipment to the group ashore. The Argentine Foreign Minister has said that the Argentine party in South Georgia will be given the full protection of the Argentine Government. Argentine warships are in the area.

"The situation which has thus arisen, while not of our seeking, is potentially dangerous. We have no doubts about British sovereignty over this Falkland Islands dependency as about the Falklands themselves.

"We remain of the view that the unauthorized presence of Argentine citizens in British territory is not acceptable. We have no wish to stand in the way of a normal commercial salvage contract, but the position of those carrying it out must be properly authorized.

"Further escalation of this dispute is in no one's interest. In these circumstances, it is clearly right to pursue a diplomatic solution of this problem. This we are doing. I hope that the Argentine Government will take the same view. ..." 6/

17. In a letter dated 1 April 1982, 7/ the Permanent Representative of Argentina notified the President of the Security Council, on the instructions of his Government and in accordance with the provisions of the Charter of the United Nations, of "the situation of grave tension existing between the Argentine Republic and the United Kingdom of Great Britain and Northern Ireland". He continued:

"On 18 March 1982, workers of Argentine nationality from a private company were transported to the South Georgia Islands by the naval transport vessel Bahía Buen Suceso, where they landed with the prior knowledge of the United Kingdom Embassy in Buenos Aires and therefore of the British Government. All this was done in accordance with a valid commercial contract between an Argentine private company and a British private company. The workers were in possession of the document known as a 'provisional

/...

certificate', the only valid document for travel to the Malvinas, South Georgia and South Sandwich Islands, in accordance with the Argentine-British joint declaration which governs the opening of communications between the mainland territory of Argentina and those islands.

"The situation of tension, which is a cause of serious concern to my Government, was created by the following acts: the uncommon presumption of the British Government in disregarding the 1971 declaration so far as the South Georgia Islands are concerned and the documents introduced under it, and the British threat to use force through the dispatch of vessels belonging to its navy. The latter was expressly admitted by the Secretary of State for Foreign Affairs of the United Kingdom in the House of Lords. In his statement of 30 March, Lord Carrington also stated that his Government was considering security measures which could not be publicly disclosed.

"The concern which these statements caused my Government was increased by news reports which appeared in the British press and were not denied, to the effect that a number of warships, some of them carrying missiles, and two nuclear submarines had been sent to the South Atlantic because of this dispute.

"The conduct of the British Government, which led to the above incidents, combined with a military presence that is unjustified and inimical to the basic principles on which international peace and security rest, is the culmination of a systematic United Kingdom policy aimed at maintaining a position of total disregard for the sovereignty of my country over the Malvinas, South Georgia and South Sandwich Islands, which the Argentine Republic has claimed, always by peaceful means, since their illegal occupation by British military forces in 1833. My Government also wishes to point out that, from the outset, the Argentine Republic has constantly reiterated its incontestable rights over the islands and has maintained its trust in the use of negotiation for a just settlement of the dispute and in the role of the United Nations in putting an end to an unjust and anachronistic colonial situation. To that end, it initiated in 1965, in compliance with resolution 2065 (XX) of the General Assembly of the United Nations, a process of negotiation which has made no progress whatever because of the persistently negative attitude of the British Government and the clearly defined subject matter of which was the dispute concerning sovereignty over these archipelagos.

"One of the many efforts by the Argentine Government mentioned above is the proposal made by the representatives of my country to the representatives of the United Kingdom at the meeting held in New York on 26 and 27 February 1982 for the establishment of a system of monthly meetings aimed at settling the dispute concerning those territories, Argentine sovereignty over which has been recognized by the great majority of the States comprising the international community.

"That proposal by the Argentine Republic received no response from the United Kingdom Government, thus demonstrating once again its indifference to considering by peaceful means and through negotiation a question which affects the territorial integrity and dignity of the Argentine nation.

"I consider it appropriate to place very special emphasis on the fact that the unilateral measures and acts of the British Government have created a situation of grave tension, the continuation of which could eventually endanger the maintenance of international peace and security."

18. In a letter dated 1 April 1982 addressed to the President of the Security Council, 8/ the Permanent Representative of the United Kingdom stated that his Government had "good reason to believe that the armed forces of the Republic of Argentina are about to invade the Falkland Islands", and requested an immediate meeting of the Security Council.

19. The 2345th meeting of the Security Council was held on the same day. During that meeting, statements were made by the two parties setting out their views on the incidents up to that date (S/PV.2345). The representative of the United Kingdom stated, inter alia, that his Government viewed the situation with the utmost seriousness, and that it called on the Security Council to take immediate action to prevent an invasion of the Territory and to maintain international peace and security. He assured the Council that his Government had conducted the recent negotiations "in perfect good faith" and stood ready to continue them in the future. What it found unacceptable was the attempt to change the situation by force.

20. In his remarks, the representative of Argentina said, inter alia, that the representative of the United Kingdom was aware of Argentina's decision to "negotiate generously and with justice" so as to "guarantee the interests of the islands". Argentina was, however, "in no way whatsoever, as we have already indicated, ready to pursue negotiations if there is no prior recognition by the United Kingdom of our sovereignty over the islands. Everything else is open to negotiation".

21. Following consultations among the members at the same meeting, the President issued a statement 9/ on behalf of the Council expressing its concern "about the tension in the region of the Falkland Islands (Malvinas)" and calling upon the Governments of Argentina and the United Kingdom "to exercise the utmost restraint at this time and in particular to refrain from the use or threat of force in the region and to continue the search for a diplomatic solution". The Council also took note of the Secretary-General's "appeal for maximum restraint on both sides".

22. By a letter dated 2 April, 10/ the Permanent Representative of the United Kingdom notified the President of the Security Council that, contrary to the call of the Council of the day before, Argentine forces were at that time invading the Falkland Islands (Malvinas) and requested an immediate meeting of the Security Council.

23. The Security Council continued its discussion of the question at its 2346th and 2347th meetings on 2 April. At its 2350th meeting, on 3 April, the Council adopted resolution 502 (1982) by 10 votes to 1, with 4 abstentions. By that resolution, the Council demanded an immediate cessation of hostilities and an immediate withdrawal of all Argentine forces from the islands, and called on the two Governments to seek a diplomatic solution to their differences and to respect fully the purposes and principles of the Charter.

24.   On 3 April, during a debate in the House of Commons, Mrs. Margaret Thatcher, Prime Minister of the United Kingdom made a statement 11/ in which she reviewed the events leading up to the situation in the Territory, and outlined the steps she intended to take.   A naval task force would be sent to the area; diplomatic efforts were to continue, with the assistance of friendly nations, and also at the United Nations; a review of all aspects of the relationship between Argentina and the United Kingdom was being undertaken, and in that regard, Argentine diplomats were to leave London within four days; economic measures, such as a "freeze" on Argentine assets in the United Kingdom and the suspension of export credits, were also being taken.

25.   In a letter dated 9 April, 12/ the Chargé d'Affaires a.i. of the Permanent Mission of the United Kingdom to the United Nations notified the President of the Security Council of the establishment of a "maritime exclusion zone" extending 200 nautical miles from the Centre of the Territory, effective 0400 Greenwich mean time on 12 April.   That action was being taken by the United Kingdom in exercise of its right to self-defence, since Argentina had not yet begun to comply with resolution 502 (1982) and was steadily reinforcing its forces in the Territory.

26.   On the same date, in a letter to the President of the Security Council, 13/ the Permanent Representative of Argentina stated that his Government had been informed of the imposition of the "maritime exclusion zone", within which any Argentine warships and naval auxiliaries would be treated as hostile and be liable to be attacked by British forces.   The Argentine Government considered that action to constitute a "blockade", and thus an act of aggression under the terms of General Assembly resolution 3314 (XXIX) of 14 December 1974.   It would thus exercise its right to self-defence under Article 51 of the Charter.

27.   On 8 April, the Government of the United States of America offered to assist the two parties in the resolution of the dispute.   Mr. Alexander M. Haig, Jr., the Secretary of State, undertook a series of visits to London and Buenos Aires to this end.   Upon returning to the United States on 14 April to brief the President, Mr. Haig issued a statement on his efforts to date, indicating that the problem was exceptionally difficult and dangerous, requiring flexibility and adjustments on both sides.

28.   On 21 April, by Communiqué No. 25, the Argentine Government made public its position on the Haig discussions, stating, inter alia, that Argentina had always been willing to take heed of the interests of the population of the islands and had made reasonable proposals to consider them; it had also not been unwilling to satisfy those British interests which were reasonable.

29.   On 26 April, at the ministerial meeting of the Organization of American States (OAS) held at Washington, D.C., Mr. Haig said that the surest guide to a peaceful settlement was through implementation of the Security Council resolution 502 (1982).   Earlier at the same meeting, Mr. Nicanor Costa Méndez, Minister of External Relations and Worship of Argentina, had called for the withdrawal of United Kingdom forces from hemispheric waters, and an end to economic sanctions by the European Economic Community (EEC).   He characterized as an act of "perfidy" the United Kingdom's recapture of South Georgia on 25 April while negotiations had still been in progress, and said that the Argentine invasion of the Territory on 2 April had been an attempt to "break the colonial knot".

/...

30.   On 29 April, in a statement to the House of Commons, 14/ Mrs. Thatcher
reiterated the hope that a negotiated settlement could be found, although in order
to strengthen diplomatic efforts military measures had to be taken. Without those
measures she doubted that the Haig initiative would have taken place so quickly.
She therefore intended to enforce a "total exclusion zone" over the same area and
as completely as the maritime exclusion zone had been enforced. The recapture of
South Georgia by British forces on 25 April had been done in exercise of the right
to self-defence under Article 51 of the Charter. On the diplomatic side, she
reaffirmed her confidence in the success of Mr. Haig's efforts.

31.   On 30 April, Mr. Haig stated that the crisis in the South Atlantic was about
to enter "a new and dangerous phase" in which large scale military action was
likely to occur. He outlined the reasons for the efforts at mediation undertaken
by the United States and the proposals put to the two parties; in his view, these
represented an estimate of what they could reasonably be expected to accept, based
on principles of the rule of law and the peaceful settlement of disputes.
Argentina's position remained that it should receive at once an assurance of
eventual sovereignty, or an immediate role leading to it, while the United Kingdom
continued to maintain the the views of the inhabitants be taken into account in any
settlement. As a result of the Argentine failure to accept a compromise, the
United States had to take steps to underscore that it could not support the use of
force to resolve disputes. Those steps included the suspension of all military
exports, the withholding of certification of eligibility for military sales and
suspension of export credits and guarantees to Argentina. The United States would
respond positively to United Kingdom requests for matériel support. It remained
ready to assist both parties in the search for an early and fair settlement.

32.   On 2 May, United Kingdom forces torpedoed and sunk the Argentine cruiser
General Belgrano in waters just outside the "total exclusion zone" (see para. 30
above). While indicating his regret for the resulting Argentine casualties,
Mr. Francis Pym, the United Kingdom Secretary of State for Foreign and Commonwealth
Affairs, said that efforts to reach a negotiated settlement were continuing,
through Mr. Haig and also on the basis of proposals put by the President of Peru.

33.   On the same date the Secretary-General, in separate meetings with Mr. Pym and
the Permanent Representative of Argentina, proposed a number of measures aimed at
achieving a peaceful solution to the conflict.

34.   On 5 May the President of the Security Council, on behalf of the members,
issued a statement 15/ expressing deep concern at the situation in the region and
at the loss of lives, and strongly supporting the efforts of the Secretary-General
with regard to his contacts with the two parties.

35.   On 8 May, the Secretary-General, having received positive responses to his
suggestions from the two parties, began a series of separate meetings with the two
sides in an effort to define point by point the elements of a mutually acceptable
text. On 20 May however, in a letter to the President of the Security Council, 16/
the Secretary-General stated that in his estimation, the time for reaching
agreement through negotiations that would restore peace in the South Atlantic was
extremely short. The efforts in which he had been engaged did not offer the
present prospect of bringing about an end to the conflict. He had thought it

essential to provide that appraisal to the Council in view of the responsibilities it bore under the Charter.

36. At its 2360th meeting on 21 May, in view of the Secretary-General's letter and at the request of Ireland 17/ and Panama, 18/ the Security Council took up the "Question concerning the situation in the region of the Falkland Islands (Islas Malvinas)". At that meeting, the Secretary-General recounted his efforts at negotiation. In his view, essential agreement had been reached by the end of the second week of May on the following points:

(a) The agreement sought would be of an interim nature, without prejudice to rights, claims or positions of the parties;

(b) It would cover: (i) a cease fire; (ii) the mutual withdrawal of forces; (iii) the termination of exclusion zones and economic measures; (iv) the interim administration of the Territory; and (v) negotiations towards a peaceful settlement;

(c) The initiation of the various parts of the agreement would be simultaneous;

(d) The withdrawal of forces would be phased and would be under the supervision of United Nations observers;

(e) The temporary administration of the Territory would be under the authority of the United Nations; the United Nations flag would be flown and Argentina and the United Kingdom would establish liaison offices on which their flags could be flown;

(f) The parties would enter into negotiations in good faith under the auspices of the Secretary-General, which they would seek to complete by 31 December 1982.

37. At that point there had still been a number of crucial differences to be resolved on which options were being considered by the two parties. However, on studying texts received between 17 and 19 May from the two parties, the Secretary-General had found that they did not reflect the progress he had thought to have been achieved in the previous exchanges. He had, however, put forward suggestions which he believed could open the way for a solution.

38. Speaking during the same meeting of the Council, the representative of Argentina observed other things:

(a) That the United Kingdom had rejected certain ideas relating to the mutual withdrawal of forces, the maintenance of communications between the islands and Argentina during the interim administration and the operation of certain services by Argentina;

(b) That Argentina had been prepared not to place any preconditions on the negotiations in view of its confidence in its legitimate authority, recognized by both OAS and the Non-Aligned Movement; however, the United Kingdom had sought to place conditions on the negotiating process by insisting on a United Nations administration which would retain a colonial administrative structure which could prejudge and place conditions on the substantive issues;

(c) That the United Kingdom did not accept any references to General Assembly resolution 1514 (XV) or the resolutions of the General Assembly on the question of the Falkland Islands (Malvinas);

(d) That the United Kingdom had attempted to divide the Territory, submitting to negotiation only one archipelago while keeping the two dependencies;

(e) That the United Kingdom wished to maintain the provisional United Nations administration indefinitely, thus drawing out the negotiations for as long as the United Kingdom desired.

39. The representative of Argentina concluded by thanking the Secretary-General for his efforts and reaffirming to the Security Council his Government's constant will to negotiate.

40. During the same meeting of the Council, the representative of the United Kingdom said that in the text submitted to the Secretary-General on 17 May his Government had shown as much flexibility as possible without compromising or abandoning certain principles. The United Kingdom had had a number of requirements:

(a) To secure withdrawal of the Argentine forces, as demanded by Security Council resolution 502 (1982);

(b) To establish a cease-fire as soon as withdrawal was agreed;

(c) To provide for the democratic administration of the islands in any interim arrangement;

(d) To ensure that the terms-of reference of the negotiations should not prejudge the outcome, whether on sovereignty or any other matter.

41. At the same time the United Kingdom had been prepared to contemplate a parallel mutual withdrawal under United Nations supervision, followed by a short interim period under United Nations administration so as to enable the diplomatic process to go ahead. It had been prepared to accept Argentine representation in the democratic institutions of the Territory disproportionate to the size of the Argentine community, as well as the presence of an Argentine observer during the interim period.

42. However, the Argentine response to the United Kingdom proposals had been unsatisfactory, especially the insistence on including South Georgia and the South Sandwich Islands in the agreement; the insistence on an unequal withdrawal of forces; the rejection of the continued functioning of the democratic institutions of the Territory during the interim period; the idea of parity in numbers of advisers between the Argentine population of 30 and the British population of about 1,800; the requirement of freedom of access to residents and property during the interim period, which would have enabled Argentina to change the demographic status of the islands; and the formulation as to how, when and by what means the negotiations should be concluded.

43. Although the United Kingdom Government was prepared to consider any avenue which promised to lead to a peaceful solution to the crisis, it could not allow itself to be inhibited from carrying out military action in accordance with its right to self-defence under Article 51 of the Charter.

44. At its 2368th meeting, on 26 May, the Security Council adopted unanimously resolution 505 (1982), by which it re-affirmed its resolution 502 (1982) and expressed its concern to achieve as a matter of the greatest urgency a cessation of hostilities and an end to the conflict between the armed forces of Argentina and the United Kingdom. The Council expressed appreciation for the efforts made by the Secretary-General to bring about agreement between the parties and to ensure the implementation of resolution 502 (1982) and thus to restore peace to the region, and requested him to undertake a renewed mission of good offices bearing in mind that resolution and the approach outlined in his statement of 21 May 1982. It urged the parties to co-operate fully with the Secretary-General in his mission and requested the Secretary-General to contact the parties with a view to negotiating acceptable terms for a cease-fire, including the possible dispatch of United Nations observers to monitor the cease-fire. Finally, it requested the Secretary-General to submit an interim report within seven days.

45. On 2 June, the Secretary-General submitted an interim report to the Security Council 19/ as requested by resolution 505 (1982). He stated that he had held extensive exchanges with the parties, seeking from each a statement of the terms it considered acceptable for a cease-fire. However, it was his considered judgement that the positions of the two parties did not offer the possibility of developing mutually acceptable terms for a cease-fire at that time. In accordance with his mandate, he would remain in close contact with the two parties.

46. At its 2372nd meeting on 3 June, at the request of Panama, 20/ the Security Council continued its consideration of the situation in the region of the Falkland Islands (Islas Malvinas). At the 2373rd meeting, on 4 June, a draft resolution 21/ proposed by Panama and Spain was put to the vote. There were 9 votes in favour, 2 against (the United Kingdom and the United States) and 4 abstentions. The draft resolution was thus not adopted owing to the negative vote of a permanent member of the Council. Under the draft resolution, the Council would have reaffirmed its resolutions 502 (1982) and 505 (1982) and the need for implementation of all parts thereof, and requested the parties to cease fire in the region immediately and initiate simultaneously all parts of those resolutions. It would also have authorized the Secretary-General to use all necessary means to ensure compliance, and requested him to make an interim report to the Council within 72 hours and to keep the Council informed as to the implementation of the resolution.

47. In a statement to the Council before the vote was taken, the representative of the United Kingdom said that he would have wished to see language appropriate to bringing about an immediate cease-fire linked inseparably to the immediate and total withdrawal of all Argentine forces from the Territory. The proposed draft did not make such a linkage and would enable Argentina to re-open the endless process of negotiation, leaving its armed forces in illegal occupation of parts of the islands. The United Kingdom would therefore vote against the draft resolution.

48. After the vote was taken, the representative of Argentina stated that under the draft resolution the Council would have assumed its minimal responsibility under the Charter for maintaining international peace and security. It would have called for a cease-fire in order to save human lives and to stop a war, so that the United Nations could serve the cause of peace. However, the United Kingdom had used its veto to prevent that and to serve its own colonial end. The United Kingdom was thus solely responsible for all the deaths, Argentine or British, which would henceforth be caused in the dispute.

49. On 14 June, at Port Stanley, Argentine forces in the Falkland Islands (Malvinas) under Brigadier General Mario Menéndez surrendered to Major-General Jeremy Moore of the United Kingdom forces, after a de facto cease-fire had occurred some hours earlier. Reporting to the House of Commons on the retaking of the Territory, Mrs. Thatcher said that she had sought from Argentina confirmation of a complete cessation of hostilities, as the victory had ended fighting in the islands but not necessarily the state of undeclared war with Argentina. Mrs. Thatcher also said that she would send Mr. Hunt back to the Territory to take over the civilian government while military affairs remained under Major General Moore. She indicated that she did not intend to allow Argentina any future voice in the Territory and that she did "not intend to negotiate on the sovereignty of the islands in any way except with the people who live there". She also ruled out any participation by the United Nations.

50. In a letter dated 17 June addressed to the President of the Security Council, 22/ the Chargé d'Affaires, a.i. of the Permanent Mission of Argentina to the United Nations transmitted Communiqué No. 166 of 16 June 1982, confirming the de facto cease-fire in the area of Port Stanley.

III. ECONOMIC CONDITIONS

51. The economy of the Territory is almost entirely dependent on sheep farming for wool production. The grasslands are generally poor, owing to difficult climatic and soil conditions, and the resulting yield per hectare is low. In 1975, the United Kingdom Government established and financed a Grasslands Trial Unit (GTU) to conduct research into the improvement of pastures and related aspects of sheep farming. The work of GTU was reviewed early in 1978 by experts from the United Kingdom, and technical alterations and changes of emphasis made in its programme. In July 1979, the staff of GTU was increased from four to six and a standing Committee of the United Kingdom Overseas Development Administration (ODA) was established to monitor GTU.

52. In 1978/79, the latest year for which figures are available, there were 659,012 sheep in the Territory, an increase of 10,646 over the record figure of the previous year. The distribution was as follows: East Falkland, 377,237; West Falkland, 213,743; and other islands, 68,032.

53. The economy depends heavily on the price of wool on the world market. Over the past few years production costs have tended to rise while the world market price has remained static. In 1980, total receipts for exports of wool amounted to £2,661,000 23/ and for hides and skins to £11,000 (£2,463,615 and £38,636,

/...

respectively, in 1979). In the recent past, expert assistance in the tanning and processing of sheepskins and hides and in the proper evaluation and preparation of wool clip for marketing has been provided to the Territory.

54. The development of the Territory has been closely linked with the Falklands Islands Company (FIC), which was registered in the United Kingdom in 1851. In 1977, FIC was purchased by the Coalite Group from Charrington's Industrial Holdings. It is the largest producer of wool in the Territory, owning almost half the sheep, and employs a large proportion of the work force and controls much of the local banking, commerce and shipping. It charters the 499 ton freighter AES, which supplies the islands four times per year. The company's turnover is approximately £3 million annually, half of which represents wool sales and the other half commerce in the islands. According to published reports, FIC accounts for less than 2 per cent of Coalite's business.

55. It will be recalled that a report prepared by Lord Shackleton, entitled Economic Survey of the Falkland Islands, 24/ was issued by the United Kingdom Government in 1976. From January to February 1976, Lord Shackleton and a team of experts carried out an economic and fiscal survey of the Territory, bearing in mind "the weakening of the Territory's economy and the decline in population" and "the present uncertain economic climate". The mission was entrusted with assessing and making recommendations concerning prospects for development in oil, minerals, fisheries, wool and alginates. The mission was further requested to advise on the need for capital expenditure over the next five years, and to assess the financial and social implications of any recommendations.

56. In the introduction to his report, Lord Shackleton stated that the terms of reference were very wide, since it was intended to provide an over-all survey of the economic prospects of the Territory in all sectors. In order to assess fully the development potential, account had to be taken of the social dimensions of the situation. However, the terms of reference had excluded any political considerations and the report was thus based on the premise that the political status of the Territory would remain as it had been over the past 150 years. It was nonetheless stated that in certain proposed areas of development, particularly those related to the exploitation of off-shore resources, "co-operation with Argentina - even participation - should, if possible, be secured".

57. Lord Shackleton suggested three measures which he considered fundamental to any major development programme:

   (a) A reversal of the outflow of funds from the Territory to the United Kingdom, to provide for investment locally;

   (b) Extension of the airport runway to handle large aircraft, at an additional investment of £5.5 million by the United Kingdom Government;

   (c) The appointment of a Chief Executive, directly under the Governor, to be responsible for economic and social development.

58.   By 1981, only the first of those measures had been implemented. Among the
other proposals made in the Shackleton report, the following were being
implemented: the construction of an all-weather Stanley-Darwin road and a school
hostel at Stanley; the provision of a new aircraft for local service, as well as an
ambulance and X-ray equipment for the medical service; the establishment of a road
construction unit under the Public Works Department; and the strengthening of GTU.
In addition, a development officer and fiscal adviser were appointed and advisory
visits had been made in various fields. On 15 June 1982, speaking in the House of
Commons, Mrs. Thatcher said that in recognition of the need for economic
development, she had asked Lord Shackleton to update his 1976 report as a matter of
urgency.

59.   Other potential areas of economic development include tourism, fisheries and
the processing of kelp into alginates. At one time, Alginate Industries, Ltd., was
making plans for the production of alginate in the Territory, but discontinued them
in 1977. In the past years, new approaches have been made to commercial
companies. The Taiyo Fishing Company of Japan and, more recently, the White Fish
Authority of the United Kingdom have been carrying out research into the fisheries
resources of the Territory. There are stocks of king crab and of krill, a small
prawn high in protein; several countries are interested in the exploitation of the
latter.

60.   Tourism, which is based on the abundance of marine and bird-life in the
Territory, including colonies of albatross, seals and geese, was the subject of a
recent study in which the Government invested some £25,000. Recent reports
indicate that Mr. Julian Fitter, the tourism expert who made the study, has set up
an organization called Falkland Wildlife to take tourists by ship to visit the
wild-life areas of the Territory.

61.   As noted above (see para. 51), the Territory specializes in the production of
wool for export and depends heavily on imported goods for the satisfaction of local
requirements. The United Kingdom continues to absorb most of the Territory's
exports and to provide most of its imports. In 1980, total imports amounted to
£259,321. Recently, attempts have been made to increase trade relations between
the Territory and the Argentine mainland and also with Chile.

62.   According to approved budget estimates for 1981/82, ordinary revenue would
amount to £2,478,311 (compared with revised estimates of £2,298,325 for 1980/81),
while expenditure would amount to £2,411,004, leaving a surplus of £67,307. The
major items of revenue were customs duties and harbour fees, internal revenue,
posts and telecommunications and municipal services. The principal items of
expenditure were aviation (£283,703), education (£256,274), medical (£269,772),
posts and telecommunications (£280,316) and public works (£598,007). From 1976 to
1980, the total amount of United Kingdom aid for development was £6.6 million, an
average of £735 per head per annum. Among the major projects financed during this
period were the electricity power station, the airport at Stanley; grants towards
the construction of an all-weather road between Stanley and Darwin and the building
of the secondary school hostel at Stanley.

63.   In 1971, the Governments of Argentina, the Falkland Islands (Malvinas) and the
United Kingdom signed a Communications Agreement at Buenos Aires, designed to

/...

improve economic, social and cultural co-operation between the Falkland Islands
(Malvinas) and Argentina. Air communications between Argentina and Stanley were
operated on a weekly basis by Líneas Aéreas del Estado (LADE), a State-owned
Argentine airline until April 1982. The permanent airport at Stanley, constructed
with United Kingdom aid at a cost of £6 million and by Argentine technicians, was
opened to traffic on 1 May 1979. The airport was designed to take aircraft up to
the size of the Hawker Siddeley HS-748 or other medium-haul aircraft.

IV. SOCIAL AND EDUCATIONAL CONDITIONS

64. The Government maintains a 170-bed general hospital at Stanley, providing
medical, surgical, obstetric and geriatric care. Of the original 27 beds, 10 have
been converted to provide hostel accommodations. The Medical Department is
responsible for public health and sanitation in the Territory and employs one
senior medical officer, two medical officers and other staff. A general
practitioner is available in the town, while a flying-doctor service reaches the
outlying farm settlements.

65. The installation at the hospital of new X-ray equipment, acquired at a cost of
£32,000 with funds from the United Kingdom, was completed late in 1980.
Expenditure on public health for the year 1981/82 was estimated at £269,772.

66. According to information submitted by the administering Power, there were
313 pupils attending the 11 government schools, which are staffed by 32 teachers.
Education is free and attendance compulsory in Stanley for children between the
ages of 5 and 15 years, and outside Stanley, for those between the ages of 7 and
15 years. Education is provided mainly at the primary level, except at the Senior
School at Stanley, which offers secondary education in a limited range of subjects
up to the ordinary level of the General Certificate of Education. In 1978,
scholarships for secondary education abroad were discontinued and in 1979, it was
announced that overseas education allowances would also be discontinued once the
current beneficiaries had completed their studies. Until April 1982 the Argentine
Government provided an unlimited number of scholarships for secondary education of
students from the Territory, although in practice few of these were taken up. It
also provided two teachers of Spanish for the schools at Stanley.

Notes

1/ The information contained in this paper has been derived from published
reports and from information transmitted to the Secretary-General by the Government
of the United Kingdom of Great Britain and Northern Ireland under Article 73 e of
the Charter of the United Nations on 27 July 1982.

2/ Official Records of the General Assembly, Twenty-fifth Session,
Supplement No. 23 (A/8023/Rev.1), vol. IV, chap. XIX, annex, paras. 4-7; and ibid.,
Thirty-third Session, Supplement No. 23 (A/33/23/Rev.1), vol. IV, chap. XXVIII,
annex I, paras. 4-7.

3/ The "camp" is used locally to describe all those areas of the Falkland
Islands (Malvinas) outside Stanley, including the settlements.

4/   Official Records of the General Assembly, Thirty-third Session, Supplement No. 23 (A/33/23/Rev.1), vol. IV, chap. XXVIII, para. 14.

5/   Parliamentary Debates, House of Commons, 3 March 1982, cols. 263-264.

6/ ˙ Ibid., 30 March 1982, cols. 163-164.

7/   Official Records of the Security Council, Thirty-seventh Year, Supplement for April, May and June 1982, document S/14940.

8/   Ibid., document S/14942.

9/   Ibid., document S/14944.

10/   Ibid., document S/14946.

11/   Parliamentary Debates, House of Commons, 3 April 1982, cols. 633-638.

12/   Official Records of the Security Council, op. cit., document S/14963.

13/   Ibid., document S/14961.

14/   Parliamentary Debates, House of Commons, 29 April 1982, cols. 980-982.

15/   Official Records of the Security Council, op. cit., document S/15047.

16/   Ibid., document S/15099.

17/   Ibid., document S/15037.

18/   Ibid., document S/15100.

19/   Ibid., document S/15151.

20/   Ibid., document S/15145.

21/   Ibid., document S/15156/Rev.2.

22/   Ibid., document S/15229.

23/   The local currency is the pound sterling.

24/   London, H.M. Stationery Office, 1976.

NITED
ATIONS

A

General Assembly

Distr.
GENERAL

A/37/193
17 August 1982
ENGLISH
ORIGINAL: SPANISH

irty-seventh session

REQUEST FOR THE INCLUSION OF A SUPPLEMENTARY ITEM
IN THE AGENDA OF THE THIRTY-SEVENTH SESSION

QUESTION OF THE MALVINAS ISLANDS

Letter dated 16 August 1982 from the Ministers for Foreign Affairs
of Argentina, Bolivia, Brazil, Chile, Colombia, Costa Rica, Cuba,
Dominican Republic, Ecuador, El Salvador, Guatemala, Haiti, Honduras,
Mexico, Nicaragua, Panama, Paraguay, Peru, Uruguay and Venezuela
addressed to the Secretary-General

Under rule 14 of the rules of procedure of the General Assembly, the Ministers
or Foreign Affairs of the countries of Latin America, who have signed this letter,
equest the inclusion in the agenda of the thirty-seventh regular session of the
eneral Assembly of a supplementary item entitled "Question of the Malvinas
slands".

Furthermore, pursuant to rule 20 of the rules of procedure, the reasons behind
ur request for the inclusion of this item are stated below.

The persistence of this colonial situation in America and the dispute between
he Argentine Republic and the United Kingdom of Great Britain and Northern Ireland
oncerning sovereignty over the Islands, on which the General Assembly has
xpressed itself in resolutions 2065 (XX), 3160 (XXVIII) and 31/49, have led to
erious armed conflict in the South Atlantic and constitute a situation that
ffects the Latin American region in particular.

The countries of America, which are peace-loving and anxious for a peaceful
ettlement of the conflict, consider that the negotiations between the Argentine
epublic and the United Kingdom of Great Britain and Northern Ireland should be
onducted under the auspices of the United Nations.

The General Assembly of the Organization, in which the international community
s represented, constitutes an appropriate forum for considering the item.

For the foregoing reasons, we request that the question of the Malvinas Islands be considered by the General Assembly, so that the latter may urge the parties to the dispute to resume, under United Nations auspices and at the earliest possible date, the negotiations with a view to a peaceful settlement.

(<u>Signed</u>)   Juan Ramón AGUIERRE LANARI
Minister for Foreign Affairs and Worship
of Argentina

Agustín SAAVEDRA WEISC
Minister for Foreign Affairs and Worship
of Bolivia

Ramiro SARAIVA GUERREIRO
Minister for Foreign Affairs of Brazil

René ROJAS GALDAMES
Minister for Foreign Affairs of Chile

Rodrigo LLOREDA CAICEDO
Minister for Foreign Affairs of Colombia

Fernando VOLIO JIMENEZ
Minister for Foreign Affairs of Costa Rica

Isidoro MALMIERCA PEOLI
Minister for Foreign Affairs of Cuba

Pedro PADILLA TONOS
Minister for Foreign Affairs
of the Dominican Republic

Luis VALENCIA RODRIGUEZ
Minister for Foreign Affairs of Ecuador

Fidel CHAVEZ MENA
Minister for Foreign Affairs of El Salvador

Eduardo CASTILLO ARRIOLA
Minister for Foreign Affairs of Guatemala

Jean Robert ESTIME
Minister for Foreign Affairs and Worship
of Haiti

Edgardo PAZ BARNICA
Minister for Foreign Affairs of Honduras

Jorge CASTAÑEDA
Minister for Foreign Affairs of Mexico

Miguel D'ESCOTO BROCKMANN
Minister for Foreign Affairs of Nicaragua

Jorge E. ILLUECA
Minister for Foreign Affairs of Panama

Alberto NOGUES
Minister for Foreign Affairs of Paraguay

Javier ARIAS STELLA
Minister for Foreign Affairs of Peru

Estanislao VALDES OTERO
Minister for Foreign Affairs of Uruguay

José Alberto ZAMBRANO VELASCO
Minister for Foreign Affairs of Venezuela

ITED
TIONS

General Assembly

Distr.
GENERAL

A/37/553
20 October 1982
ENGLISH
ORIGINAL: SPANISH

hirty-seventh session
genda item 135

QUESTION OF THE MALVINAS ISLANDS (FALKLANDS)

Letter dated 18 October 1982 from the Permanent Representative of
Argentina to the United Nations addressed to the Secretary-General

I have the honour to request you to have the attached document entitled
Question of the Malvinas Islands and the United Nations General Assembly" and its
nnexes circulated as a General Assembly document under agenda item 135.

(Signed) Carlos Manuel MUÑIZ
Ambassador
Permanent Representative

82-27968   0417u (E)

ANNEX

QUESTION OF THE MALVINAS ISLANDS AND THE
UNITED NATIONS GENERAL ASSEMBLY

I.   BACKGROUND

1.   The question of the Malvinas Islands pertains to the dispute between Argentina and the United Kingdom concerning sovereignty over the Malvinas, South Georgia and South Sandwich Islands.

2.   The dispute began in 1833, when military forces of the United Kingdom forcibly invaded and occupied those territories and ousted the Argentine authorities and population. From its independence to 1833, Argentina exercised effective sovereignty over the Islands.

These and other historical facts pertaining to the sovereign rights of Argentina are referred to in detail in annex I.

3.   Argentina never agreed to this violation of its territorial integrity. Since 1833 it has repeatedly demanded the return of the unlawfully seized territories.

4.   In 1946, the United Kingdom placed the Malvinas on the United Nations list of Non-Self-Governing Territories. Accordingly, Argentina made an express reservation on sovereignty, which was reiterated whenever the British Government reported on the Malvinas to the General Assembly.

5.   In 1964, the Special Committee on Decolonization considered the Question of the Malvinas Islands for the first time. On that occasion, Argentina

(a) Demanded the re-establishment of its territorial integrity through the return of the Malvinas, South Georgia and South Sandwich Islands;

(b) Stated that it would give special consideration to the well-being and material interests of the inhabitants of the Islands;

(c) Stressed that the indiscriminate application of the right of self-determination to territories populated by nationals of the colonial Power which had illegally occupied them by force would place the future of those territories in the hands of that Power; and

(d) Maintained that the right of self-determination should not be used to give a Power full sovereignty over an illegally held possession under the protective mantle of the United Nations.

In spite of United Kingdom opposition to entering into negotiations with Argentina on these issues and its arguments with respect to self-determination, the Special Committee, on 13 November 1964, adopted conclusions and recommendations inviting the Governments of Argentina and the United Kingdom to initiate

/...

negotiations on sovereignty which would rule out the applicability of the right of self-determination to this case. The text of this decision and those mentioned elsewhere in this note are contained in annex II.

6.   The conclusions and recommendations of the Committee were reiterated by the General Assembly in resolution 2065 (XV), adopted on 16 December 1965.

In that resolution, the General Assembly, considering that, in accordance with resolution 1514 (XV), it was necessary to bring colonialism to an end everywhere in all its forms, one of which covered the Malvinas question:

(a)   Noted the existence of a dispute between Argentina and the United Kingdom over the said Islands, and

(b)   Invited both parties to proceed without delay with the negotiations, bearing in mind the provisions and objectives of the Charter and of General Assembly resolution 1514 (XV) as well as the interests of the population of the Islands.

Thus the General Assembly expressly recognized that there was a dispute concerning sovereignty over the territory and that there were only two parties to the dispute: the Governments of Argentina and of the United Kingdom. The Assembly established further that finding a solution to the dispute was the only way to bring to an end the colonial situation in the Malvinas and ruled out the applicability of the right of self-determination to this particular special case.

7.   On the basis of resolution 2065 (XX) in January 1966, the Ministers of Foreign Affairs of Argentina and the United Kingdom signed a joint communiqué in which they agreed to conduct negotiations, which began in July and continued in November 1966 in London.

On 20 December 1966, the General Assembly adopted its first consensus on the Question of the Malvinas Islands, in which it urged "both parties to continue with the negotiations so as to find a peaceful solution as soon as possible".

The negotiations continued in 1967, and this was reported to the General Assembly. On 19 December 1967 the Assembly adopted a second consensus similar in tenor to that of 1966.

In August 1968, the Argentine and British delegations to the negotiations agreed on the final text of a Memorandum of Understanding; if the United Kingdom had not subsequently refused to implement it, it would have led to a settlement of the dispute. The Memorandum established that the United Kingdom would recognize Argentine sovereignty over the Islands when it was satisfied with the guarantees and safeguards which the Argentine Government pledged to the islanders.

8.   The United Kingdom's rejection of the Memorandum and subsequent refusal to negotiate about sovereignty resulted in five years of virtual stagnation in the negotiations.

/...

For that reason, on 15 August 1973 the Government of Argentina sent a note to the Secretary-General (A/9121) requesting the United Kingdom Government to proceed without further delay to the resumption of the negotiations called for in resolution 2065 (XX) and the subsequent consensus adopted by the General Assembly, with a view to ending the colonial situation in the territory as soon as possible.

The General Assembly recognized that the negotiations had collapsed owing to British intransigence. On 14 December 1973, therefore, it adopted resolution 3160 (XXVIII) in which it again declared the need to accelerate the negotiations envisaged in resolution 2065 (XX) in order to arrive at a peaceful solution of the conflict of sovereignty. The Assembly also reiterated that only the settlement of the conflict would put an end to the colonial situation in those territories and that there are only two parties to the dispute: the Governments of Argentina and the United Kingdom. At the same time, the Assembly again ruled out the applicability of the right to self-determination.

9. Despite resolution 3160 (XXVIII), the United Kingdom continued to refuse to negotiate over sovereignty.

This persistent intransigence caused the progressive deterioration of relations between Argentina and the United Kingdom, creating the situation outlined in document A/AC.109/L.1105, prepared by the Secretariat for the Special Committee on Decolonization.

As a result, the General Assembly was once again obliged to give special consideration to the matter. On 1 December 1976, the Assembly adopted resolution 31/49, in which it again requested the Governments of Argentina and the United Kingdom to expedite the negotiations concerning the dispute over sovereignty, as requested in resolutions 2065 (XX) and 3160 (XXVIII).

An important feature of resolution 31/49 is that it takes into account the decisions of the Movement of Non-Aligned Countries, which since 1975 has firmly supported the just claim of the Republic of Argentina for the return of the territory of the Malvinas thus putting an end to the illegal situation prevailing there. In addition, the Movement has expressed the view that the Malvinas constitute a special and particular case to which the principle of the right of colonial peoples to self-determination is not applicable. The principles and decisions adopted by the Movement of Non-Aligned Countries on the matter are contained in annex III.

It is important to note that the position held by the Movement of Non-Aligned Countries is fully in accord with that of Latin America, which also has consistently recognized Argentine sovereignty over the Malvinas and demanded the return of those territories to the national patrimony. Some of the statements of the Latin American position on the item are given in annex IV.

II. DRAFT RESOLUTION A/37/L.3

1. The cause of the Malvinas is a Latin American cause. For this reason, 20 countries (Argentina, Bolivia, Brazil, Chile, Colombia, Costa Rica, Cuba,

Dominican Republic, Ecuador, El Salvador, Guatemala, Haiti, Honduras, Mexico, Nicaragua, Panama, Paraguay, Peru, Uruguay and Venezuela) have requested the inclusion in the agenda of the thirty-seventh session of the General Assembly of a special item entitled "Question of the Falkland Islands (Malvinas)" (item 135) and have co-sponsored draft resolution A/37/L.3. The draft resolution, which is strictly in line with previous United Nations resolutions on the Malvinas, has one simple and constructive aim: the resumption of negotiations between Argentina and the United Kingdom so that a solution may be found as soon as possible to the sovereignty dispute. These negotiations should take place within the framework of the United Nations, with the assistance and the good offices of the Secretary-General, who is requested to submit a report to the General Assembly at its thirty-eighth session.

Latin America, whose position on the question of the Malvinas is of fundamental importance because the territory is situated in that region, trusts that the other regional groups will support draft resolution A/37/L.3, since it proposes the only viable alternative for a just, peaceful and permanent settlement of the question.

Annex I

HISTORY OF THE MALVINAS ISLANDS

I. DISCOVERY

The documents extant show that the islands were discovered by Spanish navigators.

1.   The islands appear on early sixteenth-century Spanish maps and planispheres. The first map is that of Pedro Reinel (1522-1523), who marked an archipelago at 53° 55' latitude south. It also appears later in the works of the chief cartographer of Charles V of Spain. Diego Rivero, who included the islands on the maps known as Castiglione (1526-1527), Salviati (1526-1527), Rivero (1527) and two planispheres of 1529, and on the Yslario de Santa Cruz (1541), the planisphere of Sebastián Gaboto (1544) and the maps of Diego Gutiérrez (1561) and Bartolomé Olives (1562).

2.   The credit for discovering the archipelago belongs to the navigator Esteban Gómez who sailed with Magellan's Spanish expedition in 1520.

Simón de Alcazaba and Alonso de Camargo also sailed in the area in 1534 and 1540 respectively. The latter were navigators of Spanish ships sailing for the Strait of Magellan, the discovery of the Strait and its proximity to the Malvinas were two of the factors on which Spain's rights to the islands were based.

In 1580, Sarmiento de Gamboa symbolically laid claim to the Strait and the nearby islands and, in 1584, founded a settlement.

The United Kingdom claims that John Davis in 1592 and Richard Hawkins in 1594 discovered the archipelago, but the English map-makers of the period did not mark the islands on their maps, nor is there any evidence to substantiate such claims of discovery. The fact of the matter is that until the middle of the eighteenth century, London was unaware of the existence of the Malvinas Islands, at most they were confused with certain hypothetical Pepys Islands.

3.   Only in 1748, at the suggestion of Admiral Anson, did England decide to send an expedition to "<u>discover</u>" and settle the islands. With that in mind, it consulted Spain in 1749 and, when it met with resistance from Madrid, abandoned its plans. That consultation shows that English recognized Spain's rights over the island and the coasts of South America.

II. SPAIN'S RIGHT OVER THE ISLANDS

These rights were granted by the papal bulls <u>Inter Coetera</u> and <u>Dudum si Quidem</u>, issued <u>erga omnes</u>, and the Treaty of Tordesillas (1497) between Spain and Portugal, and recognized by the British Crown in treaties between Spain and England.

/...

1.   The Treaty of Peace of 1604 annulled such rights as might have been acquired over the islands prior to its signature, including those based on the alleged English discovery.

2.   Under the Treaty of Madrid of 1670, it was agreed that England would retain all the lands, islands, colonies and dominions it possessed in America. That recognition of English sovereignty in North America was coupled with another provision stipulating that "the subjects of the King of Great Britain shall not sail unto and trade in the havens and places which the Catholic King holdeth in the said Indies".

3.   The Treaty of Madrid of 1713 provided that "Her Britannic Majesty has agreed to publish immediately the strongest prohibitions to all her subjects, under the most rigorous penalties, that no ship of the English nation shall venture to pass to the South Sea or to trade in any other region of the Spanish Indies". That provision prohibiting Great Britain from navigating and trading in areas not open to traffic at the end of the seventeenth century was ratified at Utrecht in 1713.

4.   Consequently, in 1749, when England tried to send its first expedition, the Malvinas Islands could not be considered res nullius, there for the taking.

III. OCCUPATION AND SETTLEMENT OF THE ISLANDS

1.   In February 1764, the French navigator Louis Antoîne de Bougainville founded Port Louis in the name of the King of France on the Eastern Malvina.

Spain formally protested to the French Government and obtained recognition of its rights of dominion. On 1 April 1767, on the order of Louis XV, de Bougainville handed Port Louis over to the Spanish authorities.

Those authorities had been appointed by a royal letter patent of 4 October 1766 placing the islands under the Captaincy-General of Buenos Aires and designating Felipe Ruiz Puente Governor. The Spanish continued to occupy Port Louis (whose name was changed to Puerto Soledad) with Spanish settlers and a military garrison.

2.   In the same year, England, which had not made any reservations concerning the transfer of Port Louis to Spain, sent a secret expedition which founded Port Egmont on Saunders Island, near the Western Malvina.

On 10 June 1770, the British garrison was ousted from Saunders Island by Spanish forces under the command of the Governor of Buenos Aires, Buccarelli. The manner in which the act was carried out provoked a protest to the Court of Madrid.

On 22 January 1771, Spain agreed to return Port Egmont to the British Crown on the express condition that that gesture - intended solely to save face for Britain - could not and should not in any way affect Spain's pre-existing right of sovereignty over the Malvinas Islands. That declaration of sovereignty was accepted without reservation by England.

/...

The 1771 agreement was apparently accompanied by a British commitment to withdraw from Port Egmont after a certain period of time. Accordingly, the English left on 22 May 1774. They returned only in 1833, when, illegally and by force, they expelled the Argentine authorities and population and seized control of the archipelago.

3. Between 1766 and 1810, the year in which Argentina broke its ties with Madrid, the islands were Spanish possessions and were administered by an uninterrupted succession of 30 Spanish governors responsible to the resident authority in Buenos Aires.

Throughout that period, England never questioned Spanish sovereignty over the Malvinas and went so far as to sign international agreements prohibiting the British from sailing in the South Atlantic (Treaty of Peace of Versailles, 1783) and settling on the coasts and islands occupied by Spain in southern America (Convention of San Lorenzo, 1790). Nor did England protest in 1776, when Spain created the Vice-Regency of the Rio de la Plata with headquarters in Buenos Aires and jurisdiction over the Malvinas.

IV. ARGENTINE RIGHTS OF SOVEREIGNTY OVER THE ISLANDS

1. Like the countries of Africa in the twentieth century, the New Latin American States in the nineteenth century for the most part drew the boundaries of their territories along the lines of the old colonial administrative divisions and proclaimed themselves sole and exclusive heirs to all titles and sovereign rights of the former metropolitan Power in those territories. The international community of the time, including England, recognized those boundaries and did not question that assertion.

2. Argentina, when it became independent in 1816, became heir to the territorial jurisdiction of the former Spanish Vice-Regency of the Rio de la Plata. As we have seen, the Malvinas were part of that Vice-Regency.

3. Consequently, as soon as it could, the Argentine Government carried out acts of possession, occupation and administration inherent in its right of sovereignty over the islands. For example:

(a) In 1820, it notified vessels operating in the waters around the Malvinas of the Argentine laws regulating hunting and fishing in the area, let it be known, that trespassers would be sent to Buenos Aires to be prosecuted, and took formal possession of the islands.

No Government objected to the assertion of Argentina's right to the archipelago or lodged any complaint about it despite the fact that the announcement was published in newspapers in England, the United States and other countries.

(b) In 1823, it appointed Pablo Areguarí Governor of the Malvinas.

(c) That same year, it granted land as well as grazing and fishing rights on the Western Malvina to Jorge Pacheco and Luis Vernet. Those two Argentines brought a number of families to the islands and after overcoming many hardships, they were permanently settled in 1826.

(d)   In 1828, it issued a decree granting concessions to Vernet on the Eastern Malvina as a demonstration of its special interest in promoting the economic development of the archipelago and declared the new settlement to be exempt from any taxes except those which might be required to maintain the local authorities.

(e)   In 1829, it established the Political and Military Command of the Malvinas, with headquarters at Puerto Soledad and jurisdiction over all the islands in the vicinity of Cape Horn in the Atlantic zone.   The above-mentioned Luis Vernet was appointed Commander.

(f)   In 1831, it seized United States fishing vessels operating in Malvinas waters in violation of Argentine legislation and rejected a protest from Washington against that enforcement of the law in its territorial waters.

(g)   In 1832, Juan Esteban Mestivier was appointed Governor of the islands and he was succeeded by Jose M. Pinedo.

V.   THE ILLEGAL OCCUPATION OF THE ISLANDS IN 1833 BY ENGLAND

1.   In 1825 England formally recognized Argentine independence.   In so doing, it made no reservation concerning Argentine sovereignty over the Malvinas.   Nor did it, up to 1829, question any of the important acts of possession, occupation and jurisdiction which, as noted earlier, the Argentine Government carried out in relation to the islands.

2.   Only in 1829 did England protest for the first time, objecting to the establishment of the Malvinas Political and Military Command.   To support its protest, it alleged supposed British rights of sovereignty founded on the "discovery and subsequent occupation of the islands".

3.   On 3 January 1833, British troops invaded the Malvinas, forcibly ousted the Argentine authorities and expelled nearly all the original inhabitants.   A few months later the British completed the occupation of the archipelago, replacing the Argentine population by officials and employees of the Crown.   Since that time, that part of Argentine territory has been a colony of the United Kingdom.

4.   Argentina never consented to the United Kingdom's aggression and illegal occupation of the islands.   Since 1833 and whenever it has been possible, the Argentine Government has formally protested to the British Government and demanded the return of the islands.   That protest against the illegal occupation of part of its territory has been reiterated in international organizations, including the United Nations.

Annex II

DECISIONS OF THE GENERAL ASSEMBLY

1.   CONCLUSIONS AND RECOMMENDATIONS ADOPTED BY THE SPECIAL COMMITTEE ON
     DECOLONIZATION ON 13 NOVEMBER 1964

(A)   The Special Committee examined the situation in the Non-Self-Governing
Territory of the Falkland Islands (Malvinas) and heard the statements of the
representative of th administering Power and the representative of Argentina;

(B)   The Committee confirmed that the provisions of the Declaration on the
Granting of Independence to Colonial Countries and Peoples apply to the Territory
of the Falkland Islands (Malvinas);

(C)   The Committee notes the existence of a dispute between the Government of
the United Kingdom and that of Argentina concerning sovereignty over the Falkland
Islands (Malvinas);

(D)   The Committee invites the Governments of the United Kingdom and Argentina
to enter into negotiations with a view to finding a peaceful solution to this
problem, bearing in mind the provisions and objectives of the United Nations
Charter and of resolution 1514 (XV) of 14 December 1960; the interests of the
population of the islands, and the opinions expressed during the course of the
general debate;

(E)   The Special Committee invites the two above-mentioned Governments to
inform the Special Committee or the General Assembly of the results of their
negotiations.

2.   RESOLUTION 2065 (XX) ADOPTED BY THE GENERAL ASSEMBLY ON 16 DECEMBER 1965

2065 (XX).   Question of the Falkland Islands
(Malvinas)

The General Asembly,

Having examined the question of the Falkland Islands (Malvinas),

Taking into account the chapters of the reports of the Special Committee on
the Situation with regard to the Implementation of the Declaration on the Granting
of Independence to Colonial Countries and Peoples relating to the Falkland Islands
(Malvinas), 15/ and in particular the conclusions and recommendations adopted by
the Committee with reference to that Territory,

Considering that its resolution 1514 (XV) of 14 December 1960 was prompted by
the cherished aim of bringing to an end everywhere colonialism in all its forms,
one of which covers the case of the Falkland Islands (Malvinas),

/...

Noting the existence of a dispute between the Governments of Argentina and the United Kingdom of Great Britain and Northern Ireland concerning sovereignty over the said Islands,

1.   Invites the Governments of Argentina and the United Kingdom of Great Britain and Northern Ireland to proceed without delay with the negotiations recommended by the Special Committee on the Situation with regard to the Implementation of the Declaration on the Granting of Independence to Colonial Countries and Peoples with a view to finding a peaceful solution to the problem, bearing in mind the provisions and objectives of the Charter of the United Nations and of General Assembly resolution 1514 (XV) and the interests of the population of the Falkland Islands (Malvinas);

2.   Requests the two Governments to report to the Special Committee and to the General Assembly at its twenty-first session on the results of the negotiations.

1398th plenary meeting,
16 December 1965.

Vote

In favour: Brazil, Bulgaria, Burma, Burundi, Byelorussian Soviet Socialist Republic, Cameroon, Central African Republic, Ceylon, Chile, China, Colombia, Congo (Brazzaville), Congo, Democratic Republic of, Costa Rica, Cuba, Czechoslovakia, Dahomey, Dominican Republic, El Salvador, Ethiopia, Gabon, Ghana, Greece, Guatemala, Guinea, Haiti, Honduras, Hungary, India, Iran, Iraq, Ireland, Israel, Italy, Ivory Coast, Jamaica, Japan, Jordan, Kenya, Kuwait, Lebanon, Liberia, Libya, Luxembourg, Madagascar, Malawi, Malaysia, Maldives, Mali, Mauritania, Mexico, Mongolia, Morocco, Nepal, Nicaragua, Niger, Nigeria, Pakistan, Panama, Paraguay, Peru, Philippines, Poland, Romania, Rwanda, Saudi Arabia, Senegal, Sierra Leone, Somalia, Spain, Sudan, Syria, Thailand, Togo, Trinidad and Tobago, Tunisia, Turkey, Uganda, Union of Soviet Socialist Republics, United Arab Republic, United Republic of Tanzania, Upper Volta, Uruguay, Venezuela, Yemen, Yugoslavia, Zambia, Afghanistan, Algeria, Argentina, Austria, Belgium, Bolivia.

Against: None.

Abstaining: Canada, Denmark, Finland, France, Iceland, Netherlands, New Zealand, Norway, Portugal, South Africa, Sweden, United Kingdom of Great Britain and Northern Ireland, United States of America, Australia.

94 votes to none, with 14 abstentions.

/...

3. CONSENSUS ADOPTED BY THE GENERAL ASSEMBLY ON 20 DECEMBER 1966

With reference to General Assembly resolution 2065 (XX) of 16 December 1965 concerning the question of the Falkland Islands (Malvinas), the Fourth Committee took note of the communications dated 15 December 1966 of Argentina and the United Kingdom of Great Britain and Northern Ireland (A/C.4/682 and A/C.4/683). In this regard there was a consensus in favour of urging both parties to continue with the negotiations so as to find a peaceful solution to the problem as soon as possible, keeping the Special Committee on the Situation with regard to the Implementation of the Declaration on the Granting of Independence to Colonial Countries and Peoples and the General Assembly duly informed about the development of the negotiations on this colonial situation, the elimination of which is of interest to the United Nations within the context of General Assembly resolution 1514 (XV) of 14 December 1960.

4. CONSENSUS ADOPTED BY THE GENERAL ASSEMBLY ON 19 DECEMBER 1967

The General Assembly, having regard to its resolution 2065 (XX) of 16 December 1965 and to the consensus approved by the General Assembly on 20 December 1966 concerning the question of the Falkland Islands (Malvinas), takes note of the communications dated 14 December 1967 from the Permanent Representatives of Argentina and the United Kingdom of Great Britain and Northern Ireland to the United Nations, addressed to the Secretary-General (A/C.4/703, A/C.4/704) and, in this connexion and bearing in mind the report of the Special Committee, on the Situation with regard to the Implementation of the Declaration on the Granting of Independence to Colonial Countries and Peoples, approves a consensus in favour of urging both parties to continue the negotiations so as to find a peaceful solution to the problem as soon as possible. It likewise urges the parties, bearing particularly in mind resolution 2065 (XX) and the consensus of 20 December 1966, to keep the Special Committee on the Situation with regard to the Implementation of the Declaration on the Granting of Independence to Colonial Countries and Peoples and the Assembly duly informed during the coming year about the development of the negotiations on this colonial situation, the elimination of which is of interest to the United Nations within the context of General Assembly resolution 1514 (XV) of 14 December 1960.

5. CONSENSUS ADOPTED BY THE GENERAL ASSEMBLY ON 16 DECEMBER 1969

The General Assembly, having regard to its resolution 2065 (XX) of 16 December 1965 and to the consensuses which it approved on 20 December 1966 and 19 December 1967 concerning the question of the Falkland Islands (Malvinas), takes note of the communications dated 21 November 1969 from the Permanent Representatives of Argentina and the United Kingdom of Great Britain and Northern Ireland addressed to the Secretary-General.

In this connexion, the General Assembly, taking account of the report of the Special Committee on the Situation with regard to the Implementation of the Declaration on the Granting of Independence to Colonial Countries and Peoples, notes with satisfaction the progress achieved in the negotiations that were reported in the notes of 21 November 1969, and urges the parties, bearing

/...

particularly in mind resolution 2065 (XX) and the consensuses mentioned above, to continue their efforts to reach, as soon as possible, a definitive solution to the dispute as envisaged in the notes referred to, and to keep the Special Committee on the Situation with regard to the Implementation of the Declaration on the Granting of Independence to Colonial Countries and Peoples and the General Assembly informed during the coming year of the development of the negotiations on this colonial situation, the elimination of which is of interest to the United Nations within the context of General Assembly resolution 1514 (XV) of 14 December 1960.

6.   CONSENSUS ADOPTED BY THE GENERAL ASSEMBLY IN 1971

The General Assembly, having regard to its resolution 2065 (XX) of 16 December 1965 and to the consensuses which it approved on 20 December 1966, 19 December 1967 and 16 December 1969, concerning the question of the Falkland Islands (Malvinas), takes note of the communications dated 12 August 1971 from the Permanent Representatives of Argentina (A/8368) and the United Kingdom of Great Britain and Northern Ireland (A/8369) addressed to the Secretary-General.

In this connexion, the General Assembly notes with satisfaction the progress achieved in the special talks on communication which took place within the general framework of the negotiations that were reported in the notes of 12 August 1971, and urges the parties, bearing particularly in mind resolution 2065 (XX) and the consensuses mentioned above, to continue their efforts to reach, as soon as possible, a definitive solution to the dispute as envisaged in the notes referred to, and to keep the Special Committee on the Situation with regard to the Implementation of the Declaration on the Granting of Independence to Colonial Countries and Peoples and the General Assembly informed during the coming year of the development of the negotiations on this colonial situation, the elimination of which is of interest to the United Nations within the context of General Assembly resolution 1514 (XV) of 14 December 1960.

7.   RESOLUTION 3160 (XXVIII) ADOPTED BY THE GENERAL ASSEMBLY ON 14 DECEMBER 1973

The General Assembly,

Having considered the question of the Falkland Islands (Malvinas),

Recalling its resolution 1514 (XV) of 14 December 1960 containing the Declaration on the Granting of Independence to Colonial Countries and Peoples,

Recalling also its resolution 2065 (XX) of 16 December 1965, in which it invited the Governments of Argentina and the United Kingdom of Great Britain and Northern Ireland to proceed without delay with the negotiations recommended by the Special Committee on the Situation with regard to the Implementation of the Declaration on the Granting of Independence to Colonial Countries and Peoples with a view to finding a peaceful solution to the problem of the Falkland Islands (Malvinas), bearing in mind the provisions and objectives of the Charter of the United Nations and of resolution 1514 (XV) and the interests of the population of the Falkland Islands (Malvinas),

/...

__Gravely concerned__ at the fact that eight years have elapsed since the adoption of resolution 2065 (XX) without any substantial progress having been made in the negotiations,

__Mindful__ that resolution 2065 (XX) indicates that the way to put an end to this colonial situation is the peaceful solution of the conflict of sovereignty between the Governments of Argentina and the United Kingdom with regard to the aforementioned islands,

__Expressing its gratitude__ for the continuous efforts made by the Government of Argentina, in accordance with the relevant decisions of the General Assembly, to facilitate the process of decolonization and to promote the well-being of the population of the islands,

1.   __Approves__ the chapters of the report of the Special Committee on the Situation with regard to the Implementation of the Declaration on the Granting of Independence to Colonial Countries and Peoples relating to the Falkland Islands (Malvinas) __60/__ and, in particular, the resolution adopted by the Special Committee on 21 August 1973 concerning the Territory; __61/__

2.   __Declares__ the need to accelerate the negotiations between the Governments of Argentina and the United Kingdom of Great Britain and Northern Ireland called for in General Assembly resolution 2065 (XX) in order to arrive at a peaceful solution of the conflict of sovereignty between them concerning the Falkland Islands (Malvinas);

3.   __Urges__ the Governments of Argentina and the United Kingdom, therefore, to proceed without delay with the negotiations, in accordance with the provisions of the relevant resolutions of the General Assembly, in order to put an end to the colonial situation;

4.   __Requests__ both Governments to report to the Secretary-General and to the General Assembly as soon as possible, and not later than at its twenty-ninth session, on the results of the recommended negotiations.

Vote

__In favour:__   Afghanistan, Albania, Algeria, Argentina, Australia, Austria, Bahamas, Bahrain, Barbados, Bhutan, Bolivia, Botswana, Brazil, Bulgaria, Burma, Burundi, Byelorussian Soviet Socialist Republic, Cameroon, Central African Republic, Chad, Chile, China, Colombia, Congo, Costa Rica, Cuba, Cyprus, Czechoslovakia, Dahomey, Democratic Yemen, Ecuador, Egypt, El Salvador, Equatorial Guinea, Ethiopia, Fiji, Gabon, German Democratic Republic, Ghana, Greece, Guatemala, Guinea, Haiti, Honduras, Hungary, Iceland, India, Indonesia, Iran, Iraq, Ireland, Israel, Italy, Ivory Coast, Jamaica, Japan, Jordan, Kenya, Khmer Republic, Kuwait, Laos, Lebanon, Lesotho, Liberia, Libyan Arab Republic, Madagascar, Malawi, Malaysia, Mali, Malta, Mauritania, Mexico, Mongolia,

/...

Morocco, Nepal, New Zealand, Nicaragua, Niger, Nigeria, Oman, Pakistan, Panama, Paraguay, Peru, Philippines, Poland, Qatar, Romania, Rwanda, Saudi Arabia, Senegal, Sierra Leone, Singapore, Somalia, Spain, Sri Lanka, Sudan, Swaziland, Syrian Arab Republic, Thailand, Togo, Trinidad and Tobago, Tunisia, Turkey, Uganda, Ukrainian Soviet Socialist Republic, Union of Soviet Socialist Republics, United Arab Emirates, United Republic of Tanzania, Upper Volta, Uruguay, Venezuela, Yemen, Yugoslavia, Zaire, Zambia.

Against: None.

Abstaining: Belgium, Canada, Denmark, Finland, France, Germany, Federal Republic of, Luxembourg, Netherlands, Norway, Portugal, South Africa, Sweden, United Kingdom of Great Britain and Northern Ireland, United States of America.

116 to none, with 14 abstentions.

RESOLUTION 31/49 ADOPTED BY THE GENERAL ASSEMBLY ON 1 DECEMBER 1976

The General Assembly,

Having considered the question of the Falkland Islands (Malvinas),

Recalling its resolutions 1514 (XV) of 14 December 1960, 2065 (XX) of December 1965 and 3160 (XXVIII) of 14 December 1973,

Bearing in mind the paragraphs related to this question contained in the Political Declaration adopted by the Conference of Ministers for Foreign Affairs of Non-Aligned Countries, held at Lima from 25 to 30 August 1975, and in the Political Declaration adopted by the Fifth Conference of Heads of State or Government of Non-Aligned Countries, held at Colombo from 16 to 19 August 1976,

Having regard to the chapter of the report of the Special Committee on the Situation with regard to the Implementation of the Declaration on the Granting of Independence to Colonial Countries and Peoples relating to the Falkland Islands (Malvinas) and, in particular, the conclusions and recommendations of the Special Committee concerning the Territory,

1. Approves the chapter of the report of the Special Committee on the Situation with regard to the Implementation of the Declaration on the Granting of Independence to Colonial Countries and Peoples relating to the Falkland Islands (Malvinas) and, in particular, the conclusions and recommendations of the Special Committee concerning the Territory;

2. Expresses its gratitude for the continuous efforts made by the Government of Argentina, in accordance with the relevant decisions of the General Assembly, to facilitate the process of decolonization and to promote the well-being of the population of the islands;

/...

3.   Requests the Governments of Argentina and the United Kingdom of Great Britain and Northern Ireland to expedite the negotiations concerning the dispute over sovereignty, as requested in General Assembly resolutions 2065 (XX) and 3160 (XXVIII);

4.   Calls upon the two parties to refrain from taking decisions that would imply introducing unilateral modifications in the situation while the islands are going through the process recommended in the above-mentioned resolutions;

5.   Requests both Governments to report to the Secretary-General and to the General Assembly as soon as possible on the results of the negotiations.

Vote

In favour: Afghanistan, Albania, Algeria, Argentina, Bahrain, Bangladesh, Benin, Bhutan, Bolivia, Brazil, Bulgaria, Burundi, Byelorussian Soviet Socialist Republic, Central African Republic, Chad, Chile, China, Colombia, Congo, Costa Rica, Cuba, Cyprus, Czechoslovakia Democratic Kampuchea, Democratic Yemen, Dominican Republic, Ecuador, Egypt, El Salvador, Equatorial Guinea, Ethiopia, Gabon, German Democratic Republic, Ghana, Greece, Guatemala, Guinea, Guinea-Bissau, Haiti, Honduras, Hungary, India, Indonesia, Iran, Iraq, Ivory Coast, Jordan, Kuwait, Lao People's Democratic Republic, Lebanon, Lesotho, Liberia, Libyan Arab Republic, Madagascar, Malaysia, Maldives, Mali, Malta, Mauritania, Mauritius, Mexico, Mongolia, Morocco, Mozambique, Nepal, Nicaragua, Oman, Pakistan, Panama, Paraguay, Peru, Philippines, Poland, Qatar, Romania, Rwanda, Sao Tome and Principe, Saudi Arabia, Senegal, Somalia, Spain, Sri Lanka, Sudan, Suriname, Swaziland, Syrian Arab Republic, Thailand, Togo, Tunisia, Turkey, Uganda, Ukrainian Soviet Socialist Republic, Union of Soviet Socialist Republics, United Arab Emirates, United Republic of Cameroon, United Republic of Tanzania, Upper Volta, Uruguay, Venezuela, Yemen, Yugoslavia, Zambia.

Against: United Kingdom of Great Britain and Northern Ireland.

Abstaining: Australia, Austria, Bahamas, Barbados, Belgium, Canada, Denmark, Fiji, Finland, France, Gambia, Germany, Federal Republic of, Guyana, Iceland, Ireland, Italy, Jamaica, Japan, Kenya, Luxembourg, Malawi, Netherlands, New Zealand, Norway, Papua New Guinea, Portugal, Sierra Leone, Singapore, Sweden, Trinidad and Tobago, United States of America, Zaire.

102 to 1 with 32 abstentions.

Annex III

STATEMENTS BY THE MOVEMENT OF NON-ALIGNED COUNTRIES

. 1975 – <u>Final Declaration of the Fifth Conference of Ministers of Foreign Affairs of Non-Aligned Countries</u>, Lima, 30 August. The following paragraph was adopted:

<u>9</u>. The Non-Aligned Countries, without prejudice to affirming the validity of the rinciple of self-determination as a general principle for other territories, trongly support in the special and particular case of the Malvinas Islands, the ust claim of the Argentine Republic, and urge the United Kingdom to actively ontinue the negotiations recommended by the United Nations in order to restore the aid territory to Argentine sovereignty and thus put an end to that illegal ituation, which still persists in the southern part of the American continent.

. 1976 – <u>Fifth Conference of Heads of State or Government of Non-Aligned Countries</u>, Colombo, Sri Lanka, 16-19 August 1976

<u>19</u>. In the special and particular case of the Malvinas (Falkland Islands), the :onference firmly supported the just claim of the Argentine Republic and urged the Inited Kingdom to actively pursue the negotiations recommended by the United Iations for the purpose of restoring that territory to Argentine sovereignty, thus :nding the illegal situation that still prevails in the extreme southern part of _he American continent.

:8. The Conference demanded the restoration of sovereignty over Guantanamo, the °anama Canal Zone and the Malvinas respectively to Cuba, Panama and Argentina, who ire the rightful owners of these territories.

:. 1978 – <u>Ministerial Meeting of the Co-ordinating Bureau of the Non-Aligned Countries</u>, Havana, Cuba, 15-20 May 1978

Political declaration

16. In the case of the Malvinas Islands, the Bureau supported the just aspiration >f the Republic of Argentina, and urged that the negotiations between the Interested parties be accelerated in order to restore said territory to Argentine sovereignty.

4.   1978 – <u>Conference of Ministers of Foreign Affairs of Non-Aligned Countries</u>,
          Belgrade, 1978

<u>124</u>. In the special and particular case of the Malvinas Islands, the Ministers
firmly support the just aspirations of Argentina for the restoration of that
territory to Argentine sovereignty and urge that the negotiations to this end be
accelerated.

5.   1979 – <u>Ministerial Meeting of the Co-ordinating Bureau of the Non-Aligned</u>
          <u>Countries</u>, Colombo, 1979

<u>93</u>.   In the special and particular case of the Malvinas Islands, the Ministers
firmly support the just aspirations of Argentina for the restoration of that
territory to Argentine sovereignty and urge that the negotiations to this end be
accelerated.

6.   1979 – <u>Final Declaration of the Sixth Conference of Heads of State or</u>
          <u>Government of Non-Aligned Countries</u>, Havana, Cuba, 3-9 September 1979

<u>168</u>. In the special and particular case of the Malvinas Islands, the Heads of Stat
or Government firmly reiterated their support for the Argentine Republic's right t
the restitution of that territory and sovereignty over it and requested that the
negotiations in this regard be speeded up.

7.   1981 – <u>Conference of Ministers of Foreign Affairs of Non-Aligned Countries</u>,
          New Delhi, 1981

<u>104</u>. In the special and particular case of the Malvinas Islands, the Ministers
firmly reiterated their support for the Argentine Republic's right to the
restitution of that territory and sovereignty over it and requested that the
negotiations with the United Kingdom in this regard be speeded up. They also
expressed the hope that the United States of America would implement and strictly
respect the Panama Canal treaties to give effect to the full sovereignty and
jurisdiction of Panama over all its national territory, as well as to the régime o
neutrality of the inter-ocean waterway.

8.   1981 – <u>Meeting of Ministers of Foreign Affairs and Heads of Delegations of th</u>
          <u>Non-Aligned Countries to the thirty-sixth session of the General</u>
          <u>Assembly of the United Nations</u> (25-28 September 1981)

COMMUNIQUE

    The Meeting firmly reiterated its support for the right of the Republic of
Argentina to the restitution of the Malvinas Islands and territorial sovereignty
over them and requested that the negotiations with the United Kingdom in this
regard be speeded up.

/..

A

**NITED
ATIONS**

General Assembly

Distr.
GENERAL

A/37/553/Corr.1
27 October 1982

ARABIC, ENGLISH, FRENCH AND
RUSSIAN ONLY

Thirty-seventh session
Agenda item 135

QUESTION OF THE FALKLAND ISLANDS (MALVINAS)

Letter dated 18 October 1982 from the Permanent Representative of
Argentina to the United Nations addressed to the Secretary-General

Corrigendum

The heading of the document should read as above.

UNITED NATIONS

GENERAL

ASSEMBLY

Distr.
GENERAL

A/37/553/Add.1
2 November 1982
ENGLISH
ORIGINAL: SPANISH

Thirty-seventh session
Agenda item 135

QUESTION OF THE FALKLAND ISLANDS (MALVINAS)

Letter dated 1 November 1982 from the Permanent Representative of
Argentina to the United Nations addressed to the Secretary-General

I have the honour to request you to have the attached letter, dated
8 June 1977, circulated as an annex to document A/37/553 and Corr.1, entitled
"Question of the Malvinas Islands and the United Nations General Assembly".

(Signed)   Carlos Manuel MUÑIZ
Ambassador
Permanent Representative

ANNEX

<u>Letter dated 8 June 1977 from the Permanent Representative</u>
<u>of Argentina to the United Nations addressed to the</u>
<u>Secretary-General</u>*

I have the honour to address Your Excellency in relation to the question of the Malvinas Islands and, bearing in mind paragraph 5 of General Assembly resolution 31/49 of 1 December 1976, to forward a copy of a joint communiqué issued in Buenos Aires and London on 26 April 1977.

I request Your Excellency to arrange for this letter and its annex to be circulated as a document of the General Assembly and brought to the attention of the Special Committee on Decolonization.

(Signed) Carlos ORTIZ DE ROZAS
Ambassador
Permanent Representative

_____

* Distributed previously under the symbol A/32/110.

Annex

Joint communiqué

The Governments of the Argentine Republic and the United Kingdom of Great Britain and Northern Ireland have agreed to hold negotiations from June or July 197 which will concern future political relations, including sovereignty, with regard to the Malvinas Islands, South Georgia and the South Sandwich Islands, and economic co-operation with regard to the said territories, in particular, and the South West Atlantic, in general. In these negotiations the issues affecting the future of the islands will be discussed, and negotiations will be directed to the working out of a peaceful solution to the existing dispute on sovereignty between the two States, and the establishment of a framework for Anglo-Argentine economic co-operation which will contribute substantially to the development of the islands, and the region as a whole.

A major objective of the negotiations will be to achieve a stable, prosperous and politically durable future for the islands, whose people the Government of the United Kingdom will consult during the course of the negotiations.

The agreement to hold these negotiations, and the negotiations themselves, are without prejudice to the position of either Government with regard to sovereignty over the islands.

The level at which the negotiations will be conducted, and the times and places at which they will be held, will be determined by agreement between the two Governments. If necessary, special working groups will be established.

———

9. Communiqué adopted by the Co-ordinating Bureau of the Non-Aligned Countries, New York, 26 April 1982

The meeting of the Co-ordinating Bureau of Non-Aligned Countries held on 26 April 1982 was convened at the request of the Permanent Representative of Argentina.

The Permanent Representative of Argentina brought to the attention of the Bureau the recent developments which have taken place in the region of the Malvinas Islands, increasing the tension existing in the area, thus gravely endangering international peace and security.

The Co-ordinating Bureau expressed its grave concern over the developments in the region of the Malvinas Islands and requested the interested parties to actively seek a peaceful solution of their dispute and refrain from any action which might endanger peace and security in the region.

The Co-ordinating Bureau reaffirmed the view that the use of force or the threat of the use of force in relations between States are acts contrary to the principles of the Movement of Non-Aligned Countries.

In conformity with the traditional support of the Movement of Non-Aligned Countries for the process of decolonization, the Co-ordinating Bureau recalled paragraph 87 of the Declaration of the Conference of Ministers of Foreign Affairs held in Lima, Peru, in August 1975, which stated:

> "The Non-Aligned Countries, without prejudice to ratifying the validity of the principle of self-determination as a general principle for other territories, strongly support, in the special and particular case of the Malvinas Islands, the just claim of the Argentine Republic and urge the United Kingdom to actively continue the negotiations recommended by the United Nations in order to restore the said territory to Argentine sovereignty and thus put an end to that illegal situation which still persists in the southern part of the American continent."

The support of the Movement of Non-Aligned Countries for Argentine sovereignty over the Malvinas Islands has been reaffirmed at subsequent summit and ministerial meetings of the Movement, including the ministerial meeting held in New York in September 1981.

In this context, the Bureau expressed its support for the efforts to achieve a just, durable and peaceful negotiated solution in accordance with the application of resolution 502 (1982) of the Security Council in its entirety, the principles and decisions of the Movement of Non-Aligned Countries and the relevant resolutions of the General Assembly.

10. Communiqué adopted by the Co-ordinating Bureau of the Movement of Non-Aligned Countries on 5 May 1982

A meeting of the Co-ordinating Bureau of the Movement of Non-Aligned Countries held on 5 May 1982, was convened at the request of the Permanent Representative of Argentina.

/...

The Permanent Representative of Argentina informed the Bureau of the developments in the region of the Malvinas Islands, since the Bureau last met on 26 April, gravely increasing the tension in the area and endangering peace and security in the region and in the world.

The Co-ordinating Bureau:

1.   Expresses regret at the mounting loss of human life in the Malvinas Islands conflict.

2.   Reiterates in all its aspects the communiqué adopted on 26 April 1982.

3.   Reiterates the communiqué's reaffirmation that the use of force or threat of the use of force in relations between States are acts contrary to the principles of the Movement of Non-Aligned Countries.

4.   Confirms the communiqué's support for Argentine sovereignty over the Malvinas Islands as reaffirmed at all summit and ministerial meetings of the Movement since the Declaration of the Conference of Ministers of Foreign Affairs held in Lima, Peru, in August 1975.

5.   Appeals once again to the parties to the conflict urgently to find a just, durable and peaceful solution in accordance with resolution 502 (1982) of the Security Council in its entirety, the principles and decisions of the Movement of Non-Aligned Countries and the relevant resolutions of the General Assembly of the United Nations.

11. <u>Documents of the Ministerial Meeting of the Co-ordinating Bureau of the Non-Aligned Countries</u> Havana, 21 May to 5 June 1982

     <u>Final communiqué</u>

25. In flagrant violation of the Charter of the United Nations and the principles of the Movement of Non-Aligned Countries, the last few years have seen an increase in the use or threat of use of force; political, diplomatic, economic, military and cultural pressures; the denial of the inalienable right of the peoples and territories under colonial and alien domination to self-determination and independence; aggression, military intervention, foreign occupation, involving the introduction and presence of foreign troops, mercenaries or irregulars under any pretext whatsoever, against the sovereignty, political independence and territorial integrity of States; interference in the internal and external affairs of States; the application of economic, political and diplomatic reprisals and other hostile measures against countries that adopt independent positions.

26. Thus, focal points of aggression and tension, such as those in the Middle East, Africa, particularly southern Africa, South-West Asia, South East Asia, the Caribbean and Central America continued to exist, while a new hotbed of tension in the South Atlantic, and conflicts between States caused further deterioration in the international situation.

7. The military operations being undertaken by the United Kingdom in the South
Atlantic through the use of a large military contingent including nuclear warships
endangers international peace and security and could cause a wider conflagration
with unforeseen consequences.

.09. At the same time, they reiterated their concern over the tension that has
continued to increase in the Caribbean, Central America and the South Atlantic,
particularly as a result of the colonialist and imperialist policy of aggression
and intervention.

.10. The Ministers reiterated the decisions of previous Non-Aligned Conferences and
Meetings in which they expressed their support for the Argentine Republic's right
to the restitution of the Malvinas Islands and sovereignty over them. They
recalled that the struggle against colonialism in all its forms is a basic
principle of non-alignment, and reaffirmed their staunch solidarity with Argentina
in its efforts to bring an end to the outdated colonial presence in the Malvinas
Islands and to prevent its re-establishment.

111. The Ministers reiterated the need for full respect for the non-aligned
principles of anti-colonialism, anti-neo-colonialism and opposition to any other
form of foreign domination, full respect for national sovereignty and territorial
integrity, peaceful settlement of disputes between States and non-use of force in
international relations.

112. The Ministers also acknowledged that the Malvinas, South Georgia and South
Sandwich Islands were an integral part of the Latin American region and that the
military actions of the United Kingdom and the overt and covert actions and
pressures of other developed countries harmed the entire region. In this
connection, they expressed their satisfaction with the solidarity and firm support
which the Latin American countries were offering Argentina in its struggle against
the British attempt to re-impose a colonial régime.

113. The Ministers denounced any attempt by the United Kingdom or any other Power
to establish military bases or impose security agreements on that Latin American
territory against the sovereign will of the Argentine Republic, as a means of
imposing imperialist domination in the area and as a serious threat to
international peace and security throughout the South Atlantic region.

114. The Ministers deplored the military operations being undertaken in the South
Atlantic, through the use of a large United Kingdom military contingent with the
support and assistance of the United States. The Ministers demanded the immediate
end of United States military support and assistance and urged the immediate
cessation of military operations. They also urged developed countries to refrain
from encouraging the continuation or escalation of military operations in the South
Atlantic.

12. <u>Final communiqué of the Meeting of the Ministers for Foreign Affairs and Heads</u>
    <u>of Delegation of the Non-Aligned Countries, held in New York from 4 to</u>
    <u>9 October 1982</u>

35.   In recalling the decisions on Latin America of the Ministerial Meeting of the
Co-ordinating Bureau in Havana, the Meeting likewise reaffirmed its decisions on
Central America, in particular on El Salvador, and reiterated its support for the
right of the Republic of Argentina to obtain the restitution of the Malvinas
Islands to its sovereignty and asked that negotiations be re-initiated, with the
participation and good offices of the Secretary-General of the United Nations,
between the Argentine Republic and the United Kingdom, with the aim of achieving as
soon as possible a peaceful and just solution to the question, taking into account
the principles and decisions of the Non-Aligned Movement and resolutions 1514 (XV),
2065 (XX), 2621 (XXV), 3160 (XXVIII), and 31/49 of the United Nations General
Assembly.

/...(

Annex IV

SOME LATIN AMERICAN DECISIONS ON THE QUESTION OF THE MALVINAS

1.   TEXT OF THE STATEMENT OF THE LATIN AMERICAN GROUP
     AT THE UNITED NATIONS OF 5 MAY 1982

The Latin American Group at the United Nations held a meeting on 4 May 1982 at
ie request of the Permanent Representative of Argentina.

The Permanent Representative of Argentina informed the Group on all armed
:tions that have taken place in the region of the Malvinas Islands between
'gentina and the United Kingdom since 25 April 1982 and have seriously affected
ace and security in the region and in the world.

In these circumstances, the Latin American Group at the United Nations, in a
iirit of assistance in the search for a peaceful solution, declares:

.   Its regret at the increasing loss of life in the region of the Malvinas
lands;

.   Its urgent call for a cessation of all hostile acts in the region of the
lvinas Islands;

.   That it urges the Governments of the Argentine Republic and of the United
ngdom to initiate negotiations, with a view to achieving a just, peaceful,
actical and lasting solution in accordance with the principles and purposes of
ie Charter of the United Nations, resolution 502 (1982) of the Security Council in
.1 its parts and the pertinent resolutions of the United Nations General Assembly.

2.   RESOLUTIONS OF THE TWENTIETH MEETING OF CONSULTATION OF MINISTERS
     OF FOREIGN AFFAIRS OF THE ORGANIZATION OF AMERICAN STATES

RESOLUTION I

Serious Situation in the South Atlantic

(Adopted it the second plenary meeting on 28 April 1982)

The Twentieth Meeting of Consultation of Ministers of Foreign Affairs,

>nsidering:

The principles of inter-American solidarity and co-operation and the need to
ind a peaceful solution to any situation that endangers the peace of the Americas;

That a dangerous confrontation has arisen between the United Kingdom of Great
ritain and Northern Ireland and the Argentine Republic, which was aggravated today

/...

by the events that have arisen from the presence of the British navy in the South Atlantic, within the security region referred to in article 4 of the ITRA;

That the primary purpose of the Inter-American Treaty of Reciprocal Assistance is the maintenance of the peace and security of the hemisphere, which, in the case that has arisen, requires ensuring the peaceful settlement of the dispute;

That to facilitate peaceful settlement of the dispute, it is urgent that hostilities cease, since they disturb the peace of the continent and may reach unforeseeable proportions;

That it is an unchanging principle of the inter-American system that peace be preserved and that all the American states unanimously reject the intervention of extra-continental or continental armed forces in any of the nations of the hemisphere;

That Argentina's rights of sovereignty over the Malvinas Islands, as stated in some important resolutions passed by various international forums, including the Declaration of the Inter-American Juridical Committee on 16 January 1976, which states: "That the Argentine Republic has an undeniable right of sovereignty over the Malvinas Islands," must be borne in mind;

That the peace efforts being made with the consent of the parties must be emphasized, and that inter-American solidarity contributes to that objective, and

Having seen:

Resolution 502 (1982) of the United Nations Security Council, all of whose terms must be fulfilled; resolution 359 of 13 April 1982, adopted by the Permanent Council of the Organization of American States, and the Declaration adopted unanimously by the Ministers of Foreign Affairs at the opening meeting of the Twentieth Meeting of Consultation (Doc.14/82), and in conformity with the Inter-American Treaty of Reciprocal Assistance,

Resolves:

1.   To urge the Government of the United Kingdom of Great Britain and Northern Ireland immediately to cease the hostilities it is conducting within the security region defined by article 4 of the Inter-American Treaty of Reciprocal Assistance and also to refrain from any act that may affect inter-American peace and security.

2.   To urge the Government of the Argentine Republic likewise to refrain from taking any action that may exacerbate the situation.

3.   To urge those Governments immediately to call a truce that will make it possible to resume the normal conduct of negotiations aimed at a peaceful settlement of the dispute, taking into account the rights of sovereignty of the Argentine Republic over the Malvinas Islands and the interests of the islanders.

/...

4.   To express the willingness of the Organ of Consultation to lend support, through whatever means it considers advisable, to the new initiatives being taken at the regional or world level, with the consent of the Parties, with a view to the just and peaceful settlement of the problem.

5.   To take note of the information received about the important steps taken by the Secretary of State of the United States of America and to express its hope that they will make an effective contribution to the peaceful settlement of the conflict.

6.   To deplore the adoption by members of the European Economic Community and other States of coercive measures of an economic and political nature which are prejudicial to the Argentine nation and urge them to rescind those measures, and to state that they constitute a serious precedent, inasmuch as they are not covered by resolution 502 (1982) of the United Nations Security Council and are incompatible with the Charters of the United Nations and of the OAS and with the General Agreement on Tariffs and Trade (GATT).

7.   To instruct the President of the Twentieth Meeting of Consultation to take immediate steps to transmit the appeal contained in paragraphs 1, 2 and 3 of this resolution to the Governments of the United Kingdom of Great Britain and Northern Ireland and the Argentine Republic and also to inform them, on behalf of the Foreign Ministers of the Americas, that he is fully confident that this appeal will be accepted for the sake of peace in the region and in the world.

8.   To instruct the President of the Twentieth Meeting of Consultation to present this resolution formally to the President of the United Nations Security Council forthwith, so that he may bring it to the attention of the members of the Council.

9.   To keep the Twentieth Meeting of Consultation open for the specific purpose of monitoring strict compliance with this resolution and to take such additional measures as it deems necessary to restore and preserve peace and settle the conflict that has arisen by peaceful means.

RESOLUTION II

RESOLUTION ENTITLED "SERIOUS SITUATION IN THE SOUTH ATLANTIC" WHICH WAS ADOPTED IN WASHINGTON, D.C. ON 29 MAY 1982 BY THE TWENTIETH MEETING OF CONSULTATION OF MINISTERS OF FOREIGN AFFAIRS OF THE STATES PARTIES TO THE INTER-AMERICAN TREATY OF RECIPROCAL ASSISTANCE

The Twentieth Meeting of Consultation of Ministers of Foreign Affairs,

Whereas:

Resolution I of the Twentieth Meeting of Consulation of Ministers of Foreign Affairs, adopted on 28 April 1982, decided to keep the Twentieth Meeting of

/...

Consultation open, for the specific purpose of monitoring strict compliance with that resolution, and to take such additional measures as it deemed necessary to restore and preserve peace and settle the conflict that had arisen by peaceful means;

That resolution urged the Government of the United Kingdom immediately to cease the hostilities it was conducting within the security region defined by article 4 of the Inter-American Treaty of Reciprocal Assistance and also to refrain from any act that might affect inter-American peace and security, and urged the Government of the Argentine Republic to refrain from taking any action that might exacerbate the situation;

The same resolution urged the Governments of the United Kingdom and the Argentine Republic to call a truce that would make it possible to resume the normal conduct of negotiations aimed at a peaceful settlement of the dispute, taking into account the rights of sovereignty of the Argentine Republic over the Malvinas and the interests of the islanders;

While the Government of the Argentine Republic informed the Organ of Consultation of its full adherence to resolution I and acted consistently therewith, British forces carried out serious and repeated armed attacks against the Argentine Republic in the zone of the Malvinas, within the security region defined by article 4 of the Inter-American Treaty of Reciprocal Assistance, which means that the United Kingdom has ignored the appeal made to it by the Twentieth Meeting of Consultation;

Following the adoption of resolution I, the Government of the United States of America decided to apply coercive measures against the Argentine Republic and is giving its support, including material support, to the United Kingdom, thereby contravening the spirit and the letter of resolution I;

As a culmination of their repeated armed attacks, the British forces have since 21 May 1982 launched a large-scale military attack against the Argentine Republic in the area of the Malvinas which affects inter-American peace and security;

The deplorable situation created by the application of political and economic coercive measures, which are not based on present-day international law and are prejudicial to the Argentine people, by the European Economic Community - with the exception of Ireland and Italy - and other industrialized States, is continuing;

The purpose of the Inter-American Treaty of Reciprocal Assistance is to assure peace, by every means possible, to provide effective reciprocal assistance in dealing with armed attacks against any American State and to ward off threats of aggression against any of them;

The Twentieth Meeting of Consulation of Ministers of Foreign Affairs,

Resolves:

/...

1.   To condemn most vigorously the unjustified and disproportionate armed attack perpetrated by the United Kingdom and its decision, which affects the security of the entire American continent, arbitrarily to declare an extensive area, of up to 12 miles from the American coasts, as a zone of hostilities, actions aggravated by the fact that when these events occurred all prospects of negotiation in pursuit of a peaceful settlement of the conflict had not been exhausted.

2.   To reiterate its firm demand that the United Kingdom cease immediately its belligerent action against the Argentine Republic and order the immediate withdrawal of all its armed forces stationed there and the return of its fleet to its usual stations.

3.   To deplore the fact that the attitude of the United Kingdom has caused the negotiations for a peaceful settlement that were conducted by Mr. Javier Pérez de Cuéllar, Secretary-General of the United Nations, to fail.

4.   To express its conviction that it is essential to reach as speedily as possible a peaceful and honourable settlement of the conflict, under the auspices of the United Nations, and in that connection, to acknowledge the praiseworthy efforts and good offices of Mr. Javier Pérez de Cuéllar, Secretary-General of the United Nations, and to lend its full support to the task entrusted to him by the Security Council.

5.   To urge the Government of the United States of America to order the immediate rescission of the coercive measures applied against the Argentine Republic and to refrain from providing material assistance to the United Kingdom, in observance of the principle of continental solidarity enshrined in the Inter-American Treaty of Reciprocal Assistance.

6.   To urge the members of the European Economic Community and the other States that have taken them to rescind immediately the coercive economic or political measures taken against the Argentine Republic.

7.   To request the States parties to the Inter-American Treat of Reciprocal Assistance to give the Argentine Republic such support as each of them deems appropriate in order to assist it in this serious situation, and to refrain from any act that might jeopardize that objective.

If expedient, this support may be arranged with adequate co-ordination.

8.   To reaffirm the basic constitutional principles of the Charter of the Organization of American States and of the Inter-American Treaty of Reciprocal Assistance, particularly those referring to the peaceful settlement of disputes.

9.   To keep the Organ of Consultation available to assist the parties in dispute with their peace-making efforts in any way that may support the mission entrusted to the Secretary-General of the United Nations by the Security Council, and to instruct the President of the Meeting of Consultation to keep in continuous contact with the Secretary-General of the United Nations.

/...

10. To keep the Twentieth Meeting of Consultation open for the purpose of monitoring strict and immediate compliance with this resolution and to take, if necessary, any additional measures that may be agreed upon to preserve inter-American solidarity and co-operation.

3. DECLARATION OF THE INTER-AMERICAN JURIDICAL COMMITTEE
ON THE PROBLEM OF THE MALVINAS

The Inter-American Juridical Committee

Recalling its resolution of 18 February 1974 in which it expressed its concern "because territories occupied by foreign Powers still remain in American lands, despite the repeated claims of Latin American States calling for their return since they constitute an integral part of their national territories";

Recalling its declaration of 1 February 1972 with respect to the presence of British warships in the Caribbean Sea, stating that "Naval or air manoeuvres conducted in or over territorial waters of American States or waters adjacent to such waters, without prior consent, by warships or military aircraft of foreign States constitute threats to the peace and security of the continent and flagrant violations of the international standards on non-intervention";

Recalling the just title the Argentine Republic possesses to sovereignty over the Malvinas, based on the international norms in force when the dispute began; that the archipelago appears in the nautical charts of the South Atlantic prepared by the cartographers of the Casa de Contratación of Seville (1552-1523) in connexion with the voyage of Magellan; that the first effective occupation of the aforementioned islands by a group of French settlers ended with the agreement of 1767 by which they handed over those islands to the Spanish authorities under the Government and Captaincy-General (Capitanía General) of Buenos Aires; that the occupation of the Malvinas by the English was only partial, since it was confined to Port Egmont, and temporary, since after eight years (1766-1774) it was abandoned; that by decree of 10 June 1829 the Government of the United Provinces of the River Plate (Provincias Unidas del Río de la Plata) established a political and military government in the Malvinas under the Civil and Military Commandant Luis Vernet; that on 3 January 1833 the English corvette Clio forcibly drove out the Argentine authorities there established and unlawfully occupied the islands on behalf of the United Kingdom of Great Britain and Northern Ireland; that the Argentine Government has consistently maintained its claim to its rights from the first moment of the dispute (note from the Argentine Minister in London of 17 June 1823) and ever since;

Recalling United Nations resolution 2065 (XX), adopted at the twentieth session of the General Assembly in 1965, in which it invited the Governments of Argentina and the United Kingdom of Great Britain and Northern Ireland to proceed without delay with the negotiations aimed at settling the dispute concerning sovereignty over the Malvinas, bearing in mind the interests of the population of the islands and United Nations resolution 3160 (XXVIII), adopted at the twenty-eighth session of the General Assembly in 1973, in which, having expressed its gratitude to the Government of Argentina for its continuous efforts to promote the well-being of the population of the islands, it declared the need to accelerate the negotiations between the two Governments in order to arrive at a peaceful solution of the conflict of sovereignty between them concerning those islands;

Recalling that, in compliance with those resolutions, the Argentine Government concluded with the Government of the United Kingdom of Great Britain and Northern Ireland various agreements on co-operation and took measures concerning communications, supplies, social welfare and infrastructure maintenance works favourable to the interests of the population of the islands, which earned the praise of the United Nations General Assembly (3160 (XXVIII));

Considering the recent dispatch, supported and encouraged by the Government of the United Kingdom of Great Britain and Northern Ireland, of the so-called "Shackleton Mission" to the Malvinas with the declared purpose of making an "economic and fiscal evaluation" of the archipelago and surrounding areas;

Considering that the opposition of the Government of the United Kingdom of Great Britain and Northern Ireland to continuing bilateral negotiations in so far as they relate to settling the dispute regarding sovereignty over those islands, because it considers them "sterile", and the proposal to limit them to an agenda on "economic co-operation" amount to bringing the question back to the old argument, advanced by that Government in its diplomatic note of 1887, in which it told the Argentine Government that it considered the discussion closed;

Considering the recent statements of the British Foreign Secretary in the House of Commons to the effect that the British warship Endurance was in the vicinity of the islands and that two other ships were ready to sail there;

Considering that the withdrawal of the Heads of Mission of both Governments is causing a state of tension in relations between the two countries;

Noting that the scope of United Nations resolutions 2065 (XX) and 3160 (XXVIII) involves a commitment accepted by the Governments of Argentina and the United Kingdom to speed up the process of re-establishing legitimate sovereignty over the territory of the Malvinas, a legal framework within which the two governments are required to act, for which reason the unilateral breaking off of the negotiations by the United Kingdom consitutes a violation both of the resolutions cited and of the spirit of the commitment undertaken;

Reaffirming that the authentic ideals of our republics demand the ending of any occupation, usurpation, enclaves and other form of colonial domination remaining in the Americas,

Declares:

1.   That the Argentine Republic has an indisputable right of sovereignty over the Malvinas and that the basic question to be solved is accordingly that of the procedure to be followed for the recovery of its territory;

2.   That the "Shackleton Mission", sponsored by the Government of the United Kingdom of Great Britain and Northern Ireland, amounts to making a change unilaterally and therefore contravenes United Nations resolutions 2065 (XX) and 3160 (XXVIII);

3.   That the presence of foreign warships in waters adjacent to American states and the intimidatory announcement by British authorities of the dispatch of other ships constitute threats to the peace and security of the continent and flagrant violations of international norms on non-intervention;

4.   That all of this amounts to hostile conduct designed to silence the claims of the Government of Argentina and to obstruct the conduct of the negotiations recommended by the General Assembly of the United Nations.

Rio de Janeiro, 16 January 1976

(Signed)   Reynaldo GALINDO POHL
Jorge A. AJA ESPIL
José Joaquín CAICEDO CASTILLA
Antonio GOMEZ ROBLEDO
José Eduardo do PRADO KELLY
Américo Pablo RICALDONI
Alberto RUIZ-ELDREDGE

UNITED
NATIONS

A

General Assembly

Distr.
GENERAL

A/37/582
29 October 1982

ORIGINAL: ENGLISH

Thirty-seventh session
Agenda item 135

QUESTION OF THE FALKLAND ISLANDS (MALVINAS)

Letter dated 28 October 1982 from the Permanent Representative
of the United Kingdom to the United Nations addressed to the
Secretary-General

I have the honour to refer to agenda item 135 (Question of the Falkland
Islands (Malvinas)), which is scheduled for debate in the plenary commencing on
2 November. In view of the fact that the document circulated at the request of the
Permanent Representative of Argentina under the symbol A/37/553 and Corr.1 repeats
numerous tendentious claims which have been refuted in earlier documents, I have
the honour to attach copies of letters dated 28 April 1982 (annex I) and
13 August 1982 (annex II) addressed to the President of the Security Council and
the Secretary-General, respectively.

I should like to emphasize one point in particular. The annex to the letter
from the Permanent Representative of Argentina, under the heading "Background",
claims in three places that the General Assembly has "ruled out the applicability
of the right of self-determination to this particular special case". The decisions
in question are the Committee of 24's conclusions and recommendations of
13 November 1964 and the General Assembly's resolutions 2065 (XX) of
16 December 1965 and 3160 (XXVIII) of 14 December 1973. However, it will be seen
from the texts themselves (reprinted in annex II to the Argentine document) that
none of them contains anything to support the Argentine allegation. In fact, all
three decisions draw their inspiration from resolution 1514 (XV), which declares in
its operative paragraph 2 that: "All peoples have the right to self-determination;
by virtue of that right they freely determine their political status and freely
pursue their economic, social and cultural development". The same part of the
Argentine document refers also to the Declarations of the Movement of Non-Aligned
Countries. Significantly, however, it fails to draw attention to the fact that the

82-29327   0560h (E)

most recent communiqué of the meeting of the Ministers for Foreign Affairs and heads of delegation of the non-aligned countries, held in New York earlier this month, made specific mention in the context of the Falkland Islands dispute of the principles of the non-aligned movement: as everyone knows, the non-aligned principles include the non-use of force, the settlement of disputes exclusively by peaceful means, and self-determination.

These are no doubt the reasons why the Argentine document seeks to obscure the essential facts by insisting that the dispute is exclusively about sovereignty and that there are only two parties to it, the Islanders being excluded. The position of the United Kingdom does not depend on sophistry of this kind, but on basic Charter principles, notably the United Kingdom's clear obligation under Article 73 to recognize the interests of the inhabitants of the Falkland Islanders as paramount.

I have the honour to request that this letter and its attachments be circulated as a document of the General Assembly under agenda item 135.

(Signed)   J. A. THOMSON

/...

ANNEX I

Letter dated 28 April 1982 from the Permanent Representative
of the United Kingdom of Great Britain and Northern Ireland
to the United Nations addressed to the President of
the Security Council

I have the honour, with reference to the letter from the Permanent
Representative of Cuba dated 26 April 1982 to which was attached a communique by
the Coordinating Bureau of the Movement of Non-Aligned countries, to state the
following.

The United Kingdom shares the concern of the Coordinating Bureau over
developments in the region of the Falkland Islands. As resolution 502(1982)
adopted by the Security Council on 3 April 1982 makes clear, the Argentine invasion
of the Falkland Islands in defiance of the Security Council's call on 1 April that
force should not be used, caused the current breach of the peace in the region.
This breach of the peace will not be brought to an end before Argentina can be seen
to have complied with operative paragraph 2 of that resolution by withdrawing all
its forces from the Falkland Islands. Argentina's use of force was not only
contrary to the principles of the Movement of Non-Aligned countries, as the
communique notes, but also to paragraphs 3 and 4 of article 2 of the Charter of the
United Nations - the fundamental principles of peaceful settlement of disputes and
non-use of force.

With regard to the question of self-determination, I wish to draw Your
Excellency's attention to the following points. Self-determination is usually
referred to these days in the United Nations not as a principle, but rather as an
"inalienable right": in other words, it is a right which cannot be taken away.
This right derives principally from the Charter and the Covenants on Human Rights.
Article 1(2) of the Charter refers to self-determination of "peoples" and
article 73 recognises "that the interests of the inhabitants" of territories such
as the Falkland Islands are paramount. Article 1 of the two International
Covenants on Human Rights contains the following provision:

"1. All peoples have the right to self-determination. By virtue of that
right they freely determine their political status and freely pursue their
economic, social and cultural development." (emphasis added)

/...

Paragraph 3 of the same article establishes that the duty to promote the realisation of this right is imposed upon all states parties and not only upon those administering territories.

The Falkland Islanders are a people. The United Kingdom ratified both the Human Rights Covenants on their behalf. They are a permanent population. Over half of the people can trace back their roots on the Island to 1850. They have no other home. They have as is well known expressed their wishes regarding their political status in free and fair elections, the last having been held as recently as October 1981. The consistent practice of the United Nations shows that there is no minimum figure for a population to qualify for the right to self-determination: it suffices to cite the case of St Helena, another South Atlantic island with about 4000 people whose right to self-determination has been consistently upheld. The United Kingdom cannot accept that the right of self-determination as enshrined in the Charter and the Human Rights Covenants is subject to a special exception in the case of the Falkland Islands. This conclusion is confirmed by the Friendly Relations Declaration, adopted by consensus in 1970.

Turning to the question of sovereignty, the United Kingdom, whilst fully maintaining its position, acknowledges that its sovereignty has been disputed by Argentina on the basis of certain events in 1833. Attached to this letter is a memorandum setting out the history of settlement of the Falkland Islands. This shows that France has maintained a colony for about 3 years, Spain for at most about 41 years, the United Kingdom 158 years and Buenos Aires about at most 6 years. In particular, the present population of the Falkland Islands has been there, generation after generation, for the last 149 years, maintaining a viable pastoral economy and distinctive way of life. And whereas the French, Spanish and Buenos Ayrean colonies were very small (under 100 people), the only significant permanent population has been that from the mid-19th century to the present day, averaging just under 2000 persons.

Whilst no doubt much time and energy could be spent in reviewing the history of the Falkland Islands between the first settlement in 1764 and 1833, and whilst the United Kingdom is confident about the strength of its legal case over that period, these factors cannot be allowed to override the right of self-determination. In 1833, the age of the railway was just opening in Europe and it hardly seems appropriate to decide issues involving the welfare of people alive in the latter part of the 20th century on the basis of (disputed) events in the early part of the 19th century or even the 18th century. If the international community were to discount 149 years of history, there would hardly be an international boundary which did not immediately become subject to dispute.

I should be grateful if you would arrange for this letter and the enclosure to be circulated as documents of the Security Council.

I avail myself of this opportunity to renew to Your Excellency the assurances of my highest consideration.

(Signed)   A D PARSONS

/...

Appendix

History of the settlement of the Falkland Islands

14 August 1592	The English ship Desire, captained by John Davis, was driven off course in a storm to "certaine isles never before discovered .... lying 50 leagues or better from the ashore east and northerly from the (Magellan) Straits".
27 January 1690	Captain John Strong of the British ship Welfare, made the first recorded landing on the island. He gave the name "Falkland" to the sound between the two main islands in the group, after Viscount Falkland who was the treasurer of the British Royal Navy. The islands were uninhabited.
1700 – 1710	The Falkland Islands were visited by French seal hunters, from St Malo (hence the French name of Les Isles Malouines). No settlements were established.
31 January 1764	A Frenchman (Louis Bougainville) established a settlement at the west end of Berkely Sound (northwest of modern Stanley). The settlement was called Port Louis.
June 1764	A British expedition left to found a settlement.
August 1764	Formal possession of the islands was announced in the name of King Louis XV of France.
January 1765	The British expedition surveyed West Falkland and established a post at Port Egmont. Commodore Byron took formal possession of all the Islands for King George III.
June 1765	Commodore Byron reported that he had "coasted the islands for 70 leagues and saw no evidence of anyone being there".
January 1766	A second British expedition, led by Captain Macbride completed the settlement at Port Egmont and erected a block house for the defence of the settlement. In December 1766, he discovered the existence of the Bougainville settlement and gave the settlers formal notice to leave British territory.

/...

April 1767	France relinquished its claim to the islands to Spain in return for a financial indemnity. Spain re-named Port Louis as Puerto de la Soledad.
November 1769	The Captain of a British frigate ordered a Spanish ship to move away from Port Egmont. The Governor of the Spanish colony called on the British settlers to leave and the British captain warned the Spaniards to leave within 6 months.
4 June 1770	A Spanish frigate entered Port Egmont and was joined two days later by 4 Spanish ships to expel the British settlers.
10 June 1770	The British settlers capitulated and set sail for the United Kingdom. The United Kingdom protested to the Government of Spain.
22 January 1771	Spain issued a declaration in response to the British protest, agreeing to restore to the United Kingdom the possession of Port Egmont. The Spanish declaration stated that the restoration of Port Egmont to British possession "cannot nor ought in any wise to affect the question of the prior right of sovereignty to the Malouines Islands, otherwise called Falkland's Islands". The British accepted this declaration, together with full performance of the Spanish undertakings, as satisfaction for the injury done to the United Kingdom on 10 June 1770.
September 1771	Port Egmont was formally restored to the United Kingdom.
May 1774	The British establishment at Port Egmont was closed for reasons of economy. The British commanding officer left the British flag flying and a plaque declaring the Falkland Islands "to be the sole right and property" of King George III.
1777	The buildings at Port Egmont were destroyed by the Spanish.
1784	Spanish colony had 82 inhabitants (including 28 convicts).
June 1806	The Spanish settlement at Soledad was abandoned. Islands uninhabited.

9 November 1820	Col. Jewett paid a brief visit and took formal possession of the Falkland Islands on behalf of the newly independent government in Buenos Aires, without establishing a settlement. He found many vessels engaged in sealing including several British and US vessels.
1823	An attempt by Don Jorge Pacheco of Buenos Aires to establish a settlement failed.
5 January 1828	The government in Buenos Aires issued a decree establishing a colony at Soledad. Mr Vernet, a Hamburg merchant of French descent, and naturalised citizen of Buenos Aires was given three years to establish a colony and provision was made in case the population should extend to other islands.
10 June 1829	A decree was issued by the government of Buenos Aires asserting sovereignty, as successor to Spain, over the Falkland Islands.
30 August 1829	Mr Vernet established the colony, with only 20 men in whom he had confidence, according to his own account.
19 November 1829	The British Charge d'Affaires at Buenos Aires delivered a formal protest against the above decree on the grounds that "an authority has been assumed, incompatible with His Britannic Majesty's rights of sovereignty over the Falkland Islands. These rights founded upon the original discovery and subsequent occupation of the said islands, acquired an additional sanction from the restoration by (Spain) of the British settlement in the year 1771 ...."
25 November 1829	The Minister of Foreign Relations of Buenos Aires acknowledged receipt of the protest.
1831	Vernet's colony numbered about 100 persons.
July 1831	Three US sealing vessels were seized by Mr Vernet, who subsequently took one of them, the schooner "Harriet" to Buenos Aires where it was declared a prize by the government.
November 1831	The US consul denied that Mr Vernet had any right to capture and detain US vessels engaged in the fisheries at the Falkland Islands and remonstrating against all measures, including the decree of 10 June 1829, asserting a claim to the

	Falkland Islands. A formal protest was made in respect of the "Harriet" and two other vessels, the "Superior" and the "Breakwater".
December 1831	The Minister at Buenos Aires replied that an enquiry was being undertaken, but that the protest could not be admitted because the US consul did not appear to have been* specially authorised.
June 1832	The US ship "Lexington" under Captain Silas Duncan arrived at the Falkland Islands and destroyed the colony set up by Buenos Aires. The colonists fled. Some were captured and taken by the "Lexington" to Montevideo. Duncan declared the islands free of all government.
20 June 1832	The US Charge d'Affaires in Buenos Aires addressed a Note to the Minister responsible for foreign affairs about the seizure of the three US vessels. On instructions, the Charge denied "the existence of any right in this Republic to interrupt, molest, detain or capture any vessels belonging to citizens of the United States ...." The US government demanded restitution of all captured property and an indemnity, pointing out "that the citizens of the United States have enjoyed the rights of free fishery in these regions unmolested ...."
September 1832	Governor appointed ad interim by Buenos Ayrean government.
December 1832-3 January 1833	Captain Onslow of HMS Clio occupied Port Egmont. On reaching Soledad, Captain Onslow found a detachment of 25 Buenos Ayrean soldiers and their schooner "Sarandi". A mutiny had previously occurred at Port Louis while the "Sarandi" was at sea and the mutineers had killed the Governor. The Commander of the Argentine schooner had placed the mutineers in irons aboard a British schooner and they were, at his request, taken to Buenos Aires. Most people elected to be repatriated: 18 were persuaded to stay behind. Not a shot was fired on either side. Captain Onslow re-asserted British sovereignty, by raising the flag.
22 January 1833	The Minister at Buenos Aires protested to the British Charge d'Affaires.

/...

May 1833	The United Kingdom rejected the protest and affirmed that the Falkland Islands belonged to the Crown.
1833	Buenos Aires presented a claim to the US government in respect of USS Lexington's action. Diplomatic correspondence continued until at least 1886 but the US government rejected the claim for compensation on the grounds that it depended on the question of sovereignty.
1841	British Lieutenant Governor appointed and civil administration organised in Port Louis.
1841-2	Further protests about British settlement rejected.
1844	Capital moved to Stanley.
1845	Governor appointed. Legislative Council and Executive Council set up.
1851	Population estimated at 287 (see below).
1884-88	Further Argentine protests made and rejected.
1949	Elections to the Legislative Council instituted on the basis of universal adult suffrage.
1977	Voting age lowered to 18.
September/October 1981	General elections held for the Legislative Council.

Since the first census in 1851, the population has increased substantially, reaching a peak in the mid-1930s of some 2,400 inhabitants. Censuses have been taken every ten years and full details are in the annex to this account. The community thus established has set up its own social, economic and cultural structures within a framework which evolved in accordance with the wishes of the islanders themselves. They have freedom of expression and all of the basic rights guaranteed to them under the United Nations Charter. The United Kingdom, as administering authority, has submitted comprehensive information on the territory annually under Article 73(e) of the Charter and an up to date account based on this information is readily available in the Committee of 24's most recent working paper on the islands (document A/AC109/670 of 5 August 1981).

/...

Table

The population in the Census years 1851-1980

Year	Population
1851	287
1861	541
1871	811
1881	1,510
1891	1,789
1901	2,043
1911	2,272
1921	2,094
1931	2,392
1946	2,239
1953	2,230
1962	2,172
1972	1,957
1980	1,813

/...

ANNEX II

Letter dated 13 August 1982 from the Chargé d'Affaires a.i.
of the Permanent Mission of the United Kingdom of Great
Britain and Northern Ireland to the United Nations addressed
to the Secretary-General

I have the honour to refer to the letter of 23 July 1982 from the Chargé d'Affaires a.i. of the Permanent Mission of Argentina concerning the Falkland Islands (A/37/353). Many of the points made in the Argentine representative's letter have already been answered in earlier correspondence, and it is unnecessary for me to rehearse my Government's position in full. However, the letter asserts that the situation of the Falkland Islands is a special one "which differs from the typical case of colonialism". It goes on to claim that the principle of self-determination "is not applicable for the benefit of the occupants of a territory that is part of an independent State, from which it has been separated, against the will of its inhabitants, through an act of force by the occupying colonial Power".

The assertion that the case of the Falkland Islands differs from the typical case of colonialism may be intended as an oblique acknowledgement of the fact that the Falkland Islanders have consistently, and democratically, expressed their clear wish to remain British. This fact, which lies at the very heart of the matter, must not be lost sight of and is of crucial importance for evaluating the situation in terms of the Charter of the United Nations. The United Kingdom is justifiably proud of its record in responding to the freely expressed wishes of the peoples of non-self-governing territories by bringing the territories in question to independence or such other status as may be freely chosen by the people concerned. This policy corresponds directly to the purposes and principles

/...

enunciated in the Charter, and the United Kingdom has no intention of varying in that policy now.

The claim to set aside the right of self-determination in the case of the Falkland Islanders, on the grounds given in the Argentine letter, is therefore tendentious in the extreme and cannot be allowed to pass unchallenged.

A full statement of the history of settlement on the Falkland Islands is given in the letter of 28 April 1982 from Sir Anthony Parsons to the President of the Security Council (S/15007). Sir Anthony Parsons' letter also contains a detailed account of the right of self-determination and its place in the contemporary international system. It is noteworthy that the Argentine letter under reply not only fails to address the sovereignty question, but makes no reference at all to the Charter of the United Nations, or to documents adopted by the General Assembly by consensus, notably the Declaration on Principles of International Law Concerning Friendly Relations and Co-operation among States in accordance with the Charter of the United Nations (resolution 2625 (XXV)), which contains an important section entitled "The principle of equal rights and self-determination of peoples". Nor does the Argentine letter acknowledge contemporary documents in the field of human rights, which give a leading place to the right of self-determination. Instead, it contents itself with selective quotations from General Assembly resolutions 1514 (XV) and 1654 (XVI). Although the United Kingdom did not vote in favour of either resolution, its sympathy with their general objectives was made clear at the time of their adoption; moreover, so far as the specific issue of the Falkland Islands is concerned, the United Kingdom's position was made clear as far back as 1964, when the United Kingdom representative drew the attention of the Committee of 24 to the fact that resolution 1514 (XV) stated specifically that "all peoples have the right to self-determination", and that no fair-minded observer could construe its paragraph 6 as imposing a limitation on the universal application of the principle of self-determination, which was guaranteed under the Charter itself (A/AC.109/SC.4/SR.24).

The Argentine letter strives to create the impression that British settlement in the Falkland Islands in 1833 and thereafter took place against the will of a settled population who were forcibly displaced. In so doing it seeks to suggest that any rights of the present inhabitants stand in opposition to the rights of a dispossessed Argentine population. However, no evidence of any kind has been produced by the Government of Argentina to justify this. On the contrary, the historical evidence marshalled in Sir Anthony Parsons' letter (S/15007) shows that such occupation as there may have been of the Falkland Islands before 1833 was scattered, impermanent, almost entirely of non-Buenos-Airean origin, and did not in any sense constitute a settled population. There is no basis for seeking arbitrarily to set aside the rights of the present population of the Falkland Islands who (as was noted in Sir Anthony Parsons' letter of 30 June 1982 (A/S-12/31)) have been settled in the Islands in many cases to the seventh generation and have been conducting a peaceful and orderly existence under British authority for the past 150 years, that is to say, since well before the vast majority of contemporary international boundaries were established.

In conclusion, may I once again draw attention to the International Covenants on Economic and Social Rights and on Civil and Political Rights. Both of these Covenants have been ratified by the United Kingdom and this ratification extends also to the Falkland Islands. The common article 1 of the two Covenants declares that all peoples have the right of self-determination, and that by virtue of that right they freely determine their political status and freely pursue their economic, social and cultural development. The last paragraph of article 1 requires all States Parties, not merely those responsible for the administration of non-self-governing territories, to promote the realization of the right of self-determination, and to respect that right, in conformity with the provisions of the Charter of the United Nations. The Government of the United Kingdom looks forward to a similar endorsement by the Government of Argentina of those widely recognized principles, rather than an attempt to insinuate, as in the letter under reply, that the General Assembly has endorsed the idea of setting aside the wishes of the inhabitants of the Falkland Islands in favour of an externally-imposed interpretation of their interests. The specious argumentation about colonialism in the Argentine letter seeks to obscure Argentina's disregard of the right of self-determination, not to mention Argentina's wanton resort to the use of force in blatant disregard of the Charter, in defiance of a direct appeal by the Security Council, and in contempt of the principles to which the overwhelming majority of Member States have dedicated themselves in the conduct of their international relations.

I should be grateful if you would arrange for this letter to be circulated as a document of the General Assembly under item 133 of the provisional agenda.

(Signed)   Hamilton WHYTE
Deputy Permanent Representative

**UNITED
NATIONS**

A

 General Assembly

Distr.
GENERAL

A/37/592
2 November 1982

ORIGINAL: ENGLISH

Thirty-seventh session
Agenda item 135

QUESTION OF THE FALKLAND ISLANDS (MALVINAS)

Report of the Fourth Committee

Rapporteur: Mr. Victor G. GARCIA (Philippines)

1.   At its 4th plenary meeting, on 24 September 1982, the General Assembly, on the
recommendation of the General Committee, decided to include in the agenda of its
thirty-seventh session the item entitled "Question of the Falkland Islands
(Malvinas)". At the same meeting, the Assembly decided that the item should be
considered directly in plenary meeting, on the understanding that bodies and
individuals having an interest in the question would be heard in the Fourth
Committee in conjunction with the consideration of the item in plenary meeting.

2.   At its 10th meeting, on 29 October, the Fourth Committee granted the following
requests for hearing concerning the item:

Petitioner	Document
Anthony T. Blake and John E. Cheek	A/C.4/37/9
Susan Coutts de Maciello	A/C.4/37/9/Add.1
Bárbara Minto de Pennissi	A/C.4/37/9/Add.2
Reynaldo Ernesto Reed	A/C.4/37/9/Add.3
Alexander Jacob Betts	A/C.4/37/9/Add.4

3.   At the 12th meeting, on 2 November, following statements by the representatives of Chile, Panama, the United Kingdom of Great Britain and Northern Ireland and Argentina, the Fourth Committee heard the statements of the above-mentioned petitioners.   Mr. Cheek and Mr. Blake replied to questions put to them by the representatives of Argentina, Colombia, Venezuela, Nicaragua, Ecuador, Brazil, Cuba, Mexico, Bolivia and Panama.

4.   Summaries of the statements are contained in the record of the meeting (A/C.4/37/SR.12).

UNITED NATIONS

GENERAL

ASSEMBLY

PROVISIONAL

A/37/PV.53
4 November 1982

ENGLISH

Thirty-seventh session

GENERAL ASSEMBLY

PROVISIONAL VERBATIM RECORD OF THE FIFTY-THIRD MEETING

Held at Headquarters, New York,
on Wednesday, 3 November 1982, at 3 p.m.

President:	Mr. HOLLAI	(Hungary)
later:	Mr. TREIKI	(Libyan Arab Jamahiriya)
	(Vice-President)	

- Question of the Falkland Islands (Malvinas): /135/ (continued)

  (a) Report of the Special Committee on the Situation with regard to
      the Implementation of the Declaration on the Granting of Independence
      to Colonial Countries and Peoples

  (b) Report of the Fourth Committee

  (c) Draft resolution

82-63315/A

The PRESIDENT: I shall now call on those representatives who have asked to be allowed to speak in exercise of the right of reply.

I would remind the Assembly that, in accordance with decision 34/401, statements in exercise of the right of reply are limited to 10 minutes and should be made by representatives from their seats.

Sir John THOMSON (United Kingdom): I have asked to be allowed to speak in exercise of the right of reply to the statement made by the Argentine Foreign Minister yesterday. So much of his statement required correction that I hope I may be forgiven if I fail to discuss in detail obscure happenings in the eighteenth century, especially since I covered the main relevant points in my statement yesterday.

I disposed then of four persistent Argentine myths, namely: the myth that Argentina inherited sovereignty over the Falkland Islands from the Spanish Empire, the myth that Argentina settled the Falkland Islands after 1820, the myth that there was a settled Argentine population when Britain reoccupied the islands in 1833, and the myth that British reoccupation in 1833 was accomplished by the use of force. All of these are myths; all of them are unsupported by the facts.

Much of the statement delivered by the Foreign Minister was based on the presupposition that the Falkland Islands constituted part of the territory of Argentina in the early part of the nineteenth century. This turns out to be false. The major part of the Foreign Minister's statement therefore falls to the ground, because it is based on an unsustainable premise.

A good half of the Foreign Minister's statement was devoted to self-determination. It was dismaying to discover that his purpose was not to reaffirm the fundamental importance of self-determination. Instead he developed a complex doctrine to show that the Falkland Islands are a special exception to this basic and universal principle. In a letter circulated on 20 October Argentina even tries, although on the basis of no evidence at all, to persuade us into believing that the Assembly has previously ruled out the applicability of self-determination to the Falkland Islands. I have dealt with this specious argument in a letter distributed yesterday as document A/37/582 and do not propose to go further into it now.

The repeated Argentine claims that the General Assembly has specifically excluded the right of self-determination for the Falkland Islanders are not true. They are not even credible. They throw doubt on the credibility of

(Sir John Thomson, United Kingdom)

other Argentine statements. For instance, how genuine is their concern for the interests of the Falklanders? Anyone who listened to the testimony in the Fourth Committee yesterday will know that the Argentines aim to set themselves up as the judges of what the interests of the Falklanders are. Most people would think that the Falklanders would be the best judges of their own interests.

In his attempt to deny the Falkland Islanders' inherent right to self-determination, the Argentine Foreign Minister used two arguments, both untenable. First, he attempted to persuade us that the International Court of Justice itself had decided that the applicability of the principle of self-determination is dependent on the nature of the ties between the Territory in question and the claiming State. To do so, he plucked out of context two paragraphs in the 1975 advisory opinion on the Western Sahara. But he failed completely to make mention of the discussion of the right of self-determination in the 1971 advisory opinion on Namibia. This is the classic statement of the International Court's views on self-determination, as was reaffirmed by the Court in the 1975 opinion.

I do not propose to make copious citations from either opinion. I merely draw attention to paragraph 52 of the Namibia opinion, in which the International Court states, in the context of Article 73 of the Charter, that:

"... the subsequent development of international law in regard to Non-Self-Governing Territories, as enshrined in the Charter of the United Nations, made the principle of self-determination applicable to all of them."

In the 1975 opinion the Court declared that the provisions of resolution 1514 (XV)

"confirm and emphasize that the application of the right of self-determination requires a free and genuine expression of the will of the peoples concerned".

I imagine those were the sort of points which the representative from Zaire had in mind in the statement we have just heard.

(Sir John Thomson, United Kingdom)

Secondly, the Foreign Minister made the quite unworthy assertion that to accept the right to self-determination in the case of the Falkland Islands would set a precedent for Israeli settlements in occupied Arab territories. The comparison is far-fetched. The Israeli settlements were established in very recent years, against the direct condemnation of the overwhelming majority in the United Nations, in territories over which Israel neither claims nor exercises sovereignty and, moreover, territories which were already densely populated.

So much for the points that occupied a great deal of the Foreign Minister's statement.

What he failed to mention at all was Argentina's act of aggression in April of this year. Indeed, astonishingly, he actually referred to "British aggression". He went on to attack my Government for the establishment of a so-called military base in the Falkland Islands. The token size of the British garrison before the Argentine attack is known to all, as is its capture by vastly overwhelming Argentine forces on 2 April. Subsequent Argentine defiance of the Security Council left the United Kingdom no alternative but to act in self-defence. The presence of a larger garrison now is solely a measure of self-defence against a continuing Argentine threat. We look forward to the day when a fundamental change of Argentine policy allows the garrison to be reduced.

Finally, one word about "colonialism" and one word about the "sovereignty dispute"; both terms figure in the Foreign Minister's statement. His assertion that "the basic assumption of the decolonization process is the denial of the sovereignty of colonial Powers over Territories subject to that process" (A/37/PV.51, p. 26) will be greeted with astonishment by this Assembly, which well understands that the basic assumption of the decolonization process is not that at all, but the assertion of the rights of the peoples, notably their right to self-determination.

If there is a valid definition of "colonialism" it is that given in operative paragraph 1 of resolution 1514 (XV): "The subjection of peoples to alien subjugation, domination and exploitation..."

In relation to the Falklands, to whom does that apply? To Argentina or to the United Kingdom?

Secondly, the Foreign Minister made much of a joint communiqué agreed by his Government and my own in December 1976, and he was kind enough to have the full text circulated this morning. It can be seen that, far from supporting his assertion about the sovereignty dispute, the communiqué referred to negotiations on the following, <u>inter alia</u>: future political relations, including sovereignty; issues affecting the future of the Islands; the establishment of a framework for Anglo-Argentine economic co-operation in the South Atlantic; a stable and prosperous and politically durable future for the Islands, and so on. The communiqué clearly recognizes the need to consult the Falkland Islanders during the course of the negotiations. What the Foreign Minister referred to as 17 years of fruitless negotiations were in fact on a quite different basis from that claimed by him and on a quite different basis from what Argentina now proposes in this draft resolution. Indeed, his point demonstrates very clearly what I said yesterday, namely, that Argentina sees only one possible end to the negotiations, that is, the transfer of sovereignty from the United Kingdom to Argentina. They do not envisage a real negotiation in which the end is not predetermined. Delegations will also wish to take note of the fact that, far from being fruitless, these negotiations led to a number of useful improvements in the conditions for the Islanders, all of which were brutally interrupted and put to an end by the Argentine invasion in April of this year.

Mr. SHERMAN (United States of America): We are engaged in this debate in a serious attempt to implement the principles of the United Nations Charter by finding a peaceful and negotiated solution to the tragic conflict between the United Kingdom and Argentina over the Falkland Islands/Islas Malvinas. Our efforts to this end are not assisted by the attempt of the Soviet Union and its East German and Bulgarian clients to introduce extraneous propaganda charges unrelated to the issue at hand. True to its conspiratorial view of world events, the Soviet Union has abused this hall today with allegations that the tragedy for which both countries paid so dearly was part of a NATO conspiracy to achieve a military springboard in the South Atlantic. I submit that this interpretation is an insult to both the parties and to the nations of Latin America.

As my country learned through its extended efforts to bring the two parties to the negotiating table, the issues involved in this tragic dispute are real and of long standing. Let no one belittle them, least of all the Soviet Union, East Germany, Bulgaria and other clients, which played no role whatsoever in seeking to restore peace during the trying days of that conflict. Their effort now, when we are gathered here to put that conflict behind us once and for all, is a mindless and incredible effort to score propaganda points from the tragic conflict of interest and principle between two Member States. It perverts and stands on end truth and the search for peace to which most of us in this hall are committed.

The meeting rose at 7.05 p.m.

UNITED NATIONS

GENERAL

ASSEMBLY

PROVISIONAL

A/37/PV.55
6 November 1982

ENGLISH

Thirty-seventh session

GENERAL ASSEMBLY

PROVISIONAL VERBATIM RECORD OF THE FIFTY-FIFTH MEETING

Held at Headquarters, New York,
on Thursday, 4 November 1982, at 3 p.m.

President: Mr. HOLLAI   (Hungary)

    later: Mr. MORENO SALCEDO   (Philippines)
                     (Vice-President)

Question of the Falkland Islands (Malvinas): /135/ (continued)

(a) Report of the Special Committee on the Situation with regard to the
Implementation of the Declaration on the Granting of Independence
to Colonial Countries and Peoples

(b) Report of the Fourth Committee

(c) Draft resolution

This record contains the original text of speeches delivered in English and
interpretations of speeches in the other languages. The final text will be
printed in the Official Records of the General Assembly.

Corrections should be submitted to original speeches only. They should be
sent under the signature of a member of the delegation concerned, within one week,
to the Chief of the Official Records Editing Section, Department of Conference
Services, room A-3550, 866 United Nations Plaza, and incorporated in a copy of
the record.

82-63327/A

(<u>Mi</u>ss D<u>e</u>ver, Bel<u>g</u>ium)

to say the least, were questionable. Nevertheless, the draft resolution now before us still contains elements which we cannot support. Essentially, it is a question of the reference to a colonial situation and to the link it establishes with world peace. Moreover, the third preambular paragraph refers to three resolutions in the voting on which my country abstained. Furthermore, in keeping with Article 73, relating to Non-Self-Governing Territories, the sixth preambular paragraph should have referred not only to the interests but also to the aspirations of the population of the islands. Finally, although we are, as I said earlier, very much in favour of a resumption of negotiations, the draft resolution would have been better balanced had the reference been general instead of being limited to just one aspect.

For those reasons, my delegation will abstain in the voting on this draft resolution. It seems to us that the adoption of this draft resolution might exacerbate the differences, which would be prejudicial to the negotiations and to the peaceful settlement of the dispute, in accordance with the principles of the Charter, which we so earnestly desire.

<u>Sir John THOMSON</u> (United Kingdom): I wish to explain why my delegation is going to vote against the draft resolution before us.

I sense that many delegations here are troubled at being obliged to vote on it. There is a feeling that it is a mistake for the Argentine Government to have pressed this matter to a vote so soon after their invasion of the Falkland Islands. This invasion showed that the present Argentine régime will stop at nothing in pursuit of its claim to sovereignty. "Stop at nothing" is not an idle phrase. Neither appeals from the Secretary-General and the President of the Security Council nor a mandatory resolution of the Security Council were heeded. Even now the Argentines continue to make it clear, especially to their own public opinion, that they expect to have what they call a second round and are preparing for it. Only two days ago the official Argentine news agency attributed to a high-level source the statement that "Argentina will not alter its position regarding the cessation of hostilities in the South Atlantic". That source, the agency said, was here in Argentina's Permanent Mission to the United Nations. The official news agency said that the purpose of this statement was to deny a report that Argentina would finally declare a cessation of hostilities.

(Sir John Thomson, United Kingdom)

It is in any case impossible to accept a call for negotiations as if the Argentine invasion had never occurred. It is impossible to accept negotiations when basic principles are excluded. These principles are fundamental. They cannot be drafted or negotiated away or made to mean something else.

Mr. ADELMAN (United States of America): The United States has always supported a negotiated settlement between the United Kingdom and Argentina in their tragic conflict over the Falkland Islands (Islas Malvinas). At the outset of the conflict my Government made sustained efforts to bring the two parties to the negotiating table. We said at that time:

> "The United States stands behind the principle that the use of force to settle disputes should not be allowed anywhere, and especially in this hemisphere where a significant number of territorial disputes remain to be solved diplomatically. For the United States, the Falkland crisis has been and still is a particularly agonizing, tragic event. As the whole world knows, we have a longstanding alliance and, beyond that, the closest relations of friendship with Great Britain, the country from which our political institutions, law and language derive. But we have not forgotten for a moment our close geographical, economic and political relations with our Latin neighbours. We not only care about this hemisphere, we are part of this hemisphere, and we share many of the aspirations, goals and dreams of all nations of the Americas." (S/PV.2362, p. 92)

That is why the United States tried so hard to avoid the conflict over the Falklands, why we hoped so intensely to reduce and isolate it, and why we support any realistic diplomatic initiative which will put a just end to it. The search for a negotiated settlement to this conflict led the United States to support Security Council resolutions 502 (1982) and 505 (1982). The essential elements of those resolutions remain the framework of the search for peace. The same vital need for a negotiated solution that would put this conflict once and for all behind us underlies our vote today.

The resolution before us, in its revised and final form, expressly reaffirms the principles of the United Nations Charter concerning non-use of force in international relations. We welcome its references to cessation of hostilities and to the intention of the parties not to renew them. The cost, in blood and treasure, to both Argentina and the United Kingdom

(Mr. Adelman, United States)

dictates that force must never again be used in this dispute. We assume, therefore, in supporting this resolution a shared responsibility for preventing the use of force in the future.

The United States would not have voted for any resolution which prejudged the question of sovereignty or the outcome of negotiations. We have never taken a position on the question of sovereignty and we do not do so now. We conclude, however, that the resolution before us does not legally prejudice the position of either Argentina or the United Kingdom and, in fact, opens the way towards negotiations in good faith and without any preordained result.

Finally, in calling on the parties to negotiate, let us not forget that these islands are and have been for generations the home of a small but resolute population of island people. The United States assumes that negotiations undertaken by the United Kingdom and Argentina must necessarily take into account the aspirations of the Falkland Islanders.

In supporting this resolution, the United States affirms that this dispute, like all others, should be settled by discussion and never by force and that the fate of peoples should never be settled without due account being taken of their views, values, interests, and rights. Let these principles and those of the United Nations Charter itself governing peaceful resolution of disputes serve as a basis for negotiation to close this unhappy chapter and move forward again towards peace, understanding and development in this hemisphere.

Mr. ZAKI (Maldives): My delegation would like to record the fact that its abstention in the voting just a few moments ago on the draft resolution contained in document A/37/L.3/Rev.1 was the result of the great importance that the Republic of Maldives attaches to a principle involved in the sad episode of the question of the Falkland Islands (Malvinas). I mean the strict adherence by every member of the international community to the cardinal principle of the United Nations Charter on the non-use of force or the threat of force in international relations and the settlement

The PRESIDENT: We have heard the last speaker in explanation of vote after the voting.

(spoke in Spanish)

. I call on the representative of Argentina, who wishes to speak in exercise of his right of reply. I remind him that, in accordance with General Assembly decision 34/401, statements in exercise of the right of reply are limited to 10 minutes and should be made by representatives from their places.

Mr. AGUIRRE LANARI (Argentina) (interpretation from Spanish): The debate so happily concluded with this vote has clearly demonstrated that the objectives of Latin America and of the United Kingdom with regard to the Malvinas Islands are different and opposing. On the one hand, the Latin American countries, encouraged by a regional solidarity that has few precedents, fully support the resumption of the negotiations for the peaceful and final settlement of the sovereignty dispute. They have supported, with the backing of this Assembly, the establishment once and for all of peace and justice in the South Atlantic through the principal and most important means provided by the Charter for the settlement of international disputes.

The British objective was quite different, as was seen in the debate; the United Kingdom merely sought the consolidation of a colonial situation in a Latin American territory. With that objective in mind and through provocative declarations and tactics aimed at dragging my delegation into a climate of confrontation, it tried hard to prevent the adoption of the Latin American draft resolution. Thus it centred its statements on the recent past, grotesquely distorting history and law, and apparently closed all doors on a draft resolution that only requested negotiations between the parties within the framework of earlier decisions of this General Assembly.

To object to a draft resolution the only objective of which is the peaceful and just settlement of an international dispute is not easy. It is even less so when the draft resolution has the firm backing of a whole region. Nor is it easy to attack it because of its alleged untimely nature, because no one can accept as logical the argument that because an international conflict occurred only recently

(<u>Mr. Aguirre Lanari, Argentina</u>)

attempts should not be made to put an end to the causes of it. In fact, we
are entitled to suspect that such refusal to negotiate is not an opportunist action
but rather a firmly established principle of British foreign policy towards my
country, as demonstrated by 17 years of fruitless negotiations. We Latin
Americans are thus not surprised that only a few countries, whose special
circumstances we all know, voted against the Latin American draft resolution.

(Mr. Aguirre Lanari, Argentina)

A detailed response to the statements made by the United Kingdom delegation would merely serve to feed the undesirable climate of confrontation sought by its Government, and we will not fall into that trap. Therefore, I shall limit myself to recalling that on various occasions - the most recent of them at the beginning of this debate - in my statements I have set out with all clarity and on the basis of solid historical facts the reasons why the Malvinas Islands belong to Argentina and should be returned to it. I refer representatives to those statements and confirm them.

I do not wish to discuss the issue at greater length, because I think that if we are seeking negotiation we should not unnecessarily aggravate the situation. We should like to demonstrate with facts that we genuinely want peaceful negotiations. That is why I shall not refer to many statements made in this hall.

However, there is one that I cannot pass over in silence, in the light of history and in the interest of justice. It is not correct, as was recently claimed, that this is a single Government's cause. Those who know my country and its history realize that this is not the cause of one single Government: this is the cause of a nation. The democratic Government that will shortly be elected in Argentina will take up the banner that we whole-heartedly raise today with the same warmth, conviction and strength in defence of our rights, which are the rights of the Republic of Argentina and of Latin America.

That is why I call for the initiation of fruitful and honest negotiations, so that we may demonstrate to the world our determination and, as has been said here, so that this world parliament can foster a decision for peace and justice.

The PRESIDENT: That concludes our consideration of agenda item 135.

The meeting rose at 7.35 p.m.

NITED
ATIONS

General Assembly

Distr.
LIMITED

A/37/L.3/Rev.1
1 November 1982
ENGLISH
ORIGINAL: SPANISH

irty-seventh session
enda item 135

QUESTION OF THE FALKLAND ISLANDS (MALVINAS)

Argentina, Bolivia, Brazil, Chile, Colombia, Costa Rica, Cuba,
Dominican Republic, Ecuador, El Salvador, Guatemala, Haiti,
Honduras, Mexico, Nicaragua, Panama, Paraguay, Peru, Uruguay,
and Venezuela: revised draft resolution

The General Assembly,

Having considered the question of the Falkland Islands (Malvinas),

Realizing that the maintenance of colonial situations is incompatible with the
ited Nations ideal of universal peace,

Recalling its resolutions 1514 (XV) of 14 December 1960, 2065 (XX) of
December 1965, 3160 (XXVIII) of 14 December 1973 and 31/49 of 1 December 1976,

Recalling further Security Council resolutions 502 (1982) of 3 April 1982 and
5 (1982) of 26 May 1982,

Taking into account the existence of a de facto cessation of hostilities in
e South Atlantic and the expressed intention of the parties not to renew them,

Reaffirming the need for the parties to take due account of the interests of
e population of the Falkland Islands (Malvinas) in accordance with the provisions
General Assembly resolutions 2065 (XX) and 3160 (XXVIII),

Likewise reaffirming the principles of the Charter of the United Nations on
e non-use of force or the threat of force in international relations and the
aceful settlement of international disputes,

1.   Requests the Governments of Argentina and the United Kingdom of Great
itain and Northern Ireland to resume negotiations in order to find as soon as
ssible a peaceful solution to the sovereignty dispute relating to the question of
e Falkland Islands (Malvinas);

-29406   0568Z (E)

2.   Requests the Secretary-General, on the basis of this resolution, to undertake a renewed mission of good offices in order to assist the parties in complying with the request made in paragraph 1 above, and to take the necessary measures to that end;

3.   Requests the Secretary-General to submit a report to the General Assembly at its thirty-eighth session on the progress made in the implementation of this resolution;

4.   Decides to include in the provisional agenda of its thirty-eighth session the item entitled "Question of the Falkland Islands (Malvinas)".

UNITED NATIONS

GENERAL
ASSEMBLY

PROVISIONAL

A/37/PV.55
6 November 1982

ENGLISH

Thirty-seventh session

GENERAL ASSEMBLY

PROVISIONAL VERBATIM RECORD OF THE FIFTY-FIFTH MEETING

Held at Headquarters, New York,
on Thursday, 4 November 1982, at 3 p.m.

President: Mr. HOLLAI (Hungary)

later: Mr. MORENO SALCEDO (Philippines)
(Vice-President)

- Question of the Falkland Islands (Malvinas): /135/ (continued)

   (a) Report of the Special Committee on the Situation with regard to the
       Implementation of the Declaration on the Granting of Independence
       to Colonial Countries and Peoples

   (b) Report of the Fourth Committee

   (c) Draft resolution

   This record contains the original text of speeches delivered in English and
interpretations of speeches in the other languages. The final text will be
printed in the Official Records of the General Assembly.

   Corrections should be submitted to original speeches only. They should be
sent under the signature of a member of the delegation concerned, within one week,
to the Chief of the Official Records Editing Section, Department of Conference
Services, room A-3550, 866 United Nations Plaza, and incorporated in a copy of
the record.

82-63327/A

A recorded vote was taken.

In favour: Afghanistan, Albania, Algeria, Angola, Argentina, Austria, Benin, Bolivia, Botswana, Brazil, Bulgaria, Burundi, Byelorussian Soviet Socialist Republic, Cape Verde, Central African Republic, Chile, China, Colombia, Comoros, Congo, Costa Rica, Cuba, Cyprus, Czechoslovakia, Democratic Kampuchea, Democratic Yemen, Dominican Republic, Ecuador, El Salvador, Equatorial Guinea, Ethiopia, Gabon, German Democratic Republic, Ghana, Greece, Grenada, Guatemala, Guinea, Guinea-Bissau, Haiti, Honduras, Hungary, India, Indonesia, Iran, Iraq, Israel, Ivory Coast, Japan, Lao People's Democratic Republic, Liberia, Libyan Arab Jamahiriya, Madagascar, Malaysia, Mali, Malta, Mexico, Mongolia, Morocco, Mozambique, Nicaragua, Nigeria, Pakistan, Panama, Paraguay, Peru, Philippines, Poland, Romania, Rwanda, Sao Tome and Principe, Spain, Suriname, Syrian Arab Republic, Togo, Tunisia, Uganda, Ukrainian Soviet Socialist Republic, Union of Soviet Socialist Republics, United Arab Emirates, United Republic of Tanzania, United States of America, Upper Volta, Uruguay, Venezuela, Viet Nam, Yemen, Yugoslavia, Zambia, Zimbabwe

Against: Antigua and Barbuda, Belize, Dominica, Fiji, Gambia, Malawi, New Zealand, Oman, Papua New Guinea, Solomon Islands, Sri Lanka, United Kingdom of Great Britain and Northern Ireland

Abstaining: Australia, Bahamas, Bahrain, Bangladesh, Barbados,
Belgium, Bhutan, Burma, Canada, Chad, Denmark, Egypt,
Finland, France, Germany, Federal Republic of, Guyana,
Iceland, Ireland, Italy, Jamaica, Jordan, Kenya,
Kuwait, Lebanon, Lesotho, Luxembourg, Maldives,
Mauritania, Mauritius, Nepal, Netherlands, Niger,
Norway, Portugal, Qatar, Saint Lucia, Saint Vincent and
the Grenadines, Samoa, Saudi Arabia, Senegal, Sierra
Leone, Singapore, Somalia, Sudan, Swaziland, Sweden,
Thailand, Trinidad and Tobago, Turkey, United Republic
of Cameroon, Vanuatu, Zaire

The draft resolution was adopted by 90 votes to 12, with 52 abstentions.
(resolution 37/9)

The PRESIDENT: I shall now call on those delegations that wish to
explain their votes.*

* Mr. Moreno Salcedo (Philippines), Vice-President, took the Chair.

UNITED STATES MISSION TO THE UNITED NATIONS

799 UNITED NATIONS PLAZA
NEW YORK, N Y 1001⁷

⌐SS RELEASE

⌐R RELEASE ON DELIVERY
⌐ECK TEXT AGAINST DELIVERY

Press Release USUN 112-(82)
November 4, 1982

⌐atement by Ambassador Kenneth L. Adelman, United States
⌐presentative to the 37th Session of the United Nations General
⌐ssembly, in Plenary, in Explanation of Vote on Item 135, Question of
⌐e Falkland Islands (Malvinas), November 4, 1982

⌐. President, the United States has always supported a negotiated
⌐ttlement between the United Kingdom and Argentina in their tragic
⌐nflict over the Falkland Islands (Islas Malvinas). At the outset of
⌐e conflict, my government made sustained efforts to bring the two
⌐rties to the negotiating table. We said at that time, "the United
⌐ates stands behind the principle that the use of force to settle
⌐sputes should not be allowed anywhere, and especially in this
⌐emisphere where a significant number of territorial disputes remain
⌐ be solved diplomatically. For the United States, the Falkland
⌐isis has been and still is a particularly agonizing, tragic event.
⌐s the whole world knows, we have a longstanding alliance and, beyond
⌐at, the closest relations of friendship with Great Britain, the
⌐untry from which our political institutions, law and language
⌐erive. But we have not forgotten for a moment our close
⌐eographical, economic and political relations with our Latin
⌐eighbors. We do not only care about this hemisphere, we are part of
⌐is hemisphere, and we share many of the aspirations, goals and
⌐reams of all nations of the Americas...."

⌐hat is why the United States tried so hard to avoid the conflict on
⌐he Falklands, why we hoped so intensely to reduce and isolate it, and
⌐hy we support any realistic diplomatic intiative which will put a
⌐ust end to it. The search for a negotiated settlement to this
⌐onflict led the United States to support Security Council Resolutions
⌐02 and 505. The essential elements of those resolutions remain the
⌐ramework of the search for peace. The same vital need for a
⌐egotiated solution that would put this conflict once and for all
⌐ehind us underlies our vote today.

⌐his resolution before us, in its revised and final form, expressly
⌐eaffirms the principles of the United Nations Charter concerning
⌐on-use of force in international relations. We welcome its
⌐eferences to cessation of hostilities and to the intention of the
⌐arties not to renew them. The cost, in blood and treasure, to both
⌐rgentina and the United Kingdom dictates that force must never again
⌐e used in this dispute. We assume, therefore, in supporting this
⌐esolution a shared responsibility for preventing the use of force in
⌐he future.

The United States would not have voted for any resolution which
prejudged the question of sovereignty or the outcome of negotiations
We have never taken a position on the question of sovereignty and we
do not now do so. We conclude, however, that the resolution before
does not legally prejudice the position of either Argentina or the
United Kingdom and, in fact, opens the way toward negotiations in go
faith without any preordained result.

Finally, in calling on the parties to negotiate, let us not forget,
Mr. President, that these islands are and have been for generations
the home of a small, but resolute, population of island people. The
United States assumes that negotiations undertaken by the United
Kingdom and Argentina must necessarily take into account the
aspirations of the Falkland Islanders.

In supporting this resolution, the United States affirms that this
dispute, like all others, should be settled by discussion and never
force and that the fate of peoples should never be settled without a
account being taken of their views, values, interests, and rights.

Let these principles and those of the United Nations Charter itself
governing peaceful resolution of disputes serve as a basis for
negotiation to close this unhappy chapter and move forward again
toward peace, understanding and development in this hemisphere.

****

DECRETO-LEY Nº 2.191. — Buenos Aires, 28|2|57

VISTO el Decreto-Ley Nº 21.178|56 por el que se establecen nuevos límites para la ex-provincia de Patagonia, hoy de Santa Cruz; y CONSIDERANDO: que es necesario adoptar las medidas necesarias para el gobierno de los territorios que, en virtud de aquel acto, han quedado fuera de los límites de las provincias;

El Presidente Provisional de la Nación Argentina, en Ejercicio del Poder Legislativo, Decreta con Fuerza de Ley:

PARTE PRIMERA — DISPOSICIONES PRELIMINARES

CAPITULO I. ESTABLECIMIENTO

1. Declaración

Artículo 1º — Queda restablecido el Territorio Nacional de la Tierra del Fuego, Antártida e Islas del Atlántico Sud, cuya organización, gobierno y administración se regirá por las disposiciones del presente decreto-ley.

2. Territorios que lo forman

Art. 2º — El Territorio Nacional de la Tierra del Fuego, Antártida e Islas del Atlántico Sud comprende: la parte oriental de la Isla Grande y demás islas del archipiélago de Tierra del Fuego e Islas de los Estados y Año Nuevo, conforme a los límites fijados por el tratado del 23 de julio de 1881, las Islas Malvinas, las Islas Georgias del Sur, las Islas Sandwich del Sur y el Sector Antártico Argentino comprendido entre los meridianos 25º Oeste y 74º Oeste y el paralelo 60º Sur.

3. Personalidad jurídica

Art. 3º — El Territorio Nacional de la Tierra del Fuego, Antártida e Islas del Atlántico Sud y sus corporaciones municipales constituyen personas de derecho público, privado de existencia necesaria.

4. Ciudad capital

Art. 4º — Declárase capital del Territorio Nacional de la Tierra del Fuego, Antártida e Islas del Atlántico Sud, la ciudad de Ushuaia, en la que deberán tener asiento el gobierno local y las oficinas principales federales.

5. Divisiones

Art. 5º — El territorio será dividido en departamentos y éstos en distritos rurales y urbanos; los que, a su vez, se subdividirán en secciones.

Las jurisdicciones política, administrativa, municipal, judicial y cualesquiera otras de servicio público, se determinarán sobre la base de estas divisiones y subdivisiones.

6. Fundación de pueblos

Art. 6º — Una ley especial establecerá los requisitos que deberán cumplirse para la fundación de pueblos en tierras de propiedad particular o fiscal y las bases de un trazado urbano, en el que se preverá la transferencia a favor del territorio de las tierras necesarias para obras y servicios públicos.

La misma ley establecerá la forma de urbanizar las agrupaciones o núcleos de población existentes.

7. Denominaciones

Art. 7º — Las denominaciones de las divisiones y subdivisiones administrativas, pueblos y lugares del territorio, serán establecidas teniendo en cuenta las tradiciones nacionales y especialmente presente las locales. En ningún caso podrá darse nombres de personas, hasta pasados veinte años de su muerte.

CAPITULO II — JURISDICCION Y COMPETENCIA

1. Materias del gobierno local

Art. 8º — Serán materias del gobierno local del territorio, todas aquéllas que en virtud del presente estatuto se le confieren y todas las necesarias o convenientes a la administración general de dicho territorio.

2. Enseñanza primaria

Art. 9º — La organización, administración y funcionamiento de la enseñanza primaria en el territorio, estará a cargo de las autoridades locales por intermedio de un Consejo Escolar compuesto de seis padres de familia, de los cuales cuatro por lo menos deberán ser de nacionalidad argentina.

3. Sanidad y Asistencia Social

Art. 10. — En todo núcleo urbano se instalará un establecimiento de sanidad y asistencia social, que será colocado en lo posible bajo la dirección de las autoridades comunales. El gobierno del territorio está obligado a contribuir financieramente al mantenimiento adecuado de estos servicios.

4. Registro público oficial

Art. 11. — Se organizará un registro público oficial que tendrá a su cargo las siguientes secciones: a) Registro de la propiedad; b) Registro civil; c) Registro agropecuario (de prenda agraria), de marcas y señales, de certificados de venta de semovientes, de guías de semovientes y toda clase de frutos del país), de minas y cateos; d) De comercio, etc. Funcionará por lo menos una delegación del registro público oficial en todos los pueblos o lugares en que haya juzgado de paz.

5. Tierras y bosques fiscales

Art. 12. — Corresponde a la Nación el dominio y disposición de las tierras y bosques fiscales.

6. Minas y productos del subsuelo

Art. 13. — Corresponde también a la Nación el dominio de las minas y productos del subsuelo y a su gobierno la determinación de las condiciones de aprovechamiento de esas substancias, así como los hidrocarburos y los minerales y elementos energéticos y nucleares, cuyas condiciones de aprovechamiento serán exclusivamente fijadas por el gobierno de la Nación.

7. Presupuesto territorial

Art. 14. — Los gastos generales del territorio se atenderán con sus recursos propios y las asignaciones globales anuales que acuerde la Nación para la organización y el funcionamiento del gobierno local y para el fomento y progreso del territorio. El presupuesto de gastos debe ser preparado por las respectivas autoridades del territorio y elevado al gobierno federal para su aprobación.

PARTE SEGUNDA — GOBIERNO Y ADMINISTRACION

CAPITULO I. ORGANOS

Art. 15. — El gobierno y administración del territorio será ejercido por un gobernador, un consejo territorial y una administración de justicia. Actuará el Congreso de la Nación como legislatura local. Una vez que el registro nacional de electores cuente con más de tres mil inscriptos, cesará el consejo territorial y se instalará una legislatura local electiva.

CAPITULO II. GOBERNADOR

1. Calidades - Nombramiento - Período Incompatibilidad

Art. 16. — Para ser gobernador del territorio se requiere ser argentino nativo, y tener más de treinta años de edad. Será designado por el Poder Ejecutivo con acuerdo del Senado, por un período de tres años, pudiendo ser reelecto. Su ejercicio será incompatible con cualquier otro cargo o función.

2. Privilegios

Art. 17. — El gobernador, desde el día de su nombramiento hasta el cese de sus funciones, no podrá ser arrestado, ni detenido, ni sometido a proceso criminal por autoridad alguna, excepto el caso de ser sorprendido "in fraganti", sin previa autorización del Poder Ejecutivo Nacional.

Art. 18. — En caso de ausencia o impedimento del gobernador, lo reemplazará el secretario, y a falta de éste, el funcionario que el Poder Ejecutivo determine.

4. Residencia

Art. 19. — El gobernador tendrá residencia habitual en la ciudad capital. No podrá ausentarse del territorio por un espacio mayor de quince días sin autorización expresa del Poder Ejecutivo.

5. Deberes y atribuciones

Art. 20.— El gobernador es el jefe de la administración del territorio, la que ejercerá de acuerdo a las leyes y reglamentos vigentes. El gobernador ejercerá por sí y sin necesidad de autorización alguna los siguientes deberes y atribuciones:

1 — Es el agente directo y natural del Gobierno Federal dentro del territorio, siendo la autoridad local superior y el jefe de la administración.

2 — Ejerce la administración general del territorio, disponiendo de las atribuciones necesarias para hacer cumplir la Constitución y las leyes de la Nación, así como las disposiciones que dictare.

3 — Representa al territorio en sus relaciones con las autoridades del Gobierno Nacional y de las restantes provincias.

4 — Dicta los reglamentos, ordenanzas y disposiciones convenientes para la administración, fomento y seguridad del territorio en todo lo que sea materia de su competencia.

5 — Dispone la recaudación de los impuestos y demás rentas del territorio, y su inversión, así como la de los demás fondos que le corresponden, con arreglo al presupuesto general aprobado por la Nación, de conformidad con las leyes y reglamentaciones nacionales vigentes, rindiendo cuenta de ello.

6 — Celebra y firma, en representación del territorio, los actos y contratos necesarios para el cumplimiento de su gestión administrativa, fiscaliza su cumplimiento, así como el de las concesiones que se hubieren acordado dentro del monto y condiciones que se establecerán por ley de la Nación.

7 — Dispone y ejecuta las obras públicas locales con los fondos que acuerde el presupuesto, aplicando las disposiciones de la ley de obras públicas de la Nación.

8 — Prepara el presupuesto de gastos y cálculo de recursos del territorio, el cual deberá dividirse en dos secciones: la primera tratará de los gastos y recursos atendidos por el Tesoro Nacional; la segunda, de los gastos y recursos atendidos por los fondos propios del territorio; elevándolo para su aprobación.

9 — Interviene en la administración de las tierras y bosques fiscales otorgando inclusive las concesiones del caso, dentro de los límites fijados por el presente Estatuto y las leyes que rigen la materia o que se dicten en lo sucesivo

10. — Dicta las medidas necesarias para conservar el orden público del territorio, ejerciendo las atribuciones inherentes al poder de policía, con arreglo a las leyes de la materia.

11. — Resuelve todos los asuntos que se le plantean en el orden administrativo que no constituyan el ejercicio de una facultad reglada, sin perjuicio de los recursos jerárquicos que correspondan.

12 — Nombra y remueve:

a) Los secretarios de despacho;

b) Los funcionarios y empleados de la gobernación del territorio;

c) Personal de policía;

d) Las comisiones de fomento;

e) Con acuerdo del Consejo Territorial o de la Legislatura una vez que ésta se constituya, el contador general del territorio, los miembros del consejo escolar y el director del registro público oficial; cuando el cuerpo esté en receso el nombramiento puede hacerse en comisión, con cargo de solicitar el acuerdo en oportunidad; si no hubiera pronunciamiento sobre los acuerdos solicitaddos, éstos caducarán al final del período ordinario de sesiones, no pudiendo volverse a nombrar al funcionario que así cesara;

Los jueces de paz, secretarios y demás personal de la justicia de paz.

13 — Dispone y distribuye las fuerzas policiales que continuarán bajo el régimen establecido por las leyes nacionales, prestando el c curso de las mismas toda vez que le requerido por los tribunales del territo justicia de paz y demás autoridades con cultades para ello.

14 — Inaugura el período anual de deliberacio del Consejo Territorial o Legislatura — se su caso —, informando sobre el estado de administración local, y presenta dentro de treinta días subsiguientes el presupuesto neral de gastos y cálculo de recursos y cuenta de inversión.

15 — Asegura la regularidad y eficacia de los ser cios públicos, el progreso y desarrollo de instrucción, la educación moral y física, fomento de la industria y del comercio, higiene pública, la asistencia social, el p greso general del territorio y, en general, do lo tendiente a la efectiva prosperidad bienestar del mismo.

16 — Convoca a elecciones para la designación las autoridades electivas del territorio, conformidad con las leyes y reglamentos la materia.

17 — Toma todas las medidas conducentes a mejor solución de las cuestiones de em gencia que se refieren al interés general la población y que reclamen disposiciones i mediatas, dando cuenta, en su caso, oport namente de ello a la autoridad correspo diente.

18 — Dispone asuetos administrativos en una varias localidades o en toda la jurisdicción a su cargo en ocasión de festividades locale o en celebración de acontecimientos nacio nales.

19 — Acuerda, previo el cumplimiento de los re caudos legales correspondientes, autorizació provisional para que las sociedades o asoci ciones de utilidad pública que aún no tenga personería jurídica actúen dentro de la juri dicción del territorio.

20. — Ejerce superintendencia sobre todas las of cinas nacionales que funcionen en el territo rio, de acuerdo con las normas que dicte Poder Ejecutivo Nacional.

CAPITULO III. SECRETARIO
DEL DESPACHO

1. Número - Ramos

Art. 21.— El despacho de los negocios admini trativos estará a cargo de uno o más secretarios no brados por el gobernador. En este último caso, deslindará los ramos y las funciones de cada uno ellos y el orden en que reemplazarán al gobernado en el caso previsto por el Artículo 18º. El númer de secretarios no podrá exceder de cuatro.

2. Calidades

Art. 22.— Para ser secretario se requiere ser a gentino nativo y mayor de veinticinco años.

3. Refrendo

Art. 23.— La firma de los gobernadores será r frendada por el secretario del ramo que correspond al acto o documento a emitirse. Sin este requisi aquélla carece de eficacia.

4. Responsabilidad - Atribuciones

Art. 24.— Los secretarios son responsables de l actos que legalizan y solidariamente de los que acue dan con sus colegas. Los secretarios no pueden por solos, en ningún caso, tomar resoluciones, salvo l concernientes al orden administrativo interno de s respectivos departamentos.

5. Reemplazo

Art. 25.— En caso de ausencia o impedimento d secretario, el gobernador determinará el funcionari que se hará cargo del despacho.

Los secretarios pueden concurrir a las sesiones d Consejo Territorial o la Legislatura —en su caso— informar ante ella y tomar parte en los debates, s voto.

CAPITULO IV. CONSEJO TERRITORIAL
1. Composición - Calidades

Art. 26. — Existirá un consejo territorial formado por cinco miembros argentinos, mayores de treinta años de edad e inscriptos en el registro electoral del territorio por lo menos con dos años de antigüedad.

2. Nombramiento

Art. 27. — Los consejeros serán designados por el Poder Ejecutivo, durarán tres años en sus funciones y podrán ser reelectos.

3. Incompatibilidades

Art. 28. — El cargo de consejero es incompatible con cualquier otro rentado por el Estado, salvo el ejercicio de la docencia. Tampoco podrá ser titular de contratos de servicios públicos con el gobierno territorial y/o corporaciones municipales ni integrar sociedades beneficiarias de ese tipo de contrato.

4. Remoción - Privilegios

Art. 29. — Los consejeros sólo podrán ser removidos en sus funciones por el Poder Ejecutivo. Los consejeros, desde el día de su nombramiento hasta el cese de sus funciones, no podrán ser arrestados, ni detenidos, ni sometidos a proceso criminal por autoridad alguna, excepto el caso de ser sorprendido "in fraganti", sin previa autorización del Poder Ejecutivo Nacional.

5. Quórum - Mayoría

Art. 30. — El Consejo deberá funcionar con la presencia de no menos de tres de sus miembros y las decisiones tomarse por mayoría de los presentes, salvo disposición en contrario de este decreto-ley.

6. Funciones - Atribuciones

Art. 31. — El Consejo Territorial tendrá las siguientes funciones y atribuciones:

1. Dictar su propio reglamento interno.
2. Fijar sus días y horas de sesión.
3. Por dos tercios de votos de los presentes, corregir a cualquiera de sus miembros y/o solicitar del Poder Ejecutivo su exclusión.
4. Designar y remover el personal de su dependencia y disponer administrativamente de sus oficinas.
5. Prestar acuerdo al gobernador para el nombramiento del contador general del territorio, los miembros del consejo escolar y el director del registro público oficial.
6. Intervenir obligatoriamente en la preparación de los proyectos de ley para su elevación al Poder Ejecutivo Nacional sobre:
   a) Impuestos, contribuciones y tasas necesarias para los gastos del servicio público; su aplicación, percepción y fiscalización;
   b) Presupuesto de gastos y cálculo de recursos;
   c) Organización administrativa del territorio; creación y supresión de dependencias, atribuciones, responsabilidades, dotación de personal y régimen general del mismo;
   d) División político-administrativa y municipal del territorio;
   e) Organización de las corporaciones municipales;
   f) Administración de los servicios intermunicipales.
7. Asesorar en todos aquellos asuntos que el gobernador considere oportuno someterle.

CAPITULO V. LEGISLATURA
1. Composición - Elección - Período

Art. 32. — La Legislatura estará compuesta por cinco miembros elegidos directamente por el cuerpo electoral del territorio, que durarán dos años en sus funciones y podrán ser reelectos.

2. Calidades

Art. 33. — Para ser legislador se requiere haber cumplido veinticinco años de edad, y:
a) Ser ciudadano nativo del territorio y estar inscripto en el registro de electores del territorio por lo menos con dos años de antigüedad; o
b) Ser ciudadano y estar inscripto en el registro de electores del territorio con no menos de cuatro años de antigüedad.

3. Incompatibilidades

Art. 34. — El cargo de legislador es incompatible con cualquier otro rentado por el Estado, salvo el ejercicio de la docencia. Tampoco podrá ser titular de contratos de servicios públicos con el gobierno territorial y/o corporaciones municipales ni integrar sociedades beneficiarias de ese tipo de contratos.

4. Inmunidades

Art. 35. — Ninguno de los miembros de la Legislatura puede ser acusado, interrogado judicialmente ni molestado por las opiniones o discursos que emita desempeñando su mandato de legislador. Ningún legislador desde el día de su elección hasta el de su cese, puede ser arrestado ni sometido a proceso criminal, excepto el caso de ser sorprendido "in fraganti".

Cuando se forme querella por escrito ante la justicia contra un legislador, examinado el mérito de sumario en juicio público, podrá la Legislatura con los dos tercios de votos de los presentes suspender en sus funciones al acusado y ponerlo a disposición del juez competente para su juzgamiento. Percibirá las asignaciones que le fije la ley de presupuesto.

5. Incorporación - Juramento

Art. 36. — Los legisladores en el acto de su incorporación prestarán juramento de desempeñar debidamente el cargo y obrar en todo de conformidad con la Constitución Nacional y lo que prescribe este decreto-ley.

6. Quórum

Art. 37. — La Legislatura no podrá constituirse en sesión sino con la mayoría absoluta del total de sus miembros; pero un número menor podrá tomar medidas en la forma que determine el reglamento, a fin de asegurar la reunión del quórum, inclusive la compulsión por la fuerza pública.

7. Sesiones

Art. 38. — La Legislatura funcionará seis meses en el año, en períodos que ella determinará, iniciará automáticamente sus sesiones ordinarias el día señalado por la ley, debiendo el gobernador informar en la misma sobre la labor desarrollada en el estado general de la administración territorial. El gobernador podrá prorrogar sus sesiones ordinarias o llamar a reuniones extraordinarias cuando un interés de orden y progreso lo requiera.

8. Atribuciones

Art. 39. — Son atribuciones de la legislatura:

1. Ser juez exclusivo de la elección, derechos y títulos de sus miembros en cuanto a su validez.
2. Dictar su propio reglamento; mientras tanto regirá en lo pertinente el de la Honorable Cámara de Diputados de la Nación.
3. Nombrar sus comisiones internas.
4. Fijar sus días y horas de sesiones.
5. Sesionar pública o secretamente, si así lo resolviere la mayoría absoluta de los miembros presentes.
6. Aceptar la renuncia de sus miembros por simple mayoría de votos y, con dos tercios de votos de los presentes, corregir a cualquiera de sus miembros y hasta exclusión de su seno por las causas establecidas en el Artículo 58 de la Constitución Nacional.
7. Designar al personal de su dependencia y disponer administrativamente de sus oficinas.
8. Solicitar al gobernador los informes que estime conveniente respecto de las cuestiones de su competencia; quien podrá optar entre contestar el informe por escrito o enviar a uno de sus secretarios para que lo haga de viva voz.
9. Acusar al gobernador por mal desempeño de sus funciones directamente ante el Poder Ejecutivo Nacional, mediante el voto afirmativo de las dos terceras partes de sus miembros presentes.
10. Prestar acuerdo para el nombramiento de funcionarios en los casos que así está establecido.
11. Sancionar, supeditado a los principios contenidos en la Constitución Nacional y las disposiciones...

siciones de este decreto-ley, leyes sobre:

a) Impuestos, contribuciones y tasas necesarias para los gastos del servicio público; su aplicación, percepción y fiscalización;

b) Presupuesto de gastos y cálculo de recursos por un año o períodos superiores que no excedan de dos años;

c) Organización administrativa del territorio, creando y suprimiendo dependencias, determinando sus atribuciones, responsabilidades, dotación de personal y régimen general del mismo sobre las siguientes bases: acceso por idoneidad, escalafón, estabilidad, uniformidad de sueldos en cada categoría e incompatibilidades;

d) **Creación de dependencias autárquicas, con facultades para nombrar y remover sus empleados y administrar en legal forma los fondos que se les asignan;**

e) División político-administrativa y municipal del territorio, con vistas a una efectiva descentralización gubernamental;

f) Régimen electoral, que deberá estar basado en el sufragio universal, secreto y obligatorio;

g) Regímenes de previsión social;

h) Higiene, moralidad y salud pública; instrucción, educación y cultura general de la población; creación de nuevos centros urbanos; fomento de las actividades agropecuaria, piscicultura, pesca y caza; promoción de industrias y colonización; prestación de servicios públicos; y, en general, todo lo tendiente a la efectiva prosperidad y bienestar del territorio;

i) Determinación de bienes que deban expropiarse por causa de utilidad pública;

j) Faltas y su procedimiento;

k) Régimen de las corporaciones municipales;

l) Administración de los servicios intermunicipales; y

m) Realización de obras públicas de carácter local.

9. De la sanción de las leyes

Art. 40. — Toda ley puede tener principio en la Legislatura por proyectos presentados por sus miembros o por el gobernador.

Art. 41. — Sancionada una ley se remitirá al gobernador para su examen y si obtiene su aprobación se promulgará. Se reputa aprobada por el gobernador toda ley no devuelta en el término de veinte días hábiles.

Art. 42. — El gobernador, dentro del término indicado en el artículo anterior, podrá desechar el proyecto de ley en todo o parte. Si fuere vetado volverá a la Legislatura únicamente en su parte desechada con las objeciones formuladas y si aquélla insiste en la sanción, con dos tercios de votos de los presentes, será ley y pasará al gobernador para su promulgación. No existiendo los dos tercios para la instancia y para aceptar las modificaciones propuestas por el gobernador no podrá repetirse en las sesiones del año.

Art. 43. — En la sanción de las leyes se usará esta fórmula: "La Legislatura sanciona con fuerza de ley".

Art. 44. — El Poder Ejecutivo Nacional, por sí y sin necesidad de autorización legislativa, podrá intervenir la Legislatura para garantir la forma republicana de gobierno y a requisición de la misma para sostenerla o restablecerla.

CAPITULO VI
ADMINISTRACION DE LA JUSTICIA

Art. 45. — Un Juez Letrado conocerá y resolverá en todas las causas que en la capital de la República se atribuyen a los jueces en lo civil, comercial, correccional, criminal y del trabajo, y también en las que corresponda a los jueces federales.

Art. 46. — Conocerán en grado de apelación de las sentencias dictadas por los jueces de paz y su resolución terminará el asunto, salvo el recurso extraordinario ante la Suprema Corte.

Art. 47. — De la sentencia que dicten los jueces letrados, en ejercicio de la jurisdicción originaria, podrá apelarse ante la Cámara Federal más próxima.

Art. 48. — El procedimiento ante el Juez Letrado será el correspondiente a la materia, vigente en la capital de la República.

Art. 49. — El Juez Letrado será nombrado por el Poder Ejecutivo con acuerdo del Senado; residirá en la capital del Territorio y no podrá ser removido sino en la forma establecida para la remoción de los funcionarios de su clase en la capital de la República.

Art. 50. — Para ser Juez Letrado se requiere ser ciudadano mayor de veinticinco años de edad, y abogado con título expedido por Universidad Nacional, con cinco años, por lo menos, de ejercicio en la profesión.

Art. 51. — El Juez Letrado prestará juramento ante la Suprema Corte y le serán aplicables las disposiciones de la ley orgánica de la justicia nacional, en cuanto sea compatible con el carácter de la justicia territorial.

Art. 52. — Habrá un escribano secretario encargado de actuar en los juicios que se sigan ante el Juez Letrado.

Art. 53. — El Secretario será nombrado y removido por el Poder Ejecutivo, previo informe del Juez Letrado.

Art. 54. — El Juez Letrado ejercerá la superintendencia sobre los jueces de paz del territorio y actuará con el personal que le asigne el presupuesto territorial.

Art. 55. — La justicia de paz estará a cargo de dos jueces de paz con asiento en Río Grande y Ushuaia, cuya competencia territorial será determinada por una ley especial.

Art. 56. — Los jueces de paz deberán ser ciudadanos, mayores de edad, y saber leer y escribir.

Art. 57. — Serán nombrados por el gobernador y conservarán el cargo mientras dure su idoneidad y buena conducta.

Art. 58. — Los jueces de paz darán cumplimiento a las comisiones que les encomienden, los jueces nacionales y territoriales, además de ejercer las funciones, atribuciones y deberes que ésta y otras leyes le señalen.

Art. 59. — Los jueces de paz conocerán:

1. En los asuntos:
   a) donde el valor cuestionado no exceda de tres mil pesos, con exclusión de juicios sucesorios, asuntos de familia, concursos y quiebras;
   b) en las demandas reconvencionales, siempre que su valor no exceda de tres mil pesos; y
   c) en las demandas por desalojo, cuando no mediare contrato escrito, cualquiera fuere el alquiler;
2. En la sanción de faltas y contravenciones por infracción al Código Rural, reglamentos de faltas, ordenanzas municipales y edictos de policía.

Art. 60. — Los jueces de paz actuarán con los secretarios y personal que les asigne el presupuesto.

Art. 61. — Los secretarios y demás personal de la justicia de paz serán designados y removidos por el gobernador, a propuesta del juez de paz respectivo.

Art. 62. — El procedimiento ante los jueces de paz será verbal y actuado; resolverán a verdad sabida y buena fe guardada, exigiendo, sin embargo, la defensa y la prueba. Los jueces de paz sólo podrán ser recusados con justa causa.

Art. 63. — Cuando el valor cuestionado no alcance a doscientos pesos, las sentencias de los jueces de paz no serán apelables, lo mismo que las que se dicten en causas por contravenciones y faltas, imponiendo multas de hasta cien pesos y arrestos que no excedan de cinco días. En los demás casos, sus resoluciones serán apelables para ante el Juez Letrado territorial. El recurso deberá interponerse dentro del tercer día; será concedido en relación y sin requerir el comparendo de las partes, pero el apelante deberá presentar un memorial en primera insncia dentro de los seis días de notificado por dula de habérsele concedido el recurso y en igual azo podrá el apelado presentar ante la misma instncia un escrito sosteniendo la resolución. Se derará desierto el recurso si el apelante no presense memorial.

DISPOSICIONES COMUNES

Art. 64. — Los jueces, secretarios y demás personal tendrán las remuneraciones que le señale el esupuesto territorial. El sueldo asignado a los jues no podrá serles disminuido en forma alguna ientras duren en sus funciones.

Art. 65. — La organización y funcionamiento de justicia territorial se regirá supletoriamente por e previsiones de la ley orgánica de la justicia naonal, en cuanto sea compatible con el carácter de justicia territorial. El número de los jueces leados y de paz podrá ser aumentado por ley de uerdo con las necesidades de la zona. La organición y establecimiento de otros organismos judiales, así como la modificación de competencia en zón del monto de los juicios podrá también ser tablecido por ley dictada al efecto por la Nación.

PARTE TERCERA — REGIMEN MUNICIPAL
APITULO I — CORPORACIONES MUNICIPALES
1. Categorías

Art. 66. — Los centros de población del territorio ie cuenten con un número mayor de doscientos scriptos en el registro electoral constituirán una unicipalidad. Las ciudades de Río Grande y Ushuaia ndrán categoría de municipalidad.

En las poblaciones que no constituyan municipalidad, la administración de los servicios comunales tará a cargo de comisiones de fomento.

2. Jurisdicción y competencia.

Art. 67. — Las corporaciones municipales están specialmente facultadas para disponer dentro de us distritos sobre:

1. edificación, apertura de calles y plazas, construcción de cercos y aceras;
2. obras de vialidad y pavimentación;
3. servicios públicos urbanos;
4. higiene y moralidad;
5. tránsito urbano;
6. espectáculos públicos y festejos populares;
7. mercados, ferias y mataderos;
8. asistencia social;
9. enseñanza y cultura;
10. cementerios;
11. policía municipal; y
12. todas aquellas materias propias de la esfera municipal, siempre que no se encuentren reservadas para el Gobierno federal o del territorio.

Ningún organismo municipal podrá imponer penas e multa o arresto, sin que éstas hayan sido establecidas por la Legislatura del Territorio.

3. Rentas

Art. 68. — Para el cumplimiento de sus fines las orporaciones municipales podrán establecer el pago e impuestos, tasas, contribuciones por mejoras, derchos de inspección y todo otro considerado propio el régimen municipal. En materia tributaria tenrán las mismas fuentes que las leyes en vigor acueren a la Municipalidad de la Ciudad de Buenos Aies y las que se le asignen por leyes futuras.

4. Personal

Art. 69. — El personal que designe las corporacioes municipales no podrá ser removido sin sumario revio y audiencia del inculpado, y sólo cuando se omprobare fehacientemente inconducta notoria, inumplimiento de sus deberes, incapacidad física o aoral o inhabilidad profesional, todo de acuerdo con as leyes y ordenanzas que rijan la materia.

CAPITULO II — MUNICIPALIDADES
1. Organos - Composición - Elección

Art. 70. — La administración de las municipalidades estará a cargo de un departamento deliberatio, que ejercerá un concejo municipal compuesto de inco miembros, y un departamento ejecutivo, desmpeñado por un intendente. Serán designados en lección directa por los electores inscriptos en el

registro nacional del distrito municipal. Durarán dos años en sus funciones y podrán ser reelectos.

2. Calidades

Art. 71. — Para ser concejal o intendente se requiere ser mayor de veinticinco años y estar inscripto en el registro electoral del distrito municipal con no menos de dos años de antigüedad.

3. Prohibiciones

Art. 72. — Quienes desempeñen los cargos de concejal o intendente no podrán percibir del tesoro municipal retribución de ninguna clase. Tampoco podrán ser titulares de contratos de servicios públicos de la municipalidad ni integrar sociedades beneficiarias de ese tipo de contratos.

4. Concejo municipal

Art. 73. — Son atribuciones del concejo:

1. Juzgar de la validez de las elecciones, de los derechos y títulos de sus miembros.
2. Dictar su reglamento interno; establecer sus períodos de sesiones ordinarias, de prórroga o extraordinarias y fijar día y horas de sesión.
3. Aceptar la renuncia de sus miembros y, por mayoría absoluta del total de los integrantes del cuerpo, corregir, suspender o excluir de su seno a cualquier concejal, por mala conducta o inhabilidad física o moral, previo juicio en sesión pública en que el acusado hará oír su defensa.
4. Solicitar del intendente los informes que considere necesarios para el mejor cumplimiento de sus funciones.
5. Examinar las cuentas de la administración municipal y comunicar sus observaciones, al gobernador y a la Legislatura cuando ésta se constituya.
6. Prestar acuerdo al intendente para la designación del secretario, contador general y tesorero de la municipalidad.
7. Nombrar y remover el personal del concejo.
8. Sancionar las ordenanzas impositivas, el presupuesto general de gastos y cálculos de recursos y demás ordenanzas que fueren necesarios para la mejor administración municipal dentro de las facultades establecidas en el artículo 67.
9. Insistir por dos tercios de votos en las ordenanzas que devuelva observadas total o parcialmente, el intendente; en cuyo caso será de cumplimiento obligatorio.

5. Intendente

Art. 74. — Son atribuciones del intendente:

1. Representar a la municipalidad en los actos oficiales y legalmente en los juicios en que aquélla sea parte, por sí o por medio de apoderado.
2. Dirigir la administración municipal de acuerdo con las ordenanzas que dicte el concejo, las que deberá hacer cumplir, a cuyo efecto podrá solicitar de los jueces, las órdenes de allanamiento cuando fuera necesario.
3. Proyectar ordenanzas y remitirlas al concejo, promulgar las que éste sancione o vetarlas dentro de los cinco días en que le fuere comunicada; reglamentarlas, cumplir y hacerlas cumplir.
4. Suministrar por escrito los informes que el concejo le solicitara.
5. Convocar al concejo a sesiones extraordinarias cuando asuntos urgentes o de interés público así lo requiera.
6. Nombrar y remover al personal municipal de acuerdo a las disposiciones vigentes; y designar con acuerdo del concejo el secretario, el contador general y el tesorero.
7. Recaudar la renta municipal y efectuar las inversiones dispuestas por la rama deliberativa, dando cuenta mensualmente al concejo del movimiento de tesorería.
8. Remitir al concejo el proyecto de presupuesto de gastos y cálculos de recursos.
9. Vigilar la debida prestación de los servicios municipales y el cumplimiento de los contratos

o concesiones de servicios públicos.

Art. 75. — El intendente no podrá ausentarse de la ciudad sin permiso del concejo por un plazo mayor de un mes. En caso de ausencia o impedimento del intendente, lo reemplazará el Presidente del Concejo; a falta de éste, el concejal de más edad.

Art. 76. — El Poder Ejecutivo, por resolución fundada y previa audiencia del inculpado, podrá separar de sus cargos a los intendentes municipales, por razón de mal desempeño o inconducta notoria, cuando su remoción hubiera sido solicitada por el concejo municipal por dos tercios de votos.

6. Acefalía - Intervención

Art. 77. — En los casos de acefalía de una cipalidad, el gobernador asumirá su administración por medio de un comisionado. Las municipalidades podrán ser intervenidas con arreglo a la ley que será la nacional hasta tanto no funcione la legislatura local, o cuando esté subvertido el régimen constitucional.

CAPITULO III — COMISIONES DE FOMENTO

1. Composición - Nombramiento - Período

Art. 78. — Las comisiones de fomento estarán formadas por cinco vecinos de arraigo en el lugar, mayores de veinticinco años, que serán nombrados por el gobernador por un período de tres años, de acuerdo con las disposiciones de este decreto-ley. No percibirán retribución alguna por el desempeño de sus cargos.

2. Atribuciones

Art. 79. — Son atribuciones y deberes de las comisiones de fomento:

1. Designar de su seno un presidente, un secretario y un tesorero.
2. Preparar la ordenanza de impuestos y tasas retributivas de servicio y el presupuesto general de gastos y cálculos de recursos que someterá a la aprobación del gobernador.
3. Administrar los bienes comunales, llevar cuenta de la recaudación e inversión de la renta de acuerdo al presupuesto general de gastos vigente, de lo que dará cuenta mensualmente al gobernador del territorio.

4. Ejercer las atribuciones necesarias para la mejor administración de los intereses comunales, dentro de las materias señaladas por el artículo 67, no pudiendo otorgar concesiones por término mayor de un año sin autorización del gobernador, y de tres, sin aprobación del Concejo Territorial o la Legislatura, en su caso.

PARTE CUARTA

DISPOSICIONES TRANSITORIAS
CAPITULO UNICO

1. Fecha de vigencia

Artículo 80. — El presente decreto-ley se pondrá en vigencia el 1º de marzo de 1957 y hasta tanto no entre en funciones el gobernador del territorio, la administración del mismo estará a cargo del Interventor Federal en la provincia de Santa Cruz.

2. Instalación de la Legislatura

Art. 81. — La elección de legisladores para la primera instalación de la Legislatura, se realizará por la ley nacional de elecciones en cuanto sea apli-

cable. El Poder Ejecutivo podrá dictar todas las disposiciones que fueren necesarias para su ejecución.

3. Administración de justicia

Art. 82. — Hasta tanto no entren en funciones los jueces previstos, harán sus veces los jueces con actual jurisdicción en el territorio determinado en el artículo 29.

4. Régimen municipal

Art. 83. — La elección de concejales e intendentes municipales se hará en la época que determine el Poder Ejecutivo Nacional, conforme a la Ley Nacional de Elecciones y a las disposiciones que aquél dicte y que fueren necesarias para su aplicación. Deberá asegurarse la representación de la minoría.

5. Transferencia de oficinas

Art. 84. — La provincia de Santa Cruz y los ministerios nacionales adoptarán las medidas necesarias para transferir antes del 1º de mayo de 1957 al Territorio Nacional de Tierra del Fuego, Antártida e Islas del Atlántico Sud todas las oficinas, su personal, muebles, útiles y créditos que correspondan al gobierno local de acuerdo con las disposiciones del presente decreto-ley.

6. Gastos

Art. 85. — Los gastos que demande el cumplimiento del presente decreto-ley, se harán de rentas generales.

Art. 86. — El presente decreto-ley será refrendado por el Excmo. señor Vicepresidente Provisional de la Nación y los señores ministros secretarios de Estado en los departamentos de Interior, Educación y Justicia, Hacienda, Relaciones Exteriores y Culto, Ejército, Marina y Aeronáutica.

Art. 87. — Comuníquese, publíquese, dése a la Dirección General del Boletín Oficial y archívese.

ARAMBURU. — Isaac Rojas. — Carlos R. S. Alconada Aramburú. — Acdel E. Salas. — Roberto P. Verrier. — Alfonso de Laferrére. — Arturo Ossorio Arana. — Teodoro Hartung. — Julio C. Krause.

BIBLIOGRAPHY

BIBLIOGRAPHY

Academia Nacional de la Historia, Buenos Aires.
Exposición histórica de las Islas Malvinas,
Georgias del Sur y Sandwich del Sur. Organi-
zada por Humberto E. Burzio. Buenos Aires,
1964.

Academia Nacional de la Historia, Buenos Aires.
Los derechos argentinos sobre las Islas Mal-
vinas. Conferencias pronunciadas por Enrique
Ruiz-Guiñazú [et al.]. Buenos Aires, 1964.

Alcedo y Herrera, Dionisio de.
Piraterías y agresiones de los ingleses y de
otros pueblos de Europa en la América
española desde el siglo XVI al XVIII. Madrid,
Impr. de M.G. Hernández, 1883.

Almeida, Juan Lucio.
Qué hizo el gaucho Rivero en las Malvinas.
Buenos Aires, Plus Ultra, 1972

Altamira, Luis Roberto.
Primeras capillas y templos de las Islas
Sansón y Patos (Malvinas) sus capellanes y
párrocos. Córdoba, Imprenta de la Universidad, 1947.

Altamira, Luis Roberto.
"Primeras capillas y templos de las islas
Sansón y Patos (Malvinas); sus capellanes y
parrocos," **Revista de la Universidad Nacional
de Cordoba,** vol. 34 (1947), pp. 425-465.

Alurraide, Nicanor.
"El primer descubrimiento de las Islas
Malvinas," **Boletín del Centro Naval** (Buenos
Aires), vol. 84, No. 669 (1966), pp. 511-526.

Anderson, William Ellery.
    Expedition South. London, Evans Bros., 1967.

Angelis, Pedro de.
    Historical sketch of Pepys' island in the
    South Pacific [i.e. Atlantic] Ocean. Buenos-
    Aires, 1842.

"Antarctic claims-recent diplomatic exchanges
    between Great Britain, Argentina and Chile,"
    The Polar record, vol. 5, nos. 35/36
    (Jan./July, 1948), pp. 228-240.

Arce, José.
    The Malvinas; our snatched little isles.
    Madrid, 1951.

Archivo General de la Nación.
    "Informe sobre dos series documentales
    correspondientes a las Islas Malvinas,"
    **Segundo Congreso de historia argentina y
    regional**, vol. 2. Buenos Aires, 1974, pp.
    9-30.

Areco, Issac P.
    Títulos de la República Argentina a la
    soberanía y posesión de las Islas Malvinas.
    Buenos Aires, Impr. de Mayo, 1885.

"The Argentine claim to the Falkland Islands," **The
    Review** (Geneva, International Commission of
    Jurists), no. 28 (June, 1982), pp. 25-32.

Argentine Republic.
    Protestation du gouvernement des Provinces
    Unies du Rio de la Plata, par son ministre
    plénipotentiaire à Londres, sur l'arrogation
    de souveraineté dans les îles Malvines, ou
    Falkland, par la Grande Bretagne, et l'éjec-
    tion de l'établissement de Buenos Ayres à
    Port Louis. Londres, Cunningham et Salmon,
    1833.

Argentine Republic. Ministerio de Educacion.
    Bibliografía sobre las Islas Malvinas. Buenos
    Aires, Centro Nacional de Documentación e
    Información Educativa, 1982.

Argentine Republic. Comisión Nacional del
Antártico.
    Las Islas Malvinas y el sector antártico
    argentino. Buenos Aires, Ministerio de
    Relaciones Exteriores y Culto, 1948.

Argentine Republic. Congreso. Cámara de Senadores.
    Las Malvinas han sido, son y serán
    argentinas; Buenos Aires, Impr. del Congreso
    de la Nación, 1951

Argentine Republic. Dirección de Bibliotecas
Populares.
    Soberanía: contribución bibliográfica a la
    afirmación de derechos argentinos sobre las
    Malvinas, islas y sector antártico. Buenos
    Aires, La Dirección, 1975.

Argentine Republic. Dirección General de
Navegación e Hidrografía.
    Faros y señales marítimas. Pt. III: Tierra
    del Fuego, Estrecho de Magallanes, Canales e
    Islas adyacentes, Islas Malvinas y Antártida
    Argentina. 2a ed. actualizada hasta el 15 de
    abril de 1957. Buenos Aires, Gurfinkel hijos
    S.R.L., 1957.

Argentine Republic. Ministerio de Relaciones
Exteriores.
    Papers relative to the origin and present
    state of the questions pending with the
    l ited States of America, on the subject of
    tne Malvinas, (Falkland Islands,) laid before
    the legislature of Buenos-Ayres by the
    government of the province charged with the
    direction of the foreign relations of the
    Argentine Republic. Buenos-Ayres, Printed at
    the office of the Gaceta mercantil, 1832.

Baquero Lazcano, Emilio.
    El archipiélago de las Malvinas y la
    soberanía. Córdoba, Secretaría de Informa-
    ción de la Presidencia de la República
    Argentina, Impr. de la Universidad, 1952.

Barcia Trelles, Camilo.
El problema de las islas Malvinas. Madrid,
Editora nacional, 1943.

Barnard, Charles H.
A narrative of the sufferings and adventures
of Capt. Charles H. Barnard, in a recent
voyage round the world, including an account
of his residence for two years on an
uninhabited island. New York, J.C. Callender,
1836.

Barnes, Robert.
The postal service of the Falkland Islands,
including South Shetlands (1906-1931) and
South Georgia. London, Lowe, 1972.

Basílico, Ernesto.
La Armada de obispo de Plasencia y el descu-
brimiento de las Malvinas. Buenos Aires,
Centro Naval, Instituto de Publicaciones
Navales, 1967.

Basilico, Ernesto.
"Las Islas Malvinas y las Islas Sansón en el
Islario General de Alonso de Santa Cruz,"
Boletín del Centro Naval (Buenos Aires), vol.
83, no. 664 (julio/set., 1965), pp. 321-341.

"La Batalla de las Malvinas (8 de diciembre de
1914)," **Guardacostas,** vol. 6, no. 22 (1970),
pp. 80-84.

Beck, Peter J.
"Cooperative confrontation in the Falkland
Islands dispute; the Anglo-Argentine search
for a way forward, 1968-1981," **Journal of
Interamerican Studies and World Affairs,** vol.
24, no. 1 (Feb., 1982), pp. 37-58.

Beltrán, Juan Gregorio.
El zarpazo inglés a las islas Malvinas.
Buenos Aires, M. Gleizer, 1934.

Bennett, Geoffrey Martin.
Coronel and the Falklands. New York,
Macmillan, 1962.

Borrello, Angel V.
  Sobre la Geología de las Islas Malvinas.
  Buenos Aires, Ed. Culturales Argentinas,
  Ministerio de Educación y Justicia, Dir.
  General de Cultura, 1963.

Bossi de Rocca, Giuliana.
  "La soberania argentina en las Islas
  Malvinas," **Nuestra soberania**, vol. 3, no. 9
  (set.-oct., 1980), pp. 51-56.

Boyson, V. F.
  The Falkland Islands. With notes on the
  natural history by Rupert Vallentin. Oxford,
  Clarendon Press, 1924.

"The British title to sovereignty in the Falkland
  Islands Dependencies," **The Polar record**, vol.
  8, no. 53 (May, 1956), pp. 125-151.

Brown, V. L.
  "Anglo-Spanish relations in America in the
  closing years of the colonial era," **Hispanic
  American Historical Review**, vol. 5 (Aug.,
  1922), pp. 387-445.

Brunet, José.
  "La iglesia en las Islas Malvinas durante el
  período hispano (1767-1810)," **Archivum**, vol.
  8 (1966), pp. 135-169. See also **Missionalia
  hispánica**, vol. 26, no. 77 (1969), pp. 209-
  240. See also **Revista de la Universidad
  Nacional** (Córdoba), vol. 12, nos. 4/5 (1971),
  pp. 7-65.

Brunet, José.
  "La iglesia en las Islas Malvinas durante el
  período hispano 1767-1810; los capellanos
  franciscanos," **Anuario: Instituto de Investigaciones Históricas** (Rosario), no. 10
  (1968/69), pp. 35-89.

Buenos Aires. Biblioteca Nacional.
  'Las Malvinas'; bibliografía. Buenos Aires,
  1982.

Burns, Alan Cuthbert.
"The Falkland Islands and Argentina," In his
**In defence of colonies: British colonial
territories in international affairs.**
London, Allen and Unwin, 1957, pp. 237-243.

Burzio, Humberto F.
"El acto de soberania del coronel de marina
David Jewett," **Boletin de la Academia
Nacional de la Historia** (Buenos Aires), vol.
43 (1970), pp. 283-287.

Bustos Berrondo, Raul.
Huellas en los mares del Sur. Buenos Aires,
Ediciones Peuser, 1959.

Caillet-Bois, Ricardo R.
Un capítulo de la historia de las Malvinas;
Bougainville y la negociación franco-
española. Buenos Aires, Imp. A. Baiocco y
cia., 1940.

Caillet-Bois, Ricardo R. and Humberto F. Burzio.
El Episodio ocurrido en Puerto de la Soledad
de Malvinas el 26 de agosto de 1833; testi-
monios documentales. Buenos Aires, 1967.

Callet-Bois, Ricardo R.
"Las Islas Malvinas," **Historia de la nación
argentina**, vol. 7, 2a. sec. Buenos Aires,
1950, pp. 369-413.

Caillet-Bois, Ricardo R.
Las Islas Malvinas; una tierra argentina.
2. ed. corr. y aumentada. Buenos Aires,
Ediciones Peuser, 1952.

Caillet-Bois, Ricardo R.
"La toma de posesión de las Islas Malvinas,
en 1820, documentada por el periodismo anglo-
hispano," **Boletin del Instituto de Historia
Argentina**, vol. 7/8, nos. 11/13 (1966), pp.
219-222.

Calvi, Mario J.
Malvinas el mito destruido. 2a. ed. Buenos
Aires, Ediciones Devoto, 1982.

Canclini, Arnoldo.
   "Las Malvinas," **Investigaciones y ensayos,**
   vol. 10 (enero-junio, 1971), pp. 387-432.

Carril, Bonifacio del.
   "Creación del primer gobierno político en el
   archipielago de Malvinas," **Boletin de la
   Academia Nacional de la Historia** (Buenos
   Aires), vol. 43 (1970), pp. 167-171.

Carril, Bonifacio del.
   El dominio de las islas Malvinas. Buenos
   Aires, Emecé Editores, 1964.

Carril, Bonifacio del.
   La cuestión de las Malvinas. Buenos Aires,
   Emecé, 1982.

Carril, Bonifacio del
   The Malvinas/Falklands Case. Buenos Aires,
   CIGA, 1982.

Cawkell, M. B. R., D. H. Maling and E. M. Cawkell.
   The Falkland Islands. London, Macmillan; New
   York, St. Martin's Press, 1960.

Chavez, Fermín.
   "Las Malvinas; 'las llaves de los mares del
   sur," **Crisis** (Buenos Aires), vol. 3, no. 35
   (1976), pp. 36-38.

Cichero, Felix Esteban.
   Las Malvinas; grieta en el mapa argentino.
   Buenos Aires, Editorial Stilcograf, 1968.

Clapperton, Chalmers Moyes and David E. Sugden.
   Scenery of the South: Falkland Islands, South
   Georgia, sub-Antarctic islands. Aberdeen, David
   E. Sugden, 1975.

Clifford, Miles.
   "The Falkland Islands and their dependencies," **The Geographical Journal,** vol. 121,
   no. 4 (Dec., 1955), pp. 405-416

Codazzi Aguirre, Juan Andrés.
Escudo para las islas Malvinas y adyacencias.
Rosario, Escuela de Artes Gráficas del
Colegio Salesiano San José, 1969.

Cohen, Jonathan G.
"Les îles Falkland (Malouines)," **Annuaire
français de droit international**, 1972, pp.
235–262.

Colección de documentos relativos a la historia de
las Islas Malvinas. Introd. de Ricardo R.
Caillet-Bois. Buenos Aires, Universidad de
Buenos Aires, Departamento Editorial, 1957–
1961.

Collection of voyages chiefly in the southern
Atlantick Ocean. Published from original
M.S.S. by Alexander Dalrymple. London,
Printed for the author; sold by J. Nourse,
1775.

Corominas, Enrique Ventura.
Como defendí Malvinas. Buenos Aires, El
Ateneo, 1950.

Cortesão, Armando.
Portvgaliae monvmenta cartographica. Lisboa,
1960.

Couyoudmjian Bergamali, Ricardo.
Manuel José dé Orejuela y la abortada
expedición en busca de los cesares y
extranjeros, 1780–1783," **Historia** (Santiago
de Chile), vol. 10 (1971), pp. 57–176.

Crosby, Ronald K.
El reto de las Malvinas. Buenos Aires,
Editorial Plus Ultra, 1968.

Crosby, Ronald K.
El reto de las Malvinas. 2. ed. corr. y
actualizada. Buenos Aires, Plus Ultra, c1975.

Davenport, Frances Gardiner.
European Treaties bearing on the History of
the United States and its Dependencies to
1648. Washington, Carnegie Institution,
1917.

Destéfani, Laurio H.
"El coronel de marina D. David Jewett y el
crucero corsario de la fragata 'Heroina',"
**Boletin de la Academia Nacional de la
Historia** (Buenos Aires), vol. 43 (1970), pp.
277-282.

Destéfani, Laurio H.
El descubrimiento de las Islas Malvinas
(Aporte para un estudio crítico). Buenos
Aires, Tall. Graf. de la DIAB, 1981.

Destéfani, Laurio H.
"Evacuación española de las Islas Malvinas,"
Investigaciones y ensayos, vol. 4 (enero-
junio, 1968), pp. 269-291.

Destéfani, Laurio H.
"Jacinto de Altolaguirre: primer gobernador
criollo de las Islas Malvinas: 1781-1783,"
Investigaciones y ensayos, vol. 14 (enero--
junio, 1973), pp. 205-221.

Destéfani, Laurio H.
Las Malvinas en la época hispana (1600-1811).
Buenos Aires, Corregidor, 1981.

Destéfani, Laurio H.
Malvinas, Georgias y Sandwich del Sur; ante
el conflict con Gran Bretaña. Buenos Aires,
1982.

Díaz de Molina, Alfredo.
Las Islas Malvinas y una nueva diplomacia.
Buenos Aires, Editorial Platero, c1976.

Díaz Molano, Elías and Esteban Homet.
Tierras australes argentinas; Malvinas,
Antártida. Buenos Aires, Sociedad Geográfica
Americana, 1948.

Dickens, P. D.
"The Falkland Islands dispute between the
United States and Argentina," **Hispanic
American Historical Review,** vol. 9 (Nov.,
1929), pp. 471-487.

Discovery reports. v. 1+
Cambridge [Eng.], The University Press, 1929+`

Economist Intelligence Unit, ltd., London
Economic survey of the Falkland Islands.
Prepared by the Economist Intelligence Unit,
ltd.; presented to the Secretary of State for
Foreign and Commonwealth Affairs. London,
E.I.U., c1976.

Economist Intelligence Unit, ltd., London.
Relevamiento económico de las Islas Malvinas:
Informe Shackleton (vol. II): julio 1976.
Buenos Aires, Instituto Argentino de Estudios
Estratégicos y de las Relaciones Inter-
nacionales, 1976 or 1977.

Eisenhower Fellows from Argentina.
La cuestión de las Islas Malvinas; The
Malvinas Islands case. Buenos Aires? 1982.

Falkland Islands.
Census of the Falkland island, 3rd April,
1881. Stanley? 1881.

Falkland Islands.
Report on census, 1901. Stanley, 1901.

Falkland Islands.
Report on census, 1911. Stanley? 1911.

Falkland Islands.
Report on census, 1921. London, Waterlow &
sons, limited, 1922.

Falkland Islands.
Report on census, 1931. Stanley, Falkland
Islands, Government printing office, 1931.

Falkland Islands.
    Report on census, 1962. Stanley, Govt.
    Print. Off., 1962?

Falkland Islands.
    The Falkland islands gazette. v. 1+ , Jan.
    1, 1891+ Stanley, 1891+

Falkland Islands. Laws, statutes, etc.
    Ordinances of the colony of the Falkland
    islands, enacted during the year 1923, 1926,
    1927 together with the rules, regulations,
    etc., etc., made during that year. Stanley,
    Government printing office, 1923-27.

Falkland Islands. Laws, statutes, etc.
    Ordinances, orders, proclamations, etc.
    Stanley? Govt. Print. Off., n.d.

Falkland Islands. Laws, statutes, etc.
    A revised edition of the ordinances of the
    colony of the Falkland islands. Prepared
    under the authority of "The new edition of
    the ordinances ordinance, 1911", by Frederic
    George Thomas. London, Stevens & sons,
    limited, 1913.

Falkland Islands. Laws, statutes, etc.
    The laws of the colony of the Falkland
    Islands and its dependencies, containing the
    ordinances and subsidiary legislation and a
    selection from the imperial legislation in
    force on the 31st day of December 1950. Rev.
    ed. prepared under the authority of the
    Revised edition of the laws ordinance, by R.
    W. S. Winter Esq. and Sir Henry Webb. London,
    Printed by Bacher, Govt. printers, 1951.

Falkland Islands. Registrar General.
    Report of 1953 census. Stanley, Govt. Print.
    Off. 1954.

"The Falkland Islands," **Department of State Bul-
    letin,** vol. 82, no. 2063 (June, 1982), pp.
    81-88.

"The Falkland Islands," **New English Review,** (Apr.,
1948),pp. 336-341.

"The Falkland Islands," **Survey of current
affairs,** vol. 12, no. 5 (May, 1982), pp.
149-155.

"The Falkland Islands," **Survey of current
affairs,** vol. 12, no. 6 (June, 1982), pp.
180-188.

"Falklands crisis," **Proceedings** (Assembly of
Western European Union), 28th sess., 1st part
(June, 1982), pp. 56-73.

Falkner, Thomas.
A description of Patagonia, and the adjoining
parts of South America; containing an account
of the soil, produce, animals, vales,
mountains, rivers, lakes, &c. of those
countries; the religion, government, policy,
customs, dress, arms, and language of the
Indian inhabitants; and some particulars
relating to Falkland's Islands. Hereford,
Printed by C. Pugh; London, T. Lewis, 1774.

Ferns, Henry Stanley.
Argentina. New York, Frederick A. Praeger,
1969.

Ferrer Vieyra, Enrique.
Problemática jurídica de las Malvinas y de la
Antártida argentina. Córdoba, Dirección
General de Publicaciones de la Universidad
Nacional de Córdoba, 1982.

Festari, Gian Battista.
"La controversia anglo-argentina per le
Maluine," **Storia e politica internazionale.**
Rassegna... dell'Istituto per gli studi di
politica internazionale. Milano, 1941, pp.
407-414.

Fitte, Ernesto J.
    "La Academia Nacional de la Historia y el
    sangriento episodio del año 1833 en
    Malvinas," **Boletín de la Academia Nacional de
    la Historia** (Buenos Aires), vol. 25 (1972),
    pp. 471-486.

Fitte, Ernesto J.
    La agresión norteamericana a las Islas
    Malvinas; crónica documental. Buenos Aires,
    Emecé, 1966.

Fitte, Ernesto J.
    Una aventura de náufragos en las Islas
    Malvinas. Buenos Aires, 1959.

Fitte, Ernesto J.
    Crónicas del Atlántico Sur; Patagonia,
    Malvinas y Antártida. Buenos Aires, Emecé
    Editors, 1974.

Fitte, Ernesto J.
    "Cronología marítima de las Islas Malvinas,"
    Investigaciones y ensayos, vol. 4 (enero-
    junio, 1968), pp. 153-189.

Fitte, Ernesto J.
    "La comandancia político-militar de
    Malvinas," **Boletín de la Academia Nacional de
    la Historia** (Buenos Aires), vol. 43 (1970),
    pp. 156-166.

Fitte, Ernesto J.
    La disputa con Gran Britaña por las islas del
    Atlántico Sur. Buenos Aires, Emecé Editores,
    1968.

Fitte, Ernesto J.
    "La Junta de Mayo y su autoridad sobre las
    Malvinas," **Historia**, vol. 12, no. 46 (enero-
    marzo, 1967), pp. 22-37

Fitte, Ernesto J.
    "Las Malvinas bajo la ocupación britanica,"
    Investigaciones y ensayos, vols. 6-7 (enero-
    dic., 1969), pp. 63-87. See also **Historia** ,
    vol. 12, no. 48 (1967), pp. 3-22.

Fitte, Ernesto J.
"Las Malvinas después de la usurpación,"
Historia, vol. 12, no. 48 (julio-set., 1967),
pp. 1-22.

Fitte, Ernesto J.
"Las Malvinas en 1820," **Boletín de la
Academia Nacional de la Historia,** vol. 43
(1970), pp. 271-276.

Fitte, Ernesto J.
"Sangre en Malvinas: el asesinato del
comandante (Esteban José Francisco)
Mestivier," **Investigaciones y ensayos,** vol.
12 (1972), pp. 121-166.

Fleischer, Friedrich Wilhelm.
Sturmfahrt der "Tinto." Oldenburg i. O., G.
Stalling, 1933.

Fonseca Figueira, José Antonio da.
Cómo los poetas les cantaron a las Malvinas.
Buenos Aires, Plus Ultra, c1978.

Fordham, Angela.
Falkland Islands; a bibliography of 50
examples of printed maps bearing specific
reference to the Falkland Islands. London,
Map Collectors' Circle, 1964.

Foulkes, Haroldo.
Las Malvinas; una causa nacional. Buenos
Aires, Ediciones Corregidor, 1978.

Foulkes, Haroldo.
Las Malvinas; una causa nacional. 2da. ed.
act. Buenos Aires, Ediciones Corregidor,
1982.

Freedman, Lawrence.
"The War of the Falkland Islands, 1982,"
Foreign Affairs, vol. 61, no. 1 (Fall, 1982),
pp. 196-210.

Gandía, Enrique de.
   "Un caso de asilo en las Malvinas," **Revista
   del Instituto de Historia del derecho Ricardo
   Levene,** no. 14 (1963), pp. 165-172.

García, Eduardo Augusto.
   "La cuestión de las Malvinas en el derecho
   internacional," **Boletín del Museo Social
   Argentino,** vol. 46, no. 339 (abril-junio,
   1969), pp. 135-140. See also **Ibid.,** vol. 49,
   no. 353 (oct.-dic, 1972), pp. 369-374.

García G., Rigoberto and Margarita Pulido.
   La cuestión de las Malvinas (Falklands).
   Stockholm, Institute of Latin American
   Studies, 1982.

García Pulido, José.
   Un repaso al pasado ... al presente y al
   futuro. Resistencia, Argentina, Librería Casa
   García, 1979.

Geoghegan, Abel Rodolfo.
   "Bibliografía de las Islas Malvinas;
   suplemento a la obra de José Torre Revelo,
   1954-1975," **Historiografía,** vol. 2 (1974),
   pp. 165-212.

Gil Munilla, Octavio.
   Malvinas, el conflicto anglo-español de
   1770. Sevilla, Escuela de Estudio Hispano-
   Americanos, 1948.

Goebel, Julius.
   The struggle for the Falkland Islands; a
   study in legal and diplomatic history. Port
   Washington, N.Y. Kennikat Press, 1971.

Gómez Langenheim, Antonio.
   Elementos para la historia de nuestras islas
   Malvinas. Buenos Aires, "El Ateneo," 1939.

Gómez Langenheim, Antonio.
   La tercera invasion inglesa. Buenos Aires,
   Editorial Tor, 1934.

González Balcarce, Luis.
"La cuestión Malvinas; evolución de una
política," **Revista de la Escuela Superior de
Guerra** (Buenos Aires), vol. 52, no. 414
(1974), pp. 73-97.

González Costa, Carlos.
El problema de las islas Malvinas; de pal-
pitante actualidad por la apelación ante la
Sociedad de las Naciones Unidas. La Plata,
Argentina, Casa Peuser, 1964.

[Gower, Erasmus]
An account of the loss of His Majesty's
sloop, Swift, Port Desire, on the coast of
Patagonia, on the 13th of March, 1770; and of
other events which succeeded, in a letter to
a friend. London, Printed by W. Winchester
and son, 1803.

Great Britain. Antarctic Place-Names Committee.
Gazetteer of the British Antarctic territory,
South Georgia and the South Sandwich Islands;
by the Foreign Office. London, HMSO, 1962.

Great Britain. Antarctic Place-Names Committee.
Gazetteer of the Falkland Islands dependencies. 2d ed. London, HMSO, 1959.

Great Britain. Antarctic Place-Names Committee.
Gazetteer of the Falkland Islands dependencies. London, Foreign Office, 1955.

Great Britain. Antarctic Place-Names Committee.
Gazetter of the Falkland Islands dependencies. Supplement. 1st-2nd; Mar. 3, 1958-Sept.
21, 1959. London, Foreign Office, 1955.

Great Britain. Antarctic Place-Names Committee.
Gazetter of the Falkland Islands dependencies
(South Georgia and the South Sandwich
Islands). London, HMSO., 1977.

Great Britain. Central Office of Information.
Reference Division.
The Falkland Islands and dependencies.
London, 1982.

Great Britain. Central Office of Information.
Reference Division.
     The Falkland Islands dependencies. London,
     1958.

Great Britain. Colonial Office.
     Annual report on the Falkland Islands and
     dependencies. 1947+ London, HMSO., 1948+

Great Britain. Colonial Office.
     Annual report on the social and economic
     progress of the people of the colony of the
     Falkland Islands and its dependencies. 1931-
     1938. London, HMSO., 1932?-1940.

Great Britain. Colonial Office.
     British islands in the southern hemisphere,
     1945-1951. London, HMSO., 1951.

Great Britain. Discovery Committee.
     "Discovery" expedition, first-[second] annual
     report. 1926-1927/28. London, 1927-29.

Great Britain. Foreign and Commonwealth Office.
     Falkland Islands and dependencies, report.
     1919-1930. London, HMSO., 1920-1931

Great Britain. Foreign Office.
     British and Foreign State Papers. vol. 22
     (1833-1834). London, James Ridgway and Sons,
     Piccadilly, 1847.

Great Britain. Foreign Office.
     Papers relative to the late negotiation with
     Spain; and the taking of Falkland's Island
     from the English. London, Printed for J.
     Almon, 1777.

Great Britain. Foreign Office. Historical Section.
     Falkland Islands, Kerguelen. London, HMSO.,
     1920.

Great Britain. Interdepartmental Committee on
Research and Development in the Dependencies of
the Falkland Islands.
>   Report of the Interdepartmental Committee on
>   Research and Development in the Dependencies
>   of the Falkland Islands, with appendices,
>   maps, &c. London, HMSO., 1920.

Greenway, M. E.
>   The geology of the Falkland Islands. London,
>   British Antarctic Survey, 1972.

Greno Velasco, José Enrique.
>   "El informe Shackleton sobre las islas
>   Malvinas," **Revista de política internacional,**
>   no. 153 (aug., 1977), pp. 31-56.

Groussac, Paul.
>   Las islas Malvinas. Buenos Aires, Talleres
>   gráficos argentinos L.J. Rosso, 1936.

Groussac, Paul.
>   Les îles Malouïnes, nouvel exposé d'un vieux
>   litige. Paris, A. Pedone, 1910.

Hadfield, William.
>   Brazil, the River Plate, and the Falkland
>   Islands; with the Cape Horn route to
>   Australia. Including notices of Lisbon.
>   Madeira, the Canaries and Cape Verds. London,
>   Longman, Brown, Green, and Longmans, 1854.

Hague. International Court of Justice.
>   Antarctica cases (United Kingdom **v.**
>   Argentina; United Kingdom v. Chile) Orders of
>   March 16th, 1956; removal from the list.
>   Hague, 1956.

Hernández, José.
>   Las Islas Malvinas; lo que escribió Hernández
>   en 1869 respecto a este territorio argentino
>   y las noticias que acerca de su viaje a las
>   islas le comunicó Augusto Lasserre.
>   Compilación, sumarios y notas de Joaquín Gil
>   Guiñón. Buenos Aires, J. Gil, 1952.

Hernández, Pablo José and Horacio Chitarroni.
    Malvinas: clave geopolítica. Buenos Aires,
    Ediciones Castañeda, c1977.

Hickey, John.
    "Keep the Falklands British? The principle
    of self determination of dependent
    territories," **Inter American Economic
    Affairs**, vol. 31, no. 1 (Summer, 1977), pp.
    77-88.

Hidalgo Nieto, Manuel.
    La cuestión de las Malvinas, contribución al
    estudio de las relaciones hispano-inglesas en
    el siglo XVIII. Madrid, CSIC, Instituto
    Gonzalo Fernández de Oviedo, 1947.

Hilditch, A. Neville.
    Coronel and the Falkland Islands. London,
    Oxford University Press, 1915.

Hirst, Lloyd.
    Coronel and after. London, P. Davis, limited,
    1934.

Holmberg, Adolfo María Dago.
    ?Cree Ud. que los ingleses nos devolverán las
    Malvinas? Yo, no. Buenos Aires, Editorial
    Grandes Temas Argentinos, c1977.

Hough, Richard Alexander.
    The long pursuit. New York, Harper & Row
    1969.

International American Conference, 9th, Bogota,
1948. Delegation from Argentina.
    Las Malvinas son argentinas. Bogota,
    Editorial "Cahur", 1948?.

International Bureau of the American Republics,
Washington, D.C.
    Commercial directory of British, Dutch,
    Danish, and French colonial possessions in
    Central and South America and the West
    Indies. Washington, Gov't print. Off., 1892.

Irving, John James Cawdell.
    Coronel and the Falklands. London, A.M.
    Philpot, ltd., 1927.

Johnson, Richard.
    "The future of the Falkland Islands," **The
    World Today,** vol. 33, no. 6 (June, 1977), pp.
    223-231.

Johnson, Samuel.
    Thoughts on the late transactions respecting
    Falkland's Islands. Dublin, Printed for J.
    Williams, 1771.

[Johnson, Samuel]
    Thoughts on the late transactions respecting
    Falkland's Islands. London, Printed for T.
    Cadell, 1771.

[Johnson, Samuel]
    Thoughts on the late transactions respecting
    Falkland's islands. London, printed, New-
    York, Re-printed, by H. Gaine, at his book-
    store and printing-office, at the Bible and
    crown, in Hanover-square, 1771.

Kirkpatrick, Frederick Alexander.
    A History of the Argentine Republic.
    Cambridge, University Press, 1931.

Labougle, Raúl de.
    La cuestión Malvinas en las Naciones Unidas.
    Buenos Aires, Casa Pardo, 1965.

Lamberg, Robert F.
    "Territorial Tensions in Latin America,"
    Swiss Review of World Affairs, vol. 32, no. 4
    (July, 1982), pp. 14-15.

Lambertie, Charles de.
    Voyage pittoresque en Californie et au Chile;
    Îles Malouïnes; terres Magellaniques; détroit
    de Magellan; Terre-du-Feu; Terre-des États;
    Cap-Horn; etc. Paris, Ledoyen; Ronmazières
    près Chabanais, L'auteur, 1853.

Larson, Everette E.
A Selective Listing of Monographs and
Government Documents on the Falkland/Malvinas
Islands in the Library of Congress.
Washington, D.C., Library of Congress, 1982.

Latella, José Rodolfo.
"'Islas Malvinas' para los argentinos;
antecedentes históricos y jurídicos que nos
otorgan justo título de soberanía," **Revista
del Circulo Militar,** año. 63, vols. 228/230,
no. 670 (1963), pp. 72-78.

Laver, Margaret Patricia Henwood.
An annotated bibliography of the Falkland
Islands and the Falkland Islands dependen-
cies: (as delimited on 3rd March, 1962).
Cape Town, University of Cape Town Libraries,
1977.

Leguizamón Pondal, Martiniano.
"Las Malvinas se están despoblando," **Anales
de la Academia Argentina de Geografía,** vol. 2
(1958), pp. 140-147.

Leguizamón Pondal, Martiniano.
Toponimia criolla en las Malvinas. Buenos
Aires, Editorial Raigal, 1956.

Levene, Ricardo.
La política internacional argentina en 1833
ante la invasión de las Islas Malvinas.
Buenos Aires, 1949.

López, Francisco Marcos.
Quiebra y reintegración del derecho de
gentes; Gibraltar, Belice, Las Malvinas.
Guatemala, Sección de Impresos de la
Secretaría de Información de la Presidencia
de la República, 195-.

Macdonald, Frederick Charles.
Bishop Stirling of the Falklands; The
adventurous life of a soldier of the cross
whose humility hid the daring spirit of a
hero and an inflexible will to face great
risks. London, Seeley, Service and Co., 1929.

Mackinnon, [Laughlan Bellingham].
Atlantic and transatlantic: sketches afloat
and ashore. New York, Harper & brothers,
1852.

Mackinnon, Laughlan Bellingham.
Some account of the Falkland Islands, from a
six month's residence in 1838 and 1839.
London, A. H. Baily and co., 1840.

"Las Malvinas," **Estrategia,** vol. 1, no. 6 (1970),
pp. 75-129.

Malvinas Islands. Statement by the Representative
of Argentina, H.E. Dr. José María Ruda,
before the Subcommittee III of the Special
Committee on the situation with regard to the
implementation of the declaration on the
granting of independence to colonial
countries and peoples. New York, 9 Sept.,
1964. (Typewritten)

Manning, William Ray.
Diplomatic correspondence of the United
States: Inter-American Affairs, 1831-1860.
vol. 1: Argentina. Washington, Carnegie
Endowment for International Peace, 1932.

Martin, R[obert] Montgomery.
History of the British possessions in the
Indian & Atlantic oceans; comprising Ceylon,
Penang, Malacca, Sincapore, the Falkland
Islands, St. Helena, Ascension, Sierra Leone,
the Gambia, Cape Coast Castle, &c., &c.
London, Whittaker & co., 1837.

Martínez Moreno, Raúl S.
La cuestión Malvinas; nuevo enfoque
histórico-jurídico, la documentación extraída
del Archivo Histórico de Madrid. Tucumán,
Facultad de Derecho y Ciencias Sociales,
Universidad Nacional de Tucumán, 1965.

Martínez Moreno, Raúl S.
"Nuevo enfoque histórico-jurídico de la
cuestión Malvinas, a traves de documentación
extraida de España en enero de 1965," **Revista de
la Universidad Nacional de Córdoba**, ser. 2, vol.
6, nos. 3/5 (1965), pp., 505-543.

Martínez Moreno, Raúl S.
La soberanía argentina en las Islas Malvinas.
Con un apéndice conteniendo: 1. El pleito
argentino en la IX Conferencia Internacional
de Bogotá. 2. Documentación. Tucumán,
Secretaría de Educación, Universidad Nacional
de Tucumán, Instituto de Derecho Público,
1948.

Martinic Beros, Mateo.
Crónica de las tierras del sur del Canal
Beagle. Buenos Aires, Santiago de Chile, Ed.
Aguirre, 1973.

Massini Ezcurra, Hernán.
El mar y la jurisprudencia. Buenos Aires,
Dirección General de Personal Naval, D.I.N.,
1974.

McWhan, Forrest.
The Falkland Islands to-day. Stirling, Scot.,
Stirling Tract Enterprise, 1952.

Melli, Oscar Ricardo.
"Colonización argentina de las islas
Malvinas," **Nuestra Historia**, vol. 2, no. 4
(1969), pp., 195-204.

Metford, J.
"Falklands or Malvinas? The Background to the
dispute," **International Affaïrs**, vol. 44, no.
3 (1975), pp. 463-481.

Migone, Mario Luis.
33 años de vida malvinera. Buenos Aires, Club
de Lectores, 1948.

Moneta, José Manuel.
        ?Nos devolverán las Malvinas? Los actuales
        problemas malvineros. Buenos Aires, Artes
        Gráficas Super, 1970.

Monroe, James.
        Message from the President of the United
        States, to both Houses of Congress, at the
        commencement of the First Session of the
        Eighteenth Congress. Washington, Gales &
        Seaton, 1823.

Montarcé Lastra, Antonio.
        Redención de la soberanía, las Malvinas y el
        diario de doña María Sáez de Vernet. 2d. ed.
        Buenos Aires, Editorial Pompeya, 1964.

Monteiro, Palmyra V. M.
        A catalogue of Latin American flat maps,
        1926-1964. v. 2: South America, Falkland
        Malvinas Islands, The Guianas. Austin, The
        University of Texas, c1967.

Moore, David Moresby.
        The vascular flora of the Falkland Islands.
        London, British Antarctic Survey, 1968.

Moreno, Juan Carlos.
        La recuperación de las Malvinas. Buenos
        Aires, Plus Ultra, 1973.

Moreno, Juan Carlos.
        Nuestras Malvinas. La Antártida. 7. ed.,
        aumentada y actualizada. Buenos Aires, El
        Ateneo, 1956.

Moreno, Juan Carlos.
        Nuestras Malvinas y La Antártida. Viaje de
        estudio y observación. 4 ed. Buenos Aires,
        Junta de Recuperación de las Malvinas, 1948.

Muñoz Azpiri, José Luis.
        Historia completa de las Malvinas. Buenos
        Aires, Oriente, 1966.

Norris, Andrew and David Beech.
   Falkland Islands: the "Travis" franks and
   covers. London, Harmers of London Stamp
   Auctioners, 1977.

Notta, Julio.
   "Mar argentino; ?un nuevo Kuwait? Los
   yacimientos de petróleo en las Malvinas y la
   Antártida," **Crisis,** vol. 3, no. 35 (1976),
   pp. 3-10.

Observations on the forcible occupation of the
   Malvinas, or Falkland Islands, by the British
   government, in 1833. London, Charles Wood and
   Son, 1833.

Palacios, Alfredo Lorenzo.
   Las islas Malvinas, archipiélago argentino;
   Buenos Aires, Editorial Claridad, 1934.

Pedrero, Julián.
   América, las Malvinas y el derecho internacional. Buenos Aires, 1954.

Penrose, Bernard.
   An account of the last expedition to Port
   Egmont in Falkland's Island, in the year
   1772. Together with the transactions of the
   company of the Penguin shallop during their
   stay there. London, J. Johnson, 1775.

Pereira Regoy Lahitte, Carlos T.
   "Los franciscanos en las Islas Malvinas,"
   Nuevo Mundo, vol. 1, no. 1 (1971), pp. 167-
   172.

Pereya, Ezequiel Federico.
   Las Islas Malvinas, soberanía argentina;
   antecedentes, gestiones diplomáticas. Buenos
   Aires, 1968.

Pernety, Antonie Joseph.
   Histoire d'un voyage aux isles Malouines,
   fait en 1763 & 1764; avec des observations
   sur le détroit de Magellan, et sur les
   Patagons. Nouvelle edition. Paris, Chez Sail-
   lant & Nyon, 1770.

Pernety, Antonie Joseph.
Journal historique d'un voyage fait aux iles
Malouînes en 1763 & 1764, pour les recon-
noître, & y former un établissement; et de
deux voyages au détroit de Magellan, avec une
rélation sur les Patagons. Berlin, Chez E. de
Bourdeaux, 1769.

Pernety, Antonie Joseph.
The history of a voyage to the Malouine (or
Falkland) Islands, made in 1763 and 1764,
under the command of M. de Bougainville,
knight of the Order of St. Lewis, in order to
form a settlement there: and of two voyages
to the Streights of Magellan, including an
account of the Patagonians. London, Printed
for G. Lister 1787.

Petersen, Neal H.
"Background on the Falkland Islands Crisis,"
Department of State Bulletin, vol. 82, no.
2063 (June, 1982), pp. 88-89.

Phipps, Colin.
What future for the Falklands? London, Fabian
Society, 1977.

Pitt, Barrie.
Coronel and Falkland. London, Cassel, 1960.

Pitt, Barrie.
Revenge at sea. New York, Stein and Day,
1964.

Pizarro, Ricardo Carreras.
"El problema de las Islas Malvinas," **Revista
de economía**, vol. 3, no. 1 (1951), pp. 27-45.

Plaza, Juan.
Malvinas: nuestra próxima recolonización de
las islas. Buenos Aires, 1970.

Quesada, Hector Cipriano.
Las Malvinas son argentinas, recopilación de
antecedentes. Buenos Aires, 1948.

Quesada, Vicente Gregorio.
　　Recuerdos de mi vida diplomática. Misión en
　　Estados Unidos (1885-1892). Buenos Aires,
　　Menéndez, 1904.

Quirós, César.
　　Hipólito Bouchard y los granaderos del
　　general San Martín. Las Malvinas; su defensa
　　gaucha. Buenos Aires, 1966.

"La question des îles Falkland (Malouines)," **Notes
　　et Etudes Documentaires**, 3490 (mai 13, 1968),
　　Problèmes d'Amérique Latine, 8, pp. 35-40.

Ramos Giménez, Leopoldo.
　　Las Islas Malvinas y la Antártida Argentina,
　　atlas documental. Buenos Aires, Impr.
　　"Abaco," 1948.

Randle, Patricio H.
　　La guerra inconclusa por el Atlántico Sur.
　　Buenos Aires, OIKOS, 1982.

Reportaje a las Malvinas; las Malvinas en las
　　Naciones Unidas. Buenos Aires, Artes Gráficas
　　Rioplatense, S.A., 1982.

Roberts, Brian.
　　"Chronological list of Antarctic
　　expeditions," **The Polar Record**, vol. 9, nos.
　　59 and 60 (May and Sept., 1958), pp. 97-134,
　　191-239.

Roberts-Wray, Kenneth Owen.
　　Commonwealth and colonial law. New York,
　　F.A. Praeger, 1966, esp. pp. 865-868.

Rodríguez Berrutti, Camilo Hugo.
　　Malvinas, última frontera del colonialismo:
　　Hechos, legitimidad, opinion, documentos.
　　Buenos Aires, Editorial Universitaria de
　　Buenos Aires, 1976.

Ros, Enrique J.
"Las conclusiones y recomendaciones del comité especial de las Naciones Unidas para la aplicación de la resolución 1514 (XV) en el caso de las islas Malvinas; su análisis," **Revista de derecho internacional y ciencias diplomaticas**, vol. 13, nos. 25/26 (1964), pp. 83-103.

Roth, Roberto.
Después de Malvinas qué? Buenos Aires, Ediciones La Campana, 1982.

Roucek, Joseph Slabey.
"The geopolitics of Antarctica and the Falkland Islands," **World Affairs Interpreter**, vol. 22, no. 1 (1951), pp. 44-56.

Rubin, Seymour J.
"The Falklands (Malvinas), International Law, and the OAS," **American Journal of International Law**, vol. 76, no. 3 (July, 1982), pp. 594-595.

Rudge, Antônio.
"Malvinas, as ilhas da discórdia," **Manchete**, vol. 21, no. 1189 (1975), pp. 52-59.

Ruiz-Guiñazú, Enrique.
Proas de España en el Mar Magallánico. Buenos Aires, Peuser, 1942.

Russell, Herbert.
"Limitations of modern sea war," **Proceedings** (Annapolis, United States Naval Institute), vol. 51, no. 270 (1925), pp. 1546-1548.

[Sachse, Willi Richard]
Der Admiral; Leben und Tod derer vor Falkland [von] Jan Murr [pseud.]. Berlin, Verlag Junge Generation, c1935.

Sayán Vidaurre, Alberto.
　　Para la inmediata restitución de las
　　Malvinas, gestión ante el embajador de los
　　Estados Unidos de América en la República
　　Argentina. Buenos Aires, Unión Nacional y
　　Democrática Interamericana, 1943.

Schmidt, Walther.
　　"Las Malvinas, die Falklandinseln," **Wissen
　　und Wehr,** (1941), pp. 24-29.

Séve de Gaston, Alberto.
　　"Cronología de los principales aconteci-
　　mientos referentes a la cuestión Malvinas
　　acaecidos durante los años 1966 y 1967,"
　　**Revista de derecho internacional y ciencias
　　diplomáticas** (Rosario), vols. 15/16, nos.
　　29/32 (1969), pp. 158-164.

Shackleton, Edward Arthur Alexander.
　　"Prospect of the Falkland Islands," **The
　　Geographical Journal,** vol. 143, no. 1 (March,
　　1977), pp. 1-13.

Silenzi de Stagni, Adolfo.
　　Las Malvinas y el petróleo. Vol. 1.　Buenos
　　Aires, El Cid Editor, 1982.

Skottsberg, Carl Johan Fredrik.
　　The wilds of Patagonia; a narrative of
　　Swedish expedition to Patagonia, Tierra del
　　Fuego and the Falkland Islands in 1907-1909.
　　London, E. Arnold, 1911.

Snow, William Parker.
　　Two years' cruise off Tierra del Fuego, the
　　Falkland Islands, Patagonia, and in the river
　　Plate; a narrative of life in the southern
　　seas. London, Longman, Brown, Green,
　　Longmans, & Roberts, 1857.

Solari Yrigoyen, Hipólito.
　　Así son las Malvinas. Buenos Aires, Librería
　　Hachette, 1959.

"The South Atlantic Crisis: Background,
consequences, documentation," **Department of
State Bulletin**, vol. 82, no. 2067 (Oct.,
1982), pp. 78-90.

Spencer-Cooper, Henry Edmund Harvey.
The battle of the Falkland Islands, before
and after. London, New York [etc.] Cassell
and company, ltd., 1919.

Strange, Ian J.
The Falkland Islands. Newton Abbot, David and
Charles; Harrisburg, Pa., Stackpole Books, 1972.

Suárez Danero, Eduardo María.
Toda la historia de las Malvinas. 2. ed.,
aumentada con nuevas notas y una cronología.
Buenos Aires, Editorial Tor, 1964.

Sulivan, Sir Batholomew James.
Derrotero de las islas Malvinas. Santiago de
Chile, Imprenta nacional, 1882.

"La soberanía argentina en las Islas Malvinas y el
derecho interamericano," **Revista de derecho
internacional y ciencias diplomaticas**
(Rosario), vols. 3/4, nos. 5/10 (1951/1953),
pp. 439-560.

Tapia, Augusto.
Sobre los rasgos principales de la glaciación
actual en la Isla Laurie Archipiélago de las
Orcadas del Sur. Buenos Aires, Tall. gráf.,
Ministerio de Agricultura, 1925.

Taylor, Margaret Stewart.
Focus on the Falkland Island. London, Hale,
1971.

Tesler, Mario.
"El apresamiento de la goleta 'Rampart' y sus
implicaciones diplomáticas; un viaje a las
Islas Malvinas," **Historia** (Buenos Aires),
vol. 11, no. 43 (1966), pp. 78-98.

Tesler, Mario.
      El gaucho Antonio Rivero; la mentira en la
      historiografía académica. Buenos Aires, A.
      Peña Lillo, 1971.

Tesler, Mario.
      Malvinas, cómo EE. UU. provocó la usurpación
      inglesa. Buenos Aires, Editorial Galerna,
      1979.

The World and its peoples: Paraguay, Argentina,
      Chile, Falkland Islands. New York, Greystone
      Press, 1966.

Torre Revello, José.
      Bibliografía de las Islas Malvinas; obras,
      mapas y documentos; contribución. Buenos
      Aires, Impr. de la Universidad, 1953.

Torre Revello, José.
      "Historia del archipiélago malvinero,"
      Humanitas (Monterrey), no. 3 (1962), pp.
      413-530.

Torre Revello, José.
      La promesa secreta y el convenio anglo-
      español sobre las Malvinas de 1771; nuevas
      aportaciones. Buenos Aires, Impr. de la
      Universidad, 1952.

Torre Revello, José.
      "El último governador español de las Islas
      Malvinas," **Revista del Instituto de Historia
      del Derecho** (Buenos Aires), no. 11 (1960),
      pp. 165-168.

Trehearne, Mary.
      Falkland heritage: a record of pioneer
      settlement. Ilfracombe, Stockwell, 1978.

Troiani, Osiris.
      Martin de Hoz en Londres. Operación
      malvinas I. Buenos Aires, El Cid Editor,
      1982.

Verner, Rudolf Henry Cole.
    The battle cruisers at the action of the
    Falkland Islands. London, J. Bale, sons &
    Danielsson, ltd., 1920.

Volkov, Aleksandr Vasil'evich.
    Argentina, Peru, Chili, Folklendskie Ostrova.
    Moskva, 1957.

Waldock, C. H. M.
    "Disputed sovereignty in the Falkland
    Islands dependencies," **British Year Book of
    International Law,** (1948), pp. 311-353.

Walton, Eric William Kevin.
    Two years in the Antarctic. New York,
    Philosophical Library, 1955.

Weber, Hermann.
    "Falkland-Islands" oder "Malvinas"? der
    Status d. Falklandinseln im Streit zwischen
    Grossbritannien u. Argentinien: e.völker-
    rechtl. Frankfurt am Main, Metzner, 1977.

Whitington, G. T.
    The Falkland Islands, &c., &c., comp. from
    ten years' investigation of the subject.
    London, Smith, Elder, & co. [etc], 1840.

Wood, Chester Clark.
    "Background of Coronel and Falklands,"
    Proceedings (Annapolis, United States Naval
    Institute), vol. 60, no. 377 (1934), pp.
    939-946.

Zavala Ortiz, Miguel Angel.
    "Islas Malvinas," **Estrategia,** no. 45 (marzo-
    abril, 1977), pp. 33-39.

Zorraquin Becú, Ricardo.
    Inglaterra prometió abandonar Las Malvinas:
    estudio histórico y jurídico del conflicto
    anglo-español. Buenos Aires, Librería
    Editorial Platero, 1975.

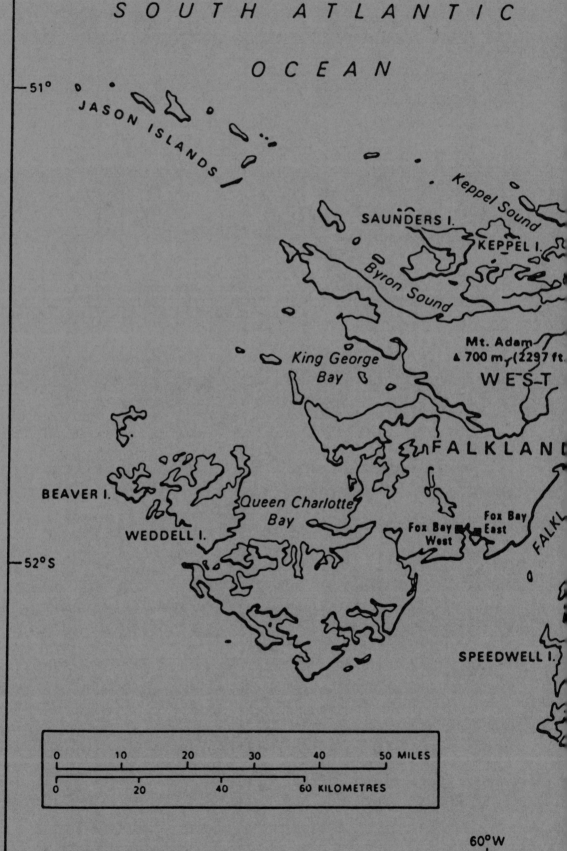